THE BOOK OF MISO

Praise for

THE BOOK OF MISO

"A CONTEMPORARY CLASSIC."
East West Journal

"Crammed full of historical information, traditional and Western recipes, explicit instructions for homemade miso in Japanese life."
Library Journal

"The most impressive single book on food that I have ever seen."
Dr. Eugene N. Anderson, Jr.
Professor of Anthropology (Chinese food and nutrition)
University of California, Riverside

"Numerous excellent illustrations . . . Useful as a guide for food technologists, home economists, dieticians, and others interested in fermented soybean products."
Food Technology

"WONDERFULLY ENTERTAINING AND COMPREHENSIVE."
Mother Earth News

"THE DEFINITIVE SOURCE ON THE SUBJECT."
Alternatives

Putting Hatcho Miso to Bed

THE BOOK OF
MISO

Savory, High-protein Seasoning

VOLUME I

WILLIAM SHURTLEFF & AKIKO AOYAGI

Illustrated by Akiko Aoyagi

Ten Speed Press
A Soyfoods Center Book

BY THE SAME AUTHORS

THE BOOK OF TOFU (Ten Speed Press; Ballantine Books)
TOFU & SOYMILK PRODUCTION (Soyfoods Center)
MISO PRODUCTION (Soyfoods Center)
THE BOOK OF TEMPEH (Harper & Row)
TEMPEH PRODUCTION (Soyfoods Center)
THE SOYFOODS INDUSTRY AND MARKET: DIRECTORY AND DATABOOK (Soyfoods Center)
HISTORY OF SOYBEANS AND SOYFOODS (Soyfoods Center)
THE BOOK OF KUDZU (Soyfoods Center)

TEN SPEED PRESS
P.O. Box 7123
Berkeley, California 94707

You may order single copies prepaid direct from the publisher for $11.95 (paper-
bound) or $16.95 (cloth-bound), plus $1.00 for postage and handling. (California
residents add 6% state sales tax; Bay Area residents add 6½%.)

Library of Congress Catalog Number: 76-19599
Cloth edition ISBN: 0-89815-098-1
Paper edition ISBN: 0-89815-097-3

Cover illustration by Akiko Aoyagi

Book design and typography by Beverly Stiskin

Printed in the United States of America

10   9   8   7   6   5   4   3   2   1

For all the world's children
whose lives are filled with hunger...
and can't understand why.

And for all beings
who are dedicated to doing something about it.

Contents

PART I

Miso: Savory, High-Protein Seasoning

PART II

Cooking with Miso

PART III
The Preparation of Miso

What is Miso?

MISO (pronounced MEE-so, and also known as "fermented soybean paste") is a savory, high-protein seasoning made from soybeans, grain (usually rice or barley), salt, water, and *Aspergillus oryzae* culture. Miso has no equivalent in the West—which may be one reason it has caught on here so quickly. Its range of flavors and colors, textures and aromas is as varied as that of the world's fine cheeses and wines. Miso's texture resembles that of a soft peanut butter. Its many warm colors range from deep chocolate browns, reddish browns, and russets, through ambers, clarets, and cinnamon reds, on up to creamy beiges and sunlight yellows for some sweeter, more modern varieties. To the sensitive palate, no two of the many miso varieties taste the same. The darker, more traditional types have flavors and aroms that are deep, rich, and hearty, almost meaty at times, making them ideal for the preparation of savory meatless dishes; the lighter, more modern misos are subtly sweet and delicately refreshing. The wonderfully fragrant aroma of traditional miso has been compared with that of freshly ground coffee.

Miso is one of East Asia's most important soyfoods. In Japan, over 70 percent of the population starts each day with a health-giving, nutritious, and warming cup of miso soup instead of coffee. Its alkalizing effect wakes up the body and mind, providing it with a steady supply of high-quality energy that lasts all morning. Miso can be used as an all-purpose seasoning in many of the same ways as salt, yet because it contains only 5.5 to 13 percent sodium chloride (versus 99 percent in table salt) it can serve as the key seasoning in moderate- or low-salt diets that are still rich in flavor. But miso is much more than just a seasoning. Highly nutritious, it is such a concentrated source of protein, vitamin B-12, and other essential nutrients, that the Japanese consider it to be a basic staple and full-fledged "food," although typically only several tablespoons are used per person each day. Moreover, like yogurt, miso is a living, cultured food containing lactic acid-forming bacteria (such as *Pediococcus halophilus* and *Lactobacillus delbrueckii*) plus other health-giving microorganisms and digestion-aiding enzymes. Traditional misos can be stored for months without refrigeration. And in 1983, a month's supply of natural miso for a person in North America using it twice daily (1½ tablespoons a day) costs as little as $2.55.

Miso is prized by cooks for its almost unlimited versatility. It can be used like bouillon or a rich meat stock in soups, meatless gravies, or stews; like soy sauce or *shoyu*, Worcestershire sauce, or ketchup in sauces, dips, and dressings; as an unmatched thickener in barbecue sauces; like cheese in casseroles and spreads; like chutney or relish as a topping for grains, fresh vegetable slices or open-faced sandwiches; as a gravy base with sauteed or steamed foods; or even like vinegar as a pickling medium. Used in many of these ways for centuries in Japanese kitchens, it has set its distinctive mark of fine flavor on the entire panorama of Japanese cuisine and added zest and variety to a diet that has long consisted primarily of grains, land-and-sea vegetables, and tofu.

There are six basic types of miso among which are found more than 28 distinctly different varieties. The three basic traditional types are rice, barley and soybean miso, the first two made from soybeans, salt and the respective grain, the last made from soybeans and salt alone. Two "special" types, finger lickin' and sweet simmered miso, contain bits of chopped vegetables, nuts and/or seasonings and are delectably sweet and chunky. Finally, there are a number of "modern" misos developed since 1959, including dehydrated and low-salt/high-protein varieties.

The progenitor of present-day miso originated in China some 2,500 years ago. Called *chiang* (pronounced jang), it was brought to Japan during the 7th century by Buddhist priests. During the following centuries, Japanese craftsmen transformed *chiang* into miso and shoyu (all-purpose Japanese soy sauce), two unique and distinctive foods which are now quite different from their Chinese counterparts. Indeed the word "miso" was first coined in Japan and its many varieties were created and developed there. *Chiang* or Chinese-style miso continues to be widely used throughout its mother country and at least five varieties are now available in the West, as are a number of types of *jang* or Korean-style miso.

First introduced to America on a small scale in the early 1960s, miso is now becoming better known and appreciated. High-quality varieties are available throughout the United States at reasonable prices in most natural and health food stores, co-op markets, Japanese and Chinese grocery stores, and a growing number of supermarkets. Some stores carry as many as 15 different varieties sold in both bulk and prepackaged 1- to 2-pound quantities. Various types of American-made miso are now being marketed, and many people—especially those in communities—have taken to preparing their own at home.

We feel that miso has come to the West to stay, and that in the near future it will come to be considered an essential element in America's evolving cuisine, a basic seasoning, of which several varieties will be found in well-stocked kitchens throughout the country. It can—and should—play an increasingly important role in the cookery and nutrition of people around the world.

Preface

To the Second Edition

SINCE THE publication of the first edition of *The Book of Miso* in September 1976 there have been many promising developments in the work to introduce this fine fermented soyfood to America. That month we bought a large Dodge van, painted a sign on one side reading "Tofu and Miso America Tour," then traveled 15,000 miles around America presenting 70 public programs for groups that had invited us. At each we talked about miso, showed color slides, and served samples—usually peanut miso on apple slices.

Increasingly we received letters from people interested in making miso on a community or commercial scale, so in August 1977 our Center published *Miso Production: The Book of Miso, Volume II.* Many new factors joined in helping to make miso more popular: the burgeoning macrobiotic, natural foods, and vegetarian movements; the sustained media interest which produced eleven major articles between 1976 and 1972; the many new cookbooks and cooking articles that included miso recipes; the rapid rise of emigration from East Asia during the 1970s; the active Soyfoods Association of North America, founded in July 1978; and *Soyfoods* magazine.

Soon a new generation of miso companies grew up in North America, led by Japanese-owned Miyako Oriental Foods in Los Angeles (1976), but soon followed by North America's first Caucasian-run miso operations: Ohio Miso Co. in Monroeville, Ohio (1979), Shin-Mei-Do on Denman Island, B.C., Canada (1979), American Miso, Inc. in Rutherfordton, North Carolina (1981), South River Miso Co. in Conway, Massachusetts (1982), Imagine Foods/Moniteau Farm in Jamestown, Missouri (1982), and General Oriental Foods in Holmdale, New Jersey (1982). Note that most of these new miso companies are located in rural areas, following an ancient East Asian tradition.

The American miso market has grown dramatically in the years since 1975, with both imports and domestic miso production expanding. Between 1975 and 1982, imports rose 109 percent, from 459 to 959 tonnes (metric tons), while production in the continental U.S. jumped a remarkable 525 percent from 120 to 750 tonnes and production in Hawaii grew 18 percent from 543 to 640 tonnes. Thus by early 1983 Americans are consuming an estimated 2,349 tonnes of miso, more than twice as much (and in the continental U.S. three times as much) as eight years earlier.

In 1976 most of the miso was purchased as miso itself, but by the late 1970s a rapidly growing proportion came to be sold as an ingredient in other popular American foods such as dehydrated instant miso soups, miso-flavored seasonings for dips and salad dressings, bottled miso dressings, brown rice pilaf seasoned with miso, miso-seasoned corn chips, and the like. These new products helped miso to reach a broad spectrum of Americans, who were formerly unaware of this savory seasoning.

The growing concern with excess salt consumption that began in the late 1970s led to a shift toward lower salt misos. In the process many people came to realize that

miso, containing an average of only 12 percent salt (versus 99 percent for straight table salt) plus a host of natural flavor enhancers, is an excellent way to help *reduce* salt intake with no sacrifice in flavor.

In July 1980 our book was published in a handsome German edition, *Das Miso Buch.* Then in March 1981, based on the popularity of the first edition of our work, Ballantine Books published an updated mass-market edition; by late 1982 the two American editions had sold more than 70,000 copies, helping to spread the good word.

With all these changes that have taken place, combined with the extensive additional research that we have done on the history of miso (it was first mentioned by a Westerner in 1597!) as well as on its nutritional value, biochemistry, production, cookery, etc., we and our new publisher felt that it was time for a second edition. Changes and updates have been made throughout the book, but the most extensive ones are to be found in the chapters on History of Miso (Appendix A), Chinese, Korean, and Indonesian Misos (Appendix B), People and Institutions Connected with Miso (Appendix C), Miso Companies in the West (Appendix D), the Bibliography, and Soybeans, Protein, and World Hunger (Chapter 1).

We are happy to see that miso is finding its rightful and enriching place in America's evolving new cuisine—more natural, healthful, light, traditional, and diverse.

The Soyfoods Center
Lafayette, California
February 1983

Preface

To the First Edition

I RECEIVED MY first introduction to fine miso while working as a cook at California's Tassajara Zen Mountain Center. It was there that I first participated in the preparation of miso—we made a 50-gallon vatful once each year—and learned its many uses as a seasoning. But it was only while living in Japan and working together with Akiko on *The Book of Tofu* that we both really discovered the enormous wealth and variety contained in the world of miso and began to recognize the great value this savory soyfood has to offer the world. This learning experience was an adventure and not the least of its many pleasures was shopping for the different varieties of miso needed to prepare our recipes.

Throughout Japan, thousands of small shops specialize in the sale of miso (and miso pickles), and a sampling of forty to fifty varieties will generally be available. Each is displayed in a 5-gallon cedar keg ringed with broad hoops of braided bamboo and marked in bold black characters with the miso's name, price, and province of origin. The hues and shades create a festival of autumn-maple colors, and the total atmosphere has all the warmth and rustic beauty of a Florentine cheese shop or a small wine cellar in the French countryside.

We enjoyed learning the names of Japan's traditional favorites and their distinguished makers, and slowly developed the ability to judge quality and character. Using miso as a seasoning in our daily cookery, we found it made many of our Western-style dishes even more delicious. Its versatility seemed almost unlimited and its deep, rich flavors served to enrich and add variety to our meatless diet. In fine restaurants, we enjoyed a wide variety of different dishes featuring miso and found that it had long been important in the two main schools of Japanese haute cuisine: Zen Temple Cookery and Tea Ceremony Cuisine. I soon came to understand that, for many Japanese, miso is the very epitome of the satisfying flavors and aromas of home cooking; the mere mention of mother's or grandma's miso soup can evoke all the warm feelings that come to most Westerners at the thought of a loaf of home-baked bread, piping hot from the oven.

As our interest deepened, we began to visit, learn from, and eventually become friends with a number of the more than 2,400 master craftsmen who make Japan's miso. Working in shops which are usually located adjacent to their homes, many of these men honored the traditional spirit of fine craftsmanship in a way that transformed daily work into an art and spiritual practice. We were drawn to their handsomely crafted tools, their high-roofed shops with massive arching rafters, and their huge cedar vats—often more than 150 years old—that stand taller than a man. In the morning air, billows of steam would rise from the great iron caldron and large cedar steamer in which half a ton of soybeans and rice were being cooked. When

freshly harvested *koji* (rice or barley covered with a cottony mycelium of fragrant white mold) was removed from its granite-hewn incubation room, it would fill the entire shop with an incomparable lingering aroma, rich and subtly sweet, like that of freshly-roasted chestnuts or coffee.

I was eventually given the opportunity to do an informal apprenticeship with Mr. Kiyoshi Tsujita, an exemplary miso master living quite near our home. A strong traditionalist and purist at heart, he made the most delicious miso—and the *only* brown-rice miso—that we had ever tasted. Studying with him and watching him at work, I began to appreciate the mysteries of the fermentation process, the complexities of its chemistry and microbiology, and the harmony of its interaction with the great movements of the four seasons. He stressed that the essence of his art could not be transmitted in words, for it was linked to one's local climate and the soil in which soybeans, rice, and barley grow; embodied in the strains of microorganisms which for generations had permeated the air, wood, and rock walls of a shop; half hidden in the muscles and bones, feeling and intuition of each craftsman. It was a total understanding, rooted in a particular place and in a man who becomes imbued with it like one who, unbeknownst to himself, becomes wet by walking through a mist. As in the ancient wine chateaux throughout Europe, it reflected a tradition and culture that took centuries to mature.

Nevertheless, he wanted to help both Akiko and me to understand his craft and convey its fundamentals to people in the West. He therefore encouraged us to begin making our own miso and helped us get started. Under his tutelage, we prepared many small batches and, for more than a year, patiently endured the suspense of waiting, wondering how they would turn out. When we seemed pleased with the results, he teased us with the Japanese proverb saying that, naturally, every person likes his own homemade miso best!

Over a period of some four years, Akiko and I had the opportunity to visit miso shops throughout Japan and study the preparation of most of the main traditional varieties. Though ordinarily quite protective of their traditional secrets, the shops' masters were pleased to see our sincere interest in their work and, without exception, spared no time or effort in showing us everything we wanted to see, answering all our questions, and in some cases, later carrying on a detailed correspondence.

Early in the spring of 1973, we made our first contact with country-style miso, a tradition started hundreds of years ago by Buddhist priests in their temples and rural peasants in their farmhouses, and which still accounts for an estimated 17 percent of all Japanese miso production. At the Banyan Ashram, a community of young people living a simple life of meditation and farming on tiny Suwanose Island, we learned how to make barley koji (mold barley) in the ancient way by "catching" natural wild mold spores floating in the air. Invited one sunny April morning to join in the work, we used a large wooden mortar and heavy pestles to mash koji and cooked soybeans together. In an atmosphere of down-home merriment, everyone lent rhythm to the pounding by clapping, stomping, and chanting. The women packed the mashed ingredients into tall earthenware crocks, which were then ceremoniously sealed. We were urged to return for the grand opening when the fermentation had finished, but warned not to be late, since even fifty gallons of homemade barley miso wouldn't last long in a large community of hungry, hard-working men and women.

As our book began to take form, we traveled to Taiwan and Korea to visit local miso makers at their work, study new varieties of Chinese- and Korean-style miso in sprawling outdoor marketplaces, and sample miso cuisine at restaurants representing the full gamut of provincial cooking styles.

In the fall of 1974, we traveled deep into the mountains of the northeast provinces to visit one of Japan's "long-life" villages, where many people live past the age of ninety and most families still prepare their own miso using an ancient method. Upon arrival we were invited to join our host family in a light meal featuring farmhouse-style *Dengaku*; fresh homemade tofu was pierced with bamboo skewers, coated on both sides with homemade miso, and grilled around a bed of live coals in the open-hearth fireplace. We were deeply touched to discover that both the miso and tofu had been made entirely from soybeans grown in the village fields, and the mere fragrance of that sizzling *Dengaku* made our 600 mile trip well worthwhile. As we studied the miso-making process, we could not help but notice how vigorous and healthy the villagers seemed, and how this simple life close to nature had made each person the master of many useful arts. Here we first came to realize how miso could make a major contribution to the life of self sufficiency.

While Akiko worked with miso in day-to-day cookery, I spent considerable time studying Western and Japanese literature on miso fermentation and visiting Japan's most modern research institutes and factories. I discovered that during the past few decades a revolution has taken place in miso manufacturing as the use of large-scale, automatic machinery, quick fermentation in heated rooms, and high-speed polyethylene packaging have made it possible to mass-produce miso at low cost and distribute it throughout the nation and even the world. The uniqueness and character of traditional provincial varieties are gradually being lost and the new factories have become a threat to the very existence of Japan's many small shops and their high-quality natural products.

Continuing our daily experimentation with miso cookery, we eventually prepared more than 600 recipes, from which we chose our favorites for use in this book. In the mornings and evenings we practiced meditation; our days were given over to writing and research, artwork and cookery.

Despite the joy we found in our work, though, one almost unbearable reality has been constantly before us: in a world blessed with an abundance of food, indeed more than enough for everyone, millions of people are now faced with perpetual hunger, severe protein malnutrition, and starvation. Yet the use of miso allows each of us to do our small part in making better use of the earth's precious food reserves by enjoying soy and grain proteins directly and thereby avoiding the colossal waste inherent in the Western pattern of feeding these proteins to livestock. How fortunate, we feel, that miso offers us its fine flavor and remarkable nutritional value together with a time-tested promise to help make the world a better home for all.

Tokyo, Japan
June 1976

Acknowledgments

ALL BEINGS, past and present, have shared in the creation of this book, yet to some we wish to express special thanks: Mr. Kiyoshi Tsujita, mentor and friend, who taught us the art of traditional miso making and supplied us with the finest brown-rice miso we have ever tasted; Mr. Wataru Kawamura, Japan's "miso sensei," who introduced us to the romance of miso history and its place in the heart of the people; Messrs. Hideo Ebine, Masahiro Nakano, Kazuo Shibasaki, Clifford W. Hesseltine, and Ms. Hwa L. Wang, miso researchers from East and West, who have pioneered the way in scientific exploration of the mysteries of miso fermentation; Messrs. Kiyoshi Kaneko and Choichi Kato, directors of Japan's two Hatcho miso companies; Messrs. Shigeru Honda and Keinosuke Ishino, owners of Kyoto's two famous sweet white miso shops; Messrs. Kojiro Ikeda and Yanosuke Kanemitsu, makers of fine barley miso; Messrs. Soichi Nishida, Nobushi Takeyama, and William Higa, makers respectively of red, sweet red, and mellow white miso; Messrs. Shigeo Sasaki, Kenichiro Sasaki, and Hiroshi Haga, of the Sendai Miso Co.; Mr. Yojuro Watanabe, production manager at Japan's largest miso factory; Messrs. Yasu Niimi and Akira Chiba, makers of fine koji starter; Messrs. Denei Fujimori and Zenichi Matsushita of the Japanese National Miso Association; Mr. Kinichiro Shibata, producer of commercial miso pickles;

Mmes. Saiyo Miura and Kazuko Shinya, who taught us how to make farmhouse *tama-miso* in remote Ugemura village; the members of Banyan Ashram, who taught us the preparation of sweet-potato miso using wild mold spores; Mr. Akiyoshi Kazama who kept us well informed on the world of international miso trade; Mr. Masahiro Miyashita of Kikkoman International, who provided us with extensive information about shoyu; Bob Gerner and Gordon Bennett who gave us support and advice; Messrs. Junsei Yamazaki, Noboru Muramoto, Wally Gorell, Thom Leonard and Blake Rankin, who have helped to get the word out; and makers of *chiang* and *jang* throughout Taiwan and Korea who gave generously of their time and experience.

Finally, we would like to give particular thanks to: Herman and Cornellia Aihara, Michio and Aveline Kushi, and Pierre Gaevert, who were instrumental in preparing the way; Frances Moore Lappé, Lester R. Brown, E. F. Schumacher, and Stephen Gaskin, whose teachings have inspired our work; Ty Smith and Paul Discoe, whose initial encouragement gave birth to this book; Bobbie and Lawton, Fumio and Kinjiro, for their love and generosity; Beverly, for her inspired design; and Nahum Stiskin, our friend and publisher, whose vision and ceaseless striving for excellence have won our deepest admiration.

10

PART I

Miso:
Savory, High-Protein
Seasoning

1
Soybeans, Protein and World Hunger

URING THE past decade, the population/food crisis has suddenly emerged as the most serious problem facing mankind. We are now experiencing the greatest famine in history and the situation is clearly getting worse. Experts estimate that starvation and malnutrition-caused diseases are now taking the lives of between five and 20 million people each year (15,000 to 60,000 *daily*), and half of the victims are children under five. According to the United Nations Food and Agricultural Organization (FAO), an additional 400 to 500 million children (more than twice the population of the United States) living in the sixty poorest countries suffer from such severe chronic malnutrition that their growth and mental capacity are permanently retarded. And more than one-quarter of the earth's present four billion inhabitants confront inescapable hunger during some part of each year. At this turning point in history, we have, for the first time, rounded the bend on three dangerous exponential curves—population, resource-and-energy consumption, and pollution—and are heading almost vertically upward at a dizzying pace. These cold statistics add up to immense human suffering, which is quickly becoming the dominant reality of daily life for poor people throughout the world.

In the least developed nations, where population generally doubles every 20 to 25 years and most of the good land is already intensively cultivated, food supplies cannot possibly keep up with demand. As the gap between the poor and rich nations widens, and the latter use increasingly large quantities of already scarce corn, soy, wheat, and oats to fatten their livestock, the price of these basic foods is pushed out of reach of the destitute and hungry. What once were local short-term famines now threaten to engulf entire nations, leading to social and political chaos. Already millions find themselves trapped in unimaginable squalor. And poverty, illiteracy, and malnutrition transferred from generation to generation in an accelerating downward spiral continually degrades the quality of individual lives and must soon have grave consequences for all people everywhere.

We in the affluent West have been fortunate. We have forgotten how it *feels* to be always hungry, for hunger has remained a news item from faraway countries. Most of us have been spared—perhaps unfortunately—the terrible and unforgettable experience of witnessing firsthand a death by starvation. And slowly many of us have allowed ourselves to become numbed—even apathetic—to the painful reality of what is happening all around us in the world. Often quite unconsciously, many have already given up the situation as hopeless, and this attitude has emerged as one of the primary forces allowing the problem to grow worse. Some feel there is not enough room in the lifeboat to save the drowning, not realizing that the earth presently produces more than enough food for everyone. Others believe it is already too late and that there is nothing they could do to make a difference, forgetting that the way they eat—which only they can change—may be one of the basic causes of worldwide food shortages. Still others argue pessimistically that to help in any way would only stimulate snowballing population growth which would ultimately make the problem even worse and simply delay the day of reckoning; they fail to understand that the easiest—if not the only—way to lower birth rates is to ensure adequate food supplies and improve living standards.

Discarding false or unexamined myths and assumptions can lead from a sense of hopelessness and helplessness to a genuine, realistic commitment to change. The present food/population crisis, if neglected, will not somehow work itself out or gradually go away. It will only get worse and worse. In our small and increasingly interdependent global village, the burden of suffering will eventually be visited upon everyone. Will we continue to live as a privileged and wealthy minority, consuming vastly more than our share of precious food (and energy) resources, until we are a tiny island in a sea of hunger, compelling the deprived, in desperation, to force us to stop? Or will we start now to really care and, thus, to work for change? These are life and death matters on which the balance of this century will turn.

Soybeans: Protein Source of the Future

Experts studying the world food crisis are quick to emphasize that the key nutrient in shortest supply is protein. World hunger is primarily protein hunger and most starvation—especially among children—is caused not by a lack of calories but of this relatively costly and scarce nutritional component. Thus it is often said that the food crisis is more specifically a protein crisis, and that if the protein gap could be filled, the most difficult part of the problem would be solved. While these experts agree that the situation admits of no easy solution, they also are virtually unanimous in their opinion that soybeans will be the protein source of the future. Why? Because soybeans can produce more usable protein per acre of land than any other known crop—33 percent more on the average (360 percent more under ideal conditions) than second-place rice and twenty *times* as much as if the land were used to raise beef cattle or grow their fodder. This fact becomes increasingly important as farmland grows more and more scarce.

Soybeans have served as the protein backbone of the East Asian diet for over 2,000 years and today—used in the form of tofu, miso, shoyu, soymilk, tempeh, fresh green soybeans and a host of other delicious foods—they are an integral part of the diet of more than one billion people. Containing 34 to 36 percent high-quality protein—more than any other plant or animal food—plus all of the eight essential amino acids, they are rightfully known throughout the Orient as "the meat of the fields." From the body's point of view, the amount of usable protein contained in ½ cup dry soybeans (1 cup cooked) is no different from that contained in 5 ounces of steak. And low-cost, low-calorie soybean foods contain no cholesterol and almost none of the saturated fats so abundant in most animal-derived products.

Americans are often surprised to learn that their country is the world's largest soybean producer, accounting for about 67 percent of the planet's total yearly output. In 1975, over 600,000 U.S. soybean farmers planted a total of 54 million acres and sold their crop for $7.5 billion. Soybeans are one of our largest and most important farm crops, second only to corn (and ahead of wheat) in total dollar value, and third in total acreage. Exporting about half of the domestic crop, America is the largest international supplier, providing 70 percent of the total trade. These beans are our biggest farm export, worth over $5 *billion* in 1975.

Institutionalized Protein Waste

But what happens to all these soybeans and the 18 *million* tons of protein they contain? Virtually all of the non-exported crop is sent to huge factories where the soy oil—which contains no protein—is extracted with hexane solvent. Then, approximately 95 percent of the protein-rich meal left over is fed directly to livestock. The soybeans exported to Russia, Europe, Poland, Iran, and other countries now building up their livestock herds follow the same route. Only in East Asia are large quantities of soybeans transformed into high-protein foods. If all of this U.S. soy protein were used directly, it could fulfill about 25 percent of the yearly protein requirements of every person on the planet.

The system responsible for this immense waste is the feedlot, which was designed after World War II in an era of huge farm surpluses as a way of transforming excess grains and soy into more "profitable" meat. Although we now live in an era of famine with reserves at a precariously low level, an astonishing 50 percent of all U.S. farmland is still used to grow crops that end up being fed to animals. In addition to soybeans, we feed livestock a full 78 percent of our cereal grains including about 90 percent of our corn, oats, and barley, and 24 percent of our wheat, all of which could, of course, serve as foods for human beings. As a result, the average American now consumes the equivalent of 2,000 pounds of grain and soybeans annually, 200 pounds of which is used directly, while the remaining 90 percent is consumed in the form of meat, poultry, dairy products, and eggs. But the average person in developing countries consumes only 400 pounds per year, virtually all of which is used directly in meatless diets. Thus, the birth of one typical American baby has *five* times the adverse effect on precious world food reserves (not to mention water, fertilizer, energy, and land resources) as the birth of a child in Asia, Africa, or Latin America.

And as other countries become affluent, they quickly follow the American pattern. Resource geographer Georg Borgstrom estimates that the developed world, with 28 percent of the world's population, consumes some two-thirds of world grain production and three-fourths of the world's fish catch (much of which is purchased from protein-starved Latin America and used to feed cats and dogs as well as livestock). In fact, the rich use practically as much cereal grains to feed animals as the poorer half of mankind eats directly as food. The 6 percent of the world's population who live in the United States eat 30 percent of the world's meat and drink half its milk. Our beef consumption has jumped from 50 pounds per capita in 1950 to 124 pounds in 1975, and our total intake of beef, pork, and poultry averages 11 ounces daily (254 pounds a year). Moreover, we consume $25 billion worth of alcoholic beverages (made largely from grains) at an annual cost of $120 per person. Thus, while population still accounts for the major part of rising food demand, it is often said that a ravenous new rival, affluence, has emerged to further increase food shortages.

As a result, livestock and pets in wealthy countries are in direct competition for basic foods with hungry people throughout the rest of the world. On the international grain markets, U.S. livestock farmers, supported by the growing demand for meat, can always outbid representatives from poor grain-eating countries. Thus, basic foods go to cows and pigs, chickens and turkeys, instead of to the people who need them most. America's 90 million dogs and cats alone consume an annual $1.5 billion worth of pet food containing enough protein to feed 4 million human beings. In his authoritative *Nutrition and our Overpopulated Planet*, Sohan Monocha concludes that "animals in developed countries eat a better, more nutritionally balanced diet than two-thirds of the human population in poorer countries." Until quite recently, though, cattle were grazed on land unfit for farming or fed vegetable refuse (such as cornstalks) that could not be eaten by people; at present only 30 percent are still raised in this way. Every effort (legal, political, and personal) should be made to return to this system as soon as possible, and consumers who feel they need beef should insist on the grass-fed variety.

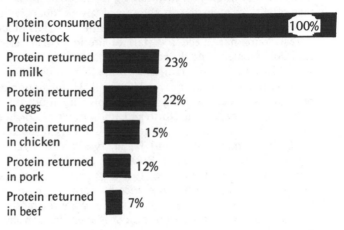

Food Energy

Food is a form of energy, and in a sense, the fundamental energy crisis is getting human beings enough food calories and protein. All food is ultimately derived from plants, which do the primary work of energy transformation that makes other life forms possible. Without plants we would have sunlight, water, air, and earth—but no food. As energy flows through a food chain, about 80 to 90 percent is degraded to useless heat at each step of the chain as explained by the second law of thermodynamics and illustrated here. The shorter the food chain between plants and man, the less the energy lost as heat and the greater the food calories available. Most people in the world—and especially those living in areas which have long been densely populated—eat low on the food chain, avoiding meat and eating plants directly. About 70 percent of the world's protein presently comes from plants and only 30 percent from animal-derived products, yet in affluent countries, these figures are often reversed. In developing countries, cereal grains alone generally provide 65 to 70 percent of the protein intake and 70 to 80 percent of the calories. This traditional grain-centered diet will support about seven times the population as its meat-centered counterpart.

The process of running grains and soybeans through animals and then eating the animals is so inefficient, uneconomical, and energy-expensive as to be virtually inexcusable. Clearly, the earth cannot support this level of waste. On the average, it takes about 7 pounds of grain- or soy protein to make 1 pound of livestock protein, but in the case of the feedlot steer, the least efficient converter, it takes a full 15 pounds. In other words, 93 percent of the protein fed to a steer is lost to human consumption, being used instead to support the animal's metabolism or build inedible parts of its body. The "return on investment" for other livestock products is shown below:

Fig. 1. Protein Consumed vs. Protein Returned

Protein consumed by livestock	100%
Protein returned in milk	23%
Protein returned in eggs	22%
Protein returned in chicken	15%
Protein returned in pork	12%
Protein returned in beef	7%

In her incisive million-copy best seller, *Diet for a Small Planet*, Frances Moore Lappé describes the basic situation vividly: "To imagine what this means in practical everyday terms, simply set yourself at a restaurant in front of an 8-ounce steak and then imagine the room filled with 40 to 50 people with empty bowls in front of them. For the 'feed cost' of your steak, each of their bowls could be filled with a full cup of cereal grains."

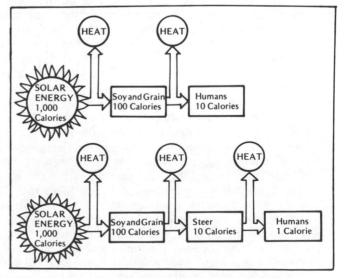

Fig. 2. Energy Flow through Food Chains

Soy Protein for a Hungry Planet

Experts studying the world food crisis generally agree that the easiest and quickest way that we in affluent countries can do something concrete to help is to greatly reduce our consumption of livestock products—especially meat. Each person that cuts his or her consumption of grain-fed beef by only one pound frees 15 pounds of grains and soybeans to be used directly as food. And a reduction in American meat consumption of only 10 percent would free 12 million tons of these basic foods per year, enough to meet the annual grain requirements of about 60 million people in less developed countries.

The key to making the transition toward a balanced meatless diet while still maintaining an adequate intake of high-quality protein lies in the use of soy products served together with the very grains that are now fed to livestock. Cereal grains have been the staff of life in virtually every traditional society, and the god of food has usually been more specifically the god of grain, as with the Roman deity Ceres, from whom we derive the word "cereal." Throughout most of East Asia, rice has long been the primary food. It was wheat in Europe, corn in North and South America, sorghum in Africa and parts of Asia, barley in Tibet, oats in Scotland, millet in northern China and Japan, rye in Mediterranean countries, and buckwheat in Russia. To this day, wheat and rice remain the primary foods for two-thirds of the human population, followed in importance by corn, sorghum, and barley in that order. Cereal grains and soy are the most democratic of foods, for nature produces them in such abundance that there is enough to go around at prices everyone can afford. And because soy products—such as miso—contain an abundance of the very amino amino acids lacking in grains, their use as a regular part of a grain-based diet can raise the quality of the protein combination to the same level as that found in most meats, while boosting the total available protein by as much as 40 percent (see p. 23). For these reasons, it is particularly important that people in protein-scarce developing countries learn to use soy.

Relying more on plant protein and less on meat can do wonders for your food budget, health, weight, conscience and ecological environment, which is perhaps why an estimated 10 million Americans have now turned to meatless diets and why the number is rapidly increasing. Since plant foods have no cholesterol and very little saturated fats or harmful environmental contaminants (DDT, etc.), your intake of these substances will be greatly reduced, as will your susceptibility to heart disease and cancer (see p. 28). In a world plagued by malnutrition and starvation, 67 percent of all Americans report that they are trying to lose weight, and a recent Public Health Survey shows that 25 to 45 percent of all U.S. adults are more than 20 percent overweight (i.e., "obese"); vegetarians, on the other hand, are found to be 20 pounds below the national average. Animals will be grateful to you for not eating them and hungry people everywhere will thank you for taking no more than your share.

While their American counterparts have sold their beans to be used for oil and fodder, farmers throughout East Asia have long used homegrown soybeans as a basic daily protein source. Recently, however, a Tennessee-based new-age community called *The Farm* has taken the historic step of cultivating soybeans for use primarily as a food staple in the vegetarian diet of its 850 members. The 200 acres they planted yielded 65 tons, most of which was made into soymilk at their soy dairy or tempeh in their incubators; some of the crop, however, was shared with people in famine-stricken areas around the world in an attempt not only to help but also to educate them in the many wonders of soy. Thanks to *The Farm's* ongoing efforts to teach other Americans about soybeans, small communities across the country are starting to grow them for home consumption.

South American nations have recently turned to soy farming on a massive scale. In 1974, Brazil (with extensive financial and technical aid from Japan) passed China to become the world's second largest producer, and Argentina is actively following Brazil's lead. In Mexico, soy imports jumped from 2 million bushels in 1971 to 30 million in 1975. Until recently most of the beans have been used for fodder or exported, but in 1975, representatives from numerous Latin American countries met in Mexico with experts from around the world to discuss ways of using soy proteins directly to help feed local populations. The first conference of its kind, this historic event will undoubtedly have important implications for people in all developing countries.

Soybeans and Agriculture

Food production can be increased either by expanding farm acreage or by increasing per-acre yields. Virtually all advances during the past quarter century have come in the latter area, largely through the use of genetically engineered hybrid seeds and fossil fuels in the form of mechanization, irrigation, chemical fertilizers, pesticides, and herbicides. The result has been a 60 percent increase in U.S. farm output since 1950. However in developed countries, the intensive use of agrichemicals is now considered to have reached a point of diminishing returns. This represents a basic change in the nature of the food problem and, as agricultural economist Lester R. Brown says, "points to the urgency of a radical shift in the traditional approach to its solution—the need to concentrate much more effort than in the past on slowing the growth in world *demand* for food." With all the major resources used to produce food—water, fertilizer, energy, and land—now scarce, and the worldwide demand from burgeoning populations of people and livestock unceasing, it is believed that food prices will continue to skyrocket.

A related question that many farmers in developed countries now raise is no longer "How much food can we produce?" but "What are the environmental consequences of doing so?" Large corporations, determined to apply the principles of industry to agriculture, have been grossly negligent of the health of our soil. Believing they have emancipated themselves from dependence upon nature, agribusiness technologists have come to view soil simply as a mixture of nitrogen, phosphorous, and potassium rather than as a living, fragile substance replete with microorganisms, humus, and organic matter. Corporate executives involved in large-scale farming seem not to take the time to understand the needs of the land and its natural cycles. A growing number of farmers, however, prompted by soaring energy costs (the price of nitrogen fertilizer alone more than quadrupled between 1971 and 1980) and a solid intuition that we can't remain insensitive to the quality of our soil without eventually suffering the consequences, are taking new interest in traditional organic techniques.

Chemical fertilizers, now applied at the average level of 150 pounds per acre, were virtually unused before 1940. Up until that time, farmers practiced crop rotation, planting legumes—such as soybeans—every three years to regenerate soil nutrients and help control monoculture insect populations. Rhizobia bacteria living in the legumes' root nodules capture atmospheric nitrogen and "fix" it in the soil; this nitrogen (the main component in protein) serves as a source of free natural fertilizer that nourishes the plant and future crops. When chemical fertilizers (anhydrous ammonia or amonium nitrate) are applied to the soil, plants utilize only about 50 percent of their nitrogen, the rest being lost to seepage and runoff which often pollute local waterways. Yet the nitrogen fixed by bacteria is used completely and there is no resulting pollution. Soybeans can fix about 100 pounds of nitrogen per acre, the chemical equivalent of which would cost about $30. The American Indians apparently recognized the soil enriching value of legumes, for they generally planted beans in alternate rows with corn. The corn, which has a hearty appetite for nitrogen, sucks up the excess nitrogen as fast as the legumes can produce it, thereby signalling the latter to produce much more total nitrogen than if there were no intercropping. Some farmers and gardeners now use soy to yield a triple bonus: first, free fertilizer; second, high-protein beans; and finally, humus-forming organic matter when the plants are turned under in the fall as green manure. Most important, organic gardeners using natural fertilizers (manure and compost) find they can obtain soybean yields of 50 bushels or more per acre, almost twice the national average, accompanied by substantial savings from not using chemicals. And soybeans have such a hardy resistance to disease and insects, that avoiding the use of toxic pesticides often makes little or no difference in crop yields, while not using herbicides helps keep the root bacteria alive and vital.

Throughout the world, there is a movement away from the energy-expensive, environmentally damaging agricultural methods now popular in industrial countries. The fact that it often costs *ten times* as much to grow an acre of "green revolution" rice as an acre of the traditional crop is bringing this lesson home to poor farmers everywhere. Soybeans thrive in virtually any climate from tropical Brazil to Japan's snowy Hokkaido, and they are as well suited for use in small vegetable gardens as on huge farms. Due to their unique ability to nourish both the soil and human beings, they are bound to play a key role in the planet's emerging agriculture.

Soyfoods: Modern and Traditional

We in the West must learn to use soybeans directly as foods. And with soy oil now facing severe competition from low-cost Malaysian and African palm oil, with growing popular resistance to the wasteful and expensive feedlot system, and with the expanding need for low-cost protein foods in developing countries, the time is ripe for the influential American Soybean Association, the food industry, and concerned invividuals to begin to take a serious interest in developing these foods.

Advanced Western technology is already being used to manufacture a number of new fabricated soy products: protein concentrates, isolates, spun fibers, and textured vegetable proteins (TVP). The latter are now widely used as meat extenders or, in combination with numerous artificial coloring and flavoring agents, as simulated meats: sausages, bacon bits, chicken, and the like. Although these products still utilize less than 2 percent of all United States soy protein, their domestic consumption is expected to increase 10-fold from 500 million pounds in 1972 to 5 billion pounds by 1985. Yet the technology and cost required to produce such products places them out of reach of the poor in developing countries who need them most, while their synthetic qualities generally limit their appeal to the growing number of Westerners interested in natural foods.

In both the developed and developing nations, there is a growing interest in methods of production employing decentralized, small-scale technology and simple, honest craftsmanship. Mass production and heavily centralized technology have created work that is mechanical and monotonous, overcrowded cities to the point of breakdown, caused severe industrial pollution, and led in many cases to massive unemployment. Most of East Asia's soyfoods are still produced in small shops which use little energy and require a minimum of capital investment to start. Traditional miso-making is a fine example of such a craft, providing truly enjoyable work that nourishes and enlivens; a beautiful mode of self expression, self discipline, and self sufficiency. Compatible with the basic needs and aspirations of human beings, it is well suited to be a model of craftsmanship for future generations.

Deeper Causes of World Hunger

We have seen in the above discussion how soybeans offer great promise to meet great needs as a key protein source for the future on our small planet, and how each of us, by moving away from meat-centered diets that support the highly wasteful feedlot system, can take a significant first step toward alleviating world food shortages. Yet we must understand that this is only a first step. As Frances Moore Lappé says so well in *Diet for a Small Planet* (Ballantine Books, 1982, revised edition) the notion of "meatless, guiltless" can be a seductively simple escape preventing further involvement. For even if the practice of feeding basic foods to animals were abandoned altogether, there would be no automatic guarantee that the vast amounts of grains and soybeans thereby released for direct consumption would actually become available to the poor at prices they could afford. Thus, if we are really serious about bringing an end to hunger and starvation on our planet, we must make an even deeper commitment to understand the larger forces that cause hunger and to do something, each in our own way, to stop them. What *are* these forces causing hunger and what *can* we do?

Population: At the present population growth rate of 1.64 percent, the population of the planet will double every 43 years. Many of the poorer nations, with growth rates of 3 percent, double every 23 years and therefore (theoretically) increase a staggering nineteenfold every century. During the 1970s, the rate of increase began to slow, perhaps for the first time in history—a promising sign. Yet each morning 178,000 new faces appear at the breakfast table and each year there are 64 million more passengers on spaceship earth. Roughly 85 to 90 percent of all new babies are born in the have-not countries, and the fastest growing populations are the ones that are the most miserable. In 1789, the English clergyman-economist Thomas Malthus accurately foresaw our predicament: "The power of population is so superior to the power of earth to provide subsistence" that man will succumb to "gigantic inevitable famine." In his excellent book *The Twenty-Ninth Day,* Lester Brown, president of the Worldwatch Institute, shows how population growth is putting increased stresses on the earth's four major biological systems that support all life: croplands, oceanic fisheries, grasslands, and forests. In each area, as demand exceeds sustainable yield, populations begin to undercut their own well being and threaten their future survival. In economic terms, they consume principal as well as interest. Brown urges governments to make a multi-pronged attack on the population problem by making family planning services universally available, liberating women from traditional roles, meeting basic social needs such as health care, nutrition, and illiteracy that are usually associated with reduced fertility, educating people about the consequences of rapid population. Brown points out that governments such as China and Singapore that have moved on all these fronts at once have been extremely successful in slowing population growth. And, of course, each of us can make a vital contribution to population control by limiting our own family size to two children or less.

Many citizens in the affluent nations tend to think of the population problem as being confined primarily to developing countries where the increase in human numbers is the highest. Yet in terms of resource consumption and pollution, the problem is actually *more* severe in the industrial nations with slower populations growth. Twenty-five percent of the passengers on spaceship earth traveling in the first class and tourist compartments consume 80 percent of the yearly supply of food, energy, and mineral resources, while contributing 75 percent of the pollution. The remaining 75 percent of the passengers traveling in the hold without adequate food, water, or shelter are beginning to get upset. It should be clear, then, that as a precondition to helping the third-class passengers, those traveling in the luxurious quarters should take all possible measures to bring their own population growth to zero while sharply limiting their consumption and waste.

While virtually all experts agree that every effort must be made on every level by almost every country to reach zero population growth as soon as possible, not all agree that high birth rate is a primary cause of hunger. In their brilliant and pioneering work, *Food First* (Ballantine Books, 1979), Frances Moore Lappé and Joseph Collins make a strong case that both hunger and population growth, rather than being causes, are symptoms of the same deeper disease—the insecurity and poverty of the majority resulting from the control over national productive resources by a small and wealthy power elite. High birth rates are seen as symptomatic of the failures of a social system, reflecting people's need to have many children in an attempt to provide laborers to increase their meager family income, to provide old-age food security, and to compensate for the high infant death rate, the result of inadequate nutrition and health care. Thus parents who are in a tragic double bind—acting quite rationally in having large families yet knowing full well they may not be able to feed them— often have no interest in birth control programs. As Lappé and Collins point out: "To attack high birth rates without attacking the causes of poverty that make large families the only survival option is not only fruitless, it is a tragic diversion our planet simply cannot afford."

Affluence: We have seen above how people (including the upper classes in less developed countries), as they become more affluent, tend to increase their consumption of foods derived from animals. In 1979, to produce these products, roughly 35 percent of the world's grain harvest (including 79 percent of the U.S. grain harvest) was fed to livestock, yet could have been used as human food. Thus while population growth accounts for about two-thirds of the annual growth in world food demand, this affluent pattern of feeding livestock grain and soy via the feedlot system accounts for the remaining one-third.

Narrow Focus on Increasing Productivity: The standard analysis that hunger is a result of food scarcity has inevitably led to programs to increase food production, generally through technological modernization. Yet when new agricultural technology enters a system based on severe economic and power disparities, it selectively benefits the rich and powerful, who have the money, land, intelligence, credit worthiness, and political influence to take fullest advantages of the new opportunities. In the end, the rich get richer and the poor poorer. A major study by the International Labor Organization (confirmed in a similar study by the United Nations Institute for Social Development) documents that in seven South Asian countries comprising 70 percent of the rural population of the nonsocialist world, while there has been a rise in per capita grain production, the food consumption of the rural poor is less than it was ten to twenty years ago; more people are more hungry and poorer than ever before. In many cases the so-called Green Revolution, expected to abolish hunger, has actually made it worse. Farm mechanization has left large numbers of farm workers without jobs and the high cost of the "inputs" necessary to grow the special new hybrid seeds—inputs such as irrigation, chemical fertilizers and pesticides, farm machinery, and the seeds themselves—have caused small farmers to go bankrupt or forced them to sell their farms to the landed elite. Not only are the poor left without a source of income, the large landowners often move the land out of basic food production and start to grow export cash crops such as grapes for wine or even flowers, which greatly increase per-acre profits.

International Food Exploitation: Large agribusiness corporations from the industrialized countries have recently begun to buy up huge quantities of basic foods from the less developed countries to sell in supermarkets at home. They have turned the planet into a Global Farm to supply a Global Supermarket, where the poor must compete with affluent foreigners for food grown in their own countries. By 1976 over 50 percent of the winter and early spring fruits and vegetables sold in U.S. supermarkets were grown in Latin America on land formerly used to feed local people. This system also puts U.S. farm workers out of work.

Land Monopolization and Misuse: In many less developed countries a small and wealthy percentage of the population owns most of the land. Based on a study of 83 developing countries, slightly more than 3 percent of all landowners controlled almost 80 percent of the farmland. The landed elite prevent land reform and redistribution by using their great political power. Yet where land redistribution has taken place, farmers who own their land are found to produce two to three times as much food per acre as tenant farmers and sharecroppers, who have no incentive to make long-term agricultural improvements on the land. All efforts must be made to give farmers control over their own land and to remove the obstacles that prevent them from growing the food they need.

Cash Crop System of Export Agriculture: The finest land in less developed countries is now widely used to grow export cash crops (coffee, sugar, cocoa, bananas, etc.) instead of growing food for the people. This system generally benefits the rich, while the poor go hungry. Clearly, agriculture must become, first and foremost, a way for people to produce the food they need and only secondly a source of foreign exchange.

An in-depth discussion of each of these problems and their complex interrelationships is given in *Food First.* Read this book! Called "One of the most stimulating books in years" by the *New York Times Book Review,* it has been highly praised by the emerging American hunger movement and by Third World leaders alike as offering a penetrating new perspective and dispelling traditional myths that prevent us from grasping how hunger is generated. While challenging the basic assumption that the main causes of hunger are too many people and not enough food, the authors show that hunger exists in the face of plenty and is caused primarily by social, economic, and political structures that block development and prevent people from democratically controlling the resources that would allow them to produce their own food. An important part of our work is to see that our own government stops its support of foreign elites and their partners, multinational corporations, that increasingly represent primary causes of the problem, then commits itself, as we each must commit ourselves, to putting an end to worldwide hunger and starvation at the same time that we put an end to the proliferation of nuclear weapons, nuclear power, and deadly environmental chemicals. Our work is cut out for us, and it will not be short or easy. But what joy in such a great and noble challenge.

Going Beyond Ourselves

An ancient Chinese proverb reminds us that "A time of crisis is a time of great opportunity." Outmoded lifestyles and patterns of thought are beginning to crack under the strain of change so rapid it borders on discontinuity, and overlapping crises are forcing us to totally re-evaluate the very basis of our being. At the still point within us all a new vision of reality, richly detailed yet strikingly simple, is beginning to take form. In part it is the holistic and contemporary view of ecology, mother of all the sciences, that sees the perfect interconnectedness of all things, the jewelled matrix form-and-energy body of the world. In part it is the holy and ancient understanding of the spiritual paths that points to an underlying oneness in which the impossible union of opposites is made real. Our expanding vision must inevitably be a call to action, and it is abundantly clear that nothing less than selfless service and loving kindness—which accord with the truth of our oneness—are suited to the immense task we face. The child wasting in the forgotten village is our child; thus do we realize that we are all brothers and sisters. We must bring food. Watch in the years to come how selflessly soybeans offer themselves to help us feed a hungry world.

2
Miso as a Food

ALTHOUGH SOYBEANS are a treasure trove of high-quality protein and other nutrients, only a portion of these are available to the body when the whole beans are served in their baked, boiled, or roasted forms. However through the process of natural fermentation, soybeans undergo a total biochemical transformation in which virtually all of their complex protein, carbohydrate, and lipid (oil or fat) molecules are broken down into readily digestible amino acids, simple sugars, and fatty acids. Most important, the process of leisurely fermentation unfolds a panorama of delicious new flavors and aromas.

Rich in High-quality Protein

The 21 amino acids which constitute all protein are the building blocks of the body: in children and adolescents they are essential for providing new tissue for growth, while in adults they supply the material for routine body maintenance. Eight (or occasionally ten) of these amino acids are termed "essential" because if they are available from the food a person eats, the body can manufacture the others. Because soybeans—and miso contain the eight essential amino acids, they are known as sources of "complete protein."

The protein value of a food depends on both the quantity and quality of the protein in that food: Miso is unusually high in both.

Protein *quantity* is a measure of the percentage by weight of the protein actually present in a food. The average of all miso varieties is about 12 to 13 percent, and certain types (such as Hatcho) containing a large percentage of soybeans exceed 20 percent. These figures compare very favorably with common Western protein sources such as chicken (21%), beef or cottage cheese (20%), hamburger or eggs (13%), and whole dairy milk (3%).

Protein *quality* is a measure of the percentage of pro-

tein in a food that can actually be utilized by the body. Usually expressed in terms of Net Protein Utilization (NPU), it depends primarily on the configuration of essential amino acids in the food and on the food's digestibility. It is now becoming widely recognized that there is no fundamental difference between animal and vegetable protein: it is simply a question of degree. All foods, animal and vegetable, can be ranked on a simple scale which shows their protein quality or NPU. Generally speaking, animal foods have relatively high NPU ratings. Eggs, for example, with an NPU of 94, have the highest quality protein of any known food. This means that of the 13 grams of protein present in 100 grams of eggs, 94 percent (12.2 grams) can actually be utilized by the body. Other animal foods with high NPU ratings are milk (82), fish (80), cottage cheese (75), cheeses (70), beef and hamburger (67), and chicken (65). But a number of plant foods are also high on the scale. Rice, with an NPU of 70, contains the highest quality protein of any basic plant food. Soybeans (NPU = 61) and barley (NPU = 60) are also both relatively high. Miso, however, has NPU ratings of up to 72, *higher than any of its constituent ingredients!* This is largely because in the production of miso, rice (or barley) and soybeans are *combined*. Due to the fact that soy and grain proteins *complement* each other, the NPU of the resultant combination is higher than that of either of the individual foods, and the final product contains all of the eight essential (plus nine non-essential) amino acids in a configuration which is highly utilizable by the human body (fig. 4). Moreover, the process of fermen-

Fig. 4. Amounts of Essential Amino Acids and Their Percentages of Minimum Daily Requirements in 100 Grams of Miso (Source: *Japanese Scientific Research Council*)

Amino Acids	MDR (gm)	Red (Rice) Miso (gm)	MDR (%)	Barley Miso (gm)	Hatcho (Soybean) Miso (gm)
(Methionine-Cystine)	1.10	.29	26	.27	.45
Lysine	.80	.57	71	.65	1.36
Tryptophan	.25	.19	76	.16	.33
(Phenylalaline-Tyrosine)	1.10	1.09	99	1.23	2.10
Valine	.80	.80	100	.79	1.21
Methionine	.20	.20	100	.17	.25
Leucine	1.10	1.37	125	1.28	1.68
Isoleucine	.70	.92	131	.94	1.18
Threonine	.50	.71	142	.74	1.03
Phenylaline	.30	.57	190	.63	1.25
Protein	61.5	13.5	22	12.8	21.0

Note: Amino acids in shortest supply are listed first. Those in parentheses are important combinations of essential and semi-essential amino acids with common properties. Thus 100 grams (5½ tablespoons) of red miso (13.5% protein) contains .29 grams of the sulfur-containing amino acids (methionine-cystine), or 26 percent of the minimum adult daily requirement of 1.10 grams.

tation renders each of the basic component foods more digestible and, therefore, increases their individual NPUs. Because red miso, the most common variety (made with rice and soybeans), contains 13.5 percent protein and has an NPU of 72, one hundred grams of this product can supply us with 9.7 grams of usable protein—more than from an equal weight of hamburger (13% protein; NPU = 67).

Miso has long been a key source of protein in the Japanese diet. It presently accounts for up to 25 percent of the protein consumed in some inland rural areas and more than 8 percent for the population as a whole. The average Japanese enjoys about 16 pounds of miso each year, or about 19 grams (3½ teaspoonsful) per day.

A Powerful Protein Booster

We saw above how the combination of two foods whose proteins are complementary—such as soybeans and grains—can lead to an increase in NPU and therefore create extra usable protein at no extra cost. Yet miso *itself* is also ideal for use in combining proteins. Because it contains an abundance of precisely the amino acids lacking in other basic foods (especially wheat, corn, sesame, and even rice), the addition of as little as several teaspoons of miso to preparations containing these foods can result in large increases in usable protein. Thus miso is not only a good source of pro-

tein, but also a protein booster. Herein lies one of its basic advantages over salt as a daily seasoning.

Miso has long been considered an important nutritional complement to rice in East Asia's grain-based diet. Similarly, the use of miso with whole-wheat bread in the form of a spread, for example, or with noodles, pizza, bulgur, or other Western-style grain dishes, can increase the sum of the protein available by as much as 30 to 40 percent.

Aids Digestion and Assimilation

Miso is prized for its ability to aid in the digestion and assimilation of other foods. At least four digestive agents are contained in all non-pasteurized miso: natural digestive enzymes, lactic acid-producing baceris (*Lactobacillus* and *Pediococcus* species), salt-resistant yeasts, and the mold and other microorganisms present in koji. Only the very heartiest microorganisms are able to survive the rigors of several years' fermentation in the presence of salt. Thus they and their enzymes are well suited to continue their work in the large and small intestines where they break down or digest complex proteins, carbohydrates, and fats into simpler, more easily assimilable molecules. In Japan, commercially available digestive enzymes are often made from the same type of koji used to make miso.

Pasteurization of miso, however, destroys most of the beneficial, digestion-aiding lactic-acid forming bacteria and their enzymes, while also decreasing some of miso's natural flavor and aroma. Most of the miso (except most Hatcho miso and a few natural imports) sold in sealed plastic bags has been pasteurized to stop the natural fermentation and its production of carbon dioxide, which would cause the bag to swell and eventually burst. Most miso sold in small plastic cottage-cheese style tubs with a pop-off lid or in bulk is *not* pasteurized. In each case, check the label to be sure . . . if you care.

Lactic acid bacteria play the key role in making both yogurt and miso aids to digestion. Studies in the early 1900s by Metchnikoff and many recent studies by Japanese scientists have suggested that either the beneficial effects of the lactic acid bacteria in aiding digestion or the effect of the lactic acid they produce in altering the pH in the intestines may be a basic cause for the association of yogurt with long life and good health. It is well known that the use of penicillin or other antibiotics kills the beneficial microflora that ordinarily live in the human digestive tract. A quick, easy, and healthful way to replenish them after use of antibiotics is by drinking a cup of miso soup.

The process of lengthy aging in cedar vats—in effect, "external" digestive systems—breaks down 80 to 90 percent of miso's basic nutrients into their simpler forms. When the human system tries to do the same job (in a much shorter time) it is not as successful: roasted soybeans are only 60 percent digestible and whole boiled soybeans 68 percent. By eating miso, the body's energy ordinarily needed to digest soybeans is freed to work on other foods. The fermentation process also serves to eliminate the factors in whole

Fig. 5. Composition of Nutrients in 100 grams of Miso*

Sources: Standard Composition of Japanese Foods (Norinsho 1964; JDAC 1964), the Japanese National Miso Association Nutrient Tables, and Data Supplied by Miso Producers.

Type of Miso	Food Energy	Moisture	Protein	Fat	Carbo-hydrates (incl. fiber)	Fiber	Ash	Sodium Chloride	Calcium	Sodium	Phosphorous	Iron	Vit. B₁ (Thiamine)	Vit. B₂ (Riboflavin)	Vit. B₃ (Niacin)
	Calories	Percent	Percent	Percent	Percent	Percent	Percent	Percent	Mg	Mg	Mg	Mg	Mg	Mg	Mg
Red Miso	153	50	13.5	5.8	19.1	1.9	14.8	13.0	115	4600	190	4.0	0.03	0.10	1.5
Light-yellow Miso	155	49	13.5	4.6	19.6	1.8	12.8	12.5	90	4100	160	4.0	0.03	0.10	1.5
Mellow Red Miso	162	42	11.2	4.2	27.9	1.3	14.5	13.0	81	3200	135	3.5	0.04	0.10	1.5
Mellow Beige Miso	165	44	13.0	4.2	29.1	1.2	8.5	7.0	80	2500	133	3.5	0.04	0.10	1.5
Mellow White Miso	215	57	12.3	1.4	27.5	1.3	4.9	9.1	31	3200	138	1.3	0.03	0.10	1.5
Sweet Red Miso	168	46	12.7	4.0	31.7	1.4	8.1	6.0	75	2100	134	3.0	0.03	0.08	3.0
Sweet White Miso	178	47	11.1	1.9	35.9	1.0	7.5	5.5	70	2100	120	4.0	0.04	0.10	1.5
Barley Miso	154	48	12.8	5.0	21.0	1.9	14.9	13.0	116	4600	190	3.5	0.04	0.10	1.5
Mellow Barley Miso	160	46	11.1	5.0	29.8	1.3	14.6	10.0	86	3500	139	3.6	0.04	0.10	1.5
Hatcho Miso	224	40	21.0	10.2	12.0	1.8	16.8	10.6	154	4100	264	7.1	0.04	0.13	1.3
Soybean Miso	180	48	19.4	6.9	13.2	2.2	13.0	11.2	140	3800	240	6.5	0.04	0.12	1.2
Tamari Miso	160	61	16.3	5.7	11.4	1.6	11.7	9.8	138	3600	220	6.3	0.04	0.11	1.1
Kinzanji Miso	172	58	11.3	2.0	30.1	2.1	5.1	8.0	95	2800	131	3.5	0.04	0.10	1.5
Peanut Miso	432	17	16.1	27.6	37.1	1.3	4.8	7.0	80	3100	180	5.6	0.04	0.10	1.3
Akadashi Miso	169	44	16.0	4.1	31.9	1.4	10.8	8.0	75	2800	135	3.6	0.05	0.10	1.4
Dehydrated Miso	303	5	32.2	9.0	35.8	3.6	26.6	18.5	180	7500	320	8.0	0.05	0.15	2.0
Low-salt/High-protein Miso	140	53	17.6	6.4	24.0	1.9	13.1	6.3	112	4600	180	4.0	0.03	0.11	1.6

Note: Values for each product vary widely depending on the maker; many of those listed are averages. The Standard Tables of Food Composition contain detailed data for red, light-yellow, sweet white, soybean, and dehydrated varieties. The Miso Association tables contain moisture, protein, fat, carbohydrate, and ash data for barley, mellow barley, mellow red and beige, and sweet red. Hatcho, peanut, and mellow white data were obtained from the makers. All other figures were derived by inter-polation.

soybeans that may cause flatulence, and to inactivate trypsin inhibitors, substances found in all fresh and uncooked dried soybeans which prevent the full utilization of soy nutrients by the body.

Adds Flavor to Low-Salt Diets

A growing number of Western doctors and nutritionists are coming to favor a relatively low-salt diet as one of the simplest ways of combatting high blood pressure, hypertension and, in some cases, obesity. Most people use salt to accentuate the flavors inherent in foods. But, because miso, which contains an average of only 12 percent salt, has its own rich flavor, it can actually impart all of the desired taste and aroma with the addition of considerably *less* salt than would ordinarily be used if the food were seasoned with salt alone.

In our ongoing study of American eating patterns, we have noticed repeatedly that Americans tend to be extremists. For example, they consume either a high-salt diet or a salt-free or low-salt diet. Yet common sense and an abundance of scientific evidence show that *moderation* in the use of salt (as of many other ingredients and nutrients) is the healthiest way. Mankind's traditional diet based on grains and vegetables, when prepared with little or no added salt is simply too bland to be enjoyed day after day. Equally important is the *quality* of the salt we use. Natural sea salt supplies us with an abundance of trace elements (micronutrients) so essential for good health and metabolic balance. Moreover, recent experiments suggest that the fermentation process actually changes the effect of salt on the human body: rats have been shown to be able to tolerate a considerably higher salt intake in the form of miso than in the form of table salt. The Japanese, who may have developed an intuitive understanding of these phenomena during their long contact with fermented soybean seasonings, now obtain less than 10 percent of their total salt intake from table salt; miso supplies 20 percent, shoyu 30 percent, and *tsukemono* (salt-pickled vegetables) 40 percent.

People on a very low salt diet might consume 1 tablespoon per day of red, barley, or Hatcho miso (the equivalent of ½ teaspoon salt): an average intake is 4 tablespoons (equivalent to 2 teaspoons salt). Low-salt/high-protein miso (p. 44) lends itself particularly well to salt-restricted diets.

Miso's salinity is four times that of sea water, but because the salt is mellowed by the presence of amino acids and natural oils, miso does not taste particularly salty. And if the salt is removed, what remains tastes remarkably sweet.

A Key to Low-fat Cookery

Miso contains an average of 5 percent natural oils—mostly unsaturated and completely free of cholesterol. These give miso its savory flavor and aroma. And because they are primarily soy oils, unrefined and unprocessed, they are rich in lecithin and linoleic acid which help disperse accumulations of cholesterol and other fatty acids in the circulatory system.

In the West, our total intake of fats (a high proportion of them saturated) is about three times that of Japan. The fact that the Japanese have fewer problems with heart disease, high blood pressure, arterio- and atherosclerosis, and overweight than people in any other part of the world has often been attributed to their low consumption of fats. One of the keys to this low-fat cookery lies in the use of miso (and shoyu) in place of salt. Since we in the West generally use salt as our basic seasoning, we tend to also use fairly large amounts of oil or butter—as in dressings, sauces, or sautéed dishes—to soften the salt's intrinsic sharpness. Yet miso's saltiness is mellowed by the natural (unsaturated) oils and amino acids already present in it, and by the slow process of fermentation. Thus miso can be used in place of salt to prepare a host of delicious Western-style dishes—ranging from miso French dressings to savory white sauces—each using less than one-half the amount of fats called for in standard recipes.

An Excellent Seasoning for Weight-watchers

A welcome addition to the diet of weight watchers, miso has one of the highest known ratios of protein to calories found in any natural food: a typical portion (1 tablespoon) contains a total of only 27 calories or as little as 11 calories per gram of protein. By comparison, brown rice contains 45, bread 34, and eggs 12 calories per gram of protein. Stated slightly differently, a 100-gram portion of red miso (containing 150 calories) will fulfill 30 percent of the daily male adult protein requirement while costing only 5 percent of the typical calorie allotment. And we saw above how using miso in place of salt can help to reduce fat intake; this is an additional aid in helping us watch our weight, since the reduction of only 1 tablespoon of oil from a dish means a decrease of some 153 calories.

While carbohydrates are a food's main source of "fattening" calories, those same calories also provide us with energy. As a result of the process of fermentation, miso's carbohydrates are largely in the form of simple, easily digestible sugars and contain relatively little fiber or cellulose. Thus miso can serve as a concentrated source of stamina.

A Vegetarian Source of Essential Vitamin B-12

B-12 is one of the vitamins most commonly deficient in the diets of those vegetarians who exclude dairy products as well as meat from their diet. Until as recently as 1977, many nutritionists believed that *only* foods of animal origin contained vitamin B-12, the most concentrated sources being beef liver, tuna, eggs, and Swiss cheese. Recent research, however, has shown that there are a number of excellent vegetarian sources of vitamin B-12 including fermented soyfoods (tempeh, natto, miso, and shoyu), sea vegetables, and some single-cell proteins. By far the best soyfood source is *tempeh* (see our *Book of Tempeh*,

Harper & Row, 1979); a typical 100-gram (3½-ounce) serving of tempeh sold in the U.S. contains from 3.9 to 8.8 micrograms of vitamin B-12. Since the official U.S. recommended daily allowance (RDA) of B-12 for adults is 3 micro grams (National Academy of Sciences, 1980) one serving the tempeh can provide 130 to 294 percent of the RDA. A study in Japanese by Dr. Jusaku Takahashi in 1955 showed that light-yellow miso contained 0.17 micrograms of vitamin B-12 per 100 grams, or 2.8 percent of the RDA. A typical serving of 1 tablespoon (18 gm) of this miso would provide 0.5 percent of the RDA.

In each of the above foods, vitamin B-12 is produced by certain bacteria or molds, as it is in the rumen of livestock from which most people who are not complete vegetarians obtain their daily allotment in the form of meat or dairy products. It is important to note that many nutritionists feel that the U.S. RDA for vitamin B-12 of 3 micrograms per day is too high. The corresponding figure set by the prestigious United Nations Food and Agricultural Organization is 2 micrograms. An intake of 0.6 to 1.2 micrograms per day is generally considered sufficient for normal blood formation and good health but it will not replenish liver stores if they are depleted. We must also recall that, for centuries, Japanese Buddhist monks, who consume no foods of animal origin but obtain their vitamin B-12 from miso, natto, shoyu, and sea vegetables, have been renowned for their good health, vigor, and longevity.

Low in Phytic Acid

Raw soybeans (like most cereal grains) contain a relatively large amount (1.4 percent on a dry basis) of phytic acid, the principal source of the phosphorus in most seeds. Phytic acid and its phytate salts can have adverse nutritional effects because of its ability to chelate or bind various important minerals (especially calcium, zinc, and iron), reducing their availability to the body and thereby leading to possible nutritional deficiencies in humans and other nonruminants. Fortunately cooking the soybeans destroys some (14 percent) of the phytic acid, and the phytase enzymes, produced by the *Aspergillus* mold during the fermentation, break down much (35 percent) of the rest of the phytic acid into inositol and phosphorus, both useful nutrients. The result is that the miso's nutritional value is doubly enhanced (Wang et al. 1980; Cheryan 1980).

May Protect from Cancer

In September 1981 the *Asahi Shimbun*, Japan's equivalent of *The New York Times*, published a front page story entitled "Unexpected Virtue of Miso Soup: It lowers the Death Rate from Cancer, Heart Disease, and Liver Disease." The article was based on a major study conducted on 265,000 people over a period of 13 years by Dr. Hirayama and the prestigious and impartial National Cancer Center. The study showed that Japanese who drink miso soup every day have 32 to 33 percent less stomach cancer

mortality than those who do not drink it at all (the most likely group to develop stomach cancer) and 8 to 18 percent less than those who drink it "sometimes" (*Asahi Shimbun* 1981; see also English translation, Shurtleff 1982). MacDonald and Deuck (1976) similarly found that shoyu apparently protects rats from stomach cancer.

Promotes Long Life and Good Health

In the following sections we will introduce a number of personal and cultural testimonies from Japan concerning the health-promoting value of miso. Because most of these lack scientific verification they should not be accepted uncritically, yet they may provide promising leads for further scientific investigation.

Although the Japanese are well aware that miso is an excellent source of essential nutrients, they prize it even more for properties which are not easily defined or measured, but which are believed to promote good health and long life. After centuries of experimentation using intuitive and systematic methods based on a holistic view of life, people have found that eating miso together with a diet low in animal foods is an effective way to improve one's physical constitution and internal environment.

In his delightful and remarkably comprehensive *We Japanese*, written in 1937, Mr. Atsuharu Sakai begins his chapter on miso by saying: "It is generally believed in Japan that miso (bean paste) is responsible in great measure for the generally sound physical health of the Japanese." In recent years, scientific studies have been conducted in order to isolate the causes of longevity in Japanese communities where many of the inhabitants live to be over one hundred. One finding that has received considerable publicity concerns the high correlation between long life and the regular consumption of miso—most of which is homemade and served in soups. One well-known researcher, Dr. Akitani Kondo, found a village near Mount Fuji where the people drank an average of six bowls of miso soup daily; the per capita miso consumption was 200 grams, a national record! When we visited a "long-life" village located deep in the mountains west of Tokyo and asked a number of the villagers what they felt were the secrets of health and long life, the most frequent responses were: hard work in the fields, clean mountain air, a diet of grains and vegetables—and plenty of miso soup. (It is interesting to note that the centenarians living in the Balkans and Eastern Europe give almost the same advice except that they recommend another fermented food: yogurt.)

Recent Western laboratory experiments offer scientific explanations for the fact that traditional Oriental cultures have shown such a strong resistance to disease. Of the 161 strains of aerobic bacteria isolated in miso, almost all have been found to be antagonistic to *Escherichia coli* and *Staphylococcus aureus*—two organisms responsible for food poisoning. And specific miso bacteria are thought, by analogy, to be useful as controllers of disease-causing agents. In 1972, Drs. H. L. Wang and C. W. Hesseltine of the Northern Regional Research Center of the U.S. Department of Agriculture (p. 259) demonstrated that the molds of tempeh, shoyu, and wine-fermented tofu (doufu-ru), each fermented soybean products, inhibited the growth of harmful bacterial cultures. Yokotsuka and others in Japan have likewise shown that the compounds produced by the miso mold, *Aspergillus oryzae*, also have antibacterial activity.

Countless laboratory tests have checked for the existence of mycotoxins and especially aflatoxins (toxins caused by harmful molds) in miso. None have been found (Manabe and Matsuura 1968; Matsuura 1970; Manabe et al. 1972; Wang and Hesseltine 1979). Likewise the extremely low levels of nitrosamines in miso and shoyu (generally less than 1 part per billion) are of no conern (Nagahori 1980). For more on aflatoxins and nitrosamines, see Appendix A.

The Perfect (Alkaline) Coffee Substitute

We consider a morning cup of miso soup to be the perfect coffee substitute. Coffee hits the nervous system with a jolt of acidic caffeine (often amplified in effect by white sugar) that snaps open droopy eyes and provides a quick shot of speedy energy, followed, unfortunately, by a depressing drop in energy and further sleepiness that requires more coffee to stave it off. Miso soup, on the other hand, as well as being a source of abundant nutrients, wakes up the nervous system gently yet effectively by alkalizing the blood stream, then providing a steady flow of energy throughout the morning. We have many friends who have kicked the coffee habit with miso soup and discovered how great it feels to be *really* awake.

Throughout East Asia, miso's alkalizing (and cleansing) effect are considered to be extremely important in the development of an alkaline constitution, which is widely believed to promote resistance to disease. In standard East Asian nutritional sourcebooks, basic foods are categorized as either alkaline or acidic. This information is common knowledge throughout the culture since it is considered one of the basic principles of maintaining good health. Most of the foods which we moderns consider special treats (sweets, alcohol, meat) are listed as acidic; taken in excess, they are said to weaken the constitution. With the consumption of sugar and liquor climbing to dangerously high levels in many affluent nations, the use of alkaline miso could at least provide a counterbalance until better eating patterns are resumed; thereafter, it could be used to promote good health.

A well-known Japanese proverb states that a bowl of miso soup each day keeps the doctor away, and traditional folk wisdom abounds with sayings about the value of miso as a medicine used to cure colds, improve metabolism, clear the skin, and help develop resistance to parasitic diseases. Miso soup is often used quite specifically in the same way Westerners use Alka-Seltzer or milk of magnesia to settle an upset stomach, ameliorate a hangover, or get rid of acid indigestion.

May Prevent Radiation Sickness

In recent years, Japanese doctors and scientists have begun to consider the possibility that miso may also be an effective agent in preventing radiation sickness. Interest in this subject was stimulated by a book called *Physical Constitution and Food* written in 1965 by Dr. Shinichiro Akizuki, director of the Saint Francis Hospital in Nagasaki. Born with a congenitally weak constitution, Dr. Akizuki has devoted his career to researching the use of food as preventive medicine, placing special emphasis on a holistic (rather than symptomatic) approach to healing, and on traditional natural foods native to Japan. Throughout his intensive experimentation and research—which included the study of Japanese folk medicine, "long life" villages, and modern nutritional science—he continually applied the findings to his own life in an attempt to develop a strong physical constitution or *taishitsu*. This latter concept, which in Japanese means literally "the quality of the body" and has a somewhat deeper meaning than its English equivalent, soon became the key to his work. As miso soup and brown rice became the central foods in his diet, he experienced a steady rejuvenation accompanied by physical strength, vigor, and resistance to disease. Soon not only his family but also his entire hospital staff and patients were including miso soup and brown rice in their daily meals. A lengthy and detailed examination of the results led him to write:

> I feel that miso soup is the most essential part of a person's diet ...I have found that, with very few exceptions, families which make a practice of serving miso soup daily are almost never sick ... By enjoying miso soup each day, your constitution will gradually improve and you will develop resistance to disease. I believe that miso belongs to the highest class of medicines, those which help prevent disease and strengthen the body through continued usage... Some people speak of miso as a condiment, but miso brings out the flavor and nutritional value in all foods and helps the body to digest and assimilate whatever we eat... I use and have deep respect for modern medicines such as antibiotics and modern surgical techniques, yet they must only be employed when absolutely necessary. Of prime importance is the development of a strong constitution through proper eating. The basic condition of a person's constitution determines whether or not he will be only mildly and temporarily affected by diseases, or be seriously and chronically affected.

In 1945, when the atomic bomb fell on Nagasaki, Dr. Akizuki's hospital—located only one mile from the epicenter of the blast—was left in ruins. Fortunately, he and his nurses and co-workers were not in the building and were uninjured. Throughout the following two years, though, Dr. Akizuki and his staff worked daily in prolonged close contact with fallout victims in areas of Nagasaki which were heavily damaged and highly radioactive. Nevertheless, neither he nor his associates suffered from the usual and expected effects of radiation. Dr. Akizuki was extremely interested in this phenomenon, which he hypothesized may well have been due to the fact that he and his staff had been drinking miso soup regularly. But he felt that only a thorough scientific study of the phenomenon could provide the full answer.

In 1972, a number of Japanese scientists, including Dr. Morishita Keiichi (p. 256) doing agricultural research stimulated by Dr. Akizuki's writings, discovered that miso contained dipicolinic acid (*zybicolin* in Japanese). Produced by miso and natto yeasts, it is an alkaloid which chelates (grabs onto) heavy metals such as radioactive strontium and discharges them from the body. The discovery received front-page coverage in Japan's major newspapers.

In 1978, we received the following letter from a woman in America:

> My mother just underwent six weeks of radiation treatments for cancer. The doctors told me she would be very ill and uncomfortable from the aftereffects of the radiation. I gave her miso soup and other miso recipes and she experienced almost no aftereffects. The doctors couldn't believe it. When I told them about the miso they laughed it off—but I'm convinced.

We feel that phenomena such as this deserve careful study by doctors in America, a country where over 25 percent of the population now dies of cancer.

Neutralizes the Effects of Smoking and Air Pollution

There is a traditional saying in Japan that smokers should drink miso soup, and some authorities contend that the amino acids contained in miso are effective in neutralizing the harmful influences of tobacco and in eliminating them from the bloodstream. In her book *Miso Cookery*, Tatsumi Hamako relates the following story:

> Since I was a little girl, my grandmother emphasized repeatedly that each morning's miso soup and pickles should be carefully and tastefully prepared, especially if they were to be served to someone who smokes. She said that miso is a solvent for nicotine and helped to carry it out of the body.
>
> One day she placed 2 or 3 drops of miso soup in the small, ½-inch-deep metal bowl of a clogged, long-stemmed Japanese pipe (*kiseru*). She held the metal bowl over a charcoal fire until we could hear the sound of the miso soup simmering. After about one minute, all of the liquid had evaporated and only the nicotine which had dissolved in the miso soup was left in the bowl. This condensed into a small pellet and suddenly jumped out. When we placed the pipe to our lips, we found that it now drew freely and easily. But at other times, when we tried using water or *bancha* tea in place of miso soup to clear the congested pipe, the nicotine refused to dissolve. Even if we blew vigorously on the pipe, we could not clear it. I realized that what grandmother had been saying was true.

A kiseru

It is said to be common knowledge among Japanese traffic policemen that the consumption of miso soup each day ameliorates the effects on the body of auto exhaust pollutants. Even today, in many areas where the police department provides communal lunches, a conscientious effort is made to include miso soup.

So if you have to smoke or breathe polluted air, at least protect yourself by drinking miso soup too.

A Seasoning of Unlimited Versatility

Even if there were only one variety of miso, its uses would invite endless experimentation. Yet each of the many miso varieties has its own unique flavor and aroma, color and texture, and each can lend the crowning touch to a wide variety of your favorite Western-style and Oriental dishes. The more than 400 recipes in the following pages give only an inkling of the many possibilities.

In a vegetarian diet, often characterized by the simple, light flavors of grains, land and sea vegetables, and soyfoods, miso has long served to add depth of flavor and savory richness.

A Traditional Natural Food

Capable of being stored without refrigeration, even in semitropical climates, miso is a traditional, natural food. Many commercial varieties are still prepared in small-scale shops using traditional technologies and without chemical additives.

An Inexpensive Delicacy

Miso is a remarkably inexpensive food, even in the West where prices of the best imported varieties are of necessity higher than they are in Japan. The per capita cost of a month's supply of top-quality miso (1½ tablespoons per day) in San Francisco, Boston, or New York need not exceed a few dollars (fig. 13, p. 48). And if the miso is prepared at home using ingredients now readily available throughout the United States, it will cost only a fraction as much.

A Key to the Vegetarian Transition

Polls taken in 1980 show that there are ten million people in the United States who eat no meat, and that the number is rapidly increasing. Recently, doctors and nutritionists have joined the bandwagon. Their arguments:

1. **Physiology**: Man's digestive system, like that of the anthropoid apes, is fundamentally different from that of carnivores. The latter have very short bowels (3 times the body's length) for rapid expulsion of putrefying meat, stomachs with ten times as much hydrochloric acid as non-carnivores for processing saturated fats and cholesterol, and sharp elongated canines for tearing flesh. Man, however, has a long bowel (12 times the body's length) ideal for the slow diges-

tion of plant foods; his dental structure is that of a strictly herbivorous animal with molars designed for grinding grains and nuts and his incisors for slicing vegetables and fruits.

2. **Heart Disease**: Over 54 percent of all deaths in the United States are caused by cardiovascular illnesses which are practically unknown in societies where meat consumption is low. About 40 percent of the fat in our diet comes from meat, and 40 percent of this is the saturated, cholesterol-producing type. A recent study of Seventh Day Adventist vegetarians

Fig. 6. Intestinal Cancer vs. Meat Consumption Among Females (*Sources: Scientific American, Nov. 1975*)

showed that they had only 40 percent the incidence of heart disease as the general population, and those that ate neither eggs nor dairy products had only 23 percent. Heart specialists estimate that if we were to reduce our saturated fat intake by 35 to 50 percent, our heart attack rate could be cut in half.

3. **Cancer**: The graph (Fig. 6) reprinted from the prestigious *Scientific American* magazine, shows the striking relationship between cancer of the large intestine and meat consumption among women in 23 countries; the writers explain that "an alternative explanation attributes cancer . . . to a low consumption of cereals. The two hypotheses are hard to distinguish from each other because high meat consumption and low cereal consumption tend to go together." Large studies of Mormons (who characteristically eat little meat) show an incidence of cancer 50 percent below the norm.

4. **Longevity**: Repeated studies by anthropologists throughout the world show that vegetarians live longer and are generally healthier than meat eaters. The long-lived Hunzas are almost total vegetarians.

5. **Arthritis**: Widely recommended dietary cures for this painful ailment call for strict avoidance of meat.

6. **Obesity**: Vegetarians in America are 20 pounds below the national average weight, while those following a standard meat-centered diet are 12 to 15 pounds above their ideal weight. Obesity is now considered a major cause of heart disease and many other illnesses.

7. **Stamina**: Numerous studies of athletes show that vegetarians have much more stamina than meat eaters, are able to perform endurance tests several times longer before exhaustion, and take less than one-fourth the time to recover from fatigue. A growing number of world record and Olympic medal holders are vegetarians. And for strength — look at the elephant, the bull, or the gorilla.

But . . . in the face of all this evidence, many people still ask, where will I get that meaty flavor I love?

From miso.

3
The Miracle of Fermentation

THE KEY TO the art of making fine miso lies in the process of fermentation, a process which, throughout its long and varied history around the world, has served three fundamental purposes: the improvement of a food's digestibility; the transformation of its flavor and aroma, color and texture; and its preservation without refrigeration. Watching the drama enlarged a thousandfold and presented in time-lapse color photography, one witnesses a near-miraculous world in which tiny spores burst into blossom like elegant and complex flowers, enzymes reach out inquisitively like long fingers melting solid particles at their touch, and populations of mold explode until they have totally enveloped the foods—or "substrates" —which support their life.

Just as Western craftsmen have fermented milk to form cheese and yogurt, or grapes to form wine, Eastern craftsmen have fermented soybeans and grains to form miso, shoyu, and tempeh. In each case, the *dramatis personae* are myriads of microorganisms which serve as the vital essence and force of the living fermentation process. These tiny creatures work best at their own unhurried pace, timed by the great rhythmic movements of the four seasons and the delicate biochemical changes occurring in their "household." Man serves his highest function by understanding the laws of change written into these life processes and providing the optimum conditions for their natural unfoldment. He thus becomes a partner with the Master Alchemist in creating a masterpiece of fine flavor.

All natural miso is prepared in basically the same way, using a two-part fermentation process. *To prepare rice miso, for example, rice is soaked overnight, drained, and then steamed. Cooled to body temperature, it is mixed with a small amount of "koji starter" consisting of spores of the mold *Aspergillus oryzae (Ass-per-JIL-us oh-RAI-zee)*. Every craftsman prizes and guards his favorite strains of this

*For a more detailed discussion of the microbiology and biochemistry of miso fermentation, see Appendix C.

mold, since they are essential to imparting a unique character to his miso. Some strains have been in the custody of family-run shops for generations: they permeate the tools, the vats, the very air. Molds are used in East Asia to activate the fermentation for miso, soy sauce, rice wine, and vinegar, just as they are used in the West to make Brie, Roquefort, Camembert, Bleu, and other mold-ripened cheeses.

The inoculated rice is spread in shallow wooden trays and incubated in a warm, humid room for about 45 hours. Here it becomes bound together by a bloom of fragrant white mold. This mold-covered grain is called *koji*. The function of the koji molds is to produce enzymes that will later break down proteins, starches, and fats into more readily digestible amino acids, simple sugars, and fatty acids.

The first fermentation complete, the koji is crumbled to break up the mat-like mycelium, thereby giving the koji an appearance similar to rice crispies that have been dusted with flour. It is then combined with cooked soybeans, a little of the soybean cooking liquid, salt, and a small amount of mature miso from a previous fermentation. This "seed miso" introduces distinctive yeasts and bacteria from the shop's miso lineage while making it possible to complete the next step in a shorter time.

The ingredients are mashed together (traditionally underfoot, like grapes for wine, in shallow wooden tubs), then packed into 6-foot-deep cedar vats. Covered with a layer of sheeting and a wooden pressing lid topped with heavy weights, they now begin their second fermentation. While enzymatic digestion gets underway, a small amount of liquid rises to the surface creating a sealed, airtight environment that prevents the entry of contaminating microorganisms. Once the complex soy and grain nutrients have been broken down into their simpler forms, yeasts and bacteria propagate. The bacteria, primarily lactic acid-formers such as *Pediococcus halophilus* and *Lactobacillus delbrueckii*, transform simple sugars into various organic acids which impart a unique flavor to the miso and help prevent spoilage. The yeasts react with sugars to produce alcohols, contributing to the miso's aroma. Eventually, alcohols and acids react with one another to produce esters, which become the chief components of the miso bouquet. Time mellows the sharpness of the salt and harmonizes it with the other deepening flavors. Slowly the color of the mixture turns from its initial light tan or yellow to rich shades of brown.

The character of a miso is determined largely by the proportions of koji and salt to soybeans. Misos made from a mixture in which koji predominates tend to be sweet since the koji enzymes break down the abundant grain carbohydrates into simple sugars. The use of a relatively large proportion of salt slows down the fermentation process and the resulting lengthy aging yields a product having a dark color

and deep, rich flavor. By contrast, a miso low in salt and rich in koji requires only a short fermentation and its sweet flavor is usually accompanied by a light color.

In large tile-roofed, almost window-less buildings that serve to insulate the miso from extremes of heat and cold, fermentation continues throughout the year with the greatest activity during the warm months and almost none at all during the dead of winter. When, after one to three summers, the miso has come to maturity, it contains an immense number of vital and very beneficial microorganisms and enzymes. These are present in the natural miso you serve, ready to continue their work of aiding digestion within the human body.

Miso Aging (from *Miso Daigaku*)

THE MIRACLE OF FERMENTATION   29

4

The Varieties of Miso

THE MOST COMMON classification divides the world of miso into three basic groups: *regular miso*, consisting of three types—rice, barley, and soybean—is used primarily in cooking and, in Japan, particularly in soups; *special miso*, consisting of two types—finger lickin' and sweet simmered miso—is used primarily as a topping for grain dishes, fresh vegetable slices and tofu, and is usually not cooked; and *modern miso* consisting of a group of products developed since the end of World War II. Each type is represented by a number of unique varieties (fig. 7), for every batch of miso differs according to the proportions of ingredients used, the cooking methods employed, and the duration and temperature of fermentation. Each craftsman, professional or amateur, produces miso which is an expression of his tradition, his mastery of the craft and, in the case of natural miso, the dominant and subtle climatic factors affecting the environment in which he lives. As is the case with the world's fine cheeses or wines, individual representatives of the same miso variety, each often bearing the name of its birthplace, differ according to their region and year of origin: a red (rice) miso made in Sendai, for example, is not the same as one made in Tokyo, while one shop's barley miso of 1980 "vintage" may be distinctly different from that made the year before using identical ingredients.

In recent years, the number of miso varieties has steadily increased. Many unknown several generations ago outside the immediate region in which they have traditionally been prepared are now available throughout the country and even in the West.

An Overview

Before we go on to a discussion of the classical varieties and their major subdivisions, it might be best to begin with an overview. The world of miso lends itself to just such a perspective since all varieties share six principle attributes: method of fermentation, flavor, color, texture, cost, and region of origin.

Natural vs. Quick Miso: Natural miso, universally regarded as having the finest flavor, is prepared in the traditional way and has three basic characteristics: it is fermented slowly and leisurely (usually for six months to three years) at the natural temperature of its environment; it is made from only natural ingredients and contains no defatted soybean meal (an inexpensive substitute for whole soybeans) or chemical additives (except, in some cases, ethyl alcohol, p. 243); and it is never pasteurized. Most natural misos have a distinctive texture imparted by clearly visible chunks of whole soybeans and koji. About 97½ percent of Japan's miso is made with whole beans, 70 percent contains no chemical additives, 50 percent is not pasteurized, and 35 percent is fermented under natural conditions. Since some of the varieties which are not pasteurized *do* contain additives, only about 25 percent of Japan's total output is estimated to be *completely* natural. The three varieties most widely prepared in the traditional way (red, barley, and Hatcho) are called for in the majority of recipes in this book.

When measuring the age of natural miso, the Japanese (and Chinese) use an unusual system which has caused some confusion in the West. In the Orient, the age of miso—and of people— is calculated in the same way we reckon the age of race horses; regardless of the actual date of production or "birth," the miso becomes one year older on the first day of each new year. Thus New Years, the most important holiday of the year in East Asia, is everyone's and everything's birthday. And miso started in the fall of one year and harvested 12 months later is called "two-year-miso," since it has been in existence during two calendar years. "Three-year" barley and Hatcho miso are often actually aged for only 18 months.

Quick miso, a 20 to 30 percent less expensive modern product, is fermented for a short time (generally about three weeks but sometimes for as little as three days) in a temperature-controlled, heated environment. The short fermenta-

Fig. 7. The Varieties of Miso

GROUP	TYPE	VARIETY	FLAVOR	COLOR	FRAGRANCE AND AROMA	NATURAL AGING TIME	JAPANESE NAMES AND SUB-VARIETIES	PLACE OF PRODUCTION	PROTEIN %	CARBO-HY-DRATE %	SALT %	DRIED KOJI (LBS.)	SALT (LBS.)
REGULAR MISO	Rice Miso	Red Miso (incl. Brown-rice Miso)	Deep rich saltiness	Reddish brown to russet	Deep fermented aroma	6 to 12 months	Aka-miso, Genmai Miso, Sendai, Sado, Echigo, Tsugaru	Tohoku, Niigata, Sado, Hokkaido, Hokuriku, Chugoku	13.5	19.1	13.0	8.5	4.4
		Light-yellow Miso	Mature rounded saltiness with subtle tartness	Bright light yellow	Light refreshing fragrance	1 to 2 years	Shinshu Miso, Akita Miso	Nagano, Tokyo Area, Akita	13.5	19.6	12.5	7	4.1
		Mellow Red Miso	Deep semi-sweetness	Yellowish red	Rich fragrance	3 to 6 months	Amakuchi Aka-miso, Gozen Miso	Urban Centers	11.2	27.9	13.0	14	4.0
		Mellow Beige Miso	Light semi-sweetness	Yellow to tan	Light mild fragrance	5 to 20 days	Amakuchi Tanshoku Miso, Aijiro Miso, Mochigomé Miso	Nagano, Tokyo Area, Urban Centers	13.0	29.1	7.0	12	4.7
		Mellow White Miso	Rich, heady mellowness	Light beige	Subtly sweet, fermented fragrance	4 weeks	Shiro-koji Miso	Hawaii	12.3	27.5	9.1	15	3.4
		Sweet Red Miso	Rich, deep sweetness	Lustrous reddish brown	Savory and sweet	10 to 30 days	Edo Ama-miso	Tokyo	12.7	31.7	6.0	13	2.2
		Sweet White Miso	Light, rich dessert-like sweetness	Ivory to yellowish white	Light, sweet springtime fragrance	1 to 4 weeks	Shiro Miso, Saikyo Miso, Fuchu Miso, Sanuki Miso	Kyoto, Hiroshima, Takamatsu	11.1	35.9	5.5	20	2.4
	Barley Miso	Barley Miso	Deep rich saltiness	Dark reddish brown	Prominent barley aroma	1 to 3 years	Karakuchi Mugi Miso	Kyushu, Saitama	12.8	21.0	13.0	10	4.6
		Mellow Barley Miso	Deep, rich subtle sweetness	Yellowish brown to russet	Subtle barley fragrance	10 to 20 days	Amakuchi Mugi Miso	Kyushu, Chugoku, Shikoku	11.1	29.8	10.0	17	4.8
	Soybean Miso	Hatcho Miso	Mellow richness, subtly tart	Chocolate brown	Distinctive rich, deep aroma	18 to 36 months	Hatcho Miso, Waka-Hatcho, Sanshu Miso	Aichi, Okazaki	21	12	10.6	0	2.0
		Soybean Miso	Mellow saltiness	Dark reddish brown	Prominent soy aroma	1 year	Ichi-nen Mamé Miso, Nagoya Miso	Aichi, Mie, Gifu	19.4	13.2	11.2	0	2.1
		Tamari Miso	Deep saltiness	Dark brown	Deep, heavy soy aroma	1 year	Tamari Miso	Aichi, Mie, Gifu	20	12.3	11.3	0	2.4
SPECIAL MISO	Finger Lickin' Miso	Kinzanji Moromi Hishio Namémiso Natto Goto	Rich fermented sweetness	Golden brown to dark amber	Deep barley fragrance	20 to 60 days	Namémiso	All Japan	11	30	8	20	3
	Sweet Simmered Miso	Peanut Walnut Sesame Yuzu Kinomé Red -snapper Tekka	Sweet and varied	Varied	Varied		Nerimiso	All Japan, Homes, Restaurants	14	37	7	—	—
MODERN MISO	Modern Miso	Akadashi Miso	Rich, mellow sweetness	Dark reddish brown	Savory sweet aroma		Akadashi Miso	Aichi, Kyoto	16	31.9	10	—	—
		Dehydrated Miso	Varied	Varied	Varied		Kanso Miso, Kona Miso	Tokyo	32.2	35.8	18.5		
		Low-salt/ High -protein Miso	Mild saltiness	Tan	Mild aroma		Gen-en Miso	Tokyo	17.6	14.0	6.3		

tion does not allow it to develop the full mellowness of flavor and aroma, deep color, and long-lasting properties characteristic of natural miso. Hence, various chemicals and synthetics (bleaches, food colorings, sweeteners, vitamins, and monosodium glutamate) are occasionally added together with preservatives (ethyl alcohol or sorbic acid). Most quick miso is also pasteurized to prevent its microorganisms from producing carbon dioxide which would cause the plastic bags in which it is packaged to swell and sometimes explode. Pasteurization, like overcooking, causes a further decline in the miso's flavor and aroma, and, by killing the microorganisms which would otherwise aid digestion in the human body, lowers the miso's nutritional value. Most quick miso has a smooth texture since the soybeans and koji are ground together usually twice, once in the vats to shorten the fermentation time and again later during pasteurization. Prepared with a large proportion of koji and small amount of salt to further accelerate fermentation, quick miso is also usually quite sweet. First manufactured on a large scale during the 1960s, it is now mass-produced in modern factories, as described in Chapter 10.

Like quick miso, naturally fermented varieties are also now available in 1- to 2-pound polyethylene bags which allow for better distribution. To prevent swelling, virtually all miso (except Hatcho) sealed in bags is pasteurized and/or contains ethyl alcohol or sorbic acid preservative. If packed in bulk

kegs or cottage cheese-type containers, pasteurization and additives become unnecessary.

Salty vs. Sweet Miso: All misos can be grouped according to their salt content as shown in figure 8.

Varieties containing 10½ to 14 percent salt are generally low in carbohydrates (20% or less) and have a savory, rather salty flavor. At the other extreme, those containing less than 7 percent salt are generally rich in carbohydrates (30 percent or more) and enjoy a heady sweetness. Note that all misos are assumed to be salty unless specifically designated otherwise. When thinned in ½ cup water, 2 teaspoons of salty miso produce about the same strength broth as 3 to 4 teaspoons mellow or 5 to 6 teaspoons sweet miso. (Mellow red miso, which contains 13 percent salt, falls outside its proper domain; due to its abundant carbohydrates, it actually has a flavor similar to that of mellow barley miso.)

Japan's sweetest misos are found in Kyoto, her ancient capital, and Tokyo, her present-day metropolitan center. As one moves from modern urban areas to more traditional farming and fishing districts, the preferred miso grows saltier and more of it is made at home. Consumption patterns demonstrate that urban office workers, young people, and the upper classes prefer the sweeter varieties, whereas farmers, laborers, and elderly adults prefer the saltier. As one might expect, the consumption of sweet miso has increased and that of salty miso has decreased since the end of World War II, paralleling Japan's rapid urbanization and industrialization. The Western pattern of sugar consumption (now over 14 tablespoons per person daily in the U.S.) has also strongly affected Japanese tastes. And the shorter fermentation time needed by the sweet misos has been an added incentive for manufacturers to emphasize their production.

Sweet miso is most commonly used in toppings, spreads, sauces, and vegetable side dishes; salty miso is preferred in soups, as a pickling agent for vegetables, and with seafoods. One tablespoon of sweet miso and 1½ teaspoons of salty miso each contain approximately ¼ teaspoon of salt.

Because the natural sugars with which it abounds tend to ferment quite quickly, forming alcohols, sweet miso has a short shelf life and is therefore difficult to export. Salty miso, on the other hand, can be stored indefinitely even at room temperature.

The sweetness or saltiness of a miso has no hard-and-fast relationship to its color. Generally, though, saltier varieties tend to be darker since both salinity and depth of color are directly related to length of fermentation.

Red vs. White Miso: Like wines, all misos can be divided into reds (actually russets and warm chestnut browns) and whites (soft light-yellows and creamy beiges). Most red miso, like red wine, obtains its coloration from natural changes requiring lengthy aging, whereas white miso is generally prepared by quick, temperature-controlled fermentation. In general, rice miso tends to be lighter in color than barley miso, and barley miso tends to be lighter than soybean miso.

The great majority of Japan's white miso is made with rice koji and contains a large proportion of carbohydrates and

Fig. 8. The Percentage of Salt in Different Miso Varieties

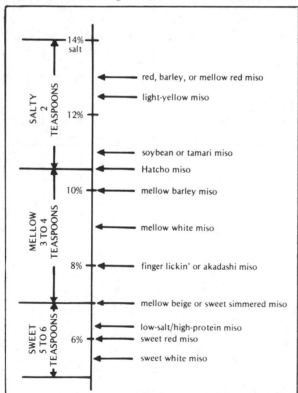

relatively little salt; hence, most white miso is rather sweet. The soybeans used are carefully selected to exclude dark varieties, dehulled to give them an even lighter coloration, and then pressure cooked under water (rather than in steam) for a relatively short time; in some cases a small amount of bleach is added to the cooking and/or soaking water. After cooking, all water is immediately expelled (with the loss of valuable nutrients), and the beans are cooled rapidly in a partial vacuum inside the pressure cooker to further minimize oxidation and browning. Yellow riboflavin food coloring (vitamin B_2) is sometimes added before fermentation to give the bleached end-product a more natural-looking luster. Packed into vats and well sealed, the miso is fermented quickly in a warm environment. Very light-colored sweet varieties are often shipped to retailers before the end of fermentation; they come to maturity en route and on the shelves in order to minimize darkening and spoilage. Varieties sealed in bags may have bleach added just before packaging.

Most white miso is a very modern product. The ancient sweet white miso of Kyoto was not nearly as white as its present descendants, since it was prepared by natural fermentation without bleaches or pressure cooking, and contained less carbohydrates. Recently, the consumption of light-colored miso has grown rapidly with the increase in the number of large-scale miso factories which find it more profitable to produce, and under the influence of modern advertising which has worked to create the image that "white" (as in white rice, white bread, and white sugar) is beautiful. Like most sweet miso, and for the same reasons, white varieties have a short shelf life and are difficult to export.

NOTE: In Japan, the term "red miso" (*aka* miso), used in its usual narrow sense, refers only to salty red rice miso. However, in its broad sense it may refer to any miso with a reddish or dark brown color. The term "white miso" (*shiro* miso) usually refers only to Kyoto-style sweet white miso; "light-colored miso" (*tanshoku* miso) is generally used to refer to all yellowish or whitish varieties. Occasionally the term "black miso" is used to refer to the darker varieties of soybean miso.

Chunky and Koji vs. Smooth Miso: Chunky miso (*tsubu miso*) is any variety in which the shape of the soybeans (and usually of the koji grains) is still visible. It is the oldest form of miso and comprised virtually all that made before 1945. During the mixing and mashing of ingredients before the fermentation of natural miso, almost all of the koji and at least half of the soybeans were left in their natural form. The koji gradually dissolved as the miso aged, but the beans generally retained their individual form, even after three years of fermentation, thereby lending the finished miso a distinctive, flavor-enhancing texture.

In koji miso, the form and texture of the koji grains are still visible. Prepared by mashing the cooked soybeans thoroughly before they are combined with the koji and salt, koji miso, with its distinctive texture, is usually quite young (12 to 18 months). It nevertheless retains a strong appeal among miso connoisseurs.

Smooth miso is that which has been blended or ground to a homogeneous purée. First prepared after 1945, it now comprises about 80 percent of all miso sold in Japan. It derives much of its appeal from the fact that the Japanese have traditionally ground their miso with a little water before adding it to soups; smooth miso saves modern cooks the time and trouble. In factories making quick miso, this smooth-textured product is an inevitable result of the production process since all of the ingredients are ground anyway, once to shorten the fermentation time and then again to reinforce the effects of pasteurization.

Expensive vs. Inexpensive Miso: In Japan, miso varieties sold in polyethylene bags through supermarkets and grocery stores are the least expensive. The same miso automatically rises in price when it is sold out of open-top kegs at traditional miso retail outlets. To avoid pasteurization and the use of preservatives, much natural miso is still sold in the latter way, but many varieties of even natural (unpasteurized) miso now contain ethyl alcohol preservative and can be found in natural food stores for relatively low prices packaged in polyethylene bags.

In general, rice miso is less expensive than barley miso, and barley miso is less expensive than soybean miso. The least expensive misos, often characterized by a soft texture due to the addition of extra water, are usually quick misos made by large-scale production methods. More expensive misos are frequently natural varieties made by small, tradition- and quality-oriented companies.

In February 1983 miso prices in Japan ranged from about $0.51 per pound for quick light-yellow miso to about $1.35 per pound for Hatcho, sweet white, and other fine natural misos. The average price per pound of quick miso was $0.57 compared with $0.82 for natural varieties. At the same time in the United States, imported natural miso packaged in polyethylene bags sold at natural food stores for the following average prices per pound: red miso $1.77, brown-rice miso $2.11, barley miso $1.96, Hatcho miso $2.35, and finger lickin' miso (including natto miso) $2.36.

Miso from the Provinces: In Japan, the many varieties of miso are often grouped according to the provinces or regions in which they are produced. Like many of the world's wines and cheeses, the majority of Japan's traditional misos bear the name of their birthplace as shown in figure 9a. A miso having a history deeply rooted in the provinces is often called *tochi* miso, or "miso of the land," and is especially prized.

If one travels the entire length of the Japanese archipelago from southwest to northeast—a distance of about 1,360 miles—one would find that as the climate changes from warm to cold, the preferred miso generally changes from sweet to salty and consumption tends to increase. In the southern third of Japan, barley miso is preferred; in the central third, soybean miso; and in the northern third, rice miso (fig. 9b).

Hokkaido Miso (salty)
Tsugaru Miso (salty)
Akita Miso (salty)
Yamagata Miso (salty)
Echigo Miso (salty)
Sado Miso (salty)
Toyama Miso (mellow)
Kaga Miso (salty)

Fuchu Miso (sweet)
Hiroshima Barley Miso (mellow)
Kyushu Miso (mellow)
Nagasaki Barley Miso (mellow)

Sendai Miso (salty)
Tochigi Miso (salty)
Shinshu Miso (salty or mellow)
Edo Amamiso (sweet or mellow)

Aijiro Miso (mellow)
Hatcho and Sanshu Soybean Misos (mildly salty)
Kyoto Shiro Miso (sweet)
Awa Miso (mellow)
Gozen Miso (mellow)
Sanuki Miso (sweet)

Rice Miso (salty, red)
Rice Miso (salty, mellow)
Rice Miso (mellow, yellow)
Barley Miso (mellow)
Soybean Miso
Rice Miso (sweet, white)
Rice Miso (salty, red)
Rice Miso (mellow, yellow)

REGULAR MISO

Our overview complete, let us proceed to the three major groupings outlined at the start of this chapter. The first group, regular miso, constitutes about 90 to 95 percent of all commercial miso prepared in Japan. The three basic types— rice, barley, and soybean miso—are classified according to the basic raw material or substrate used for the koji. The production of rice miso predominates (81% of yearly output in this category), followed by barley (11%) and soybean (8%). Each type may be further divided on the basis of flavor into sweet, mellow, and salty, and then subdivided on the basis of color into red, light-yellow, and white varieties (fig. 7, p. 32).

The following three types and 12 varieties of miso are widely available throughout Japan. Within each variety are hundreds of sub-varieties which differ according to the maker, process, ingredients, and locality of origin.

Rice Miso
(Komé Miso)

Prohibitively expensive as recently as 50 to 100 years ago, rice miso now accounts for 81 percent of the miso sold in Japan. In fact, today all miso is assumed to fall under this classification unless otherwise stated, just as all miso is assumed to be salty-tasting unless specifically called sweet; hence salty red rice miso is simply called "red miso." Very rich in glucose and other natural sugars, rice serves as the basis of the koji used in most of Japan's sweet, quick, and white misos. The finest salty rice misos have traditionally been produced in the cold provinces north of Tokyo noted for yield-

ing high-quality rice.

The scarcity of rice miso in traditional Japan is thought to be due to the fact that rice — and especially the polished or milled rice from which most rice miso has always been made — was a food reserved for the aristocracy and samurai. Feudal peasants were required to send the rice they grew to their lords, leaving them with only barley, although in some areas, the farmers were allowed to collect broken rice kernels to prepare their miso. Thus, part of the present popularity of rice miso in Japan is an expression of the ancient tendency to regard rice and rice miso as foods of the upper classes.

Variety	Native Region	Soy-beans	Rice	Salt	Natural Fermentation
Red Miso (incl. Brown-rice miso)	Northeast provinces	10	8.5	4.4	1-3 years
Light-yellow	Shinshu	10	7.0	4.1	1-3 years
Mellow Red	Urban centers	10	14.0	4.0	4-7 weeks*
Mellow Beige	Urban centers	10	12.0	4.7	3-4 weeks*
Mellow White	Hawaii	10	15.0	3.4	4-6 weeks
Sweet Red	Tokyo (Edo)	10	13.0	2.2	2-5 weeks
Sweet White	Kyoto	10	20.0	2.4	1-4 weeks
					*Quick fermentation only

Red Miso *(Aka Miso):* Fermented naturally for one to three years or by temperature-controlled methods for three to four months, red miso has a rich-and-savory salty flavor with subtly sweet undertones. Deeply fragrant, its color ranges from lustrous russet to dark reddish brown; its texture from chunky-and-soft to smooth-and-firm. It takes its Japanese name *(Sendai miso)* from the city in the northeastern provinces which has served as the center of red miso production since ancient times.

Of all types of regular miso, whether rice, barley or soybean, red miso has the lowest proportion of carbohydrates (19.1%), the second highest proportion of protein (13.5%), and the highest proportion of salt (13%). Thus the natural product can be stored for several years at room temperature and, in most cases, the flavor will actually improve over time. A popular and versatile miso, it is well suited for use in all types of cookery. An estimated 75 percent of all the rice miso now sold commercially in Japan, and virtually all the rice miso prepared in farmhouses, is red (or light-yellow, as described below).

Well known sub-varieties of red miso are listed in figure 10; their places of origin are shown on the map on page 35. Of particular historical interest is the delicious Sado miso, which was developed about 350 years ago on Sado Island in the Japan Sea far to the north of Tokyo. Centuries ago, a famous shipping route led from Osaka around the southern tip of Honshu to Sado Island, and then on to Japan's northernmost island, Hokkaido. Ships transported Sado miso to Hokkaido where it was too cold to make a local variety, and on the return voyage brought back high-quality Hokkaido soybeans, which were used in subsequent batches of Sado miso. Sado islanders now grow their own fine beans, and their miso is known for its subtly-sweet flavor and koji texture.

A sub-variety of rice miso that has recently won considerable favor in the West is brown-rice miso. It has a delectable natural flavor, deep and mellow, and a satisfying fragrance. This miso is endowed with real character, is loaded with nutrients found in the rice's bran layers, and is priced quite reasonably. Its fermentation time is 6 to 18 months. At present a number of Japanese producers make brown-rice miso (see Appendix E); the product most widely sold in America is made by Sendai Miso-Shoyu. Most red miso has always been made with white rice because: 1) the surface layers of brown rice are so nutritious that alien microorganisms as well as the koji mold spores tend to thrive and produce off-flavors; 2) preventing this phenomenon requires delicate temperature control during koji preparation; 3) the koji mycelium has difficulty penetrating the bran layers and therefore in breaking down the central portions of the rice kernels; 4) most modern Japanese prefer the flavor of white to brown rice. The rice used to make brown-rice koji is polished very slightly to aid penetration of the mycelium; about 2½ pounds of bran are removed from each 100 pounds of unpolished grain as compared with 10 pounds when making white rice. In some cases, the rice is also split before being steamed. The preparation of the koji is identical to that using white rice except that the temperature is kept within a narrower range of the ideal at each step in the process.

Light-Yellow Miso *(Shinshu Miso):* Shinshu refers to the ancient province north of Tokyo—now Nagano prefecture—where this popular variety was first developed. Originally resembling Sendai red in proportion of basic in-

gredients, color, and flavor, Shinshu contained slightly less salt and therefore enjoyed a subtle and highly prized tartness. Whereas Sendai miso was generally chunky, Shinshu was smooth, and some varieties were prepared with black soybeans. Traditional Shinshu, usually fermented for at least one year, is still made in farmhouses in its native locality but is no longer widely available on a commercial basis. Akita miso, its close relative, has a sweeter flavor and lighter color (see chart below).

Modern Shinshu, which we call light-yellow miso, is a quick miso the best examples of which have a mature and mellow salty flavor, and a subtle tart quality. Light and refreshing in aroma, its color ranges from light yellow to yellowish brown, and its firm texture is almost always smooth. Low in carbohydrates (19.6%) and quite high in both salt (12.5%) and protein (13.5%), it keeps for up to two months at room temperature, but for longer storage must be refrigerated. Prepared by temperature-controlled fermentation in only three to four weeks, light-yellow miso is Japan's least expensive variety. Some varieties may contain bleach and vitamin B_2 food coloring.

According to popular tradition, the original Shinshu miso was developed about 450 years ago by Takeda Shingen, a great and powerful samurai living in the Nagano area. This progenitor of modern Shinshu was prepared commercially in farmhouses as early as 1924 (using sodium sulfite bleach), but large-scale production and distribution did not start until after 1945. Most light-yellow miso is still produced in Nagano, although 95 percent of it is shipped throughout the rest of Japan and accounts for over 20 percent of all miso consumed in the nation. Especially popular in Tokyo and central Japan, it is used in all types of cooking. The most widely available miso presently produced in the United States falls under this category. Light-yellow miso may be substituted for red or barley miso in any of the recipes in this book.

Fig. 10 Famous Sub-varieties of Salty Rice Miso

	Japanese Name	Koji (% by wt. of soybeans)	Salt (% by wt. of miso)	Characteristics
Red miso	Sendai	60	13.6	Chunky texture, soybeans cracked coarsely, deep-red color, long aging
	Echigo	60-65[1] 80-120[2]	14.0 12.2	Chunky texture with white koji mosaic on fine-grained soybean base
	Sado	60-65	15.4	Chunky or smooth texture, long aging
	Tsugaru	50	14.6	Deep-red color, long aging
Light-yellow miso	Shinshu	60-90	13.0	Radiant light-yellow color, smooth texture
	Akita	80-100	12.3	Yellowish gold color midway between Shinshu and Sendai; relatively low salt content
		1) Niigata type	2) Joetsu type	

Mellow Red Miso *(Amakuchi Akamiso):* A close relative of red miso, this variety is prepared with exactly the same amount of salt (13.0%) but a much larger percentage of koji and thus of carbohydrates (27.9% vs. 19.1%), resulting in a slightly sweeter flavor. The traditional representative of this category is Gozen miso, a specialty of the city of Tokushima on Shikoku Island. Fermented naturally for six to 12 months, it attains a deep reddish-brown color. Since World War II, a number of quick varieties have been developed, which are prepared with pressure-steamed ingredients and fermented without the use of additives in a temperature-controlled environment for three to six months.

Mellow Beige Miso *(Amakuchi Tanshoku Miso):* This broad category is a catch-all for the many quick, light-colored misos developed as imitations of modern Shinshu but forbidden by law to use the Shinshu name. *Amakuchi* means "moderately sweet" and *Tanshoku* means "light-colored," indicating that these products are midway in flavor between sweet and salty, and in color between red and white. By 1969 this miso (together with its close relatives mellow red miso and light-yellow Shinshu) accounted for a full 70 percent of all misos sold in Japan, but its popularity is now waning as traditional varieties return to favor.

Mellow beige miso was explicitly designed to use proportions of raw materials that would minimize both the fermentation time and the cost of ingredients, and thereby maximize profits. Thus, typical products are relatively rich in carbohydrates (29.1%), and low in salt (7.0%) and protein (13.0%). The light color is produced by pressure-boiling and short fermentation (3 to 4 weeks) in a temperature-controlled environment, often together with the use of bleach and food coloring.

The traditional representatives of this category are Aijiro miso and Kyushu miso, neither of which is now widely available. Aijiro, made only in Shizuoka prefecture, was first created about 350 years ago as an imitation of Kyoto's sweet white miso, but it is not quite as sweet.

A unique sub-variety of mellow beige miso is Glutinous-Rice Miso *(mochigomé miso).* Prepared with 3 parts soybeans and 7 parts glutinous rice, it has a thick smooth texture, light yellow color, and fairly sweet flavor. First developed during the 1970s, it is sold only by the Hinode Miso Co.

Mellow White Miso *(Shiro Koji Miso):* The rich natural flavor of this variety is nicely harmonized with a subtly sweet fermented fragrance, reminiscent of *amazaké.* Unlike its slightly sweeter relative, sweet white miso, this mellow miso is a completely natural product, fermented at the temperature of its environment and prepared without pasteurization, preservatives, or bleach. Made only in Honolulu, it is now widely available on the American mainland where it is reasonably priced ($1.29 per pound) and generally sold in white cottage cheese-type containers bearing the name "Shiro White Miso." It is not available in Japan.

Midway between red and sweet white miso in salt content, it is highly versatile and can be substituted for either in most recipes in this book; use twice as much mellow white as red miso or two-thirds as much as the sweet miso called for. A good approximation of sweet white miso's flavor can be obtained by mixing ½ teaspoon honey with 4 teaspoons mellow white miso. By using a pinch of salt instead of the honey you can approximate the flavor of light-yellow miso.

Sweet Red Miso *(Edo Miso* or *Edo Ama-miso):* Endowed with a rich, slightly savory aroma and a deep, mellow sweetness, Edo miso contains a large proportion of carbohydrates (32%) and is relatively low in salt (6%) and protein (12.7%). Ranging in color from light reddish brown to lustrous russet, its traditional texture was always chunky, but many contemporary products are smooth and soft. Because virtually all varieties, even though they now contain preservatives, begin to change flavor after two to four weeks unless refrigerated, Edo miso is difficult to export.

Edo, the ancient name of modern Tokyo, is also the title of an era which began in 1603. It is said that Ieyasu Tokugawa, Japan's ruling shogun at the time, developed Edo miso in order to combine the best features of Hatcho miso, his hometown favorite, and Kyoto's sweet white miso, very popular at the time among the upper classes. In the days before the Japanese had access to sugar, Edo miso was a widely used sweetening agent. Today it is most popular in soups, where it is often mixed with red miso. Mixed with *azuki* beans, it becomes the filling for *Kashiwa Mochi* (p. 155), a famous confection served each year on Boy's Day. It is also used in Dengaku (p. 144), Nuta (p. 96), Sweetened Tekka Miso (p. 67), and nabé dishes such as Doténabé (p. 142). In Western-style preparations, it is delicious in spreads, dips, and dressings.

Most of Japan's sweet red (Edo) miso is still produced and consumed in the Tokyo area. To this day, it is made by an ingenious method of natural temperature-controlled fermentation: the miso is packed into vats while the soybeans are still hot, and the vats are wrapped with heavy rice-straw mats to keep in the heat. Although fermented for as few as ten to 20 days in summer and four to five weeks in winter, this miso enjoys a deep reddish color thanks to a unique cooking method in which the beans are boiled for a long time, allowed to stand overnight in the cauldron, then reheated before going into the vat.

A fairly good approximation of Edo miso's flavor can be obtained by mixing 3 parts red miso with 1 part honey.

Sweet White Miso *(Shiro Miso, Kyoto Shiro Miso,* or *Saikyo Miso):* Also known as "Kyoto white miso" or simply "white miso," this variety is made by combining as much as 4 parts by weight of rice koji with only 2 parts soybeans and 1 part salt. Deliciously sweet, it is so smooth it can be spread like butter on pancakes or bread. Its light refreshing flavor goes well with fresh fruits and crisp vegetables, and lends a rich, mellow quality to desserts. Ranging in color from ivory to light yellow, its fragrance is reminiscent of springtime.

Highest of all misos in carbohydrates (36%) and lowest in salt (5.5%) and protein (11.1%), its abundance of natural sugars hastens the fermentation process so that the average *natural* aging period is only three weeks, becoming as short as one week during the summer and as long as one to two months during winter. Many makers now calculate the fermentation time to include the time in transit to food stores and sitting on the shelves. If allowed to stand unrefrigerated for more than one week in summer or one month in winter, it develops a slightly alcoholic or sour flavor and reddish color. Refrigerated, however, it will keep for two months or more. Difficult to export, many varieties—whether sold in open-top kegs or sealed polyethylene bags—have been pasteurized and contain preservatives plus small amounts of bleach; some contain 2 to 3 percent added sweeteners from refined grain sugars (*mizuamé*).

Costing 63 to 83 cents per pound, this is one of Japan's most expensive misos. It is used as a pickling agent for fish and vegetables, as a topping for the grilled tofu dish Dengaku, in a special New Year's soup, Ozoni (p. 105), in Japanese confections (mixed with *adzuki* beans), and in a wide variety of *aemono* or salad dressings, sauces and spreads. Except in the Kyoto area, it is used rather infrequently in soups.

For centuries a famous product of Kyoto, it is a featured ingredient at many of the city's restaurants offering Zen Temple Cookery or Tea Ceremony Cuisine. Two large, well-known Kyoto companies, Honda and Ishino (p. 239), account for most of the nation's production. One delicious variety sold as "Hanabishi Shiro Miso" is now widely available in the United States. Produced by Nakamuraya & Co., it is pasteurized and contains preservatives and bleach. Well known sub-varieties of sweet white miso include Hiroshima's Fuchu Miso and Takamatsu's Sanuki Miso.

The commercial preparation of sweet white miso involves a rather complex process which is said to be a well guarded secret of its Kyoto manufacturers. Many Tokyo shops have tried to duplicate it but none have succeeded. Due to its short shelf life, this miso was traditionally prepared in shops only during the cold months (from October until March) without preservatives or bleaches. It is still made in farmhouses in Wakayama prefecture, especially during March and April. In modern factories, it is prepared in the general manner described previously for white miso except that, like sweet red (Edo) miso, it is packed into the fermentation vats while the mixture is still quite hot.

Since this miso can be prepared very quickly, it is an excellent variety to try making at home. A fairly good approximation of its flavor can be obtained by mixing 2 parts by volume of light-yellow miso, 1 part honey, and 1 part water.

Barley Miso
(*Mugi Miso*)

Most barley miso is darker, saltier, and aged longer than rice miso. Generally sold in the traditional chunky or koji form, its distinctive texture is one of its preferred characteristics. Each barley grain has a clearly visible dark line—known in Japanese as its "loincloth"—running the length of the kernel: this line gives the miso a unique appearance. The koji is prepared from polished or pearled barley—either the regular (*O-mugi*) or "naked" (*Hadaka-mugi*) varieties—which are higher in protein (11% vs. 7.5%) and lower in carbohydrates (67% vs. 73%) than polished rice. Therefore barley miso is generally not as sweet as its rice counterpart and takes a longer time to ferment.

At present, barley miso comprises only 11 percent of the miso sold in Japan. Nevertheless, since low-cost barley was once widely grown throughout the warmer parts of the country, and since the Chinese ideograph for the word *koji* is composed of characters meaning "barley" and "chrysanthemum," many miso scholars believe that barley miso was Japan's most popular variety from ancient times up until 50 to 100 years ago. Other authorities contend, however, that miso has always been made using the predominant grain of each region and that in most areas rice and rice miso have always been produced in greater quantities. In any event, although a large amount of farmhouse miso is still made with barley koji and many farmers believe that barley and barley miso are foods which promote long life and good health, barley miso has nevertheless gradually decreased in popularity during the past century.

Barley miso's decline has been most pronounced among urbanites and young people. Japanese miso makers, scholars, and cooks suggest a number of possible reasons for this phenomenon: 1) Barley, which even now sells for only 40 percent the cost of rice, has long been considered a poor man's grain. The miso made from it seems to have acquired low-class associations, and as people move upward socially and economically, they tend to use less and less of it, preferring rice miso instead; 2) Barley miso's heady flavor and earthy aroma, its high salt and low sugar content, no longer suit the more refined tastes and needs of urbanites; and its dark color is considered to be outdated; 3) Its chunky texture makes it inconvenient for use in creamy-smooth miso soups since it must be hand-ground and strained before use; 4) Koji-textured barley miso, made from regular barley rather than the softer "naked" barley, is said to leave a slight residue on the tongue from the firm "loincloth" line.

Yet, in parts of Japan where barley fields are still more common than rice paddies and the traditional culture has retained its vitality, barley miso continues to be produced and enjoyed in large quantities. In urban areas, mellow barley miso is swiftly taking the place of its saltier traditional counterpart; a typical Tokyo miso retail store offering 40 varieties of miso will generally have only one barley miso, and it will likely be mellow.

An estimated 80 percent of all Japan's barley miso is still prepared by natural fermentation, and most of the salty varieties are made only during the cold months, from November to April, when the new-crop barley is at its best flavor, the water is clear and delicious, and the air is cold and free of contaminating microorganisms.

The traditional home and present center of barley miso production is the southern third of the Japanese archipelago, and particularly the southernmost main island, Kyushu, where barley miso became popular in about 1600 and 75 percent of Japan's total output new originates. In the various provinces of Kyushu, the following percentages of all miso produced are barley miso: Kagoshima 100, Kumamoto 80, Nagasaki, Saga and Oita 70, and Fukuoka 50. Likewise in Yamaguchi and Hiroshima prefectures located at the southern end of Japan's main island in the Chugoku region, the proportion of miso which is barley miso is respectively 50 and 30 percent. Two of the traditional barley miso areas, Saitama prefecture located near Tokyo and Shikoku island, now produce only small amounts.

Variety	Native Region	Soy-beans	Barley	Salt	Fermen-tation
Barley Miso	Southern Japan	10	10	4.6	1-3 years
Mellow Barley Miso	Southern Japan	10	17	4.8	10-14 days

Barley Miso *(Karakuchi Mugi Miso):* Although the name of this particular variety is identical to that of the larger category described above, the "barley miso" called for in recipes always refers specifically to this product. Its relatively high salt content (13% or more) is mellowed by lengthy natural fermentation and harmonized by the barley's underlying subtle sweetness to give the miso a deep rich flavor. Many connoisseurs in fact contend that fine barley miso actually tastes *sweeter* than Sendai rice miso! Low in carbohydrates (21%) and high in protein (13%), it is fermented naturally for at least one full year, at the end of which time it has acquired its characteristic reddish-brown color, chunky texture, and prominent fragrance. When aged for three years, the color turns a deep chocolate brown, the texture becomes more homogeneous, and the flavor grows richer, subtler, and more elaborate. Although barley is generally less than one-half as expensive as rice, lengthy fermentation makes this miso more expensive than most varieties of rice miso: natural three-year barley miso (*sannen-miso*), at more than $1 per pound, is one of Japan's most expensive varieties.

Most of the natural barley miso now exported to the United States is this salty product. It is strongly favored by the American macrobiotic community, which has been one of the main influences working to popularize the use of miso in the West. Barley miso is used in soups and a wide variety of other types of cookery.

Mellow Barley Miso *(Amakuchi Mugi Miso):* Although this variety has a pleasant sweetness, the koji from which it is prepared demands a fairly high minimum level of salt for proper fermentation. Hence it is impossible to make this miso as sweet as the sweet white or sweet red rice misos. Compared with the latter variety, mellow barley miso contains almost twice as much salt (10.0% vs. 6.0%), and a little less carbohydrates (30% vs. 32%) and protein (11.0% vs. 12.6%). The color ranges from light yellow for the quick varieties to reddish brown for those produced naturally. The texture is usually chunky. It has a distinctive flavor characteristic of both the koji and soybeans, and a light fermented aroma.

Popular on the island of Kyushu—and especially in Nagasaki and Kumamoto—for over 350 years, it is known in some areas as "10-day miso" due to its short natural fermentation time of one to two weeks. At present, most mellow barley miso is prepared on a large scale using temperature-controlled fermentation, typically for 20 to 35 days in a warm room and then 15 to 20 days at room temperature, or in some cases for as few as four to six days. Although it generally contains preservatives and bleach (some varieties also contain 1% honey), this quick miso spoils rather quickly and changes color unless refrigerated. It is therefore difficult to export. Used mostly in cooked vegetable dishes and as a topping for Dengaku (p. 144), it is also combined with salty barley miso in the preparation of soups.

Soybean Miso
(*Mamé Miso*)

Soybean miso is fundamentally different from rice and barley miso in that it contains no grain; its koji is made exclusively from soybeans. Due to a consequent lack of carbohydrates and a moderately high salt content, soybean miso requires lengthy aging, most of which is still done in the slow, natural way.

Much of Japan's earliest farmhouse and commercial miso was probably of this type. In the clear, cold uplands of northern Japan, it is still prepared in the ancient way, with wild mold spores and cooked soybeans that are crushed and shaped into large balls (*miso-dama*). The balls are wrapped or tied with rice straw and hung outdoors under the eaves or indoors over an open-hearth fireplace or wood-burning kitchen stove. After a month or so when the balls are covered with mold, they are crushed, mixed with salt and water, and fermented in kegs or crocks (p. 193).

Commercial soybean miso was developed and is still most widely prepared and consumed in central Japan, in Aichi, Mie, and Gifu prefectures. It presently constitutes 8 percent of all miso sold in the nation as a whole. Since it is impossible to vary the ratio of grains in the basic ingredients, the different varieties have a relatively narrow range of flavors and aromas. All are fermented naturally for at least one year. The darker ones are occasionally called "black miso" (*kuro miso*), and all are frequency called Sanshu miso, the ancient name of central Japan.

Variety	Native Region	Soy-beans	Salt	Fermentation
Hatcho Miso	Okazaki near Nagoya	10	2.1	18-36 months
Soybean Miso	Central Japan	10	2.1	8-12 months
Tamari Miso	Central Japan	10	2.5	10-12 months

Hatcho Miso *(pronounced hot-cho):* No other miso in Japan is endowed with such a lofty and aged tradition. For centuries, Japanese poets, connoisseurs, and statesmen have celebrated Hatcho's ineffable savory aroma, deep mellow sweetness, and uniquely astringent flavor, each faintly reminiscent of chocolate; these lend the miso a sense of what the Japanese call *shibui*, a term which in its broader aesthetic usage refers to subdued yet refined tastefulness which borders on subtle, almost severe beauty. Other "shibui" things include a Zen brush painting, a sparse haiku, a tart—almost puckery—autumn persimmon.

Dark cocoa brown, Hatcho has a slightly chunky texture that in most cases is so firm you can cut it with a knife. Higher in protein (21.0%) and lower in carbohydrates (12.0%) and water (40%) than any other miso, it nevertheless contains less salt than either red or barley miso (10.6% vs. 13%).

Although any maker of Hatcho-type miso is legally allowed to use the traditional name for his product, only two companies, Hayakawa and Ota (p. 238), both of which claim to have been founded over 600 years ago (p. 219), are generally recognized as Japan's originators and present manufacturers of the real thing. Both are located in the same block, or *cho*, on the banks of the Yahagi River in the town of Okazaki near the bustling city of Nagoya (see map, frontispiece). Hat-cho, or "Eighth-street" miso, takes its name from this location. The Tokugawa family, which founded Japan's feudal shogunate in 1603 and moved its capital to Edo (now Tokyo), originally resided in this area. Very fond of their native miso, they imported it by boat to their new capital where, as it happens, it never became widely popular.

八丁味噌

In making Hatcho miso, a unique species of mold, *Aspergillus hatcho* said to flourish in the Okazaki area, was traditionally used in place of the regular *Aspergillus oryzae.* The fermented soybean koji is mixed with salt and a relatively small amount of water (see p. 210), then packed into huge cedar vats, some of which are 150 to 200 years old. Their thick cedar staves bound together with wide and beautifully woven hoops of braided bamboo, typical vats are 6 feet deep and 7 feet in diameter, with a capacity of 4 to 5 tons (1,600 gallons). A heavy wooden pressing lid is placed on top of the miso, and at least 100 large rocks, equal in their total weight to the weight of the miso, are then piled on (see frontispiece). Even with this enormous pressure, however, the mixture contains so little moisture that virtually no liquid (*miso-damari*) rises to the surface!

Because all Hatcho miso must age through at least two full summers, the youngest batches, which start to ferment in the late spring, are about 16 months old; older batches, begun in early fall, have been aged for at least 24 months. Hatcho makers say that the miso begins to reach its best flavor only after 24 months and peaks at three *full* years, but miso this old is very uncommon at present. Yet due to the unusual Japanese way of measuring a miso's age, Hatcho which is actually only 18 to 24 months old is often sold as "three-year" miso.

Since all Hatcho is prepared by lengthy natural fermentation, it costs about 79 cents per pound, or roughly 40 percent more than most rice miso. The oldest batches, which have had a large proportion of their protein broken down into amino acids, are valued for their medicinal properties. Only about 1 to 2 percent of the miso produced each year in Japan is Hatcho, and about half of the total is employed in the production of akadashi miso (see below). Most often used in soups, Hatcho is usually mixed with 3 parts red, light-yellow, or sweet rice miso to soften its astringent qualities. It is also the key ingredient in Tekka Miso (p. 66), and small chunks of the well-aged product can be served as is, to be enjoyed as a rich and mellow hors d'œuvre. When used in place of red or barley miso—as called for in most of the recipes in this book—the quantity should be increased by 15 to 20 percent to impart the equivalent degree of saltiness.

In recent years a product called "Young Hatcho Miso" (*Waka-Hatcho*) has begun to be sold. Prepared by the traditional Hatcho companies, it differs from the true Hatcho in that it is aged through only one full summer (usually for a total of 12 to 14 months) and has a lighter weight on the vat's pressing lid. Slightly less mellow in flavor, lighter in color, softer in texture, and about 15 percent less expensive, it is often preferred to true Hatcho by students of macrobiotics who feel that the latter is too *yang* due to its lengthy aging in such a warm climate.

Hatcho is said to be the Emperor's favorite miso, and he takes it with him on overseas trips. Formerly certain fine producers of miso, shoyu, and other foods received the honor of being supplier to the Imperial Household, but recently a more democratic approach has been adopted. No company is allowed to be a special supplier to the Emperor, even if they offer their goods for free, since the resulting publicity is considered to give them an unfair advantage over competitors. The Emperor must buy and pay for his beloved Hatcho miso just like everyone else.

Hatcho has been taken on all six Japanese expeditions to the South Pole, and is considered an essential food by many athletes and mountain climbers who use it as a condensed source of protein and energy. Regarded also as a key ingredient in Tea Ceremony Cuisine (*kaiseki ryori*), it is now widely available in the West and is the only miso sold in sealed bags that is not pasteurized and contains no alcohol.

Fig. 11. Supplier to the Imperial Household

Hatcho has been taken on all six Japanese expeditions to the South Pole, and is considered an essential food by many athletes and mountain climbers who use it as a condensed source of protein and energy. Regarded also as a key ingredient in Tea Ceremony Cuisine (*kaiseki ryori*), it is now widely available in the West and is the only miso sold in sealed bags that is not pasteurized and contains no alcohol.

Soybean Miso *(Mamé Miso or Ichi-nen Mamé Miso):* Also called "one-year" or "regular" soybean miso to distinguish it from other soybean misos, this variety is prepared like Hatcho except that the minimum aging requirement is one year rather than two and the usual *Aspergillus oryzae* mold is used to make the koji. Compared to Hatcho, its flavor is less rich; its color is redder; its texture is softer due to its higher water content (48% vs. 40%); and its price is about 30 percent lower. Much of this miso is used as a substitute for Hatcho in akadashi (see below). About 80 to 90 percent of the soybean miso made in Japan is of this type. The term "Nagoya Miso," the name of the most popular brand, is often used as a synonym for "soybean miso."

Tamari Miso: Prepared in miso- and shoyu shops in central Japan since 1500, this is the miso-like residue that remains after producing tamari-shoyu, an early prototype of modern shoyu. (Tamari-shoyu is made from a pure soybean koji, while modern shoyu is made with a koji consisting of equal parts soybeans and roasted wheat.)

In making tamari miso, soybean koji prepared as for Hatcho or regular soybean miso is mixed with the usual amount of salt plus about five times as much water. The resulting mash, called *moromi*, has a consistency like that of applesauce; it is placed into a huge cedar vat in the center of which is stacked a series of inverted, bottomless wooden kegs which form a hollow cylinder (fig. 12). The base of the cylinder is joined to an inverted V-shaped trough that is permeated with small holes and connected at one end to a spigot at the bottom of one side of the keg. Liquid tamari from the moromi mash quickly collects in and fills the cylindrical core. Each day some of this tamari is ladled over the surface of the moromi to stimulate fermentation and, since the usual pressing lid is not used, to prevent the formation of mold. After 10 months or more of natural fermentation, the spigot is opened and the thick, richly-flavored tamari runs out. Traditionally it was the well-drained *moromi* remaining in the vat that was sold as tamari miso. At present, however, most of the moromi is ladled into cloth sacks and hydraulically pressed to extract its full content of liquid tamari; the pulpy dry residue is then discarded or used as cattle fodder. Hence, tamari miso is now quite rare, although not extinct.

Long regarded as a very high-class food, tamari miso has a subtle natural sweetness and a distinctive flavor similar to that of fine, natural Chinese soy sauce. However, because it contains no grain koji and is fermented for a relatively short period of time, it has rather little aroma. Generally used in miso soups, it is also popular as a relish-like topping or dip for fresh vegetable slices. For a description of the liquid tamari, see pages 184 and 222.

Trough (inverted)

Fig. 12. Tamari miso vats

Front view (cross-section)

Side view (cross-section)

SPECIAL MISO

Special misos are different from their regular counterparts in four basic ways: 1) In addition to the usual miso ingredients (soybeans, koji, and salt), they contain chopped vegetables, nuts, seeds, seafoods, or natural seasonings and spices which impart a distinctive chunky texture; 2) They are generally quite sweet and, unless refrigerated, have a relatively short shelf life; 3) Generally served at the dining table for use as a topping or seasoning, they never appear in miso soups and are further cooked in only a few special dishes such as Dengaku (p. 144) and Broiled Miso (p. 71); 4) They are usually sold in small quantities (200 grams) from 2-quart crocks rather than large kegs at prices slightly higher than even the most expensive regular misos. The two basic types are finger lickin' miso and sweet simmered miso.

Finger Lickin' Miso
(Namémiso)

Each variety of namémiso—a word derived from the verb nameru meaning "to lick"—is prepared by fermenting a small amount of finely-chopped salt-pickled vegetables and spicy seasonings (about 10%) with whole cooked soybeans (15%) and a large proportion (75%) of a unique whole-grain koji usually containing barley or wheat. The resulting consistency is similar to that of apple sauce but slightly chunkier, and the color is generally a warm light brown. The high proportion of grain carbohydrates which are broken down into sugars gives this miso its characteristic rich sweetness and heady, delectable aroma.

Now available in different parts of the United States, finger lickin' miso seems particularly well suited to Western tastes. In Japan, the different varieties are favorite toppings for crisp vegetable slices, hot rice or rice porridge, Ochazuke, regular or deep-fried tofu, crackers and canapés, rice balls and mochi, baked potatoes and other root vegetables, and even some aemono salads. Finger lickin' miso is also delicious in Western-style sauces and dressings, especially with sesame tahini and seasonings such as orange juice, garlic, onion, gingerroot, shoyu, and/or honey. The following varieties, which retail for an average of $1.50 per pound in Japan, are listed in order of their availability and popularity there: refrigerated, each will keep for three to six months.

Kinzanji Miso: Kinzanji is made from a special koji containing *both* whole-grain barley and soybeans. (In most misos, it will be remembered, either grains or soybeans but never both are used in the koji.) The individual barley grains are abundant and clearly visible, and the soybeans, which have been roasted, cracked and dehulled, give the finished product a slightly nutty aroma and chunky texture. Most Kinzanji contains minced eggplant, gingerroot, white *uri* melon, *kombu* and burdock root; some varieties may contain *daikon* and cucumbers, plus green beefsteak leaves and seeds, *sansho* green pepper, and slivered *togarashi* red peppers used to enhance the fragrance. These vegetables and seasonings are added either at the start of or halfway through the natural six-month fermentation process. Traditional Kinzanji contained equal portions by weight of soybeans and barley, but many modern varieties contain four times as much barley as soybeans in order to give a sweeter product, and reduce the cost, time, and difficulty of preparation. For even greater sweetness some makers add rice koji to the original mixture, and *mizuamé* (barley- or millet jelley) at the end; the *mizuamé* also improves luster. Modern varieties may contain brown food coloring, and pasteurization or preservatives are often used to increase shelf life. Two types of Kinzanji are available, one quite sweet and the other rather mild.

Several theories are offered to account for this miso's origin. The first traces it to *Kinzanji*, the Temple of the Golden Mountain, one of China's five great Sung dynasty Zen centers. According to popular oral tradition, the Zen priest Kakushin brought a prototype back with him from China in 1255 A.D. and taught the method of its preparation to the people of Yuasa in Wakayama prefecture, where the same ancient technique is employed to this day. Yuasa has since become a famous center of shoyu production as well, and legend has it that shoyu's earliest progenitor was discovered as the dark, fragrant liquid left over at the bottom of the Kinzanji barrel! The Osaka-Wakayama area is the present center of Kinzanji production, yet manufacturers in Shizuoka prefecture to the north have developed ten new varieties plus a ready-made dried koji for use in preparing a homemade type.

A second theory suggests that some of the earliest types of Chinese chiang (see Appendix A), containing pieces of fish or meat fermented with grains and soybeans, were actually prototypes of Kinzanji, and that all the devotedly vegetarian Japanese had to do was substitute vegetables and seasonings for the meat and fish. In fact, the earliest *hishio* (the progenitor of Japanese shoyu; see below) was probably very similar to Kinzanji. The basic method for preparing this Kinzanji is believed to have been transmitted not by a priest but by a book, the *Ch'imin Yaoshu*, written in China about 550 A.D., which when translated and circulated widely in Japan had a profound influence on Japanese fermented food preparation and agricultural methods. This theory places the origin of Kinzanji 400 years after the time of Kakushin and fails to establish its famous link with the origin of shoyu. A third theory suggests that Kinzanji originated from the practice of soaking vegetables in *hishio* to make "vegetable hishio" (*kusa hishio*).

Four close relatives of Kinzanji are *Sakura Miso, Shiina Miso, Hamana Miso,* and *Bonito Miso. Sakura* — which means "cherry" —has a deep red color and is prepared from barley koji plus *mizuamé* and sugar; a modern miso with the same name is described on page 43. *Shiina*— which means "China," in honor of the fact that most finger lickin' miso originated there—and *Hamana* contain soybeans, wheat-(or barley-) and rice koji, plus diced eggplants, beefsteak seeds, and gingerroot. Some varieties contain *amazaké* (p. 162). Fermented for 20 days during the winter, they are prepared and sold mostly in Fukui prefecture. Bonito (*Katsuo*) Miso, a specialty of Tosa City on the island of Shikoku, substitutes chunks of raw bonito for the usual vegetables. It is occasionally used in soups.

Moromi Miso: Moromi is the mash from which shoyu is made. It consists of a koji made of soybeans, cracked roasted wheat, salt, and water. After a natural fermentation period of one year, it is ordinarily ladled into cloth sacks and pressed to yield the liquid shoyu.

The earliest moromi miso, developed during the 16th century in Kyushu and Shikoku by shoyu makers, was simply shoyu moromi (made with whole rather than cracked roasted wheat) taken from the fermentation vats either before or after the shoyu was filtered off. To develop their own version, all that miso makers had to do was reduce the amount of water used in the mash, add chopped, salt-pickled vegetables, and substitute miso starter (*Aspergillus oryzae* mold) for the shoyu starter to activate the fermentation. The resulting product, from which the liquid was never filtered or pressed, was dark brown and had a consistency like that of applesauce.

Today, most moromi miso contains chopped eggplants, cucumbers, and gingerroot; Nagasaki's delicious Batten Moromi also contains short sections of *wakame* midrib (*kuki-wakame*). Two varieties of moromi, prepared by miso makers, are available; one is quite sweet and slightly pink, the other tan and mild. Retailing for about 80 cents per pound, both are most widely served on fresh cucumber slices.

Hishio: The word *hishio* (pronounced HEE-shee-oh) is the Japanese pronunciation of the Chinese character *chiang*, and the present-day product is thought to bear a close resemblance to this progenitor of all Japanese miso and shoyu (see Appendix A). Commercial hishio is generally prepared from drained, unpressed shoyu moromi to which are added salt-pickled vegetables (eggplant, white *uri* melon, and gingerroot); the mixture is then further fermented by natural methods for 20 to 60 days, usually during the months of March and April. Traditional farmhouse hishio—still widely prepared in the Osaka, Chugoku, and Shikoku areas (see map, inside cover) where it is also known as *namémono* or *o-namé*—is generally prepared by fermenting the vegetables together with a barley koji from the beginning, and often contains soybeans which have been split and dehulled. Both commercial and farmhouse hishio, prized as gift items in Japan, are now available at only the best miso shops.

Namémiso: Closely related to the three varieties described above, namemiso is characterized by the presence of 3-inch-long strips of *kombu* together with diced pickled eggplants, gingerroot, and *uri* melons. Some varieties contain only wheat or barley koji and no soybeans.

Natto Miso: Prepared in the area of Nagasaki since the 1700s, natto miso contains a relatively large proportion of soybeans which gives it an appearance similar to the famous sticky fermented soybeans called *natto*, although there are no real *natto* in natto miso. Containing whole soybeans, barley koji, slivered kombu, gingerroot, and, in some modern varieties, *mizuamé* (a natural honeylike sweetener extracted from rice, millet, or barley), this miso is ferment-

ed at the natural temperature for about 30 days. One delicious and very popular variety, now widely available in the United States, is free of preservatives, artificial or refined sweeteners, and all other additives—proving that it can still be done. We would prefer to see this and all similar misos labeled as "Finger Lickin' Miso;" we feel the general term is more appealing and less confusing.

Goto Miso: A *to* is a Japanese unit of measure equal to 4¾ gallons, and the word *go* means "five." This miso is prepared by combining one *to* of each of the following five ingredients: cooked soybeans, rice koji, sake lees, salt, and sugar. The fermentation requires only ten days.

Relatives of finger lickin' miso: The numerous varieties of farmhouse miso enriched or extended with potatoes, sweet potatoes, *kobocha* or corn (or with koji made from these foods), and the farmhouse miso in which vegetables are buried and pickled are closely related to finger lickin' miso (see p. 192).

Sweet Simmered Miso
(*Nerimiso*)

Sweet simmered miso is prepared by combining regular miso with a mixture of sweetening (sugar, honey, or *mizuamé*), a little water or sake, and nuts, seeds, minced vegetables, seafoods, or seasonings. The mixture is cooked in a skillet and stirred constantly until it attains the same degree of firmness as regular miso. The most widely available commercial variety is peanut miso, which is chock full of whole peanuts, roasted sesame seeds and, in special cases, raisins; the use of *mizuamé* imparts a thick taffy-like consistency and deep amber color, while the peanuts and sesame boost the protein level to over 16 percent. Commonly sold in 3½-ounce sealed polyethylene bags or rectangular containers, it is now also available commercially and at school cafeterias in tiny ¾-ounce packets which provide a single serving for only 5 cents and are used as a sandwich spread as well as a topping for rice, tofu, and fresh vegetable slices. Other readily available commercial varieties include walnut, sesame, *yuzu*, *kinomé*, and red snapper. Since these and numerous other varieties are also prepared non-commercially in homes and restaurants, a detailed discussion of sweet simmered miso is given in the recipe section (p. 60).

MODERN MISO

Three varieties of miso, all developed since 1945, fall under this classification. They are composed of traditional misos processed or mixed in unique ways. When two or more varieties of miso are combined, the resulting commercial product is designated as "mixed miso" (*chogo-* or *awasé miso*), the best known example of which is akadashi, described below. Modern miso represents about 5 percent of all miso consumed today in Japan.

Akadashi Miso: This dark reddish-brown and rather sweet miso is prepared by combining 1 part Hatcho miso with 2 parts of various other misos (mellow beige, sweet white, and/or one-year soybean). Many varieties also contain caramel syrup, *mizuamé*, refined sugar, monosodium glutamate, shoyu, and sorbic acid preservative. The mature misos and other ingredients are simply mixed, puréed or blended, pasteurized, and packaged; the process takes less than two days since no additional fermentation is required. Hatcho akadashi miso, the finest variety, is guaranteed to contain authentic Hatcho miso, whereas less expensive varieties often substitute regular soybean miso. *Sakura* (cherry) and *Kyozakura* are types of akadashi containing about two-thirds sweet white miso.

Some Japanese say that the word *akadashi* originated in Kyoto and initially referred to any soybean miso that had a strong aroma; it is said that geishas would grind the soybean miso finely in a *suribachi* (serrated earthenware mortar), then rub it through a sieve to make a tasty miso soup. In Kyoto, the soybean miso first came to be mixed with sweet white miso to make the forerunner of today's akadashi.

Richly fragrant and hearty-tasting, akadashi is very popular in most Japanese urban centers even though its price is fairly high (48 to 73 cents per pound). Its name—literally "red dashi"—comes from a traditional, deep-red miso soup prepared with Hatcho miso, often containing oysters, and highly prized for its wonderful flavor (see p. 104).

Dehydrated Miso (Freeze-dried or Spray-dried): Called *Kanso Miso* or *Kona Miso* in Japan, this variety, developed in 1959, has become quite popular since the late 1970s, especially as the main ingredient in instant miso soups (now available at natural food stores and supermarkets throughout the U.S.), and also in the soup for instant Miso Ramen noodles. One popular natural instant miso soup, brand-named Miso Cup, contains a mixture of dehydrated onions, parsley, sea vegetables (wakame), and miso. In Japan, the most popular varieties contain slivered freeze-dried leeks, plus dried wakame and wheat gluten (or deep-fried tofu); many Japanese and supermarket products also contain chemical additives such as monosodium glutamate, sodium succinate, and inosinic acid. The mixture is sealed in tiny one-or-two serving packets (9 grams make an 8-ounce cup of instant miso soup) and five to ten packets are sold together in a foil package or box. At least three varieties are available to make red, white, or akadashi miso soup. The soup, prepared by simply mixing the contents of one packet with hot water, is ready in less than a minute at a very small cost per serving. Ideal for backpacking and camping, this miso also makes an excellent seasoning; we like to keep some in a shaker and sprinkle it on salads, sandwiches, brown rice, noodles, or crisp-fried tempeh, or to mash it with tofu for use as a spread or dip.

Of the 560,000 metric tons of miso made in Japan in 1979, no more than 2½ to 3½ percent end up dehydrated. Of the 10,000 to 15,000 tons of dehydrated product, an estimated 80 percent is freeze dried and 20 percent is spray dried. Yamajirushi is the largest maker of freeze-dried miso and Marukome and Nagatani-en are the biggest makers of spray-dried miso.

Initially, most of the dehydrated miso in Japan was made by spray drying. Miso (containing 50 percent solids) is mixed with enough water to give a slurry containing only 10 percent solids; this is blown in a fine spray from an atomizer into the top of a 150-foot-tall tower filled with circulating hot air. The miso dries as it falls. The spray inlet temperature is $482^{\circ}F$ ($250^{\circ}C$) and the exit temperature is 167 to $176^{\circ}F$ ($75\text{-}80^{\circ}C$). In recent years, freeze-drying has come to be more widely used than spray drying. Regular miso is spread to a depth of about 1 inch (2-3 cm) on large stainless steel trays, which are slid into shelves in a large vacuum chamber. First the miso is quick frozen at a very low temperature ($-22^{\circ}F$ or $-30^{\circ}C$), then dried using a strong vacuum (0.5 to 0.8 mm of mercury or torr) at a relatively low drying temperature ($104^{\circ}F$ or $40^{\circ}C$) for 10 to 15 hours, to yield dehydrated miso containing only 4 to 5 percent moisture, but 32.2 percent protein, 18.5 percent salt, and 35.8 percent carbohydrates. Though slightly more expensive, freeze-drying gives a finished product with a noticeably better flavor and aroma (some of which are lost at the high temperatures used for spray drying), that is slightly more nutritious and dissolves more readily in water. Freeze-drying is labor intensive, has a long drying time, and uses expensive, complex equipment with a small capacity but low noise level. Spray-drying is easy to mechanize, has a short drying time, and uses simple, inexpensive equipment with a large capacity, but which is very noisy.

Low-salt and Salt Free Miso *(Gen-en Miso and Mu-en Miso):* Typical low-salt miso is made by pressure-steaming dehulled, defatted soybeans, hydrolizing them with enzymes, then mixing them with an equal weight of mature red or light-yellow miso and fermenting the mixture at $86^{\circ}F$ to $95^{\circ}F$ for three to five days. First developed in 1959 the resulting product contains only 5.1 percent sodium chloride together with 17.6 percent protein and 53 percent moisture. Since its low salt content requires that the fresh miso be stored at below $50^{\circ}F$, it is usually freeze-dried and sold in 7-ounce bottles for about $1.70. Generally used as a health food, the dehydrated form contains 14 percent sodium chloride, 26.4 percent protein, and 6 percent moisture.

Some varieties, typically containing 5 percent salt and prepared like light-yellow miso using an 80-day fermentation, contain 3 to 3.5 percent alcohol as a preservative and are sold pasteurized in cans. Other methods of making low-salt miso include substituting ethyl alcohol for part of the salt (2 to 5 percent), adding *Saccharomyces rouxii* yeasts to

generate natural alcohol as in wine, or reducing the moisture content to 40 percent (Koyama 1976).

Salt free miso, which typically contains 3.5 percent alcohol, has a very noticeable alcohol flavor and aroma that we find unappetizing, except when it is masked by seasonings as for use in dressings or sauces. A canned salt-free red miso contains 53.7 percent moisture, 13.9 percent protein, 6.7 percent fats, and 24.2 percent carbohydrates including the 3.5 percent ethanol (ethyl alcohol), and 189 calories per 100 grams. Nagano Miso Co. in Japan reportedly holds the only patents on salt-free miso. Made by sterilizing koji, then mixing it with a little ethyl alcohol and cooked soybeans (without subsequent fermentation), the product, called JEPRON, contains 3 times the free amino acids of regular miso and costs about 50 percent more. Protein content ranges from 12 to 20 percent. Gold in color and rich in flavor, it can be used like miso in many recipes— yet is totally salt free. In 1982 some 250 metric tons a month were being made in Japan.

Total production of both these types of miso is still very limited, but the appeal is growing since the Japanese per-capita salt consumption is the highest in the world, 30 grams per capita in northern Japan and 18 grams in the rest of Japan, as compared with 11 grams in the United States. It is now well known that excess salt consumption can cause high blood pressure (hypertension). These products may eventually even find a market in the West.

New American Misos: American miso makers in homes, communities, and commercial shops have had good results making new types of miso using peanuts, garbanzo beans (chickpeas), black soybeans, azuki beans, common beans *(Phaseolus vulgaris,* incl. pinto, navy, kidney, great northern, etc.), *natto* (fermented soybeans), okara (soy pulp), green lentils, or green peas, as the protein source in place of regular soybeans. They have also made koji from corn (dent or flint), millet, wheat, or buckwheat. In 1982 Imagine Foods in Missouri introduced a miso in which kelp replaces some of the usual salt. Who, we wonder, will be the first to introduce miso in cubes like bullion or powdered miso in a shaker, perhaps mixed with herbs and/or spices.

A product resembling miso, produced in America by Loma Linda Foods and widely used by Seventh-day Adventists, is called *Savorex.* Made from extract of brewer's yeast, vegetable flavoring, and salt, it imparts a rich and meaty flavor. In 1983 it was sold in 9-ounce plastic containers for the equivalent of $3.61 per pound, or almost twice as much as popular natural misos.

PART II

Cooking with Miso

Getting Started

5

VIRTUALLY ALL OF THE basic types of Japanese miso described in Chapter 4, plus several new American-style misos (such as corn-soy miso or peanut miso) are now available at reasonable prices in most parts of the United States. Look for them at natural and health food stores, Japanese or other Oriental food stores, and at some supermarkets. As the amount of miso imported and made domestically continues to grow, new types continue to appear. Most miso is presently sold in 1-to 2-pound sealed polyethylene bags, cottage cheese-type containers, or small plastic tubs, although at many natural food stores it is sold in the traditional way out of wooden kegs (fig. 14). Occasionally it is sold in jars or even plastic squeeze tubes. Dehydrated miso—generally in the form of instant miso soups—are packaged in foil envelopes. If your local store does not carry miso, you may wish to give the manager the name and address of one of the makers or importers listed in Appendix D.

Buying and Storing Miso

What are the most important things to look for when buying miso? First, buy small quantities of a number of different varieties in order to become familiar with their flavors and colors, textures and aromas. Compare imported and domestic products and learn to recognize which types go best with your favorite recipes. People interested in natural foods will probably prefer traditional natural un-

pasteurized misos, which now compare very favorably in price with the more modern, quick varieties. Labels such as the one below should contain all the basic information relevant to natural miso:

Variety	Red Miso *(Sendai Akamiso)*
Type (optional)	Rice Miso *(Komé Miso)*
Texture	Chunky
Ingredients (incl. additives)	White rice and whole soybeans organically grown, unrefined sea salt, well water, alcohol, miso culture
Pasteurization	No
Temp.-controlled Fermentation	No
Age	At least 12 months
Weight	16 ounces
Maker	Nakamura Miso Co. 160 Westlake Blvd. Berkeley, CA 94706

Fig. 14. *Miso packaging*

All varieties should be stored in a cool, dark place. Sweet misos should always be refrigerated; during warm weather, it is best—but not absolutely necessary—to also refrigerate other varieties in order to prevent the growth of surface mold. Miso purchased in polyethylene bags should be kept tightly closed; expel all air from the bag, fold over the mouth, and secure with a rubber band. Miso purchased in bulk out of kegs can be packed firmly into an earthenware, glass, or tupperware container with plastic wrap, wax paper, or butcher paper pressed firmly over the entire miso surface; or it can be stored tightly enclosed in plastic wrap bound with a rubber band, or simply left in the store's small paper carton and refrigerated. During warm weather, a thin layer of harmless, almost tasteless mold may form on the air-exposed surfaces of unrefrigerated natural misos—those which contain no preservatives and are not pasteurized. Don't worry; simply scrape off the mold and discard it just before use or mix it into the body of the miso. Sweet misos may develop an alcoholic fragrance, and light-colored misos may darken, if allowed to stand open for too long; light cooking will remove the alcohol, and the darkening in no way affects the flavor.

Using Miso as a Seasoning

Miso may be used in place of salt or shoyu in most recipes. It has a more mellow and varied flavor than shoyu, and imparts added body to broths and sauces. The following quantities impart approximately the same "saltiness" and can therefore be used interchangeably as explained on page 33:

½ teaspoon salt
2 teaspoons shoyu
1 tablespoon salty miso (see chart p. 33)
1½ to 2 tablespoons mellow miso
2½ to 3 tablespoons sweet miso

To use miso sold in a polyethylene bag, cut across one of the bag's upper corners to make a ¾-inch-long opening. Then simply squeeze the bag (as you would apply icing to a cake using a pastry bag) to give a neat, smooth bead.

One tablespoon of miso weighs 17.3 gm.

Remember that natural miso is a living food containing many beneficial microorganisms which are easily killed by prolonged cooking. Whenever possible add the miso to soups or other preparations just before they are removed from the heat or use the miso in ways that require no cooking.

Basic Ingredients

We recommend the use of whole, natural foods. Since cans and bottles tend to contribute to environmental clutter, the recipes in this book call for ingredients which can be purchased free of non-biodegradable packaging. The rarer ingredients used in Japanese-style recipes are defined in the Glossary at the end of this book. Many basic Oriental foods are now widely available at natural food stores and supermarkets, as well as at Japanese and Chinese markets. Or contact the Japan Food Corporation with offices in San Francisco, Los Angeles, New York, Chicago, Houston, Columbia (Md.), and Sacramento (Calif.). The following ingredients, listed alphabetically, are those we consider basic to miso cookery:

Flour: Since all-purpose white flour contains only about 75 percent of the protein, 36 percent of the minerals, and 25 percent of the vitamins found in natural whole-wheat flour, we generally prefer to use the latter for baked goods, sauces, and the like. However, in tempura batters and pie crusts where lightness is essential, we recommend the use of unbleached white flour or a mixture of equal parts whole-wheat and white flours.

Honey and Sugar: Most of the recipes in this book that use sweetening call for honey, used in the minimum amounts we consider necessary to create the desired flavor and "balanced" by the miso's salt. One teaspoon honey imparts the same sweetness as 2 teaspoons of sugar, and in most recipes the two can be used interchangeably. Since honey is about twice as expensive as sugar, the net cost ends up being the same. But honey is a whole, natural food with a mild flavor, whereas natural unrefined sugar (available in Japan but not in America) has a dominant molasses taste and white sugar is now widely recognized as being bad for both body and mind. (We feel it is important that decreases of meat in the diet be accompanied by proportional decreases of sugar usage, and that in general, grains, vegetables, and fruits be used as natural sweetening agents.)

The first sugar arrived in Japan in 753 A.D., brought by the Chinese Buddhist priest Ganjin on the same boat said to have brought the first Chinese miso. Yet sugar was virtually unknown in Japan until the late 1500s, and not until 1776 was the first sugar refinery established. Although Japan still has the lowest sugar consumption of any industrialized country in the world, the per capita figure jumped from 28.5 pounds in 1955 to 64.0 pounds in 1975. (The latter figure is only 57 percent of America's 112 pounds—14 tablespoons per day—for the same year.) In Japan, sugar is used mostly in cooking, where it is balanced by the saltiness of miso or shoyu; its use in desserts, treats, and "junk foods" is now rapidly increasing as Western dietary patterns become popular. Honey is only rarely used in Japanese cookery.

Oil: For best flavor, use cold-pressed, natural vegetable oils. For sautéing and salad dressings, we prefer soy, corn, or "salad" oil—often mixed with small amounts of sesame oil; for deep-frying, rapeseed or soy oil. Olive oil works well in Western-style dressings. Sesame oil, especially popular in Chinese dishes, is now widely available in the West. No recipes require the use of hydrogenated oils or animal fats.

Rice: Polished or white rice contains an average of only 84 percent of the protein, 53 percent of the minerals, 38 percent of the vitamins and 30 percent of the dietary fiber found in natural brown rice. We prefer the flavor, texture, and nutritional superiority of the natural food. Yet brown rice is not flawless. Compared to white rice, it takes more time and fuel to cook (unless it is pressure cooked), and contains more mineral-binding phytic acid, and has extra oils which grow rancid faster in tropical climates.

In Japan, virtually everyone (including Zen monks) now eats white rice. The trend began in the early 1600s when it became a status symbol enjoyed first by the aristocracy and finally, in the early 1900s, by everyone. During World War II, time and energy could not be spared for polishing and, therefore, everyone ate brown rice. Today, however, the thought of un-polished rice triggers in most adults an almost Pavlovian response recalling the horrors of the war. Yet, the Japanese macrobiotic community has done excellent work in promoting the many virtues of brown rice and now, especially among the alternative lifestyle-sector of the younger generation, it is the symbol of a new, more natural and healthful way of living and eating.

Salt: Natural, unrefined sea salt contains an abundance of essential minerals which are lost during the refining process. Its flavor is richer and more concentrated than that of pure-white, refined table salt.

Shoyu and Soy Sauce: The skillful use of authentic shoyu and miso is the key to most Japanese cookery. An all-purpose seasoning, shoyu contains 6.9 percent protein and 18 percent salt; natural shoyu has been a mainstay of Japanese cooking for more than 500 years. We use shoyu, the Japanese word for "soy sauce," to distinguish this fine product from the modern nonfermented chemical or synthetic soy sauces now widely used in the West. There are five different varieties of Japanese shoyu; their composition of nutrients and relative importance in Japan are shown in the table below. Two of these varieties, regular shoyu (which includes natural shoyu) and tamari shoyu, bear special mention.

Natural Shoyu: This traditional product is always brewed using a natural (rather than temperature-controlled) fermentation process, generally for 12 to 18 months. The finest varieties are prepared from whole soybeans, natural salt, and well water fermented together in huge cedar vats. All types also contain *koji* starter *(Aspergillus oryzae)* and roasted cracked wheat. All natural shoyu presently available in the West—some of which is sold as *Tamari*—is imported from Japan. Actually, Japanese *tamari*, the progenitor of shoyu, is a different product (see below).

Shoyu: At present, this is the standard regular shoyu sold in Japan. A high quality product now produced on a large scale in the U.S., its flavor, aroma, and color are quite similar to those of the finest natural shoyu, and its price is considerably lower. Using techniques based on the traditional method but first developed during the 1950s, it is generally prepared from defatted soybean meal and brewed in large tanks for about 4 to 6 months under conditions of strictly controlled temperature and humidity.

Tamari Shoyu: This type of shoyu, a close relative of Chinese soy sauce, is made with a large percentage of soybeans (85-100 percent) and little or no wheat (0-15 percent). Produced and consumed mostly in Central Japan (Aichi, Mie, and Gifu prefectures), it constitutes only 2.2 percent of all Japanese shoyu. Tamari shoyu has a slightly darker color, richer consistency, and distinctively deeper flavor than regular shoyu, though its aroma is more subdued; since it contains little or no wheat it lacks the subtle alcohol bouquet found in regular shoyu. Many Westerners and some Japanese producers distinguish between *tamari shoyu*, which contains a small amount of wheat, and *tamari*, which contains no wheat (but may contain up to 0.15 percent roasted barley flour). According to some reports, the koji used to make tamari or tamari shoyu uses *Aspergillus tamarii* rather than *A. oryzae* as the primary microorganism. In Japan, the production of tamari shoyu is over five times as great as that of tamari. Whereas some 3,500 companies make regular shoyu, only about eight make tamari shoyu (or tamari).

Varieties, Compositions, and Production of Japanese Shoyu

English Name	Japanese Name	Be	NaCl % (W/V)	Total nitrogen % (W/V)	Reducing sugar % (W/V)	Alcohol % (V/V)	pH	Color	Annual production %
Regular shoyu	Koikuchi shoyu	22.5	17.6	1.55	3.8	2.2	4.7	Deep brown	85.4
Light-colored shoyu	Usukuchi shoyu	22.8	19.2	1.17	5.5	0.6	4.8	Light brown	11.7
Tamari shoyu	Tamari shoyu	29.9	19.9	2.55	5.3	0.1	4.8	Dark brown	2.2
Clear shoyu	Shiro shoyu	26.9	19.0	0.50	20.2	Trace	4.6	Yellow to tan	0.4
Rich shoyu	Saishikomi shoyu	26.9	18.6	2.39	7.5	Trace	4.8	Dark brown	0.3

Source: Adapted from Fukushima, 1979

A close relative of tamari shoyu is *miso-damari*—also called *uwahiki* which is the tamari-like liquid that accumulates in *any* variety of miso during fermentation. Thicker and richer than tamari, it is gathered only in very small quantities and is not sold commercially. A delicious by-product of most homemade miso (it rises to the surface in summer and settles in winter), it may be used like shoyu and is especially delicious with hors d'oeuvres.

Chinese Soy Sauce: This traditional Chinese product, which has a stronger and saltier flavor than shoyu, is also made by natural or temperature-controlled fermentation. Although some varieties are excellent, they are not widely available in the West. Our Chinese recipes call for this product. If unavailable, substitute shoyu.

Chemical or Synthetic Soy Sauce: This domestic product, sold under various Chinese brand names, is what most Westerners mean when they speak of soy sauce. It is not brewed or fermented but is prepared from hydrolyzed vegetable protein (HVP) by the reaction of defatted soybeans with hydrochloric acid. Its flavor and coloring come from additives such as corn syrup and caramel. Since it takes only a few days to prepare, the production costs are quite low. Some varieties may contain sodium benzoate or alcohol preservatives.

Soybeans: Inexpensive, whole dry soybeans are now available in the West at most natural and health food stores; buy in bulk for substantial savings. For detailed information, see *The Book of Tofu.*

Tempeh: A cake of cultured soybeans with a flavor and texture remarkably similar to that of Southern fried chicken. Tempeh has twice as much protein as hamburger and is the world's best source of vegetarian vitamin B-12. For details, see our *Book of Tempeh* (Harper & Row, 1979).

Tofu: Also known as soybean curd, this delicious protein backbone of the traditional Oriental diet is low in cost, calories and fats, and entirely free of cholesterol. Remarkably versatile, tofu is now available throughout America in more than 10 different forms, all of which are described in detail in *The Book of Tofu.* The main varieties called for in the following recipes are:

Tofu: The most widely available product sold in waterpacked 12-ounce cakes containing 7.8 percent protein.

Firm Tofu (Chinese-style Doufu or Dow-foo): A firm product resembling Japanese tofu that has been pressed (p. 55). Good for use in deep-frying, stir-frying, and salads.

Deep-fried Tofu Cutlets(Thick Agê): Whole cakes of tofu that have been pressed and deep-fried until golden brown; 10 percent protein.

Deep-fried Tofu Burgers (Ganmo): Tofu-and-vegetable patties that look like large hamburgers; 15 percent protein.

Deep-fried Tofu Pouches (Agê): Each 6- by 3- by ¼-inch-thick pouch can be opened and stuffed with fillings; 19 percent protein.

Silken Tofu (Kinugoshi): A custard-like variety made without the separation of curds and whey; 5½ percent protein.

By an unusual quirk and accident of history, the word "tamari" has come to be widely known in the West, where it is frequently misused to refer to natural shoyu. In about 1960, when the Lima Foods company of Belgium started importing the first natural shoyu from Japan, they asked Georges Ohsawa, leader of the international Macrobiotic movement, what they should call the product to distinguish it from both regular commercial shoyu and from "chemical soy sauce," an inexpensive unfermented product described below. Ohsawa suggested that Lima Foods call the new product "natural shoyu," since that was its name in Japan. Lima Foods said the word "shoyu" seemed somewhat difficult to pronounce (in French and Dutch) and asked for alternative names. Ohsawa mentioned that words like "tamari" and "murasaki" were also used to refer to soy sauce in Japan. Lima Foods liked the word "tamari," finding it short, distinctive, and easy to pronounce. So they decided to call their natural shoyu "tamari." Ohsawa eventually came to use this terminology in his teaching and writing, and it was picked up and popularized by the Western Macrobiotic movement that has played a key role in introducing the product to the West. Little did any of them foresee the confusion that would result from this misnomer as people in the West became familiar with both natural shoyu and real tamari, and as distributors began to sell both of these fine seasonings.

In Japan, tamari is now rarely used in its natural form, being generally made into *sashimi-damari* by mixing it with miso-damari (see below), *mizuamé*, cane sugar, caramel, and often preservatives. Although not widely used in Japan, it remains fairly popular in Kyoto and central Japan, where it is used as a seasoning for *sashimi* (raw fish). In ancient times, tamari was widely used in its natural form and highly prized as a fine seasoning, having much the same flavor as best-grade Chinese soy sauce. Today, an increasing amount is made synthetically.

Tofu

Silken tofu (kinugoshi)

Firm tofu (Chinese-style)

Deep-fried tofu pouches

Deep-fried tofu cutlets

Deep-fried tofu burgers (ganmo)

The Japanese chef (like most Japanese craftsmen) uses only a small number of relatively simple tools in his work. While the recipes in this book can be prepared using only the utensils found in most Western kitchens, the following tools may make cooking with miso somewhat easier and more enjoyable. Most of these tools are inexpensive and are available at many Japanese and Chinese hardware stores, as well as at some large Japanese markets.

Bamboo colander: Usually round and slightly concave, a typical *zaru*, made of thin strips of woven bamboo, is about 12 inches in diameter. It is used for draining and straining, and as a serving tray for such foods as tempura.

Broiling screen: This double-layer, 8-inch-square screen rests atop a stove burner and is used for broiling. Both layers are made of thin metal sheets, the bottom one perforated with 1/8-inch, and the top with 3/8-inch holes. The top layer slides out for easy cleaning. Broils foods faster and with less fuel than a Western oven broiler.

Charcoal brazier: Made of baked earthenware, the *konro* or *shichirin* is used for grilling and broiling, as well as for heating *nabé* dishes (p. 139) or the family teapot. When preparing *nabé*, you may substitute a tabletop gas burner, heating coil, or chafing-dish warmer.

Chinese bamboo steamer: Although most varieties of *seiro* are round and are set into a *wok* during steaming, some types are rectangular. They are made of slatted or woven bamboo with 1/4-inch gaps between the bottom slats. This design allows steam to rise through the steamer's lid and prevents it from collecting and dripping on the steaming foods. Two to four steaming compartments may be stacked in layers during steaming.

Cutting board: A board about 19 by 9 by 1 to 2 inches thick, the *manaita* is designed to be set across the kitchen sink and hung on the wall when not in use.

Japanese grater: A metal tray about 9 inches long, the *oroshi-gané* has many sharp teeth protruding from its upper surface. Since there are no holes in the grater, the grated foods collect in the trough at one end.

Japanese vegetable knife: One of the finest knives ever designed for cutting vegetables, the *hocho* makes the art of cutting and slicing a true joy. Most varieties are quite inexpensive. The finest of these knives are handmade and bear the stamp of the craftsman on the blade near the knife's wooden handle.

Pressing sack: A simple cloth sack about 15 inches wide and 15 inches deep made of coarsely woven cloth is very helpful in squeezing and crumbling tofu.

Sudaré: A bamboo mat about 10 inches square used for rolling sushi and other foods. A small bamboo table mat makes a good substitute.

Suribachi: An earthenware grinding bowl or mortar with a serrated interior surface, the usual *suribachi* is 10 inches in diameter and 3½ inches deep, and is accompanied by a wooden pestle (*surikogi*).

Tawashi scrub brush: Made of natural palm fiber, the *tawashi* is the perfect utensil for scrubbing root vegetables or

Vinegar: Use either Western-style cider or white wine vinegar, or the milder, subtly-sweet Japanese rice vinegar *(su)*. The latter is especially tasty in salad dressings, sweet-sour sauces, and sushi rice. For 1 teaspoon rice vinegar, substitute ¾ teaspoon cider or mild white vinegar.

NOTE: Monosodium glutamate—also known as MSG or *ajinomoto*—is a crystalline, pure-white powder widely used to intensify the flavor of protein foods by exciting the taste buds. But MSG's ability to overexcite nerve endings may also cause brain damage, especially in infants, who do not have a well-developed blood-brain barrier to inhibit MSG from travelling freely to the brain. A committee of scientists selected by the U.S. Food and Drug Administration has advised that MSG should not be given in any amount to children under 12 months of age, and U.S. baby food manufacturers have recently agreed to omit MSG from their products.

In 1968 Dr. Ho Man Kwok, reporting in the prestigious *New England Journal of Medicine*, found MSG to be responsible for what has come to be known as the Chinese Restaurant Syndrome, characterized by headaches, a burning sensation at the back of the neck, chest tightness, and nausea, experienced by some people after eating foods highly seasoned with MSG.

This highly refined chemical additive, which is the sodium salt of glutamic acid, differs in chemical structure from natural glutamic acid. Originally extracted from the sea vegetable kombu (*Laminaria*) it is now generally produced by fermentation and hydrolysis of molasses or of glucose from tapioca, cornstarch, potato starch, etc. We and many other people interested in healthful, natural foods, strictly avoid use of this controversial substance. It does not appear in any of the recipes in this book.

Fig. 15. Oriental Kitchen Tools

Bamboo colander

Broiling screen

Charcoal brazier

Chinese bamboo steamer

Cutting board

Japanese grater

Tawashi

Hocho

Pressing sack

Paddles & spoons

Lid

Wok

Draining rack

Sudaré

Wok support

Ladle & spatula

Suribachi

Cooking chopsticks

Mesh skimmer

Thermometer

washing pots. It is inexpensive and outlasts most synthetic brushes.

Wok set: Popular now in the West, the wok is the Orient's standard utensil for deep-frying, stir-frying, steaming, and sautéing.

1. *The wok:* The wok itself is a metal pan about 13 inches in diameter and 3½ inches deep. When placed atop a special circular support, it may be used with electric ranges. Surprisingly low in cost and now widely available in the West, its design has numerous advantages over that of a regular flat-bottomed skillet, especially when deep-frying: a) It provides the maximum oil surface and depth with the minimum necessary oil volume (3 to 5 cups); b) Each piece of food can be slid gently down the wok's sides rather than dropped with a splash into the oil; c) Freshly-fried foods can be drained into the pan on an inobtrusive rack which saves oil and allows more thorough draining when the foods are later placed on absorbent paper; d) The wok's rounded bottom and thin metal sides allow for quick heating and oil temperature adjustment; e) During stir-frying and sautéing, the wok's large surface area allows each piece of food to have maximum contact with the bottom of the pan, yielding crisp-textured foods in minimum cooking time; f) Cooked foods can be scooped out easily and thoroughly and, when all is done, the wok is easier to clean or wipe free of oil than angular, flat-bottomed pots. After sautéing or stir-frying, wash the hot wok immediately with water and a scrub brush (do not use soap), place it back on the fire until the inside is just dry, then wipe it quickly with a dry dishtowel.

2. *Wok support:* Used in most Chinese kitchens to give the wok stability and focus the strong fire at its base.

3. *Stir-frying ladle and spatula:* In Chinese kitchens, these large, sturdy tools are used during stir-frying. The ladle is employed to measure (by eye) and add all liquids and seasonings to foods cooking in the wok.

4. *Long cooking-chopsticks:* Shaped like regular Japanese wooden chopsticks but about 10 to 14 inches long and often joined with a string at one end, these *saibashi* are used mostly during deep-frying for turning foods in the hot oil or transferring cooked foods to the draining rack. Substitute a pair of long cooking tongs.

5. *Draining rack:* A semi-circular rack, the *hangetsu* is attached to the wok during deep-frying so that excess oil from the draining foods drips back into the wok.

6. *Mesh skimmer:* Used for skimming debris from the surface of the hot oil during deep-frying and for removing very small deep-fried foods.

7. *Wooden lid:* Used when simmering foods, the lid fits inside the wok's rim.

8. *Deep-frying thermometer:* Use a regular Western-style deep-fat thermometer that measures temperatures up to 380°.

Wooden spatulas, rice paddles, and spoons: These utensils make the work of sautéing, stirring, and serving easier and more enjoyable.

BASIC PREPARATORY TECHNIQUES

The following preparatory techniques will be referred to in many of the recipes in this book. We list them all here for easy reference.

Salt-rubbing

This process softens and seasons vegetables (and *konnyaku*) without cooking.

Place thinly sliced vegetables into a bowl and sprinkle with salt. Rub the salt into the vegetables with your fingertips until the vegetables are fairly soft, then let stand for 15 to 20 minutes. Fill the bowl with water and rinse away the salt. Empty vegetables into a strainer or colander and drain briefly. Wrap vegetables in a clean cloth and squeeze gently to expel excess moisture.

Rinsing and Pressing Leeks or Onions

This is a quick and easy method for neutralizing the harsh and evoking the mild, sweet flavors of these vegetables. Slice leeks or onions into thin rounds or slivers. Combine with several cups water in a small bowl and soak for 2 or 3 minutes. Pour into a cloth-lined strainer, gather the cloth's corners to form a sack, and press vegetables gently between your palms. Use immediately or refrigerate in a covered container.

Soaking Burdock Root

Burdock root has a slightly harsh, alkaline flavor that is easily removed by proper cutting and soaking. If unsoaked, burdock will lose its white color and turn a dark reddish brown soon after it is cut and exposed to the air.

Holding the root under running cold water, scrape off its dark peel with a knife or scrub it off with a scrub brush (*tawashi*). Cut the root into 2-inch lengths and submerge the lengths in cold water. Cut one section at a time into matchsticks and return these immediately to the water. Soak for about 10 minutes, then change the water and soak for 20 to 40 minutes more. Soaking time can be decreased by using warm or hot water, but some of the burdock's flavor will be lost. Drain quickly before sautéing.

Reconstituting Dried Sea Vegetables, Wheat Gluten, and Kampyo

Dried Hijiki: Immerse in several cups (warm) water and allow to soak for 20 to 30 minutes. Stir gently, then lift *hijiki* carefully out of water so that any grit stays at bottom of bowl. Place *hijiki* in a colander or strainer and press lightly to rid it of excess moisture. Note: ¼ cup (27 gm) dry *hijiki* yields 1 cup (200 gm) reconstituted.

Dried Wakame: Rinse *wakame* once, then soak for 15 to 30 minutes. Strain, reserving the nutritious liquid for use in stocks. Remove the midrib of each leaf only if it is unusually large. Squeeze *wakame* firmly, place in a compact mound on a cutting board, and cut at ½-inch intervals. (Place fresh *wakame* in several quarts of water, rinsing and squeezing 2 or 3 times to rid it of excess surface salt.) Note: 25 gm dried *wakame* yields 1 cup (125 gm) reconstituted.

Agar *(Kanten):* Tear agar bar crosswise into halves and soak in 1 quart water for several minutes. Lift out agar and squeeze firmly. Change water and resoak briefly. Squeeze again, then tear into small (1-inch) pieces.

Dried Wheat Gluten: Soak for several minutes in water. Press lightly with fingertips to expel excess moisture before use.

Kampyo: Soak for 15 minutes in water to cover seasoned with a pinch of salt. Drain briefly, then rub lightly with salt.

Parboiling

To parboil vegetables, drop them into more than enough boiling water to cover, and cook until just tender. When parboiling green vegetables, add about ¼ teaspoon salt for each 2 cups water to help the vegetables retain their color. Vegetables that are easily overcooked may be plunged into cold water as soon as they are done. Length of cooking depends both on how finely the ingredients have been cut and on whether they will be cooked again. Shredded or slivered vegetables, or leaves that will be simmered again in a seasoned liquid, may be parboiled for 30 to 60 seconds; boil for 30 to 60 seconds more if they will not be recooked. Small rectangles of *konnyaku* and root vegetables should be parboiled for 1 to 2 minutes. Larger pieces may be boiled for as much as 3 to 4 minutes.

Cutting Vegetables

Most of the cutting techniques used in the recipes presented in this book are familiar to any Western cook. A few, however, deserve special mention. The Japanese pay great attention to the way in which each ingredient is cut, because careful cutting not only lends beauty to the preparation when it is served but also assures that each uniform piece will be cooked to precisely the desired degree of tenderness.

Cutting vegetables into small rectangles: Cut thick vegetables (carrots, *daikon*, etc.) into 1½-inch lengths, then cut each section vertically into thirds. Now place each piece on its largest surface and cut lengthwise into small rectangles about 1/8 inch thick.

Cutting into matchsticks: This technique is used with long, thin root vegetables. Cut crosswise into 2-inch lengths; then stand each piece on end and cut vertically into 1/8-inch-thick pieces. Stack these on top of one another and cut lengthwise into 1/8-inch-wide strips the size of wooden matchsticks. Slivering or cutting *julienne* are variations on this basic technique.

Cutting into half moons: Use with long, thick roots or

tubers. Cut lengthwise into halves, then cut each half crosswise into pieces about ½ to ¼ inch thick.

Cutting into ginkgo leaves: Cut lengthwise into quarters, then cut crosswise into thin pieces.

Using Sesame Seeds

When roasted and ground, sesame seeds have a wonderful nutty flavor and aroma, and almost every Japanese kitchen is equipped with a *suribachi* and *surikogi* (a serrated earthenware bowl and wooden pestle, p. 51) used for grinding them. Small quantities of seeds can also be ground in a pepper grinder, a spice or coffee mill, or a special grinder that fits over the mouth of a jar of sesame seeds and is sold at Japanese hardware stores. If you are using ½ cup or more of seeds, you can grind them in a hand mill or meat grinder, or, in some cases, purée them in a blender with a dash of oil or shoyu. You may wish to make enough to last for several days or to use in Sesame Salt (p. 58). Grind the seeds with a firm but light touch until they are well crushed but not oily.

Two parts of ground roasted seeds impart about the same flavoring as 1 part pre-packaged sesame butter or *tahini.*

(Proper care of the *suribachi* is very important. Before use, scrub the suribachi with hot water and douse with boiling water. Dry with a dishcloth, then turn the bowl upside down and dry thoroughly with one edge raised to allow air to circulate. After use, fill the *suribachi* with hot water and soak for 1 hour; then scrub and dry as above.)

Heat a heavy skillet until a drop of water flicked across its surface evaporates instantly. Add seeds and reduce heat to low. Shaking the pan and stirring seeds constantly, roast for about 3 minutes or until seeds are fragrant and light brown and just begin to pop. (A seed pressed between the thumb and little finger should crush easily.) Transfer about ½ cup seeds at a time to the *suribachi* and grind with the pestle until no more than 10 to 15 percent of the seeds remain whole. For best flavor and aroma, use seeds immediately. To store, allow leftover seeds to cool, then seal in an airtight container in a cool, dry place. Prepare just enough for a week.

Toasting Nori

Wave a sheet of *nori* over medium heat for about 30 seconds or until crisp and slightly green.

Preparing a Steamer

Chinese Bamboo Steamer: Set the steamer over a wok filled with water to a depth of about 1½-inches. Bring water to a boil over high heat, then reduce heat to medium. Place the food in the steamer, cover with the bamboo lid, and steam for the required length of time. The woven bamboo lid prevents dripping by allowing steam to pass out. With this tool, several layers of food can be steamed at one time.

Covered Pot Steamer: Fill a 10- to 12-inch-diameter pot with water to a depth of about 1 inch. Bring to a boil over high heat, then reduce heat to low. Into the pot place a collapsible French steamer, a colander, or a plate set on top of an inverted bowl. Now put in the food to be steamed. (In many cases, tofu will be wrapped in a *sudaré* bamboo mat before insertion.) Place a single layer of absorbent toweling or paper over the mouth of the pot to prevent moisture from dripping onto the food, then cover the pot. Steam as directed.

PREPARING TOFU

The following procedures are used regularly in cooking with tofu. Try to master them from the outset, since each gives the tofu a unique consistency and texture.

Draining Tofu

Place the tofu in a 1- or 2-quart flat-bottomed container. Cover well and refrigerate for 1 to 2 hours or, for a firmer texture, overnight.

If set on a small colander or folded towel placed into the container beforehand, the tofu will drain even more thoroughly.

If two cakes are stacked one on top of the other, the one on the bottom will be almost as firm as if it were pressed (see below).

If the tofu was purchased in a sealed plastic tub, prick a tiny hole in bottom of tub, drain out any water, and place tofu and tub in container as described above.

Pressing Tofu

*Towel and Fridge Method: Wrap the tofu firmly in a small terry-cloth or cotton towel folded into fourths, and set on a plate in a refrigerator for 1½ to 2 hours or overnight. To decrease the pressing time, drain the tofu beforehand, place a 2- or 3-pound weight on top of the tofu, and replace the damp towel with a dry one after about 30 minutes. Or cut the cake horizontally into halves before pressing and place in the towel as illustrated.

*Slanting Press Method: Wrap the tofu in a towel or bamboo mat *(sudaré)* (or sandwich the tofu between bamboo mats) and place on a cutting board, tray, or large plate next to the sink; raise the far end of the board several inches. Set a 2- to 4-pound weight on the tofu and let stand for 30 to 60 minutes.

*Sliced Tofu Method: Cut the tofu crosswise into ½- to ¾-inch-thick slices and arrange on two towels placed on a raised cutting board. Cover the slices with a double layer of towels and pat lightly to ensure even contact. Allow to stand for 30 to 60 minutes. This method is commonly used when preparing tofu for deep-frying. For faster results, top with a cutting board and 5-pound weight and change the towels after 10 minute intervals.

Squeezing Tofu

Place drained, parboiled, or pressed tofu (or doufu) at the center of a large dry dishtowel and gather its corners to form a sack. (Or use a tofu pressing sack [p. 51] if available.) Twist sack closed, then squeeze tofu firmly, kneading it for 2 or 3 minutes to expel as much water as possible. Squeeze lightly enough so that no tofu penetrates the sack. Empty the squeezed tofu into a mixing bowl.

Scrambling Tofu

Place tofu in an unheated skillet. Using a (wooden) spatula, break tofu into small pieces. Now cook over medium heat for 4 to 5 minutes, stirring constantly and breaking tofu into smaller and smaller pieces until whey separates from curds. Pour contents of skillet into a fine-mesh strainer; allow curds to drain for about 15 seconds if a soft consistency is desired, or for about 3 minutes for a firmer consistency. Spread curds on a large plate and allow to cool to room temperature.

Crumbling Tofu

Combine 12 ounces tofu and 1 cup water in a saucepan. With a wooden spoon or spatula, break the tofu into very small pieces while bringing the water to a boil. Reduce heat and simmer for 1 to 2 minutes. Place a colander in the sink and line with a large cloth (or a tofu pressing sack). Pour the contents of the pan onto the cloth, gather its corners to form a sack, then twist closed. Using the bottom of a jar or a potato masher, press the tofu firmly against the bottom of the colander to expel as much water as possible. Empty the pressed tofu into a large bowl and allow to cool for several minutes. Now break the tofu into very small pieces, using your fingertips or a spoon.

Dousing Deep-fried Tofu

Place uncut pieces of deep-fried tofu in a strainer or colander. Bring 2 or 3 cups of water to a boil in a saucepan. Douse first one, then the other side of the tofu. Allow to drain for about 1 minute before using.

Or, holding individual pieces of tofu with chopsticks or tongs, dip tofu quickly into boiling water, then drain in a strainer.

Broiling Deep-fried Tofu

*If using a *stove-top burner* or bed of *live coals*, skewer tofu with a long-tined fork and hold just above the flames until lightly browned on both sides and fragrant.
*If using a regular *bread toaster*, simply drop in the deep-fried tofu and toast. Fast and easy. Serve immediately.
*If using an *oven broiler*, place tofu on a sheet of aluminum foil and broil under a high flame until lightly browned on both sides.
*If using a grill over a *barbecue* or *brazier*, or a Japanese-style broiling screen set over a stove-top burner, broil the tofu over high heat for 30 to 60 seconds on each side until speckled and fragrant. Turn with chopsticks or tongs. In our opinion, this method—used with a charcoal fire—gives the finest flavor and aroma.
*If using a *dry skillet*, preheat skillet over medium heat and drop in tofu. Pressing tofu down with chopsticks or fork, rub tofu over entire bottom of skillet until tofu is fragrant and lightly browned. Turn and brown second side.

The following stocks, sauces, toppings, dressings, rice and noodle dishes, and other basic preparations are often served with miso. They play important supporting roles in miso cookery, so we have grouped them all together here. They will be called for frequently in later recipes.

The different varieties of fresh *dashi* (Japanese soup stock) serve as the basis for a wide variety of miso preparations and are easily made from natural ingredients. An instant dried dashi (dashi-no-moto) is now available in the West. Refrigerated in a sealed container, fresh dashi will last for 2 to 3 days without appreciable loss of flavor. Western-style vegetable or vegetable bullion stocks make satisfactory substitutes.

Number 1 Dashi *(Ichiban Dashi)*   MAKES 3 CUPS

This preparation is a cornerstone of Japanese cooking. The amount and variety of bonito flakes used vary slightly from chef to chef, as does the (often highly secret) method of preparation. For best flavor use flakes which have been shaved just before use.

3 cups water, Kombu Dashi, or Niboshi Dashi
¼ to 1 cup bonito flakes (15 to 30 grams)

Heat the water until quite hot in a small saucepan. Add bonito flakes and bring to a boil. Turn off heat and allow to stand for 3 minutes, or until flakes settle; skim off foam. Filter the dashi through a (cloth-lined) strainer placed over a saucepan. Press flakes with the back of a spoon to extract remaining dashi, then reserve flakes. (Some cooks add fine-textured flakes to simmered broths, *nabé* dishes, and miso soups together with the dashi, or simply omit straining.)

For a richer flavor, use a relatively large amount of flakes, simmer flakes for 2 or 3 minutes, and allow the dashi to stand (covered) for 15 to 30 minutes before straining.

Number 2 Dashi *(Niban Dashi)*   MAKES 2½ CUPS

The basic dashi ingredients are generally reused at least once to make a milder-flavored "Number 2" dashi. Thereafter the kombu may be slivered and simmered in shoyu and *mirin* to make *tsukudani* (a garnish for rice), pressure cooked with brown rice (p. 57), or cut into strips, each of which are tied into a simple loop and simmered in Oden (p. 141) or Nishimé (p. 143); whole pieces are sometimes used to prepare vinegar- or *nukamiso* pickles.

Whereas Number 1 Dashi is featured primarily in Clear Soups, this stock is generally used when simmering vegetables, with miso soups, or in noodle broths.

2½ cups water
Bonito flakes and *kombu* reserved from Number 1 Dashi

Combine all ingredients in a small saucepan and bring just to a boil. Remove *kombu* immediately, then simmer for 1 more minute. Strain and allow to cool.

Two tablespoons of fresh bonito flakes may be added to the boiling water after removing the *kombu;* reduce heat to lowest point and simmer for 5 minutes before straining. Leftovers may be reboiled in 1¼ cups water to make Number 3 Dashi.

Kombu Dashi *(Kombu Stock)*   MAKES 3 CUPS

Used in many homes as the basis for Number 1 Dashi (see above), this stock is featured in its own right in Zen Temple Cookery. *Kombu's* flavoring components (such as glutamic acid) reside mostly on its surface; be careful not to remove them by washing. Since they and the *kombu's* nutrients pass quickly into the stock, lengthy cooking is unnecessary, and actually leads to a decline in flavor.

1 strip of *kombu*, about 3 by 7 inches, wiped lightly with a moistened, well-wrung cloth
3 cups water

Combine *kombu* and water in a saucepan and bring just to a boil. Turn off heat, remove *kombu,* and reserve for use in other cooking. Use dashi as required or, if preparing Number 1 (or *Niboshi*) Dashi proceed to add bonito flakes (or *niboshi*) immediately.

For a more pronounced flavor but somewhat more viscous consistency, score *kombu* surface across grain at ½-inch intervals; simmer for 3 to 5 minutes before removing; double the amount of *kombu* if desired.

VARIATIONS

*Cold Water Method: Combine water and *kombu* and allow to stand for at least six hours, and preferably overnight. Remove *kombu* and use dashi as required. (Some cooks bring the stock just to a boil before removing the *kombu*.) The lengthy soaking is often said to make best use of the *kombu's* nutrients and give the finest flavor.
*Shiitake & Kombu Dashi: Select 2 or 3 *shiitaké* mushrooms, preferably ones having thick, partially opened caps and whitish (rather than darkish or yellowish) gills. (Or use ¼ cup dried stems or broken pieces.) Rinse briefly under running water, then soak either in cold water with the *kombu* or for 30 minutes in hot, freshly prepared Kombu Dashi. Strain dashi before use; do not squeeze *shiitaké* to extract absorbed dashi lest stock turn a dark brown.

Soybean Stock   MAKES 1 QUART

Prepare Pressure Cooked Soybeans (p. 129) doubling the amount of water used. (At the end of cooking, about 1 quart cooking liquid should remain for each cup soybeans.) Strain stock before serving beans.

Shiitaké Dashi *(Mushroom Stock)*

The preparation of Shiitaké Dashi as an integral part of the process for making miso soup is described on page 105. In Chinese Buddhist vegetarian restaurants and temples, a soybean & *shiitaké* stock is prepared by adding 1 to 2 cups washed and drained *shiitaké* stems or pieces to the ingredients for Soybean Stock (see above). The *shiitaké* are usually removed before serving the beans.

Niboshi Dashi *(Sardine Dashi)*   MAKES 3 CUPS

3 cups water or Kombu Dashi (p. 57).
¼ to ½ cup tiny (2-inch-long) dried sardines

Combine ingredients and bring to a boil over medium heat. Reduce heat to low and simmer for 3 to 5 minutes, skimming off any foam that rises to the surface. Strain through a (cloth-lined) sieve, reserving fish for use in other cookery. Use dashi as required or, if preparing Number 1 Dashi, proceed to add bonita flakes immediately.

Brown Rice   MAKES 4 CUPS

The Japanese say that when cooked, both regular and *sushi* rice are at their peak of flavor when the rice at the bottom of the pot is golden brown and slightly crisp. And even moderns prize the aroma of rice cooked in a heavy iron pot over a wood fire.

2 cups brown rice, rinsed and soaked overnight in 2 2/3 cups water

In a heavy covered pot, bring water and rice to a boil over high heat. Reduce heat to low and simmer for 45 to 50 minutes, or until all water is absorbed or evaporated. Uncover pot, remove from heat, and stir rice thoroughly with a wooden spoon. (If a slightly drier consistency is desired, transfer rice to a wooden bowl before stirring). Allow to cool for several minutes, then cover pot (or bowl) with a double layer of cloth until you are ready to serve.

To pressure cook: Rinse and drain 1 cup rice. Without soaking, combine in a pressure cooker with 1 cup water. Bring to pressure (15 pounds), reduce heat to low, and simmer for 25 minutes. Allow pressure to come down naturally for 10 to 15 minutes. Open pot and mix rice well. Allow to stand uncovered for 3 to 5 minutes, then cover with a cloth as above.

Brown Rice Porridge   SERVES 2 OR 3

Called *Congee* in China and *Okayu* in Japan, this is a popular main course at breakfast in many homes and temples. Easy to digest, rice porridge is considered the ideal food for sick people, and nursing mothers sometimes skim the creamy liquid from the porridge's surface to feed their babies as a breast milk supplement. In China, rice porridge is often served garnished or seasoned with *chiang* (p. 227), as are the hundreds of varieties of rice gruel. The latter, a close relative of Japan's *Zosui* (p. 122), is prepared by cooking vegetables (often leftovers) with rice porridge and seasoning the mixture with miso or soy sauce.

½ cup brown rice, soaked overnight in 4½ cups water

Prepare as for brown rice, setting lid slightly ajar and simmering for about 90 minutes, or until rice develops a porridge-like consistency. Serve immediately, seasoned with Sesame Salt (p. 58) or salt- or miso-pickled vegetables. If desired, add crumbled *nori* and minced leeks.

Or combine 1¼ cups (leftover) cooked rice with 3½ cups water and, without soaking, proceed as above.

To pressure cook: Rinse and drain ½ cup rice. Without soaking, combine in a pressure cooker with 2½ cups water. Bring to pressure (15 pounds), reduce heat to low, and simmer for 45 minutes. Allow pressure to come down naturally for 10 to 15 minutes. Open pot and mix porridge well. Allow to stand uncovered for 3 to 5 minutes before serving.

Sushi Rice
(Rice in Vinegar Dressing)
MAKES 2½ CUPS

1 cup (brown) rice, soaked in 1½ cups water overnight in a heavy 2- to 4-quart pot
Vinegar Dressing:
  2½ tablespoons (rice) vinegar
  1½ teaspoons honey
  2 teaspoons *mirin* (optional)
  ½ teaspoon salt

Bring soaked rice to a boil in a covered pot. Reduce heat to low and simmer for 40 to 50 minutes, or until all water has been absorbed and rice is quite light and dry. (If using white rice, simmer for only 15 to 20 minutes). Remove rice from heat and allow to stand for 5 minutes. Transfer hot rice to a large wooden bowl, platter, or other non-metallic container and immediately sprinkle on the dressing. With a wooden spoon, chopsticks, or a wide fork in one hand, and a fan or flat pot lid in the other, mix the rice vigorously while fanning to cool it as quickly as possible. Fan and stir for about 3 minutes, then allow rice to cool to room temperature.

For variety, prepare Unsweetened Sushi Rice by omitting the honey and *mirin* in the dressing, and by increasing the vinegar to 4 tablespoons and the salt to 1½ teaspoons.

Paper-thin Omelets
MAKES ABOUT 8

These omelets may be made into an envelope or purse (*chakin*) used to contain Sushi Rice or they may be cut into thin strips called "threads of gold" and scattered over the top of Sushi Rice.

4 eggs
¼ teaspoon salt
1 teaspoon ground roasted sesame seeds (p.54) (optional)
1 to 2 teaspoons oil

In a small bowl, combine eggs, ¼ teaspoon salt and sesame; mix well. Heat a small skillet and coat lightly with oil, pouring off any excess. Pour about one-eighth of the egg mixture into the skillet, swishing it around quickly so that it just covers the bottom of the pan. Cook over high heat for about 20 to 30 seconds on one side only to form a thin omelet. Transfer omelet to a plate and allow to cool. Prepare 8 omelets, oiling the pan lightly after every 3 or 4. Sliver to use as a garnish.

Noodles
SERVES 2 OR 3

4½ to 5 ounces dry buckwheat or whole-wheat noodles (*soba* or *udon*)

Bring 2 to 3 quarts of water to a rolling boil over high heat. Scatter noodles slowly over surface of water and return to the boil. Lower heat until water is boiling actively but does not overflow. Cook uncovered for about 5 minutes, or until noodles are tender but not soft. Pour noodles into a colander placed in the sink and drain briefly, then transfer to a large container filled with circulating cold water. Stir noodles with chopsticks for several minutes until they cool to temperature of water, then transfer noodles back into colander; drain well and serve.

Sesame Salt (Gomashio)
MAKES ABOUT ½ CUP

A delicious all-purpose seasoning for grains, salads, beans, eggs, cereals, and sautéed vegetables, Sesame Salt is generally made with about 7 parts whole sesame seeds to 1 part salt. Please begin by studying instructions for preparing ground roasted sesame seeds (p. 54).

2 teaspoons sea salt
5 tablespoons white or black sesame seeds

Heat a heavy skillet. Pour in the salt and roast, stirring constantly, for about 1 minute. Add the sesame seeds and roast until done. Grind the salt-sesame mixture in a *suribachi* or hand mill as for Ground Roasted Sesame Seeds (p. 54). Store in an airtight container.

Ketchup-Worcestershire Sauce
MAKES 6 TABLESPOONS

¼ cup ketchup
2 to 3 teaspoons Worcestershire sauce

Combine ingredients, mixing well.

6

Recipes from East & West

MISO'S EXQUISITE flavor and deep aroma, complex orchestrations brought to perfection over the centuries, evoke and accentuate the subtlest nuances of taste. Its warm colors have long been artfully used in a cuisine which demands that the eye as well as the palate find satisfaction. Its yielding texture has been prized for being gentle on the tongue.

Our 400 recipes hope to demonstrate that miso is, indeed, an all-purpose seasoning. *Arranged with our personal favorites at the beginning of each section,* they are meant to serve as an introduction to basic principles. The possibilities are limitless, as are the wonderful flavors you will discover as you begin to create new recipes based on your own favorite dishes.

FAVORITE MISO RECIPES

Among the many recipes in this book, there are certain ones we enjoy again and again, and like to serve to guests as an introduction to miso cookery. Most take little time to prepare and use readily available ingredients. This chart gives suggestions for their use in a weekly menu.

	Breakfast	Lunch	Dinner
Sun.	• Basic Miso Soup (p. 110)	• Floating Cloud Miso Dressing (p. 83) on your favorite salad • Mushroom Casserole with Miso, (p. 133)	• Peanut Miso (p. 62) or Walnut Miso (p. 61) on brown rice or on Apple Slice Hors D'oeuvres (p. 75) • Miso Mushroom Saute (p. 65)
Mon.	• Eggs Cooked Over Brown Rice with Miso (p. 151)	• Gaucamole with Miso (p. 74) as a dressing or dip; or • Miso-Sesame-Avocado Spread (p. 79)	• Baked Potatoes in Miso Gravy (p. 133) or • Potatoes with Miso White Sauce au Gratin (p. 134)
Tues.	• Deep-fried Tofu & Wakame Miso Soup (p. 102)	• Cucumber Slices Topped with Finger Lickin' Miso (p. 77) • Grilled Cheese Sandwich on Miso-Garlic Brean (p. 81)	• Miso Spaghetti Sauce (p. 114) • Grilled Corn-on-the Cob with Miso (p. 144)
Wed.	• Instant Miso (Better 'n Coffee) Soup (p. 109)	• Velvet Zucchini Miso Soup (p. 110) • Miso-Cream Cheese Dip (p. 74)	• French Onion Soup with Miso (p. 107) or • Miso Onion Soup Casserole au Gratin (p. 133) .
Thurs.	• Brown Rice or Brown Rice Porridge with Miso Toppings (p. 119)	• Miso Onion Sauce or Mushroom Sauce (p. 113) or Miso White Sauce (p. 114) over cooked vegetables or potatoes • Miso Paté (p. 79)	• Stir-fried Rice with Almonds and Miso (p. 120) • Miso Barbecue Sauce (p. 118) on tofu burgers or tempeh burgers
Fri.	• Scrambled Eggs with Miso, Onions, (p. 151)	• Stir-fried Buckwheat Noodles with Miso (p. 123) • *Amazaké* (p. 162) or Potato Salad with Sour Cream and Miso (p. 86)	• Rich Noodle Casserole with Miso-Sour Cream & Chives (p. 133) • Baked Apples Filled with Sesame-Raisin Miso (p. 153)
Sat.	• Thick Winter Squash Soup with Miso (p. 107)	• Tabbouli with Miso (p. 126) • Miso French Dressing (p. 84) with your favorite salad	• Miso & Nutritional Yeast Gravy (p. 113) over cooked grains or vegetables, or fried tempeh or tofu • Dengaku (p. 144)

Miso Toppings

Together with miso soup and *aemono*, the following are among the most popular ways of using miso in Japanese cookery. As versatile as they are delicious, Sweet Simmered Miso, Sautéed-, Mixed-, Broiled-, and Yubeshi Miso are each easy to prepare and well suited for use in a wide variety of Western-style dishes. All varieties make excellent toppings for grain, tofu, and fresh or cooked vegetables.

SWEET SIMMERED MISO
(*Nerimiso*)

Nerimiso derives its name from the verb *neru* which means "to simmer, stirring constantly, until smooth and thick." Prepared by combining miso with honey or sugar, water or dashi, seasonings and/or sake, and in most cases, nuts, diced vegetables, or seafoods, some varieties—such as peanut, walnut, and *yuzu*—are sold commercially, but most are made at home or in Zen temple restaurants, where they are said to have originated. Sweet Simmered Miso is generally prepared as a preserved food meant to be served over a period of several weeks. One or two cups are usually prepared at a time and are kept in a small attractive container, often an earthenware crock. At mealtimes, it is served as a seasoning at the table and used as a convenient topping for rice or rice porridge, chilled or deep-fried tofu, *mochi*, curries (it replaces chutney), oatmeal and other hot breakfast cereals, sweet or Irish potatoes (baked, broiled, mashed, or tempura), fresh vegetable slices, and a variety of cooked vegetables. The sweeter varieties make delicious spreads for toast or sandwiches, waffles, crêpes and pancakes, and steamed vegetables (such as cauliflower or broc-

coli). Small (1-teaspoon) portions are served on tiny ceramic dishes as accompaniments for Japanese-style tea and cakes, or as hors d'oeuvres together with sake or beer. Sweet Simmered Miso is also used as an ingredient in cooked preparations such as Miso Oden (p. 141), Eggplants Shigiyaki (p. 146), Dengaku (p. 144), and Aemono (p. 91). Unlike regular miso, it is never used in soups.

In restaurants, Sweet-Simmered Miso is often prepared in quantities of several quarts or more; cooked in a double boiler, it is stirred for as long as 1 to 2 hours to develop cohesiveness and luster, and improve its shelf life and flavor. After cooling, it becomes somewhat firmer than regular miso, often developing a consistency similar to that of peanut butter; some makers use *mizuamé* as the sweetener to create an even firmer consistency, closer to that of taffy.

Since imported varieties are relatively expensive, several natural food companies in the United States are now beginning to prepare their own Sweet Simmered Misos (using peanuts, walnuts, or cashews as the main ingredient) packaged in small transparent cottage cheese-type containers for nationwide distribution. Actually, any natural food store could offer its own varieties prepared fresh, refrigerated and sold in bulk. A sample large-scale recipe for Peanut & Sesame Miso is given on page 62.

We generally keep a cup of each of 3 or 4 types of Sweet Simmered Miso in the refrigerator at all times. Their flavors seem to marry and improve over a period of several weeks, and they keep their peak for a month or more if well sealed after each use.

Vary the amount of sweetening to taste. If *mirin* is unavailable, use a mixture of honey and sake (or white wine).

Red Sweet Simmered Miso
MAKES ½ CUP

This is the simplest and most basic form of Sweet Simmered Miso; all other recipes may be thought of as variations or elaborations on this fundamental theme. By adding different ingredients and seasonings (sesame, gingerroot, grated lemon rind, etc.) to those listed below, you can create a wide array of delicious toppings.

5 tablespoons red or barley miso
1½ to 2½ tablespoons honey
1 tablespoon water; or 1½ teaspoons each water and white
  wine (or sake or *mirin*)

Combine all ingredients in a small earthenware pot or a skillet and bring to a boil. Simmer for 2 to 3 minutes over low heat, stirring constantly with a wooden spatula or spoon, until mixture begins to thicken. Remove from heat and allow to cool to room temperature before serving. Cover and refrigerate unused portions.

VARIATIONS: Prepare as above

*Rich Red Sweet Simmered Miso: A favorite for use in Miso Oden (p. 141)
  6 tablespoons red, barley, or Hatcho miso
  2 tablespoons honey
  ¼ cup *mirin*
  2 tablespoons sake
*Chinese-style Sweet Simmered Miso: Topping for the popular noodle dish *Cha-chiang Mien*
  3 tablespoons red or barley miso (preferably chunky)
  1½ tablespoons soy sauce
  1 to 1½ tablespoons honey
  1 teaspoon (peanut or salad) oil
  ½ teaspoon sesame oil
  1 tablespoon sake or white wine
  2 tablespoons ground roasted seasame seeds (p. 54) or
    1½ tablespoons sesame butter (optional)
*Hatcho Sweet Simmered Miso: Use Hatcho miso and reduce the amount of sweetening by about one-third. This preparation has a deep, chocolate-brown color and savory aroma.
*Sake Lees Sweet Simmered Miso: Add 3 to 4 tablespoons sake lees; reduce the honey to 1½ teaspoons and omit the water.
*Crunchy Granola Miso: Prepare ½ cup Red Sweet Simmered Miso (using a relatively small amount of honey) and allow to cool to room temperature. Combine with ½ to 2/3 cup granola, mixing well.

Thyme

*Herb Sweet Simmered Miso: Just before removing miso from heat, stir in ½ to 1 teaspoon of any of the following fresh or dried herbs: thyme, basil, oregano, *sansho* pepper, rosemary, or mint.
*For use in Dengaku (p. 144), divide Red Sweet Simmered Miso into two equal portions. To one portion add ½ to 1 teaspoon hot mustard or ½ teaspoon *sansho* pepper.

White Sweet Simmered Miso   MAKES 1¼ CUPS

This recipe, a specialty of Kyoto's 400-year-old Naka-mura-ro restaurant, is used as the topping of Japan's most famous Tofu Dengaku. In springtime, ground *kinomé* is mixed with the miso, or individual sprigs of *kinomé* are used to garnish the Dengaku portions. The use of egg gives White Sweet Simmered Miso a rich, smooth texture.

1 cup sweet white or 2/3 cup mellow white miso
3 tablespoons *mirin*
1½ tablespoons sake
1 egg yolk
3 tablespoons ground roasted sesame seeds (p. 54) or 1½
  tablespoons sesame butter or *tahini*

Prepare as for Red Sweet Simmered Miso (see above).

VARIATION: Prepare as above

*Sweet White Sweet Simmered Miso (Makes ½ cup)
  ¼ cup sweet white or 2½ tablespoons mellow white miso
  1½ to 2 teaspoons honey
  2 teaspoons *mirin*
  1 egg yolk
  Dash of *sansho* pepper (optional)
For use in Dengaku (p. 144) or hors d'oeuvres (p. 76), or as a topping for deep-fried foods, divide the prepared miso into two equal portions. To one, add any of the following: ½ to 1 teaspoon grated gingerroot; 2 to 3 tablespoons thinly sliced leeks or green onions; 3 to 4 tablespoons ground roasted sesame seeds (p. 54) or sesame butter; 1 to 2 tablespoons bonito flakes and 1½ teaspoons water.

Walnut Miso   MAKES 1 CUP

One of our favorite miso preparations, Walnut Miso is often served in Zen temple restaurants and is sold commercially in Japan. Delicious as a topping for crisp apple slices (p. 75).

1 cup walnut meats, preferably large pieces
¼ cup red, barley, or akadashi miso
2 to 3 tablespoons honey or *mizuamé*
1 tablespoon water or 1½ teaspoons each water and white
  wine (or sake)

Prepare as for Red Sweet Simmered Miso (see above).

VARIATIONS

*Sauté walnuts in 1 tablespoon oil for 1 minute before adding remaining ingredients. Or pre-roast walnuts until fragrant in a dry pan or oven and, if desired, add ¼ cup sesame butter to the ingredients listed above.
*Cashew-, Almond-, or Pecan Miso: Substitute ¾ to 1 cup of any one of these for the walnuts.
*Sunflower Seed Miso: Sauté ½ cup sunflower seeds in 1 teaspoon oil for 1 to 2 minutes; then add miso and other ingredients and proceed as above.

Peanut Miso

MAKES ½ TO ¾ CUP

1 cup peanuts, lightly roasted, if desired
¼ cup red, barley, or Hatcho miso
1½ to 3 tablespoons honey or *mizuamé*
2 tablespoons water; or 1 tablespoon each water and sake, wine, or *mirin*

Prepare as for Red Sweet Simmered Miso (see above).

VARIATIONS

*Peanut & Raisin Miso: Use ¼ cup each peanuts and raisins, and 2 to 3 teaspoons honey. Add 1 to 2 tablespoons (whole or ground) roasted sesame seeds, if desired. This delicious product is sold commercially in Japan and America.
*Use akadashi miso and reduce the honey to 1½ teaspoons.
*Sauté peanuts briefly in oil before adding the remaining ingredients; serve garnished with a sprig of *kinomé*.
*Use ¼ cup sweet white miso, omit the honey and add ¼ to ½ teaspoon salt.

Sesame

Peanut & Sesame Miso

MAKES 1 GALLON

Here is a sample recipe that could be used by natural food stores, restaurants, or communities that would like to begin commercial production of Sweet Simmered Miso.

16 cups whole roasted peanuts, or substitute walnuts, cashews, or sunflower seeds
4 cups red or barley miso
1 cup roasted sesame seeds (whole or ground)
1 to 2½ cups honey
½ to 1 cup malt syrup
½ cup water

Combine all ingredients in a heavy 1½- to 2-gallon pot and bring to a boil. Simmer, stirring constantly for 5 to 10 minutes, or until mixture begins to thicken. Pour into a large crock or wide-mouth jar and allow to cool to room temperature. Cover and refrigerate.

For variety, add 2 cups raisins and reduce the honey to taste.

Sesame Miso

MAKES ¾ CUP

The use of freshly-ground roasted sesame seeds gives the finest flavor and aroma. If desired, use black seeds with Red or Hatcho Sweet Simmered Miso, but always use white seeds with White Sweet Simmered Miso. Excellent as a topping for sauteed or steamed vegetables such as *daikon*, turnips, eggplants, or burdock root. Sesame Miso thinned in water during cooking also makes a delicious sauce.

¼ cup sesame butter, *tahini*, or ground roasted sesame seeds (p. 54)
1/3 cup red, barley, or Hatcho miso
1 to 2 tablespoons honey
1 tablespoon water; or 1½ teaspoons each water and sake (or white wine)
1 to 2 teaspoons grated orange, lemon, or *yuzu* rind (optional)

Prepare as for Red Sweet Simmered Miso (see above).

VARIATIONS

*For the sweet, chocolate-like flavor of Chinese *T'ien Mien Chiang* or Peking Duck Dipping Sauce (p. 70), use akadashi instead of the red miso.
*To the basic recipe add ¼ cup whole or chopped nutmeats (almonds, walnuts, etc.)
*To ¼ cup Red or White Nerimiso, add 1 to 2 tablespoons ground roasted sesame seeds or sesame butter, and ½ to 1 teaspoon grated gingerroot.

Yuzu

Yuzu Miso

MAKES 1 CUP

This recipe comes from Tokyo's 370-year-old tofu restaurant, Sasa-no-Yuki, where the miso is served over warm pieces of silken tofu and also sold in small ceramic jars for home use. The fragrant rind of the *yuzu* (citron) is preserved for about 1 year in *shochu*—a popular and very potent type of spirits related to gin—before being used in the miso. The chefs prepare about 35 pounds of *yuzu* miso at a time, stirring the mixture in a heavy pot for 1½ to 3 hours over low heat to develop a dark lustrous color. Some commercial varieties, most of which are a creamy beige, contain *yuzu* rind which has been immersed for 1 year in a crock of sugar before being diced and simmered with sweet white miso. In grating fresh *yuzu* at home, it is important to use only the yellow or green surface layers of the well-washed rind. If the deeper white layers are used, the miso may become bitter.

½ cup (light) red or barley miso
6 to 6½ tablespoons sugar or 3 tablespoons honey
6 tablespoons water
½ teaspoon grated *yuzu* rind, or substitute 1 to 2 teaspoons
   grated lemon, lime, or orange rind

Prepare as for Red Sweet Simmered Miso (p. 60) except add the *yuzu* rind just before removing miso from heat.

For a darker color, simmer for a longer time. For a lighter color, substitute sweet white miso for the red and reduce sugar to 1½ tablespoons. The addition of 1 tablespoon *mirin* gives a nice luster without lengthy cooking.

VARIATIONS

*Tipsy Wintertime Yuzu Miso: Prized for its subtle bitterness, this preparation makes a fine topping for cooked vegetables and broiled tofu. In traditional Japanese homes, the *yuzu* and sake are simmered in a small earthenware teapot set over the mouth of a large iron tea kettle heated by a charcoal fire in the living room *hibachi* brazier.

During December or January, choose a well-ripened, yellow *yuzu*, wash well, and cover with sake or white wine in a small lidded pot. Place pot over a double boiler and simmer until *yuzu* dissolves. (If double boiling is inconvenient, use a mixture of equal parts sake and water and simmer over low heat, stirring occasionally.) Remove *yuzu* seeds, then stir in sweet white miso and a little sugar. Simmer over low heat, stirring occasionally, until well thickened.

Lemon or Lime Miso

MAKES ¼ CUP

¼ cup red, barley, or Hatcho miso
1½ to 3 teaspoons honey
1 tablespoon water
1 teaspoon lemon (or lime) juice
1 teaspoon grated lemon (or lime) rind

Combine the first three ingredients in a skillet and proceed as for Red Sweet Simmered Miso (p. 60). After removing from heat, stir in lemon juice and rind, allow to cool to room temperature. Delicious with sliced bananas, apples, and most deep-fried foods.

A softer version can be prepared by mixing 2 teaspoons lemon juice with 2 tablespoons Red Sweet Simmered Miso. Or prepare as for Tipsy Wintertime Yuzu Miso (above).

Tangy Mustard Miso

MAKES 1 CUP

2 tablespoons red, barley, or Hatcho miso
2 tablespoons vinegar
½ teaspoon hot mustard
1 tablespoon oil
Dash of pepper (optional)

Prepare as for Red Sweet Simmered Miso (p.60) but simmer for only 30 to 60 seconds. For variety, add 1 tablespoon ground roasted sesame seeds.

Kinomé

Kinomé Miso
(Miso with Fresh Sansho Leaves)

Also called *sansho* miso, this green and refreshingly fragrant miso is a springtime favorite. When *kinomé*, the fresh sprigs of the *sansho* tree, emerge early each April, this miso is widely enjoyed as a topping for Tofu Dengaku (p.144), in *aemono* (p. 91) or on butter-fried mushrooms.

¼ cup (about 60) *kinomé* leaves (not sprigs)
5 tablespoons sweet white miso
1½ teaspoons honey
2 tablespoons water
1 teaspoon shoyu (optional)
1½ teaspoons *mirin* or sake (optional)
Dash of *sansho* pepper (optional)

Place leaves in a strainer, douse with boiling water, and drain well. Grind leaves thoroughly in a *suribachi* (or mortar), or mince with a knife. Combine the next five ingredients in a small saucepan and prepare as for Red Sweet Simmered Miso (p. 60). Add contents of saucepan and pepper, if desired, to ground *kinomé* in *suribachi;* mix well.

VARIATION

*Jade-Green Miso: Collect 4 ounces of the tender tips of *(horenso)* spinach and/or *daikon* leaves. Mince thoroughly, then grind almost to a paste in a *suribachi* or mortar. Pour in 1 cup water and, using your fingertips, free the ground leaves from the grooves in the bowl. Now pour the contents of the *suribachi* into a fine sieve set over a small saucepan and rub the leaves through the sieve with the back of a large spoon. Heat contents of saucepan over high heat until puréed leaves float to the surface, then reduce heat to low and simmer for 1 minute. Pour contents of pan into a cloth-lined strainer; drain well. Using a small spoon, carefully remove green purée (called *aoyosé*) from cloth. Add 1 teaspoon *aoyosé* to Kinomé Miso, stirring well, until the miso has turned a delicate green.

A simpler version of *aoyosé* may be prepared by parboiling and draining the greens, then pressing them with your fingertips; grind in a *suribachi* or rub through a strainer, then mix with the miso.

In many recipes *aoyosé* is used together with *kinomé* to give the miso a richer color. It is stirred into the miso just before the miso is mixed with the *kinomé*.

Egg Yolk Miso

MAKES 1 CUP

6 tablespoons sweet white or ¼ cup mellow white miso
2 egg yolks
1 tablespoon honey
5 tablespoons dashi (p.56), stock, or water
Dash of *sansho* pepper (optional)

Prepare as for Red Sweet Simmered Miso (p. 60)

For use in Tofu Dengaku (p. 144), divide the prepared miso into 2 equal portions. To one add 1 teaspoon *aoyosé* (see preceeding recipe) and 60 *kinomé* leaves prepared as for Kinomé Miso. Stir in these ingredients just after removing miso from the heat.

Garlic Miso

MAKES ¼ CUP

Often cooked without thinning the miso with water or sake, this preparation has a very firm texture: refrigerated, it will stay fresh for several months. Considered by many Japanese to promote good health, it is usually served as a topping for hot rice; the heat gives it a softer consistency.

3 cloves of garlic, thinly sliced or crushed
¼ cup red, barley, or Hatcho miso
2½ to 4 teaspoons honey
2 teaspoons sake, white wine, or water (optional)

Prepare as for Red Sweet Simmered Miso (p. 60), but simmer over very low heat for 8 to 10 minutes, or until quite firm.

Gingerroot Miso

MAKES ½ CUP

2 to 3 teaspoons grated gingerroot
5 tablespoons red, barley, or Hatcho miso
1 to 1½ tablespoons honey
2 teaspoons sake, white wine, or water

Prepare as for Red Sweet Simmered Miso (p. 60). Serve with Dengaku (p. 144), as a cracker spread, with deep-fried foods, or as a topping for rice.

To obtain a somewhat similar flavor, simply mix ½ teaspoon grated gingerroot juice with ¼ cup Red Sweet Simmered Miso.

Leek or Onion Miso

MAKES ½ CUP

This miso is especially popular in Japanese villages where it is used as a topping for baked potatoes—and as a cure for colds.

6 tablespoons barley or red miso
6 tablespoons diced or grated leek, scallion or onion
2 tablespoons bonito flakes (optional)

Prepare as for Red Sweet Simmered Miso (p. 60) but cook for only 1 to 2 minutes. Or simply mix all ingredients without cooking.

VARIATIONS

*For a sweeter version of the above, mix 1 part Red Sweet Simmered Miso (p. 60) with 1 part minced leeks or onions. Excellent as a topping for Dengaku (p. 144).
*Red-Pepper & Leek Miso: This popular Korean preparation called *doen jang* is usually prepared with Red Pepper Miso *(kochu jang;* p. 231) and served as a zesty topping for cooked rice. Omit the bonito flakes in the basic recipe above and add ¼ teaspoon red pepper or tabasco sauce and 1 teaspoon (sesame) oil.

Beefsteak Leaf Miso *(Shiso Miso)*

MAKES ½ CUP

1 tablespoon butter
3 tablespoons red or barley miso
1 tablespoon honey
4 tablespoons water
¼ teaspoon 7-spice or minced red pepper
¼ cup minced green beefsteak leaves

Melt the butter in a skillet. Add the next four ingredients and cook, stirring constantly, for 3 to 5 minutes or until fairly thick. Mix in the beefsteak leaves and cook for 1 minute more.

Or, substitute ¾ cup beefsteak seeds for the leaves. Sauté in the butter for 1 minute before adding remaining ingredients.

Vinegar Miso

MAKES 3/8 CUP

This miso is generally prepared without cooking and used in various forms as a dressing for *aemono* (p. 91). Only when the miso is heated or cooked is Vinegar Miso considered a type of Sweet Simmered Miso.

3 tablespoons red or barley miso
3 tablespoons vinegar or lemon juice
1 tablespoon honey

Heat the miso until just warm in a small saucepan. Remove from heat and mix in vinegar and honey, stirring until smooth.

Allow to cool before serving. Use as a topping for fresh or cooked vegetables, or deep-fried foods, or as a dressing for *aemono*.

Variations containing sweet white miso, *mirin*, mustard, sesame, walnuts, peanuts, or chives may be prepared as above using the ingredients found in the recipes beginning on page 91.

Sweetened Mustard Vinegar Miso   MAKES ½ CUP

3 tablespoons red, barley, or Hatcho miso
1½ teaspoons honey
1 tablespoon oil
¼ cup water
1 tablespoon vinegar
½ teaspoon hot mustard

Combine the first four ingredients in a saucepan or skillet and bring to a boil. Simmer, stirring constantly, for 3 to 4 minutes, or until as firm as regular miso. Remove from heat, stir in vinegar and mustard, and allow to cool. Delicious with Chilled Noodles (p. 126).

Kanro Hishio   MAKES ½ CUP

Kanro means "sweet morning dew." This product, sold commercially in Japan, is a specialty from the city of Choshi, famous for its fine shoyu and hishio.

½ cup hishio (p. 43)
2 tablespoons *mizuamé* or honey
1 teaspoon sake or white wine (optional)

Prepare as for Red Sweet Simmered Miso (p. 60).

Red Pepper-Miso with Burdock Root   MAKES ¾ CUP

At Tokyo's famous *Yabusoba* noodle restaurant, a dab of this tangy miso is served on a tiny wooden dish as an accompaniment for green tea.

1 teaspoon oil
6 tablespoons minced burdock root, soaked for 10 minutes in water, and drained
2½ tablespoons red miso
2½ tablespoons sweet red miso
2 tablespoons sugar or 1 tablespoon honey
2 tablespoons water or the starchy water remaining after boiling *soba* buckwheat noodles
1/8 to ¼ teaspoon 7-spice red pepper, minced chili peppers, or tabasco sauce

Heat a skillet and coat with the oil. Add burdock root and sauté for 2 or 3 minutes. Add remaining ingredients and cook over low heat, stirring constantly, for about 5 minutes. Allow to cool before serving.

If sweet red miso is unavailable, substitute red or barley miso and increase the amount of sugar by 1½ tablespoons.

Burdock

MISO SAUTÉ
(Abura Miso)

Originally a Chinese-style preparation featuring fresh vegetables sautéed in sesame oil, Miso Sauté serves as a delicious topping for brown rice or rice porridge, fresh or cooked vegetable slices, and chilled or deep-fried tofu. Refrigerated and well-sealed, unused portions will keep for up to 1 week. In each of the following recipes, up to one half of the oil may be sesame, which lends a nutty flavor and savory aroma. Experiment with other vegetables and nuts, or even with fruits.

Plain Miso Sauté   MAKES ¼ CUP

1½ tablespoons (sesame) oil
4½ tablespoons red, barley, or Hatcho miso

Heat a skillet and coat with the oil. Add miso and sauté over low heat for about 1 minute, or until miso just begins to stick to skillet. Allow to cool before serving. Delicious on cucumber slices.

Mushroom Miso Sauté   MAKES ½ CUP

2 tablespoons oil
10 mushrooms, thinly sliced
1 tablespoon red, barley, or Hatcho miso
1 teaspoon honey

Heat a skillet or wok and coat with the oil. Add mushrooms and sauté over medium heat for about 1 minute or until tender. Reduce heat to low, add miso and honey, and cook, stirring constantly, for about 1 minute more, or until mushrooms are evenly coated with miso. Allow to cool to room temperature before serving.

For variety, substitute butter for one-half of the oil, and sauté over low heat adding ¼ cup chopped walnut meats. Or use sweet white miso and reduce the honey to ½ teaspoon.

OTHER TYPES OF VEGETABLE MISO SAUTÉ

Each of the following recipes is prepared in basically the same way as Mushroom Miso Sauté. Use 1½ to 2 tablespoons oil, 1 to 1½ tablespoons miso, and 1 to 1½ teaspoons honey.

*Lotus root: Sauté 1½ cups ginkgo leaves of lotus root over low heat for about 5 minutes, or until tender but still crisp. Proceed as above.

*Kabocha: Use ¼ onion cut into thin wedges and 1½ cups thinly sliced pieces of *kabocha*, squash, or pumpkin. Sauté over medium-high heat for 4 to 5 minutes, or until softened. Add 1 tablespoon sesame butter, *tahini*, or ground roasted sesame seeds (p. 54) together with the miso and honey.

*Eggplant: Use 1 diced onion and 1½ cups 2-inch matchsticks of eggplant. Sauté just until all oil is absorbed, then add miso and honey.

*Sweet potato: Use 1¼ cups of sweet potato, yam, or Irish potato cubes. Sauté over high heat for 3 to 5 minutes until softened. If desired, sauté ½ diced onion and ½ thinly sliced carrot for 3 to 4 minutes before adding potatoes.

*Burdock root: Use 1½ to 2 cups matchsticks of burdock root, soaked (p. 53), and 1 carrot cut into matchsticks or grated. Sauté burdock root over high heat for 8 to 10 minutes, or until softened. Add carrot and sauté for 5 minutes more, or until both vegetables are tender. If desired, add 1 to 2 tablespoons roasted sesame seeds together with the miso and honey.

*Onion: Use 2 onions, cut into thin wedges, and 1 carrot, thinly sliced, slivered, or grated. Sauté both vegetables together over medium heat for 5 to 6 minutes, or until carrot is tender. Proceed as for Mushroom Miso Sauté.

*Gingerroot: Sauté 2 tablespoons grated gingerroot for about 1 minute.

*Celery: Sauté 1 cup diced celery or celery root for 2 minutes over high heat, or until softened. Add miso and honey and proceed as above.

Lemon-Walnut-Mushroom Miso Sauté

MAKES ¾ CUP

1½ teaspoons oil or butter
4 (*shiitaké*) mushrooms, thinly sliced (about 1/3 cup)
1 tablespoon minced lemon, lime, or *yuzu* rind
¼ to ½ cup chopped walnut meats
1/3 cup red, barley, or Hatcho miso
1½ to 2 tablespoons honey
2 to 3 tablespoons water

Prepare as for Mushroom Miso Sauté (p. 65) but sauté mushrooms for 2 minutes, then add lemon rind and walnuts, and sauté for 1 minute more.

Crumbly Tekka Miso

MAKES 1½ CUPS

The word *tekka* is composed of the Chinese characters for "metal" and "fire": this all-purpose condiment was traditionally simmered for a long time on a metal griddle or in a heavy iron pot. A favorite topping for brown rice, rice porridge, rice patties, and regular or deep-fried tofu, it is also served as is, as an hors d'œuvre with sake, beer, or wine. Several commercial varieties are now available at Japanese natural food stores and miso retail stores, and every good chef

has his or her own unique recipe. Crumbly Tekka Miso is prepared without sweetening and generally features chunky Hatcho miso and finely shaved burdock root; it is sautéed in sesame oil, often for as long as several hours, to create its dry, crumbly texture. Most varieties also contain roasted soybeans.

In Japan, this preparation is known formally as *Konjo Tekka Miso*. The word *konjo* means "root nature" and refers to those qualities in a great man which carry him through the most difficult situations. It is said that this miso was first developed during World War II for use as a seasoning with brown rice—which took the place of the usual white rice since it was less expensive, more nourishing, and did not require the time, energy, and manpower necessary for polishing. Eating this miso was believed to help a man develop his "root character". Today, tekka is widely regarded as one of Japan's finest and most high-class miso preparations, prized for its flavor and aroma, its long lasting qualities and versatility, and its medicinal properties (which make it a popular gift to friends who are sick). In Zen temples, it is often served as a condiment with each meal of the day.

3 tablespoons sesame oil
½ cup minced burdock root, soaked in cold water for 15 minutes and drained
6 tablespoons minced carrot or slivered, reconstituted *kombu*
¼ cup minced lotus root or whole peanuts
1 teaspoon grated gingerroot
¼ cup roasted soybeans (optional)
1 cup Hatcho, red, or barley miso
Dash of (7-spice) red pepper (optional)

Heat a large skillet or wok and coat with the oil. Add burdock root and sauté over high heat for 1 minute. Reduce heat to medium, add carrot and lotus root, and sauté for 2 to 3 minutes. Mix in gingerroot, miso and, if used, soybeans and red pepper: sauté for 2 minutes more. Reduce heat to low and cook, stirring constantly with a wooden spatula, for 20 to 30 minutes, or until miso is crumbly and fairly dry. Allow to cool before serving. Refrigerate unused portions in an airtight container.

VARIATION

*If roasted soybeans are unavailable, wash ¼ cup whole soybeans and soak in water for 30 minutes. (Or, for a firmer texture, omit soaking.) Drain beans thoroughly, then pat dry with a towel. Dry-roast in a heavy skillet until lightly browned and speckled, then add ¼ cup water and steam over low heat for 15 minutes. Add soybeans to miso together with carrots, and proceed as above.

Fine-textured Crumbly Tekka Miso

MAKES 2 CUPS

3 to 4 tablespoons (unrefined) sesame oil
¼ cup grated carrot
¼ cup grated lotus root
¼ cup grated burdock root
¼ cup black sesame seeds, ground to a paste; or sesame butter
¼ cup bonita flakes
2½ teaspoons minced gingerroot
1 cup (chunky) Hatcho miso

Heat a skillet and coat with the oil. Add the next six ingredients and sauté for about 5 minutes. Add miso, stirring well until evenly mixed with other ingredients. Reduce heat to very low and cook, stirring occasionally, for 20 to 30 minutes, or until miso is quite dry and slightly crumbly.

Moist Tekka Miso with Orange Rind

MAKES 3½ CUPS

5 tablespoons sesame oil
2 cups minced onion
2/3 cup minced burdock root
2/3 cup minced lotus root
2/3 cup minced or grated carrot
1 cup red, barley, or Hatcho miso
1 cup water
1 tablespoon grated gingerroot
1 teaspoon grated orange rind

Heat a heavy skillet and coat with the oil. Add onions and sauté for 5 minutes. Add consecutively burdock root, lotus root, and carrot, sautéing each lightly as you add it. Thin miso with the water and add, then stir in gingerroot and orange rind. Reduce heat to low and cover pan. Simmer, stirring occasionally, for 30 to 40 minutes, or until firm.

Sweetened Tekka Miso

MAKES 1¼ CUPS

The most popular form of *tekka* miso, this sweetened variety generally contains the same ingredients as Crumbly Tekka Miso plus honey; the miso is cooked only until smooth and firm.

1 tablespoon oil
2/3 cup thin rounds or matchsticks of burdock root, peeled, soaked in cold water for 15 minutes, and drained
½ carrot, cut into matchsticks
½ cup diced or slivered lotus root (optional)
1/3 cup Hatcho, red, or akadashi miso
2 tablespoons honey
1 tablespoon sake or white wine
2 tablespoons ground roasted sesame seeds (p. 54), sesame butter or *tahini*; or ¼ cup poppy or hemp seeds
¼ cup roasted soybeans (or see the variation to Crumbly Tekka Miso, p. 66)

Heat a wok or skillet and coat with the oil. Add burdock root and carrot, and sauté over medium-high heat for 3 or 4 minutes. Reduce heat to low, then stir in the next four ingredients and sauté for 3 or 4 minutes more. Stir in soybeans and remove from heat. Transfer to a bowl and allow to cool. Use as an all-purpose condiment or topping.

VARIATION
*Tekka Miso from Hatcho Sweet Simmered Miso
    ¼ cup soybeans
    1 tablespoon sesame oil
    ½ cup thin rounds or matchsticks of burdock root, prepared as above
    ¾ cup Hatcho Sweet Simmered Miso (p. 61)
    1 tablespoon ground, roasted sesame seeds
    1 tablespoon *mirin*

Roast soybeans as described in the variation under Crumbly Tekka Miso (p. 66). Sauté burdock in oil for 4 minutes, then add cooked beans and sweet simmered Miso, and sauté for 3 or 4 minutes more. Stir in sesame and *mirin*, and remove from heat.

Carrot & Red Pepper Miso Sauté

MAKES ¾ CUP

Many delicious varieties of Miso Sauté may be prepared without the use of sweetening using the basic techniques given in the following two recipes.

3 tablespoons sesame oil
¼ teaspoon minced red peppers, Chinese red-pepper *chiang*, or tabasco sauce
1 carrot, grated fine
1 tablespoon grated gingerroot
¼ cup red, barley, or Hatcho miso

Heat a wok or skillet and coat with the oil. Add the red pepper and sauté for 15 seconds. Add grated carrot and gingerroot and sauté for 1 minute more. Stir in miso and sauté for 6 more minutes. Remove from heat and allow to cool before serving.

Onion-Sesame Miso Sauté

MAKES ½ CUP

1 tablespoon sesame oil
½ cup minced wild onions, scallions, leeks, or onions
3 to 4 tablespoons sweet red miso
Dash of 7-spice red pepper, tabasco sauce, or paprika

Heat the oil over high heat in a wok or skillet. Add onions and sauté for about 1 minute. Stir in the miso and red pepper, reduce heat to low, and sauté for 2 or 3 minutes more.

Onion Miso Sauté with Orange

MAKES 1½ CUPS

2 tablespoons sesame oil
4 onions, thinly sliced
3 tablespoons red, barley, or Hatcho miso
¼ cup water
1 teaspoon grated orange rind
¼ cup grated cheese (optional)

Heat a skillet and coat with the oil. Add onions and sauté for 5 minutes. Stir in miso and water, cover, and simmer for 8 to 10 minutes. Add orange rind and, if used, grated cheese; remove from heat. For best flavor, allow to stand for 6 to 8 hours. Delicious on brown rice, tofu, or toast.

Sesame-Leek Miso Sauté

MAKES 1¼ CUPS

2 tablespoons sesame oil
2 cups chopped leeks or scallions, separated into whites and greens
6 tablespoons water or stock
4 tablespoons red, barley, or Hatcho miso

Heat a skillet or wok and coat with the oil. Add greens and sauté for 30 seconds. Add whites and sauté for 30 seconds more. Add 4 tablespoons water, cover pan, and simmer for 5 minutes. Thin miso in remaining 2 tablespoons water, add to vegetables, and simmer for 2 or 3 minutes.

Spicy Eggplant-Miso Sauté

MAKES 1½ CUPS

2 tablespoons oil
1¾ cups unpeeled, diced eggplants
3 tablespoons red, barley, or Hatcho miso
2½ teaspoons honey
2 tablespoons water
2/3 cup leeks or scallions, cut into ½-inch lengths
¼ teaspoon (7-spice) red pepper or tabasco sauce

Heat a skillet or wok and coat with the oil. Add eggplants and sauté over low heat for 3 to 4 minutes. Add miso, honey, and water and cook, stirring constantly, for 2 to 3 minutes. Mix in leeks, season with red pepper, and cook for 1 minute more.

For variety, omit leeks and serve skewered on food-picks as a hot or cold hors d'œuvre.

Garlic & Green Pepper Miso Sauté

MAKES ½ CUP

1 tablespoon oil
½ clove garlic, crushed or minced
1 or 2 green peppers, thinly sliced
2 tablespoons barley, red, or Hatcho miso
1½ teaspoons honey
3 tablespoons water

Heat a wok or skillet and coat with the oil. Add garlic and sauté over high heat for about 15 seconds. Add green peppers and sauté for 1 minute more. Reduce heat to medium, stir in

remaining ingredients and cook, stirring constantly, for 2 more minutes. Allow to cool before serving.

Spicy Burdock Miso Sauté

MAKES 1¼ CUPS

1 tablespoon sesame oil
1¼ cups shaved or slivered burdock root
1 teaspoon grated gingerroot; or ½ teaspoon grated lemon rind; or 1 tablespoon minced *umeboshi*
3 tablespoons red, barley, or Hatcho miso
1 tablespoon sesame butter or *tahini*
5 tablespoons water
Dash of (7-spice) red pepper

Heat a skillet or wok and coat with the oil. Add burdock and sauté for 5 minutes. Combine the next four ingredients, mixing well, then add to contents of skillet. Cover and simmer for 15 minutes over very low heat, stirring occasionally. Season with the red pepper and allow to cool. Serve as a topping for cooked Brown Rice (p.119).

Green Pepper Miso Sauté

MAKES 2/3 CUP

1 tablespoon oil
1 green pepper, diced
¼ cup red, barley, or Hatcho miso
2 tablespoons sake or white wine
3 to 4 tablespoons water
1½ teaspoons honey
1 teaspoon grated *yuzu*, lime, or lemon rind (optional)

Heat a wok or skillet and coat with the oil. Add green pepper and sauté for 1 minute. Mix in the next four ingredients and sauté for about 1 minute more. Remove from heat and stir in grated citrus peel. Serve as a sauce for croquettes, tofu (regular or deep-fried), baked potatoes, or sautéed vegetables.

For variety, substitute *sansho* pepper or beefsteak seeds for the citrus peel.

Beefsteak Seed Miso Sauté
(Shisonomi Abura Miso)

MAKES ½ CUP

1 teaspoon oil
¼ cup beefsteak seeds or buds, rubbed with salt, then rinsed well
¼ cup red, barley, or Hatcho miso
1¼ to 1½ tablespoons honey
1 teaspoon shoyu
1 tablespoon water or dashi (p.56)

Heat a skillet and coat with the oil. Add beefsteak seeds and sauté for 1 minute. Add remaining ingredients and proceed as for Mushroom Miso Sauté (p. 65), sautéing for 9 to 10 minutes more.

Banana Miso Sauté

MAKES 2 CUPS

1 tablespoon butter or oil
2 bananas, cut into thin rounds
½ cup chopped walnut or almond meats (optional)
1 tablespoon sweet white or 2 teaspoons mellow white miso
½ teaspoon honey (optional)

Prepare as for Mushroom Miso Sauté (p. 65), sautéing the walnuts, if used, with the bananas.

For richer color and flavor, use 1 tablespoon red or barley miso and 1½ teaspoons honey.

Spicy Korean Miso Sauté

MAKES ¾ CUP

2 tablespoons sesame oil
1 clove of garlic, crushed
1 tablespoon grated gingerroot
2 green peppers, minced
½ small onion, diced
Dash of minced red pepper, tabasco sauce, or 7-spice red pepper
3 tablespoons red, barley, or Hatcho miso
2 teaspoons soy sauce
1 tablespoon sake or white wine

Heat a wok or skillet and coat with the oil. Add the next five ingredients and sauté for 2 minutes. Stir in the miso, soy sauce, and sake, return just to the boil, and remove from heat. Allow to cool before serving. Delicious as a topping for fresh cucumber, celery, or tomato slices; for noodles or deep-fried tofu.

Vinegar Miso Sauté (Abura-su Miso)

MAKES ½ CUP

The addition of vinegar to many varieties of Miso Sauté gives a tangy flavor which is particularly well suited to deep-fried foods.

1 tablespoon oil
1 small onion or leek, thinly sliced
1 clove of garlic, crushed or minced
1½ tablespoons red, barley, or Hatcho miso
1½ teaspoons honey
1 tablespoon vinegar

Heat a wok or skillet and coat with the oil. Add onion and garlic and sauté over high heat for 2 minutes. Reduce heat to low, mix in miso and honey, and simmer for 1 minute more. Remove from heat, mix in vinegar, and allow to cool.

VARIATIONS

*Mustard-Vinegar Miso Sauté: Add ½ teaspoon hot mustard together with the vinegar.
*Substitute for the onions an equal volume of thinly sliced green peppers, mushrooms, or bamboo shoots.
*Add vinegar to taste to any of the previous recipes for Miso Sauté.

Oregano

MIXED MISO
(Awasé Miso)

These simple but delicious recipes, requiring no cooking, are quick and easy to prepare. A number of closely related dishes are given at Vinegar Miso Dressings (p. 91). Unseasoned mixed misos are described on page 44.

Mixed Red Miso Toppings

MAKES ABOUT ¼ CUP

In Japan, many of the following mixtures, prepared with shoyu rather than miso, are widely used as dipping sauces. The simplest of all types of miso recipes, these are extremely versatile, adapting themselves readily to experimentation with your favorite herbs and spices. All varieties may be served as toppings for rice or rice gruel, regular or deep-fried tofu, fresh vegetable slices, *mochi*, and baked or broiled potatoes.

Combine ¼ cup red, barley, or Hatcho miso with any one of the following, mixing well. Cover and refrigerate unused portions.
  *Garlic: 2 cloves of garlic, grated or crushed
  *Bonito: ¼ cup bonito flakes and, if desired, 1½ tablespoons *mirin*
  *Umeboshi Salt Plums: 1½ tablespoons minced *umeboshi* (about 10) and, if desired, 2 tablespoons bonito flakes
  *Wasabi: 1 teaspoon freshly grated *wasabi*, *wasabi* paste, or Western-style horseradish and, if desired, 1½ teaspoons honey
  *Gingerroot: 2 teaspoons grated gingerroot
  *Daikon: 4 to 6 tablespoons grated *daikon* and, if desired, 2 tablespoons bonito flakes
  *Leek: ¼ cup diced or grated leeks or scallions and, if desired, 1½ tablespoons bonito flakes
  *Citrus: 1 to 2 teaspoons grated or slivered lemon, lime, or *yuzu* rind
  *Herb: ½ to 1 teaspoon dill, marjoram, oregano, thyme, basil, or tarragon
  *Mustard: ½ to 1 teaspoon hot mustard and 2 tablespoons *mirin*, sake, or white wine
  *Lemon: 2 to 2½ tablespoons lemon (or lime) juice or vinegar and, if desired, 2 tablespoons sake or white wine
  *Sesame: 1½ tablespoons sesame or nut butter and, if desired, 1½ tablespoons honey and 4 teaspoons sake or white wine
  *Sesame-Bonito-Citrus: 1 tablespoon each sesame butter and bonito flakes (or grated cheese) and ¼ teaspoon grated lemon rind; serve in a hollowed half-lemon rind

Mixed White Miso Toppings

MAKES ABOUT ¼ CUP

¼ cup sweet white or 2½ tablespoons mellow white miso
½ to 1 teaspoon honey
Seasonings (optional): Choose one

 ¼ teaspoon grated lemon or orange rind and 1 teaspoon
   lemon juice
 1 tablespoon finely minced mint or green beefsteak
   leaves and ½ teaspoon water
 1 tablespoon each Parmesan cheese and parsley, and 1
   teaspoon water

Combine all ingredients, mixing well. Try with thinly sliced cucumbers or tomatoes, canapés or crackers, apple wedges or banana rounds.

Subtly Sweet Leek Miso

MAKES 1 CUP

1 cup leeks, sliced into very thin rounds
¼ cup barley or red miso

Combine ingredients, mixing well (with chopsticks) for several minutes. For best flavor, refrigerate for 1 to 2 days before serving. Excellent as a topping for Furofuki Daikon (p. 140) or baked potatoes. Or serve in small portions as an hors d'œuvre with drinks. A favorite in Japanese farmhouses where it is said to warm the body while providing strength and stamina.

 For a richer flavor, use ¼ cup each leeks and miso, and 1½ tablespoons bonita flakes.

Natto-Miso Topping

SERVES 2

½ cup natto (fermented soybeans)
2½ tablespoons red, barley, or Hatcho miso
1½ tablespoons bonito flakes
1½ tablespoons thinly sliced leeks, minced onions, or daikon leaves
1/3 teaspoon hot mustard
1½ tablespoons green nori flakes or crumbled toasted nori (p. 54) (optional)

Combine all ingredients, mixing well (with chopsticks) for several minutes to develop cohesiveness. Serve as a garnish for brown rice or rice porridge, or as a spread for crackers or canapés.

Homemade Akadashi Miso

MAKES ¼ CUP

2 tablespoons Hatcho miso
2 tablespoons red or light-yellow miso
1 tablespoon honey or mizuamé
½ to 1 teaspoon shoyu

Combine all ingredients, mixing well. For a smoother texture, rub through a sieve.

Cheese Miso

MAKES ¼ CUP

¼ cup finely grated (firm) cheese or Parmesan
1 tablespoon red, barley, or Hatcho miso
1 tablespoon butter (optional)
Seasonings (optional): Choose one
2 teaspoons minced onion, leek, or chives
1 to 2 tablespoons bonito flakes
½ clove crushed garlic
Dash of pepper, 7-spice red pepper, or tabasco sauce

Combine the cheese, miso and, if desired, the butter and seasoning. Mix lightly so that grated cheese retains its texture. Serve as a topping (or filling) for broiled or baked potatoes, sliced cucumbers, canapés, mochi, brown rice, or deep-fried tofu.

Peking Duck Dipping Sauce
(Homemade T'ien Mien Chiang)

MAKES ½ CUP

 This recipe, used by many Chinese-style restaurants in Japan, yields a sauce closely related to Sweet Wheat-flour Chiang (t'ien mien chiang), but with a slightly sweeter flavor and softer consistency. It is often used as an all-purpose cooking seasoning in sauces and stir-fried dishes, as well as with Peking Duck and Pancake Rolls.

¼ cup Hatcho miso
1½ teaspoons sesame oil
½ teaspoon vegetable oil
¾ teaspoon sake or white wine
1 teaspoon shoyu
1½ tablespoons honey
2 tablespoons water

Combine all ingredients, mixing until smooth. Refrigerate unused portions in a sealed container.

Peking Duck Dipping Sauce
(from Sweet Wheat-flour Chiang)

MAKES 3/8 CUP

¼ cup Sweet Wheat-flour Chiang (t'ien mien chiang)
1 teaspoon sesame oil
1½ teaspoons honey
1 teaspoon mirin, sake, or white wine

Combine all ingredients, mixing well.

Homemade Korean Red-pepper Miso (*Kochu jang*)

MAKES 3/8 CUP

¼ cup Hatcho or red miso
½ teaspoon powdered red pepper or tabasco sauce
1 tablespoon soy sauce
1 tablespoon honey
1 teaspoon sesame oil

Combine all ingredients, mixing well. A favorite with Korean-style five-color rice (*Bibimpap*, p. 123).

Rich & Savory Bonito-Miso Topping

MAKES 3 TABLESPOONS

2 to 3 tablespoons bonita flakes
1 to 1½ tablespoons red, barley, or Hatcho miso
1 tablespoon minced leeks or scallions
¼ teaspoon grated gingerroot

Combine all ingredients, mixing well. A favorite topping for tofu or deep-fried foods.

Savory Broiled Miso

SERVES 1

Use 1 to 2 teaspoons of any of the following:
   A chunky, natural Hatcho, barley or red miso
   Any dark-colored Sweet Simmered Miso (p. 60)
   Any variety of Mixed Miso, expecially varieties containing bonito flakes (p. 69)
   Subtly Sweet Leek Miso (p. 64)
   Cheese Miso (p. 70)

If using a stove-top burner, charcoal brazier, or bed of live coals: Spread miso in a layer about 1/8 inch thick on a thin cedar plank, the lid of an earthenware bowl, in a clam or scallop shell, or in the concave surface of a large wooden or metal spatula or spoon (fig. 16). Holding the miso (with tongs) 1 to 2 inches above the open fire and moving it back and forth slowly, broil for 15 to 30 seconds (checking miso every 5 seconds) until it is fragrant and lightly speckled. If broiling miso on a lid, place lid on its matching (empty) cup or bowl to help retain miso fragrance. If using a shell, serve in the shell. Or scrape miso from the plank, spatula, or spoon into a small shallow dish. Serve immediately.

If using an oven broiler: Spread miso as above on a piece of aluminum foil or directly onto canapés, buttered crackers, toast, thinly-sliced, steamed potatoes, deep-fried tofu, or eggplants. Broil and serve as above.

Fig. 16. Broiling Miso

BROILED MISO
(*Yakimiso*)

When broiled or grilled over an open fire, miso develops a delightful aroma and flavor, and in Japan, the use of cryptomeria or Japanese cedar *(sugi)* as the broiling plank imparts an additional subtlety to the fragrance. Served as a topping for hot rice or rice gruel, regular or deep-fried tofu, canapés, broiled potatoes or cucumber slices, broiled miso transforms the simplest dishes into gourmet delights. It may also be served as is, as an hors d'œuvre with sake or beer, or added to chilled summertime soups.

VARIATIONS

*Skewered Broiled Miso: Shape miso into 1½-inch-diameter balls, adding bonito flakes or grated cheese if necessary to give a firmer texture. Pierce with a skewer, chopsticks, or a fork, and broil over an open fire.
*Broiled Citrus Miso: Prepare Yuzu- or Lemon Miso (p. 62) and pack firmly into a hollowed half yuzu or lemon rind. Broil slowly over a bed of live coals until fragrant.
*Broiled Miso & Leek Broth: This preparation is a Japanese folk remedy said to cure colds and fevers. Combine broiled red miso with 1 tablespoon thinly sliced leeks. Stir in ½ cup boiling water, adding a little at a time until smooth. Serve hot.

Fig. 17. Hoba Miso

Hoba Miso (Miso & Vegetables Broiled on Magnolia Leaves)

SERVES 2

The word *hoba* refers to the huge oval leaves of the wild *ho* tree *(Magnolia hypoleuca)*. Often attaining a length of over 16 inches, the dried leaves have a delightful aroma that permeates the miso as the latter broils. This preparation is famous in and around Japan's mountain village of Takayama. In restaurants, it is usually prepared over a small tabletop charcoal brazier (fig. 17); in farmhouses, over the dying coals in the open-hearth fireplace located at the center of the main room. The fragrance of the woodsmoke is said to be one of the keys to its fine flavor.

1 large dry magnolia leaf, at least 12 inches long and 5 inches wide
2 to 3 tablespoons red, barley, or Hatcho miso
2 to 4 tablespoons grated *daikon*
½ leek, sliced into very thin rounds
4 (fresh *shiitaké*) mushrooms, thinly sliced
Seasonal wild vegetables, thinly sliced; or nuts (optional)
1 teaspoon oil (optional)

Place leaf with concave side facing upward atop a glowing charcoal brazier or barbecue, then place other ingredients at center of leaf. Broil, stirring occasionally with chopsticks, for 5 to 6 minutes, or until miso begins to simmer. While continuing to broil, transfer hot miso-vegetable mixture a little at a time from leaf and use as a topping for cooked Brown Rice, Rice Patties (p. 121), thin cucumber slices, or Ochazuké (p. 123). Or eat as is in small amounts as an hors d'œuvre with drinks.

A fairly good facsimile of this dish can be prepared using aluminum foil in place of the leaf and broiling in an oven broiler. In some parts of Japan, dry buckeye leaves are also used.

Kaiyaki-miso

Kaiyaki-miso (Miso Sautéed with Vegetables in Scallop Shells)

SERVES 4

This close relative of Hoba Miso is ideal for use at barbecues or campfire dinners.

4 teaspoons (sesame) oil
2 green *(togarashi)* peppers, minced
¼ cup diced eggplant
8 green beans, slivered
¼ cup slivered burdock root or carrot
2 teaspoons minced or grated gingerroot or garlic
2 green beefsteak or fresh basil leaves, slivered
4 to 6 tablespoons Hatcho, red, or barley miso
¼ cup bonito flakes (optional)

Place 4 scallop shells over a charcoal brazier, on a barbecue grill, or directly atop the dying coals of a campfire. Divide the oil among the shells and heat, then add equal amounts of the next six ingredients to each shell. Sauté, stirring occasionally, for 4 to 6 minutes, or until all vegetables are tender. Stir in miso (and bonito flakes) and cook for 2 minutes more. Without removing shells from fire, transfer hot miso-vegetable mixture a little at a time from shell and use as a topping as for Hoba Miso.

Fuki-no-to Miso (Butterbur-buds Broiled Miso)

MAKES 1¼ CUPS

The butterbur or bog rhubarb *(Petasites japonicus)* is an edible wild mountain plant whose budding forth from the frozen earth heralds the coming of spring. While the mature stems also make a delicious food, the young buds which emerge from the base of the plant close to the ground are used to create the unique, subtly bitter flavor and aroma of this popular preparation.

½ cup red or barley miso
½ cup bonito flakes
¼ cup minced walnuts or sesame butter
1½ tablespoons honey or mirin (optional)
5 butterbur buds, with outer layers carefully removed and reserved
1½ tablespoons honey or *mirin* (optional)

Combine the first three (or four) ingredients, mixing well, and divide into two equal portions. Dice buds and mix with one portion of the miso, then use the mixture to prepare Broiled Miso (p. 71). (For a mellower flavor, allow the miso-buds mixture to stand in a cool place for 10 days before broiling.)

Divide second portion of miso mixture into fifths, shape into small balls, and wrap each in butterbur's outer layers. Place into a preheated steamer and steam for 15 minutes, then set in a cool dry place and allow to stand for 6 months. Remove leaves and discard. Cut miso balls into thin rounds and serve as hors d'œuvres, in miso soups, or as a topping for Ochazuké (p.123) or brown rice.

YUBESHI MISO
(Miso-stuffed Citrus)

The word *yubeshi*, which originated in China, is written with three ideographic characters: the first means *yuzu* (the fragrant East-Asian citron); the second refers either to a treat or confection or, more specifically, to *mochi* (steamed and pounded glutinous rice); the third means child. *Yubeshi* has long been made in Japanese farmhouses during the cold months, especially just before New Year's. *Yuzu* (or lemon) halves are stuffed with a miso mixture, steamed, and hung in the shade to dry. The miso and citrus gradually become permeated with each other's fragrance, and the finished product is firm enough to be sliced into thin rounds. There are two basic types of *yubeshi:* that which contains *mochi* has a relatively mild and sweet, rather spicy flavor, and is excellent for use as an hors d'œuvre or confection; that which contains mostly miso is generally used as a topping, but can also be served in very thin slices as an hors d'œuvre. The preparation of the former, less common variety, will be described under hors d'œuvres (p. 76).

Fig. 18. Yubeshi Miso

Yubeshi Miso Topping
MAKES ½ CUP

½ cup red, barley, or Hatcho miso
2 tablespoons bonito flakes, or substitute grated cheese
2 tablespoons sesame butter, minced walnuts, or ground roasted sesame seeds
2 large *yuzu* or lemons, washed, cut crosswise (or vertically) into halves, the fruit scooped out and reserved

Combine the first three ingredients, mixing well, and use to stuff the yuzu or lemon halves. Rejoin halves and tie with 4 long strips of cloth (or rice straw) as shown in figure 18. Place into a pre-heated steamer and steam for 40 minutes. Hang (under the eaves) in a shady, well-ventilated place and allow to dry for at least 1, preferably 3 to 4 weeks. Cut crosswise into ¼-inch-thick rounds (or scoop out the miso filling) and serve as a topping for grain or tofu dishes, thinly sliced cucumbers, tomatoes, or apples, crackers or canapés.

VARIATIONS

*Quick Yubeshi: Add ½ teaspoon grated *yuzu* or lemon peel to the above ingredients. Omit steaming. Wrap miso-stuffed citrus with plastic wrap and refrigerate for 1 or 2 days. To serve, scoop out fragrant miso and discard citrus halves.
*Use as the filling: miso, grated gingerroot, (7-spice) red pepper and, if desired, minced walnuts. For a sweeter version, add a little honey.

Miso in Dips & Hors D'oeuvres

Most of the recipes in this section make use of nut butters and dairy products, are uniquely Western and, we feel, exemplify miso's delicious versatility.

MISO IN DIPS

Miso-Cream Cheese Dips

MAKES ¾ CUP

4 ounces cream cheese, softened with 1½ to 3 tablespoons warm water
2 teaspoons red or barley (or 4 teaspoons mellow white) miso
½ small onion, grated or minced
1 tablespoon butter, softened
¼ cup grated cheese
2 teaspoons sake or white wine

Combine all ingredients, mixing well until thoroughly blended and smooth. For best flavor, refrigerate in a sealed container for 5 to 7 days. Serve with crackers, chips, fresh vegetable slices, celery stalks, or apple wedges. Also delicious as a spread for sandwiches or canapés.

VARIATIONS

Add any of the following ingredients to the softened cream cheese and miso; serve immediately:

*Tangy: 2 tablespoons grated cheese, 1 teaspoon minced onion, and 4 teaspoons mayonnaise
*Curry: ½ teaspoon curry powder
*Sesame: 1½ tablespoons sesame butter or *tahini* and a dash of tabasco sauce or red pepper
*Lemon: 2 to 3 teaspoons lemon juice plus 1 tablespoon warm water to soften the cream cheese, ½ teaspoon grated lemon rind, 3 tablespoons mayonnaise, 1 tablespoon minced parsley, and a dash of pepper
*Sweet Miso and Sesame: See Miso-Stuffed Celery (p. 77)

Guacamole with Miso

MAKES 1 CUP

1 well-ripened avacado, peeled and seeded
¼ tomato, diced
2 teaspoons lemon juice
½ clove garlic, crushed
1½ tablespoons red or barley (or 2½ tablespoons mellow white) miso
2 tablespoons sesame butter or *tahini* (optional)
2 tablespoons minced onion
Dash of paprika or ¼ teaspoon tabasco sauce
1 to 2 tablespoons minced parsley

Combine the first eight ingredients; mash together with a fork until smooth. Serve as a dip, spread, or dressing; garnish with the parsley. Flavor improves if sealed and refrigerated for one hour or more.

Miso-Cottage Cheese Dip

MAKES ½ CUP

6 tablespoons cottage cheese
1½ teaspoons red or barley (or 1 tablespoon mellow white) miso
2 teaspoons minced parsley
Dash of pepper
1 tablespoon minced onion, or ½ clove of garlic, crushed (optional)

Combine all ingredients, mixing well. Excellent on hors d'œuvre crackers or as a sandwich spread.

Cream Cheese-Miso Dip with Nuts and Raisins

MAKES 1 CUP

4 ounces cream cheese softened with 1 tablespoon warm water
4 tablespoons sweet white or 2½ teaspoons red miso
2 tablespoons butter
¼ cup chopped walnuts or almonds
¼ cup raisins

Combine all ingredients, mixing well. Serve with crackers, tomato and cucumber slices, or celery stalks. Good also as a sandwich spread.

Tofu-Miso-Sour Cream Dip   MAKES 1½ CUPS

12 ounces tofu, drained and mashed
1½ tablespoons red or barley (or 3 tablespoons mellow
    white) miso
5 tablespoons sour cream
1 teaspoon lemon juice or vinegar
1 tablespoon minced parsley or chives
Dash of pepper

Combine all ingredients, mixing well. Delicious with crackers
or fresh vegetable slices.

Soy Jalapeño with Miso   MAKES 1¼ CUPS

1 cup cooked soybeans (p.129), well drained and mashed
¼ onion, minced
2 tablespoons red, barley, or Hatcho miso
1 teaspoon oil
½ clove garlic, crushed
1 tablespoon lemon juice or vinegar
½ to ¾ teaspoon tabasco sauce or powdered red pepper

Combine all ingredients and mash until smooth or run
through a hand mill or meat grinder. Serve as a dip or spread.
Especially good with taco chips.
    For variety, substitute pinto beans for one-half the
cooked soybeans.

Tangy Miso-Tahini Dip   MAKES 1 CUP

2 teaspoons red, barley, or Hatcho miso
½ cup tahini or sesame butter
¼ cup lemon juice
1½ cloves garlic, crushed
¼ cup water

Combine all ingredients, mixing well. For a sweeter flavor,
add 2 teaspoons honey. To make a sauce, add ¼ cup more
water.

MISO IN HORS D'ŒUVRES

    Miso is perhaps at its best when used in the preparation
of Western-style hors d'œuvres. See also Dengaku (p. 144),
Eggs Pickled in Sweet White Miso (p. 159), and other miso
pickles (p. 156). Finger Lickin' Miso (p. 41) and Sweet
Simmered Miso (p. 60) are often served in quantities of 1 to 2
teaspoons on a small dish as an accompaniment for drinks.

Miso Walnuts, Cashews, or Almonds   SERVES 3 TO 4

½ cup unsalted walnut, cashew, or almond meats
1½ teaspoons red or barley miso, dissolved in 3 tablespoons
    water

Heat a heavy skillet, drop in nuts, and dry-roast over medium
heat, stirring constantly, for about 3 minutes, or until fragrant. Add dissolved miso and sauté for 30 seconds, or just
until all liquid has evaporated. (Slight overcooking may cause
the miso to burn.) Allow to cool before serving.
    For a crunchier texture, toast in a medium oven for
about 20 minutes, or until fragrant.

Crackers with Cream Cheese, Egg & Miso Topping   MAKES 10 TO 15

2 hard-boiled eggs, separated into yolks and whites
2 ounces cream cheese
1½ teaspoons red or barley (or 3 teaspoons mellow white)
    miso
1 tablespoon minced parsley
Dash of pepper or paprika
10 to 15 hors d'œuvre crackers

Combine egg yolks with the cream cheese, miso, parsley, and
pepper; mash well. Slice egg whites into thin rounds and place
one round on each cracker. Top with a dab of the cream
cheese-miso mixture.

Mushroom Hors D'œuvre with Miso Marinade   SERVES 2 TO 4

1 tablespoon red, barley, or Hatcho miso
2½ to 3 tablespoons (rice) vinegar
1½ teaspoons honey
1 tablespoon sesame butter (optional)
20 (shiitaké) mushrooms, washed and drained

Combine the first four ingredients in a shallow pan, mixing
until smooth. Broil mushrooms for 1 minute on each side, or
until speckled and fragrant, then add immediately to miso-
vinegar mixture; marinate for 30 minutes. Serve skewered on
foodpicks or mounded on lettuce leaves with a little marinade
poured over the top.

Apple Wedges with Miso Toppings   SERVES 4

2 apples, cut into thin wedges
¼ cup Peanut Miso (p. 60), Orange-Sesame Miso (p. 115),
    Walnut Miso (p. 61), Sesame Miso Spread (p. 81), or
    your favorite variety of Finger Lickin' Miso (p. 41)

Arrange apple slices on a serving platter and top each with a ½
teaspoon dollop of the miso.

Apple & Banana Hors D'œuvre with Miso Topping

SERVES 4 TO 6

1 banana, cut diagonally into 1-inch-thick ovals
1 apple, cut into thin wedges
Sweet Miso & Tahini Topping:
   2 tablespoons *tahini* or sesame butter
   1 teaspoon honey
   1 teaspoon red, barley, or Hatcho miso
   2 to 3 tablespoons raisins
   2 to 3 tablespoons chopped almonds or walnuts

Arrange fruit slices on a serving platter. Mix topping ingredients and spoon in dollops (or spread) onto slices.

Sliced Bananas with Peanut Butter-Miso Topping

SERVES 2

2 bananas, cut diagonally into long, thin ovals
1½ tablespoons peanut butter
1 teaspoon red or 2 teaspoons sweet white miso
2 tablespoons wheat germ
1½ tablespoons raisins

Arrange banana slices on a serving platter. Combine peanut butter and miso, mixing well, and place in dabs atop bananas. Sprinkle with wheat germ and dot each dab with 3 or 4 raisins just before serving.

   For added richness, combine 1 tablespoon each grated coconut and minced nutmeats with the peanut butter and miso.

Canapés with Miso Spreads

MAKES 30

30 pieces of buttered (whole-grain) bread or toast, each 2 inches square
Spreads: About 2 to 3 tablespoons each
   Sweet Simmered Miso (pp. 60 to 65; Sesame, Peanut, Red Pepper, or Subtley Sweet Leek Miso)
   Finger Lickin' Miso (p. 42)
   Miso Mayonnaise (p. 84)
   Sweet White Miso & Butter Spread (p. 80)
   Cheese Mixed Miso (p. 10)
Canapé Toppings:
   ½ cucumber, sliced into thin ovals
   1 green pepper, cut lengthwise into quarters
   1 hard-boiled egg, thinly sliced
   1 tomato, thinly sliced
   ½ carrot, sliced into thin ovals
   8 green peas, parboiled (optional)
   1 small potato or sweet potato, boiled and thinly sliced

Use each of the five types of miso as a spread for one-fifth of the bread slices. Place the toppings individually or in combinations on the bread to form canapés. If desired, pierce each canapé with a foodpick. Arrange on large serving platters.

VARIATION

*Deep-fried Tofu & Miso Hors d'œuvre: Cut any variety of deep-fried tofu into thin strips or bite-sized pieces. For best flavor, broil quickly until speckled and fragrant. Top each piece with any of the above miso spreads and canapé toppings. Serve skewered with foodpicks.

   The ingredients may also be rolled up in an opened deep-fried tofu pouch, fastened in 3 or 4 places with foodpicks, and cut crosswise into small cylinders.

Tomato Hors D'œuvre with Sesame Miso

SERVES 8 TO 12

¼ cup sesame butter or *tahini*
2 teaspoons red, barley, or Hatcho miso
2 tablespoons mayonnaise
1 clove of garlic, crushed
½ teaspoon honey
1 teaspoon sake or white wine
1 to 2 teaspoons water (optional)
3 tomatoes, cut into ½-inch-thick rounds

Combine the first seven ingredients, mixing well. Arrange tomato slices on a serving platter and top each slice with a dollop of the sesame miso.

   This topping is also delicious on other fresh vegetable slices and canapés; or use as a sandwich spread.

Spicy Yubeshi Miso Hors D'œuvre

MAKES 1 CUP

   Please begin by reading about Yubeshi (p. 76). This traditional preparation, a specialty of Japan's southernmost main island, Kyushu, is now sold commercially throughout Japan and looks remarkably like a 5-inch-long sausage. Whereas the traditional product was steamed in bamboo leaves and packed (and occasionally sold) in the joined halves of a citrus, its modern counterpart is plastic-wrapped, but is still very delicious.

6 tablespoons glutinous rice flour (*shiratama-ko*)
2½ tablespoons water
3 tablespoons red, barley, or Hatcho miso
1 tablespoon honey
Dash of (7-spice) red pepper or tabasco sauce
½ teaspoon grated gingerroot
2 teaspoons sesame butter or *tahini;* or 3 to 4½ teaspoons minced walnuts
¼ teaspoon grated *yuzu,* lemon, or orange rind

Combine the flour and water, and mix for several minutes to develop a smooth dough of earlobe consistency. Mix in remaining ingredients and knead with a rubber spatula (or your hands) for several minutes more. Form mixture into a 1½-inch-diameter sausage shape and wrap in corn leaves or cellophane. (Or pack into a cup or small bowl and cover with cellophane.) Place into a preheated steamer and steam for 20 minutes, then allow to cool to room temperature. Slice into thin rounds (or serve in cup accompanied by a small knife or spoon). Use like cold cuts as an hors d'œuvre topping for crackers, thin vegetable slices, or canapés, or as a garnish for rice.

For variety, wash 2 *yuzu* or lemons, cut into halves, scoop out the fruit and reserve. Fill with the (unsteamed) miso mixture and proceed as for Yubeshi Miso (p. 73).

Cucumber and/or Jicama Slices Topped with Finger Lickin' Miso   SERVES 4

Crisp, juicy, and unbelievably delicious, *jicama* is a root vegetable from Latin America now widely available in the United States and quite inexpensive. Heart-shaped and 5 to 7 inches in diameter, its peel is the color of a potato's. Best fresh, it may also be cooked lightly.

1 large cucumber, cut into diagonal slices and/or
¼ jicama, cut into sticks for dipping
3 to 6 tablespoons finger lickin' miso

Top each slice with a dab of the miso. Serve chilled, arranged on a platter. As delicious as they are easy to prepare.

Fresh Cucumber Slices with Miso Topping   SERVES 2

In Japan, a popular hors d'œuvre called *Morokyu* is prepared by slicing fresh cucumbers on the diagonal to form thin ovals, then spreading one surface of each with moromi miso. Other varieties of Finger Lickin' or Sweet Simmered Miso may also be used. The following cooked topping takes longer to prepare but is well worth the time and effort.

1 tablespoon oil
2 inches of leek or ¼ onion, thinly sliced
1 tablespoon red, barley, or Hatcho miso
1 tablespoon grated gingerroot
1 (*shiitaké*) mushroom, thinly sliced
1 large cucumber, cut into thin diagonal slices

Heat a wok or skillet and coat with the oil. Add the next four ingredients and sauté over low heat, stirring constantly, for 3 to 4 minutes. To serve, allow to cool, then spread on sliced cucumbers.

Stuffed Eggs with Miso and Sesame   MAKES 8 HALVES

4 eggs, hard-boiled and cut lengthwise into halves
2 teaspoons red, barley, or Hatcho miso
4 teaspoons sesame butter or grated cheese
2 tablespoons minced onion
Paprika (optional)

Remove egg yolks and mash together with the miso, sesame butter, and onion. Form the mixture into 8 balls, and use as a stuffing for the egg halves. If desired, top with paprika.

Hors D'œuvre with Miso-damari   SERVES 4

2 hard-boiled eggs, shelled and cut lengthwise into halves
1 cucumber, cut into long, thin diagonals
1 small tomato, cut into ½-inch-thich rounds
2 deep-fried tofu cutlets or burgers, cut into bite-sized pieces
2 tablespoons miso-damari (pp. 50 and 219)

Arrange the first four ingredients on a serving platter, then top each with a sprinkling of the *miso-damari*.

Miso-Stuffed Celery Hors D'œuvre

Peanut Butter & Miso:
    2 tablespoons peanut butter
    2 to 3 teaspoons red, barley, or Hatcho miso
    1 teaspoon grated onion and juice
Cream Cheese, Sweet Miso & Sesame:
    2 tablespoons cream cheese
    2½ tablespoons sweet white miso
    ½ teaspoon shoyu
    1 tablespoon ground roasted sesame seeds (p. 54)
      or sesame butter
Cream Cheese, Miso & Lemon:
    2 tablespoons cream cheese
    1 tablespoon red, barley, or Hatcho miso
    1 teaspoon lemon juice
    2 tablespoons mayonnaise
6 large celery stalks

Combine the ingredients for each of the three stuffings, mixing until smooth. Stuff celery stalks, then cut stalks into 2-inch lengths and serve as hors d'œuvres. If desired, top with a sprinkling of paprika.

Celery stalks are also delicious served with most types of Sweet Simmered Miso (p. 60), Vinegar Miso (p. 91), Peanut Butter-Miso (p. 80), Sesame Miso Spreads (p. 81), or Cream Cheese-Miso Dips (p. 74).

Crunchy Miso - Soynut Butter Balls   MAKES 12

1/3 cup Miso-Soynut Butter (p. 80), cooled to room temperature
¼ cup raisins
¼ cup (roasted) sunflower seeds, chopped nuts, or ground roasted sesame seeds
2 tablespoons roasted soy flour *(kinako)* or ¼ cup shredded coconut

Combine the first three ingredients, mixing well. Shape mixture into 12 small balls, then roll each in roasted soy flour. Chill briefly before serving.

Lotus Root Hors D'œuvre Stuffed with Miso-Cream Cheese

MAKES 12

1 lotus root, 4 inches long and 2 inches in diameter, peeled
1 ounce cream cheese
1 teaspoon red, barley, or Hatcho miso
1 teaspoon minced onion
½ teaspoon minced parsley
1/8 teaspoon curry powder

Trim both ends of lotus root, revealing hollow tubules. Cut into 2-inch lengths and simmer in water to cover for 15 to 20 minutes, or until tender; then drain and allow to cool to body temperature. Combine remaining ingredients, mixing well. Press mixture into tubules using your finger tips or a spatula. Cut each section of lotus root crosswise into 6 thin discs and spread any remaining filling in a thin layer over one surface of each disc. Serve chilled.

For variety, substitute 1 mashed hard-boiled egg for the cream cheese. Omit curry powder, and add a dash of pepper and 2 teaspoons mayonnaise.

Nori-wrapped Cucumbers with Sour Cream & Miso

MAKES 12

¼ cup sour cream
1 teaspoon red, barley, or Hatcho miso
Dash of pepper
3 sheets of nori, toasted (p. 54)
1 cucumber, cut into long slivers

Combine the first three ingredients, mixing well, and spread in an even layer over one surface of each nori sheet. Now arrange cucumber slivers in a row along the near edge of each sheet. Roll up from the near edge so that the cucumbers form the central core. Cut the rolls crosswise into fourths; serve immediately.

For variety, use slivers of cheese and agé (deep-fried tofu) together with the cucumbers.

Miso-filled Beefsteak Leaf Hors D'œuvre

SERVES 2

This popular Japanese hors d'œuvre, now available commercially, is prepared with red beefsteak leaves which have been salt-pickled (p. 158) to give them a softer flavor and texture. The filling may be made with Peanut Miso (p. 62).

1½ tablespoons sweet white miso or 2 teaspoons red miso
1½ tablespoons sesame butter or whole roasted peanuts
½ teaspoon honey
6 green beefsteak leaves

Combine the first three ingredients, mixing well, and divide into six equal portions. Place one portion at the center of each leaf near one end, then roll up leaf firmly so that miso-sesame mixture fills rolled cylinder. Skewer with foodpicks, if desired, and serve arranged on small plates.

Sashimi Konnyaku

SERVES 4

Cut and served in this way, konnyaku is made to resemble one of Japan's culinary specialties, sashimi, or fresh uncooked fish cut into thin slices and served with a dipping sauce or topping. In Zen temples and shojin temple·restaurants, the konnyaku is prepared in prefect resemblance of fresh squid.

10 to 12 ounces konnyaku, cut crosswise into ¼-inch-thick strips and parboiled in lightly-salted water
¼ cup Tangy Mustard Vinegar Miso (p. 92), or 2 to 3 tablespoons Wasabi Mixed Miso (p. 69)

Arrange konnyaku strips in a flower-petal pattern on a serving platter. Place the dipping sauce and a serving spoon in a cup at center of platter. Invite each guest to serve himself.

Miso Pastry Twists

MAKES ABOUT 40

Made with unsweetened pie crust, these have a slightly salty flavor; serve as you would potato chips, or use as the accompaniment for sweet fruits or desserts.

3 tablespoons red, barley, or Hatcho miso
6 tablespoons water
5 ounces butter, chilled
2¼ cups flour, approximately
1 egg yolk

Combine miso and water, mixing well. Cut butter into 2 cups flour until butter pieces are the size of peas. Gently stir in thinned miso to form a moist dough. Wrap in a very lightly dampened towel and refrigerate for 1 hour.

Roll dough out thin, and fold into thirds. Sprinkle lightly with flour, and repeat 4 times to give a 12-layer pastry dough. Finally, roll dough into a long rectange ¼ inch thick and about 3 inches wide. Cut crosswise into ¾-inch-wide strips. Twist each strip once and brush with egg yolk. Arrange strips on lightly oiled baking pans. Bake in a 390° oven for 4 minutes, then reduce heat to 300° and bake for 8 to 10 minutes more, or until strips are nicely browned.

For variety, replace one-half the miso with grated cheese. Sprinkle ¼ cup minced walnuts over dough before final folding.

Miso in Spreads & Sandwiches

Whether used with nut butters or dairy products, creamy avocados or butter, high-protein tofu or cooked soybeans, miso adds richness of flavor to many of your favorite sandwich fixin's. Thinned slightly, miso spreads make excellent dips; creamed with hot stock or broth, they make savory sauces.

MISO IN SPREADS

Miso Paté
MAKES 1½ CUPS

Remarkably similar in flavor and texture to its liver-based counterpart, this recipe combines wheat, sesame butter, and miso to yield maximum protein value (p. 23).

2 cups broken pieces of (dry) whole-wheat bread
½ cup water or stock
½ cup sesame butter
1½ tablespoons red, barley, or Hatcho miso
1 small onion, minced
1 tablespoon (sesame) oil
1 clove of garlic, crushed or minced
¼ cup minced parsley
Dash each of thyme, rosemary, and sage

Combine bread and water, mashing well with fingers. Mix in remaining ingredients and allow to stand for at least 1 hour, preferably 1 full day. Serve as a spread on crackers, canapés, or bread.

For a firmer consistency, bake in a loaf pan at 350° for 1 to 1½ hours, or until surface is nicely browned.

Tofu-Miso Paté
MAKES 1¾ CUPS

12 ounces tofu, lightly pressed (p. 55)
5 teaspoons red, barley, or Hatcho miso
¼ cup sesame butter or ½ cup ground roasted sesame seeds (p. 54)
3 tablespoons minced parsley
1 tablespoon dill seeds, minced
2 tablespoons chopped green onion
1 clove of garlic, crushed
¼ teaspoon nutmeg

Preheat oven to 350°. Combine all ingredients, mixing well, and press into a loaf pan. Bake for 15 to 20 minutes, or until lightly browned. Serve as a spread. Also delicious unbaked.

Hard-boiled Egg & Miso Spread
MAKES ½ CUP

2 hard-boiled eggs, mashed with a fork
1 teaspoon red or barley (or 2 teaspoons mellow white) miso
2 tablespoons mayonnaise
1 tablespoon minced parsley
Dash of pepper or paprika

Combine all ingredients, mixing well. For variety, add ½ teaspoon curry powder.

Miso-Sesame-Avocado Spread
MAKES ¾ CUP

2 teaspoons red, barley, or Hatcho miso
6 tablespoons sesame butter
½ avocado, peeled and seeded
¼ tomato, minced
1 tablespoon minced onion
1 tablespoon lemon juice
½ clove of garlic, crushed
1 tablespoon minced parsley or ¼ cup alfalfa sprouts

Combine the first seven ingredients; mash together until smooth. Serve topped with a sprinkling of the parsley or sprouts.

Sweet Carob-Sesame-Miso Spread

MAKES 1/3 CUP

1 tablespoon carob powder
4 to 5 teaspoons water
2 to 3 tablespoons sesame butter or *tahini*
2 teaspoons sweet white or 1½ teaspoons mellow white miso
1 teaspoon honey

Combine carob powder with water, mixing until smooth, then stir in remaining ingredients. Nice on toast or unsalted crackers.

Walnut Miso Spread or Topping

MAKES 1 CUP

1 cup walnut meats, lightly roasted and ground to a paste
¼ cup red, barley, or Hatcho miso
3 to 4 tablespoons water

Combine all ingredients, mixing well. Serve as a spread with sandwiches or crackers, or as a topping with cooked vegetables or tofu.
    For variety, add ½ teaspoon grated orange or lemon rind.

Miso - Soynut Butter

MAKES ½ CUP

    This delicious spread tastes like a cross between sesame and peanut butter but is less expensive and higher in protein. Produced commercially, it would surely sell well at natural- and health food stores.

2½ tablespoons oil or butter
½ cup roasted soy flour *(kinako)*
1 teaspoon red, barley, or Hatcho miso
1 tablespoon honey
1½ to 2 tablespoons water

Heat the oil in a skillet, then turn off heat. Add remaining ingredients, mixing until smooth. Delicious on crackers, canapés, or fresh vegetable slices.

Sweetened Peanut Butter-Miso Spread

MAKES ¾ CUP

¼ cup peanut butter
1 tablespoon red, barley, or Hatcho miso
1 tablespoon honey
¼ cup diced apples
2 tablespoons sunflower seeds or minced nutmeats
2 tablespoons raisins
1 teaspoon sake or white wine (optional)

Combine all ingredients, mixing well. Serve on buttered whole-wheat bread.

VARIATION

*Omit raisins, sunflower seeds, and apple. Use 4 teaspoons miso; serve in vegetable sandwiches with lettuce, cucumbers, tomatoes, sprouts, and cheese. For more zest, add 1 tablespoon diced onion and/or parsley; nice on canapés. For more tang, add 2½ tablespoons vinegar.

Savory Peanut Butter-Miso Spread

MAKES ½ CUP

¼ cup peanut butter
2 teaspoons red, barley, or Hatcho miso
1 teaspoon Worcestershire sauce
2 tablespoons butter, softened

Combine all ingredients, mixing well.

Miso Cheese Spread

MAKES 1 CUP

1 tablespoon butter
1 tablespoon red, barley, or Hatcho miso
6 ounces grated cheese
¼ cup milk (soy or dairy)
1 egg, lightly beaten
Dash of mustard
¼ teaspoon crushed garlic or 1 tablespoon minced parsley
    (optional)

Melt butter in a skillet. Stir in miso, then add remaining ingredients, mixing well. Cook, stirring constantly, for 1 to 2 minutes, or until cheese just melts. Serve on buttered toast or canapés. Brown under a broiler, if desired.

Sweet White Miso & Butter Spread

MAKES 3/8 CUP

2 tablespoons butter
¼ cup sweet white or 2½ tablespoons mellow white miso

Combine butter and miso, mixing well. Serve as a spread for hors d'œuvre crackers and sandwiches topped with fresh vegetables and cheese, or as a topping for pancakes and waffles.

Sesame-Miso Spread

MAKES ½ CUP

4 or 5 tablespoons sesame butter
1 tablespoon red, barley, or Hatcho miso
½ teaspoon grated lemon or *yuzu* rind (optional)
3 tablespoons water

Combine all ingredients, mixing well. Nice on freshly sliced cucumbers, crackers, or open-faced sandwiches.

Sweetened Sesame-Miso Spread

MAKES ½ CUP

¼ cup sesame butter or *tahini*
2 to 4 teaspoons red, barley, or Hatcho miso
1½ to 2 tablespoons honey
Dash of cinnamon, (7-spice) red pepper, or tabasco sauce
1 to 1½ tablespoons water

Combine all ingredients, mixing well. Serve on bread, toast, or deep-fried tofu. Or use as a topping for Dengaku (p. 144).

Tahini-Miso Spread

MAKES ABOUT ¼ CUP

¼ cup *tahini*
1 tablespoon red, barley, or Hatcho miso
1 teaspoon honey
¼ to ½ teaspoon grated orange or lemon rind

Combine all ingredients, mixing well. Serve as a sandwich spread.

Tangy Soybean-Sesame-Miso Spread

MAKES 1½ CUP

1 cup cooked soybeans (p.129), drained and mashed
1/3 cup sesame butter
1½ tablespoons red, barley, or Hatcho miso
2 tablespoons lemon juice
1/3 cup diced raw onion
1 clove of garlic, crushed or minced
1 tablespoon honey
Dash of pepper

Combine all ingredients, mashing together until smooth. For best flavor allow to stand for at least 8, preferably 24, hours before serving.

VARIATIONS

*Rich and Crunchy Spread: Omit lemon juice, onion, and garlic. Add several tablespoons each sunflower seeds, raisins, and diced apple, and ½ teaspoon grated orange peel.
*Garbanzo or Navy Bean Spreads: Substitute an equal volume of either of these cooked beans for the soybeans in the basic recipe or variation.
*Lentil-Miso Spread: Prepare lentils as in thick Lentil-Miso Soup (p. 111). For a smoother texture, purée in a handmill or blender. To each cup of purée add 2 teaspoons red miso, a pinch of nutmeg and minced parsley and, if desired, sesame butter or ground roasted sesame seeds. Mix well and chill to thicken. Serve on buttered whole-wheat bread or toast.
*Azuki-Miso Spread: Prepare Azuki-Vegetable Soup with Miso (p. 111) except use only 2½ cups water. Serve on Chapaties (p. 128) or as a sandwich spread.

MISO IN SANDWICHES

The many spreads we've described above can serve as the makings for a sandwich in themselves. Any of the following types of miso or miso mixtures can be used with thinly sliced vegetables, cheese, sprouts, or (deep-fried) tofu on buttered whole-grain bread or toast. Try using ketchup, mayonnaise, and/or mustard together with the miso. Or use Finger Lickin' Miso or diced miso pickles like relish.

*All types of regular red or white miso
*Sweet Simmered Miso (p.60), Finger Lickin' Miso (p. 41), Miso Sauté (p. 65), Mixed Miso (p. 69) or Broiled Miso (p. 71)
*2 parts sesame or nut butter and 1 part miso
*6 parts red or barley miso and 1 part grated gingerroot (or diced leeks or scallions)

Grilled Cheese Sandwich on Miso-Garlic Bread

SERVES 4

Miso-Garlic-Butter Spread:
   1½ teaspoons red, barley, or Hatcho miso
   ¼ teaspoon crushed garlic
   ¼ cup melted butter
   ½ teaspoon grated lemon peel or grated onion (optional)
4 large slices of French or sourdough bread
½ cup grated or ¼ cup Parmesan cheese
4 teaspoons minced parsley

Combine spread ingredients, mixing well, then brush onto surface of bread. Top with a sprinkling of the cheese and parsley. Toast in a medium broiler or oven until nicely browned.

For variety arrange tomato (and deep-fried tofu) slices on the bread before sprinkling with cheese. Or soften the butter, mix with the other spread ingredients, and serve on canapés.

Grilled Cheese and Tomato Sandwich

MAKES 5

½ cup grated cheese
1 tablespoon red, barley, or Hatcho miso
1 tablespoon minced onion
1 tablespoon minced parsley
1 clove of garlic, crushed
5 pieces of buttered (whole-grain) bread
2 tomatoes, cut into thin rounds

Combine the first five ingredients, mixing well, and spread on the buttered bread. Top with tomato slices and broil under medium heat for 4 to 5 minutes, or until fragrant and nicely browned. Serve sizzling hot.

Fried Egg Sandwich with Deep-fried Tofu and Miso

MAKES 1

4 teaspoons butter
2½ to 3 ounces deep-fried tofu, cut into thin strips
1 egg
Dash of pepper
1 teaspoon red, barley, or Hatcho miso
1½ teaspoons ketchup (optional)
1 large piece of (whole-wheat) toast

Melt 1 tablespoon butter in a skillet. Arrange tofu strips in a single layer on bottom of skillet, then break egg over the top. Cover and fry until egg is firm, season with pepper, cover, and remove from heat. Combine remaining 1 teaspoon butter with miso and, if desired the ketchup; mix well and spread on one surface of toast. Top with the tofu-fried egg placed sunny side up and serve immediately.

For added color and flavor, top with a sprinkling of minced parsley or grated cheese.

Deep-fried Tofu Burger

MAKES 1

Spread both surfaces of a 3- to 4-ounce deep-fried tofu burger with a thin layer of red, barley, or Hatcho miso. Broil tofu briefly on both sides if desired, then use in place of meat in a hamburger or cheeseburger, accompanied by all of your favorite trimmings.

Miso Dressings with Salads

Smooth sour-cream dressings and nut-butter favorites; tangy French- or citrus dressings; thick and creamy tofu- or yogurt dressings. Miso makes each of them a little more delicious, and can help to keep your intake of fats to a minimum as explained on page 25.

WESTERN-STYLE DRESSINGS

Floating Cloud Miso Dressing   MAKES ABOUT 1 CUP

One of our very favorites; the key to the flavor lies in the miso-sesame oil-garlic combination.

6 tablespoons vegetable oil
¼ teaspoon sesame oil
2 tablespoons (rice) vinegar or lemon juice
2 tablespoons red, barley, or Hatcho miso
¼ cup water
½ clove of garlic, crushed
Dash of powdered ginger
Dash of dry mustard

Combine all ingredients; whisk or shake well. Good on all tossed green salads, especially those with Chinese cabbage. Tomatoes and (deep-fried) tofu make excellent accompaniments. Try marinating hot green beans or artichoke hearts overnight in this dressing, then serving them drained and chilled on lettuce. Also great on cooked broccoli.

Miso-Cheese Dressing   MAKES ABOUT 1 CUP

½ cup oil
3 tablespoons vinegar
1½ tablespoons red, barley, or Hatcho miso
2 tablespoons Parmesan cheese
2 tablespoons water
1 tablespoon minced onion
1½ tablespoon minced green pepper
1 clove of garlic, crushed
¼ teaspoon (7-spice) red pepper or tabasco sauce

Combine all ingredients and allow to stand for at least 1 hour. Shake thoroughly before serving.

Lemon-Mustard-Miso Dressing   MAKES ½ CUP

3 tablespoons red, barley, or Hatcho miso
2 tablespoons oil
1 tablespoon lemon juice
1/8 teaspoon lemon rind
½ teaspoon hot mustard
1½ teaspoons honey
1½ teaspoons minced onion (optional)

Combine all ingredients, mixing well. Delicious with 1 small head of torn butter lettuce and 6 thinly-sliced fresh mushrooms; serves 2.

Miso-Sour Cream Dressing   MAKES ¾ CUP

3 tablespoons sour cream
1 tablespoon red or barley (or 2 tablespoons mellow white) miso
1½ tablespoons cream cheese or Roquefort cheese, softened
¼ cup oil
2 tablespoons lemon juice
1 tablespoon minced onions or chives

Combine all ingredients, mixing well. Good on steamed cauliflower or green beans. Or try on tossed green salads with thinly sliced beets.

Cream Cheese-Miso Mayonnaise Dressing   MAKES ABOUT ½ CUP

¼ cup mayonnaise
1 tablespoon red or barley (or 2 tablespoons mellow white) miso
2 tablespoons lemon juice
1½ tablespoons cream cheese, softened
1 tablespoon sesame or peanut butter
1½ teaspoons grated onion and juice

Combine all ingredients, mixing well. Especially good with asparagus, cauliflower, broccoli, or artichoke hearts salads.

Tangy Peanut Butter-Miso Dressing   MAKES ¼ CUP

2 tablespoons peanut butter
4 teaspoons vinegar
1 tablespoon red, barley, or Hatcho miso
2 tablespoons oil
1½ teaspoons honey

Combine all ingredients, mixing well.

White Sesame-Miso Dressing   MAKES 3/8 CUP

2 tablespoons sweet white or 1½ tablespoons mellow white
   miso
2 tablespoons sesame butter or *tahini*; or 3 tablespoons
   ground roasted sesame seeds (p. 54)
2 teaspoons *mirin*, sake, white wine, or water
½ teaspoon honey
1 teaspoon shoyu or ¼ teaspoon salt

Combine ingredients, mixing well. Try with (1 pound) parboiled spinach, or an apple-and-raisin salad.

Parsley

Miso French Dressing   MAKES 3/8 CUP

The use of miso, which has a much mellower saltiness
than plain salt, makes it possible to reduce the proportion of
oil in the traditional recipe and also to take full advantage of
the fine miso flavor. Good for those who like their salads with
plenty of dressing but must still watch their intake of fats.

4 tablespoons oil
2 tablespoons lemon juice or vinegar
2½ to 3 teaspoons red, barley, or Hatcho miso
1 teaspoon minced parsley
½ teaspoon dill or caraway seeds
Dash of pepper

Combine all ingredients, whisking or shaking well just before
dressing salad.

VARIATIONS

*Substitute for the miso 1½ tablespoons any variety of Sweet
Simmered Miso (pp. 60 to 65), or 2 tablespoons sweet white
miso.
*For zest, add ½ clove of crushed garlic and a dash of dry
mustard or gingerroot.
*For richness and variety, add small amounts of your favorite
herbs, Roquefort cheese, Worcestershire or chili sauce, or
chutney.

Tangy Miso-French Dressing   MAKES ¾ CUP

4 tablespoons oil
3½ tablespoons red, barley, or Hatcho miso
3½ tablespoons vinegar
2½ tablespoons lemon juice
¾ teaspoon hot mustard
½ clove of garlic, crushed (optional)
Dash of pepper

Combine all ingredients, mixing well. Use in small amounts.
Especially tasty with a salad of lettuce, jicama, cucumbers,
and deep-fried tofu.

Miso-Vinegar Dressing with   MAKES 1/3 CUP
   Gingerroot

2 tablespoons red, barley, or Hatcho miso
2 tablespoons vinegar
2 teaspoons (sesame) oil
1 tablespoon juice pressed from grated gingerroot
Dash of (7-spice) red pepper or tabasco sauce

Combine all ingredients, mixing well. Delicious served over
fresh tomato and cucumber slices, with parboiled bean
sprouts, or with *wakame* and deep-fried tofu.

Miso-Mayonnaise Dressings   MAKES 1/3 TO ½ CUP

The combination of miso, mayonnaise, and lemon juice
(or vinegar) yields a wide variety of dressings and sauces.
Experiment using the following guidelines to develop your
own combinations, or try a few of our favorites listed below.

To ¼ cup mayonnaise add:
   Miso: Choose one
      1 teaspoon red, barley, or Hatcho miso for tossed
         green salads. Use 1 to 2 tablespoons with fresh
         vegetable slices and as much as 3 tablespoons with
         noodle salads.
      2 to 3 teaspoons sweet white or mellow white miso,
         Sweet simmered Miso (p. 60), Finger Lickin' Miso
         (p. 42), or Miso-Nut Butter Spreads (p. 80).
   Vinegar or Lemon Juice: Use 2 parts for every 3 parts
      miso.
   Pepper: A dash of white, black, or red is essential.
   Other Seasonings: ½ to 2 teaspoons of minced onion, hot
      mustard, crushed garlic, grated gingerroot, or your
      favorite herbs or spices.
   Sesame or Nut Butters: Use 1 part to every 1 part red
      miso.
   Dairy Products: 1 to 2 tablespoons cream cheese, sour
      cream, or grated cheese adds richness and flavor.
   Sweetenings: The occasional use of 1 to 2 teaspoons
      honey goes nicely with red miso.

We have found the following combinations to go particularly well with certain salad ingredients. Mix miso and
other ingredients with ¼ cup mayonnaise; dress salad just
before serving. Serves 4 to 6.

*Basic: Use with your favorite tossed green·salads or cooked vegetables (asparagus, broccoli, cauliflower, bean sprouts)

  1 teaspoon red, barley, or Hatcho miso
  1 teaspoon lemon juice
  1 to 2 teaspoons water or stock
  Dash of paprika or pepper

*Cheese-Garlic: Try with lettuce-cucumber-and-tomato salads

  2 to 3 teaspoons red miso, or 4 to 6 teaspoons Sesame Miso (p. 62)
  2 to 3 teaspoons lemon juice
  2 tablespoons grated cheese
  ½ clove of garlic, crushed
  Dash of pepper
  ½ teaspoon caraway or dill seeds (optional)

*Tangy Onion: Nice with buckwheat noodle or macaroni salads

  3 tablespoons red, barley, or Hatcho miso
  3 tablespoons lemon juice
  4 tablespoons vinegar
  2 teaspoons minced onion
  1 to 2 tablespoons oil (optional)

*Sweetened: Delicious with salads of chilled cooked vegetables, especially pumpkin, squash or *kabocha*, potatoes, asparagus, or deep-fried tofu

  2 tablespoons red, barley, or Hatcho miso
  1 tablespoon lemon juice or vinegar
  ½ to ¾ teaspoon honey

*Sesame: Nice over lettuce-egg-and-tomato salads

  1 tablespoon red, barley, or Hatcho miso
  1 tablespoon sesame butter, *tahini,* or ground roasted sesame seeds (p. 54)
  2 tablespoons vinegar or lemon juice
  ½ teaspoon honey

*Rich & Creamy Nut Butter: Often prepared from leftover Miso-Nut Butter spreads; try with apple or tomato wedges, or fresh cucumber slices

  ¼ cup Miso-Nut Butter Spread (any variety) (pp. 80 to 81)
  3½ tablespoons lemon juice
  Dash of pepper

Creamy Tofu Dressings & Dips with Miso

MAKES ABOUT 1 CUP

Here is a wonderful way to introduce both tofu and miso into your daily menu served with salads, hors d'œuvres, or even as a sandwich spread. Quick and easy to prepare, the possible variations are virtually unlimited. Each is thick, rich, and full of flavor, yet remarkably low in fats and calories. The perfect answer for those who love dressings but dislike their typical oily qualities.

6 ounces tofu
1½ to 2 tablespoons lemon juice or vinegar
2 tablespoons oil
1 tablespoon red, barley, or Hatcho miso; or 2 tablespoons mellow white miso
Choice of seasonings (see below)

Combine all ingredients in a blender and purée for 20 seconds, or until smooth. (Or mash all ingredients and allow to stand for 15 to 30 minutes before serving.) If desired, serve topped with a sprinkling of minced parsley or a dash of pepper. Refrigerated in a covered container, these preparations will stay fresh for 2 to 3 days; the consistency will thicken (delectably).

SEASONINGS: Use any one of the following

*Curry: ½ teaspoon curry powder and 2 tablespoons minced onion. Top with a sprinkling of 1 tablespoon minced parsley.

*Dill: ¼ to ½ teaspoon dill seeds. If desired, add 1 clove of minced garlic. Top with a sprinkling of parsley.

*Onion: ¼ cup diced onion. Excellent on all types of deep-fried tofu and with many vegetable dishes.

*Cheese and Garlic: ¼ cup Parmesan or grated cheese and ½ clove of garlic (or ¼ onion), minced. Serve topped with a sprinkling of minced parsley.

*Gingerroot: 1 teaspoon grated or 1½ teaspoons powdered gingerroot and a dash of (7-spice) red pepper or tabasco sauce. Try over tomato & cucumber salad. Top with a sprinkling of parsley.

*Avocado: 1 well-ripened avocado, peeled, seeded, and mashed. For tang, add a few drops of tabasco and 2 tablespoons minced onion.

*Carrot: ¼ cup grated carrot and 2 teaspoons minced onion. Top with a sprinkling of parsley.

*Sesame: 2 tablespoons sesame butter or *tahini* and, if desired, 1 clove of crushed garlic.

*Walnut: ¼ cup each walnut meats and ketchup. Try over a salad of hard-boiled eggs, asparagus, and tomato wedges.

*Sweetened: Use white miso plus 1½ to 3 teaspoons honey. Nice with tomatoes.

*Herb: ½ teaspoon fresh or dried herbs (oregano, marjoram, caraway, basil).

Basil

Tofu Mayonnaise with Miso

MAKES ABOUT 1 CUP

At last a delicious homemade mayonnaise that is low in fats and calories, entirely free of cholesterol-rich eggs, and takes only a minute to prepare. Commercial mayonnaise, by comparison, is required by law to contain at least 65 percent fats—and most homemade varieties have even more. The following recipe, which serves 4 to 6, contains a total of only 466 calories, whereas an equal weight (9.1 ounces) of commercial mayonnaise contains 1820 calories, or *four* times as many!

6 ounces tofu, drained and pressed (p. 55) if desired
1½ to 2 tablespoons lemon juice or vinegar
2 tablespoons oil
2 tablespoons sweet white miso; or 4 teaspoons mellow white miso; or 1 tablespoon light-yellow miso; or 1½ teaspoons red miso and ¼ teaspoon salt
Dash of pepper (optional)

Combine all ingredients in a blender and purée for about 20 seconds, or until smooth. Store as for Creamy Tofu Dressings (above).

Soymilk Mayonnaise Dressing

MAKES 1 CUP

½ cup soymilk
½ cup oil
3 tablespoons lemon juice or 2½ tablespoons vinegar
2 tablespoons sweet white miso; or 4 teaspoons mellow white miso; or 1½ teaspoons red miso and ¼ teaspoon salt

Combine soymilk and ¼ cup oil in a blender and purée for 1 minute. Slowly add remaining oil in a thin stream. When mixture is fairly thick, add lemon juice and miso, and purée for 30 seconds more. For variety add minced onions, garlic, grated gingerroot, paprika, or your choice of herbs or seasonings. Or add any of the combinations of ingredients used in the variations to Creamy Tofu Dressings (above).

Miso-Yogurt Dressing

MAKES ABOUT ½ CUP

½ cup yogurt
4 teaspoons red or 8 teaspoons sweet white miso
1 tablespoon orange juice
2 tablespoons (olive) oil
Dash of pepper
½ teaspoon fresh herbs (tarragon, basil, thyme) (optional)

Combine all ingredients; whisk well. Good with both tossed green and fruit salads.

Sweet Mustard-Vinegar Miso Dressing

MAKES ½ CUP

2 tablespoons sweet white or 4 teaspoons mellow white miso
2 tablespoons vinegar or lemon juice
3 tablespoons oil
½ teaspoon powdered hot mustard
Dash of paprika or (7-spice) red pepper

Combine all ingredients, mixing well. Try with a salad of (Chinese) cabbage, apples, raisins, and walnuts.

Sweet Miso Marinade

MAKES ¾ CUP

6 tablespoons sweet white or ¼ cup mellow white miso
2 tablespoons ketchup
2 tablespoons lemon juice
2 tablespoons oil
1 tablespoon grated or minced onion
Dash of (7-spice) red pepper

Combine all ingredients, mixing well. Use as a marinade for fresh vegetables.

WESTERN-STYLE SALADS

Potato Salad with Sour Cream and Miso

SERVES 3 OR 4

4 small potatoes, boiled or steamed in the skins until tender, cubed (2 cups)
2 tablespoons butter
¼ cup chives
½ cup sour cream
1½ tablespoons red, barley, or Hatcho miso
1½ cucumbers, sliced into very thin rounds
Dash of pepper or paprika

Place hot cubed potatoes into a bowl and top with butter and chives; mix lightly until butter has melted. Combine sour cream and miso, mixing well, then use to dress potatoes. Allow to cool, then mix in cucumbers. Serve chilled, topped with a sprinkling of pepper.

Carrot, Raisin & Walnut Salad
with Tofu and Miso

SERVES 4

1 cup grated carrots; or diced apple or celery
½ cup raisins
½ cup (roasted) walnut meats, diced
1½ tablespoons red, barley, or Hatcho miso
1 teaspoon honey
1 teaspoon white wine or sake
2 tablespoons sesame butter
4 lettuce leaves (optional)

Combine all ingredients, mixing well. If desired, serve mounded on lettuce leaves.

For a milder, slightly sweeter flavor, substitute for the red miso and honey: 3 to 4 tablespoons sweet white miso and ½ teaspoon shoyu.

Carrot & Raisin Salad
with Miso-Mayonnaise Dressing

SERVES 5

2 carrots, grated
¾ cup raisins
¾ to 1 cup diced apple or persimmon (optional)
½ cup walnut meats
1/3 cup mayonnaise
2 tablespoons sweet white miso; or 1 tablespoon red miso and 1 teaspoon honey

Combine all ingredients, mixing lightly.

Fresh Vegetable Slices
with Tofu-Miso Dressing

SERVES 3

3 tablespoons red, barley, or Hatcho miso
2½ tablespoons vinegar or lemon juice
1 tablespoon honey
2 tablespoons oil
2 tablespoons minced parsley
Dash of paprika
12 ounces tofu
3 large lettuce leaves
2 tomatoes, cut into thin wedges
2 cucumbers, cut into thin diagonals
2/3 cup peanuts

Combine the first seven ingredients and mash together well (or purée in a blender). Place lettuce leaves in individual salad bowls, arrange sliced tomatoes and cucumbers on leaves, and spoon on the dressing. Top with peanuts just before serving.

Crispy Sprout Salad
with Tofu-Miso Dressing

SERVES 3 TO 4

2 cups alfalfa sprouts
1 carrot, grated
¼ cup (roasted) sunflower seeds
¼ cup raisins
1 cup Creamy Tofu Dressing with Miso (p. 85)

Combine the first four ingredients, toss lightly, and serve topped with dollops of the dressing.

Cucumbers with Walnut-
Vinegar Miso Dressing

SERVES 2

1 cucumber, sliced into thin rounds; or 20 to 30 green beans, parboiled
Dressing:
    1½ teaspoons red, barley, or Hatcho miso
    1 teaspoon vinegar
    ¼ cup chopped (roasted) walnut meats
    1 tablespoon *tahini* or sesame butter

Combine the cucumber rounds and dressing; mix lightly. Serve immediately.

Tomato-Cucumber Salad
with Tangy Miso Dressing

SERVES 3 OR 4

This simple but delicious salad shows how Japanese-style *aemono* dressings can be used with fresh Western-style salads.

1 tomato, cut into ½-inch cubes
2 cucumbers, sliced into thin rounds
6 tablespoons Sweet Sesame-Vinegar Miso Dressing (p. 93)

Combine all ingredients, mixing lightly. Serve immediately.

For variety, add fresh mushrooms, green beans, grated carrot or reconstituted *wakame.*

Tomatoes with Sesame-Miso
Mayonnaise

SERVES 4

2 tomatoes, cut into wedges
2 tablespoons mayonnaise
1 to 1½ tablespoons red, barley or Hatcho miso
½ clove of garlic, grated or crushed
1 tablespoon sesame butter or *tahini*
1 teaspoon honey or lemon juice

Arrange tomato wedges on individual plates. Combine the next 5 ingredients, mixing well, then spoon over tomatoes. Serve topped with a sprinkling of parsley.

For a milder dressing, use ¼ cup mayonnaise, 3 to 4 teaspoons Sweet Simmered Miso (p. 60), 2 tablespoons sesame butter, 2 teaspoons water, and a dash of pepper.

Tofu-Miso Salad
with Walnuts and Apple
SERVES 4 TO 5

8 ounces tofu pressed (p. 55); or 7 ounces firm tofu
1 tablespoon red miso
2 tablespoons sesame butter
1 tablespoon lemon juice
2 tablespoons honey
½ cup raisins
1 cup walnut meats
1 apple, diced

Combine the first five ingredients, mashing and mixing well. Add the raisins, walnut meats, and apple, mixing lightly. Serve as is, or chill for several hours.

Fruit Salad
with Miso-Cream Cheese Balls
SERVES 3

3 ounces cream cheese
2½ tablespoons sweet white miso
¼ cup minced walnut meats or sunflower seeds
2 lettuce leaves
1 apple or pear, cut into ½-inch cubes
3 tablespoons raisins
2 tablespoons mayonnaise
2 tablespoons lemon juice

Combine the first three ingredients, mixing well, and shape into about 25 small balls. Arrange lettuce leaves on plates and mound with apples, raisins, and cream cheese-miso balls. Combine mayonnaise and lemon juice to make a dressing; pour over salad and serve immediately.

Fruit Salad
with Sweet Miso-Mayonnaise Dressing
SERVES 4

1 grapefruit, sectioned
1 orange, sectioned
1 apple, cut into ½-inch cubes
1 banana, sliced into thin rounds
6 prunes, seeded and minced
Dressing:
    1 tablespoon sweet white miso
    2 tablespoons mayonnaise
    1 tablespoon grapefruit- or apple juice

Combine the fruits in a serving bowl; toss lightly with the dressing.

Apple-Raisin Salad
with Sesame-Miso Dressing
SERVES 4

1½ to 2 large apples, cut into thin wedges
3 tablespoons raisins
¼ cup chopped walnuts
¼ cup chopped celery or sliced cucumber (optional)
3/8 cup White Sesame-Miso Dressing (p. 84)

Combine all ingredients, mixing lightly.

Macaroni Salad
with Miso Mayonnaise
SERVES 4 TO 5

5 to 6 ounces (1¼ cups) dry macaroni, cooked (3 cups)
2 cucumbers, sliced into thin rounds
2 small tomatoes, cut into wedges
White Miso & Mustard Mayonnaise Dressing:
    ¼ cup sweet white miso
    ¼ cup mayonnaise
    1½ tablespoons lemon juice
    ½ teaspoon hot mustard
    1 tablespoon finely minced or grated onion
    Dash of pepper
4 lettuce leaves
Parsley sprigs

Combine the first three ingredients with the dressing; mix lightly. Chill for several hours, then serve mounded on lettuce leaves and garnished with parsley.

    For variety, add 9 ounces cubed deep-fried tofu, ½ cup raisins, and 3½ ounces fresh or reconstituted *wakame* (or grated carrot); double the amount of dressing. Or substitute for the macaroni an equal weight of noodles (whole-wheat, buckwheat, rice-flour, or transparent).

Buckwheat Noodle Salad
with Miso Mayonnaise
SERVES 4

3 ounces (*soba*) buckwheat noodles (or spaghetti), cooked (p. 58), cooled, and cut into 3-inch lengths
1 large tomato, diced
1½ cucumbers, cut into thin rounds
2/3 cup diced celery
½ cup grated cheese or walnut meats; or 2 diced hard-boiled eggs (optional)
Dressing:
    ¼ cup mayonnaise
    1½ tablespoons red, barley, or Hatcho miso
    1 teaspoon lemon juice
    Dash of pepper
4 lettuce leaves
¼ cup parsley

Combine the first four (or five) ingredients with the dressing; mix lightly. Arrange lettuce leaves in individual bowls, mound with the salad, and top with a sprinkling of parsley.

    For variety, add 5 ounces diced deep-fried tofu.

Wakame

Fresh Sea Vegetable Salad
with Miso-Mayonnaise
SERVES 4

1 cup fresh or reconstituted *wakame* (p. 54), cut into 2-inch
    lengths
1 green pepper, thinly sliced
1 cucumber, thinly sliced
7 ounces deep-fried tofu, lightly broiled if desired, cut cross-
    wise into thin strips
Rich Miso-Mayonnaise Dressing:
    ¼ cup mayonnaise
    6 tablespoons red, barley, or Hatcho Miso
    ¼ cup lemon juice
    Dash of pepper
1 tomato, cut into thin wedges
4 lettuce leaves

Combine the first five ingredients and the dressing; mix lightly. Arrange tomato wedges on lettuce leaves in a large salad
bowl. Top with the salad mixture and chill for several hours
before serving.
    If *wakame* is unavailable, substitute 1 large diced apple
or tomato.

Wakame Salad
with Miso-Cream Cheese Dressing
SERVES 4

1 cup fresh or reconstituted *wakame* (p. 54), chopped
1 cucumber, thinly sliced
4 lettuce leaves, torn into small pieces
Dressing:
    2 teaspoons red, barley, or Hatcho miso
    2 ounces cream cheese mixed with 2 tablespoons warm
        water
    ¼ cup mayonnaise
    1 tablespoon lemon juice
    ½ teaspoon grated lemon rind
    Dash of pepper
1 small tomato, cut into thin wedges
¼ cup sunflower seeds

Combine the first three ingredients and the dressing; toss
lightly and place into individual bowls. Garnish with tomato
wedges and top with a sprinkling of sunflower seeds.

Land-and-Sea Vegetable Salad
with Mustard Lemon-Miso Dressing
SERVES 3

1 cup fresh or reconstituted *wakame* (p. 54), cut into 1½-
    inch lengths
1 cucumber, cut into thin rounds
1 tomato, cut into thin wedges
1¼ cups thin rounds of jicama, turnip, *daikon*, or celery root
2 ounces deep-fried tofu, broiled if desired, thinly sliced
Dressing:
    2 tablespoons sweet white miso
    3 tablespoons lemon juice
    1 teaspoon honey
    ¼ teaspoon hot mustard

Combine the first five ingredients with the dressing, mixing
lightly; serve immediately.

Green Beans
with Miso-Sour Cream
SERVES 2 OR 3

1½ cups green beans (stringed, split lengthwise into halves,
    and cut diagonally into 2-inch lengths)
¼ cup water
2 tablespoons sour cream
1 tablespoon red, barley, or light-yellow miso
Dash of pepper

Combine beans and water in a small saucepan and bring just
to a boil. Reduce heat to low, cover, and cook for about 10
minutes, or until liquid has evaporated and beans are just
tender; remove from heat. Combine sour cream, miso and
pepper, mixing well. Stir in green beans. Serve cold as a salad
or hot as a dinner vegetable.
    Any of the following, steamed until tender, make ex-
cellent substitutes for the green beans: *(kabocha)* pumpkin,
winter squash or zucchini seasoned with a little dill; Irish or
sweet potatoes, celery, bean sprouts, or eggplant.

Fresh Vegetable & Raisin Salad
with Mustard Vinegar-Miso Dressing
SERVES 3

2 tomatoes, diced
1½ cucumbers, cut into thin rounds
1 cabbage leaf, shredded
½ cup diced celery
2 to 4 ounces deep-fried tofu, diced (optional)
¼ cup raisins
Dressing:
    2 tablespoons red or barley miso
    2 tablespoons vinegar
    1½ tablespoons lemon juice
    ½ teaspoon mustard
    1 tablespoon oil (optional)
    Dash of pepper
3 lettuce leaves

Combine the first six ingredients with the dressing; mix lightly. Serve immediately, mounded on the lettuce leaves.

Refreshing Potato Salad with Miso Dressing

SERVES 5 OR 6

1¼ pounds potatoes, halved or quartered and steamed for 30 minutes
1½ tablespoons red, barley, or Hatcho miso
¼ cup lemon juice
Dash of pepper
¼ cup mayonnaise
1 tablespoon honey
1½ to 2 cucumbers, sliced into thin rounds
¼ cup chopped parsley
1 cup mandarin orange or tangerine sections, chopped apples, or tomato wedges
¼ cup raisins (optional)

Break or cut freshly steamed potatoes into bite-sized pieces and place in a serving bowl. Combine miso, lemon juice and pepper, mixing well, then pour over the potatoes. Toss lightly and allow to cool for 20 to 30 minutes. Mix mayonnaise and honey, then stir into the potatoes together with the cucumbers and parsley. Add orange sections and, if used, the raisins; mix gently. Chill before serving.

Tofu & Tomato Salad with Walnut-Lemon Miso

SERVES 3

12 ounces tofu, scrambled (p. 55)
1½ tablespoons Lemon-Walnut-Miso (p. 66) or Sesame Miso (p. 62)
3 tablespoons mayonnaise
3 tablespoons minced parsley
1 tomato, cut into thin wedges
¼ cup chopped walnut meats (optional)
Dash of pepper

Combine tofu, miso, and mayonnaise in a serving bowl; mix well. Add parsley, tomato and nutmeats, mixing lightly. Season with a sprinkling of the pepper. Chill before serving.

Cottage Cheese & Tomato Salad with Miso Dressing

SERVES 3 OR 4

1 cup cottage cheese
1 small tomato, cut into wedges
1 cucumber, cut into thin rounds
3½ cups sprouts (parboiled mung or soy; or fresh alfalfa)
Dressing:
    ¼ cup oil
    2 tablespoons vinegar
    2 tablespoons red, barley, or Hatcho miso
    Dash of (7-spice) red pepper or tabasco sauce
    1 clove of garlic, crushed (optional)
3 or 4 lettuce leaves

Combine the first four ingredients and the dressing; mix lightly. Serve mounded on lettuce leaves, if desired.

Quick Potato Salad with Miso Dressing

SERVES 2

2 potatoes or sweet potatoes (12 ounces), boiled or steamed and cut into 1-inch cubes
½ cup Sweetened Miso Mayonnaise Dressing (p. 85)
½ cup parsley

Combine potatoes and miso mayonnaise, mix lightly and chill for at least 1 hour. Served topped with the parsley.

Tomato Slices Mounded with Miso-Cottage Cheese

SERVES 3

2 tomatoes, cut into ½-inch-thick rounds
½ cup cottage or ricotta cheese
5 tablespoons sweet white miso or White Nerimiso (p. 61)
2 to 2½ tablespoons lemon juice
Dash of pepper or paprika
Minced parsley or chives (optional)

Arrange tomato slices on a serving plate. Combine the next three ingredients, mixing well, then mound on the tomato slices. Serve topped with a sprinkling of the pepper and parsley.

Vegetable & Tofu Salad with Peanut Butter-Miso Dressing

SERVES 2 OR 3

½ carrot, cut into large matchsticks and steamed
15 green beans, steamed and cut diagonally into halves
4 to 5 ounces deep-fried tofu, cut into thin bite-sized rectangles
¼ cup Tangy Peanut Butter-Miso Dressing (p. 84)

Combine all ingredients, mixing lightly. If tofu is unavailable use 1¼ carrots and 35 green beans.

Fresh Vegetable Salad with Miso Mayonnaise

SERVES 4

1 tomato, cut into wedges
2 cucumbers, sliced into thin rounds
1/3 cup raisins
1 green pepper, thinly sliced
3 lettuce leaves, torn into small pieces
Mustard-Miso Mayonnaise Dressing:
    ¼ cup mayonnaise
    1½ tablespoons lemon juice
    ¼ teaspoon hot mustard
    1½ tablespoons red, barley, or Hatcho miso

Combine the first five ingredients with the dressing; toss lightly. For best flavor, chill for several hours before serving.

AEMONO AND THEIR DRESSINGS

Next to miso soups, *aemono* are the most popular way of using miso in Japanese cookery. These unique preparations are a favorite among most Western visitors to Japan, not only because of their fine flavor and the artistic way in which they are served, but also because of the way in which they make creative use of the tastiest and freshest seasonal vegetables, including those from wild upland meadows and the sea. Aemono trace their origins to the two schools of Japanese haute cuisine: Zen Temple Cookery *(Shojin Ryori)* and Tea Ceremony Cuisine *(Kaiseki Ryori),* which were founded and developed by men who treasured a life of elegant simplicity and refined frugality. Early temple cooks, monks, and tea masters knew of no better union of joy and economy than to roam Japan's mountains early each spring in search of edible wild buds and fronds, tender sprigs, and leafy shoots. These became the ingredients and garnishes for the finest of Japan's many *aemono.*

The word *aemono* means "dressed things," and these preparations might be described as Japanese-style salads of mixed foods in thick, rich dressings. Whereas the vegetables in Western-style salads are often light, crisp and fresh, those in aemono generally have a softer texture imparted by parboiling, simmering in sweetened shoyu broths, or rubbing with salt. Fresh vegetables, *konnyaku,* deep-fried tofu, and various seafoods are also used.

In Japanese, aemono dressings are known as *ae-goromo,* a word derived from *koromo,* the robes worn by Buddhist priests. Whereas many Western-style dressings are light "negligee" which help to preserve the crisp quality of tossed green salads, the Japanese "robes" generally have plenty of body. This helps them to unite and bind various soft vegetable pieces while simultaneously evoking and harmonizing their individual flavors.

The most common ingredients in aemono dressings are miso, vinegar, nut-and-seed butters, tofu and, in some cases, relatively large amounts of sweetening. In the many dressings that contain vinegar, use rice vinegar for a milder, gentler flavor and Western-style fruit-based vinegar for additional tang and zest. Since oil is virtually never used in aemono dressings, they are low in calories and highly digestible. Dairy products—such as mayonnaise, cottage, cream-, or regular cheese—so widely used in Western dressings are virtually never employed. Yet because of the richness of the dressing, aemono are typically served in very small portions (often no more than 3 or 4 tablespoons) and are meant to accompany main dishes which they complement in color, taste, and texture. On Western menus they may be served either as first courses or as salads. Moreover, many aemono dressings, sometimes seasoned with herbs and spices, go well with Western-style salads, too.

There are fourteen basic aemono dressings which feature miso (and a number of others in which shoyu or salt provide the seasoning). Most are closely related to Sweet Simmered Miso except that they are almost always prepared without cooking. Each aemono preparation takes its name from the name of its dressing: thus, a lotus root salad with vinegar-miso dressing would be called Lotus Root Vinegar-

Miso Ae. The basic dressings are listed here in the approximate order of their popularity.

Red Miso Dressing   MAKES ¼ CUP

This and the following preparation are known collectively in Japanese as *awasé-miso* or "uncooked mixed miso." They contain almost the same ingredients in the same proportions as their close relatives red and white *nerimiso.* Rather than being used directly as *aemono* dressings, they are generally mixed with vinegar, mustard, sesame, and other ingredients, thereby serving as the foundation for a wide variety of dressings.

2½ tablespoons red or barley miso
1 to 2 tablespoons (natural) sugar or 1 to 3 teaspoons honey
1½ to 3 teaspoons water or dashi (p. 56)
1 teaspoon sake, white wine, or *mirin*

Combine all ingredients, mixing well.

White Miso Dressing   MAKES ¼ CUP

3 tablespoons sweet white miso
½ teaspoon sugar or ¼ teaspoon honey
2 teaspoons water or dashi (p. 56)
2 teaspoons sake, white wine, or *mirin*

Combine all ingredients, mixing well.

Vinegar Miso Dressing *(Sumiso)*   MAKES ¼ CUP

These tangy preparations are delicious with almost all varieties of aemono as well as with Western-style salads, thin slices of fresh vegetables, and even deep-fried foods. Experiment adding your favorite herbs and spices. For a more vivid flavor use a slightly smaller quantity of cider vinegar or lemon juice in place of the traditional rice vinegar. In each preparation, the trick is to use just enough vinegar to give the desired tang, but not so much as to make the consistency too thin. All vinegar miso dressings can be divided into two basic types: those which contain more miso than vinegar have a richer flavor and more body, while those containing more vinegar are tangy and more delicate in consistency.

2 tablespoons red, barley, or Hatcho miso
1 tablespoon vinegar or 2½ teaspoons lemon juice
2 to 3 teaspoons (natural) sugar or 1 to 1½ teaspoons honey
2 teaspoons *mirin* or 1 teaspoon sake (or white wine)
  (optional)

Combine all ingredients, mixing well.

VARIATIONS

*Tangy: A favorite with sea and wild mountain vegetables

2 tablespoons vinegar
1 tablespoon red, barley, or Hatcho miso
1 to 2 tablespoons dashi (p. 56), stock, or water
*Sweet White Vinegar Miso Dressing: Nice with steamed cauliflower
    2 tablespoons sweet white miso
    1½ tablespoons vinegar or lemon juice
    1 teaspoon sugar or ½ teaspoon honey
*Miso Sambaizu: Sweet and zesty
    2 tablespoons red miso
    5 tablespoons vinegar
    2½ tablespoons dashi (p. 56), stock, or water
    2½ tablespoons (natural) sugar or 4 teaspoons honey
*Mix ¼ cup Red Miso Dressing (p. 91) with 1 tablespoon vinegar

Mustard-Vinegar Miso Dressing
(Karashi Sumiso)
MAKES ½ CUP

This preparation is generally made with sweet white miso, and may or may not contain sugar, sake or *mirin.* Various forms can be prepared simply by adding a small amount of hot mustard to any of the different recipes for Vinegar Miso Dressing given above. This dressing is a favorite with sea vegetables (such as *wakame*), green beans, eggplants, cabbage, steamed (*kabocha*) squash or pumpkin sprinkled with minced parsley, thinly sliced *konnyaku*, and deep-fried tofu.

3 tablespoons sweet white or 2 tablespoons mellow white miso
3 tablespoons vinegar
1½ to 3 teaspoons (natural) sugar or ¾ to 1 teaspoon honey
1 teaspoon *mirin* (optional)
¼ teaspoon hot mustard

Combine all ingredients, mixing well.

VARIATIONS

*Tangy Mustard Vinegar Miso: Made with red miso, this is a popular topping for *Sashimi Konnyaku* (p. 78)
    2 tablespoons red miso
    1 tablespoon vinegar
    4 teaspoons (natural) sugar or 2 teaspoons honey
    ½ teaspoon *mirin*
    ¼ teaspoon mustard
*To 5 tablespoons Vinegar Miso Dressing add ½ to 1 teaspoon hot mustard.

Sesame, Walnut, or Peanut Miso Dressings
(Goma Miso or Kurumi Miso)
MAKES 6 TABLESPOONS

In Japan these dressing are generally prepared by grinding roasted seeds or nuts to a paste in a *suribachi*, then adding the remaining ingredients and mixing them together with the pestle until smooth. White sesame seeds should be used with white miso; either white or black seeds with red miso. Although freshly roasted and ground sesame yields the best flavor and aroma, sesame butter or *tahini* may be more convenient. This dressing goes well with spinach, chrysanthemum leaves, boiled *daikon*, turnips, celery, or even apples.

2 tablespoons sweet white or 4 teaspoons mellow white miso
3 tablespoons ground roasted sesame seeds (p. 54), sesame butter, or *tahini*
1 teaspoon sugar or ½ teaspoon honey
1 tablespoon sake, *mirin*, water, or dashi (p. 56)
¼ teaspoon salt

Combine all ingredients, mixing well.

For variety substitute for the sesame seeds: ground walnuts or peanuts, or your choice of nut butters. In Japan, Walnut Miso Dressing is especially popular.

Sesame-Vinegar Miso Dressing
(Goma Sumiso)
MAKES 3/8 CUP

This preparation and its popular relatives, containing walnuts or peanuts in place of sesame, combine the tangy flavor of vinegar miso with the richness of nut butters. In some preparations the sesame flavor is featured, while in others the miso is accentuated. One of Japan's most widely-used dressings for *aemono*, it goes especially well with green beans, cucumbers, mushrooms, deep-fried tofu, and all sea vegetables. Or try it with Western-style apple-walnut-celery salads.

2 tablespoons red, barley, or Hatcho miso
2 tablespoons vinegar
2 tablespoons ground roasted sesame seeds (p. 54), sesame butter, *tahini*, or walnuts
1 tablespoon (natural) sugar or 1½ teaspoons honey

Combine all ingredients, mixing well.

VARIATIONS: Prepare as above

*Peanut-Vinegar Miso Dressing:
    1 tablespoon sweet white or 2 teaspoons mellow white miso
    2 tablespoons vinegar
    20 peanuts, chopped fine; or 3 tablespoons peanut butter
    2 teaspoons honey
    ½ teaspoon shoyu

*Sweet Sesame-Vinegar Miso Dressing: Nice with Western-style green salads.

 3 tablespoons sweet white or 2 tablespoons mellow
    white miso
 1½ tablespoons vinegar
 1 tablespoon sesame butter or *tahini*, or 1½ table-
    spoons ground roasted sesame seeds (p. 54)
 ¼ teaspoon honey

*Try reversing the proportions of miso and sesame.

Tofu Miso Dressing
(Shira-ae and Shirozu-ae)

SERVES 4

In *shira-ae*-type *aemono*, the dressing itself often forms the basis and bulk of the salad, and the vegetables are used subordinately to add texture, flavor and color. Tofu plays the leading role, supported by white miso, ground roasted sesame seeds and, sometimes, vinegar. This dressing goes especially well with cooked carrots, *konnyaku*, and mushrooms. Or use lotus root, burdock, sweet potatoes, eggplants, or your favorite wild mountain vegetables. The vegetables are often simmered in a sweetened shoyu broth before being mixed with the dressing. The amounts of sweetening, *mirin*, and vinegar should be adjusted carefully to suit the flavoring given to the vegetables and other basic ingredients. A well-made Tofu Miso Dressing has a texture similar to that of very firm cottage cheese.

 3 to 6 tablespoons roasted sesame (p.54), or 1½ to 3 table-
    spoons sesame butter or *tahini*
 6 ounces tofu, pressed or squeezed (p. 55)
 3 tablespoons sweet white or 2 tablespoons mellow white
    miso
 1 to 3 tablespoons sugar or 1½ to 4½ teaspoons honey
 1 to 2 teaspoons *mirin* (optional)

Place the hot, freshly roasted sesame seeds into a *suribachi* and grind to a smooth paste. Add tofu and re-grind. Add miso, sugar and *mirin*, and grind for several minutes more to develop cohesiveness. Then add the cooked vegetables to be used, mixing lightly. Serve immediately.

To prepare Tangy Tofu & Miso Dressing *(Shirozu-ae)*, add 2 tablespoons vinegar or lemon juice and 2 to 3 drops of shoyu to the completed dressing just before mixing in the vegetables.

If using sesame butter or *tahini* in place of sesame seeds, the dressing may be prepared by simply combining all ingredients in a bowl and mixing with a (wooden) spoon for about 3 minutes to develop cohesiveness.

Egg Yolk-Vinegar Miso Dressing
(Kimi Sumiso)

MAKES ½ CUP

This rich, light-yellow dressing is generally used with the same ingredients as Tofu Miso Dressing or with light-colored foods such as white mushrooms, asparagus, okra, or shrimp.

 2 hard-boiled eggs, separated into yolks and whites
 1 tablespoon sweet white or 2 teaspoons mellow white miso
 2½ teaspoons vinegar or lemon juice
 ¼ teaspoon honey
 2 teaspoons dashi (p. 56) stock, or water

Press firm egg yolks through a sieve, then combine with all remaining ingredients except the egg whites, which are diced and used in the salad itself. Try with 5 grilled *(shiitaké)* mushrooms, and top with 1 tablespoon minced parsley.

Gingerroot Miso Dressing

MAKES 2 TABLESPOONS

 1½ tablespoons red, barley, or Hatcho Miso
 1 teaspoon grated gingerroot or its juice
 2 teaspoons (natural) sugar or 1 teaspoon honey (optional)

Combine all ingredients, mixing well. Excellent with green beans, snow peas, crisp green vegetables, or deep-fried tofu.

Kinomé Miso Dressing

MAKES 1/3 CUP

 10 to 15 individual *kinomé* leaves (not sprigs)
 5 tablespoons sweet white or 3 tablespoons mellow white
    miso
 1 teaspoon sugar or ½ teaspoon honey (optional)
 1 teaspoon *mirin*

Place *kinomé* in a strainer or colander and douse with boiling water. Drain well, then transfer to a *suribachi* and grind thoroughly. Add the remaining ingredients and grind to a smooth paste. For a richer green, add 1 to 2 teaspoons *aoyosé* (p. 63). Try with regular or deep-fried tofu, celery cut into very thin diagonals, bamboo shoots, or turnips cut into paper-thin rounds.

Chive-Vinegar Miso Dressing

MAKES ¾ CUP

2 tablespoons red or barley miso
2 tablespoons vinegar
¼ cup minced chives, *nira*, or *asatsuki*
2 to 3 teaspoons sugar or 1 to 1½ teaspoons honey

Combine all ingredients, mixing well.

Leek Miso Dressing

MAKES ¼ CUP

4 tablespoons thinly-sliced leeks
1 tablespoon barley, Hatcho, or red miso

Combine ingredients, mixing well. For best flavor, cover and refrigerate for 1 to 2 days. Goes nicely with 2 cups steamed and cubed potatoes, sweet potatoes, or *kabocha*; or try with deep-fried tofu, steamed green beans, or spinach.

Yuzu Miso Dressing *(Yuzu Miso Ae)*

Prepare Yuzu Miso (p. 62) or Lemon Miso (p. 63), and allow to cool thoroughly. Use as is, or mix 3 parts with 1 part vinegar. Serve as for Kinomé Miso Dressing.

Sake Lees & Miso Dressing *(Kasumiso)*

MAKES ¼ CUP

2 tablespoons sake lees
2 teaspoons red or 4 teaspoons mellow white miso
1 teaspoon honey or 2 teaspoons (natural) sugar
2 tablespoons water

Combine all ingredients, mixing well. Delicious with parboiled or steamed *(horenso)* spinach or chrysanthemum leaves; use 10 ounces fresh.

AEMONO THEMSELVES

When preparing *aemono*, be sure that your vegetables contain no excess surface moisture when mixed with the dressing; drain them well and pat lightly with a dry cloth just before they are to be dressed. Parboil vegetables for only as long as is necessary to make them tender while still preserving some of their crispness (and most of their vitamins). Use lightly salted water for green vegetables, and plunge into cold water immediately after parboiling to preserve their emerald color. Use the seasoning quantities in the basic dressing recipes as guidelines, adjusting them to suit your ingredients and taste. Use seasonal ingredients and whatever is on hand. In Zen temples, even trimmings and peelings are sometimes creatively incorporated.

Cucumber Salad with Vinegar-Miso Dressing *(Sunomono)*

SERVES 4

3 cucumbers, sliced into thin rounds
1 teaspoon salt
3 tablespoons (rice) vinegar
2 teaspoons red, barley, or Hatcho miso
2 teaspoons (natural) sugar or 1 teaspoon honey
¼ teaspoon grated gingerroot

Place cucumber slices in a bowl, sprinkle with the salt, and allow to stand for 1 to 2 hours. Drain and squeeze out excess liquid. Combine vinegar, miso, sugar, and gingerroot in a serving bowl; add cucumbers and mix well. Serve chilled.

For variety, add to the dressing 1/3 cup reconstituted *wakame*, raisins, or cooked transparent noodles.

Pumpkin or Squash with Mustard-Vinegar Miso Dressing

SERVES 2 OR 3

9½ ounces *(kabocha)* pumpkin or squash, steamed and cut into 1-inch cubes
Mustard Vinegar-Miso:
   1½ tablespoons red, barley, or Hatcho miso
   2 tablespoons vinegar
   1 teaspoon (natural) sugar or ½ teaspoon honey
   ¼ teaspoon hot mustard
   ½ teaspoon *mirin*, sake or white wine
   2 tablespoons minced parsley

Combine well-cooled squash with the dressing, mixing lightly. Refrigerate for several hours before serving.

Refreshing Wakame Salad with Lemon

SERVES 4

1 cup fresh or reconstituted *wakame* (p. 54), cut into 1-inch lengths
Dressing:
   1½ teaspoons red, barley, or Hatcho miso
   1 tablespoon vinegar
   1 tablespoon dashi (p. 56), stock, or water
   ¼ teaspoon grated lemon rind

Combine *wakame* and dressing, mixing lightly; serve immediately.

Wakame & Cucumber Salad with Peanut-Vinegar Miso Dressing

SERVES 2 OR 3

2 tablespoons vinegar
1 tablespoon red, barley, or Hatcho miso
2 tablespoons peanut, sesame, or walnut butter
1 cucumber, sliced into thin rounds
1/3 cup fresh or reconstituted *wakame* (p. 54), cut into 1½-inch lengths

Combine the first three ingredients in a serving bowl, mixing well. Add cucumbers and *wakame*, mixing lightly. Serve immediately.

Wakame Salad with Vinegar Miso Dressing

SERVES 3

½ cup fresh or reconstituted *wakame* (p. 54), thinly sliced
½ large tomato, cut into thin wedges, or 2 Chinese cabbage leaves, thinly sliced
1 cucumber, cut into thin rounds
1 to 2 ounces deep-fried tofu, thinly sliced
3/8 cup Sesame-Vinegar Miso Dressing (p. 92), or ¼ cup Vinegar Miso Dressing (p. 91)

Combine all ingredients, mixing lightly. For best flavor, allow to stand for several hours before serving.

Konnyaku & Carrot Salad with Tofu Miso Dressing (Shira-ae)

SERVES 4

1 piece of *konnyaku*, cut into small rectangles and parboiled
1 carrot, cut into small rectangles
½ cup dashi , stock, or water
3 tablespoons sugar
½ teaspoon salt
½ teaspoon shoyu
¼ cup sesame seeds, roasted and ground to a paste (p. 54), sesame butter, or *tahini*
4 ounces tofu, pressed (p. 55), or 3 ounces firm tofu
2 tablespoons sweet white or 4 teaspoons mellow white miso
4 sprigs *kinomé* (optional)

Combine *konnyaku*, carrots, dashi, 1 tablespoon sugar, salt and shoyu in a small saucepan. Simmer until all liquid has been absorbed or evaporated, then allow to cool to room temperature. To the ground sesame seeds (in a *suribachi*), add tofu, miso and the remaining 2 tablespoons sugar; mix together (with a wooden pestle). Stir in the vegetables and serve each portion garnished with a sprig of *kinomé*.

Carrot-Daikon-Konnyaku Salad with Tofu Miso Dressing (Shira-ae)

SERVES 4

¼ carrot, cut into matchsticks
4 ounces *daikon*, cut into small rectangles
½ piece of *konnyaku*, cut into small rectangles
1¼ teaspoons salt
3 (*shiitaké*) mushrooms, cut into thin strips
2 teaspoons shoyu
4 teaspoons *mirin*
1 tablespoon roasted sesame seeds, sesame butter or *tahini*
8 ounces tofu, pressed (p. 55), or 6 ounces firm tofu
3 tablespoons sweet white or 2 tablespoons mellow white miso
1 teaspoon (natural) sugar or ½ teaspoon honey

Combine carrot, *daikon* and *konnyaku* in a small bowl. Rub with 1 teaspoon salt, rinse and press (p. 53). Heat an unoiled skillet or wok, drop in *konnyaku* and cook for several minutes, stirring constantly, until it becomes quite dry and begins to shrink; set *konnyaku* aside and allow to cool.

Combine mushrooms, shoyu and 1 teaspoon *mirin* in a small saucepan. Simmer until most of the liquid has been absorbed or evaporated, then drain and allow to cool to room temperature.

Combine sesame seeds and ¼ teaspoon salt in a *suribachi* and grind until seeds are slightly oily (p. 54). Add tofu, miso, sugar and 1 tablespoon *mirin*, and mix with the sesame using the wooden pestle. Stir in the *daikon*, carrot, *konnyaku* and mushrooms just before serving.

Vinegared Shira-ae (Shirozu-ae)

SERVES 2

6 ounces tofu, pressed (p. 55) and mashed
1 tablespoon sesame butter or *tahini*
1 tablespoon lemon juice
1½ tablespoons vinegar
1 tablespoon red or 2 tablespoons mellow white miso
1 teaspoon sake or white wine
1 cucumber or small carrot, sliced into thin rounds
2 hard-boiled eggs, chopped
¼ cup walnut meats
¼ cup raisins
2 tablespoons minced cucumber pickles (optional)

Combine the first six ingredients, mixing until smooth. Gently stir in the remaining ingredients. Serve immediately.

Green Beans and Carrots with Tofu-Miso Dressing (Shira-ae)

SERVES 4 TO 5

16 green beans, parboiled (p. 54) and cut into thin strips
1 carrot, cut into matchsticks and parboiled (p. 54)
4 teaspoons shoyu
4 teaspoons (natural) sugar or 2 teaspoons honey
4 tablespoons sesame butter, *tahini*, or ground roasted sesame seeds (p. 54)
12 ounces tofu, well pressed (p. 55), or 9 ounces firm tofu
4½ tablespoons sweet white or 3 tablespoons mellow white miso
1 tablespoon sake, white wine, or *mirin*

In a small saucepan combine green beans, carrots, shoyu, and sugar. Simmer over low heat until liquid has been absorbed or evaporated, then cool to room temperature. To the sesame butter (or ground sesame seeds in the *suribachi*), add tofu, miso and sake. Grind all ingredients together with the wooden pestle, or mix together with a spoon. Stir in the green beans and carrots. Serve immediately.

Green Beans with Vinegar Miso Dressing

SERVES 2

1½ tablespoons red, barley, or Hatcho miso
1 tablespoon vinegar
1½ tablespoons (natural) sugar or 2½ teaspoons honey
1 clove of garlic (or *myoga*), crushed or minced
25 green beans, parboiled (p. 54), and sliced diagonally into thin strips; or substitute 70 whole, parboiled snow peas

Combine the first four ingredients to make a dressing and mix lightly with the freshly cooked beans; allow to cool before serving.

Green Bean & Tofu Salad with Gingerroot Miso Dressing

SERVES 3

5 ounces green beans, parboiled (p. 54) and cut crosswise into halves; or substitute whole, parboiled snow peas
5 ounces deep-fried tofu, cut into small rectangles
2 tablespoons Gingerroot Miso Dressing (sweetened; p. 93)
1/3 cup peanuts or roasted soybeans

Combine crisp green beans, deep-fried tofu, and the dressing in a serving bowl; mix lightly. Top with peanuts just before serving.

Spinach with Sesame Miso Dressing

SERVES 4

1 pound (*horenso*) spinach
3 tablespoons sweet white or 2 tablespoons mellow white miso
1½ tablespoons sesame butter or *tahini*, or 3 tablespoons ground roasted sesame seeds
1 tablespoon (natural) sugar or 1½ teaspoons honey
1 to 3 teaspoons water

Bring 1 quart lightly salted water to a boil. Drop in spinach, return to the boil, and simmer for 1 to 2 minutes. Drain spinach briefly in a colander and douse with cold water. Press spinach firmly in one hand to form a compact cylinder then cut crosswise into 1-inch lengths.

Combine miso with remaining ingredients in a large bowl, mixing well. Now stir in spinach. For best flavor, allow to stand for several hours before serving.

Leek & Wakame Nuta

SERVES 2

Nuta is such a popular type of *aemono* that many Japanese actually use the two words interchangeably. *Wakame* and leeks (preferably the tender young variety known as *wakegi*) are used in most versions. Other popular ingredients include short-necked clams, sardines, squid, yellowtail, tuna, and a number of wild mountain vegetables such as *udo* and bracken ferns. Moist, cool and refreshing, *nuta* is generally prepared with a Miso Vinegar Dressing or occasionally with Sweet Simmered Miso.

2 leeks or 6 scallions, cut into ½-inch lengths
½ cup fresh or reconstituted *wakame* (p. 54), cut into 1½-inch lengths
2 ounces deep-fried tofu (*agé*), lightly broiled if desired and thinly sliced
Sweet White Vinegar-Miso Dressing (p. 92)

Cut leek pieces lengthwise into halves and parboil very briefly. Drain well, pat dry with a towel, and combine with the *wakame*, agé, and dressing; mix lightly. Serve immediately.

Onion Sesame-Miso Ae

SERVES 3 OR 4

3 onions, cut into thin wedges
¼ teaspoon salt
1½ tablespoons red, barley, or Hatcho miso
1½ tablespoons sesame butter or *tahini*

Bring ½ cup water to a boil in a small saucepan. Drop in the onions, season with the salt, and simmer for 5 minutes. Pour contents of saucepan into a strainer set over a bowl, and allow onions to drain well. In a large bowl combine miso, sesame butter, and 4½ tablespoons of the drained cooking liquid; mix well. Add onions and toss lightly. Serve immediately.

Turnips (kabu)

Miso in Soups & Stews

The great majority of Japan's miso (an estimated 80 to 85 percent of total yearly production) is used in the preparation of miso soup, and a recent survey showed that 73 percent of all Japanese—whether rich or poor, farmers or urbanites—enjoy miso soup at least once a day. Indeed, for most Japanese, the words miso and miso soup are practically synonymous.

Generally called *miso shiru* or *o-miotsuké*, but also known in better restaurants as *miso-jitaté*, miso soup became popular in Japan about 700 years ago, when samurai warriors who had siezed power from the traditional nobility developed a national cuisine reflecting the simplicity and frugality of their new life-style. Grains were given the leading role at each meal, supported by miso soup, cooked vegetables, tofu, and occasionally fish and shellfish. Today, miso soup is an indispensable element in the traditional Japanese breakfast, where it is accompanied by a large bowl of rice or rice porridge, usually garnished with salt-pickled vegetables, *umeboshi* (salt plums), and/or *nori*.

To prepare miso soup, fresh (or lightly sautéed) vegetables are simmered until just tender in dashi, the all-purpose soup stock; ingredients such as regular or deep-fried tofu and *wakame* are added as the vegetables near completion. Finally the miso is added (about 1 tablespoon per serving), and the soup reheated until the first bubble appears. Poured into lacquerware bowls, sprinkled lightly with a seasoning or garnish and covered with a lid, it is generally served steaming hot, while its aroma and flavor are at their peak. Plucking them out of the bowl with chopsticks (never a spoon), each person first enjoys the tofu and vegetables, then downs the warming broth.

One of the few peoples in the world to start off the day with soup, the Japanese point to the fact that miso soup is quick and easy to prepare; it is often ready to serve within 5 minutes after the cook starts work—a key factor during the busy morning meal. Almost any ingredient goes well in it and, being cooked only briefly, they all retain their health-giving vitamins, crispness, and delicate flavor. For the Japanese, the hearty aroma of this filling soup is as appetizing as that of coffee for many Westerners, while its mellow, subtly pungent flavor and low-calorie warmth help to start the day off right. By alkalizing the blood, miso soup is said to wake up the nervous system and offer abundant nourishment, stamina, and energy that last all morning. An aid to digestion and assimilation, it is also said to relieve acid indigestion and settle an upset stomach. Sake-lovers are unanimous in their assertion that miso soup does wonders for a hangover.

True enough, a typical serving is remarkably rich in essential nutrients. The tofu and miso together provide about 9 to 12 grams of protein (roughly one-sixth of the adult daily requirement), plus important polyunsaturated oils. The *wakame* and tofu supply abundant calcium and other minerals; the fresh vegetables offer vitamins; and the miso supplies salt.

In most rural farmhouses, a large kettle of miso soup is prepared each morning and reheated before lunch and dinner. This practice simplifies the work of the housewife in preparing meals, and many claim that as the flavors intermingle and marry, the soup becomes even more delicious. On winter evenings, the family will often have dinner around the open-hearth, sunken fireplace at the center of the main room, with the pot of simmering soup, suspended above the live coals from an overhead hook, serving as the center of conviviality and warmth. Miso soup is one of the most commonly served foods in Japan's many "long-life" villages where it is considered essential to good health and longevity; in some areas, the villagers are reported to consume an average of 4 to 6 cups daily. In most of Japan's Zen temples, miso soup is served with each meal, often using miso prepared by the monks; at breakfast and lunch it accompanies rice or rice porridge and cooked or salt-pickled vegetables, while at dinner it is mixed with leftovers to make a richly flavored gruel.

One of Japan's truly seasonal preparations, miso soup is served throughout the year. By using fresh vegetables, sprouts, sprigs and even flowers, the sensitive cook is able to reflect in a dark lacquerware soupbowl the great rhythms and cycles of the natural world. And by choosing from and combining the multitude of different types of fine miso, giving each combination the perfect accent with the proper choice of seasonings and garnishes, it is quite easy to prepare a different type of miso soup every day of the year. In fact, a number of Japanese cookbooks contain easy-to-follow charts suggesting ingredients for breakfast and dinner each day of the week throughout the four seasons (see p. 101), and cookbooks devoted exclusively to the preparation of miso soups group recipes as spring, summer, fall, and winter preparations. In Japan's most popular book on miso cookery, 76 of the 131 pages describe the preparation of miso soups. Several of Japan's largest miso makers have gone so far as to provide a free service whereby any cook can dial a widely advertised phone number and listen to a recording of "the miso soup of the day," featuring seasonal ingredients and the miso with which they best harmonize.

Likened to a haiku in a lacquerware bowl, miso soup is surrounded by a veritable mystique. It has been noted that in the writings of almost every great Japanese author and poet, there can be found a section of reminiscences about its ineffable aroma filling the air on unforgettable childhood mornings. Mr. Wataru Kawamura, Japan's best known writer on the subject, whose works include *An Encyclopedia of Miso Soups* and *Miso Soups Throughout the Provinces*, feels that it epitomizes Japanese character and culture. Describing himself as "a scholar not of miso, but of miso soup," Mr. Kawamura points out that even the thought of the piping hot broth has the power to touch Japanese heartstrings. The contemporary wanderer and poet Nanao Sasaki has written: "Everything starts from miso soup in good morning. Miso soup is made of shiny spider web..." The Japanese National Miso Association now uses as the motto for its letterhead: "A Happy Family is One that Starts the Day with Miso Soup." And many writers — both Japanese and foreign — have commented on the similarity between its essence and that of Zen: a certain simple yet deeply satisfying flavor that can be enjoyed day after day. Of course, miso soup is an integral part of the life of monks in their temples and tea masters in their hermitages, who delight in the flavor of a soup prepared with homemade miso and seasonal delicacies gathered wild from nearby mountains.

Japan's great master of Tea Ceremony Cuisine, Mr. Kaichi Tsuji, writes eloquently about miso soup: "Its taste must be subtle, complex, and compact—all within what is appropriate to the tea ceremony. A fine *misoshiru* is like the trailing reverberations of a great temple bell. Its goodness lies in its aftertaste, which invites the guest to a second bowl ... Its flavor is indeed the flavor of Japan."

A well-known Japanese proverb says that only when a young woman has mastered the art of making fine miso soup is she ready to become a bride. For although it is remarkably simple to follow the basic recipe and come up with a tasty result, to learn to prepare the very finest miso soup is deceptively difficult and requires years of practice. Yet many find that the joy lies in the learning, and claim that each day's effort allows the cook to express culinary mastery and love while serving as a nutritional key-stone for a healthy family.

Numerous Japanese restaurants specialize in the preparation of miso soup (p. 240), and virtually every restaurant

offers at least several varieties as standard fare. In recent years, modern technology has yielded a number of new forms, some sold through coffee-like vending machines and others in sealed foil packages as "instant miso soup," now widely available even in the West. The latter contain either regular or dehydrated miso (p. 44), plus dehydrated dashi, *wakame*, and tofu with freeze-dried vegetables. These lightweight, inexpensive products are ready to serve as soon as they have been mixed with hot water and are well suited for back packing, camping, and picnicking.

Although miso is used to season soups in China and Korea, too, the resulting dishes are completely different from Japanese miso soup and play a much less important role in the national cuisine. The Chinese variety, *chiang t'sang*, is usually made with a chicken broth and contains fish and vegetables sautéed in sesame oil. The fiery Korean *daen jang chigé* contains diced tofu, leeks, chunks of beef, and plenty of red pepper.

Since the 1960s, miso soup has come to be widely enjoyed in the West, particularly among those interested in natural foods. New variations on the traditional Japanese motif are beginning to appear using Western ingredients matched to Western tastes: some like to substitute cottage cheese for tofu or drop in an egg, add their favorite herbs or serve the soup chilled on hot summer afternoons. Winning growing acceptance among doctors and nutritionists alike, miso soup is rapidly finding a new home in America.

Basic Ingredients

Every miso soup is composed of four principal elements: dashi, miso, vegetables or other solids, and garnishes or seasonings.

Dashi: The Japanese consider a richly-flavored, fragrant dashi to be the indispensable foundation of a fine miso soup. Most dashi is prepared with *kombu* (dried kelp) together with either freshly-shaved bonita flakes or tiny dried sardines *(niboshi)*. In Zen Temple Cookery, the dashi is made with either *kombu* or a combination of *kombu* and *shiitaké* mushrooms (p. 57). In the West, vegetable or vegetable bouillon stocks are also used. Surprisingly delicious flavors result from the combination of 1 part stock with 1 part herb or peppermint teas or (home-extracted) vegetable juices (carrot, tomato, cabbage, etc.).

Miso: All varieties of regular miso are used in miso soups. Red, barley, and Hatcho miso are by far the most popular. Broiled miso is sometimes used to add savory aroma to chilled soups; sweet white and sweet red varieties are used only on special occasions. (Finger Lickin' and Sweet Simmered Miso are never used.) In most home cookery only one type of miso is used at a time, although restaurant chefs and cookbooks often call for the simultaneous use of two or occasionally even three types. Just as in the blending of fine coffees, the combination of fundamentally different misos (red and white, sweet and salty, rice and barley, etc.) produces delightful harmonies of flavor and aroma. The five most popular mixtures are:

4 parts red or light-yellow and 1 part Hatcho
3 parts red and 2 parts sweet white
1 part red and 9 parts sweet white
1 part light-yellow and 1 part sweet barley
1 part red and 1 part barley

For each cup of dashi or stock, use about 1 to 1½ tablespoons red, barley, or Hatcho miso; 2 tablespoons mellow miso; or 2 to 3 tablespoons sweet white or sweet red miso.

Vegetables, etc.: The English language has no good equivalent for the Japanese term *mi*—literally "fruits"—which refers to all of the basic solids in a soup. One of Japan's largest food and housekeeping magazines recently conducted a nationwide survey to find out which "fruits" were used most frequently in daily miso soups. The top 25 favorites, with relative popularity, are listed below. Note the total absence of meat, fish, or poultry, and the low position of two types of shellfish:

Daikon	19.6	Onion	3.7
Leek	19.1	Burdock root	3.4
Tofu pouches	16.2	Eggplant	3.2
Wakame	15.7	Mushrooms	3.1
Tofu	13.8	Turnip (kabu)	2.9
Chinese		Lotus root	2.5
Cabbage	8.5	Bean sprouts	2.4
Potato	7.7	Wild vegetables	2.3
Spinach	5.8	Corbicula (shellfish)	2.0
Cabbage	4.3	Sweet potato	1.6
Wheat gluten	4.2	Spring chrysanthemum	1.1
Carrot	3.9	Short-necked clams	0.8

Other popular ingredients are listed in the chart on page 101. Unlisted ingredients which are also used include:

Yuba (fresh or dried)
Tempura dumplings and skimmings
Snow peas
Noodles (all types)
Natto and *Hamanatto*
Cottage cheese
Ginkgo nuts

Most soups contain a combination of two or three of these "fruits", with one given the leading role and others used to complement and support it. All are sliced or diced fine so that they will cook quickly. An average serving contains about 1 to 1½ ounces (30 to 40 grams) of solids, and a thick soup 2½ times this much. In choosing ingredients, a skilled cook considers:

What locally grown vegetables are fresh and in season?
Which of these will harmonize best with the color and flavor of the miso to be used?
How much should be used together with a given amount of a particular miso?
Will they sink or float on the surface to complement the garnish?
Should they be cut into tree-leaf (maple, ginkgo) or blossom (cherry, plum) shapes to express the sense of the season; or do they lend themselves to cutting into loops, interlocking rings, pine-needle, or fan shapes?
Does the color and shape of the vegetable suit the color and design of the bowl to be used?

Seasonings and Garnishes: The proper seasoning or garnish provides the crowning touch. True to their name, many Japanese seasonings are strictly seasonal; they are used fresh and prized for their transiency. Many of the favorites are shown in the chart on page 101.

Although Western herbs and spices are not widely used in Japan, we have found them remarkably well suited for use in miso soups. For best fragrance, use them freshly picked, crushed, or ground. Parmesan and grated cheeses as well as sesame- and nut-butters also add delicious flavor and richness. Occasionally miso soups are spiked with a little sake or white wine, and thickened with *kuzu* (kudzu powder) or arrowroot.

Principles of Preparation and Serving

*Miso is always mixed with hot broth and sometimes puréed or ground before being added to a soup. In the following recipes, for the sake of brevity, we will simply call for the miso to be creamed. However any of the following four techniques may be used:

Vegetables cut for miso soup

1. *Creaming:* Place miso in a small cup. Remove about ½ cup hot dashi or stock from the saucepan and, adding a little at a time, stir into the miso; then add the cream back into the soup. Dip the cup into the soup to retrieve all the miso. This quick-and-easy technique allows the texture of the miso to appear in the soup.

2. *Puréeing:* Place miso in a small sieve or woven bamboo miso strainer (below). Partially immerse sieve in

Miso-koshi

broth and press miso through sieve with the back of a (wooden) spoon. If desired, add to the soup any particles of koji or soybeans remaining in the sieve. This technique yields a satin-smooth soup even when made from chunky miso.

3. *Grinding:* Combine miso and a small amount of hot broth in a *suribachi* (mortar) and grind to a smooth paste with a wooden pestle. Pour through a sieve (or directly) into the hot broth. Using a rubber spatula or wooden spoon, retrieve any miso remaining in *suribachi*, then rinse out *suribachi* with a little of the hot soup. This technique is used with (home-made) miso containing firm chunks of koji or soybeans.

Mad monks grinding miso

4. *Mincing:* Place very firm miso in a small mound on a cutting board and mince with a sharp knife. This technique, used exclusively with Hatcho miso, is usually followed by puréeing or creaming.

*Overcooking spoils the miso's prized aroma while also destroying microorganisms and enzymes which aid digestion. Remove soup from heat just before it comes to a boil and, for best flavor, serve immediately.

*For breakfast miso soup or when the ingredients are primarily vegetables, the Japanese use a relatively large amount of red or barley miso to create a rich, hearty broth. At dinnertime or when the ingredients are primarily tofu or seafoods, less miso is generally used to yield a more delicately flavored broth which allows the character of the individual ingredients to shine forth. Better restaurants generally serve a dinner miso soup prepared with a somewhat mild broth containing relatively few solid ingredients; the dinnertime miso soup served in private homes, however, can often resemble a hearty Western-style stew, served at the table in a casserole, earthenware *nabé*, or cast iron pot.

*During the warm half of the year (April to September), red or barley miso is generally used and the total amount of solid ingredients is kept relatively small; in midsummer, chilled miso soup is a favorite at lunch or dinner. During the cold seasons, the amount of solid ingredients increases and thick, sweet miso soups are served more frequently: in midwinter, a thick-as-a-stew miso soup may serve as the main course. During March-April and September-August, the months preceeding and following the equinoxes, mixtures of salty and sweet miso are enjoyed.

*Miso soup is generally served at the end of formal Japanese meals.

Fig. 19. Miso Soups Throughout the Four Seasons (FROM: *Miso Cookery Throughout the Twelve Months*)

Spring

Day	Meal	Main Ingredient	Supporting Ingredient	Miso	Seasoning
Sunday	Breakfast	deep-fried tofu	chrysanthemum leaves	sweet white miso	*yuzu* or lemon rind
	Dinner	egg tofu	*junsai*	red miso	*sansho* pepper
Monday	Breakfast	small turnips	chrysanthemum leaves	sweet white miso	mustard
	Dinner	mackerel or sardines	leek or wild onion	red miso	*sansho* pepper
Tuesday	Breakfast	onions	*wakame*	red miso	mustard
	Dinner	grilled tofu	burdock & deep-fried tofu	red miso	gingerroot juice
Wednesday	Breakfast	fish sausage	trefoil	sweet white miso	horsetails
	Dinner	bamboo shoots	*wakame*	sweet white miso	*kinomé*
Thursday	Breakfast	egg & dry sardines	trefoil	red miso	*yuzu* or lemon rind
	Dinner	*kampyo*	deep-fried tofu	red miso	butterbur sprouts
Friday	Breakfast	Osmund fern	deep-fried tofu	light-yellow miso	*sansho* pepper
	Dinner	young burdock	pork	light-yellow miso	gingerroot juice
Saturday	Breakfast	clams	*udo* or *nanohana*	red & white miso	*sansho* pepper
	Dinner	eggs	leeks	sweet white miso	curry powder

Summer

Day	Meal	Main Ingredient	Supporting Ingredient	Miso	Seasoning
Sunday	Breakfast	eggplant	*wakame*	red miso	cucumber or myoga
	Dinner	loach	burdock root	red & white miso	*sansho* pepper
Monday	Breakfast	egg	fresh greens	white & yellow miso	gingerroot juice
	Dinner	white gourd-melon	chicken	red & yellow miso	*sansho* pepper
Tuesday	Breakfast	green beans	deep-fried tofu	white & yellow miso	ground sesame
	Dinner	tomato & milk	green pepper & onion	sweet white miso	minced parsley
Wednesday	Breakfast	*kabocha*	*wakame*	red miso	7-spice red pepper
	Dinner	ground sesame	cucumber	broiled miso	7-spice red pepper
Thursday	Breakfast	cabbage	*tororo kombu*	sweet white miso	red pepper powder
	Dinner	taro	fried tofu, *shiitaké* & carrot	light-yellow miso	7-spice red pepper
Friday	Breakfast	potato	*daikon* & *wakame*	red miso	*daikon* leaf tips
	Dinner	corbicula (shellfish)	leeks	light-yellow miso	beefsteak leaf
Saturday	Breakfast	cucumber	beansprouts	Hatcho miso	hot mustard
	Dinner	fresh *shiitaké*	rice-flour dumplings	sweet white miso	hot mustard

Fall

Day	Meal	Main Ingredient	Supporting Ingredient	Miso	Seasoning
Sunday	Breakfast	*hijiki*	deep-fried tofu	red miso	7-spice red pepper
	Dinner	*matsutaké* mushrooms	*myoga* buds	red miso	*yuzu*
Monday	Breakfast	cabbage	deep-fried tofu	light-yellow miso	pepper
	Dinner	pork	grilled eggplants	sweet white miso	*myoga* or beefsteak buds
Tuesday	Breakfast	tofu	*nameko* mushrooms	Hatcho miso	hot mustard
	Dinner	taro	chicken	white & red miso	*sansho* pepper
Wednesday	Breakfast	cucumber	tomato	sweet white miso	*wasabi*
	Dinner	*shimeji* mushrooms	tofu & chrysanthemum leaves	white & red miso	*yuzu*
Thursday	Breakfast	sweet potato	deep-fried tofu	light-yellow miso	pepper
	Dinner	grilled eggplant	roasted sesame	sweet white miso	trefoil
Friday	Breakfast	*kabocha*	fried tofu & *shiitaké*	red miso	beefsteak seeds
	Dinner	fish	burdock root	white & red miso	*sansho* pepper
Saturday	Breakfast	*nira* chives	egg	white & red miso	gingerroot juice
	Dinner	mackerel	spinach & *wakame*	red miso	*sansho* pepper

Winter

Day	Meal	Main Ingredient	Supporting Ingredient	Miso	Seasoning
Sunday	Breakfast	*mochi*	*daikon*, carrot & *shiitaké*	red miso	*yuzu*
	Dinner	*junsai*	glutinous yam	Hatcho miso	green *nori* flakes
Monday	Breakfast	tofu	milk & *asatsuki* chives	light-yellow miso	pepper
	Dinner	peanuts	*aona* greens	red miso	crumbled *wakame*
Tuesday	Breakfast	small turnips	deep-fried tofu	red miso	hot mustard
	Dinner	dried-frozen tofu	chrysanthemum leaves	white & red miso	hot mustard
Wednesday	Breakfast	Chinese cabbage	deep-fried tofu	light-yellow miso	pepper
	Dinner	taro & *konnyaku*	burdock, leek, & sake lees	light-yellow miso	7-spice red pepper
Thursday	Breakfast	*daikon*	leeks	sweet white miso	butter or red pepper
	Dinner	pork	*konnyaku*	red miso	*sansho* pepper
Friday	Breakfast	tofu	bean sprouts	red miso	slivered leeks
	Dinner	tofu	salmon roe	sweet white miso	Mandarin orange peel
Saturday	Breakfast	oyster & tofu	leeks	red miso	*sansho* pepper
	Dinner	dried slivered *daikon* & *shiitaké*	chrysanthemum leaves	red miso	*sansho* pepper

Beefsteak leaves

Deep-fried Tofu & Wakame Miso Soup
SERVES 2 OR 3

This is one of Japan's favorite and most traditional miso soups. The *wakame* supplies an abundance of calcium and other minerals, while the deep-fried tofu and miso provide protein and unsaturated oils. Requiring less than 3 minutes to prepare, this soup is particularly popular at breakfast.

1¾ cups dashi (p. 56) or stock
¼ to 1/3 cup fresh or reconstituted *wakame* (p. 56), cut into 1-inch lengths
1 to 2 ounces deep-fried tofu, cut crosswise into thin strips
2 tablespoons red, barley, or Hatcho miso
1 tablespoon thinly sliced leeks and/or a dash of 7-spice red pepper

Bring dashi to a boil in a saucepan. Add *wakame* and deep-fried tofu, and simmer for 1 minute. Add miso creamed in a little of the hot broth and return just to the boil. Serve immediately, garnished with the leeks.

White Miso Soup with Tofu, Nori & Spinach
SERVES 2

This recipe is a specialty of Fugetsu, a Japanese natural-food restaurant in Berkeley. The key is the combination of sweet white miso with a little salt. The broth is kept warm in a double boiler and simply poured over the other ingredients in a bowl for each new serving.

1½ cups Number 1 Dashi (p. 56)
¼ cup sweet white miso
¼ teaspoon salt
1½ to 2 ounces tofu, cut into 3/8-inch cubes
3 to 4 tablespoons steamed or parboiled spinach, well drained
2 tablespoons thinly sliced green onions
2 pieces of *nori*, each 1½ inches square

Bring the dashi to a boil in a saucepan. Add the creamed miso and salt and return just to the boil. Divide the tofu, spinach, and green onions among individual warmed bowls and pour on the hot broth. Float a square of *nori* in the soup and serve immediately.

Nori & Deep-fried Tofu Miso Soup
SERVES 2

1¼ cups dashi (p. 56)
1½ ounces deep-fried tofu, cut into 3/8-inch cubes
¼ cup thinly sliced rounds of leek
1½ tablespoons red, barley, or Hatcho miso
½ sheet of *nori*, torn into small pieces; or 2 tablespoons rinsed and diced fresh *nori*

Bring dashi to a boil in a small saucepan. Add tofu, leeks, and miso creamed in a little of the hot broth; return to the boil. Stir in *nori*, return just to the boil, and serve.

Kabocha

Refreshing Pumpkin Miso Soup
SERVES 2

1¼ cups (*kabocha*) pumpkin or squash (1-inch chunks)
2 cups dashi (p. 56), stock, or water
2 tablespoons akadashi or red miso
1 green beefsteak leaf, thinly sliced

Combine pumpkin and dashi in a small saucepan and bring to a boil. Cover and simmer for about 15 minutes, or until pumpkin is tender. Stir in miso creamed in a little of the hot broth and return just to the boil. Serve garnished with the beefsteak leaf.

Miso Soup with Sake Lees (Sakenokasu-jiru)
SERVES 2

Available in the West at most Japanese food markets, sake lees may be added to any miso soup to impart a rich flavor, heady aroma, and thick texture: use 2 to 3 parts (by volume) lees to 3 parts miso, or about 1 tablespoon per serving.

1½ cups dashi (p. 56), stock, or water
2 Chinese cabbage leaves, thinly sliced
2/3 cup diced sweet potatoes, yams, or Irish potatoes
1 to 2 ounces deep-fried tofu (optional)
2 tablespoons red, barley, or Hatcho miso
1½ to 2 tablespoons sake lees

Bring dashi to a boil in a small saucepan. Add Chinese cabbage, sweet potatoes and, if used, the tofu. Return to the boil and simmer for 5 minutes. Combine the miso and sake lees, cream with a little of the hot broth, and stir into the soup. Return just to the boil. Serve piping hot.

For a softer texture and lower alcohol content, simmer the lees with the vegetables before adding the miso.

Miso Soup with Potato, Wakame & Tofu
SERVES 4

4 cups water or stock
¼ cup bonito flakes
1 small potato, cut into ½-inch cubes
¾ cup fresh or reconstituted *wakame* (p. 54), cut into 1½-inch lengths
2 ounces deep-fried tofu, thinly sliced (optional)
5 tablespoons red, barley, or Hatcho miso
¼ cup thinly-sliced leeks

Bring water to a boil in a small saucepan. Add bonito flakes, turn off heat and allow to stand for 3 to 4 minutes. (Strain if flakes are coarse.) Return broth to a boil, add potatoes and cook for 8 to 10 minutes, or until potatoes are tender. Add *wakame*, tofu, and miso creamed in a little of the hot broth. Return just to the boil and remove from heat. Top with a sprinkling of the leeks and serve hot or cold.

Gingerroot-Onion Miso Soup
SERVES 3

2 teaspoons oil or butter
½ clove of garlic, crushed or minced
1 onion, thinly sliced
2 cups water or stock
2 tablespoons sweet white or 4 teaspoons mellow white miso
1 tablespoon red, barley, or Hatcho miso
½ teaspoon grated gingerroot

Heat a small pot or saucepan and coat with the oil. Add garlic and sauté for 30 seconds, then add onion and sauté for 5 minutes more. Add water and bring to a boil; cover and simmer for 3 minutes. Add both varieties of miso dissolved in a little of the hot broth, stir in gingerroot, and return just to the boil. Serve piping hot.

Picnic Miso Soup
SERVES 3

3 tablespoons red, barley, or Hatcho miso
2 tablespoons bonito flakes or grated cheese
Dash of pepper (7-spice, red, or black)
1 to 2 ounces deep-fried tofu, cut crosswise into thin strips
12 inches dry *wakame*, cut into 1-inch lengths; or 3 cakes of dried wheat gluten
2 to 3 tablespoons thinly-sliced leeks; or minced chives or parsley
2 cups hot or boiling water

Combine miso, bonito flakes, and pepper, mixing well, then shape into 3 balls. Skewer and broil each ball over a burner (as for Broiled Miso, p. 71) until well browned and fragrant. Place balls and the next three ingredients into a picnic container. Take the hot water in a thermos or heat water at the picnic site. To serve, divide all solid ingredients among 3 bowls, pour in the hot water, and mix until miso dissolves. Cover and allow to stand for several minutes before serving.

Curried White Miso Soup with Onion and Egg
SERVES 2

1¼ cups dashi (p. 56) or stock
1 small onion, sliced very thin
¼ cup sweet white or 2½ tablespoons mellow white miso
½ teaspoon curry powder
1 egg, lightly beaten

Combine dashi and onion in a small saucepan, bring to a boil, and simmer, covered, for 3 minutes. Add miso and curry powder creamed in a little of the hot broth; return to the boil. Stir in egg a little at a time. Remove from heat and serve immediately.

Natto & Chinese Cabbage Miso Soup
SERVES 2 OR 3

1¼ cups dashi (p. 56), stock, or water
2 (Chinese) cabbage leaves, cut lengthwise into halves, then crosswise into 1½-inch-wide strips
1 tablespoon red, barley, or Hatcho miso
2 tablespoons sweet white or 4 teaspoons mellow white miso
½ cup *natto*
¼ cup thin rounds of leek or scallion
Dash of 7-spice red pepper

Bring dashi to a boil in a saucepan. Add Chinese cabbage, cover, and simmer for 2 or 3 minutes. Add miso creamed in a little of the hot broth. Add *natto* and return just to the boil. Sprinkle on leeks and remove from heat. Serve seasoned with a sprinkling of the red pepper.

Daikon & Onion Miso Soup
SERVES 3 TO 4

2 to 3 teaspoons oil
1 onion, thinly sliced
1 cup thin half-moons of *daikon* (p.54)
2 cups water, stock, or dashi (p.56)
4 tablespoons red, barley, or Hatcho miso
2 tablespoons thinly sliced leek or scallion greens (optional)

Heat a skillet or casserole and coat with the oil. Add onion and sauté for 3 minutes. Add *daikon* and water, and bring to a boil. Reduce heat to low and simmer, covered, for 15 minutes. Add miso creamed in a little of the hot broth and return to the boil. Serve garnished, if desired, with a sprinkling of leek slices.

Akadashi Miso Soup   SERVES 2 OR 3
with Tofu and Mushrooms

Akadashi or "red dashi" was originally the name of a miso soup containing a mixture of soybean (usually Hatcho) miso and one or two rice misos. It originated in central Japan and was prepared in either of two ways: 1) The firm soybean miso was minced on a bread board, mixed with the softer rice miso(s) and tied in a small piece of coarsely-woven cloth to form a sack, which was then immersed in hot dashi until the miso flavor and color had permeated the broth; 2) The red and minced soybean misos were combined with bonita flakes in a *suribachi* and ground until smooth; hot water was stirred in and the mixture allowed to stand until strained for use as the broth. After World War II, "akadashi" came to refer to a new variety of miso (p. 44). Yet the colorful and tasty soup is still a favorite in many of Japan's finest restaurants, where it may be prepared with either the modern or traditional misos. Since the basic ingredients are added to the broth *after* the miso, only those requiring very little cooking are used.

1¼ cups dashi (p. 56) or stock
2 teaspoons Hatcho miso
1 tablespoon red miso
1 teaspoon sweet white miso (optional)
6 ounces tofu, cut into 3/8-inch cubes
1/3 cup *nameko* mushrooms and their liquid
3 sprigs of trefoil, cut into 1-inch lengths

Bring dashi to a boil in a small saucepan. Add misos creamed in a little of the dashi and return to the boil. Add tofu and mushrooms, and return again to the boil. Serve garnished with trefoil.

If *nameko* mushrooms are not available, sauté 6 thinly sliced fresh mushrooms in butter until tender and add to dashi together with tofu. If desired, substitute dry wheat gluten cakes for the tofu; season with *sansho* green pepper.

Hiyashi-jiru   SERVES 2 OR 3
(Broiled Miso in Chilled Soup)

1½ cups dashi (p. 56) or stock, cooled
1½ to 2 tablespoons Savory Broiled Miso (p. 71; use red miso)
½ cup thinly sliced cucumber
½ cup diced tomato
2 green beefsteak or mint leaves, minced (optional)

Cream the miso in a little of the dashi, then add remaining dashi, stirring until smooth; cover and refrigerate until chilled. Refrigerate vegetables in separate containers. Divide vegetables among individual bowls and pour on the chilled broth. Serve immediately.

Tororo-jiru with Sweet White Miso   SERVES 5 TO 6

This unusual Japanese delicacy bears some resemblance to a chilled Western-style consommé. The ingredients are traditionally mixed in a *suribachi* rather than a blender.

2½ cups dashi (p. 56) or stock, cooled to room temperature
7½ tablespoons sweet white or 5 tablespoons mellow white miso
10½ ounces glutinous yam, peeled and grated
1 egg
1 sheet of *nori*, toasted (p. 54) and crumbled (optional)

Combine the first four ingredients in a blender and purée for about 1 minute. Serve as is or chilled, topped with a sprinkling of *nori*.

Onion-Miso Soup with Tofu and Eggs   SERVES 3

2 cups dashi (p. 56), stock, or water
1 onion, thinly sliced
2½ to 3 tablespoons red, barley, or Hatcho miso
4 to 6 ounces regular or deep-fried tofu, cut into 3/8-inch cubes
2 or 3 eggs, lightly beaten if desired (optional)
Dash of black or 7-spice red pepper

Combine dashi and onion in a small saucepan, bring to a boil, and simmer, covered, for 4 to 5 minutes. Add the miso creamed in a little of the hot broth, then the tofu and eggs. (For an egg-flower soup, swirl broth while adding lightly beaten eggs.) Return just to a boil over high heat, season with pepper, and serve immediately. Or allow to cool to room temperature and serve topped with 1 tablespoon minced parsley.

Miso Soup with Buckwheat Noodles   SERVES 2
and Eggs

2 teaspoons (sesame) oil
1 small onion, thinly sliced
1½ cups water, stock, or dashi (p. 56)
2 ounces *(soba)* buckwheat noodles, broken into 4-inch lengths and cooked (p. 58)
3 tablespoons red, barley, or Hatcho miso
2 eggs
1 tablespoon minced parsley (optional)

Heat a skillet and coat with the oil. Add onion and sauté for 5 minutes, then add water and bring to a boil. Add cooked noodles and return to the boil. Stir in miso creamed in a little of the hot broth. Now increase heat to medium-high and carefully break in the eggs, keeping the yolks whole. Cook for 1 minute more, or until whites are just firm. Serve immediately, garnished with parsley.

Miso Ozoni

SERVES 3

Ozoni is a soup containing *mochi* (pounded rice cakes) served daily in Japan during the week of festivities that begins on New Year's Day. Neither the usual cooked rice nor miso soup are served throughout this period; Ozoni takes their place and is eaten with special, thick chopsticks *(zoni-bashi)* which help to pluck out the soft mochi while also serving as a symbol of the holiday season. In the Kyoto area, freshly-prepared *mochi* dumplings are served in a rich soup made with sweet white miso and generally containing taro, *daikon*, carrot, grilled tofu, and a garnish of grated bonita flakes. The *mochi* partially melts in the hot soup, imparting to it a thick, almost creamy consistency. In country farmhouses, the *mochi* is often broiled and—to prevent its dissolution—added at the last minute to soups prepared with red miso. Fresh or broiled *mochi* may be added to many of the miso soups given in this section. Or try this country-style preparation:

2 cups dashi (p. 56) or stock
1 leek, cut diagonally into ½-inch-thick ovals, separated into greens and whites
7 ounces deep-fried tofu, thinly sliced
3 tablespoons red, barley, or Hatcho miso
3 cakes of *mochi* (each 2 by 1½ by ½ inches), broiled until speckled then pierced in several places with a chopstick or fork

Combine dashi, leek greens, and deep-fried tofu in a saucepan and bring to a boil. Add leek whites and stir in miso creamed in a little of the hot broth; return just to the boil. Pour into individual bowls, add *mochi*, and serve immediately.

Red & White Miso Soup with Swirled Eggs and Chives

SERVES 2

1¼ cups dashi (p. 56) or stock
1 teaspoon butter or oil
2/3 cup chopped chives or *nira*
1 tablespoon red, barley, or Hatcho miso
1½ tablespoons sweet white or 1 tablespoon mellow white miso
1 egg, lightly beaten
¼ to ½ teaspoon grated gingerroot or ½ teaspoon powdered ginger

Heat dashi in a small saucepan over medium heat. Meanwhile heat a skillet and coat with the butter. Add chives and sauté for 20 to 30 seconds. Add to dashi and bring to a boil. Add miso creamed in a little of the hot broth and return to the boil. Stir in eggs a little at a time, then remove from heat. Serve immediately, topped with a dab of gingerroot.

For a richer flavor and thicker consistency, combine with the eggs before stirring into the soup: 1½ teaspoons sake or white wine and 1 teaspoon *kuzu* (kudzu powder) or cornstarch, dissolved in 1 tablespoon water.

Mushroom Miso Soup

SERVES 2

1½ tablespoons butter
6 mushrooms, thinly sliced
1 small onion, thinly sliced
2 cups dashi (p. 56), stock, or water
3 tablespoons akadashi or 2½ tablespoons red miso
2 tablespoons minced parsley or thinly sliced leeks

Melt the butter in a heavy skillet. Add mushrooms and onion, and sauté until onions are just transparent. Add dashi and bring to a boil. Add miso creamed in a little of the hot broth and return just to the boil. Serve hot garnished with parsley.

Mushroom & Tofu Miso Soup

SERVES 6

The following is a description of the method used to prepare the daily miso soup in a large, well-known Japanese restaurant. Each ingredient has been reduced to about one-eighth its usual quantity. Notice the integrated preparation of both Number 1 and Number 2 Dashi along with a basic *shiitaké* dashi.

1½ cups (5 ounces) dried *shiitaké* mushrooms, soaked for 10 hours (overnight) in 2 cups water
½ cup (¾ ounce) round-herring flakes *(urume iwashi)*
½ cup (medium salty) light-yellow miso
1/3 cup Hatcho miso
5½ cups water
60 (canned) *nameko* mushrooms
12 ounces silken (or regular) tofu, cut into ½-inch cubes
18 trefoil leaves (including stems)

Pour mushrooms into a colander set over a pot. Press mushrooms gently but firmly against bottom of colander to expel remaining liquid, then reserve mushrooms for use in other cooking.

Bring mushroom soaking water *(shiitaké dashi)* to a boil over high heat. Skim off any foam that may develop, then add herring flakes and return to the boil. Reduce heat to low, simmer for 5 minutes, and turn off heat.

Meanwhile, combine light-yellow and Hatcho miso with ¾ cup warm water in a mixing bowl. Mix well until miso is dissolved. Pour herring-*shiitaké* dashi through a fine-mesh strainer set over the mixing bowl and press herring flakes in strainer to expel all liquid.

Now combine herring flakes with 2 cups water in a saucepan to make a Number 2 Dashi. Bring this dashi to a boil and reduce heat to low; cover pan and simmer for 5 minutes.

While Number 2 Dashi is simmering, pour miso-dashi mixture through a fine-mesh strainer set over the pot. Remove particles of miso grain left in strainer and combine with 2 cups warm water. Mix well, then pour back through strainer into pot, reserving grain particles for use in other cooking.

Pour Number 2 Dashi through strainer into pot, discarding herring flakes. Now bring dashi in pot just to a boil, add *nameko* mushrooms and tofu, and remove from heat. Serve piping hot, garnished with trefoil leaves.

Butter & Lemon Soup with Sweet Miso

SERVES 3 OR 4

2½ tablespoons butter
1 onion, minced
½ cup corn or green peas, parboiled
2 cups hot water or stock
2 teaspoons lemon juice
6 tablespoons sweet white or ¼ cup mellow white miso
Dash of pepper (optional)

Melt the butter in a heavy skillet. Add onion and corn, and sauté for 4 to 5 minutes. Stir in the hot water and bring to a boil. Add lemon juice and miso, creamed in a little of the hot broth, and return just to the boil. Serve hot, seasoned with pepper.

Sweet White Miso Potage

SERVES 2 OR 3

2 tablespoons butter
½ cup minced onion
1½ tablespoons whole-wheat flour
2 cups dashi (p. 56), stock, or water
6 tablespoons sweet white or ¼ cup mellow white miso
Dash of pepper
1 tablespoon minced parsley

Melt butter in a skillet. Add onion and sauté for 4 to 5 minutes. Reduce heat to low, add flour and sauté for 1 minute more. Add dashi a little at a time, stirring constantly until smooth. Mix in miso dissolved in a little of the hot broth, season with pepper, and return just to the boil. Serve topped with a sprinkling of parsley.

JAPANESE-STYLE MISO STEWS

In addition to its daily use in soups, miso is also employed as the essential seasoning in a number of stew-like preparations, most of which are made with soybeans or tofu and have enough body and protein to serve as a main course. Kenchin-jiru, Tanuki-jiru, and Gôjiru are the three most famous representatives of these dinnertime specialties.

Kenchin-jiru

SERVES 5

1½ tablespoons sesame oil
18 ounces tofu, pressed (p.55) and broken into small pieces
½ cup shaved burdock root
1 cup half-moons of *daikon*
5 *shiitaké* or cloud-ear mushrooms, thinly sliced
1 to 1¼ cups large irregular chunks of sweet potato, yam, or taro
½ cup carrot (cut into ginkgo leaves; p. 54)
½ cake of *konnyaku*, broken into small pieces and lightly salted
2¼ cups dashi (p. 56), stock, or water
5 tablespoons red, barley, or Hatcho miso
¼ teaspoon salt
2 teaspoons sake or *mirin*
Garnishes: 7-spice red pepper, slivered leeks, crumbled *nori*, and/or grated lemon or *yuzu* rind

Heat the oil in a heavy-bottomed saucepan. Add consecutively: tofu, burdock root, *daikon*, mushrooms, sweet potato, carrot, and *konnyaku*, sautéing each over medium heat for about 1 minute. Reduce heat to low, and add broth, miso, salt, and sake. Cover pan and simmer for 30 to 40 minutes, or until *daikon* is transparent. For best flavor, allow to stand for 6 to 8 hours, then serve individual portions topped with a sprinkling of the garnishes.

VARIATION

*Tanuki-jiru *(Badger's Soup):* Omit all vegetables except the burdock root and carrot, and triple the amounts of both of these. Use barley miso.

Gôjiru

SERVES 4 TO 6

This thick miso soup prepared with *gô*, a purée of well-soaked soybeans, is a wintertime favorite in Japan's snowy northeast provinces. It can be prepared using a wide range of vegetables, seasonings, and garnishes; experiment with whatever is available, in season, or simply appealing.

½ cup soybeans, rinsed and soaked for 8 to 10 hours in 1 quart water
4½ cups water, stock, or dashi (p. 56)
2 tablespoons oil
1 onion, thinly sliced; or 1 leek, cut into 2-inch lengths
½ carrot, cut into thin half moons
2 ounces deep-fried tofu, cut into thin strips
3 mushrooms, thinly sliced
2 inches *daikon*, cut into half moons; or ½ cup chopped celery
1 potato, sweet potato, yam, or taro, diced
5 to 6 tablespoons red, barley, or Hatcho miso

Rinse, then drain beans in a colander. Combine beans and ¾ cup water in a blender and purée at high speed for about 3 minutes, or until smooth.

Heat a heavy pot and coat with the oil. Add the next six ingredients and sauté for 5 to 10 minutes, or until potatoes are softened. Add soybean purée and remaining 3¾ cups water, bring to a boil, and simmer uncovered for 10 to 15 minutes, stirring occasionally. Add miso thinned in a few tablespoons of the hot broth and simmer for 1 minute more. Serve immediately or, for a richer, sweeter flavor, allow to cool for at least 6 hours.

VARIATIONS

*Any of the following garnishes or seasonings may be added to the soup with the miso or sprinkled on top of individual servings: 7-spice red pepper, green *nori* flakes, *sansho* pepper; minced trefoil, sake lees, slivered *yuzu* or lemon rind; pepper, crushed garlic, croutons, sage, or thyme.
*Experiment using other vegetables such as green beans, celery (including leaves), snow peas, *kombu*, or shelled green soybeans. For extra richness, try adding 2 lightly beaten eggs or 2 thinly sliced, deep-fried potatoes together with the miso.

WESTERN-STYLE SOUPS AND STEWS

Miso can be used to combine the functions of a hearty bouillon- or meat broth and a savory seasoning. Try substituting about 1 tablespoon of red, barley, or Hatcho for each ½ teaspoon salt in your favorite recipes. To keep the miso aroma, flavor, and nutrients at their peak of goodness, remember to add the creamed miso just before the end of cooking.

Thick French Onion Soup with Miso   MAKES 4 CUPS; SERVES 4

Our favorite Western-style soup with miso, this dish reaches its peak of flavor after lengthy cooking and when allowed to stand overnight for the flavors to marry. It can, however, be served before the marriage night, while piping hot, and is still guaranteed to delight the senses of even Monsieur Brillat-Savarin.

2 tablespoons oil
6 onions, thinly sliced
3 tablespoons red, barley, or Hatcho miso, dissolved in 2 cups warm water
1 tablespoon butter
2 ounces cheese, grated or minced

Heat a large casserole or heavy pot and coat with the oil. Add onions, cover, and simmer over very low heat for 3½ hours, stirring every 20 to 30 minutes. Mix in dissolved miso and butter, return just to the boil, and remove from heat. Allow to cool, then refrigerate overnight. Stir in the cheese, bring to a boil and simmer, stirring constantly, for about 1 minute, or until cheese melts. Serve hot or, for a richer, sweeter flavor, allow to cool to room temperature.

For variety, add 10 ounces diced deep-fried or regular tofu, 1 more tablespoon miso and, if desired, 2 lightly beaten eggs 15 minutes before adding miso.

Thick Winter Squash Soup with Miso   SERVES 4 OR 5

1½ tablespoons oil
1 pound seeded *(kabocha)* pumpkin, squash, or zucchini, cut into ½-inch squares
2 onions, thinly sliced
2 cups water or stock
¼ teaspoon nutmeg or cinnamon
1 clove garlic, minced
4 tablespoons red, barley, or Hatcho miso
3 tablespoons parsley, minced
½ cup croutons or dry bread pieces
2 tablespoons ground roasted sesame seeds (p. 54) (optional)

Heat the oil in a casserole or large pot. Add pumpkin and onion, and sauté for 3 minutes. Add water, cover, and bring to a boil. Reduce heat to low and simmer for 25 minutes. Stir in nutmeg, garlic, and miso thinned in a little of the hot soup, and return just to the boil; remove from heat. For best flavor, allow to cool to room temperature, then serve cold or reheated, topped with parsley, croutons and, if used, the sesame seeds. Also nice pureed in a blender.

For a slightly richer flavor, add 2 tablespoons butter and/or finely-shaved bonito flakes together with the miso.

Tomato & Cottage Cheese Soup with Miso   SERVES 2

1 tablespoon butter
2 small tomatoes, peeled and thinly sliced
½ onion, thinly sliced
1 green pepper, seeded and diced
1 bay leaf (optional)
1 cup water or stock
1½ tablespoons red, barley, or Hatcho miso
6 tablespoons cottage cheese
Dash of pepper
Dash of oregano (optional)
3 to 4 tablespoons Parmesan cheese

Melt butter in a skillet. Add the next four ingredients and sauté for 3 minutes, or until tomato dissolves. Add water and bring to a boil. Stir in miso dissolved in a little of the hot broth. Add cottage cheese, mixing lightly, and return just to the boil. Remove from heat. Remove bay leaf and serve hot, seasoned with the pepper and oregano and topped with a sprinkling of the cheese.

Thick Corn & Tomato Soup with Miso SERVES 2

1 tablespoon oil
1½ small onions, thinly sliced
½ cup corn kernels
1 large tomato, diced
1 cup milk (soy or dairy)
2½ tablespoons red, barley, or Hatcho miso
Dash of pepper or a dab of mustard
¼ teaspoon oregano or marjoram
1 tablespoon minced parsley

Heat a pot and coat with the oil. Add onion and corn and sauté for 4 minutes. Add tomato and sauté for 2 to 3 minutes more. Stir in the milk and miso, and season with pepper and oregano. Cook for about 1 minute, whisking or stirring constantly, but do not bring to a boil. Remove from heat and allow to cool to body temperature. Transfer to a blender and purée until smooth. Return to the pot and bring just to a boil. Serve hot or cold, topped with a sprinkling of parsley.

Creamy Corn & Cheese Soup with Miso SERVES 3

1 tablespoon oil
1 onion, minced
1 cup grated carrot
1 cup fresh corn kernels
2 cups water or stock
1 cup grated cheese
2 tablespoons red, barley, or Hatcho miso
1½ tablespoons sweet white or 1 tablespoon mellow white
   miso
Dash of pepper
1 tablespoon minced parsley

Heat a heavy pot or deep skillet and coat with the oil. Add consecutively: onion, carrot and corn, sautéing each for 3 minutes. Stir in water, cover, and bring to a boil; simmer for 10 minutes. Add cheese and both varieties of miso creamed in a little of the hot broth. Return just to the boil, then season with pepper and top with parsley. Serve hot or cold.

   For extra protein and flavor, add 5 to 10 ounces diced tofu (deep-fried or regular) together with the miso, increasing the miso by 1½ to 3 teaspoons.

Refreshing Yogurt Soup with Miso SERVES 2

1 tablespoon butter
1 small onion, thinly sliced
1 green pepper, sliced into thin rings
1 cup dashi (p. 56) or stock
1½ tablespoons red, barley, or Hatcho miso
¼ cup yogurt
Dash of pepper

Melt the butter in a skillet. Add onion and green pepper, and sauté for 3 minutes. Add dashi and bring to a boil. Stir in miso creamed in a little of the hot broth, then mix in yogurt and return to the boil. Season with pepper and serve immediately.

Vichyssoise with Miso SERVES 4

2 tablespoons butter
1 cup minced leek whites and/or (wild) onions
2 potatoes, thinly sliced
2 cups water or stock
2 tablespoons red, barley, or Hatcho miso
1½ cups cream or rich soymilk
Dash of pepper
Chopped chives or watercress (optional)

Melt the butter in a skillet. Add leeks or onions and sauté for 3 minutes. Add potatoes, water and miso (creamed in a few tablespoons of the water). Simmer, covered, for 15 minutes, then cool briefly. Purée in a blender until smooth. Add cream and pepper and purée again. Chill thoroughly. Serve topped with the chives.

Potato & Onion Soup with White Miso SERVES 2

4 small potatoes (2½-inch diameter), peeled and cut into
   halves
1 small onion, thinly sliced
2 cups water or stock
1 bay leaf
5 tablespoons sweet white or 3 tablespoons mellow white
   miso
2 tablespoons Parmesan cheese
Dash of pepper
1 tablespoon parsley

Combine the first four ingredients in a saucepan and bring to a boil. Cover and simmer over low heat for 1 hour. Remove bay leaf, add miso creamed in a little of the hot broth, and stir in Parmesan. Season with pepper and return just to the boil. Serve chilled, topped with a sprinkling of parsley.

   For variety, substitute sweet potatoes, *kabocha*, squash, or lentils for the potatoes.

Potato, Cottage Cheese & Chive Soup SERVES 2
with Miso

   The cottage cheese in this dish works somewhat like tofu in traditional Japanese miso soups, but since some of the cottage cheese melts, it gives the soup a rich, slightly creamy consistency.

1 tablespoon butter
2 small potatoes, cut into thin rectangles (1¼ cups)
5 tablespoons chives, *nira*, or wild onions, chopped
1¼ cups water or stock
2 tablespoons red, barley, or Hatcho miso
½ cup cottage cheese

Melt the butter in a skillet. Add potatoes and ¼ cup chives, and sauté for 2 minutes. Add water and simmer for about 7 minutes. Stir in miso creamed in a little of the hot broth. Add cottage cheese, mix lightly, and return just to the boil. Serve immediately, garnished with the remaining 1 tablespoon chives.

Potato & Miso Soup with Milk, Cheese & Tofu

SERVES 3

1½ tablespoons butter
1 potato, cut into pieces 3 inches long and ½ inch square
5 ounces deep-fried or 12 ounces regular tofu, cut crosswise into thin slices
1 cup dashi (p. 56), stock, or water
2 to 2½ tablespoons red, barley, or Hatcho miso
1 cup milk (soy or dairy)
2 tablespoons minced leeks, scallions, or onions
Dash of pepper
¼ cup grated cheese or parboiled green peas (optional)

Melt the butter in a skillet. Add potato pieces and sauté for 5 minutes, then transfer to a separate container. Add tofu to skillet, sauté for 3 minutes, and remove from heat.

Bring dashi to a boil in a small saucepan. Add the miso creamed in a little of the hot dashi, then add potatoes, tofu and milk. Return just to the boil before removing from heat. Sprinkle on leeks, pepper, and cheese. Serve immediately.

Instant Miso (Better 'n Coffee) Soup

SERVES 1

½ cup very hot or boiling water
Miso: Choose one
    2 teaspoons red, barley, Hatcho, or light yellow
    4 teaspoons mellow white
    6 teaspoons sweet white

Place miso in a cup or small bowl and add hot water a little at a time, stirring until smooth. Serve immediately; a good way to start the day off right!

Cream of Mushroom Soup with Miso

SERVES 3

2 tablespoons butter
2 cups diced mushrooms (about 16)
½ cup thinly sliced onion
¼ cup chopped celery
1 cup water or stock
2 tablespoons minced parsley
5 to 6 teaspoons red, barley, or Hatcho miso
1½ tablespoons white wine or sake
Dash of pepper
½ cup Miso White Sauce (p. 114)

Melt the butter in a saucepan. Add mushrooms and sauté for 2 to 3 minutes. Add onion, celery, water, and 1 tablespoon parsley; cover and bring to a boil. Simmer over low heat for 20 minutes. Remove from heat, uncover, and allow to cool briefly. Transfer to a blender, add miso, white wine and pepper, and purée until smooth. Return to saucepan, stir in white sauce, and bring just to a boil. Serve hot or chilled, garnished with the remaining 1 tablespoon parsley.

For variety, add 12 ounces diced regular tofu or 5 ounces deep-fried tofu together with the white sauce. For best flavor, allow to stand overnight, then serve chilled.

Mushroom & Onion Soup with White Miso

SERVES 2

2 tablespoons butter
6 mushrooms, diced (½ cup)
½ onion, thinly sliced
1¼ cups water or stock
2 tablespoon sweet white or 4 teaspoons mellow white miso
1 tablespoon red, barley, or Hatcho miso
2 tablespoons Parmesan cheese
Dash of pepper
1 tablespoon minced parsley

Melt the butter in a skillet. Add mushrooms and onions, and sauté for 4 minutes. Add water and bring to a boil. Add miso creamed in a little of the hot broth, then stir in Parmesan; season with pepper and return just to the boil. Serve topped with a sprinkling of parsley.

Almost Pudding Soup with Miso

SERVES 3

1½ teaspoons butter
½ cup minced onion
1½ cups diced whole-wheat bread
2 cups milk (soy or dairy)
2½ tablespoons red, barley, or Hatcho miso
1 small egg
Dash of freshly-grated nutmeg
1 tablespoon minced parsley

Melt the butter in a skillet, add onions and sauté for 5 minutes. Add bread pieces and 1½ cups milk, and bring just to a boil. Remove from heat, cover, and allow to stand for 20 minutes. Mix well with a whisk or fork to give a smooth texture. Combine miso and egg with remaining ½ cup milk, mixing well, then stir into soup. Return to heat and bring just to a boil, whisking constantly. Mix in nutmeg and serve hot or cold, topped with a sprinkling of parsley.

For use as a dessert, add ¼ to ½ cup raisins together with the nutmeg.

Tomato Juice & Onion Soup with White Miso

SERVES 3

1 tablespoon oil
1 small onion, thinly sliced
2 mushrooms, thinly sliced
¾ cup tomato juice
1 cup dashi (p. 56), stock, or water
2 tablespoons sweet white or 4 teaspoons mellow white miso
1 teaspoon red, barley, or Hatcho miso
1 tablespoon minced parsley

Heat a saucepan and coat with the oil. Add onion and mushrooms, and sauté for 5 minutes. Add dashi and tomato juice, bring to a boil, and simmer for 3 minutes. Add creamed miso and return just to the boil. Serve hot or chilled topped with a sprinkling of parsley.

Carrot Juice Soup with Miso
SERVES 2 OR 3

2 teaspoons oil
¼ onion, thinly sliced
¼ cabbage leaf, shredded
¼ carrot, grated or cut into thin rounds
1 small potato, yam, or sweet potato, diced into ¼-inch
  cubes
¾ cup carrot- or tomato juice
¾ cup water or stock
4 teaspoons red, barley, or Hatcho miso
3 tablespoons Parmesan cheese
Dash of oregano or pepper
1 tablespoon minced parsley

Heat a skillet and coat with the oil. Add the next four ingredients and sauté for 2 minutes. Add juice and water, bring to a boil, and simmer, covered, for 20 minutes. Add miso creamed in a little of the hot broth; stir in Parmesan, season with oregano, and return just to the boil. Serve topped with a sprinkling of parsley.

Chilled Cucumber & Yogurt Soup with Miso
SERVES 2

1 cucumber, sliced into thin rounds
2 tablespoons minced onion
1½ cups stock or water
1½ tablespoons red, barley, or Hatcho miso
Dash of pepper
2 tablespoons flour
½ bay leaf or 1 clove
½ cup yogurt
½ teaspoon caraway seeds or 1½ teaspoons grated lemon
  rind, dill, or chives

Combine cucumber, onion, and ½ cup stock in a saucepa Bring to a boil, cover, and simmer for 15 minutes. Allow i cool for 10 minutes. Stir in miso and pepper, transfer to blender, and purée until smooth.

Combine flour and ¼ cup stock, mixing well, then gradually add the remaining ¾ cup stock, stirring until smooth. Combine with the cucumber purée in a saucepan, add bay leaf, and bring to a boil. Cover and simmer for 2 to 3 minutes. Cool to room temperature and remove bay leaf. Mix in yogurt and caraway. Serve chilled.

Chilled Cucumber & Tahini Soup with Miso
SERVES 2

1¼ cups dashi (p. 56) or stock
1 tablespoon red, barley, or Hatcho miso
1½ tablespoons sweet white or 1 tablespoon mellow white
  miso
1 tablespoon *tahini* or sesame butter
1 cucumber, sliced into thin rounds
Dash of (7-spice) red pepper or tabasco sauce (optional)

Bring dashi to a boil in a small saucepan. Add miso and *tahini*,

both creamed in a little of the hot broth. Add cucumber and return to the boil. Serve chilled, seasoned with the red pepper.

VARIATION

*Chilled Cucumber & Tomato White Miso Soup. Omit red miso and *tahini*. Use ¼ cup sweet white miso. Add 1 small tomato (cut into wedges) together with cucumber. Season with black pepper and garnish with minced parsley.

Basic Miso Soup
SERVES 4 TO 6

Featuring the most widely used and inexpensive vegetables, this easy-to-make recipe is a favorite year-round, day after day.

2 teaspoons oil
1 cup sliced onions
1 cup sliced carrots
2 cups chopped cabbage
4 cups water or stock
3½ tablespoons red, barley, or Hatcho miso
2 tablespoons minced parsley or scallions

Heat the oil in a wok or heavy pot. Add onion and carrots and sauté for 3 to 4 minutes. Add cabbage and sauté for 2 minutes more. Add water, cover, bring to a boil, and simmer for 15 minutes. Stir in miso creamed with a little of the broth, then remove from heat. Serve topped with a sprinkling of parsley. Delicious hot or cold. Chilled, pureed leftovers are especially tasty.

For variety, add 1 cup diced potatoes together with the carrots.

Velvet Zucchini Miso Soup
SERVES 4

A wonderful way to make use of the summer garden's overflowing zucchini crop and to cool and refresh the body on hot summer afternoons or evenings. Leftovers may be frozen indefinitely.

1 tablespoon oil
½ onion, sliced
1¼ cups chopped celery (2 stalks)
2½ cups diced zucchini
3 cups water or stock
3½ tablespoons red, barley, or Hatcho miso
2 tablespoons minced parsley

Heat the oil in a wok or heavy pot. Add onion and sauté for 2 to 3 minutes. Add celery and zucchini and sauté for another 2 to 3 minutes. Add the water or stock, cover, and simmer for 5 minutes, then remove from heat. Stir in miso creamed with a little of the cooking broth. Allow to cool briefly, then puree in a blender until smooth. Serve chilled, topped with a sprinkling of the parsley. In colder months, this recipe is also nice served unpureed and piping hot.

Onion Soup with Ketchup & Miso

SERVES 2 OR 3

1 tablespoon butter
1 onion, thinly sliced
1¼ cups water or stock
4 teaspoons red, barley, or Hatcho miso
3 tablespoons ketchup or tomato paste
Dash of pepper
2 tablespoons Parmesan cheese
1 tablespoon minced parsley

Melt the butter in a skillet. Add onion and sauté for 5 minutes, then add water and bring to a boil. Stir in miso creamed with ketchup, add pepper and cheese, and return just to the boil. Serve topped with a sprinkling of parsley.

Quick Cream of Onion Soup with Miso

SERVES 3

2 tablespoons oil
3 onions, thinly sliced
2½ cups water or stock
3 tablespoons whole-wheat flour
3 tablespoons red, barley, or Hatcho miso
Dash of pepper
1 tablespoon minced parsley

Heat a pressure cooker and coat with the oil. Add onions and sauté for 3 minutes. Add 2 cups water, cover, and bring to full pressure (15 pounds). Reduce heat and cook for 5 minutes, then allow pressure to come down naturally.

Meanwhile, heat a skillet and coat with remaining 1 tablespoon oil. Add flour and sauté for 2 minutes, or until fragrant. Slowly add ½ cup water, stirring constantly, to make a thick sauce. Add miso and pepper, mixing until smooth. Open pressure cooker, mix sauce into onions, and bring just to a boil. Serve hot or, for a richer flavor, allow to stand overnight and serve reheated or cold, garnished with parsley.

Azuki-Vegetable Soup with Miso

SERVES 4 TO 6

1 cup azuki beans, rinsed and drained
3 cups water
1 tablespoon oil
1 onion, thinly sliced
1 small carrot, cut into matchsticks or grated
4 tablespoons red, barley, or Hatcho miso
2 tablespoons honey
2 tablespoons sesame butter
¼ teaspoon cinnamon or nutmeg

Combine beans and water in a pressure cooker. Bring to full pressure (15 pounds), reduce heat to low and cook for 40 minutes. Remove from heat and allow to stand for 15 minutes while pressure comes down naturally.

Heat a skillet and coat with the oil. Add onions and carrot, and sauté for 5 minutes; remove from heat. Add miso, honey, sesame butter, cinnamon, and several tablespoons hot cooking liquid from the beans. Mix thoroughly, then stir miso-vegetable mixture into the beans in the cooker. For best flavor, allow to cool, then refrigerate for at least 8, preferably 24, hours. Serve cold or reheated.

Thick Lentil or Split Pea Soup with Miso

SERVES 4 OR 5

1 cup lentils or split peas, rinsed and drained
5 to 5½ cups water or stock
2 tablespoons oil
½ cup thinly sliced onions
½ cup thinly sliced carrots or diced yams
¾ cup chopped celery (with leaves)
1 clove of garlic, crushed
3½ tablespoons red, barley, or Hatcho miso, creamed with ¼ cup water
2 tablespoons butter
½ teaspoon oregano, thyme, or rosemary
Dash of black or red pepper; or ½ teaspoon nutmeg
2 to 4 tablespoons ground roasted sesame seeds (p. 54) (optional)
1 tablespoon minced parsley

Combine lentils and water in a large pot and soak overnight. Bring to a boil and simmer for about 2 hours, stirring occasionally, until quite thick. (Or reduce water to 2½ cups and pressure cook at 15 pounds for 20 minutes.)

Meanwhile, heat a skillet and coat with the oil. Add onions, carrots, celery and garlic, and sauté for about 5 minutes. Add ¼ cup water, cover, and simmer for 10 to 15 minutes, or until water has been absorbed or evaporated.

When soup has finished cooking, stir in miso, butter, oregano, and sautéed vegetables. Cover and allow to stand for at least 10 minutes; serve topped with a sprinkling of sesame and parsley. (For a richer flavor, refrigerate overnight and serve as is or reheated.)

Creamy Cauliflower & Tofu Soup with Miso

SERVES 4

1 tablespoon oil
1 onion, thinly sliced
1½ to 2 cups cauliflowerets, parboiled (p. 54)
2 tablespoons butter
2 tablespoons whole-wheat flour
1 cup milk
½ cup water
2 ounces cheese, grated or finely diced
12 ounces regular or 5 ounces deep-fried tofu, cut into small rectangles
2 tablespoons light-yellow or red miso
Dash of pepper

Heat a casserole and coat with the oil. Add onion and sauté for 3 minutes, or until lightly browned. Add cauliflower and sauté for 1 minute more, then turn off heat.

Using the butter, flour, and milk, prepare a white sauce (p. 114). Add the sauce and water to the casserole, cover, and simmer over low heat for 5 minutes. Add cheese and tofu, increase heat to medium, and cook for 3 minutes. Stir in the miso thinned in a little of the cooking broth, season with pepper, and return just to the boil. Serve hot or, for a richer, sweeter flavor, allow to cool before serving.

Miso Stew

SERVES 4 TO 5

This hearty dish resembles a very thick miso soup prepared with sautéed vegetables.

1½ tablespoons sesame oil
3 onions, cut into thin wedges
½ carrot, cut into half moons
2 potatoes or 4 taro cut into irregular chunks (1½ cups)
1½ cups sliced (Chinese) cabbage or 1 cup thin rounds of
  daikon
3 cups water or stock
5½ tablespoons red, barley, or Hatcho miso
2 tablespoons minced parsley (optional)

Heat a heavy pot or skillet and coat with the oil. Add the four vegetables consecutively, sautéing each for about 1 minute. Add the water and bring to a boil. Reduce heat to low, cover, and simmer for 15 minutes. Stir in miso creamed in a little of the hot broth and return just to the boil. For best flavor, allow to cool for 6 to 8 hours. Serve as is or reheated, garnished with the parsley.

For added body and protein, substitute for the potatoes 12 to 18 ounces regular or 5 to 7 ounces deep-fried tofu. Use other seasonal vegetables.

Open-hearth fireplace

Miso in Sauces

Whether Western-style or Oriental, Near Eastern or Latin American, any sauce is enhanced by the presence of miso. Creamy Tofu Dressings also work well, especially with grains and vegetables.

Miso & Nutritional Yeast Gravy   FOR 2 to 3 SERVINGS

¼ cup butter or margarine
¼ cup nutritional yeast (we prefer the good-tasting Red Star brand)
¼ cup whole-wheat flour
2 tablespoons red miso, dissolved in 1½ to 1¾ cups hot water

Melt the butter in a skillet. Add nutritional yeast and mix well for 30 seconds. Add flour and sauté for 1 minute. Add the hot miso-water mixture a little at a time, stirring constantly to create a thick, creamy consistency. When all is added, bring just to the boil, then remove from heat. Delicious served over cooked grains (brown rice, noodles, millet), baked potatoes, cooked vegetables (broccoli, cauliflower, etc.), or fried tempeh or tofu.

Miso Onion Sauce   SERVES 4

3 tablespoons (sesame) oil
4 onions, thinly sliced
2½ to 3 tablespoons red, barley, or Hatcho miso, thinned in 2/3 cup water

Heat the oil in a large, heavy skillet. Add onions and sauté for 5 minutes. Add thinned miso, cover pan, and simmer for 30 minutes, or until most of the liquid has been absorbed or evaporated. For best flavor, allow to stand for 6 to 8 hours. Serve as is or reheated. Delicious over grain dishes, toast, steamed vegetables, or tofu. Or serve as a side dish.

This sauce may also be prepared by starting with Thick French Onion Soup (p. 107); add the miso dissolved in 3 tablespoons (rather than 2 cups) warm water.

VARIATION

*Seasoned Onion Sauce with Nut Butters: Thin your favorite nut butter with a small amount of water or stock and, if desired, some lemon or orange juice, and add to 2 parts Onion Sauce. Season with herbs, 7-spice red pepper, shoyu, or miso.

Garnish with thinly sliced green onions or parsley. For variety, add large chunks of nuts, diced cheese, or sprouts.

Miso-Gingerroot Ankaké Sauce   MAKES 1 CUP

2/3 cup dashi (p. 56), stock, or water
4 to 4½ tablespoons red, barley, or Hatcho miso
1 tablespoon honey or 2 tablespoons (natural) sugar
2 teaspoons arrowroot, cornstarch, or kuzu (kudzu powder) dissolved in 2 tablespoons water
2 teaspoons freshly grated gingerroot

Combine dashi, miso, and honey in a small saucepan. Bring to a boil, then stir in dissolved arrowroot and gingerroot. Cook for about 1 minute or until thick.

Miso-Lemon Ankaké Sauce   MAKES 1¼ CUPS

1 cup dashi (p. 56), stock, or water
2½ tablespoons red, barley, or Hatcho miso
1½ teaspoons honey or 1 tablespoon (natural) sugar
2 teaspoons cornstarch, arrow root, or kuzu (kudzu powder), dissolved in 1½ tablespoons water
½ teaspoon grated lemon rind

Combine dashi, miso, and honey in a small saucepan, mixing well. Bring to a boil, stir in dissolved cornstarch and lemon rind, and cook for about 1 minute more until thick. Serve over cooked vegetables, tofu, or broiled mochi.

Miso-Mushroom Sauce   FOR 3 SERVINGS

1½ tablespoons butter
½ teaspoon minced or crushed garlic
1 tablespoon minced onion
½ teaspoon grated gingerroot
5 mushrooms, thinly sliced
1/3 cup ketchup
1 tablespoon red, barley, or Hatcho miso
Dash of pepper

Melt the butter in a skillet. Add garlic, onion and gingerroot, and sauté for 1 minute. Add mushrooms and sauté for 2 minutes. Stir in ketchup and miso, season with pepper, and sauté for 1 minute more. Delicious with most grain dishes, especially tacos or tortillas, and with deep-fried or barbecued foods.

Miso White Sauce

MAKES 1 CUP

Also known as Cream- or Béchamel Sauce, this traditional Western favorite acquires a distinctive flavor and creaminess when seasoned with miso. Season lightly for use with vegetables and more prominently for use with tofu dishes.

2 tablespoons butter or oil
2 tablespoons (whole-wheat) flour
1 cup milk (soy or dairy) or stock
3 to 4 teaspoons red, barley, or Hatcho miso; or 2 to 2½ tablespoons sweet white or mellow white miso
Dash of pepper, paprika, or cayenne
1 tablespoon minced parsley (optional)

Melt the butter (or heat oil) in a skillet. Add flour and, stirring constantly, cook over low heat for 1 to 2 minutes, or until four is well blended and its raw taste has vanished. Add ½ cup milk (or stock) a little at a time, continuing to stir, then mix in the miso and slowly add the remainder of the milk. Increase heat to medium and cook, whisking or stirring, for 3 to 4 minutes more, or until sauce develops a smooth, thickened consistency. Stir in pepper (and parsley) and remove from heat.

VARIATIONS

***Cheese-Miso White Sauce:** Sauté 1 clove of crushed garlic in butter for 30 seconds before adding flour. Add ½ teaspoon dry mustard and ½ cup grated cheese several minutes before removing from heat.
***Lemon-Miso White Sauce:** Add 2 teaspoons lemon juice (and ¼ teaspoon grated lemon rind) about 1 minute before removing from heat.
***Herb Sauce:** Add or substitute for the parsley any of the following, preferably fresh: thyme, basil, oregano, or beefsteak leaves.
***Mushroom-Miso White Sauce:** Just after adding the last of the milk, add ¼ diced onion and 6 thinly-sliced mushrooms. Stirring constantly, simmer over low heat for 4 to 5 minutes. Then add 1 teaspoon lemon juice, the pepper, and 1 tablespoon white wine or sake.
***Sesame-Miso White Sauce:** Add 1 tablespoon sesame butter or *tahini* several minutes before removing from heat. Delicious over steamed cauliflower, mushrooms, chard, Brussels sprouts, or celery. Serve topped with a sprinkling of parsley.
***Tofu-Miso White Sauce:** Use 4 teaspoons red miso. Add 12 ounces regular tofu (mashed) or 7½ ounces deep-fried tofu (diced) about 2 minutes before removing from heat.
***Brown Sauce:** Prepare as for a white sauce except cook the flour until it is lightly browned and fragrant.

Miso-Spaghetti Sauce

SERVES 3 OR 4

2 tablespoons oil
2 small onions, thinly sliced
1 clove of garlic, crushed
10 mushrooms, thinly sliced
5 tomatoes, diced,
3 green peppers, diced
½ carrot, grated or thinly sliced
2 cups water or stock
2 bay leaves
4½ tablespoons red, barley, or Hatcho miso
1 tablespoon butter
Dash of pepper
Dash of oregano and/or basil
1/3 cup grated or Parmesan cheese

Heat a heavy pot and coat with the oil. Add onions and garlic and sauté for about 3 minutes. Add the next four ingredients and sauté for 4 minutes more. Add water, drop in bay leaves, and bring to a boil. Simmer uncovered for 10 minutes. Mix in miso and next three ingredients; simmer, stirring every 5 minutes, for 1 hour. For best flavor, allow to stand for 6 to 8 hours. Remove bay leaves and serve hot or cold over buckwheat noodles or spaghetti. Top with cheese.

VARIATIONS

***With Soybeans:** Add together with the miso in the basic recipe: 1 cup stock (soybean cooking liquid or mushroom soaking water), 1½ tablespoons additional red miso, and 2¼ cups cooked soybeans (p. 129). Proceed as above; serve topped with an additional 3 tablespoons grated or Parmesan cheese. Also delicious served chilled as a dish in its own right.
***With Tofu:** Add 12 to 24 ounces diced regular tofu (or 5 to 10 ounces deep-fried tofu) together with the miso; simmer covered. Mix in ½ cup additional grated cheese just before removing from heat.

Miso Taco or Pizza Sauce

MAKES 1¼ CUPS

2/3 cup ketchup
1¼ cup grated cheese
2 tablespoons red, barley, or Hatcho miso
2 tablespoon minced onion, leek, or scallion
1 teaspoon grated gingerroot (optional)
1 teaspoon sake or white wine
Dash of tabasco sauce
Dash of pepper
1 tablespoon water

Combine all ingredients, mixing well. For best flavor, allow to stand for at least several hours before serving. Spread 3 to 4 teaspoons on each of 12 crisp buttered tortillas before topping with shredded lettuce, diced tomatoes, grated cheese, and your choice of other ingredients. Or use with pizza.

Quick Spaghetti Sauce with Miso & Tofu

SERVES 3 OR 4

1½ tablespoons oil
1 clove of garlic, crushed or minced
2 onions, diced
2 leaves of (Chinese) cabbage, thinly sliced
1 tomato, diced
1 cup ketchup
¼ cup water
2 green beefsteak leaves, minced, or 1 teaspoon grated gingerroot
10 ounces deep-fried or regular tofu, cubed
½ cup chives or *nira*
1/3 cup grated cheese
3 tablespoons butter
Dash of pepper
2 tablespoons red, barley, or Hatcho miso
½ cup Parmesan cheese
¼ cup minced parsley

Heat oil in a pot. Add the next four ingredients and sauté for 5 to 7 minutes, or until soft. Add ketchup, water, and beefsteak leaves, and simmer for 5 minutes. Add tofu, chives, and grated cheese, and simmer for 4 minutes more. Stir in the butter, pepper and the miso creamed in a little of the hot sauce. Stirring constantly, simmer for 1 more minute. For best flavor, remove from heat and allow to stand for 6 to 8 hours. Serve reheated or as is, topped with the cheese and parsley.

Pineapple Sweet & Sour Sauce with Miso

MAKES 1½ CUPS

1¼ cup pineapple chunks, drained
2½ teaspoons honey
3 tablespoons vinegar
½ cup water
3 tablespoons red, barley, or Hatcho miso
2 tablespoons ketchup
½ teaspoon grated gingerroot or 1 teaspoon powdered ginger
1 tablespoon cornstarch

Combine all ingredients in a saucepan, mixing well. Bring to a boil and cook, stirring constantly, for about 1 minute, or until thick. Delicious served over vegetables sautéed with a little garlic, or over brown rice, buckwheat noodles, or deep-fried tofu.

Orange-Sesame Miso Sauce

MAKES ½ CUP

3 tablespoons red, barley, or Hatcho Miso
1½ tablespoons sesame butter
1½ to 2 teaspoons honey
1 tablespoon sake or white wine
2 tablespoons water or dashi (p. 56)
¼ to ½ teaspoon grated orange rind
1 egg yolk (optional)

Combine all ingredients in a small saucepan or skillet. Simmer for 2 to 3 minutes over low heat, stirring constantly with a wooden spoon or spatula, until mixture has a slightly firmer consistency than that of regular miso. Serve hot or cold. Delicious as a topping for Furofuki Daikon (p. 140), fried eggplant slices, or crisp apple wedges; a dipping sauce for Miso Oden (p. 141); or slightly thinned as a sauce for potatoes, (kabocha) pumpkin, okra, or squash.

Garbanzo-Tahini Sauce with Miso (*Hummus bi Tahina*)

MAKES 4 CUPS

1 cup garbanzo beans, soaked for 3 hours in 3½ cups water
½ cup tahini
1 to 2 cloves of garlic, minced or crushed
2½ tablespoons lemon juice
2 tablespoons red or barley (or ¼ cup mellow white) miso
Dash of pepper and/or tabasco sauce
3 tablespoons minced parsley and/or a dash of paprika

Combine beans and soaking water in a pressure cooker, bring to full pressure (15 pounds), and simmer for 30 minutes. Remove from heat and allow to stand for 10 minutes while pressure returns to normal. Combine hot beans and remaining cooking liquid in a blender with the next five ingredients; purée until smooth. Serve hot or cold, topped with a sprinkling of parsley and/or paprika. Excellent served over rice, millet, buckwheat groats, or steamed greens. Also makes a delicious dip.

Sweet White Miso Sauce

MAKES 1 CUP

½ cup sweet white miso
½ cup water, stock, or dashi (p. 56)
1 tablespoon honey
¾ teaspoon sesame oil
¾ teaspoon tapioca, arrowroot, or cornstarch, dissolved in 1 tablespoon water
1 teaspoon sake or white wine (optional)

Combine all ingredients in a heavy saucepan, bring to a boil, and simmer, stirring constantly, for 3 minutes, or until slightly thick. Delicious served over Grilled Tofu & Vegetables (p. 146) or Brussels sprouts.

Miso-Cream Cheese Sauce   MAKES ½ CUP

4 ounces cream cheese
2 teaspoons red or barley (or 4 teaspoons mellow white)
   miso
1 tablespoon Worcestershire sauce
3 tablespoons water or milk

Combine all ingredients and beat or blend together until smooth. Delicious over cooked vegetables such as broccoli, squash, or cauliflower.

Miso Gravy   MAKES 1½ CUPS

2 tablespoons butter
1 small onion, minced
3 tablespoons (whole-wheat or barley) flour
1½ tablespoons red, barley, or Hatcho miso
1 cup water
Dash of pepper

Melt 1 tablespoon butter in a skillet. Add onion and sauté for 5 minutes, or until soft and lightly browned. Add remaining 1 tablespoon butter; when melted, add flour and sauté for 2 to 3 minutes. Add miso and sauté for 30 seconds more. Now add the water a little at a time, stirring constantly; bring to a boil, season with pepper, and simmer for 1 minute. Delicious over steamed cauliflower or broccoli.

    For a richer flavor use 2½ tablespoons miso. Serve as a topping for brown rice or deep-fried tofu.

Spicy Indoneisan Peanut Sauce with Miso (Gado-gado Sauce)   MAKES 2 CUPS

3 tablespoons oil
1 cup roasted (unsalted) peanuts
1 clove of garlic, crushed or minced
¼ to ½ teaspoon (7-spice) red pepper or tabasco sauce
1½ teaspoons honey
2½ tablespoons red, barley, or Hatcho miso
1½ cups stock, water, or (coconut) milk
¼ onion, minced
1 teaspoon minced parsley

Heat a wok or skillet and coat with 2 tablespoons oil. Add peanuts and sauté for 3 to 5 minutes, or until browned and fragrant. Mix in the next five ingredients and bring to a boil, then remove from heat and allow to cool briefly. Meanwhile, heat the remaining 1 tablespoon oil in a skillet. Add onion and sauté for 5 minutes, or until well browned. Transfer cooled peanut sauce to a blender and purée until smooth. Pour into a serving container, mix in sautéed onion, and top with a sprinkling of parsley. Serve hot or chilled over cooked rice or noodles, or lightly steamed vegetables (especially cabbage, cauliflower, or broccoli).

    If Indonesian spices (kenchur, asam, or danjelpur) are available, add together with the red pepper.

Korean-style Miso Dipping Sauce   MAKES ¼ CUP

1½ tablespoons red, barley, or Hatcho miso
½ teaspoon sesame oil
¼ teaspoon crushed or minced garlic
1 tablespoon water
Dash of (7-spice) red pepper or tabasco sauce

Combine all ingredients, mixing well. Serve with broiled or deep-fried foods. Excellent with vegetarian Shish Kebab (p. 144).

Tangy Miso Chirizu Dipping Sauce   MAKES 1/3 CUP

2 tablespoons red, barley, or Hatcho miso
4 teaspoons lemon juice
2½ tablespoons grated daikon
2½ tablespoons thin rounds of leek or scallion
Dash of 7-spice red pepper or tabasco sauce

Combine all ingredients, mixing well. Serve with regular or deep-fried tofu, all nabé preparations, tempura, or croquettes.

Apple & Onion Curry Sauce with Deep-fried Tofu and Miso   SERVES 3 OR 4

7½ ounces deep fried tofu cutlets, burgers, or pouches, diced; or 18 ounces regular tofu
1 apple, diced
2 potatoes, diced (1¾ cups)
1 cup water or stock
3 tablespoons butter
1 clove of garlic, crushed
1 teaspoon grated or 1½ teaspoons powdered gingerroot
1½ onions, minced
5 to 6 mushrooms, thinly sliced
1½ to 2 teaspoons curry powder
2 tablespoons whole-wheat flour
3 to 3½ tablespoons red, barley, or Hatcho miso
1 tablespoon honey
2 tablespoons ketchup
Sambals: Sliced bananas, grated coconut, raisins, diced apples, peanuts or almonds, chopped hard-boiled eggs, and chutney

Combine the first four ingredients in a heavy pot or casserole and bring to a boil. Cover and simmer over low heat. Meanwhile melt the butter in a skillet. Add garlic and gingerroot, and sauté for 30 seconds. Add onions and mushrooms, and sauté for 5 to 6 minutes more. Mix in curry powder and flour, and cook, stirring constantly, for 1 minute. Cream miso with about 1/3 cup broth removed from the pot, then stir into the curried mixture together with the honey and ketchup to form a smooth, thick sauce. Now mix sauce into contents of pot, cover, and simmer for 20 to 30 minutes, stirring occasionally. Serve over brown rice or buckwheat noodles, topped with the sambals.

    For a more elaborate sauce, add diced lotus root, cooked lentils, sweet potatoes, *kabocha*, or squash. To serve as an entrèe without grains, reduce the amounts of miso and curry powder by about one-fifth. Try substituting 1½ cups cooked soybeans for the tofu.

Tangy Miso, Ketchup & Lemon Sauce

MAKES ¾ CUP

½ cup ketchup
2 tablespoons red, barley, or Hatcho miso
1½ tablespoons lemon juice
1 tablespoon minced onion
1 tablespoon minced parsley
Dash of pepper

Combine all ingredients, mixing well. Serve with deep-fried, broiled, or barbecued foods. Also good with shrimp cocktail or seafoods.
　　For variety add any of the following: ¼ teaspoon hot mustard, 1 teaspoon horseradish, ½ teaspoon crushed anise or ground roasted sesame seeds, or 1 tablespoon minced parsley.

Sesame-Miso Sauce

MAKES 2/3 CUP

　　This recipe is good for use with vegetables such as cauliflower, spinach or turnips; use the hot cooking water as the basis of the sauce.

2 tablespoons red, barley, or Hatcho miso
1 tablespoon sesame butter
½ cup hot vegetable cooking liquid, stock, or dashi (p. 56)
½ teaspoon grated lemon or *yuzu* rind

Combine the first three ingredients, mixing until smooth. Pour over cooked vegetables and top with a sprinkling of the lemon rind.

Miso-Sesame Lyonnaise Sauce

MAKES 1½ CUPS

2 tablespoons sesame oil
2 onions, minced
2 tablespoons whole-wheat flour
1 cup stock, water, or dashi (p. 56).
¼ cup white wine or sake
3 tablespoons red, barley, or Hatcho miso
Dash of pepper
1 tablespoon minced parsley

Heat a skillet and coat with the oil. Add onions and sauté for 5 minutes, or until lightly browned. Stir in flour and sauté for 2 minutes more. Add stock a little at a time, stirring until smooth. Stir in wine and cook, stirring constantly, for 3 minutes. Add miso creamed in a little of the hot sauce, season with pepper, and return just to the boil. Serve topped with a sprinkling of parsley.

Sesame, Onion & Miso Sauce

MAKES 2/3 CUP

2 to 3 teaspoons sesame oil
1 onion, minced
2 tablespoons sesame (or peanut) butter
2 tablespoons red, barley, or Hatcho miso, thinned in 2½ tablespoons water
1 teaspoon white wine, sake, or *mirin* (optional)

Heat a skillet or wok and coat with the oil. Add onion and sauté for 4 to 5 minutes. Combine sesame butter and thinned miso, mix briefly, and stir into onion. Add wine (if used), mix well, and remove from heat. Serve as a topping for Brown Rice (p. 57), Rice Patties (p. 121), or steamed vegetables.

Creamy Sesame-Miso Sauce

MAKES ½ CUP

3 tablespoons sweet white or 2 tablespoons mellow white miso
1½ tablespoons sesame butter or *tahini*
3 tablespoons milk (soy or dairy)
1½ tablespoons vinegar

Combine all ingredients, mixing well. Serve with cooked vegetables (especially good with spinach, cauliflower, chard, or broccoli).

Peanut Butter-Miso Sauce

MAKES ½ CUP

1 to 1½ tablespoons red, barley, or Hatcho Miso
2 tablespoons peanut butter
2 to 3 tablespoons hot vegetable cooking liquid, stock, or dashi (p. 56)
1 teaspoon grated lemon or *yuzu* peel, or ½ teaspoon lemon juice

Prepare and serve as for Sesame-Miso Sauce, above. If desired, reduce the amount of water and use as a cracker spread or filling for celery stalks.

Tomato & Cheese Sauce with Miso

MAKES 1¼ CUPS

2 tablespoons butter
1¼ cups chopped fresh tomatoes
½ onion, minced
1½ tablespoons red, barley, or Hatcho miso
¾ cup grated cheese
¼ teaspoon oregano or basil
¼ teaspoon paprika
Dash of pepper

Melt the butter in a skillet. Add tomatoes and onion and sauté for 2 minutes, then cover and simmer for 3 minutes. Uncover and continue to simmer, stirring occasionally, for 15 minutes more, or until sauce is well thickened. Add miso creamed in a little of the hot sauce, then stir in remaining ingredients and remove from heat.

Miso-Gingerroot Sauce

MAKES 2 CUPS

5 tablespoons red, barley, Hatcho miso
3 to 4 teaspoons honey
1 cup dashi (p. 56), stock, or water
2 teaspoons arrowroot, cornstarch or *kuzu* (kudzu powder),
   dissolved in ¼ cup water
1 tablespoon grated gingerroot
Dash of (7-spice) red pepper

Combine the first three ingredients in a small saucepan and bring to a boil. Stir in dissolved arrowroot and grated gingerroot and cook for about 1 minute, or until thickened. Season with red pepper. Delicious with steamed or sautéed vegetables (cauliflower, cabbage, chard, broccoli, squash), deep-fried foods, or tofu.

Gingerroot-Miso Barbecue Sauce

MAKES ⅓ CUP

1½ teaspoons oil
½ teaspoon minced gingerroot
3½ tablespoons red, barley, or Hatcho miso
¼ cup water, stock, or dashi (p. 56)
2½ teaspoons honey
1½ tablespoons *mirin*, dry sherry, or white wine
Dash of 7-spice red or *sansho* pepper (optional)

Heat a wok or skillet and coat with the oil. Add gingerroot and sauté for 1 minute, or until just fragrant. Add the next four ingredients and cook, stirring constantly, for 3 minutes, or until mixture has the consistency of a thick sauce. Stir in the pepper, if used, and remove from heat. Allow to cool before serving with deep-fried tofu, barbecued foods, tempura, or fresh vegetable slices.

Korean-style Miso Barbecue Sauce

MAKES ¼ CUP

3 tablespoons red, barley, or Hatcho miso
1 tablespoon honey
1 clove of garlic, crushed
1 tablespoon diced leeks or onions
1 tablespoon ground roasted sesame seeds (p. 54), or 2 teaspoons sesame butter or *tahini*
2 teaspoons sesame oil
¼ teaspoon (7-spice) red pepper or tabasco sauce
Dash of white pepper

Combine all ingredients, mixing well. Delicious with (grilled) deep-fried tofu.

Miso Shish Kebab (or Barbecue) Sauce

MAKES ¼ CUP

In Japan, a close relative of this preparation is used with the popular chicken shish kebab called *yakitori*.

2 tablespoons red, barley, or Hatcho miso
1 teaspoon oil
½ teaspoon honey
¼ teaspoon grated gingerroot
¼ to ½ clove garlic, crushed
2 tablespoons water

Combine all ingredients, mixing well. Use as a marinade and/or basting sauce with your favorite preparations, or with Shish Kebab (p. 144).

Miso-Ketchup Barbecue Sauce

MAKES ⅓ CUP

2 tablespoons red, barley, or Hatcho miso
2 tablespoons ketchup
¼ small onion, diced
1 tablespoon melted butter
1 tablespoon sake or white wine
½ clove of garlic, crushed
¾ teaspoon honey
Dash of (7-spice) red pepper or tabasco sauce

Combine all ingredients in a skillet, mixing well. Cook over medium heat for about 1 minute. Serve hot or cold. Excellent over croquettes or deep-fried tofu.

Miso Teriyaki Sauce

MAKES 1 CUP

Generally used in Japan to baste broiled fish, this savory sauce is now used by many Westerners with shish kebab and other barbecued preparations. Also good as a dip for fresh vegetables or a topping for deep-fried tofu.

6 tablespoons red, barley, or Hatcho miso
3 tablespoons sake or white wine
1 tablespoon sesame or vegetable oil
1 teaspoon grated gingerroot or 1½ teaspoons powdered ginger
2 cloves of garlic, crushed
3 tablespoons brown sugar or 1½ tablespoons honey
¼ teaspoon dry mustard (optional)

Combine all ingredients, mixing well. Marinate foods (green peppers, onions or leeks, deep-fried tofu, tomatoes, mushrooms, etc.) for at least 1 hour before skewering and broiling. Use remaining sauce to baste.

Miso with Grains, Beans & Tofu

Miso evokes and accentuates the simple, satisfying flavors of grains and beans (pulses), mankind's most basic foods. Inexpensive and easy to prepare, these dishes can be enjoyed day after day and serve as the center of a healthful diet. Using miso and soybean products together with grains can increase the total protein content of each dish by more than 30 percent (p. 23). See also Miso in Baked Dishes (p. 133) and Miso in Sandwiches (p. 81).

MISO WITH BROWN RICE

For most of recorded history, unpolished rice has served as the staff of life for more than one-half of the world's population. Fortunately, its health-giving virtues are now gaining greater and greater recognition in the West.

Brown Rice or Rice Porridge with Miso Toppings

MAKES 1 SERVING

In Japan, this is the most popular way of serving rice seasoned with miso. Quick and easy to prepare, the many variations of this tasty dish can be enjoyed daily throughout the four seasons.

1 to 1½ cups cooked Brown Rice or Rice Porridge (p. 57; unseasoned)
1 to 2 teaspoons of any one of the following:
　Red, barley, or Hatcho miso
　Finger Lickin' or akadashi miso
　Sweet Simmered Miso (p. 60)
　Miso Sauté (p. 65)
　Mixed Miso (p. 69)
　Broiled Miso (p. 71)
　Yubeshi Miso (p. 73)
　Soybean & Miso Garnish (p. 130)
　Miso pickles, minced or thinly sliced (p. 156)

Place rice in a bowl and top with a bead or dab of the miso. Mix well or, if using chopsticks, take a small piece of miso together with each biteful of rice. Chew well for best flavor and nutrition.

Brown Rice Topped with Miso Sauces

Serve cooked hot or cold brown rice topped with any of the miso sauces and garnishes listed on page 124 for use with noodles.

Rice Jambalaya with Miso

SERVES 3 OR 4

3 tablespoons butter
3 ounces mushrooms, thinly sliced
5 ounces deep-fried tofu, cubed; or substitute an equal weight of sliced mushrooms
½ onion, thinly sliced
2 green peppers, thinly sliced
¼ cup diced celery
1 tomato, diced
1½ tablespoons red, barley, or Hatcho miso
Dash of (7-spice) red pepper or tabasco sauce
¼ teaspoon paprika
½ cup brown rice, cooked (p. 57); or use 1¼ cups leftover rice
2 tablespoons minced parsley

Preheat oven to 300°. Melt 1½ tablespoons butter in a skillet. Add mushrooms and deep-fried tofu, and sauté for 2 minutes. Add the next four ingredients and sauté for 2 minutes more. Mix in miso, red pepper, and paprika, then remove from heat. Combine with cooked rice, 1 tablespoon parsley, and the remaining 1½ tablespoons butter. Mix well and spoon into an oiled casserole or loaf pan. Cover and bake for 45 to 60 minutes. Serve hot or cold, topped with the remaining 1 tablespoon parsley.

119

Deep-fried Miso-Rice Balls with Sweet & Sour Sauce

SERVES 3 OR 4

1 cup brown rice, cooked (p. 57) and cooled to body or
    room temperature
¾ cup chopped leeks or scallions
2 tablespoons red, barley, or Hatcho miso
¼ cup sesame butter or *tahini*
2 teaspoons grated gingerroot
1 clove of garlic, crushed
½ cup cornstarch, arrowroot, or *kuzu*
Oil for deep-frying
1½ cups Pineapple Sweet & Sour Sauce (p. 115)

Combine the first six ingredients, mixing well. Shape into
1½-inch-diameter balls (20 to 25) and roll in cornstarch. Heat
the oil to 350° in a wok, skillet, or deep-fryer. Drop in balls (8
to 10 at a time) and deep-fry until crisp and golden brown (p.
147). Drain well, then top with the hot sauce. Serve immediately or, for a richer, sweeter flavor, allow to stand for 6
to 8 hours.

Stir-fried Rice with Almonds and Miso

SERVES 4

2 tablespoons oil
1 clove of garlic, minced
½ cup almonds, slivered
½ leek, chopped fine
2 eggs, lightly beaten
1 cup brown rice, cooked (p. 57) and cooled
2 tablespoons red, barley or Hatcho miso, creamed with 1
    tablespoon water
Dash of pepper (optional)

Heat 1 tablespoon oil in a wok or large skillet. Add garlic and
almonds, and sauté for 2 to 3 minutes until browned. Add
leeks, sauté for 1 minute more, then remove from heat and
transfer to an empty bowl. Re-heat wok and coat with remaining 1 tablespoon oil. Add eggs and scramble for 1 minute
until just firm. Mix in rice and sauté for 1 minute, then add
almond-leek mixture and sauté for 2 minutes more, or until
crumbly. Mix in miso and pepper and cook for 2 minutes.
Delicious hot or cold.

Brown Rice Porridge with Miso and Vegetables

SERVES 3 OR 4

½ cup brown rice
4½ cups water
1 tablespoon (sesame) oil
½ onion, thinly sliced
½ small carrot, slivered or diced
½ cup diced or slivered celery or *daikon*
1 tablespoon red or barley miso, dissolved in ¼ cup water
½ cup fresh or reconstituted *wakame* (p. 54), thinly sliced
    (optional)
Miso Pickles (p. 156) or Sesame Salt (p. 58)
Crumbled toasted *nori* (optional)

Combine rice and water in a heavy pot, cover, and bring to a
boil. Reduce heat to very low, and simmer for 90 minutes
with lid set slightly ajar.
    Meanwhile, heat a skillet and coat with the oil. Add
onion and sauté for 2 minutes. Add carrot and celery, and
sauté for 5 minutes more. Add dissolved miso together with
wakame, if used. Bring just to a boil, turn off heat, and cover.
    When porridge is ready, stir in miso-vegetable mixture
and simmer for 5 minutes. Serve individual portions seasoned
with miso pickles or sesame salt and, if desired, the *nori*.

VARIATIONS

Pressure Cooked Porridge: Combine rice with 2½ cups
water in a pressure cooker and bring to full pressure (15
pounds). Reduce heat to very low and simmer for 45 minutes.
Turn off heat and allow to stand for 10 minutes while pressure returns to normal. Open cooker and stir in miso and
vegetables. Allow to stand for 5 to 10 minutes. Mix well
before serving.
Porridge with Miso and Soybeans: Combine rice with 2¾
cups water and ¼ cup dry soybeans, soaked for at least 3
hours in water to cover, then drained. Proceed as for Pressure
Cooked Porridge, above. After opening cooker, stir in 1½
tablespoons red miso, 1 tablespoon butter, and 1 tablespoon
minced parsley. Let stand for several minutes before serving.

Creamy Rice Porridge with White Miso and Broccoli

SERVES 4

2 tablespoons butter
1 onion, minced
1½ cups cooked Brown Rice (p. 57)
2 cups water
2 cups chopped broccoli (4½ ounces)
¼ cup sweet white or 2½ tablespoons mellow white miso,
    dissolved in 3 tablespoons water

Melt the butter in a heavy (earthenware) pot. Add onion and
sauté for 3 minutes. Add brown rice and water, and bring to a
boil. Add broccoli and return to the boil, then simmer, covered, for 15 minutes, stirring occasionally. Stir in creamed miso
and return just to the boil. Delicious hot or cold.

Sang Chu

SERVES 3 TO 5

One of Korea's most popular national dishes, Sang Chu is composed of rice and a spicy garnish wrapped in a crisp lettuce leaf; held in the fingers, it is eaten like a sandwich. In the following recipe, we substitute tofu (or scrambled eggs) for the usual hamburger or pork miso.

1 tablespoon sesame oil
1 clove of garlic, minced
12 ounces tofu, crumbled (p. 56); or 3 eggs, scrambled (without salt)
3 tablespoons red, barley, or Hatcho miso
1 teaspoon juice pressed from grated gingerroot
1/3 cup chopped leeks or scallions
¼ teaspoon red pepper powder
12 to 15 (butter) lettuce leaves
3 to 5 thin lemon wedges
6 to 10 thin tomato wedges, sprigs of parsley, spring chrysanthemum leaves, or cheese slices
2 to 2½ cups cooked Brown Rice (p. 57)

To prepare garnish, heat a skillet and coat with the oil. Add garlic and sauté for 30 seconds. Add tofu (or eggs) and sauté for 2 minutes. Add gingerroot juice and miso, sauté for 30 seconds more, and remove from heat. Stir in leeks and red pepper, mash all ingredients together thoroughly, and spoon into a small bowl.

Place bowl at the center of a large serving plate and surround with lettuce leaves. Top leaves with lemon and tomato wedges. Serve as a main course or hors d'œuvre accompanied by a serving bowl mounded with the rice.

Hold a lettuce leaf in the palm of one hand, spoon about 2 tablespoons of rice onto the leaf's center, and top the rice with a tablespoon of garnish. Squeeze a little lemon juice over the garnish and/or top with a tomato wedge. Fold ends and sides of leaf over filling.

Other popular Korean garnishes include Red-Pepper & Leek Miso (*doen jang;* p. 64) and Red-pepper Miso (*kochu jang;* p. 71). Try also Finger Lickin' Miso.

Egg & Miso Domburi

SERVES 4 TO 5

1 tablespoon oil
2/3 cup grated carrot
1 small onion, minced
1 cup green peas or minced green peppers
3 tablespoons red, barley, or Hatcho miso, thinned in ¼ cup water
2½ teaspoons honey or 1½ tablespoons natural sugar
1½ cups brown rice, cooked (p. 57).

Heat a skillet or wok and coat with the oil. Add carrot, onion

and green peas, and sauté for 4 to 5 minutes. Add thinned miso and honey, and cook, stirring constantly, until most of the liquid has been absorbed or evaporated. Add eggs and cook, stirring constantly, for about 2 minutes, or until firm. Divide hot rice among large individual bowls and spoon on the egg-and-miso topping. Serve hot or cold.

Fig. 20. Rice Patties

Rice Patties with Miso (*O-musubi* or *O-nigiri*)

MAKES 9

1½ tablespoons red, barley, or Hatcho miso
6 *umeboshi* salt plums, pitted and minced (optional)
3 tablespoons bonito flakes or grated cheese (optional)
2 cups brown rice, cooked (p. 57), then cooled for 5 minutes; or use 5 cups leftover rice
3 sheets of *nori,* toasted (p. 54) and each cut into 6 squares

Combine the first three ingredients, mixing well. (Or use only the miso.) Add to the rice, mixing lightly with a wooden spoon or spatula. Moisten hands in cold water (to prevent sticking) and shape rice into 9 triangular wedges or patties, pressing each firmly as shown in figure 20. Lay a *nori* square over both of the large surfaces of each pattie, then press edges and corners of *nori* against rice. (Keep your hands lightly moistened at all times.) Serve patties arranged on a large platter garnished with parsley sprigs or use in box lunches.

VARIATIONS

*Substitute for the red miso mixture ¼ cup Sesame Miso (p. 62), Sweet Simmered Miso (p. 60), or Finger Lickin' Miso (p. 41). If desired, mix with 10 to 15 minced green beefsteak leaves.
*Omit *nori* and roll patties in roasted (whole or ground) sesame seeds.
*Form the miso or miso mixture into 9 small balls and press one ball into the center of each rice pattie.
*Broiled Rice Patties (*Yaki-musubi*): Make rice patties using the crisp, golden-brown rice from the bottom of the cooking pot. Spread the surface of each pattie with a thin layer of miso (omitting *nori*), then broil quickly over an open flame until miso is fragrant.
*Crisp Rice Patties: Deep-fry or pan-fry patties in hot oil until crisp and golden brown (p. 147). Serve hot or cold.

Fried Miso-and-Rice Patties

SERVES 4

4 cups cooked (or leftover) Brown Rice (p. 57)
¼ cup diced leeks or scallions
¼ cup red, barley, or Hatcho miso
2 tablespoons oil

Combine the first three ingredients, mixing well, and shape into eight patties. Heat one-half the oil in a large skillet. Add four patties and fry on both sides until golden brown and fragrant. Repeat with remaining ingredients.

For variety, roll patties in 2 tablespoons roasted sesame seeds (or mix 2 tablespoons sesame butter into the miso) before frying.

Brown Rice with Mushrooms and Miso (Chameshi)

SERVES 3 OR 4

Also called *Takikomi-gohan*, this richly-flavored, popular dish is frequently prepared with chestnuts, chicken, crab, or shrimp used in place of the mushrooms and green peas.

1½ cups brown rice, rinsed and drained
12/3 cups water or green tea
5 (*shiitaké* or *matsutaké*) mushrooms, thinly sliced
½ cup fresh green peas
2 tablespoons red, barley, or Hatcho miso
2 teaspoons *mirin*, sake, or white wine
Minced parsley or trefoil (optional)

Combine all ingredients in a pressure cooker; mix briefly. Proceed as for Brown Rice (p. 57). Serve hot, topped if desired with a sprinkling of parsley.

For a simpler preparation, combine 1½ tablespoons red miso with the rice and water, and proceed as for Brown Rice.

VARIATION

*Brown Rice with Chestnuts and Miso (*Miso Kuri Kinton*): Substitute ½ cup whole or halved fresh or dry chestnut meats for the mushrooms and peas.

Thick Miso Shake with Brown Rice

SERVES 3

2 cups carrot-, tomato-, or mixed vegetable juice
¾ cup cooked Brown Rice (p. 57)
1 tablespoon red, barley, or Hatcho miso
Dash of pepper or oregano
¼ cup (toasted) wheat germ (optional)
1 teaspoon lemon juice (optional)

Combine all ingredients in a blender and purée for 2 to 3 minutes, or until creamy and thick. If desired, chill before serving.

Zosui or Ojiya (Rice Gruel)

SERVES 1 OR 2

Zosui, which means "a variety of things cooked together," is a popular way of using leftover rice (or rice porridge) and miso soup or clear soup served daily in most Japanese homes. In times of war or famine when rice was scarce, Zosui was daily fare; prepared with a large proportion of broth, it served to fill the belly and ward off hunger. Today, in times of abundance, thick Zosui served piping hot is still a wintertime favorite, prized for its ability to warm body and soul.

Known colloquially (and in Tokyo) as *Ojiya*, it originated at an early date in China, where more than 100 varieties were developed as part of that country's elaborate Congee or Rice Porridge Cuisine. During the 15th century, it became a popular dish throughout Japan, served on January 7, the last day of the New Year's season. Its preparation, using the "seven spring herbs," "newly drawn water," and miso, was transformed into a lovely ceremony linked to the zodiacal hours. One who added each freshly gathered wild herb at its propitious hour and served the dish "before the Chinese white eagle flies overhead" (a euphemism for diseases feared brought to Japan from the Chinese mainland), was said to be given by the gods an additional 8,000 years of happy life — and made instantaneously 70 years younger. To this day it is thought to be good insurance against colds and the flu, even in the midst of the influenza season. The proportions of rice and soup can be varied considerably depending on the amounts of leftovers.

1½ cups Miso Soup (p. 97)
1 cup cooked Brown Rice (p. 57) or Rice Porridge (p. 57)

Bring miso soup to a boil in a saucepan. Mix in the rice and return to the boil. Cover and simmer for 15 to 30 minutes, or until rice is soft.

For variety, just before removing from heat, stir in diced tofu, leftover vegetables or tempura, and/or eggs. Season to taste with 7-spice red pepper or grated gingerroot. Garnish with crumbled, toasted *nori*, green *nori* flakes, slivered leeks or citrus rind, or minced parsley. Serve immediately.

Miso Gruel with Leftovers

Gruel is an ancient preparation designed to create continually new and tasty combinations of foods while simultaneously preventing waste.
Combine all leftover cooked grains, vegetables, and tofu or other soybean foods in a large, heavy pot. Add enough leftover soup, stock, or water to give the consistency of a thick stew; bring to a boil and simmer for 5 to 10 minutes. Add creamed miso and, if desired, curry powder or ketchup to unify the flavors. To thicken, stir in lightly roasted wholewheat flour or barley flour and cook for several minutes more. Serve hot or cold. To use leftover gruel as the basis for full-bodied breads, knead in flour to earlobe consistency, allow to rise overnight, and bake in a slow oven for several hours.

Ochazuké with Miso Toppings · MAKES 1 SERVING

If you're in a hurry or want to make a quick, light meal (or when there is leftover rice which you don't have time to reheat), this impromptu dish is ideal. In Japan, some people also like to make Ochazuké using the rice remaining in their bowls toward the end of a meal, and many restaurants even feature Ochazuké as their specialty. Its most popular accompaniments are *takuan* (or other salt-pickled vegetables) and *tsukudani* (slivers or 1-inch squares of *kombu*, beefsteak seeds, tiny dried fish, etc., which have been simmered in a salty mixture of shoyu and *mirin*). Various types of miso are used as toppings. Although each person prepares Ochazuké at the table, using ingredients and proportions to taste, the method might look like this in recipe form:

½ to 1 cup cooked (leftover) rice
Miso Toppings (listed in order of popularity): Use 1 to 2
    teaspoons of any one of the following
        Thinly sliced Miso Pickles (p. 156)
        Broiled Miso (p. 71)
        Finger Lickin' Miso (p. 42)
        Sweet Simmered Miso (p. 60)
        Miso Sauté (p. 65)
        Hoba Miso (p. 72)
¼ to 1 cup very hot green tea
1 tablespoon crumbled, toasted *nori* (p. 54) or bonito
    flakes (optional)

Place rice in individual bowls and top with miso. Pour on hot tea, then press miso into rice with tips of chopsticks. Cover and allow to stand for several minutes. Sprinkle with *nori*, then sip the broth alternately with bites of rice.

Bibimpap · SERVES 6

This famous Korean rice dish, seasoned with fiery hot Red-pepper Miso *(kochu jang)* and topped with sautéed vegetables, is served on special occasions in much the same way as its relative, Five-Color Sushi, is served in Japan. Since the method of preparation is quite detailed and varies widely from chef to chef, we will present it here in a concise outline form.

Prepare 2 paper-thin omelets (p. 58) and reserve.
    Cut 2 cucumbers into thin rounds and rub lightly with salt. Allow to stand for 20 minutes, then rinse. Sauté rounds for 3 minutes in sesame oil together with a little minced leek, ground sesame seeds, and red pepper.
    Parboil 3 cups soybean sprouts for 10 minutes in lightly salted water. Drain sprouts, then sauté for 4 minutes in the same mixture of ingredients used with the cucumbers.
    Sauté 9 thinly sliced mushrooms (or Osmund ferns) in the same mixture to which has been added a little natural sugar and crushed garlic.
    Place 5 cups cooked brown rice in a large, shallow bowl. Atop rice arrange sautéed vegetables, slivered omelets, slivered almonds, and crumbled deep-fried *kombu* or toasted

nori. Accompany rice with a small cup filled with (home-made) Red-pepper Miso (p. 71). Invite each guest to transfer his choice of vegetables and rice to his individual plate, then top the combination with a small dab of the miso.

MISO WITH NOODLES

Noodles are among the most easily digestible of all foods and can serve as a central element in a meatless diet. For best nutritive value, look for noodles rich in whole-wheat, unrefined buckwheat, or soy flours.

Richly-flavored *soba* or fat *udon;* Italian spaghetti or crinkly Chinese *ramen;* winter noodles steaming hot or summer noodles in chilled broth; stir-fried noodles in savory sauces, and deep-fried noodles, brittle, crisp, and golden brown; homemade or leftover noodles in soups, sauces, and casseroles. Oodles of possibilities, each made more tasty and nutritious by the use of miso.

Stir-fried Buckwheat Noodles with Miso · SERVES 4

3 tablespoons oil, preferably used deep-frying oil
5 eggs, lightly beaten
¼ teaspoon salt
Pepper
1 onion, thinly sliced
10 ounces Chinese cabbage
3½ tablespoons red, barley, or Hatcho miso
6 to 7 ounces (soba) buckwheat noodles, cooked (p. 58)
¾ cup grated or Parmesan cheese (optional)

Heat 1 tablespoon oil in a wok or skillet. Add eggs, salt and a dash of pepper; scramble until eggs are fairly dry and crumbly, then transfer to a separate container and reserve.
    Heat the remaining 2 tablespoons oil in the wok. Add onion and cabbage, and sauté for 3 minutes. Add miso and cook, stirring constantly, for 1 minute more. Mix in cooked eggs, noodles and, if desired, the cheese. When noodles are heated through, remove from heat. Serve hot or cold.
    For variety, substitute 10 ounces diced deep-fried tofu for the eggs. Sauté until nicely browned and increase the miso to 5 tablespoons.

Bamboo noodle-tongs

Soybeans, Miso, and Sautéed Vegetables with Noodles

SERVES 4

2½ cups Pressure Cooked Soybeans (p. 129; unseasoned), drained
3 tablespoons red, barley, or Hatcho miso
2 tablespoons oil
1 clove of garlic, minced or crushed
1½ cups shredded cabbage
1 cup thinly sliced leeks or onions
½ cup grated carrot
6½ ounces (buckwheat or Chinese) noodles, cooked (p. 58)
1½ tablespoons shoyu
Dash of pepper

Combine cooked soybeans and miso, mixing well and mashing half the beans; set aside. Heat a large wok or skillet and coat with the oil. Add garlic and sauté for 30 seconds. Add cabbage, onions and carrot, sauté for 4 minutes more, and turn off heat. Add soybeans, mixing until evenly distributed. Stir in noodles, sprinkle with shoyu, and season with pepper; mix lightly. Delicious hot or cold.

Buckwheat Noodles in Miso-Soymilk Sauce

SERVES 2

1½ cups milk (soy or dairy)
1 small onion, diced
1 tablespoon red, barley, or Hatcho miso
2 tablespoons sweet white miso or 1 tablespoon red miso
2 tablespoons butter
½ cup grated cheese or 2½ tablespoons sesame butter
3½ ounces (soba) buckwheat noodles, cooked (p. 58) and well drained
Dash of pepper
2 tablespoons minced parsley or ground roasted sesame seeds (p. 54)
Crumbled toasted *nori* (optional)

Combine milk and onion in a large saucepan and bring to a boil over medium heat, stirring constantly. Stir in miso creamed in a little of the hot liquid. Add butter, cheese and noodles, and return to the boil, then season with pepper and remove from heat. For best flavor, allow to stand for several hours. Serve as is or reheated, garnished with parsley and, if used, the *nori*.

For variety, combine all ingredients in a casserole and bake at 350° for about 20 minutes, or until nicely browned.

Noodles Topped with Miso Sauces

SERVES 4

7 to 8 ounces buckwheat or whole-wheat noodles, cooked (p. 58)
Miso Sauce: Use 2 to 4 cups of any of the following (pp.113 to 118):
    Miso Onion Sauce
    Miso Mushroom Sauce
    Miso Spaghetti Sauce
    Miso White Sauce
    Miso Curry Sauce
    Miso Gravy
    Spicy Indonesian Peanut Sauce
    Sesame Miso Sauce
Garnishes and seasonings:
    Crumbled, Toasted Nori (p. 54)
    Sambals (p. 116)
    Roasted (whole or ground) sesame seeds (p. 54)
    Thinly sliced Miso Pickles (p. 156)
    7-spice red pepper

Arrange hot or cold noodles in individual or serving bowls. Spoon on the sauce and serve accompanied by garnish.

Deep-fried Noodles with Miso Sweet & Sour Sauce

SERVES 4

6 ounces noodles
Oil for deep-frying
3 cups Pineapple Sweet & Sour Sauce (p. 115)

Cook noodles (p. 58), then drain in a colander for about 1 hour. Heat the oil to 350° in a wok, skillet, or deep-fryer. Place about ¼ cup noodles on a spatula and slide into the oil. Deep-fry for about 30 seconds (p. 147), then turn and deep-fry for 30 seconds more, or until crisp and golden brown; drain well. Repeat until all noodles are used. Divide noodles among individual plates, top with the sauce, and serve immediately.

Also good with most of the sauces enumerated in Noodles Topped with Miso Sauces (above).

Noodles Cooked with Miso & Milk

SERVES 2

1½ cups milk (soy or dairy)
3½ ounces (*soba*) buckwheat noodles, cooked (p. 58)
2 tablespoons butter
1/3 cup grated cheese (optional)
3½ tablespoons red, barley, or Hatcho miso
2 tablespoons minced parsley or ground roasted sesame seeds (p. 54)
Crumbled, toasted *nori* (optional)

In a large pot, bring milk just to a boil over medium heat, stirring constantly. Add cooked noodles, butter, cheese, and miso creamed with a little of the hot milk. Return to the boil, then set aside to cool until milk clabbers. Serve garnished with the parsley and *nori*.

For variety, combine ¼ cup diced onion with the milk in the pot before heating.

Buckwheat Noodles
   ## with Miso Dipping Sauce

SERVES 5 OR 6

2 tablespoons sweet white miso
4 tablespoons shoyu
1 tablespoon honey
2 tablespoons *mirin*, dry sherry, or white wine
2 tablespoons sesame butter or ¼ cup ground roasted sesame seeds (p. 54)
2 cups dashi (p. 56), stock, or water
1/3 cup thinly sliced leeks or scallions
Dash of (7-spice) red pepper
8 to 10 ounces (*soba*) buckwheat noodles, cooked (p. 58)

Combine the first five ingredients in a pot or large skillet and cook, stirring constantly, for about 1 minute, or until smooth. Stir in dashi and bring to a boil. Remove from heat and allow to cool, then divide among individual bowls. Place noodles on plates or in a large bamboo colander. Invite guests to garnish dipping sauce to taste with leeks and red pepper. Dip noodles into sauce to serve.

VARIATION

*Miso Tanuki Soba: Prepare the dipping sauce using 9 to 10 tablespoons red miso, 4½ cups dashi and, if desired, 1 tablespoon natural sugar and 2 tablespoons sake, white wine, or *mirin*. Pour hot broth over noodles in individual bowls, garnish and season as above, then top each portion with ¼ cup of *agédama*, tiny particles of deep-fried tempura batter skimmed off during the deep-frying process or specially prepared for this dish.

Nikomi-udon
   ### (Homemade Noodles Simmered in Miso)

SERVES 6

In this popular miso preparation, the water in which the noodles are cooked is not discarded, but is used as the basis for a thick miso sauce that closely resembles a Western-style white sauce. For best flavor, allow this dish to stand overnight so that the noodles further contribute to the thickening of the sauce. Serve either cold or reheated.

2 cups flour, half of which is whole-wheat
8½ cups warm water
¼ teaspoon salt
5 tablespoons sweet white or 3 tablespoons mellow white miso
3 tablespoons red, barley, or Hatcho miso
3 large leeks, cut diagonally into 2-inch lengths
1½ small leeks or scallions, cut into thin rounds
7-spice red pepper
Crumbled, toasted *nori* (optional)

Put the 2 cups flour into a large bowl and, adding ½ cup water a little at a time, mix and knead to form a heavy dough. Roll out dough on a floured breadboard to 1/8-inch thickness, sprinkle surface lightly with flour, and fold lengthwise accordion fashion into quarters. Now cut dough crosswise into 1/8-inch-wide strands to make noodles. Spread noodle strips on the floured board to dry briefly.

Bring the remaining 8 cups water to a boil in a large pot. Drop in noodles and salt, and cook until until noodles float to surface. Add miso creamed with a little of the hot water, then add large leeks and simmer for 10 minutes. Remove from heat and allow to stand as long as overnight. Serve garnished with thin rounds of leeks, red pepper, and *nori*.

To save time, use about 10 ounces dried noodles in place of the homemade variety. In some parts of Japan, *daikon*, mushrooms, taro, carrots, and deep-fried tofu are parboiled or simmered in sweetened shoyu broth, then added to the noodles together with the miso. Result: A thick noodle-and-vegetable stew.

Homemade noodles

Miso Ramen

SERVES 2 OR 3

A favorite at Japan's thousands of small restaurants specializing in Chinese-style *ramen* noodles, this preparation is usually made with a chicken-based broth and served steaming hot. Sapporo Miso Ramen, the most famous variety, is named after the city in Hokkaido, Japan's northernmost island, where this dish is said to have originated.

3½ ounces (Chinese) noodles
1 tablespoon sesame oil
1 clove of garlic, minced or crushed
1½ cups bean sprouts
½ cup thinly sliced leeks or onions
3 tablespoons red, barley, or Hatcho miso
1 tablespoon shoyu
2½ cups stock or dashi (p. 56)
Dash of (7-spice) red pepper or tabasco sauce
1 tablespoon dry (cloud-ear) mushroom, reconstituted (p. 54) and minced

Cook noodles (p. 58), drain, and reserve. Heat a skillet or wok and coat with the oil. Add garlic and sauté for 30 seconds. Add bean sprouts and leeks and sauté for 3 minutes more. Dissolve miso and shoyu in ½ cup stock and add to skillet together with red pepper and mushrooms; bring to a boil. Add remaining dashi and return to the boil, stirring constantly.

Place noodles in a strainer and dip briefly into boiling water until warmed through. Mound in deep bowls, then pour on the vegetables-and-broth.

Noodles Cooked with Miso
(Misoyaki Udon)

SERVES 4

6 tablespoons sweet white miso or 3 tablespoons red miso
7 tablespoons dashi (p. 56), stock, or water
1 tablespoon shoyu
2½ tablespoon *mirin*, sake, or white wine
1½ tablespoons oil
1 small onion, thinly sliced
2 to 3 ounces deep-fried tofu or 4 to 6 mushrooms, thinly sliced
1½ teaspoons grated or minced gingerroot
3½ ounces (*udon* or *soba*) whole-wheat or buckwheat noodles, cooked (p. 58) and drained

Combine the first four ingredients, mixing well. Heat the oil in a pot or large skillet. Add onion, deep-fried tofu and gingerroot, and sauté over medium-high heat for 2 to 3 minutes. Stir in the miso-dashi mixture and cooked noodles, cover, and return to the boil. Lower heat and simmer for 10 to 15 minutes. Serve hot or cold.

Chilled Noodles with Mustard-Vinegar Miso (*Sumiso Udon*)

SERVES 4

7 ounces noodles, cooked (p. 58), drained and chilled
½ cup Sweetened Mustard Vinegar Miso (p. 65)
1 cucumber, slivered
1 tomato, cut into thin wedges
1 egg, hard-boiled and cut into thin wedges

Place chilled noodles into a large serving bowl. Spoon miso into a mound at center of noodles, then arrange garnishes around miso. Invite guests to serve themselves.

Cha-chiang Mien

SERVES 4

One of the most popular ways of using miso in Chinese-style cookery, this tasty dish is usually prepared with chiang (Chinese miso) mixed with bits of pork (or occasionally ground beef) fried in oil and served over crinkly noodles together with a wide variety of toppings and garnishes.

3½ ounces (Chinese or buckwheat) noodles, cooked (p. 58)
Garnishes: Any or all of the following
    2 cups bean-sprouts, quickly parboiled
    2 cucumbers, slivered
    2 eggs made into paper-thin omelets, cooled and slivered (p. 58)
    6 mushrooms or 2 leeks, thinly sliced and sautéed in butter
Chinese-style Nerimiso (p. 61)

Place noodles, individual garnishes and the miso in separate serving bowls. Invite each guest to serve himself with noodles and preferred garnish, then miso. Mix well.

MISO WITH OTHER GRAINS

Miso with bulgur wheat and tortillas, *mochi* and French toast; miso toppings with oatmeal, cornmeal, and cream of wheat. All offer many delicious possibilities. For corn-on-the-cob, see page 144.

In Japan, miso rice crackers (*miso senbei*) and sweet miso rolls topped with sesame seeds (*miso pan*) are both sold commercially. In each case, red miso is simply mixed with a sweetened rice-flour or wheat-flour dough and then baked.

Curried Bulgur Pilaf with Cheese and Miso

SERVES 2 OR 3

Bulgur wheat—also known as couscous—is prepared by partially cooking, drying, and then cracking whole-grain wheat. A popular ingredient in Near Eastern and North African cuisines, it needs little cooking and has a pleasant, nutty flavor. In the West, it is now widely known as Ala.

2 tablespoons butter
½ cup bulgur wheat
1 small onion, thinly sliced
1 small carrot, slivered or diced
1 cup water or stock
½ teaspoon curry powder
1½ tablespoons red, barley, or Hatcho miso
2½ tablespoons Parmesan or grated cheese
1 tablespoon minced parsley

Melt the butter in a skillet. Add bulgur and onion, and sauté for 4 to 5 minutes. Add water and curry powder, cover, and bring to a boil. Simmer for 15 minutes, or until all liquid has been absorbed. Stir in miso and cheese, and remove from heat. Serve hot or cold, garnished with parsley.

Tabbouli with Miso (*Bulgur Salad with Mint and Lemon*)

SERVES 4 TO 6

1 cup bulgur wheat or couscous
¾ cup lemon juice
¾ cup very finely minced parsley
2 tablespoons minced fresh mint, or 3 tablespoons dried mint flakes reconstituted in 2 tablespoons hot water
3 tomatoes, minced
½ green pepper, chopped fine
6 to 8 tablespoons olive oil
1 teaspoon red, barley, or Hatcho miso, dissolved in 2 teaspoons warm water

Combine the bulgur and lemon juice, mix lightly, and allow to stand for 1 hour. Stir in the remaining ingredients and, for best flavor, allow to stand for at least several hours, preferably 2 to 3 days. Delicious served chilled.

French Toast with White Miso & Raisins

SERVES 2

½ cup milk (soy or dairy)
1 egg, lightly beaten
2 tablespoons sweet white or 4 teaspoons mellow white miso
1½ teaspoons honey
¼ cup raisins
2 large slices of whole-wheat bread, cut into fourths
2 tablespoons butter
Dash of cinnamon

Combine the first five ingredients in a shallow pan, mixing until smooth. Add bread and allow to stand for 3 to 5 minutes. (For very firm or unyeasted bread, soak for 1 hour.) Melt the butter in a large skillet. Add bread, spoon on any raisins remaining in pan, and cook for 2 to 3 minutes on each side, or until nicely browned. Serve topped with a sprinkling of cinnamon.

Cornmeal Spoonbread with Miso

MAKES 1 LOAF

Rich as cheesecake, this delicious loaf separates into three decorative layers. The miso lends its own savory flavor while the combination of soy, corn, and milk boosts the total protein content by up to 13 percent.

½ cup cornmeal
¼ cup whole-wheat flour
1 teaspoon baking powder
1½ cups milk (soy or dairy)
1 egg, lightly beaten
1 tablespoon honey
1½ tablespoons red or barley (or 3 tablespoons mellow white) miso
¼ cup raisins
2 tablespoons butter

Preheat oven to 375°. Combine the first three ingredients, sifting or mixing well. Combine 1 cup milk with the next four ingredients, mixing until miso is dissolved, then stir into the flour mixture and beat until well blended. Melt butter in a loaf pan. Pour in batter and top with the remaining ½ cup milk. Bake for 45 minutes. Serve buttered, piping hot or, for a richer sweeter flavor, chilled.

Hot Cereals with Miso Toppings

MAKES 1 SERVING

1 to 1½ cups freshly cooked rolled oats, oatmeal, cornmeal, rice cream, or cream of wheat
1 to 1½ tablespoons of any of the following (pp. 61–62):
    Peanut- or Peanut & Raisin Miso
    Sesame Miso
    Walnut-, Cashew-, or Sunflower Seed Miso

Dash of salt
1 tablespoon butter (optional)
¼ cup nuts, raisins, and/or granola (optional)
¼ to ½ cup warm milk (soy or dairy) (optional)

Serve hot cereal in a large bowl, topped with a dab of miso and seasoned with salt. Add butter, nuts, and milk if desired; mix lightly.

Broiled Mochi with Sweet Miso and Nori

SERVES 2 TO 4

8 cakes of *mochi*, each about 3 by 2 by ¾ inches
8 teaspoons butter
4 teaspoons honey (optional)
2 teaspoons grated gingerroot (optional)
8 teaspoons of any one of the following:
    Sweet Simmered Miso (p. 60)
    Finger Lickin' Miso (p. 41)
    Sweet White Miso
8 pieces of *nori*, each 3 by 6 inches

Broil *mochi* cakes on both sides in an oven broiler or on a grill until cakes are crisp, nicely browned, and puffed to twice their original thickness. Slit one end of each cake and fill with butter, honey and gingerroot. Spread both sides of cakes with the miso, wrap in a sheet of *nori* (fig. 21) and serve hot.

If *nori* is not available, use miso as part of the filling. Or omit honey and grated gingerroot, and fill *mochi* with 8 teaspoons Gingerroot Mixed Red Miso (p. 69) combined with ¼ cup grated *daikon*.

VARIATION

*Mochi in Miso-Ankaké: Broil *mochi* cakes as above. Place 2 cakes in each of four bowls and top with about ¼ cup of any of the following: Miso-Gingerroot Ankaké Sauce (p. 113), Miso-Lemon Ankaké Sauce (p. 113), Miso-Gingerroot Sauce (p. 118).

Fig. 21. Broiled Mochi with Nori

Millet or Buckwheat Pilaf
SERVES 4

3 tablespoons butter
½ cup millet or buckwheat groats (kasha)
1 onion, minced
1 tablespoon red miso, dissolved in 1 cup boiling water
¼ teaspoon oregano
Dash of pepper

Melt the butter in a heavy skillet. Add millet and onion, and saute until golden brown. Add remaining ingredients, cover, and bring to a boil. Reduce heat and simmer for 30 to 35 minutes. Delicious topped with Garbanzo-Tahini Sauce (p. 115) or Gado-Gado (p. 116).

Buckwheat Groats Medley with Miso
SERVES 4

1 cup buckwheat groats (kasha)
1 tablespoon oil
1 carrot, diced, slivered, or grated
¼ cup chopped hazel- or Brazil nuts
¼ cup sunflower seeds
¼ cup roasted sesame seeds
1 banana, sliced into thin rounds
1 apple, diced
1 pear, diced
Seeds from 1 cardamom, crushed
Dash of cinnamon
1 tablespoon red or barley miso; or 2 tablespoons mellow white miso
½ cup apple juice

Dry roast buckwheat groats until fragrant and nicely browned. Heat a skillet and coat with the oil. Add groats and the next ten ingredients and sauté for 10 minutes. Dissolve miso in apple juice, add to contents of skillet, and sauté for 1 minute more. Serve hot or chilled topped with applesauce, yogurt, kefir, or ricotta cheese. Or use as is like granola.

Crisp Tortillas with Taco Sauce (*Tostadas*)
SERVES 5

Miso can serve as a delicious complement to the simple, natural flavors of these grain-based "platters" so widely used throughout Latin America and India.

10 seven-inch *tortillas*
Butter
1¼ cups Miso Taco Sauce (p.114)
2 tomatoes, diced
2½ cups shredded lettuce, sprouts, or cabbage

Heat *tortillas* in a medium oven for 5 to 7 minutes, or until lightly browned and crisp. (Or deep-fry in hot oil.) Butter one side of each *tortilla*, then spread with the sauce and top with tomatoes and lettuce.

For a meatier flavor, mix 10 to 15 ounces thinly sliced deep-fried tofu with the lettuce. Serve topped with a little grated cheese and tabasco sauce.

OTHER PREPARATIONS WITH *TORTILLAS, CHAPATIES, TACOS,* OR *PURIES*

*With Butter and Mixed Miso: Butter warm *tortillas* well, then coat one surface with a thin layer of Finger Lickin' Miso, sweet white miso, Mixed White Miso Topping with Parmesan (p. 69), or Mixed Cheese Miso (p. 70).
*Miso-filled Puries: Deep-fry *tortillas* (or puri dough) in hot oil until they swell and turn golden brown. Fill with butter, honey, gingerroot, and miso as for Broiled Mochi (p.127).
*Tacos with Miso & Salads: Bake or deep-fry *tortillas* until crisp. Top with thinly sliced lettuce, tomatoes, deep-fried tofu and grated cheese. Spoon on Floating Cloud (p. 83) or your favorite miso dressing.
*With Miso Spreads: Top individual (warm) *tortillas* with ¼ to ½ cup Azuki-Miso (p. 81) or Soybean-Sesame-Miso (p. 81), or any of your other favorite miso spreads. Roll before eating.
*Serve miso-seasoned vegetable or grain dishes atop *tortillas*.

Chinese Pancake Rolls with Miso Sauce
SERVES 4

This recipe is closely related to the famous Peking Duck also served with miso (*t'ien mien chiang*) in tender, thin pancake rolls. In China, these *chapati*-like pancakes are usually prepared in the kitchen, fried in a dry skillet and steamed in large bamboo steamers. Since the process is complex, this recipe calls for ready-made *tortillas*.

4 teaspoons oil
4 eggs, lightly beaten
1 cup thinly sliced leek rounds
1½ cups bean sprouts
2 green peppers, thinly sliced
Miso Sauce:
    3½ tablespoons red, barley, or Hatcho miso
    4 teaspoons honey
    2 tablespoons sesame oil
    1 teaspoon soy sauce
    2 tablespoons water
½ large tomato, cut into thin wedges
½ small onion, minced
12 wheat-flour *tortillas*, warmed (preferably steamed)

Heat a skillet and coat with 1 tablespoon oil. Add eggs and leeks, and scramble until firm. Transfer to a small serving bowl.

Reheat skillet and coat with remaining 1 teaspoon oil. Add sprouts and green peppers, and sauté for 2 to 3 minutes. Transfer to a second serving bowl.

Combine ingredients for the sauce in a third (small) bowl; mix well. Place tomato wedges and minced onions on small plates. Fold warm *tortillas* into quarters and place on the dining table together with the sauce and fillings. Invite each guest to open a pancake, coat upper surface with sauce, and top with fillings. Roll pancake around fillings and eat like a sandwich or *taco*.

Mock Peking Duck

MISO WITH SOYBEANS AND TOFU

The use of miso (or shoyu) is one of the keys to seasoning soybeans and the more than eight varieties of Japanese and Chinese tofu described in *The Book of Tofu*. Tofu and soybeans are also used in a number of recipes throughout the preceding sections of this book. Topped with or added to Miso Sauces, especially Sweet & Sour-, Gingerroot- or White Sauce, deep-fried or regular tofu is at its very best. For miso with high-protein soybean spreads, see page 81.

Miso-filled Rolled Breads
MAKES 2 LOAVES

Dough for 2 loaves of bread (reduce salt content to 1 teaspoon)
¼ cup red, barley, or Hatcho miso
¼ cup honey
2 tablespoons butter or sesame butter
¾ cup raisins
1 apple, cut into very thin wedges; or 1 large banana, cut into thin rounds
½ cup chopped nutmeats (walnut or almond)

Roll out dough into two long rectangles, each about 8 inches wide and 3/8 inch thick. Combine miso, honey, and butter, mixing well, then spread in an even layer over upper surface of each rectangle. Top with a sprinkling of raisins, apple wedges and, if used, nutmeats. Roll each rectangle from one end to form a compact cylinder. Place into oiled loaf pans and bake at 350° for about 45 minutes, or until nicely browned. Allow to cool thoroughly. Serve with butter.

Mock Peking Duck
SERVES 2

This delicacy is the prized creation (and most expensive item) in many fine Chinese restaurants. Thin slices of duck with lacquer-crisp skin are rolled up in paper-thin wheat-flour "doilies" (each 6 inches in diameter) or folded in steamed *litus* buns together with slivered leeks (or scallions) and *t'ien mien chiang* (or *hoishin* sauce). The following is a vegetarian version of the original using ingredients more readily available in the West.

4 *tortillas*, cut into halves and warmed in a steamer
Butter
10 ounces deep-fried tofu cutlets, cut into 4-inch-long strips
2 or 3 tablespoons *t'ien mien chiang* (homemade, p. 70 or commercial, p. 243)
1 leek or 3 green onions, cut into 4-inch slivers, soaked in water for 5 minutes and drained

Butter warmed *tortillas* lightly on one side. Divide tofu among *tortillas*, placing the strips in the center of each *tortilla* half perpendicular to the *tortilla's* cut edge. Spread the *t'ien mien chiang* on the tofu, then top with a sprinkling of the leek slivers. Roll up and, if desired, secure with a foodpick. Serve while *tortillas* are still warm.

Pressure Cooked Soybeans with Miso
MAKES 2¼ CUPS

1 cup dry soybeans, rinsed and soaked for 2 to 3 hours in 2 quarts water
2 cups water
A thin wedge of lemon or lime (optional)

Drain and rinse soaked beans, and combine with 2 cups water in a pressure cooker. Bring to full pressure (15 pounds) and simmer for 25 minutes. Remove from heat and allow to stand for 10 to 15 minutes as pressure returns to normal. Cool lid under cold running water and open.

Return cooker to stove, stir in any of the ingredients listed below, and simmer uncovered for 10 to 15 minutes, or until flavors are nicely married. If necessary, add ¼ cup water during simmering. Stir from time to time. Serve hot or cold.

*2 tablespoons red, barley, or Hatcho miso (creamed with a little of the cooking liquid). If desired, add 1 teaspoon lemon juice and/or 1 tablespoon butter. For a deliciously rich flavor, add 1 (sautéed) minced onion together with the miso and stir in ½ cup grated cheese or ¼ cup Parmesan just before removing from heat.

*1½ tablespoons red miso, 3 tablespoons sesame butter or *tahini*, 3 to 4 tablespoons dry *hijiki* or slivered *kombu* (reconstituted, p. 54), and 1 onion or ¾ cup carrot (pre-sautéed in 1 tablespoon oil, if desired). For extra sweetness, add 1½ teaspoons honey or natural sugar.

*1 to 1½ tablespoons red miso and 2 to 3 tablespoons molasses or honey.

*1 tablespoon red miso and ¼ cup sesame butter or *tahini*.

*1 tablespoon red miso and ½ to 1 cup total of the following (added alone or in combination): diced tomatoes, onions, carrots, celery, mushrooms, lotus root, burdock root, sprouts, fresh or dried *daikon*, or *kombu*. For variety add ½ teaspoon curry powder and/or 1 clove of crushed garlic.

*In any of the above recipes, after the beans and seasonings have finished cooking, try sautéing the mixture for a few minutes in a little (sesame) oil.

Corn & Soybean Succotash

SERVES 3

Here's a delicious, high-protein favorite of the American Indians with soybeans used in place of the traditional lima beans, and miso in place of salt.

2 tablespoons butter or oil
1 cup cooked soybeans (p. 129; unseasoned)
1 cup cooked fresh corn
1 tablespoon red, barley, or Hatcho miso
1/8 teaspoon paprika
1 tablespoon minced parsley

Melt the butter in a heavy skillet or pot. Add corn and beans, and sauté over low heat for 5 minutes. Mix in miso, season with paprika, and remove from heat. Top with a sprinkling of parsley.

For variety, sauté ½ minced onion together with the corn and/or add ¼ cup grated cheese together with the miso.

Boston Baked Soybeans with Brown Rice & Miso

SERVES 3

1 cup cooked soybeans (p. 129), drained
2 cups cooked Brown Rice (p. 57)
¼ cup minced onion
2½ tablespoons ketchup
5 teaspoons red, barley, or Hatcho miso
1½ teaspoons honey
2 teaspoons dry mustard
½ cup soybean cooking liquid
¾ teaspoon curry powder
½ teaspoon vinegar
2½ teaspoons Worcestershire sauce

Preheat oven to 250°. Combine all ingredients, mixing well. Place into a lightly oiled baking dish and bake covered for 30 minutes, then uncovered for 30 minutes more. Delicious hot or chilled.

Miso also makes an excellent substitute for salt in your favorite recipe for Boston Baked Beans.

Soybean & Miso Garnish

MAKES 1 CUP

2 tablespoons sesame oil
1 cup cooked soybeans (p. 129), well drained
2 tablespoons red, barley, or Hatcho miso
½ teaspoon grated gingerroot
Dash of 7-spice red pepper (optional)

Heat a skillet or wok and coat with the oil. Add soybeans and sauté for 2 to 3 minutes. Reduce heat to low, add remaining ingredients, and sauté for 2 minutes more. Allow to cool to room temperature. Serve as a garnish with brown rice or rice porridge.

Green Peppers Stuffed with Miso-Soybeans

SERVES 6

1 cup dry soybeans, cooked (p. 129) and drained
2 tablespoons red, barley, or Hatcho miso
¼ cup ketchup
½ onion, minced
2 tablespoons dark brown sugar
1½ to 2 teaspoons mustard
½ cup grated cheese
3 green peppers, seeded and parboiled in salted water for 5 minutes
1 tablespoon oil

Preheat oven to 350°. Combine the first seven ingredients, mixing well, then use to fill green pepper shells. Rub shells lightly with oil, place in an oiled pan, and bake for 20 minutes. Serve hot or chilled.

Other delicious fillings for green pepper shells include Refried Pinto Beans (p. 132), and Boston Baked Soybeans.

Savory Soybean, Corn & Miso Casserole

SERVES 4

1¼ cups cooked soybeans (p. 129), drained
1¼ cups cooked corn
1 tomato, diced
¼ cup ketchup
1½ tablespoons red, barley, or Hatcho miso
½ teaspoon honey
¼ onion, minced
¼ cup chopped peanuts or bread crumbs

Preheat oven to 350°. Combine the first seven ingredients, mixing well. Place into a lightly oiled baking dish and top with a sprinkling of peanuts. Bake covered for about 45 minutes. Serve hot or chilled.

Also delicious as a topping for plain or stir-fried brown rice (pp. 119 and 120).

Tofu with Miso Toppings

SERVES 1

6 to 8 ounces regular or 3 to 5 ounces (lightly-broiled) deep-fried tofu

Miso Toppings: Use any of the following
    1 to 2 teaspoons red, barley, or Hatcho miso
    1 tablespoon Sweet Simmered Miso (p. 60), Finger Lickin' Miso (p. 41), Miso Sauté (p. 65), Mixed Miso (p. 69), or Broiled Miso (p. 71); or, for use only with deep-fried tofu, Vinegar Miso (p. 64) or Daikon Mixed Miso (p. 69)
    1½ tablespoons sweet white or red miso

Garnishes: Use ½ to 1 teaspoon of any of the following (optional)
    Thinly sliced leeks
    Grated gingerroot
    Minced or crushed garlic
    Wasabi
    Slivered lemon, lime, or *yuzu* rind

Place tofu on a plate and coat its upper surface with your choice of topping. If desired, cut into bite-sized pieces and serve topped with the garnish.

Tofu with Miso-Onion Sauce and Cheese

SERVES 4 TO 6

2 tablespoons oil
6 onions, thinly sliced
6 tablespoons red, barley, or Hatcho miso
1½ teaspoons honey
1 tablespoon sake or white wine
24 ounces tofu, cut into bite-sized cubes
2 ounces grated cheese
2 eggs, lightly beaten
2 to 3 tablespoons Parmesan cheese (optional)

Heat a large casserole or pot and coat with the oil. Add onions, cover, and cook over very low heat for 1½ hours, stirring occasionally. Mix in miso, honey and sake, then carefully add tofu cubes, covering them by spooning onion sauce over the top. Cover pot and simmer for 10 minutes. Gently mix in grated cheese and pour egg over the top. Re-cover and simmer for 5 minutes more, or until egg is firm. Sprinkle with Parmesan if desired and allow to stand, covered, overnight. Serve as is or reheated.

Tofu with Miso White Sauce Au Gratin

SERVES 3

1 tablespoon oil
1 clove of garlic, crushed or minced
2 small onions, thinly sliced
1/3 cup grated cheese
7½ ounces deep-fried tofu, cubed; or 18 ounces regular tofu, pressed (p. 55) and cubed
1 cup Miso White Sauce (p. 114; season with 2 tablespoons red miso)
2 tablespoons Parmesan cheese
1 tablespoon bread crumbs

Preheat oven to 350°. Heat the oil in a skillet or wok. Add garlic and sauté for 15 seconds. Add onions and sauté for 3 minutes more. Remove from heat, stir in grated cheese and tofu, then spoon into a loaf pan or casserole. Pour on the white sauce and top with a sprinkling of Parmesan and bread crumbs. Bake for about 20 minutes, or until nicely browned. Delicious either hot or cold.

Steamed Miso-filled Tofu
(*Nanzenji no Tsutsumi-dofu*)

SERVES 4

24 ounces tofu
¼ to ½ cup Yuzu Miso (p. 62) or any Sweet Simmered Miso (p. 60)

Cut tofu into four 6-ounce pieces. With the sharp point of a knife, cut a section 2 inches square and 1 inch deep from the larger surface of each piece, and lift out carefully (fig. 22). Fill the "well" that remains with 1 to 2 tablespoons of the miso, then replace the small piece of tofu atop the miso. Wrap each piece of tofu in strong, absorbent paper (the Japanese use *washi* for this purpose) or in aluminum foil.

    Bring water to a boil in a steamer. Place wrapped tofu in steamer and steam for 5 to 10 minutes, or until miso is well heated. Serve hot, inviting each guest to unwrap his or her portion just before eating.

Fig. 22. Steamed Tofu

Deep-fried Tofu with Gingerroot Miso

SERVES 2 OR 3

1½ tablespoons oil
10 ounces deep-fried tofu, cut into bite-sized rectangles ½-inch thick
2 tablespoons red, barley, or Hatcho miso
1 tablespoon honey
1 teaspoon grated gingerroot
Minced parsley or whole lettuce leaves

Heat a skillet or wok and coat with the oil. Add deep-fried tofu and sauté over high heat for 3 to 4 minutes until slightly crisp and well browned. Add miso, honey, and gingerroot and cook, stirring constantly, for 2 to 3 minutes, or until all ingredients are well mixed. Serve hot or cold garnished with the parsley or placed on individual lettuce leaves.

MISO WITH OTHER BEANS

Mexican-style Pinto Beans with Miso (*Frijoles de Olla*)

SERVES 6 TO 8

2 cups pinto beans, washed and soaked overnight in 9 cups water
1 onion, minced
3½ tablespoons red, barley, or Hatcho miso
Dash of cumin seeds and/or red pepper (optional)
½ to 1 cup grated or Parmesan cheese

Place beans and water in a casserole or heavy pot and bring to a boil. Reduce heat to very low, cover, and simmer for 1½ hours. Add onion, miso and cumin seeds, then simmer for 30 minutes more, or until beans are tender. Serve in soup bowls, topped with a sprinkling of the cheese.

Refried Pinto Beans with Sour Cream and Miso (*Frijoles Refritos*)

SERVES 3

In Mexico, the leftovers from a large pot of *Frijoles de Olla* (above) are usually served at the next meal prepared in the following manner:

2 tablespoons oil
1 clove of garlic, minced or crushed
½ onion, minced
2 cups *Frijoles de Olla* (without cheese), drained of excess liquid
¼ to ½ cup grated cheese
½ cup sour cream
2 teaspoons red, barley, or Hatcho miso

Heat a skillet and coat with the oil. Add garlic and onion, and sauté for 1 minute. Add beans, mash well with a fork, and sauté for about 3 minutes, or until slightly dry and crisp. Combine cheese, sour cream and miso, mixing well, then stir into the beans and remove from heat. Delicious served as a side dish, in *tortillas* or as a spread.

Making tortillas

Miso in Baked Dishes

More of our very favorite recipes appear among the following than in any other section of this book. Almost all are Western-style preparations and many contain grains as the basic ingredient.

Rich Noodle Casserole with Miso-Sour Cream and Chives

SERVES 5 TO 6

1 cup sour cream
3 tablespoons red, barley, or Hatcho miso
2 eggs, lightly beaten
6 tablespoons minced chives
1½ cups cottage cheese
4¼ ounces (*soba*) buckwheat noodles, cooked, drained and cooled (p. 58)
2 to 3 tablespoons butter

Preheat oven to 350°. Combine the first five ingredients, mixing well, then gently stir into the cooked noodles. Place into a buttered casserole and top with dabs of the remaining butter. Bake covered for 20 minutes, then uncover and bake for about 15 minutes more, or until nicely browned.

Miso-Onion Soup Casserole Au Gratin

SERVES 5 TO 6

2½ to 3 cups bread cubes (fresh, stale, or croutons)
4 cups Thick French Onion Soup with Miso (p. 107)
6 tablespoons Parmesan or grated cheese

Combine bread and soup, mixing well, and spoon into a lightly oiled or buttered loaf pan or casserole; allow to stand for 1 to 2 hours. Preheat oven to 350°. Sprinkle casserole with cheese and bake for about 20 minutes, or until nicely browned. Serve hot or cold.

Mushroom Casserole with Miso

SERVES 5

3 tablespoons butter
4 cups sliced mushrooms (12 ounces)
6 slices of whole-wheat bread, buttered and broken into bite-sized pieces
½ cup minced onion
½ cup minced green pepper
½ cup minced celery
3½ tablespoons red, barley, or Hatcho miso
1 cup milk (soy or dairy)
4 eggs, lightly beaten
¼ cup mayonnaise
Dash of pepper

Melt the butter in a skillet. Add mushrooms and sauté for 3 minutes, then transfer to a large buttered casserole. Add bread and minced vegetables. Cream miso with a little milk, then combine with the remaining ingredients, stirring vigorously until smooth. Add to casserole and mix with vegetables and bread. Smooth surface of ingredients, cover, and refrigerate for 6 to 8 hours. Bake in a preheated 325° oven for 50 minutes.

Baked Potatoes in Miso Gravy

SERVES 6 TO 8

3¾ pounds potatoes (6 to 8), each peeled and cut into fourths
1 cup vegetable stock or water
3½ tablespoons butter
3½ tablespoons red, barley, or Hatcho miso
3½ tablespoons honey
1 tablespoon shoyu (natural soy sauce)

Preheat oven to 450°F. Place potatoes in a greased casserole. Mix remaining ingredients in a bowl or blender and pour over the potatoes. Cover and bake for 30 minutes. Mix well. Re-cover and bake for 30 minutes more. Serve hot or cold.

133

Potatoes with Miso White Sauce Au Gratin

SERVES 3

1½ teaspoons oil
1 onion, thinly sliced
1 cup Miso White Sauce (p. 114), seasoned with dill if
   desired
3 potatoes, boiled and cubed (2 to 2½ cups)
¼ cup grated cheese
1½ teaspoons butter
1½ tablespoons bread crumbs
1½ tablespoons Parmesan cheese

Preheat oven to 400°. Heat a skillet and coat with the oil. Add onions and sauté for 3 minutes. Prepare Miso White Sauce, then mix in the potatoes, onions, and grated cheese. Spoon into a buttered loaf pan or casserole, dot with butter, and sprinkle with bread crumbs and Parmesan cheese. Bake for 10 to 15 minutes, or until nicely browned. Serve hot or, for a richer flavor, refrigerate overnight and serve cold.

For variety, substitute squash or (*kabocha*) pumpkin for the potatoes.

Potatoes Baked in Miso Gravy Au Gratin

SERVES 3 OR 4

4 small potatoes, boiled in their skins until tender and cut
   into bite-sized pieces
2½ cups Miso Gravy (p. 116)
2 tablespoons Parmesan cheese

Preheat oven to 350°. Combine potatoes and gravy in an oiled loaf pan or casserole and top with a sprinkling of cheese. Bake for about 20 minutes, or until nicely browned. Delicious hot or cold.

Quiche Nicoise with Miso

SERVES 6

A 9-inch pie shell
6 tablespoons (olive) oil
1 onion, minced
4 tomatoes, diced
2 large cloves of garlic, minced
1 teaspoon basil
1 teaspoon thyme
1½ teaspoons red, barley, or Hatcho miso
Dash of pepper, coarsely ground
3 eggs
3 tablespoons tomato paste
¼ cup chopped parsely
Dash of cayenne or tabasco sauce
8 black olives, thinly sliced (optional)
½ cup Parmsan cheese

Bake pie shell at 425° for 7 minutes until partially done, then set aside. Heat a skillet and coat with 4 tablespoons oil. Add onions and sauté for 4 minutes, or until tender. Add the next six ingredients, cover, and cook over low heat for about 5

minutes. Uncover and cook 5 minutes more, or until liquid has evaporated, then set aside to cool for 10 minutes. Meanwhile, combine the eggs in a mixing bowl with the last four ingredients plus 2 tablespoons olive oil; beat until smooth. Gently stir in cooked ingredients, then spoon mixture into pie shell. Decorate, if desired, with olive slices, sprinkle with cheese, and dribble the remaining 1 tablespoon oil over the top. Bake at 375° for about 25 minures, or until quiche has set. Delicious hot or cold.

Quick Cheese & Onion Quiche with Miso

SERVES 6

2 teaspoons oil
¾ onion, thinly sliced
A 9-inch pie shell, uncooked
4 eggs, one of which is separated into yolk and white
6 ounces Swiss cheese, grated
¾ cup half-and-half cream
1½ teaspoons red miso, creamed in 1 tablespoon hot water
Dash of nutmeg

Preheat oven to 350°. Heat a skillet and coat with the oil. Add onions and sauté for about 3 minutes, or until limp. Line a 9-inch pie pan with the pastry shell, then brush lightly with egg white. Place alternate layers of onion and cheese in shell until both ingredients are used up. Mix together remaining eggs, cream, and softened miso; pour over cheese-and-onions, then top with a sprinkling of nutmeg. Bake for 45 minutes.

Miso-Noodle Gratin

SERVES 4 TO 6

5 tablespoons butter
2/3 onion, thinly sliced
4 small mushrooms, sliced
5 ounces deep-fried tofu, thinly sliced (optional)
2½ tablespoons red, barley, or Hatcho miso
7 ounces (*soba*) buckwheat noodles or macaroni, cooked
Dash of pepper
3 tablespoons whole-wheat flour
2 cups milk (soy or dairy)
2 tablespoons grated cheese
2 tablespoons bread crumbs or bread crumb flakes
2 tablespoons minced parsley

Preheat oven to 350°. Melt 4 teaspoons butter in a skillet. Add onion and sauté for 1 minute. Add mushrooms and deep-fried tofu, and sauté for 2 minutes more. Stir in 1½ teaspoons miso, the cooked noodles, and pepper; sauté for 1 minute more and remove from heat.

Using 3 tablespoons butter, the flour, 2 tablespoons miso and the milk, prepare a Miso White Sauce (p.114). Stir in the noodle-vegetable mixture, then transfer to a lightly buttered gratin dish, casserole, or baking pan. Sprinkle with cheese and bread crumbs, and dot with the remaining 2 teaspoons butter. Bake for 15 minutes, or until lightly browned. Serve topped with a sprinkling of minced parsley.

Noodles & Eggs with Miso White Sauce Au Gratin

SERVES 3

2 tablespoons butter
1 onion, thinly sliced
1 cup Miso White Sauce (p. 114; seasoned with 1½ table-
    spoons miso)
3 ounces (buckwheat) noodles, cooked (p. 58), drained, and
    cut into 4-inch lengths
3 hard-boiled eggs, shelled and cut lengthwise into halves
2 tablespoons Parmesan cheese
2 tablespoons minced parsley

Preheat oven to 350°. Melt the butter in a skillet, add onion, and sauté for 4 minutes. Remove from heat, combine with noodles and one-half the white sauce, and spoon into an oiled casserole or loaf pan. Arrange egg halves atop noodles, top with remaining white sauce, and sprinkle with Parmesan; bake for 20 minutes or until nicely browned. Delicious either hot or chilled, topped with a sprinkling of parsley.

Tomatoes Stuffed with Eggs and Miso

SERVES 4

2 large, firm tomatoes, unpeeled
2 hard-boiled eggs, diced
¼ cup bread crumbs
1 tablespoon red, barley, or Hatcho miso
1 tablespoon minced parsley
1 tablespoon butter
Dash of pepper
3 tablespoons Parmesan cheese

Preheat oven to 350°. Slice off tops of tomatoes and scoop out insides, reserving one half of the latter for use in other cooking. Combine the remaining scooped-out portion with the diced eggs and the next five ingredients. Add 1 tablespoon Parmesan cheese and mix well, then use mixture to stuff tomatoes. Place tomatoes in an oiled loaf pan, sprinkle with the remaining 2 tablespoons Parmesan, and bake for 20 minutes. Cool to room temperature before serving.

For variety, pour 1 cup Miso White Sauce (p. 114; seasoned with 4 teaspoons red miso) over tomatoes in loaf pan. Top with the Parmesan and 2 tablespoons bread crumbs, then bake until nicely browned.

Miso-Creamed Celery Casserole

SERVES 4 TO 6

2 cups sliced celery stalks and leaves
2 cups water or stock
6 tablespoons butter
6 tablespoons flour
¼ cup red, barley, or Hatcho miso
2 cups milk (soy or dairy)
Dash of pepper
4 slices whole-wheat bread (preferably several days old)
¼ cup grated or Parmesan cheese; or ¼ to ½ cup sherry,
    sake, or white wine

Combine celery and water in a saucepan, bring to a boil, and simmer uncovered for 10 to 12 minutes. Cool briefly, then purée in a blender until smooth.

Preheat oven to 350°. Melt ¼ cup butter in a large saucepan, then use the flour, 2 tablespoons miso, milk, puréed celery, and pepper to make a Miso White Sauce (p. 114); remove from heat.

Spread 2 tablespoons each butter and miso over one surface of each piece of bread. Break bread into small chunks and place into a lightly buttered casserole. Pour in white sauce and allow to stand for 1 to 2 hours. Top with the cheese or sherry, and bake uncovered for 30 minutes, or until nicely browned.

Cooked rice or noodles may be substituted for the bread, and the 2 tablespoons miso and butter may be added directly to the white sauce.

Curried Green Rice Casserole with Miso

SERVES 3

2 eggs, lightly beaten
¾ cup milk (soy or dairy)
2½ to 3 tablespoons red, barley, or Hatcho miso
2 cups cooked Brown Rice (p. 57)
½ cup minced parsley
½ cup grated cheese
1 onion, minced
¼ teaspoon curry powder
1 clove of garlic, crushed or minced
1 tablespoon butter

Preheat oven to 325°. Combine the eggs, milk and miso, mixing well, then stir in the next six ingredients. Coat a casserole or baking tin with the butter and spoon in the curried-rice mixture. Bake for about 40 minutes, or until nicely browned. For best flavor, allow to cool for 6 to 8 hours. Serve hot or cold.

For variety, sauté onion for several minutes before use and/or substitute ½ cup corn kernels for one-half the onion.

Baked Potatoes with Miso

2 potatoes, baked in their skins
2 tablespoons butter
2 teaspoons of one of the following:
    Red, barley, or Hatcho miso
    Finger Lickin' Miso (p. 42)
    Leek or Onion Miso (pp. 64 and 70)
    Cheese Miso (p. 70)
Sour cream or Creamy Tofu Dressing (with Cheese &
    Garlic, p. 85) (optional)
Minced chives, grated cheese, or parsley (optional)

Cut open the hot potatoes and spoon in butter and miso. Mix lightly, and, if desired, top with sour cream and chives. Serve hot or cold.

Or, substitute 4 teaspoons mellow white miso for the miso above.

Miso Sautéed & Simmered with Vegetables

The recipes that follow are only a few of many delicious possibilities. Experiment using our basic techniques applied to your favorite vegetable cookery.

SAUTÉED PREPARATIONS

Most types of Japanese-style miso toppings—especially Sesame Miso (p. 62), Walnut Miso (p. 61), and Miso Sauté (p. 65)—make excellent additions to sautéed vegetable dishes. Note the use of miso in the cooking technique called *nitsuké* wherein vegetables are first sautéed until just barely tender, then steamed or simmered in a little water—and miso —until done.

Mushrooms Sautéed in Miso   SERVES 2 OR 3

1 tablespoon oil
12 fresh (*shiitaké*) mushrooms, cut into halves or quarters
1 tablespoon red, barley, or Hatcho miso
1 to 1½ teaspoons honey
1 teaspoon shoyu
¼ teaspoon freshly grated or ½ teaspoon powdered ginger-root (optional)
1 tablespoon ground roasted sesame seeds (p. 54) (optional)

Heat a skillet and coat with the oil. Add mushrooms and sauté for 2 to 3 minutes. Stir in the next three (or four) ingredients and sauté for 1 minute more. Serve hot or cold, topped, if desired, with a sprinkling of sesame seeds.

VARIATION

*Eggplants Sautéed in Miso. Use 4 small Japanese eggplants, cut lengthwise into halves, then diagonally into 3/8-inch-thick slices. Sauté in 2 tablespoons oil over medium heat for 5 minutes, then reduce heat to low and proceed as above.

Miso-Cooked Carrots   SERVES 2 OR 3
with Wheat Germ and Nuts

2 tablespoons oil
1 carrot, sliced into thin rounds (1½ cups)
4 teaspoons red, barley, or Hatcho miso, thinned with 3 tablespoons water
¼ cup (toasted) wheat germ
¼ cup sunflower seeds or chopped nutmeats
½ teaspoon grated orange rind (optional)

Heat the oil in a wok or skillet. Add carrots and sauté for 3 minutes. Mix in creamed miso and cook for 4 minutes, or until liquid is absorbed or evaporated. Remove from heat and stir in remaining ingredients. Serve hot or cold.

Eggplants Szechwan   SERVES 4

3 tablespoons oil
4 small eggplants (about 12 ounces total), cut into ½-inch cubes
1 clove of garlic, minced or crushed
1½ teaspoons minced gingerroot
3 tablespoons chopped leek greens or green onions
Dash of (7-spice) red pepper or tabasco sauce
½ cup stock or water
2 tablespoons red, barley, or Hatcho miso
½ teaspoon honey
1½ teaspoons sesame oil
1½ teaspoons vinegar

Heat a skillet and coat with the oil. Add eggplants and sauté for 3 minutes, then drain briefly over skillet and transfer to a separate container. Now add to the skillet: garlic, gingerroot, 2 tablespoons chopped leek greens, and enough red pepper to give a spicy hot flavor; sauté for 15 seconds. Mix in stock, miso and honey, and bring to a boil. Add eggplants, simmer for 1 minute, and turn off heat. Sprinkle with sesame oil and vinegar, and garnish with the remaining 1 tablespoon chopped leek greens.

Eggplant with Sesame & Miso Sauce
SERVES 4

6 tablespoons oil
2½ to 3 cups eggplant (¾-inch cubes)
3 tablespoons red, barley, or Hatcho miso
2 tablespoons sesame butter
1 tablespoon honey
1 tablespoon white wine, sake, or *mirin*
6½ tablespoons stock or water
½ teaspoon grated or 1 teaspoon powdered gingerroot
4 lettuce leaves

Heat a wok or skillet and coat with 5 tablespoons oil. Add eggplants and sauté for 3 to 4 minutes, then transfer to a separate container.

Reheat skillet and coat with remaining 1 tablespoon oil. Add miso and the next 5 ingredients. Cook, stirring constantly, for 1 to 2 minutes to form a smooth sauce. Mix in cooked eggplant and remove from heat. For best flavor, serve chilled, mounded on lettuce leaves.

Cauliflower & Carrots with Miso & Cheese
SERVES 2 OR 3

2½ tablespoons butter
½ cup thin rounds of leek or scallion
2 tablespoons red, barley, or Hatcho miso
½ cauliflower, separated into flowerets, steamed for 10 minutes
1 carrot, cut into thin half moons and steamed for 15 minutes
3 tablespoons grated cheese
2 tablespoons minced parsley
Dash of pepper

Melt the butter in a skillet. Add leek rounds, miso and steamed vegetables, and sauté for 2 to 3 minutes. Turn off heat and top immediately with cheese and parsley. Season with pepper. Serve hot.

Sautéed Leeks & Carrots with Sesame Miso
SERVES 3 OR 4

¼ cup sesame butter
3 tablespoons red, barley, or Hatcho miso
2 tablespoons water
2 teaspoons oil
2½ cups thinly sliced leeks or onions
1 cup slivered or grated carrots

Combine the first three ingredients, mixing well. Heat oil in a skillet or wok. Add leeks and carrots and sauté for 4 to 5 minutes. Add sesame-miso mixture and cook, stirring constantly, for 1 minute more. Serve as is, or as a topping for grain dishes or tofu.

Green Peppers & Tofu Sautéed with Miso
SERVES 2

3½ tablespoons red, barley, or Hatcho miso
½ cup stock or water
2½ to 3 teaspoons honey
2 teaspoons sake or white wine
7 ounces deep-fried tofu, cut into ½-inch strips
2 tablespoons oil
1½ teaspoons minced garlic
5 green peppers, cut lengthwise into sixths
1 large onion, thinly sliced

Combine the first five ingredients in a saucepan and bring to a boil. Cover and simmer for 5 minutes, then remove from heat.

Heat a wok or skillet and coat with the oil. Add garlic and sauté for 30 seconds. Increase heat to high, add green peppers and onion, and sauté for 3 minutes more. Add deep-fried tofu and any remaining cooking broth, then cook, stirring constantly, for 1 minute. Serve hot or cold.

Green Beans & Onions in Spicy Miso Sauce
SERVES 3

1 tablespoon oil
1 clove of garlic, minced or crushed
½ onion, thinly sliced
20 green beans, parboiled until just tender
1½ tablespoons red, barley, or Hatcho miso, dissolved in ½ cup water or stock
¾ teaspoon honey
1½ teaspoons sake or white wine
Dash of (7-spice) red pepper or tabasco sauce
2 teaspoons cornstarch, arrowroot, or *kuzu*, dissolved in 3 tablespoons water

Heat a wok or skillet and coat with the oil. Add garlic and sauté for 30 seconds, then add onion and sauté for 4 minutes. Add green beans and sauté for 1 minute more. Stir in the next four ingredients and bring to a boil. Add dissolved cornstarch and simmer, stirring constantly, for about 1 minute, or until thick. Serve as a side dish or as a topping for (deep-fried) noodles.

Potatoes Sautéed with Miso

1½ to 2 tablespoons oil
6 small potatoes, sliced into thin rounds (3½ cups)
½ cup water
2 tablespoons red, barley, or Hatcho miso
Dash of pepper
2 tablespoons minced parsley and/or grated cheese

Heat a large skillet or wok and coat with the oil. Add potatoes and sauté for 4 minutes. Add water, cover, and simmer for 5 to 6 minutes. Mix in miso and cook, stirring constantly, for 1 to 2 minutes, or until most of liquid has evaporated. Serve seasoned with pepper and topped with parsley.

Sweet & Sour Cabbage with Miso
SERVES 2 OR 3

1½ teaspoons oil
1 red pepper, seeded and minced
11 ounces cabbage, chopped into 1½-inch squares
2½ tablespoons red, barley, or Hatcho miso
1 teaspoon honey
2 teaspoons vinegar
2 teaspoons sesame oil

Heat a wok or skillet and coat with the oil. Add red pepper and sauté for 30 seconds, or until color changes. Add cabbage and sauté for 3 to 4 minutes, then add the next three ingredients and sauté for 1 minute more. Sprinkle with the sesame oil and remove from heat. Serve hot or cold.

Land & Sea Vegetables with Miso
SERVES 4

2 tablespoons sesame oil
1 large onion, thinly sliced
1 carrot, grated or slivered
1 cup thin half-moons of lotus root
¾ cup dry *hijiki*, soaked for 15 minutes in water to cover, rinsed and drained
2½ tablespoons red, barley, or Hatcho miso
¾ cup water

Heat a skillet or wok and coat with the oil. Add onion, carrot, and lotus root and sauté for 4 minutes. Add *hijiki* and sauté for 3 minutes more. Stir in miso and water and bring to a boil. Cover and simmer for 10 minutes. Serve hot or cold.

Cultivated shiitaké

FRIED AND STIR-FRIED PREPARATIONS

Fried Eggplants Shigiyaki
(*Nasu no Nabé Shigiyaki*)
SERVES 4

One of Japan's favorite miso recipes, this is a close relative of the equally popular Grilled Eggplants Shigiyaki described on page 146. The key to the fine flavor lies in choosing tender young eggplants.

4 Japanese eggplants, each 1¼ inches in diameter, or 2 small Western eggplants
2 tablespoons red, barley, or Hatcho miso
1 tablespoon honey
1½ teaspoons sake or white wine
¼ teaspoon grated gingerroot
1 tablespoon water
3 to 4 tablespoons oil
1 to 2 teaspoons roasted sesame seeds or Parmesan cheese

Peel eggplants lengthwise so that ½-inch-wide peeled strips alternate with ½-inch-wide unpeeled strips. Soak in water for 10 minutes.

Meanwhile combine miso, honey, sake, gingerroot and water in a small skillet and simmer over low heat, stirring constantly, for 3 to 4 minutes until smooth and slightly thickened. Remove from heat.

Pat eggplants dry with a dishtowel. Cut Japanese eggplants lengthwise into halves, Western eggplants into ½-inch-thick diagonal sections. Heat the oil in a skillet. Add eggplant slices, cover, and fry for 2 minutes or until golden brown. Turn and repeat on second side. Arrange slices on a large serving plate, spread with the miso sauce and sprinkle with sesame seeds. For best flavor, serve chilled.

For variety, cut eggplants into ¾-inch-thick rounds and pierce each side in 2 or 3 places with chopsticks or a fork. Fry in oil as above, then serve topped with White Nerimiso (p. 61) or Kinomé Miso (p. 63) and, if desired, a sprinkling of roasted sesame seeds.

Fried Eggplants with Sweet Simmered Miso (*Yaki-nasu*)

SERVES 4

4 small eggplants, each about 4 inches long
1½ tablespoons sesame oil
2 tablespoons Sesame-(p. 62) or Walnut Miso (p. 61)

Cut eggplants lengthwise into halves and score the outer surfaces in a checkerboard pattern to a depth of 1/3 inch. (If using larger Western eggplants, cut into ¾-inch-thick half moons.) Heat a skillet and coat with the oil. Add eggplants and fry over low heat on both sides until nicely browned. Coat flat surface with a thin layer of miso. Serve hot or cold.

Deep-fried Tofu and Vegetables with Miso-Sweet & Sour Sauce

SERVES 4 TO 5

2 tablespoons oil
1 clove of garlic, crushed or minced
1 small onion, thinly sliced
2 tomatoes, diced; or 1 cup cherry tomatoes, cut into halves
1 green pepper, cut into 1-inch squares
1½ cups Pineapple Sweet & Sour Sauce (p. 115)
7 ounces deep-fried tofu, cut into 1-inch cubes

Heat the oil in a large skillet or wok. Add garlic and onion, and stir-fry over high heat for 2 minutes. Add tomatoes, green pepper and sauce. Cook, stirring constantly, for about 1 minute until thick. Mix in deep-fried tofu and remove from heat. Serve chilled. (To serve hot, increase amount of honey and vinegar in sauce by 1 tablespoon each.)

Fried Sweet Potatoes with Sesame Miso

SERVES 2 OR 3

1 sweet potato (6 inches long)
2 teaspoons oil
2½ to 3 tablespoons Sesame Miso (p. 62)

Steam sweet potato for 30 minutes, then cut into ½-inch-thick rounds. Heat oil in a large skillet. Add rounds and fry for 2 minutes on each side, or until nicely browned. Transfer onto absorbent paper (or a large plate) and allow to cool for several minutes. Coat one surface of each round with the miso. Serve as a side dish or hors d'œuvre.

NABÉ AND SIMMERED PREPARATIONS

Miso is used as the basis for the dipping sauce in a number of Japan's famous *nabémono*, the do-it-yourself one-pot cookery prepared at the table. In dishes known as *Miso-ni*, vegetables (or seafoods) are simmered slowly in a rich, slightly sweet miso sauce. Most Miso Sauces (p. 113) or Toppings (p. 60) can be used with excellent results over vegetables simmered until tender in dashi or stock.

Kabocha Simmered in Miso (*Kabocha no Miso-ni*)

SERVES 4

2 tablespoons sesame oil
2 onions, thinly sliced
1 pound *kabocha*, pumpkin, or squash, cubed
1 cup water
¼ cup red, barley, or Hatcho miso, thinned in ½ cup warm water

Heat a wok or skillet and coat with the oil. Add onions and sauté for 5 minutes. Add pumpkin and sauté for 3 minutes more. Stir in water and bring to a boil. Cover and simmer for 30 minutes, or until tender. Stir in thinned miso and simmer uncovered for about 5 minutes, or until liquid has been absorbed or evaporated.

VARIATION

*Other Types of Miso-ni: Substitute for the *kabocha* in the above recipe an equal weight of any of the following: potatoes or sweet potatoes, red radishes, turnips, bamboo shoots, butterbur. Serve hot or cold.

Taro or Sweet Potatoes Simmered in Miso

SERVES 4

1 pound peeled taro or unpeeled sweet potatoes, cut into bite-sized pieces
3 tablespoons red, barley, or Hatcho miso
1 to 1½ tablespoons honey
1¼ cups water, stock, or dashi (p. 56)
3 tablespoons bonito flakes

Combine all ingredients in a pot or saucepan, cover, and bring to a boil. Simmer for 15 minutes, then uncover and simmer, stirring occasionally, for 5 to 10 minutes more, or until most of the liquid has evaporated. Allow to cool before serving.

Pumpkin Simmered in Sweetened Miso

SERVES 3 OR 4

14 ounces *kabocha,* pumpkin, or squash, seeded and cut
    into 1½-inch squares
¾ cup water, stock, or dashi (p. 56)
1½ to 2 tablespoons red, barley, or Hatcho miso
2 to 3 teaspoons honey
1½ tablespoons bonito flakes (optional)

Combine *kabocha* and water in a saucepan and bring to a boil.
Cover and simmer for 10 minutes. Stir in remaining ingredients and simmer for about 8 minutes more, or until *kabocha* is tender and all but ¼ cup liquid has been absorbed or
evaporated. For richest flavor, serve chilled.

    For variety, omit bonita flakes and add 1½ tablespoons
butter and a dash of nutmeg. Serve topped with Tofu Mayonnaise (p. 86) and a little minced (fresh) basil or parsley.

Sautéed Potatoes Simmered in Sweet Miso

SERVES 2

1 tablespoon oil
4 small potatoes, cut crosswise into halves, then into thin
    wedges (1¾ cups)
1 tablespoon sweet white or 2 teaspoons mellow white miso
1½ teaspoons red or barley miso
½ teaspoon honey
2½ teaspoons sake or white wine
¾ teaspoon minced gingerroot
¼ cup water, stock, or dashi (p. 56)

Heat a skillet and coat with the oil. Add potatoes and sauté
for 3 minutes. Mix in remaining ingredients and bring to a
boil. Cover and simmer over low heat for 10 minutes. Serve
hot or cold.

    For variety, substitute eggplants or 5 ounces deep-fried
tofu for the potatoes.

Turnips with Sesame Miso Sauce

SERVES 4

6 small (*kabu*) turnips, with greens
3 cups dashi (p. 56), stock, or water
2/3 cup Sesame Miso Sauce (p. 117)

Cut turnip roots lengthwise into halves, combine with dashi
in a saucepan, and bring to a boil. Cover and simmer for 15
minutes, or until tender. Remove from heat and drain, reserving liquid for use in sauce.

    Parboil turnip greens for 2 to 3 minutes in lightly salted
water; drain in a colander. Squeeze to remove excess liquid,
then cut into 1-inch lengths. Divide leaves and turnip halves
among individual bowls and top with the sauce.

    Daikon, radishes, and other root vegetables may be
substituted for the turnips.

Furofuki Daikon

SERVES 4

8 *daikon* rounds, each 2½ to 3 inches in diameter and ¾ inch
    thick
½ cup Orange-Sesame Miso Sauce (p.115) or
    Subtly Sweet Leek Miso (p. 70)

Combine *daikon* rounds with water (or dashi; p. 56) to cover
in a saucepan, bring to a boil, and simmer for 20 to 30
minutes, or until *daikon* is very tender. Drain well and
arrange rounds on serving plates. Place a large dollop of the
miso atop each round. Serve hot or cold.

    For variety, prepare as for Miso Oden (p. 141). Cook 4
daikon rounds together with 4 taro and 4 *konnyaku* triangles
in a *nabé* pot. Place the miso sauce in a cup at the center of
pot and use for dipping.

Daikon Rounds with Orange-Onion Miso

SERVES 2 OR 3

4 teaspoons oil, one of which may be sesame
6 *daikon* or turnip rounds, each 1 inch thick and 2½ inches
    in diameter
1 cup water or stock
¼ teaspoon salt
1 onion, minced
1½ tablespoons red, barley, or Hatcho miso
1 tablespoon sesame butter (optional)
½ teaspoon grated orange rind

Heat a large skillet and coat with 1 tablespoon (regular) oil.
Add *daikon* and fry for about 2½ minutes on each side, or
until nicely browned. Add water and bring to a boil. Cover
and simmer for 30 minutes, or until only several tablespoons
of liquid remain. Sprinkle rounds with salt and transfer to
serving plates; reserve liquid in skillet.

    Heat a second small skillet and coat with 1 teaspoon
(sesame) oil. Add onion and sauté for 5 minutes, then transfer
to the first skillet. Mix in miso and, if used, sesame butter.
Bring to a boil and cook, stirring constantly, for about 1
minute. Spoon this sauce over *daikon* rounds and top with a
sprinkling of orange rind. Serve hot or cold. Also delicious on
toast.

Miso Oden

In Japan, this popular wintertime dish is sold by street venders out of pushcarts or prepared in homes, particularly on special occasions.

Choose one of the following sauces:
    Orange-Sesame Miso Sauce (p.115)
    Gingerroot-Miso Barbecue Sauce (p.118)
    Rich Red Nerimiso (p.61)
    Yuzu Miso (p.62)
12 ounces tofu (regular or grilled), cut into 1- by 3- by ½-inch strips
1 cake of *konnyaku*
4 inches large *daikon*, cut into ½-inch-thick half moons
A 5-inch square of *kombu*, wiped clean; or substitute ½ teaspoon salt

Place the miso sauce into a small heat-resistant cup. Spear each tofu strip with two (6-inch bamboo) skewers or a fork. Rub *konnyaku* well with salt, rinse, cut crosswise into ½-inch-wide strips, and skewer each piece. Parboil *daikon*, then skewer each piece.

Place *kombu* in a casserole and set the cup of miso atop it. Arrange skewered ingredients around the cup with handles of skewers resting on rim of casserole (fig. 23). Add boiling water to just cover ingredients, return to the boil over medium heat, then simmer for 3 minutes. Dip skewered ingredients into miso sauce before eating.

For variety, add parboiled skewered pieces of cauliflower, potato, sweet potato, yam, or turnip.

Eggplants & Corn Simmered in Miso

2 tablespoons oil
4 small (Japanese) eggplants, uncut and unpeeled; or 1 medium-sized Western eggplant, cut lengthwise into fourths
1 cup fresh corn kernels
1½ tablespoons red, barley, or Hatcho miso, dissolved in ¾ cup water
1 teaspoon honey
Dash of (7-spice) red pepper or tabasco sauce

Heat a heavy pot or casserole and coat with the oil. Add eggplants and fry over low heat for 7 to 8 minutes on each side. Add remaining ingredients and bring to a boil. Re-cover and simmer for 5 minutes. Serve hot.

If using Western eggplants, increase oil to 3 tablespoons. Place pieces in pot with skin down and fry for 8 minutes, then fry for 2 minutes on each of the cut surfaces. Add remaining ingredients and proceed as above.

Spinach with Miso White Sauce

¼ cup water
1 pound spinach or *horenso*, washed, tough stems removed
3½ tablespoons butter
4½ tablespoons whole-wheat flour
2 tablespoons red, barley, or Hatcho miso
1½ cups milk (soy or dairy)
Dash of pepper

Combine water and spinach in a large skillet. Bring to a boil, stirring constantly, and cook for 3 to 4 minutes, or until spinach is just tender. Drain briefly and chop into 1-inch lengths.

Using the butter and remaining ingredients, prepare a Miso White Sauce (p.114). Add spinach to the sauce and serve hot or cold.

Fig. 23. Miso Oden

Doténabé

In Japanese, a *doté* is an earthen embankment or "shoulder." The reddish-brown miso in this preparation resembles an embankment around the *nabé's* rim until, that is, it dissolves into the simmering broth. The most famous Doténabé contain oysters, for which we substitute deep-fried tofu.

2½ cups dashi (p. 56) or stock
1 small potato, cut into quarters
1/3 cup shaved burdock root, soaked (p. 53) and drained
4 *daikon* rounds, each 2 inches in diameter and ½ inch thick
¼ cup red, barley, or Hatcho miso
1 to 1½ tablespoons honey
2½ tablespoons sake, white wine, or *mirin*
1 tablespoon bonito flakes (optional)
½ cake of *konnyaku*, torn into small pieces and rubbed lightly with salt
5 ounces deep-fried tofu, cut into 8 pieces
2 hard-boiled eggs, shelled; or 4 quail eggs
1 Chinese cabbage leaf, cut crosswise into 1½-inch-wide strips
1 leek, cut diagonally into 2-inch lengths
2 to 3 teaspoons hot mustard
Dash of *sansho* pepper
1 cup cooked noodles (optional)

Combine the first four ingredients in a saucepan and bring to a boil. Cover and simmer for 15 minutes. Meanwhile combine the miso, honey, 1 tablespoon sake and, if used, the bonita flakes in a skillet. Cook over low heat, stirring constantly, for 2 to 3 minutes, or until firm.

Ring the inner rim of an 8- to 10-inch diameter casserole or *nabé* pot with a thin, 1-inch-wide layer of the miso. Transfer cooked vegetables to casserole together with *konnyaku* and the next four ingredients. Add remaining 1½ tablespoons sake and enough of the dashi to fill casserole to ¼ inch above bottom of miso ring. Place casserole on a tabletop burner, cover, and bring to a boil. Simmer for about 15 minutes, or until flavors are well married and miso has melted into broth. Invite each guest to remove ingredients with chopsticks and transfer them to an individual bowl. (Cut egg lengthwise into halves.) Spoon on a little of the hot broth and serve topped with a dab of mustard and a sprinkling of *sansho* pepper.

Toward the end of the meal, drop cooked noodles into broth remaining in casserole and simmer until heated through. Serve in individual bowls, topped with the remaining broth.

For a richer flavor, allow cooked ingredients to stand in *nabé* overnight, then serve the next day, chilled or reheated.

Konnyaku-Twists

Farmhouse Nishime with Miso
SERVES 8

A tasty Japanese vegetable stew, Nishime is a popular dish at New Year's, equinox celebrations, and other national holidays. Farmhouse Nishime often employs homemade miso as the basic seasoning, whereas in restaurants and city homes, shoyu is generally used. Both varieties are usually prepared in large enough quantities to last for up to one week, during which time the flavors marry and improve.

Many recipes include only 3 or 4 of the vegetables listed below, so omit or substitute according to what is available. Adjust the amount of cooking liquid accordingly. Some cooks prefer to cook each of the ingredients separately for a different length of time in a broth seasoned to match the food's unique character. Each cooked ingredient is allowed to marinate overnight in its own broth, but is served without broth in a bowl together with all the other ingredients.

3 cups dashi (p. 56), stock, or water
8 to 10 tablespoons red, barley, or Hatcho miso
3½ to 4½ tablespoons honey or *mirin*
3 tablespoons sake or white wine
½ teaspoon salt
1 cake of *konnyaku*, cut crosswise into ¼-inch-thick pieces
1 carrot, cut into large random chunks
½ burdock root, cut lengthwise into halves, then into 1½-inch lengths and parboiled for 10 minutes
1 large taro or potato, cut into eighths
2 inches *daikon*, cut into half moons
½ lotus root, cut into half moons
8 inches *kombu*, wiped clean with a moist cloth and cut crosswise into 1-inch-wide strips
1 small bamboo shoot, cut into large random chunks
3 *(shiitaké)* mushrooms, cut into quarters
10½ ounces deep-fried tofu, doused (p. 56) and cut into bite-sized pieces
12 ounces tofu, cut into large triangles (optional)
8 sprigs of *kinomé*

Combine the first five ingredients in a large pot or casserole and bring to a boil. Meanwhile, cut a slit lengthwise down the center of each small piece of *konnyaku* and thread one end up through the slit and back again (above). Add *konnyaku* and next eight ingredients to the broth, and return to the boil. Reduce heat to low, cover pot, and simmer for about 40 minutes. Add tofu, stir vegetables so that uppermost ones are transferred to bottom of pot, re-cover, and continue simmering until all but about ¾ cup of broth has been absorbed or evaporated. Remove from heat and allow to cool for at least 5, preferably 24 hours. Divide ingredients among individual serving bowls, pour on remaining liquid, and garnish with a sprig of *kinomé*.

Daikon

Boiled Potatoes with Onion Miso
SERVES 2

4 small potatoes, boiled in their skins until tender
¼ cup Leek or Onion Miso (p. 64 or 70)
Butter or Parmesan Cheese (optional)

Cut potatoes into bite-sized pieces (or mash). Serve hot or cold, topped with the remaining ingredients. A favorite in Japanese farmhouses.

Potatoes Simmered in Miso
SERVES 4

10 small potatoes (1 pound), peeled and cut into halves
1¾ cups water
1½ tablespoons bonito flakes
3½ tablespoons red, barely, or Hatcho miso
1 tablespoon honey
1 tablespoon *mirin*, sake, or white wine

Combine the first three ingredients in a large saucepan and bring to a boil. Cover and simmer for 20 minutes, or until potatoes are tender. Mix in the last three ingredients and simmer, uncovered, for 10 minutes more. Cover and allow to stand for at least 4 hours, preferably overnight. Serve cold or reheated.

For variety, deep-fry potatoes (without batter) before simmering. Or substitute for the potatoes 5 small taro (whole) and 2 inches lotus root, the latter cut into 3/8-inch-thick rounds.

Miso in Grilled Dishes

The process of broiling or grilling miso—especially over a barbecue, campfire, or charcoal brazier—imparts a heart-warming, savory aroma and flavor to both the miso and the food it coats. Why not start by trying a traditional Western favorite, corn-on-the-cob, then move on to shish kebab and Japan's famous Dengaku? See also Broiled Miso Toppings (pp. 71–72).

Grilled Corn-on-the-Cob with Miso   SERVES 2

This savory dish, generally prepared with shoyu rather than miso, is a favorite throughout Japan where it is served freshly grilled from small, sidewalk vending booths.

2 ears of fresh corn
2 teaspoons red, barley, or Hatcho miso
4 teaspoons butter

Grill, broil, or barbecue ears of corn until nicely speckled. Spread on miso using a small rubber spatula or a butter knife, then rebroil for about 1 minute until fragrant. Butter corn and serve piping hot.

If you prefer to steam the corn, spread on miso and butter just before serving. For variety, mix about ¼ teaspoon crushed garlic with the miso.

Shish Kebab with Miso Sauce   SERVES 4

Ingredients for Skewering: Use four or more
    5 ounces deep-fried tofu, cut into bite-sized cubes
    4 green peppers, cut into 2-inch triangles
    8 mushrooms
    1 apple, cut into bite-sized chunks or rounds
    8 chunks of firm pineapple
    4 small blanched onions
    4 small firm tomatoes
    1 celery stalk or cucumber, cut into bite-sized sections
¾ cup Miso Shish Kebab Sauce (p. 118) or 2/3 cup Teriyaki Sauce (p. 118)

Place basic ingredients in a shallow pan and pour on sauce. Marinate for 1 hour, turning ingredients several times. Skewer pieces on 4 to 8 skewers and broil for 2 to 3 minutes, basting occasionally, until nicely speckled and fragrant.

Dengaku Hoshi

Dengaku   SERVES 4

Dengaku, one of Japan's oldest and most famous types of miso cuisine, is prepared by charcoal broiling skewered, bite-sized pieces of various foods. Each piece is then coated on one or both sides with a thin layer of miso and the skewers are rebroiled briefly until the miso is speckled and fragrant. Although the best known type of Dengaku is prepared with small pieces of firmly-pressed tofu, other varieties are made with eggplants, taro, sweet potatoes, mushrooms, and a host of other tasty ingredients listed below. In restaurants, the foods are generally pierced with tiny bamboo skewers, broiled over a charcoal brazier, and topped with one or more types of Sweet Simmered Miso. In farmhouses, the tofu or vegetables are skewered on 18-inch-long slats of bamboo, which are poked at a slant into the ashes around a bed of glowing coals in the living room open-hearth fireplace. A hand's width above the embers, the foods imbibe the fragrance of woodsmoke as they sizzle and broil. Here homemade barley or red miso is often used as the topping.

The two Chinese characters which form the word *Dengaku* mean "rice paddy" and "music." It is said that the name originated about 600 years ago when an ancient form of folk drama consisting of music and dance was popular in Japan's rural villages. In one famous play using a rice paddy as its setting, a Buddhist priest mounted a single stilt (resembling a pogo stick) which was called a "heron's leg." Precariously balanced, this character was called Dengaku Hoshi, and he did a dance known as the *dengaku* or "music in the rice

144

paddy." The newly conceived grilled cuisine, initially prepared by piercing each tofu cake with a single skewer, apparently reminded the people of the dengaku dancer, and the tasty preparation soon became known as Dengaku.

Dengaku first became popular throughout Japan in the early 1600s, and by 1775 it had become fashionable for tea shops and way stations in Tokyo and Kyoto to serve this delicacy, often together with Tea Ceremony Cuisine. Until the late 1900s, many tofu shops prepared and delivered Dengaku to order.

The basic recipe that follows is that for grilled Tofu Dengaku. The use of other basic ingredients and cooking techniques are discribed as variations. Additional variations on the basic Tofu Dengaku method can be found in *The Book of Tofu.*

Miso Topping: Use a total of ¼ to ½ cup of one or more of the following types of Sweet Simmered Miso (p. 60):

 Red or White Sweet Simmered Miso
 Yuzu or Lemon Miso
 Kinomé or Egg Yolk Miso
 Seasame or Walnut Miso; or a Nut Butter Topping

12 to 24 ounces tofu, pressed (p. 55)
Garnishes (optional):
 Sprigs of *kinomé*
 Slivered *yuzu* or lemon rind
 Poppy seeds, roasted sesame seeds, or wheat germ
 Hot mustard

Prepare the miso topping(s) in advance and allow to cool. In a large skillet or pan, heat water to about the temperature of a hot bath. Drop in tofu, then cut into pieces about 2 by 1 by ¾ inches. Pierce each piece under water from one end using either 2 round bamboo skewers or 1 flat skewer. Cover a cutting board or flat tray with a dry dishtowel and raise one end of the board. Carefully place skewered tofu on cloth and allow to stand for 15 minutes, or until tofu is firm.

Holding 3 to 4 pieces of skewered tofu at a time side by side over a gas burner, broil for about 30 seconds, or until tofu is lightly speckled. (Or broil tofu on one side over a charcoal brazier or barbecue.) Turn tofu over and coat broiled side with a 1/8-inch-thick layer of topping, then broil second side. Turn again and broil miso topping until it too is speckled, then arrange garnishes, if used, atop miso. Repeat with remaining ingredients. If desired, use a different miso topping with each set of tofu pieces. Serve hot with the meal or as an hors d'œuvre.

Tofu Dengaku is also prepared with grilled or deep-fried tofu.

OTHER INGREDIENTS AND METHODS OF PREPARATION

*****Eggplant:** Cut small Japanese eggplants into ½-inch-thick rounds (or larger Western eggplants into bite-sized half moons or wedges). Soak for 5 to 10 minutes in lightly salted water, drain well, and pat dry with a towel. Pierce both sides in several places with a fork or chop-stick, then brush with

(sesame) oil. Skewer and proceed as above. Top with Sesame (or Gingerroot) Miso and garnish with sesame or poppy seeds. Or use White Sweet Simmered Miso, Egg Yolk Miso, or Kinomé Miso and garnish with *kinomé* sprigs.

*****Sweet Potato, Taro, Daikon, Bamboo Shoots, or Irish Potato:** Cut vegetables into ½-inch-thick ovals or rounds and steam or parboil until just tender. Top with Sesame Miso or Miso Sauté (p. 65).

*****Mushroom:** Skewer large, whole (fresh *shiitake*) mushrooms and broil. Spread both sides with Sweet Simmered Miso, rebroil, and garnish with roasted sesame seeds.

*****Fresh Wheat Gluten:** Cut into tofu-sized rectangles or ½-inch-thick rounds. Broil and top with Sweet Simmered Miso or Kinomé Miso; garnish with *kinomé.*

*****Hard-boiled Eggs, Mochi, Konnyaku, or Green Peppers:** Use (chicken or quail) eggs and uncut *mochi* cakes. Cut *konnyaku* and peppers into bite-sized triangles. Skewer individually or in combinations like shish kebab. Top with Sweet Simmered Miso.

*****Leeks:** Parboil whole leeks for 2 to 3 minutes, cut into 1¼-inch sections, and skewer four sections crosswise. Broil using Walnut Miso.

*****Unskewered Dengaku:** Broil any of the above-mentioned ingredients on both sides until speckled in an oven broiler. Spread upper surface with miso and rebroil briefly.

*****Deep-fried Dengaku:** All varieties of tofu, yuba, and wheat gluten are most commonly prepared in this way, but other ingredients may also be used. Roll pieces in flour, dip in lightly beaten egg, and roll in bread crumbs. Skewer and deep-fry until crisp, then serve topped with Sweet Simmered Miso. Or skewer first, dip into tempura batter (or leave uncoated), and deep-fry.

*****Sautéed and Butter-fried Dengaku:** Sauté eggplant rounds on both sides and serve topped with Sesame Miso. Or butter-fry mushrooms or tofu on both sides and serve like eggplant.

Tofu Dengaku

Grilled Tofu & Vegetables with Miso White Sauce

SERVES 3 TO 4

At Fugetsu, a Japanese natural-food restaurant in Berkeley, this delicious preparation is served either as an hors d'oeuvre or a main course. The sauce is prepared and kept hot in a double boiler.

2 tender eggplants, cut into ¾-inch-thick rounds and brushed with oil
6 large mushrooms
12 ounces tofu, drained or pressed (p. 55)
1 cup Sweet White Miso Sauce (p. 115)
Dash of green *nori* flakes
Dash of *sansho* pepper
1 to 2 teaspoons roasted sesame seeds

Barbecue or grill eggplants, mushrooms, and tofu for about 3 minutes on each side, or until eggplants are tender and other ingredients are nicely browned. Arrange barbecued ingredients on individual plates, spoon on the hot sauce, and top with a sprinkling of green *nori*, *sansho*, and sesame seeds.

Broiled Sweet Potatoes with Miso Topping

SERVES 2

4 sweet potatoes, steamed until just tender and cut lengthwise into 3/8-inch-thick slices
2 tablespoons butter
2 tablespoons Sweet Simmered Miso (p. 60) or Finger Lickin' Miso (p. 42)

Broil sweet-potato slices until lightly speckled and just fragrant. Spread each slice with butter and a thin layer of the miso. Serve hot or cold.

Grilled Eggplants Shigiyaki (*Nasu no Shigiyaki*)

SERVES 4

The word *shigiyaki* means "grilled snipe." Old cookbooks show that this now famous eggplant dish was originally prepared by stuffing a pickled eggplant with snipe meat, capping the eggplant with a persimmon leaf, and simmering the tender morsel in a seasoned broth. The present version is a close relative of Eggplant Dengaku (p.145) and Fried Eggplants Shigiyaki (p. 138)

4 tender, young Japanese eggplants, cut lengthwise into halves (unpeeled)
1 tablespoon sesame oil
2½ tablespoons of one of the following types of Sweet Simmered Miso (pp. 60 to 65):
    Red or White Sweet Simmered Miso
    Egg Yolk, Kinomé, or Gingerroot Miso
    Sesame or Walnut Miso
Dash of *sansho* pepper

Pierce eggplant halves crosswise with metal skewers, spread cut surface with sesame oil, and broil over a charcoal fire (or stove-top burner) on both sides until nicely speckled. Spread each cut surface with a thin layer of the miso and rebroil quickly until miso is fragrant and speckled. Remove skewers, arrange on individual serving dishes, and top with a sprinkling of the pepper. Serve as a side dish or hors d'œuvre.

VARIATIONS

*Deep-fried Shigiyaki: Cut eggplants into ½-inch-thick rounds, deep-fry, and drain well. Skewer, spread one side with sweet white miso, and score miso in a crisscross pattern with a wet knife. Grill on both sides.
*Savory Shigiyaki: Cut eggplants into ½-inch-thick rounds before skewering, then score both surfaces with a knife or poke with a fork or chopstick. (If using large Western eggplants, cut into bite-sized wedges of an equivalent thickness.) Brush surfaces with oil, skewer, and proceed as above.

Miso in Deep-fried Dishes

Sweet Simmered Miso (p. 60) and most other Miso Toppings are delicious served in small quantities atop tempura or other deep-fried foods. The different varieties of deep-fried Dengaku are described on page 145.

ABOUT DEEP-FRYING

Although deep-fat frying has long been a part of Western cookery, it has never attained the degree of popularity or artistry that it enjoys throughout the Orient, and particularly in Japan. Deep-frying is as common in the typical Japanese kitchen as baking is in the West, while it is faster and uses much less fuel. In only a few minutes, it transforms the simplest fresh vegetables, pieces of tofu, and even leftovers into prize creations. The art of deep-frying is a joy to practice.

For the Japanese, whose diet is still very low in meats, deep-fried foods are an important source of both savory flavor and essential (unsaturated) oils. Some Westerners still have the image of deep-fried foods as being necessarily "greasy," while others believe that heating the oil to high temperatures impairs its nutritional value. Yet anyone who has lived in Japan or dined on tempura knows that deep-frying can yield foods that are remarkably crisp and light. And keeping the oil at its proper temperature, at 350° or less, guarantees its health-giving benefits.

In Japanese, the verb *ageru* means "to deep-fry," and *agé-mono* or "deep-fried things" are the many foods that make up this vast world. The simplest form of deep-frying is called *kara-agé* or "deep-frying without a coating or batter." The three basic types of deep-fried tofu are each prepared in this way. After mastering this technique, you should find no difficulty in preparing fine, crisp tempura.

If you wish to make deep-frying a permanent part of your repertoire of cooking techniques, it is best to start with the proper tools. Most important is the deep-frying pot. While many Westerners use a heavy 3- to 4-quart kettle, or an electric deep-fryer, most Japanese use either a wok (see p. 53) or a heavy-bottomed skillet 2½ to 3 inches deep and 10 to 12 inches in diameter.

For best results use a simple vegetable oil. Japanese prefer rapeseed oil, but Western cooks use soy, corn, or cottonseed oil. Some chefs specializing in vegetable tempura prefer a combination of oils. If 10 to 30 percent sesame oil is added to any of the above basic oils, it will give the foods a delicious, nutty flavor. Other popular combinations are: peanut or corn (70%) and sesame (30%); peanut (75%), sesame (20%), and olive (5%); cotton-seed (85%), olive (10%), and sesame (5%). For a light, crisp texture, avoid the use of animal fats in deep-frying.

Used deep-frying oil should be kept in a sealed jar and stored in a cool, dark place. When sautéing vegetables or frying eggs, you may use some of this oil to impart added flavor to the foods and help use up the oil. When deep-frying, try to use about one part fresh oil and one part used. Dark or thick used oil has a low smoke point and imparts a poor flavor. Foods deep-fried in used oil only are not as light and crisp as they could be. Pour oil from the storage jar into the deep-fryer carefully so that any sediment remains at the bottom of the jar. Then add fresh oil to fill the wok or skillet to a depth of 1½ to 2 inches.

Maintaining the oil at the proper temperature is the most important part of deep-frying. At first it may be easiest to measure the temperature with a deep-frying thermometer. More experienced chefs judge the oil's temperature by its appearance, aroma, and subtle crackling sound. If the oil begins to smoke, it is too hot. Overheating shortens the life of the oil—Japanese say it "tires" the oil— and imparts a bad flavor to the foods cooked in it. Tempura chefs drop a little batter into hot oil to test its temperature. If the batter submerges slightly, then rises quickly to the surface where it browns within about 45 seconds, the temperature is just right. If the batter sinks to the bottom and rises only slowly to the surface, the oil is not hot enough; if it remains on the surface and dances furiously, the oil is too hot. Oil which is too hot will smoke—and burn the batter—whereas that which is too cold will not give the desired crispness.

Keeping the oil clean is another secret of successful deep-frying. This is especially important when using the batter or bound-breading methods. Use a mesh skimmer, or a perforated metal spatula or spoon, to remove all particles of food and batter from the oil's surface. Most cooks skim after every two or three batches of ingredients have been cooked. Place the small particles of deep-fried batter skimmed from the oil into a large colander or bowl lined with absorbent paper, and allow to drain thoroughly. These may be used later

Deep-frying with wok

as tasty additions to soups, salads, sautéed vegetables, noodles-in-broth, or other grain dishes.

To ensure that deep-fried foods are served at their peak of texture and flavor, do your deep-frying just before you are ready to serve the meal, preferably after your guests have been seated at the table. If you have a large quantity of ingredients to deep-fry and wish to serve them simultaneously, keep freshly cooked pieces warm in a 250° oven.

After all foods have been deep-fried, allow the oil to cool in the wok or skillet, then pour it through a mesh skimmer or fine-weave strainer held over a funnel into your used-oil container. Seal the jar and discard any residue in the skimmer. Wipe all utensils with absorbent paper (washing is unnecessary) and store in a sealed plastic bag.

Crispy Lotus Root SERVES 4
Stuffed with Miso & Onion

1 teaspoon sesame oil
1 onion, minced
2 tablespoons red, barley, or Hatcho miso, creamed with 1
   tablespoon water
1 lotus root, cut into ¾-inch-thick rounds (7 or 8)
Oil for deep-frying
3 tablespoons (whole-wheat) flour
1 egg, lightly beaten
Parsley sprigs

Heat a skillet and coat with the oil. Add onion and sauté for 4 minutes. Mix in creamed miso and sauté for 1 minute more. Remove from heat and allow to cool to body temperature. Use fingertips or a spatula to fill hollows in each round of lotus root with onion-miso mixture.

Heat the oil to 350° in a wok, skillet, or deep-fryer. Dust rounds in flour, dip in egg, and deep-fry for about 3 minutes, or until golden brown (p. 147). Drain well, then cut rounds horizontally into halves exposing the snowflake pattern of the miso-filled holes. Serve garnished with parsley.

For variety, roll in bread crumbs or bread crumb flakes after dipping in eggs.

Deep-fried Lotus Root Stuffed SERVES 4
with Cheese & Miso

A traditional favorite sold in Japanese delicatessens, this dish makes an excellent hors d'œuvre and is a joy to prepare.

1 cup grated cheese
2 tablespoons red, barley, or Hatcho miso
1 tablespoon minced onion or 1 clove of garlic, crushed
   (optional)
Dash of pepper
2 lotus roots, each 5 inches long
Oil for deep-frying
2 tablespoons (whole-wheat) flour
1 egg, lightly beaten
Shoyu (optional)

Combine the first four ingredients in a large cup, mixing well. Trim ends of lotus roots revealing hollow inner tubules. Cut each root crosswise into halves, parboil for 5 minutes, and drain briefly. Holding one lotus root section with a small cloth (to protect your hands from the heat), press the large end into the cheese-miso mixture, forcing the mixture up into the tubules until it fills them. Then press the end of the lotus root against the side of the cup while sliding it out to prevent the mixture from being withdrawn by suction. Repeat with the remaining sections.

Heat the oil to 350° in a wok, skillet, or deep-fryer. Dust each lotus root section liberally with flour, dip into the egg, and deep-fry until golden brown (p. 147). Drain well, then cut crosswise into ½-inch-thick discs. Serve hot or cold, seasoned, if desired, with a sprinkling of shoyu.

VARIATIONS

*Karashi Renkon: As an alternate filling use
     6 tablespoons sweet white or 4 tablespoons mellow
       white miso
     1 tablespoon red miso
     2 tablespoons minced leek or onion
     1 teaspoon hot mustard

*Sandwiched Hors D'oeuvres: Between two rounds of stuffed, deep-fried lotus root, sandwich any of the following: slices of cheese and/or fresh vegetables; deep-fried tofu (especially burgers or pouches); gluten meat.

Creamy Corn Croquettes with Miso

SERVES 3 OR 4

Miso is the key to the flavor in these unique delicacies which have a crisp crust and soft melt-in-the-mouth center.

2½ tablespoons butter
½ cup whole-wheat flour
1¼ cups milk (soy or dairy)
2 tablespoons red, barley, Hatcho, or light-yellow miso
Dash of pepper
½ small onion, minced
½ cup fresh corn kernels
1 egg, lightly beaten
¾ cup bread crumbs or bread crumb flakes
Oil for deep frying

Use 1½ tablespoons butter, ¼ cup flour, the milk, 1½ tablespoons miso, and the pepper to make a Miso White Sauce (p. 114).

Melt remaining 1 tablespoon butter in a skillet. Add onion and corn, and sauté for 4 minutes. Mix in the miso, remove from heat, and stir into the white sauce. Allow to cool to room temperature, then cover and refrigerate for 30 minutes.

Using a large spoon or dipper, scoop out one-eighth of the vegetable-sauce mixture and drop in a ball into a bowl containing the remaining ¼ cup flour. Gently sprinkle flour over moist filling while using fingertips to form a sausage-shaped croquette about 4 inches long and 1½ inches in diameter. Carefully dip in eggs and sprinkle with bread crumbs. Repeat to make 8 croquettes, and allow to dry for 10 minutes.

Heat oil to hot (395°) in a wok, skillet, or deep-fryer. Slide in 2 croquettes at a time and deep-fry for about 1 minute or until golden brown and crisp. Drain and serve immediately, garnished, if desired, with lettuce, tomato slices, and parsley.

For an even richer texture, add ½ cup grated cheese to the white sauce.

Cheese & Miso Deep-fried Sandwich

SERVES 2

Known in Japan as *Hakata-age*, this *nori*-wrapped preparation takes its name from the well-known *Hakata* kimono sash characterized by colorful horizontal stripes. Dried-frozen (or well-pressed regular) tofu is often used in place of bread.

4 bread slices, each 3½ inches square and 3/8 inch thick
2 teaspoons red, barley, or Hatcho miso
2 cheese slices, each 3½ inches square and ¼ inch thick
6 strips of *nori*, each 3½ inches wide and 8 to 10 inches long
2 eggs, lightly beaten
¼ cup whole-wheat flour
¼ cup bread crumbs, bread crumb flakes, or ground roasted sesame seeds (optional)
Oil for deep-frying
2 to 4 parsley sprigs

Spread one surface of each bread slice with ½ teaspoon miso, then sandwich 1 slice of cheese between 2 slices of bread to form 2 sandwiches (fig. 24). Cut each sandwich crosswise into thirds and wrap each third with a strip of *nori*, moistening one end of *nori* to seal. Combine eggs and flour, mixing lightly, to form a batter. Heat oil to 350° in a wok, skillet, or deep-fryer. Dip sandwiches into batter and, if desired, roll in bread crumbs or sesame. Drop into oil and deep-fry until golden brown (p. 147). Drain well. Cut each sandwich crosswise into thirds and serve with the cut surface facing upward, garnished with parsley.

VARIATIONS

*If *nori* is not available, pierce sandwiches in 2 places with foodpicks before deep-frying in batter.
***Tofu Hakata-agé:** Cut a 12-ounce cake of well-pressed tofu (or a 5-ounce tofu cutlet) horizontally into fourths, then lengthwise and again crosswise into halves to make 16 rectangular pieces. Coat one surface of 8 pieces with a 1/8-inch-thick layer of Sweet Simmered Miso (p. 60), then top with the remaining tofu pieces. Dust each of the 8 sandwiches with flour, dip into beaten egg, and roll in bread crumbs. Deep-fry, cut, and serve as above, using lemon wedges and parsley as the garnish.

Fig. 24. Deep-fried Sandwiches

Deep-fried Potatoes in Miso & Onion Sauce

SERVES 2 OR 3

½ onion, minced
¼ cup water
Oil for deep-frying
4 small unpeeled potatoes (2-inch diameter), each cut into 4 equal-sized chunks
1½ tablespoons red, barley, or Hatcho miso
2 tablespoons Parmesan cheese

Combine onion and water in a small saucepan, bring to a boil, and simmer for 5 minutes. Meanwhile heat oil to 350° in a wok, skillet, or deep-fryer. Drop in potato chunks and deep-fry until golden brown (p. 147); drain on absorbent paper.

Stir miso into simmering onions, then add potatoes and season with pepper; simmer for 1 minute. Serve topped with a sprinkling of the cheese.

Deep-fried Potato Chunks in Miso & Ginger Sauce

SERVES 3 OR 4

2 tablespoons red, barley, or Hatcho miso
2 to 2½ teaspoons honey
½ teaspoon powdered ginger or ¼ teaspoon grated ginger-root
¼ cup water or stock
2 small potatoes (2½-inch diameter), each cut into 4 chunks and patted very dry with a dishcloth
Oil for deep-frying

Combine the first four ingredients in a small saucepan, mixing well, and set aside on a back burner. Heat oil to 325° in a wok, skillet, or deep-fryer. Drop in potato chunks and deep-fry for about 6 minutes, or until golden brown and tender (p. 147). Meanwhile bring miso-ginger sauce to a boil and simmer over very low heat. Drain potatoes briefly, dip into sauce until covered, and transfer to individual plates. Serve hot or cold.

Eggs Deep-fried in Overcoats with Miso

SERVES 3

2 tablespoons butter
½ onion, minced
½ cup carrot, grated
2 cups cubed potatoes (1-inch cubes), boiled for 20 minutes, drained and mashed
1½ tablespoons red, barley, or Hatcho miso
½ teaspoon curry powder or dash of pepper
3 hard-boiled eggs, shelled and cooled to room temperature
3 tablespoons whole-wheat flour
1 egg, lightly beaten
1/3 cup bread crumbs
Oil for deep-frying
Ketchup-Worcestershire Sauce (p. 58)
Minced parsley

Melt the butter in a skillet. Add onion and carrot, and sauté for 3 minutes. Mix with mashed potato, miso, and curry powder and divide into 3 equal portions; allow to cool to at least body temperature. Completely enfold each egg with an even covering of the potato-miso mixture, then dust with flour, dip in beaten egg, and roll in bread crumbs. Heat oil to 375° in a wok, skillet, or deep-fryer. Deep-fry coated eggs until golden brown, lift out of oil with a slotted spoon or skimmer, and drain well. Allow to cool to at least body temperature, then cut each egg lengthwise into halves. Serve topped with the sauce and a sprinkling of parsley. If desired, arrange on a bed of lettuce or shredded cabbage garnished by tomato wedges.

For variety, omit the flour and beaten eggs in the coating, and use only bread crumbs; instead of deep-frying, bake at 350° for 20 minutes, or until nicely browned.

Sweet Miso Deep-fried in Yuba or Wonton Skins

MAKES 6

6 sheets of fresh yuba, each 4 inches square; or 6 wonton skins
9 tablespoons diced fresh yuba or wonton
3 tablespoons Yuzu Miso (p. 62) or Red Nerimiso (p. 60)
Oil for deep-frying
Shoyu

In the center of each yuba square layer 1 tablespoon diced yuba and 1½ teaspoons miso, and top with ½ teaspoon more of the yuba. Fold over the four corners of the yuba or wonton to form an envelope and fasten corners with a foodpick. Heat the oil to 350° in a wok, skillet, or deep-fryer. Drop in envelopes and deep-fry, turning them from time to time with chopsticks or tongs, for about 40 seconds, or until golden brown (p. 147). Drain well and serve (on sheets of neatly folded white paper) accompanied by the shoyu for dipping.

For variety, omit diced yuba and use 1 tablespoon Mushroom Miso Sauté (p. 65) as the filling.

Miso & Eggs

The use of miso in your favorite breakfast and luncheon egg preparations provides added aroma, flavor, and protein. For hors d'œuvres see Eggs with Miso and Sesame (p. 77).

Eggs Cooked Over Brown Rice with Miso
SERVES 3

1½ tablespoons oil
1 clove of garlic, minced
½ small onion, minced
4 mushrooms, minced
1 cup cooked Brown Rice (p. 57)
1 tablespoon red or barley miso, creamed with 1 tablespoon water
3 eggs
Dash of pepper

Heat a large skillet and coat with the oil. Add garlic and sauté for 30 seconds. Add onion and mushrooms, and sauté for 5 minutes more. Mix in brown rice, sauté for 2 more minutes, then stir in slightly more than half of the creamed miso. Spread rice in an even layer over bottom of skillet. Break eggs over rice and cook, covered, over low heat for 4 to 5 minutes, or until eggs are firm. Season with pepper and top each egg with a dab of creamed miso.

Fig. 25. Gashouse Eggs

Gashouse Eggs with Miso
SERVES 1

Also known as Cockeyed Egyptians, these innovative delicacies are a nice way of combining miso and wheat proteins in a breakfast egg dish.

1 teaspoon sweet or mellow white (or ½ teaspoon red) miso
5 teaspoons butter
1 slice of whole-wheat bread
1 egg

Spread first the miso and then 1 teaspoon butter evenly over one surface of the bread. Use the mouth of a small glass to cut a hole in the center of the bread (fig. 25) and remove the round. Melt the remaining 4 teaspoons butter in a skillet, put in the bread with the buttered side up, and break the egg into the hole. Place the round (buttered-side-up) next to the bread and fry both for 2 to 3 minutes, or until bottom is nicely browned and egg is half done. Turn and repeat until second side is slightly crisp and golden brown. Serve immediately.

Poached Eggs on Toast with White Miso
SERVES 2

2 eggs, poached
2 slices of buttered whole-grain toast
1 tablespoon sweet white or 2 teaspoons mellow white miso, creamed with 1 tablespoon boiling water

Place one egg atop the buttered side of each slice of toast, then pour on miso sauce. Serve immediately.

Scrambled Eggs or Omelets with Miso
SERVES 2 OR 3

4 eggs, lightly beaten
4 teaspoons red, barley, or Hatcho miso
2 to 3 tablespoons minced onion
3½ teaspoons oil
Dash of pepper
Sprigs of parsley

Combine the first three ingredients, mixing well. Heat one-half the oil in a large skillet. Pour in half the egg-miso mixture and scramble until firm, then press surface of eggs with the back of a spatula until bottom of eggs is lightly browned and fragrant. Turn and press the second side, then remove from skillet. Repeat with remaining egg-miso mixture. Serve seasoned with pepper and garnished with parsley.

To make omelets, reduce the amount of oil slightly and cook in two batches without scrambling. If desired, serve omelets filled with 1 tablespoon Sweet Simmered Miso (p. 60) and a pinch of alfalfa sprouts.

Scrambled Eggs
with Miso, Onions, and Tofu

SERVES 3

2 eggs, lightly beaten
1½ tablespoons red, barley, or Hatcho miso
7½ ounces (deep-fried) tofu, cut into ½-inch cubes
1 tablespoon oil
1 small onion, thinly sliced
Dash of pepper

Combine the eggs and miso in a small bowl, mixing well. Add tofu and set aside.

Heat a skillet and coat with the oil. Add onion and sauté for 4 to 5 minutes. Pour in tofu-egg mixture and scramble for 2 to 3 minutes, or until eggs are firm. Season with pepper. Serve hot or cold.

Egg Foo Yung with Miso

SERVES 2

1 tablespoon red, barley, or Hatcho miso
2¾ tablespoons stock or water
2 eggs, lightly beaten
1½ tablespoons oil, one-half of which may be sesame
¾ cup mung bean sprouts
3 mushrooms, thinly sliced
½ to ¾ cup chopped leeks or minced onions
Dash of pepper

Cream the miso with a little of the stock, then add eggs and remaining stock; mix well and set aside. Heat the oil in a large skillet. Add the next three ingredients and sauté over high heat for about 1 minute, or until leeks are lightly browned. Pour in miso-egg mixture to form a round pattie and fry on both sides until golden brown. Serve seasoned with pepper.

For variety, add diced (deep-fried) tofu and/or green peppers together with the sprouts. Top with Miso-Gingerroot Ankaké (p. 113) or Gingerroot Sauce (p. 118).

Layered Japanese Omelet
with Sweet Simmered Miso

SERVES 2 OR 3

Sweet Simmered Miso makes a good filling for many Western-style omelets. This subtly-sweet vegetable omelet is composed of alternating almost-crisp and creamy-soft layers.

4 eggs, lightly beaten
1 tablespoon brown sugar or honey
2 mushrooms, minced
1/3 cup finely-minced leeks, onions, or chives
Dash of salt
¼ cup dashi (p. 56), water, or stock
2 teaspoons oil
2½ teaspoons Red Nerimiso (p. 60)

Combine the first six ingredients, mixing well. Heat a large skillet and coat with 1 teaspoon oil. Fold a 4- by 6-inch piece of cheese cloth to form a small pad, grasp with tongs or chopsticks, and use to spread oil evenly over bottom and sides of skillet (fig. 26). Pour in one-fourth of the vegetable-egg mixture, swish it quickly around skillet to make a uniformly thin layer, and cook over high heat on one side only until omelet firms. Reduce heat to low and cook until bottom is almost crisp. Roll up omelet with a spatula, remove from skillet, and coat upper surface with ½ teaspoon Nerimiso. Re-oil skillet lightly and use cloth pad to free any particles of omelet clinging to skillet's walls. Prepare a second omelet. When it has finished cooking, place the first back into skillet atop the second. Fold one edge of bottom omelet over rolled omelet and, using spatula, roll up second omelet around first. Carefully remove roll from skillet and again coat upper surface with ½ teaspoon Nerimiso. Continue in this way to prepare a single roll composed of 4 omelets. Coat the top of the finished roll with 1 teaspoon Nerimiso and allow to cool to room temperature. Cut crosswise into 1-inch-wide sections before serving.

Fig. 26. Layered Omelets

Miso in Desserts

A little miso helps to evoke the natural sweetness of most fresh fruits—especially apples. The low salt content, subtle tartness, and mellow flavor of Hatcho often gives particularly good results in baked treats. Experiment also with Sesame Miso (p. 62), sweet or mellow white miso, or red miso in your favorite recipes for Apple Brown Betty, fruit fritters or turnovers, and pies.

Before the arrival of cane sugar in Japan, sweet and Finger Lickin' misos were served together with *mizuamé* and *amazaké* as the major natural sweetenings. They were—and still are—used in confections and tea treats, the most popular of which is *Kashiwa Mochi*, described below. Miso is also a key ingredient in the crisp Tokyo dessert crackers called *Kawara Senbei*, made by baking a mixture of wheat (or rice flour) dough, sweet red miso and sugar between two small roof tiles *(kawara)*, from which the crackers take their form. Sweet red miso is also mixed with sweet azuki-bean paste and used as a filling for the widely available steamed buns called *Miso Manju*.

Baked Apples Filled with Sesame-Raisin Miso
SERVES 5

5 large (red) apples
Sesame-Raisin Miso:
    1½ tablespoons sesame butter
    ¼ cup raisins
    1 tablespoon Hatcho, red, or barley miso
    1 tablespoon butter
    3 tablespoons brown sugar or 1½ tablespoons honey
    2 tablespoons water
    1 tablespoon sake or white wine (optional)
    ¼ teaspoon cinnamon (optional)

Preheat oven to 350°. Core apples to about seven-eighths of their depth. Mix the ingredients for sesame-raisin miso, then pack the mixture firmly into the hollow of each apple. Wrap apples in aluminum foil, place on a cookie tin and bake for about 20 minutes. Serve hot or chilled.

Apple Crisp with Miso
SERVES 4 TO 6

4 apples, thinly sliced
¼ cup raisins
1 tablespoon Hatcho, red, or barley miso
½ teaspoon grated lemon rind
1 tablespoon lemon juice
1 cup rolled oats or oatmeal (uncooked)
1/3 cup whole-wheat flour
2 tablespoons brown sugar (optional)
½ teaspoon cinnamon
¼ teaspoon nutmeg
Dash of salt
¼ cup oil (one-half of which may be butter)

Preheat oven to 350°. Combine the first five ingredients, mixing well, and spoon into a lightly oiled baking dish. Combine the remaining ingredients, mixing (or rubbing between palms) until oil is evenly distributed; sprinkle over surface of apples. Bake for about 30 minutes, or until apples are tender and surface is nicely browned. Delicious hot or chilled.

Jelled Apple-Miso Dessert
SERVES 5 TO 6

5 apples, peeled and cut lengthwise into fourths
1 cup water
1 tablespoon red, barley, or Hatcho miso
½ cup raisins
1 tablespoon lemon juice
2 tablespoons honey
2 tablespoons sesame butter
¼ teaspoon cinnamon
½ bar of agar (4 to 5 grams), soaked in water for 2 minutes, squeezed firmly and torn into small pieces

Combine apples and water in a saucepan, bring to a boil, and simmer, covered, for 10 minutes. Using a fork, remove apples and transfer to a baking pan or mold. Add miso and the next five ingredients to the apple cooking liquid, mixing well. Add agar, bring to a boil, and simmer for 4 to 5 minutes, or until agar has dissolved. Pour liquid into mold and allow to cool to room temperature. Cover and refrigerate until firm, preferably for 6 to 8 hours. Serve as is or topped with yogurt.

Japanese-style Steamed Miso-Cupcakes or Spongecake (Miso-iri Mushipan)

SERVES 2 OR 3

2 eggs separated into whites and lightly beaten yolks
1 tablespoon red or barley miso, creamed with 1½ teaspoons water
2/3 cup whole-wheat flour
½ teaspoon baking powder
6½ teaspoons honey
1 tablespoon finely chopped peanuts or roasted sesame seeds
Butter

Preheat a steamer (p. 55). In a large bowl, beat egg whites until stiff. Fold in yolks, creamed miso, flour, baking powder, and 2 tablespoons honey. Spoon batter into (paper-lined) cupcake molds or a small loaf pan lined with aluminum foil. Place in steamer and, unless using a bamboo steamer, stretch a moist cloth over steamer's mouth before covering. Steam for 20 to 25 minutes. Brush surface of cakes with ½ teaspoon honey, then sprinkle with peanuts or sesame seeds. Serve hot or cold with butter.

The Japanese and Chinese prefer steaming to baking since much less fuel is needed. Of course, the cupcakes may also be baked over a pan of water if desired.

Miso Mincemeat

MAKES ONE 9-INCH PIE

The mellow, slightly tart flavor of Hatcho miso provides the key to this unique and delicious dessert preparation.

4 (tart) apples, peeled, cored, and diced
½ cup apple juice
1½ cups raisins
Grated rind of 1 orange
Juice of 1 orange
2 cups nutmeats, preferably walnuts
¼ teaspoon cinnamon
¼ to ½ teaspoon cloves, allspice, or coriander
2 tablespoons Hatcho miso, or substitute 1½ tablespoons red or barley miso

Combine the first five ingredients in a heavy pot, bring to a boil, and simmer for 30 minutes. Add the next three ingredients and the miso creamed in a little of the cooking liquid; mix well, remove from heat, and allow to cool to room temperature. Use as a filling for a 9-inch mince pie or for turnovers. Also delicious as a spread for buttered toast or served like chutney with curried dishes.

Heavenly Sweet-potato Patties with White Miso

SERVES 6 OR 12

4 (Japanese) sweet potatoes, steamed for 20 minutes and mashed (2¼ cups)
¼ cup sweet white or 2 tablespoons mellow white miso
½ cup raisins
1 tablespoon honey
3 tablespoons butter

Combine the first four ingredients, mixing well, and shape into 12 patties. Melt 1 tablespoon butter in a heavy skillet, add 4 patties, and fry for 2 to 3 minutes on each side, or until lightly browned. Repeat until all ingredients are used. Serve hot or cold.

Banana, Peanut Butter & Sweet Miso Delight

SERVES 2 OR 3

2 tablespoons peanut or sesame butter
1 tablespoon sweet white miso
¼ cup raisins
1 teaspoon honey
2 tablespoons water
2 bananas, sliced into ½-inch-thick rounds

Combine the first five ingredients, mixing well, then spoon over banana slices. Mix lightly until slices are evenly coated. Serve immediately.

Miso Rice Pudding

SERVES 3 OR 4

The rich, creamy texture of rice porridge works like milk in most pudding recipes; raisins provide most of the sweetness.

½ cup brown rice, rinsed and drained
2½ cups water
1½ tablespoons Hatcho, red, or barley miso
½ cup raisins
1 tablespoon brown sugar or 1½ teaspoons honey
1 tablespoon butter
Dash of cinnamon

Combine rice and water in a pressure cooker and proceed as for rice porridge (p. 57). After opening cooker, stir in the last four ingredients. For best flavor, allow to stand for several hours before serving.

Miso Pumpkin Pie

SERVES 6

24 ounces *kabocha* (unpeeled), cut into 1-inch cubes
2 tablespoons red, barley, or Hatcho miso
2 tablespoons honey or brown sugar
1½ tablespoons butter
Dash of nutmeg and/or allspice
Crust for an 8-inch pie

Combine *kabocha* with water to cover in a saucepan or pot, bring to a boil, and simmer for 20 minutes. Drain well, then combine with the next four ingredients and mash together. Line an 8-inch pie pan with the crust and bake in a 400° oven until lightly browned. Spoon in the *kabocha* mixture and re-bake for 20 to 30 minutes, or until nicely browned. For richest flavor, serve cold. This filling also works well in turnovers.

If pumpkin or squash is substituted for the *kabocha*, peel before boiling and drain very well; add 1 to 3 eggs to the mixture before baking.

Crêpes with Sweet Simmered Miso Filling

SERVES 2

Red Sweet Simmered Miso Filling:
   3½ teaspoons red or barley miso
   2 teaspoons honey
   ½ teaspoon butter
   1 teaspoon sake or white wine
   ½ teaspoon grated lemon or orange rind
   2 teaspoons water
7/8 cup sifted whole-wheat flour
1 egg, lightly beaten
1 cup milk (soy or dairy)
1 tablespoon oil or butter

Using the filling ingredients, prepare Red Sweet Simmered Miso (p. 60) and set aside to cool. Combine the flour, egg, milk and 1 teaspoon oil, whisking lightly to form a smooth batter. Lightly oil a large skillet, then use batter to prepare 10 to 12 crêpes. Allow crêpes to cool, then spread one surface of each with about ½ teaspoon of the miso filling. Roll crêpes before serving.

Miso Kashiwa Mochi

MAKES 8

Served once each year as a special treat on Children's Day—the fifth day of the fifth month—*Kashiwa Mochi* takes its name from the oak leaves generally used to wrap each portion. Widely prepared at commercial Japanese confectioneries, the filling is generally made of sweet white miso and puréed white kidney beans *(Ingen mamé)*, or occasionally of sweet red miso and sweet, azuki-bean paste *(an)*. Household recipes also call for a filling made with *kabocha* or chestnut purée.

7 ounces *kabocha*, pumpkin, or squash, peeled and cut into cubes
3¼ tablespoons sweet white miso
2½ teaspoons honey
1¼ cups glutinous rice flour
½ teaspoon salt
¾ cup boiling water

Steam *kabocha* for 15 to 20 minutes, then rub through a sieve. Add miso and honey, mixing well, to make a filling.

Combine flour and salt, mixing thoroughly. Gradually add boiling water while stirring vigorously for 3 minutes to develop a cohesive dough. Wrap dough in a moist cloth, place into a preheated steamer (p. 55) and steam for 20 minutes. Now transfer dough to a *suribachi* or mortar and pound for 5 to 10 minutes, or until dough develops a uniform, resilient texture. Divide dough into 8 parts and roll out each into 3½-inch rounds on a lightly floured board. Place equal portions of the filling at the center of each round, then fold over one side of the dough to form a half-moon shape. Seal edges by pinching dough with fingers. Wrap each portion in a large (6-to 8-inch-long) oak leaf, with the leaf's shiny surface touching the dough (or use a beech leaf or aluminum foil). Replace into preheated steamer and steam for 4 to 5 minutes. Allow to cool before serving.

Kashiwa Mochi

Miso Pickles

Pickled vegetables are a basic condiment in the Japanese (and Chinese) diet, where they are the single most important source of salt, providing about 40 percent of the total intake. Served at almost every meal of the day, primarily as an accompaniment for rice or rice porridge, they are enjoyed for their slightly crisp texture and deep, rich flavor. There are six basic types of Japanese pickles and each takes its name from the pickling agent: miso, salt, salted moist rice-bran, vinegar, sake lees, and koji. Some scholars believe that the earliest Japanese pickles, called *konomono* or "fragrant things," were made with miso. And to this day, miso pickles (*miso-zuké*) are believed to aid the digestive process and promote long life and good health.

Commercially prepared miso pickles—made both at specialty shops and regular miso shops—are widely available at most food stores and miso retail outlets throughout Japan. More than 12 varieties of vegetables and seeds are used, the most popular of which are *daikon*, (wild) burdock root, cucumbers, eggplants, gingerroot, carrots, *uri* melons, beefsteak seeds, and *myoga*. Fish and meat pickles, usually prepared with sweet white miso, are generally sold at fish or meat markets. In farmhouses and temples, large batches of miso pickles are still prepared each year as part of the miso-making process, with vegetables buried in the keg at the start of fermentation and usually left there until the miso is fully mature (p. 192). In urban homes, small batches are made using storebought miso and special ingredients such as eggs and egg yolks, which are then often served as hors d'œuvres. Most farmers and homemakers prefer to make their miso pickles during the fall or winter; although the process takes longer due to the cold, the pickles' flavor is said to improve and it is easier to prevent the growth of unwanted mold on the miso surface.

Over a period of many centuries, Japanese craftsmen have raised the practice of miso-pickling to the level of a fine art. The country's most famous commercial makers enjoy a wide and lofty reputation, and they guard the secrets of their trade most carefully. Traditional masters call for a lengthy pickling believed to give vegetables a mellow saltiness and tender crunchiness, while extinguishing all bitter and strong flavors (such as those found in *daikon* or burdock root), accenting subtle indwelling flavors, and, above all, evoking a

Selling miso pickles

delightful aroma—which devotees refer to as "the life" of the product.

In this section, we will first discuss the rather simple method of preparing miso pickles at home, then go on to the complete 5-step process used by most commercial makers.

The Pickling Container

156

The type and size of the container used are determined by the scale of the household pickling process:

*Large Scale (2 to 10 pounds of fresh vegetable ingredients): Use a container of 2 to 10 gallons capacity, preferably an earthenware crock, a seasoned wooden keg (such as that used for shoyu or miso), a glass container (such as an aquarium), or an enamelware pot. If none of these are available, use a polyethylene tub or bucket. This scale is recommended for ingredients requiring 1 year or more of pickling.

*Medium Scale (½ pound to 2 pounds of ingredients): For kitchen use when pickling for less than one year, use a container of 2 to 4 quarts capacity such as an earthenware crock or casserole, a glass bowl, an enamel pot or shallow pan, or a tupperware container.

*Small Scale (less than 8 ounces of ingredients): Spread the miso in a ½-inch-thick layer over a piece of plastic wrap, arrange ingredients to be pickled on the miso, and roll up into a cylinder. This technique is especially good with small amounts of long, thin vegetables such as cucumbers and burdock root. Or you can use small glass jars or tupperware containers for small-sized ingredients such as egg yolks or garlic.

Preparatory Techniques

A vegetable's water content must be reduced to aid it in absorbing the miso's flavor, while preventing it from diluting the medium with excess water extracted by the miso's salt. The following procedures are used:

*Parboiling: Used to sterilize vegetables and soften their skins. Bring lightly salted water to a boil. Drop in well-washed vegetables, return to the boil, and simmer for 1 to 2 minutes. Drain thoroughly in a colander and allow to cool to room temperature.

*Salt Pressing: Use an amount of salt equal to about 10 percent of the weight of the fresh vegetables, about 2 tablespoons for every ½ pound. Place whole or cut ingredients in a large (earthenware, wooden, glass, or enamel) flat-bottomed container and sprinkle the entire surface of each vegetable with salt. Arrange ingredients compactly in parallel rows, top with a lid or another flat-bottomed container, and press with a stone or water-filled jar (fig. 27). For ingredients weighing less than 1 pound, use a 5- to 10-pound pressing weight; for 10 pounds of ingredients, use a 30-pound weight. Press for 2 days unless otherwise stated. After pressing, drain vegetables well, discard liquid, and wipe vegetables with a dry cloth.

*Wrapping in Cheesecloth: This technique helps soft ingredients to keep their form during pickling and makes it easier to remove them from the miso bed. Simply wrap in a single or double layer of cheesecloth before embedding.

Air-drying daikon

*Air-drying: Place vegetables in a shallow colander or tie in strands with string. Place or hang in a shady location during summer, in direct sunlight in very cold weather. Cover or bring indoors at night to protect from dew.

Fig. 27. Salt-pressing

Air-drying turnips (kabu)

The Miso "Bed"

In Japanese, the pickling medium is called the "bed" and burying the vegetables in it is called "embedding." Use red or barley miso when pickling for several weeks or more; sweet white miso when the pickling time is less than one week. The latter gives a mild, subtly sweet flavor which is often given added zest by mixing in a small amount of sake, rice koji, or powdered mustard. The flavor of red miso can be enriched by the addition of (7-spice) red pepper, sake, or honey. Kinzanji and other varieties of Finger Lickin' Miso give delicious results with overnight pickles, especially egg yolks.

To prepare the bed, cover the bottom of the miso container with a ½- to 1-inch-thick layer of miso. On top of this lay a snug layer of the ingredients to be pickled, then cover with another layer of miso. Repeat until all ingredients are used. Cover the top miso layer with a double thickness of cotton cloth or a sheet of wax paper or plastic to keep out air and prevent mold formation. Store in a cool place or, if using sweet white, Finger Lickin', or small quantities of red miso, refrigerate. Large-scale containers should be further covered with a weighted pressing lid

Cleaning and Serving Pickles

Remove only as many vegetables from the miso as you need for 1 or 2 days. Using your fingers, scrape off excess miso and return it to the pickling container. Unless otherwise specified, rinse off any remaining miso under cold running water. Cut pickles crosswise or diagonally into thin slices, or mince.

Serve red-miso pickles as an accompaniment with plain or fried rice or noodles, or use as a granish for rice porridge, gruel, or tofu. Serve pickles made with sweet white or Finger Lickin' miso as an hors d'oeuvre. In Japan, thin rounds of either type are often arranged on tiny dishes (accompanied by chopsticks) and served together with green tea.

In most Zen temples (and some homes), each person reserves one fairly large slice of pickle until the end of the meal. This is held with a pair of chopsticks and used, together with a small amount of hot tea or water, to rinse out the eating bowls. The pickle is then enjoyed with the broth—and nothing has been wasted. Individuals then dry their own bowls, nestle them snugly one inside the other, and tie them into an attractive bundle, ready for the next meal. Thanks to the humble pickle, the kitchen crew is saved hours of dish washing.

When all homemade pickles have been removed from the container, the miso will be softer than usual due to the moisture extracted from the pickled vegetables. Use in cookery as you would regular miso or in the preliminary pickling of a similar second batch of vegetables (p. 161). After the removal of ingredients such as garlic or *daikon*, the miso will have been flavorfully enriched.

FOODS TO BE PICKLED

Asparagus

Peel 6 slender, young stalks and snap the tips. Cut lengthwise into halves, then into ½-inch lengths. Bring 2 cups water to a boil. Drop in asparagus and return to the boil. Drain, cool under cold running water, and pat dry with towels. Mix ½ cup sweet white miso and 1 tablespoon powdered mustard. Spread half the mixture in a shallow baking dish and cover with a double thickness of cheesecloth. Arrange asparagus in one layer on cloth, cover with a second double layer, and top with remaining miso mixture. Let stand for 3 hours at room temperature or refrigerate overnight. Serve as an hors d'œuvre.

Beefsteak Leaves

Embed green leaves (fresh or salt-pressed) in a mixture of 4 parts red miso and 1 part *mirin* for 1 to 3 days. Silver and serve as a garnish.

Beefsteak Seeds

Salt-press about ½ cup red beefsteak seeds, then tie in a small cheesecloth bag. Embed in red miso for 1 month. Use as (1) a filling for rice balls or nori-wrapped sushi, (2) a garnish for soups, vegetable pancakes and grain dishes, or (3) an ingredient in tempura.

Burdock Root and Wild Mountain Burdock

Wild mountain burdock (*Yamagobo*) is one of Japan's most popular commercial varieties of miso pickle. Smaller and more richly flavored than regular burdock, it turns a handsome yellowish gold when pickled.

Use whole roots or fairly long lengths. If pickling for less than 1 month, cut roots lengthwise into halves. Parboil for 3 minutes and salt press for 1 to 3 days, then air-dry for several hours. Embed in red miso for at least 4 months, preferably 1 to 3 years.

Carrots

Prepare as for burdock root. For a firmer texture, salt-press or air-dry for about 1 week before pickling.

Celery

Cut stalks into 1-inch lengths. Embed in red miso for 24 to 36 hours. Serve as an hors d'œuvre.

Cucumbers

Use whole cucumbers. Salt-press for 1 to 2 days, then embed in red miso for 3 to 6 months, or in sweet white miso for 5 months.

Daikon or Turnips (*Kabu*)

Use whole *daikon*. Salt-press under heavy weights for 1 week or airdry for 5 to 10 days, or until soft and well contracted. Embed in red miso for at least 4 to 6 months; if desired, for 2 or 3 years.

For faster results, cut lengthwise into halves, then crosswise into 3- to 6-inch sections. Salt-press for 1 night or air-dry for 10 days. Embed in red miso (or a mixture of ½ teaspoon 7-spice red pepper for every 2 cups red miso) for 3 to 4 months, or in moromi miso for 5 months. *Takuan*, or *daikon* which has been pickled in moist salted rice bran, can be further pickled in miso for 3 to 4 weeks.

Eggplants

For best results use (Japanese-style) small and tender whole eggplants. Salt-press for 24 hours, then embed in red miso for 4 to 8 months, or as long as 1 to 2 years. Delicious also embedded in moromi miso or Finger Lickin' Miso for 70 days.

Eggs (*Hardboiled*)

*Sweet White Miso: Use 4 eggs, shelled. For the "bed" use ¾ cup sweet white miso (mixed, if desired, with 1 to 4 tablespoons *mirin*, sake or white wine). Cut two eggs lengthwise into halves and embed with the cut surface facing upward.

Embed remaining eggs whole. Cover container and refrigerate for 1 to 7 days. Remove excess miso but do not wash. Slice whole eggs into thin rounds. Serve as an hors d'œuvre as is, or on crackers or canapés.

*Red Miso: These eggs end up firmer and saltier. Use plain red miso (or mix with sake, etc., as above). Embed eggs whole. For use as an hors d'œuvre, pickle for 5 to 6 hours and serve as is, cut into halves. For use on crackers or canapés, pickle for 10 to 12 hours, then cut into thin rounds. For use as a rice garnish, pickle for 1 to 4 days, then dice or sliver.

*Sweetened Red Miso: Use as the pickling medium: ¾ cup red or barley miso, ¼ cup sugar and 3 tablespoons sake. Proceed as for red miso above.

*Finger Lickin' Miso: Cut eggs length wise into halves, remove yolks, and bury yolks and whites in (Kinzanji or moromi) miso for 24 hours. Remove and serve as for sweet white miso, above.

Egg Yolks (*Softboiled*)

Cover the bottom of a 6-inch square container with a 1-inch-deep layer of red miso. Press the large end of an egg into the miso in 4 places to make 4 depressions, then cover miso with a layer of cheesecloth and press cloth into depressions. Prepare four 3-minute eggs. Carefully remove yolks unbroken, and place one yolk in each of the 4 depressions. Cover with a layer of cheesecloth, gently top with miso, and wait for 1½ to 2 days. Serve yolks like cheese as an hors d'œuvre (garnished with slivered green beefsteak leaves if desired) or as a garnish atop hot rice.

Garlic or Shallots

*Red Nerimiso: Peel the thin outer skin from 10 to 12 cloves of garlic and parboil cloves for 3 minutes. Cut lengthwise into halves and dry on a (bamboo) colander in the shade for 6 to 12 hours. (For added fragrance, skewer and broil dried cloves until speckled.) Embed in about 1 cup hot, freshly-prepared Red Nerimiso (p. 60) for 3 to 6 months. Cut lengthwise into very thin slices before serving.

To reduce pickling time, cut (fresh or parboiled) garlic cloves into paper-thin slices; pickle for at least 2, preferably 3 weeks.

*Red Miso: Peel garlic cloves and cut lengthwise into halves. Embed in miso for at least 4, preferably 6 months. Serve diced or thinly sliced with rice or rice gruel. In rural Japan, these miso pickles are considered an excellent source of stamina and a cure for numerous diseases.

The miso which remains after pickling garlic is most delicious; use it like Garlic Miso (p. 64) or as a topping for tofu or hot rice.

Gingerroot

Use whole mature or young gingerroot. Salt-press for 1 to 3 days. Embed in red miso for at least 1, preferably 2 years. Or, for faster results, slice fresh gingerroot diagonally into paper-thin ovals. Embed for at least 2, preferably 3 weeks.

Green Peppers

Parboil 5 or 6 green peppers for 1 minute in lightly salted water. Remove seeds and stems, then cut lengthwise into 1-inch-wide strips. Combine 8 ounces sweet white miso, 2½ tablespoons *mirin*, and 1 tablespoon sake or white wine; mix well. Embed peppers, cover, and refrigerate for 1 week. Serve as a garnish for hot rice seasoned with a little sesame salt, or as an hors d'œuvre sprinkled with a few drops of shoyu. Cook leftover miso for 5 to 10 minutes in a skillet, stirring constantly, as for Sweet Simmered Miso.

Or cut fresh green peppers lengthwise into 1-inch-wide strips and salt-press for 24 hours; embed in red miso for 2 to 3 months.

Kabocha

Cut *kabocha* into ½-inch-thick slices; peel and trim off pulpy inner edge. Parboil for 1 to 2 minutes in lightly salted water. Drain and cool under cold running water. Air-dry for several hours. Embed in red miso for 2 to 4 months. For added tang, mix ½ teaspoon (7-spice) red pepper with each 2 cups of miso used.

Kombu

Use best grade *dashi kombu*. Wipe with a moist cloth, cut into 8-inch lengths, and steam or pressure cook in a little water for 20 to 30 minutes, or until tender. Spread upper surface of each *kombu* sheet with either a mixture of 1 cup sweet white miso and 1½ teaspoons sake, or with red miso. Roll up sheets from one end, embed in the miso with which they were spread, and wait for at least 6, preferably 12 months. (If using sweet white miso, cover and refrigerate during pickling.) Cut into very thin strips and serve as a garnish with rice.

Lotus Root

Cut 3 ounces of peeled lotus root into 2-inch lengths. Simmer until just tender in a mixture of 1 cup water and 1 tablespoon vinegar, then drain well. Embed in a mixture of ¾ cup sweet white miso, 1 teaspoon hot mustard, and 1 tablespoon *mirin*, pressing miso mixture into lotus root tubules to fill them. Wait for 24 hours. Scrape off miso, wash well, and cut into very thin rounds. Serve as a garnish or hors d'œuvre.

Myoga

Cut fresh *myoga* lengthwise into halves, then embed in red miso for 5 to 7 days. Serve as a garnish with rice.

Sansho Seeds

Salt-press *sansho* seeds for 2 to 3 days, then tie in a small gauze bag and embed in red miso for 1 to 2 weeks.

Tofu

Drain and press tofu (p. 55), then cut crosswise into ½-inch-thick slices. Parboil for 3 minutes, drain, and allow to cool to room temperature. Combine for the miso bed: ½ cup red miso, ½ teaspoon each grated gingerroot and sesame oil, 1 teaspoon sake or white wine, and a dash of (7-spice) red pepper or tabasco sauce. Embed tofu for 12 to 15 hours, then remove carefully and wipe miso from tofu surface with a damp cloth. Cut into ½-inch cubes and, for best flavor, broil on both sides until nicely speckled. This preparation has a soft cheeselike consistency, rich fragrance, and mellow saltiness. Served as is, it makes a tasty garnish for rice or a savory hors d'œuvre. Mashed with thinly-sliced vegetables, it goes well on crackers. To make a sandwich spread or dip, try mixing 3 parts pickled tofu with 2 parts sesame- or peanut butter, 1 part honey, and a little lemon juice.

Or, dry very well pressed tofu in a slow oven for about 1 hour. Cut each cake crosswise into thirds and embed in the miso for 1 year. Sold commercially in Japan, this product has a much firmer consistency than that described above; its appearance and aroma resemble those of a well-aged cheese. (Some varieties are wrapped in *kombu* and beefsteak leaves, and embedded in mellow barley miso.)

For a sweeter product, sprinkle parboiled tofu slices with ¼ teaspoon salt and embed for 2 days in a mixture of 1½ cups sweet white miso and 2 teaspoons sake (or white wine). Broil and serve as above.

Uri or White Melons

Cut each melon lengthwise into halves. Salt-press for 2 to 4 days. Embed in red miso for 3 months.

Wakame

Use 1 cup fresh or refreshed (uncut) *wakame*. Embed in 2 cups red miso for 1 week or in sweet white miso for 8 to 10 days. Serve thinly sliced as a garnish for rice or rice gruel.

Watermelon Rind

Remove green skin and pink flesh. Cut rind into 1-inch squares and parboil for 2 minutes in lightly salted water. Drain well, pat dry with a towel, and embed in sweet white miso; refrigerate for 2 to 3 weeks. Serve as an hors d'œuvre or garnish, or use in fruitcakes.

DAIKON MISO PICKLES
(Commercial Process)

The following process, used by most of Japan's large commercial makers of miso pickles, is said to create a long-lasting product with the best flavor, texture, and color. All vegetables are pickled in basically the same way; only the proportion of salt used and the pickling time varies. An increase or decrease in the weight of the *daikon* (or other vegetables) should be accompanied by an exactly proportional change in the weight of the other ingredients, and of the pressing weight.

In the commercial process, up to 1,200 pounds of *daikon* are pickled at one time in large polymer or concrete tanks; more traditional makers use wooden vats with a capacity of 175 pounds. The following recipe has been scaled down for use in households or communities.

10 pounds daikon, slender varieties used whole, fat varieties
    cut lengthwise into fourths
2 pounds salt
10 pounds red or barley miso, approximately

I. SALT PICKLING (Shiozuké)

1. *First Salt Pickling (Arazuké):* Wash *daikon* thoroughly and drain well. Place in a large (18 inch diameter, 18 inch deep) sturdy wooden, crockery, or plastic tub and sprinkle uniformly with 1.2 pounds salt (12 percent of the daikon's weight). Arrange *daikon* as snugly and compactly as possible in container, then top with a sturdy (wooden) pressing lid and a 20- to 30-pound weight. Cover container with a layer of plastic wrap or paper to keep out insects and dust, and allow to stand for 15 to 20 days.

2. *Second Salt Pickling (Chuzuké):* Pour off and discard any liquid that has accumulated in the pickling container. Drain *daikon* thoroughly, then sprinkle with 0.6 pounds salt (6 percent of *daikon's* original weight). Replace lid and re-press, this time using only a 20- to 25-pound weight; allow to stand for 60 to 90 days.

3. *Washing and Pressing (Shionuki):* Wash *daikon* well with water, then place in a tub of cold running water for 15 to 20 hours, or until the residual salt content of the *daikon* has dropped to about 10 percent. (Professional pickle makers determine this by measuring the relative density of a puréed sample of the *daikon* or of the liquid pressed from them.) Drain washed *daikon* well and place into an empty tub (preferably one with small drainage holes in the lower sides and bottom). Replace pressing lid and top with a 3- to 4-pound weight for 3 to 4 hours, or until liquid equal to about 15 percent of *daikon* weight is expelled. Remove *daikon* and discard liquid.

II. MISO PICKLING (Misozuké)

4. *Preliminary Miso Pickling (Shitazuké):* Measure out an amount of miso equal to 1.5 times the weight of the pressed *daikon*. (If possible, use miso which has already been used once in step 5 below). Arrange alternating layers of miso and *daikon* in the tub used in step 1, so that each daikon is completely surrounded by miso. Spread a double layer of cloth or sheet of plastic wrap directly over miso surface, top with lightly weighted (3-pound) pressing lid (to prevent mold growth), and allow to stand for 5 to 8 days.

5. *Basic Miso Pickling (Honzuké):* Remove *daikon* from miso, reserving miso (which now contains a fairly high proportion of liquid) for use in step 4 of your next batch of pickles, after which it is discarded. Measure out an amount of fresh miso equal in weight to that used in step 4 and mix into it 0.2 pounds of salt plus 1 to 2 ounces each of any or all of the following natural organic acids: racemic (grape), glutamic, citric, malic (apple), lactic. Embed *daikon*, cover, and allow to stand for at least 60, preferably 120 to 180 days, or until you are ready to use it. Remove only as much *daikon* from miso as you plan to serve in one week or less. Scrape miso from *daikon* by hand, returning miso to pickling container. Wash *daikon* and slice into thin rounds before use. When all *daikon* has been used, reserve miso remaining in keg for step 4 of a future batch.

OTHER MISO PICKLES (Commercial Process)

Cucumbers and Uri Melons: In the first salt pickling, use an amount of salt equal to 16 percent by weight of the vegetables; in the second, 8 percent. Do basic miso pickling for at least 70 days.

Daikon Moromi Pickles: Proceed as for *daikon* pickles but wash in step 3 until only 6 percent salt remains, then pickle in moromi miso for at least 70 days.

Eggplants: In the first salt pickling use an amount of salt equal to 18 percent by weight of the vegetables; in the second, 6 percent. Do basic miso pickling for at least 120 days. (Note: burnt alum is sometimes used in place of salt in the first salt pickling.)

Gingerroot: For best results, choose large, mellow-flavored roots. In the first salt-pickling use an amount of salt equal to 20 percent by weight of the vegetables; omit the second salt pickling. Pickle for at least 90 days in sweet white or mellow barley miso.

Kombu: Use best quality, sweet kombu having a dark color tinged with black. Wash well in lukewarm water and steam for 15 to 20 minutes. Allow to cool to room temperature, then pickle (flat or rolled) in red miso for at least 120 days.

Miso pickles with tea

Koji Cookery

If you prepare your own koji at home (p.179) or purchase ready-made varieties, you may have a little left over after using it to make miso. The following recipes suggest ways of using koji in other preparations.

Amazaké

MAKES 3½ CUPS

Literally "sweet sake" (pronounced ah-mah-ZAH-kay), this creamy-thick hot rice drink has a rich, ambrosial flavor and virtually no alcohol content. A specialty at numerous teahouses and inns, it is often served with Dengaku (p. 144) and is most popular during the winter months—especially at New Year's. Rich in natural sugars (22.7% by weight vs. 34.8% in sweet white miso, 70.2% in honey, and 83.0% in *mizuamé*), it has long served as a sweetening agent in Japanese cookery. Amazaké is now being made by Grainaissance in Berkeley, CA; by Kendall Food Co. in Ashburnham, MA; by The Bridge in Middletown, CT; and by small companies in Los Angeles and Miami. All have received the eternal blessings of heaven and earth.

1 cup white, brown, or glutinous rice, washed and drained
2 cups water
2 cups firm granular rice koji

Combine rice and water in a pressure cooker and bring to full pressure (15 pounds). Reduce heat to low and simmer for 3 minutes if using white rice, or 20 minutes if using brown or glutinous rice. Remove from heat and allow pressure to come down naturally for 10 minutes. (Or cook in a regular pot as described on page 57.) Open crock, stir well, and allow to cool to 140°F. Mix in koji and pack mixture into a well-washed (or sterilized) wide-mouth jar or crock. Cover tightly and incubate at 140°F for 10 to 14 hours or at 90°F for 20 to 24 hours.

(To incubate, float the container in a large covered pot or tub partially filled with warm water, or wrap in towels and place over a hot water heater or in an insulated box next to hot water bottles.)

The fermentation is complete when the mixture has a rich, sweet fragrance and individual grains are very soft. Now stir well with a fork or several chopsticks to create a porridge-like consistency or, if using brown rice and a smooth texture is desired, purée in a blender or sieve. You now have amazaké base, which may be used in any of three ways:

*To Serve as Amazaké: Combine 1 part base with 1½ to 1¾ parts water in a saucepan and bring just to a boil. Season lightly with salt, pour into preheated cups, and top each portion with a dab of grated gingerroot.

*To Use as a Sweetener: Substitute 3½ tablespoons amazaké base for 1 tablespoon honey (or 2 tablespoons sugar) in any of your favorite preparations. Rich in enzymes, it is especially good in breads, cakes, pancakes, waffles, or muffins, where it assists in the leavening process and adds a rich moistness.

*To Make Doburoku *(grog):* Incubate for 7 to 10 more days at body temperature, or until the mixture develops a heady, slightly alcoholic aroma. Purée and serve as is, or dilute as above.

Bettara-zuké *(Daikon Pickled in Koji)*

In Japan, koji is used in the preparation of several types of pickles, including *daikon*, eggplant, and Chinese cabbage. As delectable as it is costly, *Bettara-zuké* has a unique mellow sweetness and juicy crunchiness combined with a heady aroma.

1 small *daikon*, peeled, cut lengthwise into quarters and then crosswise into fourths
2 tablespoons salt
1 cup white rice, cooked and cooled to body temperature
1 cup koji
¼ cup sake, white wine, or *shochu*
¼ teaspoon minced red peppers (optional)

Please begin by reading about Miso Pickles (p. 156). Air-dry *daikon* sections for 2 to 4 days until soft and well contracted, then salt-press using the 2 tablespoons salt. Pour off excess liquid and discard.

Meanwhile, combine warm rice, koji, and sake in a well-washed quart jar, cover tightly, and incubate at about 110°F for 2 days (or 80°F for 3 to 4 days), or until rice almost decomposes. Now combine salt-pickled *daikon* with rice-koji mixture and, if desired, sweetening and red pepper; allow to stand at room temperature for 6 to 10 days or until sweet and transparent. Remove *daikon* and scrape off koji mixture with your fingers; do not wash *daikon*. Slice into thin rounds and serve as an accompaniment for rice or as an hors d'œuvre.

Eggplants Pickled in Koji (*Nasu no Karashi-zuké*)

25 tiny Japanese eggplants (2 inches long, pick in autumn),
    caps removed, or substitute 18 ounces medium-sized
    eggplants
13 tablespoons salt
4¼ cups water
1½ cups koji
6 tablespoons mild mustard
4½ tablespoons *mirin*

Rub eggplants lightly with half the salt, then place (together with this salt) in a pickling container (p. 156); top with a pressing lid and 8-pound weight. Combine remaining half of salt with the water, mix until dissolved, and pour into pickling container. Allow to stand for 20 to 30 days. Pour off liquid and transfer eggplants to a bowl. Combine koji, mustard and *mirin*, mixing well, then stir into eggplants. Return to pickling container and press for 15 days more. Serve as for Bettara-zuké.

VARIATIONS

*For a richer flavor use: 4¼ pounds salt-pressed eggplants, 2¼ cups (7 oz.) koji, 5 tablespoons honey, ¾ to 1 cup mild mustard powder, 12 tablespoons sake or water, and 6 tablespoons shoyu. Mix all ingredients and press with a light weight for 15 days.

*Chinese Cabbage Pickled in Koji: In a pickling container, place alternating layers of Chinese cabbage (total 2 pounds) and salt (3 tablespoons). Salt-press for 2 to 3 days then discard liquid. Soak ½ cup koji in ¼ cup warm water for 15 minutes. Mix in 1 teaspoon honey, 2 tablespoons slivered *kombu*, and 1 slivered red pepper. Squeeze cabbage well to expel excess liquid then arrange alternating layers of cabbage and koji mixture in the container. Press with a light weight for 4 to 5 days. Serve as for Bettara-zuké.

Amazaké at the Nakamura-ro restaurant

PART III

The Preparation of Miso

7
Making Miso at Home and in Communities

THE JAPANESE have long taken great pride in their homemade miso. During visits to the homes of friends, both in modern high-rise apartments and traditional farmhouses, we have been surprised again and again to discover how many people even to this day make their own. After mentioning our interest in the subject, we have found ourselves ushered to the kitchen, back porch, storeroom, or barn—where our hosts would proudly reveal their cache of 3 or 4 kegs or crocks—and treated to a taste of their favorite variety, followed by a detailed description of their personal miso-making process.

Indeed, the number of families and communities in Japan preparing their own miso is on the rise. For some, this is a response to rising food prices and the commercial trend toward standardization and deteriorating quality. But many are also rediscovering how enjoyable and easy it is to prepare miso with just the right flavor by choosing their own blend of ingredients and aging it for as long as they like. At least one large company (p. 239) is now doing a booming business selling *shikomi-miso*, a 44-pound mixture of high-quality koji, cooked soybeans, salt and water, packed into a keg and ready to be aged. Available in blends that produce either red or light-yellow miso, it is 10 to 20 percent less expensive than mature commercial brands and yields a product that is guaranteed to be both free of additives and, of course, unpasteurized. Yet whether they prepare it from scratch or use the new convenience mixture, most Japanese still maintain that the ancient proverb holds true: everyone prizes most the flavor of his or her family's homemade miso.

Starting in the late 1960s, a surprisingly large number of people in the United States started preparing homemade miso. Classes have been conducted by natural food companies and Japanese-American makers, and recipes for barley and red miso have been published and distributed. Names of organizations and individuals actively interested in such work are given on page 241.

The three most important factors affecting the quality of homemade miso are: 1) the quality of the koji; 2) the use of a proper fermentation container; and 3) the maintenance of a clean environment during preparation. Working with clean hands and utensils is of the utmost importance in keeping the influence of contaminating microorganisms to a minimum. Before making your own miso, please read Appendix C in order to get a sense of the chemical and microbiological changes you will be helping on their way.

Four Decisions

Before starting your miso, you will have to make four basic decisions:

1. **The Time of Year:** For best results, make miso during the cold months when the air is relatively free of contaminating microorganisms. Such molds and bacteria increase in number during the warmer part of the year and can impart an undesirable (sour or acidic) flavor to the finished product. Late November or early March are the best times for preparing homemade koji since the weather is cold but not *too* cold. Some Japanese prefer to make their miso in the fall when the new-crop soybeans and rice are at their peak of flavor; others prefer early spring, just before the warm months when most

167

of the transformation due to fermentation takes place in the kegs. Miso prepared during the cold months will be ready by October when the heat of summer is past and fall breezes begin to chill the air. In Japan, families generally make miso only once a year, preparing one vat of each of several varieties.

2. To Make or Buy the Koji: Homemade koji can be prepared for less than one-fourth the cost of storebought varieties, but the process takes about two days and it is not always possible to get a top-quality product on the first try. Nevertheless, if the instructions contained in the second half of this chapter are followed carefully, you should get good results. Most Japanese homemade miso is presently prepared with ready-made koji: the recipes are easy to follow, take very little preparation time, and are virtually foolproof. We have therefore placed them at the start of this chapter to encourage beginners to try them first.

3. The Vat Size: We will henceforth use the word "vat" to refer to all sizes and types of fermentation containers. The total amount of miso you wish to prepare determines the size of the vat you will need. It is generally agreed that *the larger the vat, the easier it is to produce delicious miso.* Why? Because the larger the vat, the smaller the total surface area (bottom, sides, and top) of the miso in proportion to the total volume. As shown in the figure below, the miso in the larger container has only one-third as much surface area per unit volume as the miso in the smaller.

		SMALL	LARGE
Surface Area	(in²)	169	1526
Volume	(in³)	169	4578
Ratio	(S:V)	1.0	0.33

Thus large containers have a voluminous central core of miso totally sealed off from the surrounding environment; only a proportionally small surface area remains in contact with the walls, bottom, and top of the container where it is subject to gradual moisture losses through the container's pores and subtle outside (aerobic) influences. Miso in containers of only 1- to 2-quarts capacity may develop a slightly tart or alcoholic flavor, with moisture losses running as high as 5 to 7 percent of the original weight causing a concentration in salt content and an excessively "salty" flavor. For best results, your vat

should have a capacity of no less than 1 gallon, which is enough to hold 2 small-scale batches as described below. A Japanese family will typically make one 10-gallon or two 5-gallon vatfuls each year; individuals might consider pooling their efforts with friends to fill one such vat. Communities often use a wooden keg of 50 gallons capacity.

4. Batch Size: After you have determined the total amount of miso you wish to make, you are ready to decide how many individual batches will be required. The batch size is generally determined by the size of the cooking pots and mixing containers in your kitchen. Often two or three batches are needed to fill one vat. In the following section we give three batch sizes: small, medium, and large. A small batch makes about 2 quarts of miso, a medium batch 2 gallons, and a large batch 8 gallons. We have chosen a small-scale basic recipe so that the 2 cups of soybeans required can be cooked in a standard pressure cooker or 1-gallon pot found in most kitchens. However, if you have a large pressure cooker or pot, you will save time and fuel by doubling the basic recipe or using a larger batch size.

HOMEMADE MISO
(*Using Ready-made Koji*)

The following section contains recipes for six basic varieties of miso that are easily prepared at home. Each is actually only a variation on a basic theme, for in each recipe (for the same batch size) the amount of soybeans is the same (fig. 31, p. 172). The basic method calls for pressure cooking the soybeans, which takes much less time and fuel than boiling and prevents the beans from turning reddish-brown during cooking, thereby making it possible to produce light-colored misos as well as the standard darker varieties. Since a typical pressure cooker will hold just 2 cups of dry soybeans, larger batches should be prepared by multiple cooking. Overfilling may cause loose soybean hulls to clog the steam escape valve. If a pressure cooker is not available, use a pot (see Variation 1).

Using pressure-cooked soybeans, one batch of miso ingredients will be in the vat and ready to start fermentation within one hour after you begin work. The commercial miso retailed in the United States will cost you about 2½ times as much per pound as the miso in the following recipes, and 5½ times as much as miso prepared from homemade koji!

Utensils

To prepare miso on a small scale, you will need the following common kitchen utensils and a fermentation container (fig. 28):

A standard pressure cooker or pot of 1-gallon capacity

A mixing pot of 1½ to 2½ gallons capacity

A colander or bamboo *zaru*

A wooden pestle (a wooden rod about 2 inches in diameter, a tall thin bottle, or a potato masher also work well), or a grain mill or meat grinder

A measuring cup and measuring spoons

A large (wooden) spoon or spatula

A vat of at least 1-gallon capacity (see below)

A sealing sheet consisting of a 1½-foot square of butcher paper, brown kraft paper, or Japanese natural *washi* paper; or a double thickness of sturdy tightly-woven undyed cloth; or several sheets of wide *kombu;* or a piece of plastic wrap or cellophane

A pressing lid made of a piece of wood, plywood, firm plastic, or other sturdy material cut to fit inside the fermentation container atop the sealing sheet with a gap of 1/8 inch or less between the perimeter of the lid and the container's walls

A 3- to 4-pound pressing weight such as a well-washed stone or brick, or a water-filled jar

A piece of wrapping paper, newspaper, or polyethylene sheeting and a piece of string several feet long

A 3- by 5-inch index card

Fig. 28. Utensils for making miso

The key piece of equipment is the vat. The ideal small- or medium-scale vat (1- to 4-gallons capacity) is made of glazed or non-porous earthenware and is either cylindrical in shape or has a wide mouth. A traditional American crock (fig. 29), works perfectly; still used for pickling, and in natural food stores for storing and displaying grains, nuts, or dried fruits, it is available in various sizes at many natural food stores, Japanese hardware stores, or old-fashioned American hardware stores. Or order from the producer: Marshall Pottery Inc., 1400 Lake St., Marshall, TX 75670. Tel. 214-938-9201. A glass container, which has the advantage of permitting observation of the fermentation process, or an enamelware pot also work well. Small wooden kegs sometimes sold as containers for miso or shoyu are excellent for quantities of 4 gallons or more; be sure they are well seasoned and do not use them for smaller quantities since they may cause an excessive loss of moisture due to their slight porosity. Large wooden barrels (available in 30- and 55-gallon sizes for about $5.00 each from nail wholesalers or salted salmon importers) or used hogshead casks (available in 63- to 140-gallon sizes from some wineries) are ideal for community or large-scale production. Regardless of the vat's size, the diameter of its mouth should be no greater than its depth (preferably slightly less), and the miso should fill the vat to at least 80 percent of capacity.

Vats made of polyethylene or other plastics having 5- to 10-gallons capacity are now widely used in Japan, but experienced miso makers feel that natural materials yield a better flavor, and may be safer. Do not use a metal vat.

For larger batch sizes, increase the size of your utensils accordingly.

Fig. 29. Miso fermentation crocks

resembling the nap on a brand new tennis ball. This koji is used primarily to prepare homemade *Amazaké* (p. 162) but also works well in the preparation of both miso and salt-pickled vegetables.

Ingredients

Each of the basic ingredients for homemade miso is now available at reasonable prices in the United States. For a list of sources, see page 258.

Soybeans: Any variety of whole dry soybeans available at natural or health food stores, co-ops, and some supermarkets. Order in bulk for substantial savings. Soy grits (see Variation 4) may be either the coarse or fine varieties now available at better natural food stores. The larger sized and slightly more expensive "vegetable" type soybeans, bred from Japanese stock, are preferred by some to the smaller and more widely available U.S. "field" soybeans.

Corona hand-mill

Ready-made Dried Koji *(Urikoji):* This koji is prepared by drying fresh koji on large screens in an oven at 104°F. Both ready-made rice and barley koji are now available in the West at most natural food stores and at Japanese food markets (especially at New Years). The main U.S. producer is Miyako Oriental Foods in Los Angeles. In 1983 a 20-ounce tub of their white rice koji retailed for $3.46, or the equivalent of $2.77 a pound. Names of other makers, importers, and distributors are given on page 258. There are two basic types of ready-made dried koji:

Firm Granular Koji is composed of whole separate kernals of rice or barley with very little downy white mycelium visible on the surface of each grain. The beige or milky-white kernels look something like slightly puffed rice. One variety used primarily for making miso and one for salt-pickled vegetables *(tsukemono).* Miyako makes the miso type.

Soft Mat Koji is sold in sheets about 8 to 10 inches square and ¾ inch thick. It is composed of fluffy grains of steamed rice bound together by a felt-like white mycelium

Firm granular koji is the traditional form used to make miso and is still considered the best since it has more "strength" (ability to break down proteins and carbohydrates) than the soft mat variety. High-quality granular koji will have a very small percentage of "transparent" grains (those which the mycelium has not penetrated) among the milky-white majority. Individual grains, when broken in half, should show the white mycelium penetrating to the very center and not have a transparent core.

Since dried koji does not, in general, have quite as much "strength" as fresh koji, miso prepared with it takes slightly longer to come to maturity. This explains the difference in aging times between the following homemade varieties and their commercial counterparts as described in Chapter 4.

All koji should be kept well sealed in a cool dry place. For long-term storage, small quantities should be refrigerated (but not frozen). Koji with an olive-green or yellowish tint has probably stood too long in a warm place causing sporulation; it is best used whole or ground as koji starter (p. 178).

Ready-made Fresh Koji: Excellent quality fresh rice koji, produced by Miyako Oriental Foods in Los Angeles, is now widely available in the U.S. In Japan, fresh koji may be purchased directly from a koji or miso shop the day before the soybeans are cooked; it is immediately crumbled and mixed with all of the salt in the miso recipe, placed in a covered container, and stored in a cool, dry place. A given volume of fresh koji weighs about 14 percent more than dried granular koji. In the following recipes, when substituting fresh koji for dried, use only 60 percent of the required mixing liquid.

Salt: Any salt may be used, but to make miso with the best flavor and nutritional value, use sun-dried, unrefined natural sea salt, now available at some natural and health food stores and very rich in minerals (more than 63 varieties). You can prepare your own natural salt by simmering clean sea water in a large kettle until almost all of the moisture has evaporated, placing the moist salt in a cloth-lined colander or strainer, and allowing it to drain for several days; measure homemade salt by volume rather than weight when using it to make miso. (Save the liquid nigari that drips from the salt to use in preparing tofu.)

The salt in miso mellows as the fermentation proceeds; thus miso which tastes quite salty after six months may taste just right one year later. To compensate for this phenomenon, some recipes increase the proportion of salt together with the expected fermentation time. Whereas a 1-year red miso might, for example, require 2½ pounds of salt, the same product fermented for 2½ years would require 4 pounds.

People wishing to prepare low-salt misos should make either sweet red or sweet white varieties; do not simply try to reduce the salt in other types or they may spoil. As a general rule, the minimum amount of salt used with a given weight of grain or dried koji should *not fall below* the broken line in figure 30. The equation for this minimum amount is:

$$S = \frac{45 - G}{10}$$

where S is the weight in pounds of salt and G is the weight in pounds of grain or dried koji used with 10 pounds of dry soybeans. Thus a recipe calling for 10 pounds each soybeans and dried rice koji should not contain less than 3.5 pounds salt.

Fig. 30. Basic Proportions of Salt and Grain (or Dried Koji) used with 10 Pounds of Dry Soybeans for Different Miso Varieties

Water: Any water may be used for cooking the soybeans or as mixing liquid (below), but fresh pure water—from a deep well, spring, or distilled—has traditionally been considered to give the best flavor and most trouble-free fermentation. Water containing an abundance of chlorine or other chemicals may somewhat retard the activity of miso's microorganisms, while impure water may introduce contaminating microorganisms.

Seed Miso: Use any good-quality mature miso, either from a previous batch of your own making or commercial miso which has not been pasteurized and contains no preservatives. The use of a small amount of seed miso as an inoculum adds large numbers of yeasts and bacteria to the unfermented ingredients thereby enhancing the aroma and flavor of the finished product and reducing the fermentation time by up to 50 percent. It is best to use seed miso of the same variety as the miso you wish to prepare, but any miso will work.

Mixing Liquid: Either boiled water or the cooking liquid remaining after boiling the soybeans is mixed with the other ingredients to give the miso its proper moisture content. In Japan, this is called "seed water" (*tané mizu*). Fresh water, unless taken from a very pure deep well, is always boiled to assure that no contaminating microorganisms are present. From November until early April, soybean cooking liquid gives excellent results and helps make full use of the soybean nutrients. However, if the miso is prepared during the warm half of the year, water should be used since the soybean cooking liquid may encourage spoilage; in this case, cook the soybeans so that very little liquid remains at the end. If you want to try to use cooking liquid during the warmer part of the year, mix the liquid with 3 tablespoons salt as soon as it has drained from the beans, and reduce the salt added with the other ingredients accordingly.

The proper amount of liquid to be added to any given mixture of ingredients is difficult to specify exactly since it depends upon the moisture level of the koji and the moisture losses through the vat (which are determined by the vat's size and construction). If too much liquid is added, the miso can easily over-ferment and develop a strong alcoholic aroma. The miso's moisture content can be adjusted during fermentation by simply increasing or decreasing the pressing weight.

Alternate Carbohydrate Sources: For rice or barley koji, you may substitute up to 50 percent cornmeal or corn, sweet potatoes, Irish potatoes, or *kabocha;* these foods should be well steamed or boiled (see Variation 5). Wheat koji may be substituted in equal parts. See also page 44.

Alternate Protein Sources: For soybeans, you may substitute up to 100 percent broad, black, *azuki,* lima, or garbanzo beans, or others listed on page 44. Indian pulses (Bengal gram, Thur dhal, green gram, and Field beans) also work well. If 10 to 20 percent soybeans (and peanuts) are used together with these ingredients, the amino acid balance and total usable protein will be considerably enhanced (see p. 21).

Fig. 31. Proportions by Weight of Basic Ingredients for Various Homemade Misos

Type of Miso	Batch Size	Dry Soybeans		Dried Koji	Soft Mat	Firm Granular [1]	Salt		Mixing Liquid		Seed Miso (Optional)	
Red Miso	BASIC RATIO (WT)	10		8.5			4.4		11.1		0.4	
	Small Batch	13 oz	2c	11.1 oz	3.4c	2.4c	5.7 oz	8.9T	14.4 oz	1.7c	0.5oz	1T
	Medium	3 lb 4 oz	8c	2 lb 12 oz	13.4c	9.7c	22.9 oz	2.2c	3 lb 9 oz	6.9c	2.1oz	4T
	Large	13 lb	32c	11 lb 1 oz	53.5c	39.0c	5 lb 12 oz	9.0c	14 lb 7 oz	27.7c	8.3oz	1c
Barley Miso	BASIC RATIO (WT)	10		10			4.6		13.0		0.4	
	Small Batch	13 oz	2c	13 oz	3.9c	2.9c	6.0 oz	9.3T	16.9 oz	2.0c	0.5oz	1T
	Medium	3 lb 4 oz	8c	3 lb 4 oz	15.7c	11.4c	23.9 oz	2.3c	4 lb 4 oz	8.1c	2.1oz	4T
	Large	13 lb	32c	13 lb	62.7c	45.7c	6 lb 0 oz	9.4c	16 lb 14 oz	32.5c	8.3oz	1c
Light-yellow Miso	BASIC RATIO (WT)	10		8.5			4.1		11.1		0.4	
	Small Batch	13 oz	2c	11.1 oz	3.4c	2.4c	5.3 oz	8.3T	14.4 oz	1.7c	0.5oz	1T
	Medium	3 lb 4 oz	8c	2 lb 12 oz	13.4c	9.7c	21.3 oz	2.1c	3 lb 9 oz	6.9c	2.1oz	4T
	Large	13 lb	32c	11 lb 1 oz	53.5c	39.0c	5 lb 3 oz	8.4c	14 lb 7 oz	27.7c	8.3oz	1c
Sweet Red Miso	BASIC RATIO (WT)	10		13			2.2		12.3		0	
	Small Batch	13 oz	2c	16.9 oz	5.1c	3.7c	2.9 oz	4.5T	16.0 oz	1.9c	—	—
	Medium	3 lb 4 oz	8c	4 lb 3 oz	20.4c	14.4c	11.4 oz	1.1c	4 lb 0 oz	7.7c	—	—
	Large	13 lb	32c	16 lb 12 oz	81.5c	59.4c	2 lb 14 oz	4.5c	16 lb 0 oz	30.8c	—	—
Sweet White Miso	BASIC RATIO (WT)	10		20			2.4		19.2		0.4	
	Small Batch	13 oz	2c	1 lb 12 oz	8.4c	6.2c	3.1 oz	4.9T	25.0 oz	3.0c	0.5oz	1T
	Medium	3 lb 4 oz	8c	7 lb	33.7c	24.6c	12.5 oz	1.2c	6 lb 4 oz	12.0c	2.1oz	4T
	Large	13 lb	32c	28 lb	134.9c	98.5c	3 lb 2 oz	4.9c	24 lb 15 oz	48.0c	8.3oz	1C
Mellow Barley Miso	BASIC RATIO (WT)	10		17			4.8		16.3		0.4	
	Small Batch	13 oz	2c	1 lb 6 oz	6.6c	4.8c	6.2 oz	9.7T	21.2 oz	2.6c	0.5oz	1T
	Medium	3 lb 4 oz	8c	5 lb 8 oz	26.5c	19.3c	25.0 oz	2.4c	5 lb 5 oz	10.2c	2.1oz	4T
	Large	13 lb	32c	22 lb 2 oz	106.0c	77.3c	6 lb 4 oz	9.8c	21 lb 3 oz	40.9c	8.3oz	1c
Soybean Miso	BASIC RATIO (WT)	10		—			2.0		3.4		0.4	
	Medium Batch	3 lb 4 oz	8c	—			10.4 oz	1.0c	16.6 oz	2c	2.1oz	4T
	Large	13 lb	32c	—			2 lb 10 oz	4.1c	4 lb 2 oz	8c	9.4oz	1c

Notes:
1) The ready-made firm granular dried koji produced in the U.S. by Miyako Oriental Foods weights 175 grams (6.17 ounces) per cup, or 36 percent more per cup than the figures given in this table. Since the basic proportions of the table are based on weight, use either the same weight as shown in the table or 66 percent the required volume. Example: to make a small batch of red miso using Miyako firm granular dried koji, use either 11.1 ounces or 1.58 cups of this koji.
2) If using fresh koji, use 1.14 times as much by weight as the dried koji.
3) If using fresh koji, use only 40 to 60 percent as much mixing liquid; for firm granular koji, only 80 to 90 percent as much.

Homemade Red Miso
(Sendai Miso)
MAKES 6 CUPS OR 3.6 POUNDS

Basic proportions by weight: soybeans 10, dried rice koji 8.5, salt, 4.4, mixing liquid 11.1 (reduced to 6.7 if using fresh koji), seed miso 0.4.

  2 cups (13 ounces) whole dry soybeans
  3¼ cups water
  9 tablespoons (5.7 ounces) natural salt
  1 tablespoon seed miso (optional)
  1¾ cups mixing liquid
  11.1 ounces (315 grams) ready-made dried rice koji
    (about 3.4 cups well-crumbled soft mat koji or 2.4
    cups homemade or firm granular koji)

PREPARE IN ADVANCE

Carefully remove any split soybeans (their loose hulls easily clog pressure cooker), then wash beans thoroughly in pressure cooker. Add 3¼ cups water, cover pot, and soak for 3 hours, or until beans have swelled to fill hulls tightly. Skim off any hulls floating in water.

To cook beans without pressure, see Variation 1.

If using a wooden vat, fill it with water and allow it to stand overnight to seal leaks.

1) Bring cooker to full pressure over medium-high heat. When steam first begins to jiggle vent cap, turn heat *immediately* to very low (to prevent foaming over); cook for 25 minutes at 15 pounds (30 minutes at 10 pounds, or 75 minutes at 5 pounds). Remove from heat and allow to stand for 10 to 15 minutes as pressure returns to normal. Open cooker and test for doneness; each bean should be soft enough to be easily crushed between your thumb and ring finger. Re-cover cooker.

2) See that all utensils are well washed, preferably doused with boiling water. Place colander over (or into) mixing pot, pour in cooked beans, and allow to drain for 3 to 5

minutes before returning beans to cooker. Using pestle or potato masher, mash beans until only about one-third remain whole. Or run two-thirds of the beans through a grain mill or meat grinder. (For smooth miso, mash or grind all beans.) Allow beans' temperature to cool to 110°F.

3) Remove cooking liquid from mixing pot and measure out 1¾ cups, reserving any excess for use in other cooking; if insufficient liquid remains, add the necessary amount of boiled water. Combine in the mixing pot all but 1½ teaspoons of the salt and, if used, the seed miso. Add ¼ cup liquid, mixing with a wooden spoon until smooth, then stir in the remaining 1½ cups liquid. Wash hands. Using fingertips,

crumble koji into mixing pot, then stir into liquid mixture. Now add soybeans and mix all ingredients thoroughly, using first the wooden spoon, then your hands to squeeze the ingredients together. After mixing, ingredients should have about the same consistency as mature miso.

4) Wash, rinse, and dry vat. Sprinkle ¼ teaspoon salt onto your moistened fingertips and rub salt over walls of vat. Sprinkle additional ¼ teaspoon salt over bottom of vat, then spoon in miso mixture, packing it down firmly to expel air pockets. Smooth miso surface, then sprinkle on and gently rub in the remaining 1 teaspoon salt. Cover surface with seal-

ing sheet, pressing it firmly against miso to expel surface air bubbles. Top with pressing lid and weight(s).

5) Within several days, make additional batches of mixed ingredients as described above; rub salt over vat's walls before packing in mixture but do not sprinkle additional salt over surface of previous batch. When vat is at least 80 percent full and contains a minimum of 12 cups unfermented miso, sprinkle surface with salt and top with sealing sheet, lid, and weight(s).

6) Cover container with a double layer of wrapping paper and tie in place with string. On index card, write type of miso prepared, exact ingredients used, the date, and date at which miso is expected to be ready. Make a note of this latter date on your yearly calendar and tape index card to paper-wrapped vat.

HOME MADE
RED MISO
MADE MAR. 1
FINISHED OCT. 1

7) For natural fermentation, choose an unheated environment such as a garage, store-room, workshop, or barn; for faster (temperature-controlled) fermentation, see Variation 2. Choose a location that receives no direct sunlight and has adequate air circulation. Clean area well and set vat off floor on several blocks. Allow miso to ferment for at least 6 months including 1 full summer. The finest flavor will be attained after 12 months (or 18 to 24 months if seed miso is not used). Do not stir miso during fermentation.

8) As fermentation proceeds, you may wish to check the miso once every few months. However, do not open the vat more than is necessary since contact with the air encourages the growth of surface mold and contaminating organisms, and causes a slight darkening of the color and loss of aroma. If, after one month, no liquid tamari has risen to the miso's surface, increase the pressing weight. If tamari rises to a depth of more than ½ inch during the warm months, reduce the weight. To taste the miso, remove lid and sealing sheet and tilt vat so that tamari runs to one side. Using a clean spoon, open a small hole 3 to 4 inches deep at center of miso surface and retrieve a sample. Compare aroma, flavor, color, and texture with your favorite commercial miso and record your impressions on index card. If flavor is too salty or color too light, increase fermentation time. If texture is too soft, increase pressing weight and remove tamari for use in cookery (pp. 50 or 77). Overly alcoholic, acidic, or sour flavors cannot be remedied and may require that the miso be discarded. After each tasting, record date for next tasting on yearly calendar.

9) When miso is mature, remove all covering; carefully scrape off and discard any surface mold. (Although this mold is not harmful, it causes a slight decline in the miso aroma and flavor). Mix miso in container thoroughly from top to bottom to evenly distribute tamari and saltier surface layer. (Removal of tamari for use in cookery will cause a slight decline in the miso flavor.) Spoon a 1-month supply of miso into a small crock or jar and place in a refrigerator or other cool place for daily use. Smooth surface of miso remaining in container, re-cover, and weight as before. All non-sweet miso may be stored in its vat for 1 to 3 years; sweet miso should be stored in a very cool place and used within 1 to 2 months.

VARIATIONS

1) Cooking Soybeans Without Pressure: Wash beans thoroughly in cooking pot and drain well. Add 8 cups water, cover, and allow to stand for 12 to 14 hours at room temperature. (At temperatures below 50°F, increase soaking time to 18 hours.) Bring covered beans to a boil over high heat. Reduce heat to very low, set lid ajar, and simmer for about 2 hours, skimming off any foam and hulls that surface. Add 3 cups (hot) water and simmer for 2½ to 3 hours more, or until beans are soft (see Step 1). If necessary, add water from time to time so that about 2 cups cooking liquid remain when beans are done. Drain and proceed from Step 2.

2) Temperature-controlled Fermentation: Place the vat of mixed, unfermented ingredients in a warm dark place such as a water heater- or furnace room, above a stove, or in an insulated attic. During the first 2 months, choose a location

where the temperature is 70°F to 75°F. Then transfer for 2 months to a temperature of about 85°F. Finally, return to the original temperature for 2 months more. Allow the miso to stand in an unheated environment for 1 week before opening (fig. 49, p. 236). (For an even faster fermentation, place at 85°F for 1 week, 90°F for 2 to 3 months, 85°F for 1 week more, then ripen for 1 week in an unheated place.) Flavor will be improved if the miso is stirred thoroughly once or twice during this period. Fermentation time can also be decreased by packing mixed ingredients into vat while they are still hot (90°F to 100°F) and wrapping vat with several layers of thick towelling.

3) **Using Fresh Koji:** Substitute for the 11.1 ounces ready-made dried koji, 12.7 ounces fresh koji. Purchase or prepare this koji before starting to cook the soybeans, as explained on page 177. Use only 1 cup mixing liquid.

4) **Using Soy Grits:** The use of grits reduces the soaking, cooking, and fermentation times, and yields a lighter colored miso. Substitute as equal weight of grits for the soybeans in the basic recipe. a) To Pressure Cook: Soak as for whole soybeans, then pressure cook for 12 minutes. Continue as for the basic recipe. b) To Boil: Combine grits and 5 cups water in a large pot, cover, and soak for 2½ hours. Bring to a boil over low heat and simmer for 1 hour with lid slightly ajar.

5) **Using Alternate Protein and Carbohydrate Sources:** Lists of these are given to pages 44 and 171. All or part of the soybeans may be replaced by other beans. Soak, cook, and add these to the miso as for soybeans. If using alternate carbohydrate sources, add no more than 5½ ounces cooked weight and reduce the weight of koji by one half the weight of the carbohydrates added; mash well before mixing with koji. For example, to prepare a small batch of Sweet Potato Miso: Combine 5½ ounces each dried koji and mashed cooked sweet potatoes. Mix in the salt, cooked (mashed) soybeans, seed miso, and 1 cup mixing liquid (two-thirds the basic abount). Ferment as for red miso.

6) **Alternate Basic Ratios:** There are many different varieties of red miso, each determined by its ratio of basic ingredient weights. The ratio used by the Sendai Miso-shoyu Co., which makes most of the 1-year natural red miso sold in the West, is soybeans 10, koji 5.8, salt 4.5. Mr. Junsei Yamazaki (p. 241) uses 10:10:2.5 for 1-year red miso, increasing the salt to 3.5 for 2 year miso. Mr. Herman Aihara uses 10:10:3.0 for 8-month miso. Other ratios commonly employed in Japan are: a) soybeans 10, koji 6.4, salt 5.3; b) soybeans 10, koji 5.0, salt 4.1; c) soybeans 10, koji 7.2, salt 4.9. Notice that in the latter proportions, the salt is considerably higher than that used in America.

Homemade Barley Miso (Mugi Miso)

For basic ratios and amounts of raw materials, see page 172. Prepare as for Homemade Red Miso except: 1) Use barley koji instead of rice koji. 2) Increase the amount of water used in cooking the beans so that the necessary amount of mixing liquid remains when the beans have finished cooking. 3) Using natural fermentation, allow miso to ferment for at least 12 to 18 months; the finest flavor will be attained after 2 to 3

years. If using temperature controlled fermentation, reduce the above fermentation time by one half. 4) Virtually all barley miso calls for 10 parts each by weight of dry soybeans and dry koji. The ratio of salt used in America is as low as 3.5; in Japan it ranges for 4.6 to 6.0, with the latter proportion requiring 2 to 3 years fermentation.

Homemade Light-yellow Miso (Shinshu Miso)

For the basic ratio of raw materials, see page 172. Prepare as for Homemade Red Miso except: 1) After soaking, drain the beans, measure the amount of water drained, and add back an equal amount of fresh water. 2) For a lighter colored miso, rub the soaked beans between the palms of both hands to remove seedcoats before cooking. 3) Pressure cook beans to give a light color. 4) For an even lighter color (accompanied, however, by a loss of nutrients) discard all soybean cooking liquid and use boiled water as the mixing liquid. 5) Using natural fermentation, age for the same time as red miso. Using temperature controlled fermentation (to give a still lighter color) ferment for 1 week at 86°F, 3 weeks at 95°F, 1 more week at 86°F, and then allow to stand at room temperature for 1 week before serving. 6) For a slightly saltier miso, increase the ratio of salt from 4.1 to 4.5 and increase the aging time by 10 percent.

Homemade Sweet Red Miso (Edo Miso)

This is an excellent variety for those who don't want to wait more than one month to sample their homemade miso. Prepare as for Homemade Red Miso except: 1) Boil the soybeans for 8 to 10 hours, adding water as required. Or boil for 4 hours, allow to stand covered overnight, and return to the boil the next morning. Both procedures give the beans a deep reddish-brown color. 2) Drain beans for no more than 1 minute to prevent them from cooling. 3) Mash no more than 50 percent of the whole beans. 4) Mix beans with koji while beans are still quite hot (140°F to 158°F). Do not use seed miso lest the final miso sour slightly. 5) Pack the mixture into vat while mixture is still quite warm (122°F to 131°F). 6) Wrap vat with heavy towels to minimize heat loss, cover, and press as in the basic recipe. Place in a very warm environment (104°F to 113°F) for 3 weeks, then unwrap container and allow miso to ripen at room temperature for one week before serving. (Or wrap and ferment naturally for 4 to 5 weeks). Refrigerate the remaining miso to prevent spoilage.

Homemade Sweet White Miso (Shiro Miso)

Due to its high carbohydrate and low salt content, this miso takes less time to ferment than any other variety and is therefore excellent for homemade miso experimentation. Wash and cook soybeans as for Homemade Light-yellow Miso. Pack into vat while beans are quite warm and wrap as for Sweet Red Miso (above). Proceed as for light-yellow miso except: 1) Reduce fermentation time as follows: If using natural fermentation, age for 1 to 3 weeks in summer (taste frequently), 5 weeks in spring or fall, and 6 to 8 weeks in winter. If using temperature-controlled fermentation, age at 95°F for 1 to 3 weeks, or 113°F for 1 to 2 weeks. Commercial makers say this miso can be prepared in 24 hours if the basic ratio by weight is soybeans 10, dried koji 20, and salt 1.5, and if the temperature of the room is 140°F. Before serving, grind the miso in a grain mill or meat grinder to create a smooth texture.

Some makers suggest increasing the basic proportion of koji from 20 to 24 if dried rather than fresh koji is used, and increasing the proportion to 30 if the miso is prepared during the winter by natural fermentation. When using temperature-controlled fermentation, many makers mix the miso once midway through the fermentation.

Homemade Mellow Barley Miso
(Amakuchi Mugi Miso)

For the basic ratios of raw materials, see page 172. Prepare as for Homemade Red Miso except: 1) Use barley koji instead of rice koji. 2) Add enough water to the beans so that the necessary amount of mixing liquid remains when the beans have finished cooking. 3) Ferment the miso for the same lengths of time and at the same temperatures as for Homemade Sweet White Miso.

Homemade Hishio   MAKES 4½ CUPS

Also called Namé-mono or o-namé, hishio is a variety of country-style namémiso requiring a relatively short fermentation. It is generally prepared in farmhouses sometime between October and May. The koji is prepared both with and without soybeans depending on the locality. The method using soybeans is more difficult since, if the temperature rises, natto bacteria often propagate and the miso fails. In some localities, instead of stirring the miso daily, a pressing lid is used and the miso is left untouched. Hishio is thought to be the earliest ancestor of present-day shoyu.

    4 ounces eggplant, well washed
    5 ounces cucumber or uri melon, well washed
    8 tablespoons salt
    3 cups (13.4 ounces) ready-made dried wheat or barley
       koji
    2¼ cups boiled water
    2 ounces gingerroot, parboiled, and thinly sliced
       (optional)

Parboil eggplant and cucumber for about 1 minute to sterilize, then cool briefly and dice. Combine in a small bowl with 1 tablespoon salt, and gently rub salt into vegetables. Set a plate atop the layer of vegetables in bowl and place a 4- to 5-pound weight atop plate. Cover bowl with plastic wrap and press for 1 week.

On the same day vegetables begin to press, combine the koji, water, remaining 7 tablespoons salt and, if used, the gingerroot in the fermentation container. Cover container with a sheet of paper or plastic wrap held in place by a string, and place container in a clean location which receives no direct sunlight. Stir the mixture thoroughly once daily.

After 1 week, pour off all liquid from the pressed vegetables and discard. Wash hands, then squeeze vegetables firmly to expel any excess liquid. Mix vegetables into fermenting hishio. Allow hishio to ferment for 3 more weeks, stirring daily. The finished product should have a very moist texture (similar to applesauce) and pleasant, subtly sweet fragrance and flavor. Store covered in a cool place or refrigerator to prevent further fermentation.

To prepare the same miso using soybeans, use 3 1/3 cups rice koji, 1 cup soybeans and 1/3 cup salt, plus other ingredients as listed above. Cook beans, cool to body temperature and mash, then mix with the koji and cooking liquid. Add remaining ingredients and transfer to a crock. Allow to ferment, mixing daily, for about 1 to 2 weeks.

Indian Pulse & Soybean Miso

Developed in 1963 by Dr. T. N. Rao of the Central Food Technological Research Institute in Mysore, India, this flavorful product is a good example of how Japanese miso can be adapted to the tastes and ingredients of other countries. The use of a relatively small proportion of soybeans and peanuts together with local pulses greatly enhances the amino acid balance; the resultant product contains 11.2 percent protein when Bengal gram is used and 8.7 percent with Thur dhal. The percentages of salt are 5.0 and 5.4 respectively. To give a longer shelf life, powdered red peppers or chilies may be added to taste.

    2¾ pounds dehulled Bengal gram or Thur dhal, soaked
       for 15 hours in water to cover
    ½ pound whole dry soybeans, soaked for 12 hours
    ¾ pound chopped peanuts
    2½ pounds rice koji
    ¾ pound salt

Pressure-cook pulses like soybeans (25 minutes at 15 pounds), then drain and reserve. Combine soybeans and peanuts, and pressure cook as in the basic method above. Mix cooked ingredients with koji and salt (and spices if desired), add enough cooking liquid to give the desired consistency (45 to 47 percent moisture), and pack into vat. Ferment at 83°F for 5 to 10 days. Store in a very cool place, or refrigerate.

A square steamer

HOMEMADE KOJI AND KOJI STARTER

The preparation of good-quality koji is a fairly sensitive process requiring several pieces of special equipment (steamer and koji tray) that can be made or purchased without much difficulty. Don't be daunted: anyone can make good koji if he or she carefully follows the instructions given below, paying special attention to two basic points: 1) Keep your hands, all utensils, and the entire work area as clean as possible; 2) Keep the koji temperature within the recommended range throughout the 45-hour incubation period.

Most Japanese prepare koji at the same time of year they make miso, in the late fall or early spring, when the weather is cool and the number of contaminating microorganisms in the air is fairly low. The koji is generally prepared indoors in a room with a clean wooden floor. A typical batch calls for about 30 pounds of rice or barley so that the scale is considerably larger than in the following recipe. We have preferred to start with a smaller batch since the equipment is easier to obtain and you can easily increase all of the ingredients by as much as you like after your first small-scale success. The following recipe yields just enough koji for 1 medium-sized batch of Homemade Red Miso (p. 173). The amount of rice given just fills a typical steamer during one steaming.

To obtain a better perspective on the process of making koji, study the traditional miso shop method (Chapter 9), and to see how it fits into the integrated process of preparing Homemade Red Miso, study the flow chart in figure 33. The time schedule built into the following recipe ensures that all of the work can be done during ordinary waking hours. In all koji recipes, 1 pound of uncooked rice yields about 1.14 pounds of fresh koji. In the basic miso proportions on page 172, the weight of ready-made dried koji is the same as the weight of uncooked rice necessary to prepare fresh koji.

Utensils

A wooden koji tray about 16 by 10 by 2½ inches deep with a lid consisting of 1 or 2 thin boards. Japanese trays are made of cedar (*sugi*), but Douglas fir, cherry, or pine also work well. Join boards with dowels or pegs to prevent rusting. A desk or bureau drawer, a cloth-lined enamel or stainless steel tray, or a shallow fruit box may also be used.

A 1-gallon soaking container

A 1½- to 2-gallon kettle or wok. The kettle must have a flat rim and no handles rising above the rim to interfere with the steamer.

A 2- to 3-quart strainer or a cloth-lined colander

A square steamer (used with the kettle and easily made at home) or a round Chinese bamboo steamer with a woven bamboo lid (used with a wok and available at most Chinese hardware stores). Additional layers of steaming compartments may be added when using more than 6 to 8 cups of rice. The square steamer shown in figure 32 is made of ¾-inch-thick cedar boards; it is 9½ inches square and 4½ inches deep inside. Two ¾-inch-square boards near the bottom support a 9½-inch square bamboo mat which forms the steamer's floor. The base is a 13-inch-square board with a ¾-inch-diameter hole at the center. The steamer lid is composed of 2 boards reinforced on top to prevent buckling. An excellent Western-style steamer my also be improvised by placing a large colander atop several bricks or an inverted bowl inside an even larger kettle.

A steamer cloth made of coarsely-woven cotton or linen about 18 by 30 inches (or 24 inches square when used with the round steamer). Do not use ordinary dish-towel cloth; its relatively fine weave will not allow the passage of steam.

A wooden spatula or spoon

5 to 6 heavy-duty blankets (the oldest ones you have). A thick, flat cushion several feet square and a tarp may be substituted for 2 of them.

A clean linen sheet, or a piece of cotton cloth or *gyoza* mat of comparable size

A jar or bowl of several cups capacity

2 hot water bottles each wrapped in a small terrycloth towel or placed into a terrycloth sack with a drawstring mouth

2 thermometers (range 65°F to 130°F)

An incubation box, preferably one of sturdy carboard about 20 by 12 by 14 inches deep. It must be slightly larger than the koji tray. Poke a ¼-inch-diameter hole through lower left side of box, about 3 inches above the base.

Fig. 32. Utensils for making koji

Fig. 33. Miso Flow Chart

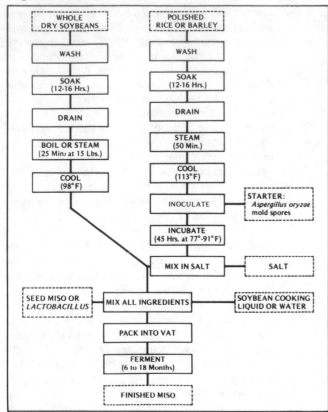

Fig. 34. Composition of Nutrients in 100 Grams of Basic Miso Ingredients

(Source: Standard Tables of Food Composition, Japan)

Ingredient	Food Energy	Protein	Fat	Carbohydrates (incl. fiber)	Ash
	Calories	*Percent*	*Percent*	*Percent*	*Percent*
Koji, Rice	334	6.0	0.7	73.4	0.4
Rice, white	351	6.2	0.8	76.9	0.6
Rice, brown	337	7.4	2.3	73.5	1.3
Barley, pearled	337	8.0	0.7	76.6	0.7
Barley, unpearled	335	10.0	1.9	71.7	2.4
Soybeans, whole	392	34.3	17.5	31.2	5.0
Soybean meal, defatted	322	49.0	0.4	36.6	6.0

softer and free of the residual "centerline" and characteristic of polished regular barley (*omugi*) so that it gives the miso what many consider to be a more agreeable texture.

Other Koji Grains: In some traditional miso shops and many farmhouses, whole wheat is used to make koji for *hishio* and Kinzanji miso. Cornmeal is also used as the koji substrate in order to create a less expensive miso. In the Shinshu area, where the latter technique originated, cornmeal is soaked in water for 1 hour, steamed for 40 minutes, cooled to body temperature, and then inoculated with starter as for rice koji. In some areas rye, oats, millet, corn kernels and even sweet potatoes are used as the substrate.

Koji Starter *(tané koji, koji kin):* Koji starter is now available from several natural food suppliers in the United States (p. 258) or in small quantities from the Northern Regional Research Center (p. 259). The best source, Westbrae, buys koji starter from Nihon Jozo Kogyo in Japan (p. 258), the producer of eight basic types: one each for red-barley, and mellow barley miso; two for soybean miso; and three for sweet white miso. Each type is available in at least one of three different forms (whole-grain, meal, or spore powder) and some types are fortified with yeasts and *Lactobacillus*. Most starters are a mixture of pure-culture mold strains, each having different capabilities in breaking down proteins, carbohydrates, and oils. Among the total of 17 different varieties and forms produced by Nihon Jozo, those most widely available in North America are the spore-powder starters for red, barley, soybean and light-colored misos, and for shoyu. Each comes sealed in a foil envelope weighing about 1½ ounces. Always keep starters well sealed in a refrigerator at 40°F to 59°F. Do not freeze.

All starter is olive green in color. The spore powder is 5 times as concentrated as the meal or whole grain forms and only 10 grams (1 tablespoon) are required to inoculate 110 pounds of (uncooked) rice. One tablespoon of the other two forms weighs 8.8 grams and will inoculate 19 pounds of rice. In cold weather or with small amounts of rice (less than 5 pounds), doubling the dosage of starter called for on the package yields good results.

If you already have a small amount of starter and wish to prepare more of your own see pages 182 and 249.

Ingredients

Rice: Most rice koji (for *amazaké* and *tsukemono* as well as for miso) is prepared from short-grain white (milled or polished) rice, most modern makers believing that the bran layers of brown rice inhibit the penetration and growth of the mycelium. For a discussion of the basic techniques and difficulties of preparing brown-rice koji, see page 36. Beginning koji makers may wish to experiment with a koji midway between the white and brown varieties by removing 50 to 75 percent of the bran layers and cracking the kernels into several pieces, thereby exposing the soft inner carbohydrate core to mycelium growth. Rice is always steamed, never boiled, to make koji; the latter process creates a wet texture which encourages the growth of undesirable bacteria. One cup raw rice (7.24 oz) yields 1.80 cups (8.25 ounces) fresh koji.

Barley *(O mugi, seimugi, hadakamugi):* For basically the same reasons that white rice is generally used to make rice koji, pearled barley (whole grains of unrolled natural barley with the bran layers removed) is used to prepare barley koji—and has been since ancient times. Barley contains slightly more protein, but slightly less carbohydrate and natural sugar than rice (fig. 34). Thus barley miso generally has a slightly higher nutritional value and is less sweet than rice miso. Other things being equal, the lack of sugars makes it necessary to ferment barley miso somewhat longer than rice miso.

Some miso makers prefer to use "naked" barley (*hadakamugi*) which is sometimes classified as a type of rye and yields miso with a unique aroma and flavor. It is also

Homemade Rice Koji
(Using Koji Starter)
MAKES 3.1 POUNDS (11 CUPS)

**6.1 cups (2.7 pounds) white rice
5/8 teaspoon (1.9 grams) spore powder koji starter or 1½
    teaspoons (4.4 grams) meal or whole-grain starter
¼ cup (lightly roasted) white or whole-wheat flour**

PREVIOUS AFTERNOON

Wash and scrub koji tray thoroughly, rinse with boiling water, and set upside-down to dry in a clean (sunny) place. Wash rice 3 or 4 times in soaking pot and soak for 12 to 16 hours in water to cover.

DAY 1:

1) 8:00 a.m.: Fill kettle (or wok) two-thirds full of water and bring to a boil. Meanwhile, transfer soaked rice to a large strainer or cloth-lined colander, rinse under cold running water, and drain well. Rinse off steamer, insert bamboo mat, and line bottom and sides with moistened steamer cloth. Place steamer and base atop kettle (or place round steamer into wok) and pour rice into steamer to a depth of about 2 inches. (For large batches of koji, if all rice will not fit into one steamer layer, either add a second layer or steam rice in several consecutive batches.) Using wooden paddle or spoon, press rice firmly into corners of steamer and smooth rice

Fig. 35a

surface (fig. 35a). Fold over ends of cloth to cover. When steam rises through rice, cover with lid (fig. b), and turn heat to medium-high. Steam for 50 minutes.

b

2) While rice is steaming, spread 2 blankets in a double layer atop a large table. Fold a clean sheet end to end and spread atop blankets.

Combine the flour and koji starter in a small cup. Mix well, cover, and place on table near blankets.

Fill a hot water bottle with boiling water; wrap in a small terrycloth towel or place in a towel sack.

3) Transfer hot steamed rice to center of sheet (fig. c). Using wooden paddle, mix rice thoroughly, breaking up all lumps, and spread to a depth of about 1 inch over a small area

c

at the center of sheet. Insert thermometer into rice and wait several minutes until temperature drops to 113°F (45°C). Sprinkle one-half of the starter-flour mixture over rice and stir vigorously with paddle until starter spores are evenly distributed throughout grain. Sprinkle on remainder of starter mixture and stir, breaking up any remaining small lumps (fig. d).

d

4) Mound and pack inoculated rice into a hemisphere at center of sheet. Insert thermometer into rice and fold edges of sheet snugly over hemisphere to form a compact bundle (fig. e). Use the 2 blankets on the table to wrap bundle firmly, to minimize heat loss. Place hot water bottle atop another thick blanket folded into fourths (or a large flat cushion). Place bundled rice directly on top of hot water bottle and cover with at least two more thick blankets. Place this entire insulated "package" in a clean, out-of-the-way place, preferably one that is fairly warm. (Avoid locations near circulating air heaters; the Japanese set their koji on boards over a warm bath.)

e

g

5) Check rice temperature every 2 to 4 hours, seeing that it stays between 77°F and 95°F (25°C and 35°C). To raise the temperature, add fresh or additional hot water bottles and/or more blankets; to lower, transfer hot water bottle to below the bottom blanket and/or remove topmost blankets. Just before retiring, check temperature and insert a fresh hot water bottle (fig. f).

up any small lumps. Shape koji into an oval mound (fig. h) 2 inches high at the highest points and slightly hollowed at the center. Insert one thermometer into koji and cover tray with

f

h

DAY 2:

6) 8:00 a.m.: Check that koji temperature is within the range prescribed above. Adjust heat to bring temperature to about 95°F. Wash hands and open bundle. The young koji should now have a pleasant aroma, and individual grains should have a white, powder-like coating and be very loosely bound together by an almost invisible mycelium. If areas of bluish-green, black, or pink molds appear, carefully remove and discard. Now mix rice thoroughly and re-bundle.

7) 10:00 a.m.: Check koji temperature, wash hands, and open bundle. Re-check aroma and appearance, then transfer koji from sheet to koji tray (fig. g). Mix koji, breaking

lid(s). Put tray into incubation box; beside tray place 2 fresh hot water bottles and an uncovered jar of hot water (to keep air humidity at 90 percent to 95 percent). Set box atop 6 to 8 thicknesses of folded blankets (or 1 or 2 thick cushions). Insert the second thermometer into the hole poked through the side of box and cover box with 2 or 3 thick blankets (fig. i). Check box air temperature from time to time; try to

i

keep it at 82°F, or at least within the range of 77°F to 91°F.

8) 2:30 p.m.: Wash hands and check that koji temperature is between 80°F and 98°F. In no case should it be allowed to fall below 77°F or rise above 104°F. Stir koji quickly but thoroughly in order to break up lumps (which can cause overheating), aid circulation, and ensure even mycelium growth. Remound koji into oval volcano shape, re-cover tray with lid set slightly ajar, and re-cover incubation box with blankets.

9) 6:00 p.m.: Check that temperature inside koji is within the range prescribed above. Stir koji thoroughly and spread it in an even layer (about 1 inch deep) over entire bottom of tray. Re-cover tray with lid set well ajar. Replenish hot water bottles and hot water in jar. (Begin to soak soybeans as described in the basic homemade miso recipe given on page 173.)

10) 10:00 p.m. (or just before retiring): Check that koji temperature is between 85°F and 96°F. If necessary, replenish hot water bottles.

DAY 3:

11) 11:00 a.m. (after 45 hours of incubation): Open box and examine koji for doneness. The individual rice grains should now be bound together with a delicate mycelium of fragrant white mold. Break open several grains (they should be soft enough to break easily) and check that the white mycelium roots have penetrated at least two-thirds of the way to the grain's center.

(If koji has a bluish-green color and a moldy or musty odor, sporulation has begun due to over-fermentation. If koji is black and slightly damp, contaminating molds have begun to grow due to overheating. In either case, place koji in a large colander, douse several times with hot water to wash off undesirable microorganisms, and re-incubate. Or discard koji and start again.)

12) Stir finished koji thoroughly, remove tray from incubation box and place in a cool, clean location for about ½ hour, or until koji temperature drops to room temperature. Measure into a large pot the amount of koji called for in the recipe you wish to prepare: a medium-sized batch of red miso, for example, requires 2 pounds 12 ounces times 1.14, or about 3 pounds 2 ounces. Mix this fresh koji with the amount of salt called for in your miso recipe, then proceed to mix with the cooked soybeans as described in variation 3 of the basic recipe for Homemade Red Miso (p. 175).

If any koji remains, transfer it to a separate container, seal well, and refrigerate; reserve for use in making *amazaké* or koji pickles (p. 162), or additional batches of miso.

STORING KOJI

If for some reason you cannot use the koji immediately, spread it in a thin layer on sheets of newspaper and allow to dry for 10 to 20 hours in a clean, warm place. Then seal and store in a cool, dry place. It will keep for 1 to 2 months in good condition, or for as long as 6 months, but with a slight decline in flavor and potency.

For even longer storage, spread the (plain or salted) koji on a clean sheet in direct sunlight (or on baking tins in a 113°F oven) until thoroughly dried. Sealed and stored in a cool, dry place, it will last for up to 1 year.

Fig. 36. Changes in Koji Temperature

1. Inoculation
2. Into crib
3. Heat generation begins
4. Stirring in crib
5. Trays into incubation room
6. First stirring
7. Second stirring
8. Trays removed

IDEAL INCUBATION AIR TEMPERATURE

Homemade Brown Rice Koji

Soak and steam very lightly polished brown rice as described above for white rice. To prevent the growth of alien microorganisms, regulate the koji temperature very carefully, keeping it about 5°F below the average temperature when using white rice. Otherwise the process is the same.

Homemade Barley Koji   MAKES 3.5 POUNDS (12.5 CUPS)
(Using Koji Starter)

To make enough fresh koji for one medium-sized batch of Homemade Barley Miso (p. 175) simply substitute polished (pearled) barley for white rice in the basic koji recipe. Prepare as for Homemade Fresh Koji except: 1) Soak the barley for only 2 to 3 hours. 2) Steam the barley for 90 minutes or until the grain becomes somewhat transparent and slightly rubbery. 3) For best results try to remove the incubating koji when the mycelium is pure white, after about 36 hours. A yellow mycelium is also satisfactory but will yield a sweeter miso. A black mycelium is unsatisfactory.

Homemade Rice or Barley Koji   MAKES 12 CUPS
(Prepared Without Koji Starter)

Preparing this koji using wild mold spores is analogous to making sourdough bread without starter. The best results are obtained in areas where the air is clear and somewhat cold, or in places such as miso shops or rooms where miso is fermenting where there are large numbers of free *Aspergillus oryzae* mold spores in the atmosphere.

In Japan, it is said that the air is much more free of undesirable organisms (that could produce toxins in fermenting koji) than most air in the U.S. or other parts of the West. Thus, unless you live in an area where the air is very clean and preferably, cold, it is better to use koji starter.

Soak and steam the rice or barley as for Homemade Rice or Barley Koji. Spread the steamed grain on a sheet and allow to stand uncovered overnight so that it "catches" wild mold spores floating in the air. Transfer grain to the koji tray and spread it in an even layer over the bottom. Place tray in incubation box and proceed as for Homemade Rice Koji. Harvest the koji after about 3 to 4 days when it is covered with a white or light-yellow mycelium.

Homemade Koji Starter

Please begin by studying the commercial process for preparing koji starter (p. 233). The best starter is prepared from homemade koji incubated under carefully controlled conditions of temperature, humidity, and cleanliness. If contaminating microorganisms enter the koji, and the koji is then made into starter, their negative effect is multiplied. Starter can also be prepared from commercial koji, but the chances of obtaining a high degree of purity are somewhat less than with the homemade variety. Traditional Japanese homemade miso was generally started either by wild mold spores (described above) or by incubating a portion of each batch of homemade koji for 5 to 7 days, until the molds sporulated, then drying the product thoroughly and storing it for later use as starter. This latter process, known as the "cut-and-dry" method, was generally carried out without the use of brown rice or wood ash now used commercially—and good results were obtained.

To make your own starter, place about ½ cup finished homemade koji in a small wooden bowl, return it to the incubator, and keep at the same temperatures required for the commercial process until the mycelium turns from white to a soft olive green. Crumble, dry in a warm oven as described, and store sealed in a cool, dry place. Use as for whole-grain starter.

HOMEMADE MISO
(*Using Homemade Koji*)

In the following recipes, the preparation of the koji is an integral part of the miso-making process.

Homemade Hatcho or Soybean Miso

MAKES 6.4 POUNDS (10.6 CUPS)

We have had excellent results with this recipe. The key lies in keeping the temperature below 100°F, lest contaminating microorganisms begin to propagate and turn the soybeans into sticky *natto*. Some makers prefer to use a special soybean koji starter, however the regular starter used for rice or barley miso also works well. Please begin by studying the process for Homemade Rice Koji (p. 179), which the following recipe closely resembles, and the process for Commercial Hatcho Miso (p. 210).

8 cups (3¼ pounds) whole dry soybeans, soaked for 10 hours and drained
½ teaspoon (1.5 grams) spore-powder koji starter or 1½ teaspoons (4.4 grams) meal- or whole-grain starter
5 tablespoons (lightly roasted) white or whole-wheat flour
1 cup (10.4 ounces) salt (increase to 1¼ cups if aging miso for 2 years or more)
2 cups mixing liquid (boiled water)
4 tablespoons Hatcho or soybean miso

Place beans in a large steamer (p. 177) and steam for 6 hours, or until individual beans are soft enough to crush easily between the thumb and small finger. Combine starter and flour in a small bowl, mixing well. Cool beans to body temperature, then transfer onto a clean sheet and sprinkle with half the flour-starter mixture. Stir beans thoroughly with a wooden spoon, then sprinkle on the rest of the mixture and re-stir until each bean is covered with the inoculum.

Transfer inoculated beans into koji tray and place into incubation box with hot water bottles and water-filled jar as for Homemade Rice Koji. Keep air temperature inside box as close as possible to 86°F (and within the range of 79°F to 89°F), and stir following the same schedule as for Homemade Rice Koji. If the temperature rises above 100°F or if the beans become sticky, immediately remove hot water bottles and jar and open lid of box until temperature and humidity drop. Then return 1 water bottle but do not return jar for at least 4 hours, or until stickiness has disappeared. Continue incubating for 40 to 50 hours, or until beans are bound together by a dense mat of fragrant white mycelium. Mash or grind two-thirds of the soybean koji and combine in a large mixing pot with the salt, mixing liquid and mature miso; mix well. Transfer to vat, cover with sealing sheet and pressing lid, and top with weights: for Hatcho miso, use a weight equal to that of the fermenting mixture; for regular soybean miso, use one-third to one-fourth the weight. Allow to stand at the natural temperature of the environment for at least 12 months or, for best flavor, for 18 months or more, including two full summers.

*Tamari Miso: Please begin by reading the description of the commercial process on page 41. Prepare as for Homemade Hatcho except increase mixing liquid to 8 or 10 cups. Ferment in a regular vat (without central core or draining trough); mix thoroughly once a day for 1 year.

To extract *tamari*, pour mature *moromi* into a coarse-weave sack or a cloth-lined colander set over a large pot. Drain, then squeeze well to extract as much of the liquid as possible. Use tamari with hors d'œuvres or as an all-purpose seasoning like shoyu. Reserve pressing residue in sack for use as a topping.

Homemade Kinzanji Miso
(Prepared with both Whole-wheat and Rice Koji)

MAKES 20 CUPS

Traditionally, Kinzanji was prepared in farmhouses during the first week of October, when there is little rain and the air is cold and clear. The koji was made from equal weights of hulled soybeans and whole wheat, the proportions still believed to give the finest flavor. However, since this relatively large proportion of soybeans invites the entry of contaminating *natto* bacteria and since it takes a long time to hull the beans by hand, some non-commercial makers prefer to use 4 parts by weight of wheat to 1 part soybeans in order to ensure success and save time.

Commercial makers say repeatedly that it is extremely difficult to obtain the true Kinzanji flavor and aroma, and not simply a miso flavor. Some makers rely on a special ready-made Kinzanji koji (which is sold commercially in Shizuoka and Aichi prefectures and will hopefully soon be available in the West), while others use rice koji to give the miso additional sweetness. Careful control of the temperature during the koji incubation is essential.

45/8 cups whole wheat
4¼ cups whole dry soybeans
1¾ pounds eggplant, cut lengthwise into halves then crosswise into slices 3/8 inch thick
7¾ ounces gingerroot, cut into very thin rounds
2 or 3 white *uri* melons or large cucumbers cut into rounds 3/8 inch thick
½ cup thinly sliced rounds of burdock root (optional)
1¼ cups salt
4¼ cups well-crumbled rice koji
2 pieces of *kombu*, each 6 to 8 inches square, rinsed (optional)
6 to 8 green *shiso* leaves (optional)

Wash 4¼ cups wheat several times in a large pot, cover with plenty of water, and soak for 24 hours; drain well.

About 1 hour before wheat has finished soaking, place soybeans into a heavy skillet or pot and roast over medium heat, stirring constantly, until fragrant and light brown. Transfer warm beans to a wooden bowl and rub vigorously between the palms of both hands to remove hulls which are then discarded. (Or place roasted beans in a winnowing basket or on a mat and crush by rolling them under a small wooden box.) Soak beans in water for 30 minutes, then drain.

Place the wheat and beans in separate steamers. Steam the beans for about 5 hours until they are soft enough to be easily crushed between the thumb and ring finger. Steam the wheat for about 90 minutes or until the skins break open.

Roast the 3/8 cup uncooked wheat in a heavy skillet until light brown and fragrant, then purée in a blender or grind in a handmill to make flour. Spread the cooked beans and wheat in a large koji tray (p. 177), then sprinkle on and mix in the roasted flour. Place tray in incubation box and cover with blankets as when preparing Homemade Koji (p. 180); allow to ferment for about 4 days. Check temperature and mold growth from time to time. When the mycelium has a sweet aroma and is basically white interspersed with tiny dots of yellow, the koji is ready to harvest. (If it has begun to turn brown and develop a strong smell, it has fermented for too long and must be discarded.)

One day before you expect the koji to be ready, combine the four vegetables and salt in a large bowl; mix well. Cover vegetables with a large plate and press overnight with a 5- to 6-pound weight. Drain off liquid from vegetables and reserve.

Crumble the finished soybean-wheat koji, spread it on a clean surface in the sunlight, and dry for 6 hours. Allow koji to cool in the shade.

In a large vat combine soybean-wheat koji with crumbled rice koji; mix well. Add drained vegetables and reserved pickling liquid and mix again. Smooth surface of mixture and cover with one layer of *kombu*. If desired, top with a layer of green shiso leaves. Set a pressing lid on top of the miso and press with a weight of 2 to 3 pounds for at least 3 weeks and as long as 6 months. The miso may be served when the *uri* melons turn amber and become slightly transparent. (If using cucumbers in place of melons, add them 1 to 2 weeks before the miso is to be harvested.)

VARIATIONS

*Roast the whole beans, remove the skins and break the beans into halves. Mix the beans and whole wheat and steam them together until the beans are soft. Mix koji starter into the cooled mixture and ferment for 45 hours to make koji. Mix with a small amount of salt and water, pack into a fermentation container and allow to ferment for 2 months. Now add the salted, drained vegetables and ferment for 4 more months. Mix in a small amount of honey or *mizuamé* just before serving to give added sweetness and luster.
*In the above method use 4 parts by weight of wheat to 1 part soybeans. Prepare a 15% salt solution (100 parts water by weight to 15 parts salt) and add this to the finished koji to obtain the desired miso consistency. Omit use of rice koji.

Homemade Natural Shoyu · MAKES 3½ GALLONS

The process for making shoyu is very similar to that for making miso except: 1) The koji is made of a mixture of equal parts soybeans and roasted cracked wheat; 2) A different species of *Aspergillus* starter is used; 3) About three times as much mixing liquid and twice as much salt are used; and 4) the liquid is extracted by pressing after fermentation. Since extracting a large percentage of the liquid (shoyu) is the most difficult part of the process, in traditional Japan, men with special portable lever presses would make the rounds of farmhouses each year to do the job.

    10 pounds (24.5 cups) whole dry soybeans
    10 pounds (22 cups) whole wheat
    1 tablespoon shoyu koji starter (*Aspergillus soyae*), or
        substitute *A. oryzae*
    8 pounds (12½ cups) salt
    28 pounds (3.4 gallons) mixing liquid (boiled or very
        pure water)

Wash soybeans, soak in water to cover for 12 hours, then drain well. Steam (do *not* boil) at 15 pounds for 75 minutes and allow pressure to come down naturally. (Or steam at atmospheric pressure for 5½ hours.)

Meanwhile, roast wheat in a heavy dry skillet until fragrant and golden brown, then grind coarsely (or crack) so that each kernel is split into an average of 4 pieces.

Allow soybeans and wheat to cool to body temperature, then combine with the starter, mixing well. Place about 3 quarts of the mixture into each of about 8 koji trays and incubate at 77°F to 86°F for 60 to 72 hours. Mix twice as for Homemade Koji and do not allow koji temperature to rise above 104°F.

Combine mixing liquid and salt in an 8- to 10-gallon vat; add koji and mix well. Leaving top open, allow to stand in a clean place at the natural temperature of the environment for exactly 12 months. Mix daily for the first three days, then once a week throughout most of the rest of the year (twice a week in summer); mixing incorporates oxygen, expels carbon dioxide, and prevents surface mold growth. (For a quicker fermentation, place vat in a heated room at 68°F to 77°F for 6 months; stir 2 to 3 times a week.) The finished *moromi* should have a deep reddish-brown color, applesauce-like consistency, and pleasant flavor and aroma.

The best way to extract shoyu from moromi on a small scale is to use a hydraulic press and press-ing sack, the type found at many tofu shops. Or, construct a pressing rack atop an empty wooden keg or sturdy pot using 4 to 6 sturdy broom handles or 2-by-4 boards laid parallel about 2 inches apart. Place a coarsely-woven sack atop the rack and pour *moromi* into sack; twist closed mouth of sack. Now have two people holding opposite ends of a sturdy wide plank place plank across top of sack and bear down with their full body weight to press liquid from sack. Repeat numerous times, squeezing neck of sack tighter from time to time, until as much liquid as possible has been extracted. Remove *moromi* residue from sack and reserve for use as a seasoning; refrigerate unused portions in a covered container. Pour shoyu into bottles and keep well sealed in a cool place. If soy oil accumulates or white mold forms on shoyu surface, remove and discard.

Homemade Namémiso · MAKES 2 GALLONS

This is the recipe for the delicious *namémiso* prepared at the Amanoya shop in Tokyo (p. 240). A typical batch of theirs is about nine times as large as the following recipe.

    ½ pound small eggplants
    1½ ounces (21/3 tablespoons) salt
    13.3 pounds (29 cups) wheat, roasted and split or cracked
    1 pound (2½ cups) whole soybeans
    1 tablespoon koji starter
    1 gallon shoyu
    ¾ cup *mirin*
    11/3 cups *mizuamé* or *bakugato* (millet or barley sugar
        syrup)
    ½ pound gingerroot, peeled and thinly sliced

Place uncut eggplants in a keg, sprinkle with the salt and press under 3- to 4-pound weight for 1 week. Drain, rinse, and cut lengthwise into halves, then into 3/8-inch cubes.

Mix wheat and soybeans and soak for 2 to 3 hours (longer in cold weather) or until soybeans just yield when pressed. Steam for 40 minutes, or until a piece of wheat broken open is no longer white inside. Cool to 80°F, then mix in koji starter. Prepare koji as for Homemade Rice Koji (p. 179). Combine finished koji with remaining ingredients and the salted eggplants. Ferment in kegs for 10 days in mid-summer, 20 days in fall or spring, and 30 days in winter.

Fig. 37. Equivalent Weights and Volumes of Miso Ingredients

Ingredient	Volume	Wt. (gm)	Wt. (oz)
Soybeans, whole dry	1 cup	185	6.52
Koji, dry soft mat (crumbled)	1 cup	94.1	3.32
Koji, dry firm granular	1 cup	129	4.55
Koji, fresh (crumbled)	1 cup	130	4.58
Salt	1 cup	290	10.2
Miso	1 cup	276	9.73
Water	1 cup	236	8.32
Rice or barley	1 cup	205	7.24
Miso	1 table-spoon	17.3	0.61

8
Japanese Farmhouse Miso

THIS CHAPTER has two basic purposes: first, to describe the traditional art of preparing country-style miso and the role of that miso in Japanese culture and cookery; and second, to present this method and its tools as a model for the preparation of miso in communities in the West on a scale 2½ times the size of the largest recipe in the previous chapter.

Most of Japan's earliest miso was prepared by farmers and Buddhist priests. Indeed, throughout most of East Asia, the appearance of miso shops and professional craftsmen has been a rather recent development. Roughly 85 percent of all the miso found in present-day Korea, for example, is still made in private homes. And until the 1940s, most Japanese farmhouses and temples were totally self-sufficient in this regard.

Although there are more miso shops in Japan than in any other country in the Far East, the tradition of farmhouse miso remains alive, especially in remote rural areas and in the northeast provinces. This miso, an estimated 132,000 tons in 1974, accounts for about 17 percent of the nation's total output, with some 35,000 tons of soybeans used each year to produce it. Arriving at the right season in rural villages in any of Japan's famous farmhouse-miso provinces (Aomori, Nakano, Fukushima, Iwate, Yamanashi), one can still witness the art, craft, and ceremony involved in the ancient process. In most of these areas, one large batch of miso is made each year in March or April, during the peach-blossom season, when the farmers are awaiting the rice planting, the water is clear and cold, the air free of molds, and the temperature just warm enough to allow for the preparation of koji. In other areas, miso is made in the fall, during the lull following the harvest, for at this time, too, the weather is favorable, and the new-crop rice and soybeans are at their peak of flavor.

Every rural family that makes miso has its own distinctive variety in which it takes great pride. From this fact stems the famous proverb *temaemiso*, which literally means simply "homemade miso," but is a compact way of saying that everyone likes his own miso best. In fact the Japanese term for self-glorification is *temaemiso;* when someone shows unusual satisfaction in something he has made or done himself, others may say in jest: "It's just like his pride in his homemade miso," or "There he goes, lining up his kegs of homemade miso."

In Japan, farmhouse miso is known as *inaka* or "rural" miso, and city dwellers speak nostalgically of the satisfying, down-to-earth goodness of the miso made in the village from which they trace their origin. During the major holiday seasons of New Year's and O-bon (all saints week), many return to the countryside to visit relatives, and most return with a large supply of farmhouse miso to help perpetuate the good memories of their visit. Although miso connoisseurs say that the finest country-style miso is made in areas where the air is clear and cold, or in the mountains where there is a sharp contrast between day- and nighttime temperatures, most Japanese simply refuse to believe that any miso can be more delicious than that prepared in their own native area.

Three different types of miso are prepared in Japanese farmhouses. The most common is either red or barley miso, prepared using a relatively large proportion of salt and the prevailing grain of the region, with a fermentation time of one to three years. In addition, many farmers also prepare one of the more than five varieties of Finger Lickin' Miso (p. 42). In a few parts of Japan, the main type is still soybean miso made with *miso-dama* or "miso balls" (p. 193). The first and third types are most widely used in miso soups and, on special occasions, in farmhouse-style Dengaku, Oden, or Nishimé. The second type is generally used as a topping for hot rice or, occasionally, as an hors d'œuvre with sake.

Part of each year's supply will usually be made with a relatively large proportion of salt and part will be made with less. The saltier varieties are used in soups throughout the summer months, since farmers feel they require an increased salt intake for their strenuous work under the hot sun. All are used abundantly, and even today miso consumption in rural Japan is about 20 percent higher than it is in the cities.

The work of preparing each year's supply is shared by the entire family, although in most villages it is primarily the responsibility of the womenfolk; the men help with the pounding and other heavy work but often know little of the technical details of the process. Always surrounded by an atmosphere of festivity, good cheer and excitement for the children, the work begins when the family's miso-making tools are brought out of storage from the barn, attic, or cellar. The huge wooden mortar and pestle used for mashing the cooked soybeans are charged with good memories of the New Year's season when they are used for pounding *mochi* (rice cakes). The main miso ingredients are gathered and made ready: home-grown soybeans often planted along the paths between the rice and barley fields, and grain freshly harvested and/or stored in the family barn. In some areas, miso making is a communal event, with an entire village or group of families coming together for 3 or 4 days and interspersing their work with song, dance, and great merriment.

Farmhouse cauldrons and dais

Together with the sense of festivity is an even deeper sense of ritual, so often found in traditional societies where food is gratefully recieved as a life-sustaining gift from mother earth and its preparation is considered a sacred act. The work is timed to begin so that the third day, when fermentation in the vats begins, is highly propitious according to the ancient lunar calendar. Before lighting the fire under the massive kitchen cauldron (used only on special occasions), the entire family is assembled and two pinches of salt are placed at the corners of the cauldron's dais or on the cauldron's rim as an act of purification and offering to the many forces, great and minute, that will carry the miso fermentation to fruition. A year or more later, when the miso vats are ready to be opened, another propitious day is chosen and the family again gathers together. A small sample of the new miso is taken as a gift to neighbors, and the family tests the flavor in a special soup at the very next meal.

The koji prepared in many farmhouses is made without the use of a special starter; the ubiquitous natural mold spores, floating in the air and present in large numbers wherever other miso is fermenting, are found to be sufficient. In areas where grains or soybeans are scarce or expensive, or to produce unique flavors, rural miso makers sometimes add cooked starchy vegetables or corn to the basic mixture or even use the vegetables as the substrate for the koji.

In many farmhouses, various vegetables (which have been previously salt-pickled under pressure to reduce their moisture content) are buried in the miso just before it begins its fermentation. The art of pickling, in all of its many forms, is highly evolved in rural Japan as is its Western counterpart, the canning of fruits and jams. Homemade miso pickles are particularly prized by nursing mothers, since they are said to aid digestion and improve the flow and quality of breast milk.

When all is done, the family gathers to seal the 20-gallon wooden kegs or 10-gallon earthenware crocks. The relatively high salt content in most farmhouse miso, the often unheated (and generally very cold) environment, and the frequent lack of "strength" in koji prepared with wild mold spores, all combine to necessitate a relatively long aging, in most cases two to three years. In recent times, as farmers have moved to the cities, farms have been left abandoned throughout the remote countryside, and in the barns on a number of these we have found large kegs of (delicious) miso which were apparently too heavy to transport to the nearest road.

Despite its survival in some parts of Japan, the traditional farmhouse method is nevertheless gradually being forgotten and is in danger of dying out completely over the next few decades due largely to the spread of commercial miso to even the most remote regions of the nation. The estimated total rural production dropped 40 percent in the short period between 1966 and 1974, and many families that formerly prepared their own koji and cooked their soybeans now prefer to buy either ready-made koji or *shikomi-miso*, a mixture of the basic ingredients pre-packed in the vat and ready to ferment. Fortunately, however, there has been a recent revival of interest in preparing farmhouse miso among young Japanese. Living in rural communities devoted to a simple life of self-sufficiency and respect for tradition, they hope to stem the tide.

Fig. 38. Farmhouse Floorplan

The kura

The Farmhouse as the Stage

Country-style miso is prepared and often fermented inside the farmhouse itself (fig. 38). The kitchen and entrance room usually have dirt floors well suited for the heavy work of pounding the beans and supporting the log fire that heats the caldron. The warm rice is usually allowed to cool on rice-straw mats spread under the eaves of an outdoor verandah or on the wide wooden step below which guests leave their shoes as they step up into the *tatami*-mat main room. The koji is often incubated at one end of this step next to the base of a huge, 2-foot-diameter wooden pillar that serves as the roofbeams' main support; there is access to this central area from both the entrance-way and the main room. In some farmhouses, the miso is fermented indoors behind the wood-burning stoves, an area warmer than the rest of the house; this arrangement not only promotes faster fermentation but makes the mature miso easier to get at from the kitchen. In other farmhouses, the miso is fermented in a nearby barn, woodshed, granary, or *kura*, the family treasure storehouse. The fireproof *kura*, with its thick earthen walls, keeps the miso cool in summer and warm in winter and thereby works like a family wine cellar to promote even fermentation. Some families may have a special *kura* (called a *miso-gura*) used exclusively for aging miso. It generally has an earth floor and a slightly moist or humid interior enviornment compared with the dry environment in the family treasure storehouse.

Tools

Most of the tools used by farmhouse miso makers are made at home by hand. Wooden tools are generally made of fragrant and durable cedar (*sugi*), which has a high resistance to salt, water, and heat. The synthesis of utility and artistry in most traditional tools makes them models of folk-craftsmanship.

Caldron: A massive iron pot 24 to 30 inches in diameter at the mouth and 18 inches deep at the center of the rounded bottom. It is set atop a stone dais over a wood-burning stove and used only on special occasions (to prepare New Year's *mochi* and festival tofu, for example); each occasion is accompanied by the salt offering described previously. Most caldrons have a heavy wooden lid, its boards joined by dovetailing.

Colanders: Made of thin strips of woven bamboo, each *zaru* is about 42 inches in diameter and 14 inches deep. Bamboo winnowing baskets are also widely used.

Koji Trays or Thick Straw Mats: Two different sets of equipment are used for incubating the koji. Four or five wooden trays, each about 2½ feet square and 3 inches deep (used in some villages to store cakes of *mochi*) are used for large batches. They are stacked atop a 2½-foot-square insulating cushion (*zabuton*) and covered with gunney sacks and/or quilts. If more heat is needed, metal or porcelain hot water bottles are placed against the boxes under the covering.

In many areas, the koji is incubated inside thick *mushiro*, or insulating mats, made of tightly-woven rice straw. They are about 3½ by 6½ feet and ½ to ¾ inch thick. The *mushiro* mats are placed on top of a thick layer of rice straw for insulation. In cold weather, 4 to 5 mats are used, and in some cases a layer of clean cloth is placed between the koji and the mats.

Ladle: A 2-quart ladle with a sturdy 3-foot wooden handle.

Pounding Miso Ingredients

Mortar and Pestle: The massive wooden farmhouse mortar, 2½ feet in diameter and about 2 feet tall, is also used for pounding steamed glutinous rice to make *mochi*. Most mortars weigh several hundred pounds and the finest varieties are made of zelkovia (*keyaki*) using only the hard, tough trunk-wood just above the roots. Wooden pestles of two designs are used for pounding miso soybeans. One is shaped like a huge mallet with a heavy, slightly rounded head; the other is simply a heavy piece of wood about 3 to 4 inches in diameter at the base and 4 feet long. It is said that in some areas, the cooked soybeans are placed in a large wooden tub and crushed underfoot by workers wearing rice-straw sandals, as was the practice in traditional miso shops.

Rice Paddle: A wooden paddle about 9½ inches long, ordinarily used for serving rice.

Soaking Keg: A 19-gallon wooden container, identical to the wooden fermentation kegs described below under "vats."

Steamers and Cauldron Steaming Lid: A typical steamer consists of 4 to 6 wooden boxes, each about 5 inches deep and either 15 to 25 inches square or 22 inches in diameter. The bottom of each box is made of bamboo slats; the boxes are usually stacked one atop the other during steaming. A notch or hole in the extended sides of each box allows for the

insertion of a long pole so that it can be lifted off without having to touch the hot wood. A flat lid covers the top box, and all are set on a steaming lid placed over the mouth of the cauldron. A 1-inch-square hole in the center of this lid allows steam to rise from the cauldron. In some cases a steam disperser is placed over this hole to allow more uniform steaming of the grain in the bottom box.

Straw Cooling Mats: Either *mushiro* mats (see above) or *gyoza* mats of about the same size and made of *igusa* reeds are spread on the floor and covered with the freshly steamed grain. Usually two, but sometimes as many as four mats are used.

Vats: Either earthenware crocks or wooden kegs make excellent fermentation containers for the miso. A typical crock is 16 to 20 inches in diameter and 20 to 30 inches deep. The inside is glazed to prevent moisture loss and the mouth is wide enough to allow the insertion of a pressing lid. A typical wooden keg is either 9½ or 19 gallons in capacity. Ordinarily used as a sake container, it is bound with hoops of braided bamboo and must be well seasoned.

Each vat has a wooden pressing lid about 1 inch thick and ½ to 1 inch smaller in diameter than the mouth of the keg. Some kegs are sealed with a tight-fitting barrelhead that is used to keep out dust. Rope may be packed into the space between the head's outer rim and the vat's mouth to create a tighter fit. Or a regular wooden lid, grooved in a circle where it touches the mouth of the vat, may serve the same purpose.

Grooved lid

Ingredients

Grain: All farmouse miso is made with the grain that is most available locally. Most families use grain they have grown themselves and which has been polished at the local rice shop. Traditionally, the word *inaka* (country-style) miso has generally connoted barley rather than rice or soybean miso. In some areas, wheat is used together with barley to give the miso a darker color.

Water: Water quality is believed to have a very important effect on the miso's flavor. Water drawn from the deep farmhouse well, whence it comes cold and pure, is preferred. It is generally boiled when used as the mixing liquid.

Koji Starter: At least four different methods are used to start koji. 1) *Natural Molds:* Perhaps the oldest, most difficult, and most time-consuming way of making koji, in which mold spores living in the air and on the koji trays or straw mats are used to inoculate the warm rice. It is said that in parts of Japan with clean air, molds that yield mycotoxins (such as aflatoxins) are rarer than in most countries. 2) *Cut-and-Dried Starter:* See page 182. 3) *Commercial Koji Starter:* Whole-grain starter purchased from the local koji maker or sake brewer. 4) *Regular Koji:* A small amount of commercial or homemade dried koji is mixed with the warm grain, which is then allowed to be inoculated further by natural mold spores; the addition of the dried koji simply hastens the process, however the results are generally not as good as when methods 2 or 3 are used.

Soybeans: Japanese soybeans are generally believed to yield the best miso. While many families grow their own, those that do not, purchase them from a local tofu or miso shop. New-crop beans have the best flavor.

Salt: Widely known as *nami-no-hana,* "the flowers of the waves," natural salt is preferred. Many farmers buy a large rice-straw sack filled with unrefined salt, allow it to drain (indoors) over a wooden tub for several weeks, and collect the liquid (*nigari*) that drips into the tub for use in making tofu. They then use the "naturally-refined" salt remaining in the sack to make their miso. Since the koji used in most farmhouse miso is not prepared under the controlled conditions prevailing in commercial shops, and since country-style miso is generally fermented for a long time, a relatively large amount of salt is used to prevent spoilage and the growth of contaminating microorganisms.

Alternate Carbohydrate and Protein Sources: Miso containing a large proportion of sweet potatoes or Irish potatoes is particularly popular (see p. 171).

Pickled Ingredients: In many farmhouses, salt-pressed vegetables are packed into the miso vat together with the basic ingredients and allowed to ferment until the miso is mature (see pp. 156 and 192).

Farmhouse Barley Miso MAKES ABOUT 16 GALLONS

The following amounts are typical of an average batch, which makes a one-year supply. Our method uses koji starter which is easiest, fastest, and guarantees the best quality. Before starting, please study Homemade Koji (p. 179) and Homemade Miso (p. 172). Many of the illustrations accompanying the basic method are adapted with permission from *Miso Daigaku.*

4½ gallons (32½ pounds) pearled barley
2 tablespoons (17.6 grams) whole-grain koji starter
5 gallons (32½ pounds) whole soybeans
1½ gallons (14.9 pounds) natural salt
3 gallons (25 pounds) mixing liquid

DAY 1:

1) Start work early in the morning. Wash and rinse the barley several times in the soaking keg placed next to your water source, then soak for 2½ to 3 hours. Fill the cauldron half full of water and cover with the steaming lid. Light a wood fire beneath the cauldron and bring the water to a boil.

2) Line each of 3 steamers with a layer of cloth. Drain barley and divide among the 3 steamers, covering the bottom of each with an even layer about 1½ to 2 inches deep. Stack steamers congruently on top of each other over the center of

the steaming lid and cover barley in top steamer with lid or a layer of heavy cloth or burlap. Measuring from the time steam begins to rise through this cloth, steam barley for 60 to 90 minutes. Have two people use two poles to lift the top two steamer boxes while a third person removes the bottom one from the cauldron lid. Re-place the top two boxes, set the bottom one atop the other two, and cover the top box with the lid or cloth; continue steaming. Transfer the bottom box to the top in this way at 20- to 30-minute intervals until all barley has been steamed. (If desired, as each bottom box is removed, sprinkle barley lightly with water to hasten cooking, and stir vigorously with the rice paddle to break up lumps.)

3) Examine grain to see that it is somewhat transparent and resilient yet fairly soft. Arrange a double thickness of cooling mats (or blankets topped with a clean sheet) in the

shade outdoors and spread barley on mats in a layer 1 to 2 inches thick. Stir barley frequently with wooden paddle to hasten cooling and drying.

4) When grain temperature drops to about body temperature, and when its moisture level has decreased to the extent that only a few kernels stick to your palm if touched, sprinkle on the koji starter. Using the wooden paddle, lightly mix starter into barley, breaking up all lumps; then mix vigorously for 5 minutes. (If preparing koji without starter or if using koji boxes, see Variation 1.) Using your fingertips, crumble any remaining small lumps of grain, then gather inoculated barley into a mound at center of mat.

5) Fold ends and sides of mat over barley to form a compact bundle into which air cannot easily enter. Spread some dry straw as insulation to a depth of about 12 inches over an area the size of one of the mats (or use a mattress, thick cushions, or air mattress). Cover with the bottom cooling mat, then place bundle on top of mat. Cover with 2 or more straw mats, blankets, or quilts. If air temperature is low, place 2 to 4 hot water bottles beneath covering mats next to barley bundle; leave them in place for 10 to 12 hours, or until koji begins to develop its own heat. Check koji temperature every few hours and, if possible, once during the night, to see that it does not drop below 77°F or rise above 90°F. Add hot water bottles or covering mats to raise temperature; remove to lower.

DAY 2:

6) Early morning: Open bundle, check temperature, and mix barley thoroughly with paddle. Re-wrap, cover, and allow to stand for 2 hours more. Now unfold mat in which barley is wrapped and spread it flat on mat resting on straw. Spread barley in a layer 2 to 2½ inches deep over upper mat and cover with 2 to 4 more mats. At about 1:00 p.m. and again at 5:00 p.m., uncover barley, check that temperature is between 80°F and 95°F, and stir well. If temperature is too low, increase thickness of barley layer and/or add additional covering mats. Crumble any lumps with your fingertips; always re-cover.

In the evening, wash soybeans thoroughly, cover with water, and soak overnight in soaking keg placed near your water source.

DAY 3:

7) Early morning: Uncover and examine koji (p. 170). If barley is covered with a bloom of fragrant white mold, koji is at its best. With your fingertips, crumble thoroughly any small lumps. Leave koji uncovered for several hours as it cools to room temperature, then re-cover with a single mat to keep out contaminating microorganisms. (If koji mold is yellow and has a slightly sweet fragrance, it is satisfactory but not ideal; treat as for white mold. If mold is black, it must be removed; see p. 181). If koji is not yet done, re-cover with mats, bring temperature up to 94°F, and allow to stand until white mold appears.)

8) After beans have soaked for about 16 hours, drain and rinse well. Combine beans and about 15 gallons water in caldron, and light a wood fire beneath it. Cover caldron, bring water to a boil, and simmer for 5 to 6 hours, or until beans are soft. Add water occasionally if necessary. Near the end, adjust water so that about 3 gallons of liquid remain after cooked beans are drained.

9) Ladle beans into 1 or 2 colanders set over caldron and/or soaking keg and allow to drain thoroughly. Meanwhile, wash fermentation keg, mortar, and pestle(s).

10) When beans have cooled to about body temperature, shake colanders briefly, then transfer about 10 percent of the cooked beans to the mortar. With one to three people working together, pound beans thoroughly; chanting or singing helps keep the rhythm if several pestles are being used together.

11) Set aside 6 tablespoons salt. Measure out 3 gallons soybean cooking liquid. Add one-tenth each of the remaining salt, the koji and the cooking liquid to the mashed soybeans in mortar. Mix ingredients together with pestles, then pound briefly. Rub 2 tablespoons of salt over bottom and sides of vat, then pack in pounded mixture. (If preparing pickles in miso, see Variation 2).

1) Making Koji Without Starter in Koji Boxes: For this method to be successful, it is very important that the air be quite clear and preferably fairly cold, and that natural mold spores be present in the environment. Straw mats may be used in place of the boxes, as described in the method given above.

Spread steamed barley on cooling mats and allow to cool to no less than 113°F. Spread warm barley in a layer 1½ inches thick over bottom of each of 3 to 5 koji boxes. Place

12) Repeat mixing and packing procedure until all ingredients have been used and vat is at least 80 percent full. Now, using a long pestle or your fists, gently pound miso in keg to mix the various layers and expel air. Using a paddle, pack miso surface firmly, then smooth and level it precisely. Sprinkle remaining ¼ cup salt over miso surface, making sure to reach edges. Top miso with unweighted pressing lid, pushing lid about ¼ inch into miso. (In some areas, sheets of *kombu, ho* leaves [*Magnolia hypoleuca*], or cloth are placed between miso and pressing lid, and lid is weighted with an 8- to 10-pound stone.) Seal mouth of vat with a barrelhead or

one box on an insulating cushion, then stack on the remaining boxes so that each box completely covers the one below it and thereby prevents heat loss. Cover top and sides of stack with several layers of thick straw matting and/or quilts and

lid. Cover, if desired, with a large sheet of paper tied in place with string. Record exact miso ingredients, date, and expected date of maturity on an index card and attach it to vat. Place vat in appropriate fermentation area and allow to stand untouched for at least 18 months, preferably 2 to 3 years. Sample flavor from time to time.

To open: Stir miso thoroughly with paddle to mix in salty surface layers. Serve, reserving and storing unused portions as for Homemade Miso (p. 174).

blankets. In cold weather, heat with hot water bottles. After the first 24 hours of koji fermentation, mix the developing koji once daily with a paddle. When koji begins to develop its own heat, stagger boxes slightly to allow the entry of oxygen and escape of carbon dioxide. The mycelium of white or yellow mold should appear after 4 to 7 days depending on the weather and the number of yeasts in the environment. Discard any koji covered with bluish-green mold. Proceed as for barley miso.

2) Making Miso Containing Miso Pickles: Miso pickles (*miso-zuké*) are prepared in most batches of farmhouse miso even though this practice is generally considered to cause a slight decline in the miso flavor.

A 19-gallon keg of miso may contain any or all of the following: 5 to 6 *daikon*, 10 small eggplants, 10 cucumbers, 15 gingerroots, 2 *kombu* rolls, 4 burdock roots and/or 5 carrots. Cut very large *daikon* lengthwise into quarters; cut regular-sized *daikon* lengthwise into halves. Use other vegetables whole. Wash and drain vegetables thoroughly, then place into separate tubs or large bowls and sprinkle with salt equal to about 7 percent of the vegetable weight. Place a pressing lid directly atop vegetables and press with a weight equal to four or five times the weight of the vegetables for about 1 week in summer and 2 weeks in winter. Rinse vegetables and discard briny pressing liquid. When one-fourth of miso has been packed into the fermentation keg, arrange one-third of each of the vegetables in a layer on top of the miso. Sprinkle vegetables with a few tablespoons of salt. When miso keg is one-half full and again when it is three-fourths full, insert layers of remaining vegetables. Cover third layer with remainder of miso. Do not stir miso after keg is full. Leave pickling vegetables untouched until miso has finished fermenting.

To use, remove vegetables from keg as they are needed. Rub excess miso from surface of each vegetable and return miso to keg. Rinse vegetables, slice into thin ovals or rounds, and serve (p. 156).

3) Making Sweet Potato Miso *(Imo Miso):* To the ingredients in the basic recipe, add 14 to 15 pounds steamed (sweet) potatoes or yams. (If desired, make potatoes into koji as for rice koji; p. 179.) Reduce the amount of salt to 4¾ quarts. Add potatoes to pounded soybeans together with koji; mash thoroughly. Pack into vats as above. Ferment for at least 5 to 6 months, starting in April or May.

In some areas, the sweet potatoes are cooked, pickled whole in salt, and mixed with commercial miso as an extender just prior to packaging. In some farmhouses, potato koji replaces the grain koji.

4) Making Date Miso *(Sotetsu Miso):* A farmhouse specialty on the island of Amami Oshima south of Kyushu. Use brown rice in place of barley to make the koji. Dry and grind to a powder 1 to 3 gallons of dried dates (the fruit of the sago palm, *Cycas revoluta*). Combine and mix with the other basic ingredients just before placing them to the vat.

NOTES AND ADDITIONAL INFORMATION

1) For a relatively sweet miso requiring only 6 to 9 months fermentation, use 65 percent of the salt in the basic recipe; for a saltier variety, increase the salt by 15 percent and age for 2 to 3 years.

2) For large-scale community production, the method used by a village we studied in Nagano prefecture might best serve as a model. Fifteen to twenty people work together. A building is equipped with a small (6 by 8 by 7-foot tall) koji incubating room containing 56 koji trays; it is similar to those in traditional miso shops. The room is kept at 77°F by a charcoal brazier throughout the koji fermentation. One part barley and 2 parts soybeans are mixed, soaked, steamed for 4 hours and made into koji. Sufficient portions of the finished soybean-barley koji is taken home by each family, mixed with salt, and fermented in kegs. Most people add only one-half the salt at the beginning and the rest 2 weeks later; some add the salt six times during the first 2 weeks. The miso is stirred daily for 6 months after which time it may be served, although most families ferment it for 1½ to 2 years to improve the flavor. Tamari is sometimes drawn from the miso in a long bamboo colander.

3) Rather than using hot water bottles, some farmers warm small batches of koji next to or under their living room *kotatsu*, a table covered with a large quilt and set over a sunken box at the bottom of which is a charcoal brazier heater. In many farmhouses, this is the only heat source for the entire family during the long, cold winter.

4) The soybeans are sometimes cooked for up to 24 hours. From morning until night, they are simmered in a covered pot over a low fire. Any logs remaining in the fire are removed and the beans are then cooked over low coals through the night.

5) In some villages, the miso is mixed once a month during the summer to prevent mold growth and hasten fermentation. The craftsman uses either his hands—well washed to the elbows—or a wooden paddle.

Farmhouse Soybean Miso made with Miso-dama
(Miso Balls)

Known as *Tama Miso* (miso made from balls), this is one of Japan's earliest farmhouse varieties. Unknown in China, the method for its preparation came to Japan from Korea where the balls (*miso-dama*) are still widely used to make both Korean miso (*jang*) and soy sauce.

In the basic process, cooked soybeans are mashed, shaped into balls, and tied with rice straw. Suspended from poles or placed on a special drying rack over the open-hearth fireplace (or the kitchen wood-burning stove), they are allowed to stand for about 30 days, or until the surface of each ball is covered with a bloom of fragrant mold. (In some areas, the balls are hung outdoors under the high farmhouse eaves for up to 60 days.) The inoculated balls are then crushed in a mortar, mixed with salt and water, and packed into vats, where the mixture is allowed to ferment for 1 year or more. Naturally, *miso-dama* are said to be quite difficult to prepare, except in areas blessed with clear, cold air in which the appropriate molds are found in abundance. Nowadays, miso made in this traditional, colorful way is gradually becoming a thing of the past.

Nevertheless, in a number of remote areas, it continues to thrive. In Nagano, Gifu, and Aichi prefectures, it is prepared in the late fall, while in Iwate and Miyagi prefectures it is made just after the spring equinox or the traditional lunar New Year, between late March and mid April. At both times in these places, the air is cold and clear enough to ensure that very few contaminating microorganisms are present, yet not so cold as to hinder fermentation.

Up until about 1600 A.D., most of the miso made in rural Japan was made from *miso-dama*. As the use of rice and barley koji grew in popularity (together with miso soup), the tradition of making pure soybean miso began to decline. Farmers began mixing rice- or barley koji with their *miso-dama* soybean koji just before the basic ingredients were packed into vats. And at a somewhat later stage, the *miso-dama* were largely abandoned in favor of rice or barley koji made in bundled straw mats or trays. At present, much of the farmhouse miso prepared with *miso-dama* contains rice- or barley koji purchased from a local koji or miso shop and mixed with the crushed balls. Adding grain koji decreases the fermentation time and increases the finished miso's sweetness and yield. Yet many farmers still prefer the flavor of the traditional product prepared with only soybeans, and we have been impressed by the flavor and aroma produced under even the simplest of brewing conditions.

We learned the following method from Mmes. Saiyo Miura and Kazuko Shinya in the remote mountain village of Kami Ugemura near Iwaizumi in Iwate prefecture. Since each family in the village makes all its own miso (as well as its own tofu), each farmhouse kitchen is equipped with a large cauldron (36 inches in diameter and 20 inches deep), a wooden tub (36 inches in diameter and 12 inches deep), and the other necessary pieces of equipment.

The following ingredients are for one batch. Four batches, usually prepared on four consecutive days, just fill a typical 48-gallon wooden fermentation keg.

9½ gallons whole soybeans, soaked overnight and drained
3½ (or as much as 4¾) gallons salt
Water

1) Combine beans in a caldron with about 20 gallons of water and simmer for 5 to 6 hours, or until soft. Place a 3-gallon bamboo basket on a draining rack set across one side of the caldron's mouth. Using a woven bamboo scoop (constructed like a concave badminton racket), ladle cooked beans

a

into the basket (fig. a), then transfer 2 basketsful of beans at a time into wooden mixing tub. Wearing (10-inch-high) woven-rice straw or rubber boots, tread beans for 15 to 30 minutes, or until thoroughly crushed (fig. b) (Or grind beans in a hand mill or pound in a mortar.) Combine remaining cooking liquid with the salt in a large crock or keg, cover, and store in a cool place.

b

2) Using both hands, shape crushed beans into slightly oval balls, each about 7 inches long.

c

3) Tie together the ends of four 3-foot-long strands of dried rice straw. Arrange strands on a clean surface in the form of a cross, place one miso ball at intersection of strands (fig. c), and tie together at top of ball to form a supportive net. After preparing about 50, hang balls indoors from sturdy horizontal poles (fig. d) suspended from the ceiling 6 to 8 feet above a heat source (open hearth fireplace at center of main farmhouse room).

4) Allow balls to ferment for about 30 days until they are covered with a bloom of light bluish-green mold and are very hard.

5) Remove straw and immerse balls in water-filled mixing tub for several hours, or until the thin, slightly dusty surface layer dissolves in the water. Discard water and drain balls well. Transfer several balls at a time to a large wooden mortar, combine with a small amount of the salted soybean cooking liquid (and if necessary a little water), and pound with a pestle to give a consistency similar to that of regular miso. Repeat until all balls are pounded and mixed.

d

6) Line the bottom of a keg with a layer of garlic leaves (or sprinkle with salt) and place in the fermentation area (*kura* or barn). Transfer pounded soybean mixture into keg and pack firmly. Smooth miso surface and top with a ½-inch-thick layer of extra salt, then a layer of garlic leaves followed by a layer of (*sasa*) bamboo leaves. Top bamboo leaves with 6 flat rocks and cover keg with a wooden lid (fig. e). (A weighted pressing lid may be substituted for the garlic and bamboo leaves.)

e

7) Allow miso to ferment for at least 1 year, preferably 3 to 4 years for best flavor. When miso is ready, discard bamboo leaves. Scoop off upper layer of garlic leaves and salt, and mix in small amounts into fodder to feed to livestock. Mix miso well. Keep keg tightly covered when not in use.

9

The Traditional Miso Shop

A N EXAMPLE OF Japan's ancient heritage of fine craftsmanship, the traditional miso shop has a charm and rustic beauty similar to that found in fine old wineries: in the morning sunlight, golden soybeans soak in great wooden tubs; steam billows up from the massive black cauldron and wooden steamers through the arching rafters fashioned from the entire trunks of huge trees; basketfuls of steaming rice are spread with wooden pushing tools over a cedar floor; in a dark, warm-and-humid incubation room, row on row of shallow wooden boxes hold mounds of rice covered with a delicate bloom of pure white mold; the subtly sweet and pervasive fragrance of koji suffuses the atmosphere as it is crumbled between a craftsman's palms; men in straw sandals mash soft, warm soybeans underfoot in wooden tubs or pound them in sturdy mortars with large wooden pestles; tall cedar vats made of thick staves stand bound together by wide-girth hoops of exquisitely woven bamboo; men tread freshly mixed miso underfoot, packing it firmly into vats; others working with wooden spades shovel mature miso into wooden buckets; wife and children standing at the doorway of their home watch the men work in the adjoining shop: all while the master craftsman carefully, patiently helps it to happen.

The traditional craftsman takes deep pride in the quality of his miso, in his work and in the lineage of masters of which he is the living descendant. In many cases his apprenticeship was long and difficult and began at an early age. His master—who was often his father—customarily yielded each secret begrudgingly only after the young disciple had fully demonstrated his capacity for hard work, selfless service and devotion to the spirit of the craft. The work of a true

master is a joy to watch. Years of patient and careful practice give rise to movements which flow effortlessly and gracefully. At one with his work, he cares, wasting nothing. He realizes that only by harmonizing his actions with the great rhythm of the four seasons and the microscopic chemical and biological forces at work within the huge fermention vats can he enable fine miso to come to fruition. His work is a process of continually learning from nature, and his miso is an expression of the depth of his understanding. On the wall behind the great iron cauldron in many shops is a small but well-kept altar, an expression of gratitude.

For many master miso-craftsmen—as for fine sword makers or potters—daily work is seen as a spiritual practice or, as the Japanese say, a Way. Focusing his full attention on every detail moment after moment, the craftsman discovers a space in which the restrictions of time and self cease to operate. Since his main concern is neither fame nor fortune, his work becomes its own fulfillment and reward.

The method for preparing miso in the traditional shop has a number of basic distinguishing characteristics: the grains and beans are cooked over (or in) a large iron cauldron heated from below by a wood or charcoal fire; all of the work is done by hand without the use of motor-driven machines; the tools and containers are handmade and handsomely crafted from natural materials; the koji is prepared in small wooden trays in an incubation room heated, when necessary, by a small charcoal burner or stove; the miso is fermented naturally in huge cedar vats and contains only natural ingredients; it is packed into (5-gallon) wooden kegs for distribution and sale.

Japan's mild, relatively humid climate has proven itself ideal for supporting the growth of fermentation microorganisms. Thanks to this natural advantage and centuries of experience, Japanese craftsmen have developed a level of technical expertise second to none.

The first Japanese commercial miso shops were in operation as early as the year 700 A.D., but up until about 1600, the great majority of miso made in the country was prepared non-commercially in private homes. As commercial miso shops developed, they used the basic farmhouse methods and tools but on an expanded scale. Some shops prepared miso only once each year, generally in the fall using new-crop soybeans and grains. Just as many farmers prepared shoyu as well as miso, so also did the earliest miso shops. Figure 39 shows the preparation of miso in a relatively large 17th century workplace. At the lower left, a fire is being stoked to heat the rice steamer above. The steamed rice is being carried in buckets to straw mats, where it is spread and cooled. After inoculation, the rice is rolled up in the mats and carried to the incubation room (upper center). The finished koji is carried out and mixed with salt in a large tub (lower right). Men bind staves with bamboo hoops to make wooden buckets in which they will sell the finished miso (upper right). The water carrier heads for the shop's well. In the storeroom, bales of rice in straw sacks and stacks of koji trays await use (upper center left).

Since earliest times, the word *kura* has been used to refer to miso shops. Ordinarily the term denotes the thick-walled storehouse or treasury in which a large and fairly well-to-do family keeps its valuables, and, in some cases, its home-made miso. Applied to miso shops, however, the term takes on a broader meaning, referring to the entire business and its tradition. It also refers to the buildings and incubation room, which are said to have their own *kura-gusé* or "unique individual characteristics." These are a product of the resident microorganisms, the buildings' structure and materials, the local climate, plus the intangible yet very real vibrations and living wisdom of all the shop's past masters. The soul and life-force of a shop, the *kura-gusé* is prized and nurtured above all, for it is believed to be the primary factor determining the quality of the miso prepared within its walls.

In most traditional shops throughout Japan, the basic tools and methodology remained virtually unchanged over a period of several centuries up until the end of World War II. At present, miso shops generally prepare miso throughout the year, either daily or at least 3 to 5 times each week. Some miso is seasonal, such as barley miso which, in many regions, is prepared only during the winter. Each master has his own preferred blend of ingredients and numerous secrets for giving a distinctive flavor, aroma, color and texture to his miso.

Today the traditional shop in its pure form is largely a thing of the past. The last examples, which were located in remote rural areas, are said to have disappeared during the mid 1950s. Although traditional tools are still widely used in modern shops, parts of the basic processes have been subject to mechanization in an effort to increase productivity and cut labor costs. The result has been what we shall call the "semi-traditional" shop. An excellent example of the use of middle-level technology, its basic characteristics are described on page 208.

In both traditional and semi-traditional shops the basic method for preparing miso is the same, and the key process is that of preparing fine koji. To master this process and make it work throughout the varying weather conditions of the four seasons requires many years of devoted study. Like the brewer of fine wines or the maker of delicious natural cheeses, the miso master is always learning. Koji is an essential part of many Japanese foods, including sake and shoyu, and a truly accomplished craftsman known for his expertise in preparing the koji for any of these is given the rare and honorific title of *toji* or "master brewer." Many *toji* are able to prepare at least seven varieties of koji, including, of course, the basic types made from white or brown rice, barley, and soybeans.

The latest statistics (1974) show that there are 2,400 commercial miso shops and factories in Japan, and they produce a total yearly output of 649,000 tons of miso retailing for 492 million dollars. Each year, they use 212,000 tons of soybeans, 101,000 tons of rice, 22,000 tons of barley, and 82,000 tons of salt. The great majority of these shops are relatively small scale, semi-traditional enterprises run by a single man and his family with the help of one or two relatives or hired craftsmen. Most shops produce several types of miso, and some also prepare special batches of koji which are sold fresh or dried as an independent item. During the cold months, a few use this koji to prepare commercial *amazaké* (p. 162).

Fig. 39. A 17th century workplace

The Miso Shop Building

Most traditional and semi-traditional shops are located adjoining the home of the miso maker. In the cities, the home and shop are often under the same roof, as in the *Tsujita* shop (fig. 40), whereas in the countryside, the home and various buildings used for miso making are usually located on the same piece of property.

15 FOOT CEILING
L = 50 FT. W = 24 FT.

Fig. 40. *Tsujita Shop Floorplan*

The main building where most of the miso preparation takes place often looks like a large barn with a massive ridgepole 20 to 30 feet above ground level and an elaborate support system of beams and rafters joined without nails and fashioned from arching tree trunks. The high roof is generally covered with tile or thatch to keep out the summer heat and snowy winter cold. The walls are made of wood or mud plaster mixed with straw. Since there are generally few windows, the interior is often fairly dark. Parts of the floor are covered with large squares of hand-cut granite or concrete aggregate and, in some shops, parts are uncovered, packed dirt. In some set-ups, the caldron, koji incubation room and vats are all located in the main building; in others the koji room is in an adjacent building. A well is generally located within the main building fairly near the caldron or the washing-and-soaking area. A storeroom for soybeans, grain, and salt is situated either in the main building or nearby.

The koji incubation room, which is located near the center of many shops, is a well-insulated chamber usually constructed of 10-inch-thick stone or packed earth blocks, or of bricks. The floor is 12 by 9 feet and the low ceiling is never higher than 7 feet. The door is often very small (3 feet high) and thick to minimize heat loss when it is opened. One foot off the floor along both walls are benches on which the koji trays are stacked during fermentation. The room is heated by

a small charcoal brazier or gas stove, and a thermometer and hygrometer (to measure humidity) hang on the wall. At the center of many—but not all—incubation rooms there is a large wooden box called a "crib." In it the koji begins its incubation before being transferred to small wooden trays.

Koji trays

The koji mixing-floor generally runs across the entire front of the incubation room and is about 12 to 14 feet from front to back (p. 208). Made of tightly fitted, smooth cedar planks, it is elevated 6 to 8 inches above the shop's floor and used as the area for cooling the freshly steamed rice and inoculating it with starter. Some small shops use a large wooden mixing box measuring 6 by 9 by 1 foot deep in place of the floor; the box can be stood against a wall and the area used for other purposes as well.

Some traditional shops employ large insulated boxes, each big enough to house four medium-sized vats (fig. 41). After the vats are packed with the unfermented miso mixture and topped with individual pressing lids, an insulated wooden lid is placed over the entire affair. The heat generated by the miso fermentation raises the interior temperature, resulting in a sort of natural temperature-controlled fermentation and a considerable reduction in the required aging time.

Fig. 41. *Insulated fermentation box*

Brooms

Fig. 42. The Smaller Tools

Buckets

Koji scraper

Rubber scrapers

Scoop

Rice-straw sandals

Stirring tool

Rack

Spade

Spatula

Scooping pans

Traditional Tools and Equipment

The refining force of centuries of daily use has given the basic miso-making tools functionality and simple beauty. Most wooden implements are made of seasoned Japanese cedar (*sugi*) which is durable in the presence of water, heat, and salt, and has a pleasant fragrance. The principal smaller tools are shown in figure 42.

The most important large-scale pieces of equipment are the caldrons, the steamers, and the fermentation vats. Figure 43 shows a shop with a large caldron topped with the soybean steamer and small caldron topped with the grain steamer. Beneath each caldron is a firebox, access to which is gained by descending a small ladder into a pit 4-feet-wide and 5-feet-deep. Logs are stacked at one end of the pit and in the center is a cinder box in which burning logs are extinguished at the end of work for reuse later. Some shops have only one caldron (in which the soybeans are boiled) and one steamer used for the grain.

Fig. 44. Steamer and cauldron

Fig. 43. Steamer and caldron

An exploded view of a steamer and cauldron is shown in figure 44. At the right are the steamer's bottom, a rack that sits on it, and a cloth that lines the rack and holds the rice. Note that the grain in the wood is radial, which enables the steamer to expand when heated. Bamboo (rather than metal) hoops are used to bind the staves so that in case the steamer catches fire, the hoops burn, the staves fall apart, and the steamer's moist contents extinguish the flames.

Two views of a fermentation vat are shown in figure 45. Capable of holding 4 to 6 tons of miso, a typical vat is 5½ feet deep and 7 feet in diameter at the mouth. Only the best quality, knot-free cedar is used, and if kept in constant use, the average vat will last 150 to 200 years; Western winery cooperage, which is equally long lasting, is usually made of white oak. Note that the wood grain of the slats is concentric with the vat to help prevent the leakage of tamari. Vats are always mounted on blocks to provide air circulation for the

Fig. 45. A fermentation vat

base and ensure their long life. In some shops, the entire wood floor is built at the level of the vat's rim to provide easy access (fig. 46). Some contain a tamari trough (see also fig. 12, p. 41) and spout by means of which tamari that settles in the miso can be extracted when fermentation is complete. The fine art of Japanese cooperage is now almost totally extinct, and new vats are virtually impossible to find. Specially ordered they cost from $2,500 to $5,000 each.

Detailed descriptions of the sizes and construction of all traditional (and modern) miso making equipment is given in our *Miso Production: The Book of Miso, Volume II*, available exclusively from our Center (see p. 277).

Fig. 46. Shop floor at vat's rim

Preparing Traditional Rice Miso

The basic ingredients required to make a 1-ton batch of miso are given below; four batches fill one vat. The work is done by a miso master and two craftsmen who assist him. The following recipe is written for a shop that might wish to make only one batch of miso. To prevent overcrowding, small shops often prepare one batch of koji on each of four consecutive days, mixing each with salt and storing it. On each of the next four days, a batch of soybeans is cooked, mixed with one-fourth of the salted koji, and packed into the vats. Eight days are therefore required to fill one vat. The basic proportions of raw materials by weight are soybeans 10, rice 10, and salt 4.4.

528 pounds (white or lightly polished brown) rice
8 ounces whole-grain (or 1.6 ounces spore powder) koji starter
234 pounds natural salt
528 pounds whole dry soybeans
15 gallons seed miso
28 to 34 gallons mixing liquid

In the afternoon or evening the miso maker measures out the rice. If it has not been cleaned, he runs it through a winnowing machine to remove chaff, straw, or other debris.

He fills the washing keg about two-thirds full of grain and adds water to cover. Working the base of the stirring tool down to the bottom of the tub, he twists it vigorously back

and forth, agitating the rice for 30 to 60 seconds until it is well washed.

Using a large, wooden scoop, he transfers the rice into two baskets set on a draining rack. Dousing each basket with 2 or 3 scoops of water, he allows the grain to drain while washing more in the keg.

Now he rinses out a deep soaking tub, inserts a wooden plug in the tub's drainage hole, and covers the hole inside the tub with a small screen. The drained rice is then emptied into the tub and smoothed. Enough water to cover is added and the rice is left to soak overnight (12 to 16 hours).

THE FIRST DAY

At 6:30 a.m. the master fills his caldron two-thirds full of water, descends the ladder into the firebox pit, and lights a wood fire. After pulling the plug in the soaking tub to drain the rice, he places the steamer and its support on the

caldron's mouth then arranges the lower cloth to cover the steamer's wooden grating. He readies the koji mixing box, lining it with a large sheet of canvas (or, if using a mixing floor, sweeps then wipes it with a moist cloth).

When the water in the caldron comes to a boil, the master scoops his soaked rice into the steamer, smooths its surface, and covers it first with the upper cloth, then with two layers of gunny sacking. The edges of the sacks are tucked down firmly around all sides of the rice to help trap the steam which, after about 15 minutes, begins to rise through the sacks; measuring from this time, the rice is steamed for 40 minutes.

The master removes the sacks and upper cloth while an assistant hooks a rack over the steamer's side and places a basket on it. Using a wooden spade, the master turns over 10 to 12 spadefuls of rice, breaking up large clumps by whacking them with the spade's flat blade. Using the scoop, he then, fills the basket with steaming-hot rice.

While an assistant carries rice-filled baskets to the mixing box, the master continues to break up the firm rice still remaining in the steamer.

Emptied from the baskets into the large (6- by 9- by 1-foot-deep) mixing box, the rice is spread evenly in a 2½-inch-thick layer and allowed to cool.

Every five minutes, the master and one assistant mix and break up the rice with their spades, aiding the cooling process. The grain's temperature is measured (by touch or with a thermometer) after each mixing.

When the temperature has dropped to about 113°F, the master places a koji tray over the mixing box and measures in the koji starter together with approximately 3½ pounds of well-crumbled rice. Slowly and carefully, he mixes the two by hand.

After he has scattered half of this mixture over the rice, his assistants, using spades, mix the rice thoroughly until the mold spores are evenly distributed. After several minutes, the remaining inoculum is sprinkled on and mixed in. From time

to time, remaining clumps of rice are broken up with the spade's flat blade. It is now about noon.

As the rice continues to cool, the crib—a heavy wooden box about 4 by 4½ by 2 feet deep which may be located either in or outside the incubation room—is lined with clean canvas. When its temperature has dropped to 95°F, the rice is mounded at one end of the mixing box by pulling the box's cloth lining toward that end. Any remaining small clumps are broken up by hand as the rice is scooped into baskets, then poured into the crib. When all of the rice is in the crib, the surface is pressed firmly by hand to compact the interior and retard cooling. When the rice temperature reaches 91°F, the edges of the canvas are folded over and the crib's contents covered with 4 layers of thick rice-straw mats which serve as

insulation. The preparation of koji, the first fermentation process, is now well underway and will continue undisturbed throughout the night.

THE SECOND DAY

At 6:30 a.m., the master preheats the incubation room to between 80°F and 86°F using a small charcoal brazier or stove. (During the summer, preheating is often unnecessary.)

At 7:00 a.m., the two assistant craftsmen uncover the rice and check its temperature, which should be about 89°F but may be as high as 100°F. Using their spades and starting at one end of the crib, they turn over the warm rice, breaking up any lumps, and shovel it to the opposite end. After reaching the bottom at the first end, they work toward the opposite end, replacing the turned rice. In this way, oxygen is incorporated to nourish the growing koji molds, carbon dioxide is expelled, and the warm rice from the crib's center is mixed with the cooler portions from the sides and bottom. When all the rice has been turned, its surface is packed, smoothed, and re-covered.

By 9:00 a.m., about 160 clean koji trays have been neatly stacked (inverted to keep out alien mold spores) near the crib. The latter is uncovered and the rice thoroughly

turned and crumbled as before. As one assistant stacks nine koji trays across a corner of the crib, the other fills them one by one with (about 3¼ quarts or 3 pounds of) warm rice, poured in so as to form a mounded oval.

With one hand, the first assistant then quickly indents the center of each mound to form the "hollow oval" pattern, which will later prevent overheating at the koji's center.

When 9 trays have been filled, hollowed, and stacked one atop the other, the master carries them to the incubation room where they are arranged in "vertical stacks" on a bench along one wall. When all of the trays are in the room (7 stacks of 22 trays each), an empty tray is inverted over the top of each stack, and the door of the room is tightly closed. The rice now continues its fermentation as it becomes koji.

After 1 hour, the master checks the room's temperature and humidity. In winter, the temperature should ideally be between 80°F and 86°F, and in no case must it be allowed to drop below 77°F. In summer, it may rise as high as 92°F but not above. The humidity should be 93 to 95 percent. To warm the room, the master stokes the brazier or stove (its fumes go out through a chimmney) and/or closes the ceiling vents; to cool it, he opens the vents or door. To raise the humidity, he sprinkles (hot) water over the floor.

At 1:00 p.m., the master and both assistant craftsmen wash their hands and test the koji's temperature (which should be about 95°F). They transfer the top tray in each stack to an empty section of the bench and stir the koji in it quickly with one hand to break up the young mycelium and thereby encourage its further growth; the mounded center is

indented to form a hollow as before. When all of the trays have been relocated and stirred, those which were formerly on the top of each stack are now on the bottom. This time the trays are arranged in "staggered stacks" to prevent the koji's overheating and provide more oxygen for growth.

At 5:00 p.m., the master and his helpers once again wash their hands, test the koji (which should be about 100°F) and check the room's temperature and humidity which should be the same as described previously. They transfer the top tray from each stack onto an empty section of bench, and arrange them now in "bricklap stacks."

This time, the koji is stirred with both hands, which work quickly from the far to the near end of each tray making about eight openings and closings.

Finally, fingertips quickly shape the crumbled koji into the "three waves" pattern. When all of the koji has been stirred and re-stacked, it is incubated untouched overnight.

At 6:00 p.m. (or several hours earlier in winter), the soybeans are washed and drained using the same tools and procedures employed earlier for the rice. They are then soaked overnight in a tub reserved for this purpose, which is slightly larger than that used for the grain.

THE THIRD DAY

The morning hours are spent steaming a second batch of rice. At 10:00 a.m., the master and both assistant crafts-men check the koji's temperature (which may have risen as high as 104°F) and appearance. A fragrant white mycelium should now bind the soft rice kernels into a cohesive, ¾-inch-thick mat. The trays are carried from the incubation room and arranged in "staggered stacks" near the koji mixing-floor. Holding the trays one by one over a basket, one craftsman uses a wooden scraper to transfer the koji from tray to basket.

When the basket is full, the koji is crumbled into a large, flat strainer held over a second basket and any lumps are rubbed through.

All of the crumbled koji is now divided among a number of 34-gallon wooden kegs, which are placed around a special tub at the center of the mixing area. The master weighs the salt in a basket, then divides it into as many portions as there are kegs. In the mixing tub, he combines one keg of koji with one portion of salt.

Using a long-handled wooden "pusher," he mixes the two ingredients, then places the salted koji back into its keg. When all of the salt and koji have been mixed, the kegs are covered and set aside.

With the koji finished and the second batch of rice steamed, the work of cooking the soybeans takes center stage. The rice steamer is removed from atop the caldron and replaced by the slightly larger soybean steamer. (In some shops the beans are boiled in the caldron.) While the fire is being stoked, the master scoops the soybeans from the soaking tub into the steamer, then places a wooden lid directly atop the beans. After about 35 minutes, steam begins to rise through the lid. Measuring from this time, the beans are steamed for 5 to 5½ hours.

Meanwhile, the assistants prepare the vat in which the miso will be fermented. After constructing a walkway or ramp halfway up the vat's side, they scrub the interior with boiling water and stiff brushes, rinse the walls repeatedly, and

drain the water from a hole at the bottom of one side (or remove it with scooping pans if there is no hole.) The hole plugged, they wipe the vat clean and dry, then sprinkle approximately 1 pound of salt over its bottom. If the vat has a tamari trough it is set in place, its spigot closed.

When the soybeans are done, any logs in the firebox are removed and placed into a covered cinder pot. The soybeans are scooped into some 10 well-washed kegs and carried to the mixing area, together with a larger keg filled with about 40 gallons of boiled water drawn from the caldron. The beans and water are allowed to cool for 5 to 6 hours, or until they can be touched without discomfort (110°F-120°F).

Now all the basic ingredients in kegs around the mixing tub are ready to be combined. One keg each of soybeans and koji are poured into the tub, filling it to about one-half its capacity. While the master mixes the ingredients with a pusher or spade, an assistant rolls up his pantlegs, washes his feet *most* thoroughly and, sometimes, dons rice-straw sandals. Using a pusher to help maintain his balance, he treads the beans and koji underfoot for 2 to 4 minutes.

In an empty keg, meanwhile, the master combines a portion (about 6 quarts) of the seed miso with some of the mixing liquid (11 to 13½ quarts). He then adds the mixture a little at a time to the tub where it is mashed underfoot together with the koji and soybeans. When about half of the soybeans have been mashed and the mixture has approximately the same consistency as mature miso, it is scooped into empty kegs, carried up the ramp, and emptied into the

vat. The mixing and mashing process is repeated until all of the ingredients have been readied and transferred. The tools are carefully cleaned with scrapers, then washed. A layer of burlap sacking or cloth is placed over the unfermented miso during the night.

Preparing Subsequent Batches

For four consecutive days, the men steam soybeans, mash them with koji, and place the mixture into the vat. The latter is filled to within 6 inches of its rim with approximately 4 tons of tan, unfermented miso.

Using a spade, the master levels the miso surface while an assistant (having taken the same sanitary measures as before) treads the miso underfoot to pack it firmly and prevent the formation of air pockets. After extensive packing and a final leveling with the spade, the master lays a plank across the vat's mouth and, kneeling on the plank, proceeds to smooth and level the miso surface with a moistened spatula until it is perfectly flat. After sprinkling 3 cups of salt over the miso's surface (as a mold deterrent), he covers it with burlap sacking (sterilized with steam) which he tucks down firmly around the edges. Both halves of the pressing lid are set atop the sacks and 16 to 18 blocks (each weighing about 55 pounds) are arranged uniformly over the sturdy cross pieces joining the boards which comprise it.

Finally, the craftsmen cover the lid with several more layers of burlap (or, more recently, polyethylene sheeting).

On a large piece of heavy-duty paper the master records the quantities of ingredients he has used, the date, and the expected date of maturity. He attaches this paper to the vat or a nearby wall. The miso is allowed to ferment untouched at the natural temperature of the environment for a minimum of 6 months, including one full summer, and generally for 12 to 18 months.

Harvesting the Miso

When the miso is ready, the craftsmen remove the weights, lid, and sacking. Any tamari that has risen to the surface is ladled into a small keg and reserved. If the vat contains a tamari trough, its spigot is opened and the tamari that has settled to the bottom of the vat is collected, usually for use a mixing liquid in subsequent miso, but also as a household seasoning.

Now a ramp, stairway, or ladder is constructed to a few

feet below the vat's rim, to which a rack is hooked. On the rack are placed several kegs. After the master and his assistants have sampled—and given their approval to—the new miso, one man mounts the ramp. Using the pusher or spade, he mixes the saltier upper layers into the body of the miso, then begins filling the kegs.

After enough miso to meet outstanding orders has been carried to the packing room, the remainder in the vat is recovered with the sacking, but without the lid or weights.

Most of the miso is transferred to 5- or 20-gallon wooden shipping kegs, each sealed with a wooden lid. A small portion is kept for home consumption and gifting purposes.

Making Koji (Using Natural Mold Spores)

In some traditional miso shops, koji starter was not employed until the end of World War II. Rather, the multitudes of naturally-existing mold spores floating in the air inside the shop were used to start the koji fermentation and about 70 hours (as compared with 45 hours using starter) were required to finish it.

On the morning of the first day, freshly steamed barley was spread over a smooth wooden mixing-floor (located in front of the incubation room) which had been carefully wiped clean with a damp cloth. Wearing a special variety of *geta* footwear with stilt-like clogs to raise his feet above the

hot barley and prevent its being mashed, the master stirred the grain with a pusher until it had cooled to the point that it could be touched without discomfort. Having removed his clogs, rolled up his pantlegs, and washed his feet, he then used his toes to flip the barley into the air with each step, thereby hastening its cooling and exposing it to more of the airborne spores. After flipping all the barley, he allowed it to stand for about 3 hours. In the early afternoon, he used the pusher to transfer the barley onto half of the floor, making a layer 6 to 8 inches thick; this helped the barley develop internal heat during its fermentation. The grain was then left to stand uncovered overnight while mold spores settled on it.

On the morning of the second day, the koji incubating room was preheated to between 78°F and 86°F. About 3¼ pounds of barley were placed into each koji tray and the trays were arranged in "vertical stacks" of ten trays each on the floor of the room. If the room or koji were cold, an inverted koji tray was placed atop the stack, and the entire stack was covered with burlap sacking and, if necessary, doused with boiling water. The koji was allowed to stand overnight in the trays, untouched.

Early on the third day, the koji in each tray was mixed by hand as described above, and the trays were then arranged in "slanting stacks." Early on the fourth day, the mixing was repeated, and at the same time on the morning of the fifth, the koji was removed from the trays and mixed with salt. Later that morning the soybeans were cooked. The mixed ingredients were in the vat by nightfall.

THE SEMITRADITIONAL SHOP

After World War II, many traditional shops began a process of modernization and mechanization in order to compete with large miso factories, increase output and lower labor costs. The resulting semitraditional shop is still much smaller than the modern miso factory, and most of its new equipment is simple and relatively inexpensive. While these electrically-powered machines make it possible to prepare miso with less work in a shorter time, though, they do give a different feeling to the work and result in a less rustic and quiet environment. But the miso-making process itself is almost identical to that used traditionally, and the use of the machines seems to have relatively little effect on the quality of the end-product. Many modernized makers have retained the spirit of traditional craftsmanship and take pride in their work. Some prepare both natural and quick miso, generally serving the former in their own homes and reserving the latter for sale to the many modern Japanese for whom flavor and quality have become less important than cost.

The transition from the traditional to the semitraditional shop was marked primarily by a change in basic equipment. The wood fires (or later fuel-oil burners) used to boil water in the caldron were replaced by a small boiler. Regulated by a time clock, it could be set to have steam ready as soon as the master began work, thereby saving him the time of lighting a fire and waiting for large amounts of water to come to a boil.

One of the boiler's pipes was run into the base of the steamer and used to cook the grain. In some shops, the steam was also used in this way to cook the soybeans, or it was run into the caldron and used to heat the water in which the beans were boiled. However, since cooking the soybeans traditionally took at least 5 hours, many semitraditional shops switched to a steam-heated pressure cooker which did the job in less than 1 hour with no decline in quality.

The time-consuming job of crumbling the finished koji by hand and rubbing it through a strainer was simplified by the use of a small crumbler.

Whereas the soybeans had formerly been mashed by treading them underfoot in a wooden tub, now they were simply run through an extruder or blender, together with a mixture of seed miso and mixing liquid. The same machine, heated by a jacket of circulating hot water, could be used later to pasteurize the miso, although many traditional masters preferred to omit this process.

The traditional wooden mixing tub was replaced by a motor-driven device. Built like a small cement mixer with a stainless steel body, it contained 4 rake-like "blades" that revolve slowly around a vertical axis to mix first the koji and salt, and later the blended soybeans and salted koji. The mixture is removed through a door at the base of the machine.

Finally, a small pneumatic filling machine was used to run the finished miso into polyethylene bags which replaced the traditional 5-gallon wooden kegs; each bag was thermally sealed with a small electric device.

Gradually, wells which were contaminated by industrial pollution came to be replaced with municipal water which almost always contained unwanted chemicals. Light-weight plastic buckets and kegs replaced their wooden forebears. Polyethylene film was used to cover the miso surface in the vats, and the koji incubation room was, in some cases, heated by a thermostat-controlled gas heater. Yet, with all these modifications, the basic process for preparing miso remained essentially unaltered in small shops. The truly fundamental changes were to begin with the rise of modern factories.

Making Hatcho Miso

The process for making Hatcho miso is a unique combination of the best of the traditional and modern techniques. Relatively large-scale, modern equipment is employed for cooking the soybeans and incubating the koji, but the fermentation of the miso takes place in huge cedar vats at the natural temperature of the environment over a period spanning at least two full summers. The finished product, although often packaged in sealed foil bags, is not pasteurized and contains no alcohol, preservatives, or other additives.

Traditionally, the cooked, mashed soybeans were shaped by hand into balls in a manner resembling the preparation of *miso-dama* (p. 193). The finished soybean koji was packed into the fermentation vats only during the cold months (from November to March), whereas now Hatcho miso is made throughout the year and four new vats are filled each week. Their lids piled high with stones, these centuries-old 6-foot-deep vats are housed in barn-like wooden buildings graced by massive arching rafters and high ceilings. The total atmosphere is a breathtaking remnant of an ancient tradition.

Until 1926, the soybean balls were placed on a bamboo gridwork in the attic and inoculated by allowing wild mold spores to settle on them. These were the famous *A. Hatcho* (or *A. oryzae* var. *hatcho*) spores. However, after 1926, regular *A. oryzae* fortified with *Lactobacillus* and purchased from specialty starter-shops in Kyoto and Toyohashi replaced the traditional product. Today, the unique Hatcho flavor comes not from the molds but from the unusual Okazaki climate (hot summers and mild winters); from the soybean koji and small proportion of water used; from the heavy pressing weight and long fermentation time employed; and from the Hatcho-makers' *kura-gusé* (p. 196). Hatcho is indeed difficult to reproduce outside its native birthplace.

Both of Japan's two Hatcho producers use basically the same methodology and equipment. The ingredients required to fill one vat are given below. The basic proportions of raw materials by weight are soybeans 10, salt 2, and mixing liquid 3.4.

5,500 pounds whole dry soybeans
3¼ cups. *A. oryzae* starter (spore powder)
27.5 pounds whole wheat, roasted then ground to a flour
1,100 pounds salt
1,850 pounds mixing liquid (water)

The dry soybeans are sorted and air-cleaned on a screen vibrator, washed in water, and soaked for 3 hours. After being drained, they weigh about 1.5 times their dry weight. The beans are transferred to a large rotary-type pressure cooker in which they are steamed for 3 to 4 hours; they then stand overnight under pressure.

The entire cooker is rotated on its horizontal axis to empty the cooked beans into a large grinder. Most (or all) of the beans are run through the machine's screw extruder into a metal die and cutter which grinds and shapes them into a three-dimensional "cross" about 2 inches thick and 2¼ inches in diameter; this shape creates a larger surface area for mold growth than if the beans were shaped into balls.

The Hatcho "cross"

Koji starter mold spores are mixed in a sifting machine with the roasted flour, and the soybean "balls" are passed under the sifter on a conveyer to inoculate them. They are then run by conveyor directly into one of several stainless steel incubating rooms, each about 30 by 50 by 7 feet high. Workers using shovels spread the balls to a depth of 1 foot over the stainless steel floors which are permeated with many tiny holes. Modern electronic temperature and humidity control equipment keeps the room's air temperature at 86°F and the temperature inside the koji at about 97°F during the 3 to 4 days of fermentation. At the interior of each ball, anaerobic *Lactobacillus* are actively producing substances which will later contribute to the miso's uniquely tart flavor. At the end of this first fermentation, the surface of each ball is covered with a pale yellowish-green bloom of fragrant mold, and the inside is mosit and brown. The koji balls (now weighing 6,600 pounds) are shoveled onto a conveyer and run between metal rollers in a crusher. In a 2½-foot-diameter, motor-driven mixer, batches of the crushed koji are mixed thoroughly with water and salt.

They are then transferred in wheelbarrows to huge cedar fermentation vats, each with a capacity of about 1,300 gallons. The miso mixture—which fills the vat to about 80 percent of capacity and weighs 9,500 pounds—is covered with a sturdy wooden pressing lid, atop which are piled large stones equal in weight to the total weight of the miso (frontispiece). In the large, unheated and uninsulated wooden buildings, the miso is allowed to ferment through at least 2 full summers. The lengthy fermentation is necessitated by the low percentage of carbohydrates and moisture in the substrate, and the heavy weight which creates a strictly anaerobic environment. The finished miso is removed from the vats on a first-in first-out basis as orders are received. If business is slow, some batches may ferment for 2½ or even 3 full years. The miso is packed into wooden or polyethylene kegs, or foil or polyethylene bags, for distribution.

Making Mellow White Miso

This process, developed in semi-traditional shops in Hawaii, is of particular interest for three reasons: 1) It allows for the preparation of a white and relatively sweet miso using only traditional, natural methods: 2) Low in salt, the miso requires only 1 month to prepare, yet is very delicious; 3) The process is easily adapted to community-scale production.

Steamed, inoculated rice is spread on 7- by 10-foot tables (made of stainless steel or wood and having a 3-inch-high rim around the perimeter), covered with canvas, and allowed to ferment at the natural room temperature—which in Hawaii is, of course, quite warm (77°F to 84°F) and humid; the mixture is stirred 2 or 3 times during the 45-hour koji incubation.

Soybeans (Kanrich variety work well) are soaked for 4 to 5 hours, then boiled for 1 hour at atmospheric pressure; they are then drained and the water discarded. The finished koji, cooked beans, and salt are mixed (without the addition of extra water), puréed in a grinder (which warms the mixture), and packed while still warm into 55-gallon wooden barrels (purchased for $5 each from a company that buys salted salmon in them). A double or triple thickness of heavy white cotton sacking (the type used to make rice sacks) is spread firmly over the miso's surface and tucked down around the edges to help minimize air contact. Atop the pressing lid is placed a 100-pound weight, and the mouth of the barrel is then covered with plastic sheeting to keep out dust. The miso is allowed to ferment at room temperature for 4 weeks. The liquid which accumulates at the surface (*miso-damari*) is removed and the miso packaged in plastic cottage cheese-type containers; no pasteurization, preservatives, or bleach need be used.

10
The Modern
Miso Factory

BEGINNING IN THE mid 1950s, a revolution began in the manufacture of miso. The application of modern technology to the entire miso-making process has resulted in the use of automated equipment, new ingredients, continuous process methodologies and packaging techniques, and new merchandising methods which have profoundly transformed the ancient craft as well as the miso itself.

By 1965, a number of the larger traditional manufacturers had amalgamated to form huge modern companies: twenty three factories had a yearly capacity of at least 4,100 tons each, and the ten largest produced 154,000 tons per year, or about 26 percent of the nation's total output. By 1974, the latter statistic had climbed to 30 percent and individual factories were turning out 264,000 pounds (twenty-two 6-ton vatsful) of miso daily! Today, the names of the "top ten" makers (p. 257) are household words in Japan, for they have been able for the first time in history to generate enough capital to do nationwide advertising via television, printed media, and billboards. Reaping the full benefits of a large-scale, low-margin enterprise, they distribute their standardized products to every part of Japan where they are sold in supermarkets and neighborhood grocery stores at heretofore unbelievably low prices. Recently, they have begun to export to North America and Europe, and one company is even starting a small branch factory in Los Angeles.

The first and perhaps most important technical innovation leading to the modern factory was the development of temperature-controlled fermentation, whereby total aging time could be reduced from one or two years to one month—and in the case of sweet misos, only three or four days! Heating the entire room in which miso was aged required, of course, extra energy expenditures, but the rapid turnover freed capital and space for additional production resulting in great savings.

Due to its quick aging, this miso was, by necessity, much lighter in color than most traditional miso. Aware of

Rotary drum incubators

the modern Japanese tendency to associate whiteness in foods (bread, rice, sugar) with newness, prestige, and good flavor, the manufacturers added bleach to their product and pressure cooked it using special techniques to make it still whiter. Moreover, by using a large proportion of rice koji, they gave the product a sweet flavor, while further helping to reduce the fermentation time and lighten the color. By the mid 1960s, the sales of light-yellow and mellow beige miso had skyrocketed.

The second great technical innovation was the development of polyethylene bags for packaging. Formerly, all miso had been sold out of kegs at special retail outlets; the shop owner weighed and wrapped the miso for each customer, which of course raised its price. Suddenly, bagged miso was found on the shelves of virtually all food stores. At first, consumers did not realize that the new product contained preservatives (and/or had been pasteurized) to keep the bag from swelling and additional bleach to keep the color from darkening. In fact, it was not until 1975 that the government—in response to growing consumer concern—required makers to list all additives on their labels. Even before this time, however, sales had begun to fall as consumer interest in natural foods gained momentum.

The inside of a modern miso factory, in sharp contrast to its traditional forbear, reminds one of scenes from a science fiction film. Long conveyors carry freshly steamed rice up three floors in a reinforced concrete building. Huge pieces of stainless steel equipment carry out their functions with stopwatch precision in a highly sanitary environment. In research and testing laboratories, scientists in white coats examine mold cultures while engineers refine statistical methods of quality control and time-and-motion studies.

The development of new machinery has played a major role in reducing labor costs and increasing production speed. Electronic feedback systems link the entire process controlling the duration, temperature, and humidity of the various cooking and fermentation processes. The largest and most important pieces of new equipment include: *rotary-type soybean pressure cookers* capable of producing temperatures of 250°F, evenly cooking over 2,500 pounds of beans at a time by slowly rotating as the steam enters, preventing browning by having all their air quickly evaporated with a vacuum pump, and unloading their contents automatically onto a conveyor; *rotary drum incubators*, horizontally-mounted metal cylinders about 12 feet long and 6 feet in diameter, that slowly revolve to mix their load of koji under carefully controlled conditions of temperature and humidity; *continuous process rice and barley steamers*, in which the grain is loaded from chutes onto a stainless-steel mesh conveyor 3 feet wide and 20 feet long and passed slowly through four pressurized steaming chambers; and *automatic packaging machines* that seal miso in polyethylene bags at the rate of 30 per minute. The final mixture of ingredients is fermented in epoxy-lined steel tanks each having a capacity of 12 tons.

A number of new ingedients, too, have come into use since the 1950s, most important of which are pure culture inocula or fortifying agents including salt resistant yeasts and *Lactobacillus*. They serve much the same function as traditional seed miso in reducing the fermentation time and imparting a better flavor and aroma to the miso. As explained in Appendix I, a number of new chemical additives (preservatives, bleach, food coloring, chemical seasonings, artificial sweeteners, and vitamins) are also now employed. Although in the late 1950s up to 30 percent of all soybeans used in Japanese miso were in the form of defatted meal, the figure has fortunately dropped to less than 2½ percent.

The trend toward large-scale production and standardization seems to be slowing in Japan as affluence creates a growing demand for high quality. Yet it remains to be seen whether small, traditional makers can weather the storm.

For detailed descriptions of the equipment and methods used in producing miso in modern factories, see our *Miso Production, The Book of Miso, Volume II.*

Rotary-type pressure cooker

Appendix A
A History of Miso and Soybean Chiang

THE HISTORY of both miso and soybean chiang is interwoven with the histories of soy nuggets (called *shih* or *tou-ch'ih* in China, *Hamanatto* in Japan, and generally "salted black beans" in the West) and soy sauce. The earliest evidence of soy nuggets is found in archaeological remains in China; they were excavated from the famous Western Han Tomb No. 1 at Ma-wang-tui, located at Ch'ang-sha, Hunan, and sealed in about 168 B.C. (Chang 1977). The earliest known literary reference to soy nuggets is found in the *Historical Records* (Chinese: *Shih chi;* Japanese: *Shiki*) by Ssu-ma Ch'ien, the great historian who died in about 85 B.C. (Watson 1961). Thus it seems likely that soy nuggets, an early ancestor of miso and soybean chiang, were known in China before the Han dynasty (206 B.C. to A.D. 220).

Soy sauce apparently originated in China at about this same time, for the earliest known appearance of the present characters of soy sauce, *chiang-yu*, is also in the *Historical Records (Shih chi)* of 85 B.C. It is not completely clear, however, if this liquid *chiang-yu* was made from a product containing soybeans; it could have been a meat or fish sauce. No clear indication of a soy sauce definitely made from soybeans appears until the time of the *Pen Ts'ao Kang-mu* in 1578 (Li 1965). This gap of 16 centuries raises many questions about the early origins of soy sauce in China. As we shall soon see, soybean chiang, a fermented soybean paste that is a close relative of miso, originated in China in the first century B.C. For most of its early history it was probably used in the form of a paste, rather than being pressed to extract a liquid soy sauce.

A single integrated history of soy nuggets, soy sauce, soybean chiang, and miso is given in the Ballantine edition of our *Book of Miso*. Our main sources of information on the early histories of chiang and miso in East Asia have been our own translations of the following works: Kawamura's *Miso no Hon* (1972; The Book of Miso), Ichiyama's *Kikkoman Shoyu Shi* (1968; History of Kikkoman Shoyu), Kawamura's *Miso Enkaku-shi* (1958; Historical Chronicles of Miso), Motoyama's *Inshoku Jiten* (1971; Encyclopedia of Food and Drink), and Morohashi's *Daikanwa Jiten* (1955; Historical Chinese Character Dictionary).

Etymology: While the general term *chiang*, referring to various pastes, appeared as early as the third century B.C., the first reference to chiang made from soybeans *(tou-chiang)* is found in the *Ch'i-min yao-shu* (Shih 1962) in A.D. 535. Since that time soybean chiang has always been known in standard Chinese (Mandarin) as *tou-chiang* ("bean chiang"); in Pinyin it is called *doujiang*. Other types

of chiang containing soybeans were also developed, as will be discussed later. As *tou-chiang* moved southward into southern China and Southeast Asia it became known as *tau cheung* in Cantonese, as *tau ch'iu* in Hokkien (from Fukien province), as *tauco* (pronounced taucho and formerly spelled tao-tjo; a corruption of the Hokkien for *tou chiang*) in Indonesian, as *tau-cheo* or *tau-chio* in Malaysian, as *tao-chio* or *tau-cheaw* in Thai, and as *tuong* (a term derived from *chiang*) in Vietnamese. To the east, in Korea, it became known as *jang*.

The Chinese word for soy sauce, *chiang-yu*, means "the liquid pressed from chiang." It clearly was derived from the earlier term *chiang*.

Pronounced *chiang* in China and *hishio* in Japan

Pronouned *chiang-yu* in China and *shoyu* in Japan

When the Chinese character *chiang* entered Japan (it first appeared in the *Man'yoshu* in A.D. 686) it was pronounced *hishio* (Pierson 1929). By 730 the character was being pronounced both *hishio* and *misho*. The present word for miso, written with the present characters, first appeared between 886 and 901. A more detailed discussion of the complex evolution of the new term will be given later.

Since miso has no close counterpart among Western foods, it has, since the time of earliest Western contact, usually been referred to in European languages by its Japanese name, *miso*. Only rarely has it been called "soybean paste." Chinese soybean chiang has never been widely known in the West, probably because it is a relatively unimportant food in China and because it is not nearly as appealing as miso to most Westerners. In 1976 Shurtleff and Aoyagi gave the first specific English names for each of the 6 basic types and 28 varieties of Japanese miso, as well as 9 varieties of Chinese chiang, 5 varieties of Korean Jang, and 4 varieties of Indonesian taucho. Miso is now known as *le miso* in French and *das miso* in German.

SOYBEAN CHIANG IN CHINA

Early Chinese Non-Soybean Chiang: Thought to have originated before the Chou dynasty (722-481 B.C.), chiang is undoubtedly the oldest condiment known to man, originally developed as a way of preserving protein-rich animal foods to be used either as seasonings or preserves. In effect, the peoples of East Asia discovered that when seafoods and meat (and, later, soybeans) were salted or immersed in a mixture of salt and rice wine (or water), their protein was broken down by enzymes into amino acids, which in turn stimulated human taste buds, augmenting the flavors of other foods. It was soon found that subsequent fermentation served to deepen and elaborate the primary flavor and aroma of the salt-pickled ingredients. The idea of combining these two distinct preservation techniques into a single process laid the foundation for the later development of miso, and enabled people long ago to break the vicious cycle of feast and famine, conserving foods from times of bounty to be enjoyed in times of scarcity.

The earliest varieties of Chinese chiang were probably made with fish, shellfish, and game. Their flesh—and in some cases bones, blood, and entrails—was ground or crushed, pickled in a mixture of salt and rice wine, and fermented in sealed earthenware vats for 100 days or more. This chiang closely resembled contemporary Asian fermented fish sauces and pastes such as the strong-smelling *nuoc mam* of Vietnam. But it was fundamentally different from modern miso (or shoyu) in that it contained no soybeans, grains, or koji. According to Shinoda (1974), Japan's most respected historian of Chinese foods, the earliest reference to koji appears in the *Shih Ching (Classic of Songs)*, the first of the Chinese Five Classics, consisting of 305 songs dating from the tenth to the seventh centuries B.C. Koji was added to pickled fish mixtures to speed the fermentation. Soybeans and grains were being used as ingredients in chiang by the first century B.C. The consistency of early chiang was probably neither as firm as that of miso nor as liquid as shoyu; rather it more than likely resembled applesauce, porridge, or the mash known as *moromi* from which today's shoyu is pressed. The various types of seafood miso (crab, shrimp, and red-snapper miso) still very popular in Japan are thought to be its direct descendants.

According to the *Daikanwa Jiten*, a remarkable dictionary showing the earliest uses of Chinese characters (Morohashi 1955), the written character for chiang made its first appearance in about the third century B.C. in two unrelated documents, the *Chou-li* (Japanese: *Shurai*) and the *Analects of Confucius (Lun yü)*. It is not clear which of these is the older. In the *Chou-li* (Rituals of the Chou Dynasty, a bureaucratic utopian vision of the administration that supposedly existed in the dynasty's royal court in the sixth to eighth centuries B.C.), chiang is mentioned several times. In the chapter "Contents of the Heavenly Palace Household" *(T'ien Kung Chia Tsai)* it is stated that "One hundred and twenty crocks of chiang were stocked for a party by the Chou government" (Biot 1851, Sun 1966). The work also states: "In preparing the eight basic

types of foods whose qualities harmonize with the four seasons, one should learn to use chiang from the hundred and twenty crocks . . . Fasting from all foods is in the spring. Fasting from soups is in the summer. Fasting from chiang is in the autumn. Fasting from drinks is in the winter . . . They selected the hundred delicacies, chiang products and rare things to make an offering." The *Chou-li* states that this chiang was made by mixing the meat of animals, birds, and fish with millet koji and salt, then pickling it in wine in a crock for a hundred days. It is quite remarkable that even at this early date the Chinese were consciously using the enzymes produced by the koji molds (whose spores fell on the substrate naturally, rather than by inoculation), to make fermented foods such as chiang and fermented grain-based alcoholic beverages (Sakaguchi 1979). It is also clear from the context that chiang was regarded as a highly prestigious food and a delicacy.

In the *Analects of Confucius (Lun yü*, Scroll 2, Chapter 10; Waley 1966; Lau 1979), chiang appears in a section where the sage is discussing proper etiquette and social behavior, the wise choice of foods, and fasting: "Foods not accompanied by the appropriate variety of chiang should not be served. Rather than using only one to season all foods, you should provide many to ensure harmony with each of the basic food types. Make grains central to your diet. Use wine in moderation to welcome guests, but by no means should you get drunk and act foolish." Confucius (c. 551-479 B.C.) did not write the *Analects* (or any other works); they were compiled by his disciples 100 to 200 years after his death.

In other texts of the same period, we learn that each of the 120 crocks mentioned above contained chiang made with a different combination of ingredients and having a distinctive flavor. One source mentions, for example, mustard chiang and says that it should be eaten only with *sashimi* (raw fish). A Chou dynasty legal document tells us that one government official was appointed director of chiang production, while another was made director of the closely affiliated bureau of medicine and foods.

The character for chiang next appears in several texts of the second or third century B.C. The *Chan Kuo*, in the section "The Intrigues of Eastern Chou," states that "Caldrons are not like pickle pots or chiang jars. If you pick up one and try to go to Ch'i, you will not get there as quick as a bird flying or a rabbit jumping or a horse galloping." This suggests that the containers in which chiang was pickled were relatively small. Five types of meat or fish chiang are mentioned in the *Li Chi* or *Record of Rituals* (Japanese: *Reiki*), the last of the Confucian Five Classics. This suggests the food's high status.

Chiang is next mentioned in the *Historical Records* (Chinese: *Shih chi;* Japanese: *Shiki*) by Ssu-ma Ch'ien, the great historian, who died in about 85 B.C. In "The Record of Prosperity" chapter it is stated that "Throughout Ta-i [possibly a district in today's Szechuan] in one year, one thousand fermented products and one thousand crocks of pickles and chiang are made. This is equivalent to a house of a thousand chariots (i.e. a dukedom)" (Watson 1961). Chiang is also mentioned in Chapter 135 (*Huo Ch'ih*

Lieh Chuan or "List of Various Products"); this is almost certainly a meat or fish chiang paste. The book also notes that in 140 B.C. a traveler in Canton ate a fermented food called *ku-chiang* prepared with a sweet wild fruit and probably resembling today's Kinzanji miso, but containing no soybeans. Since Canton was thousands of miles from the imperial capital at Chang-an and since we are told that this chiang was made in a remote town upstream from it, we may assume that the process for preparing various types of chiang was known throughout much of China before the Christian era. In this reference we also have the first known description of a chiang made without meat or fish.

The *Han Shu*, written by Pan Ku circa A.D. 90, stated in "The Collated Records of Yang Hsiung" section that the students of that age were such ignorant materialists that in the future, they might even use the sacred Taoist books "to cover chiang jars." The *Han shu* also mentioned the use of a starter *(chü)* in making two types of rice wines, *li* and *chiu*.

Early Chinese Soybean Chiang (*tou-chiang;* 100 B.C.-A.D. 599). The first reference to the use of soybeans as the basic protein source in chiang, as a substitute for the previously used meat and fish, appeared in the *Chi Chiu P'ien*, written by Shih Yu during the first century B.C. It stated, "Soy nuggets *(shih)* are made from black beans . . . chiang is made from (soy) beans and wheat flour . . . Wheat, rice, and (soy) bean gruel are what the country people and farmers eat." In the *Lun Heng*, written by Wang Chung in approximately A.D. 27-100, in the "Four Taboos" section, it is stated that "it is bad to hear thunder when making soybean chiang *(tou chiang)*." One wonders if it was believed that the thunder's static electricity affected the fermentation process.

The first detailed description of the process for making soybean chiang appeared in the *Ch'i-min yao-shu*, a remarkable ten fascicle agricultural encyclopedia, written in about A.D. 533 to 544 (Shih 1962). All of the fascicles 7 and 8 are about fermented foods and there is a long section on "Chiang." It states that the culture used for making chiang was called *huang-i* (yellow coating), *huang-cheng* (yellow mold) and *mai-yuan* (wheat must). These cultures of *Aspergillus* or *Rhizopus* molds were propagated on steamed wheat grains inoculated by spores that were airborne or attached to the leaves of certain plants (*Phragmites* or *Xanthium*). After describing the preparation of meat chiang and fish chiang, the *Ch'i-min yao-shu* stated that soybean chiang was prepared by fermenting a mixture of 30 parts presoaked steamed soybeans, 10 parts powdered wine starter, 10 parts yellow mold, and 5 parts white table salt. After incubation for three to five weeks (depending on the weather), the mixture ripened as a stock (now called chiang chiao). Thirty percent by volume of salt solution was then stirred into this and the mixture fermented for 100 days for best flavor, although it could be eaten after 20. It was thought that if a pregnant woman touched it during fermentation, it would go bad. In one place, the book advised making chiang during the twelfth and first months of the lunar calendar (January-February); in another it recommended fermentation under the hot summer sun. It also described the preparation of Chinese koji (called

ch'u or *k'u*) to produce fermented alcoholic beverages from millet or rice, and the preparation of "chiang-pickled vegetables" *(chiang tsai)*, made by pickling half-dried vegetables in fermenting or well-fermented soybean chiang (Shih 1962).

During this period the Chinese learned to preserve a number of foods by pickling them in chiang: tofu was pickled to make *chiang toufu*, white uri melon to make *chiang kua*, and pork to make *chiang jou*. The use of soybeans in all of the above preparations marked a major step in the development of today's miso and shoyu. The early mention of soybean chiang in the *Chi Chiu P'ien* and *Lun Heng*, and the detailed description of this chiang's preparation in the *Ch'i-min yao-shu* indicate that the basic techniques for making soybean chiang had probably been established before the second century B.C.

These early varieties of Chinese chiang were used primarily as a seasoning. Their consistency was midway that of today's miso and soy sauce, resembling an applesauce or porridge. Considered both nutritious and tasty, they were popular daily foods, highly esteemed by all classes of people, and used as a dressing for cooked vegetables or grains (typically mixed with other ingredients such as vinegar or a sweetener), or for pickling.

The development of fermented soyfoods, a process that depends on a rather sophisticated (intuitive and conscious) understanding of microbiology and fermentation technology, was a remarkable achievement in the early history of China. It is also remarkable that the Chinese recognized and deliberately cultivated at least two types of molds, *Aspergillus* and *Rhizopus*, and used them to produce enzymes. The *Rhizopus* processes, used with soybeans or barley to make chiang or soy nuggets (both having koji with a crumbly consistency), were never transmitted to Japan. (The Japanese, however, developed a way for making saké with *Rhizopus* that was not found in China.)

600 to 1899: During the T'ang dynasty (618 A.D.-906 A.D.) chiang was referred to as the "ruler of foods" and in one well-known ceremony, a tray bearing its many varieties was placed on the palace altar, before which the Emperor showed his respect by formally bowing in public. A special official was appointed to guard the Imperial Household's supply as it fermented so that no one could steal the secrets of its production. In the *T'ang Shu* (The Old Book of T'ang, written by Liu Hsu, A.D. 887-946) at the "Records of the Hundred Officials" chapter it is stated that "In the department of the controller of pickles are 23 chiang craftsmen, 12 vinegar craftsmen, and 12 soy nugget *(shih)* craftsmen." The *Liu Shu Ku* written by Tai T'ung of the Sung dynasty (960-1126) noted cynically, "Nowadays people let soybeans and wheat go yellow, throw in some salt and water, and consider it chiang." Here we see mention of the use of both wheat and soybeans in chiang, the forerunner of today's shoyu. An early mention of the Chinese equivalent of miso soup appears in the *T'an Yuan*, written by Huang Chien in roughly 1027 A.D. "Someone asked if the people and officials of Hsiu-shui and Ch'ing-te were clear (i.e. honest). He replied, 'they are the color of *chiang shui* ("chiang water")—not clear and not thick (i.e.

corrupt)." This *chiang shui*, pronounced *shosui* in Japanese, later became the famous Zosui, a miso porridge. During the Southern Sung dynasty (1127-1279), chiang (probably soybean chiang) was considered one of the "Seven Necessities" in China. The other six were firewood, rice (or grain), oil, salt, vinegar, and tea.

The *Pen ts'ao kang mu*, a large and famous collection of botanical and medical writings by Li Shih-chen (1578, Ming Dynasty), mentioned various types of chiang, including soybean chiang, wheat chiang, and wheat & soy chiang. It mentioned five types of illnesses for which chiang was considered a potent remedy.

The *Kuang yang tsa chi*, written by Liu Hsien-t'ing during the late 17th century stated: "So if the sage did not get his chiang, he would not eat," attesting to the continued importance of chiang in the culture.

The Twentieth Century: Surprisingly little has been published about soybean chiang in China during the 20th century, although it still plays a very important role in the diet of the people.

The Englishman Shaw (1911) in Manchuria stated that "Chinese paste (chiang) is not the same article of diet as the Japanese paste miso. It is made by farmers, and eaten with fish, meat, and vegetables, while the more expensive soy (sauce) is only made by wealthy families and restaurant keepers and is not consumed by the very poor. There are two kinds of chiang: *ta* (great) and *hsiao* (small)." For great chiang, soybeans were boiled until soft, mashed in a mortar, shaped into flat cakes, and fermented on mats for 2 months. They were then ground to a powder, mixed with salt water, and fermented in a vat, with occasional stirring, for 15 days. The same method was used for small chiang, except that equal parts soybeans and maize (corn) were used in place of just soybeans.

In 1918 Shih in China wrote in detail about "Tou Chiang or Bean Sauce" but stated that it was generally made the "Water White Bean, *Phaseolus vulgaris.*" No mention of soybeans was made in the article, which described the fermentation process in detail.

The most detailed information seen on Chinese chiang is Nakayama's *Chugoku Meisaifu* (1973), published in four volumes in Japanese. It describes the numerous types of chiang and gives many recipes. Little else is known about the present status of the chiang industry or market in China. In the USA chiang is not nearly as widely known or used as Chinese soy sauce or Japanese miso, and only a few types (such as bean sauce and hoisin sauce) are mentioned in U.S. Chinese cookbooks, and then not frequently. Apparently it does not appeal to most American palates.

One interesting innovation is that in Taiwan the okara or soy pulp remaining from manufacture of soymilk or tofu is now sometimes used as an extender for soybeans in making miso.

The main varieties of soy-based Chinese chiang today are chunky soybean chiang *(tou-pan chiang)*, hot chunky soybean chiang *(la tou-pan chiang)*, Szechuan red-pepper soybean chiang *(ssu-ch'uan tou-pan chiang)*, soy nugget chiang *(tou-ch'ih chiang)*, and black soybean chiang *(hei chiang)*.

SOYBEAN CHIANG IN KOREA AND SOUTHEAST ASIA

Dissemination of Chiang from China: By the early T'ang dynasty (618-906 A.D.), soybean chiang and soy sauce (the liquid seasoning extracted from chiang) had begun to move out of China into adjoining countries. There is considerable evidence that Buddhist priests played a key role in taking soybean chiang eastward into Korea and Japan, while Chinese traders from Canton and the surrounding Kwantung province, and from Fukien province were instrumental in disseminating it southward. As it entered new cultures, both its basic character and its name were altered slightly. Unfortunately, very little has been published about the history of soybean chiang as it entered the various countries surrounding China, except for Japan.

The various relatives of chiang in Southeast Asia are much more closely related to Chinese chiang in consistency (like applesauce) and flavor (strongly flavored) than to Japanese miso. As in China, most continue to be made noncommercially at home for home use, and they are most widely used as a base for sauces served with meat, seafood, poultry, or vegetable dishes, rather than as a soup base like Japanese miso. A detailed description of all the basic chiang-type foods with production information is given in Appendix B.

Korea: Korean records from A.D. 680 indicate that *jang* (soybean chiang) and *kan jang* (soy sauce) had entered the country in the customary exchange of gifts between ruling houses (Wang and Lee 1978). Today the main soy-based varieties of Korean jang are Korean soybean jang *(doen jang)*, red-pepper soybean chiang *(kochu jang)*, mild red-pepper soybean chiang *(may jang)*, and Japanese red jang *(wei jang* or *ilbon jang)*. Traditional Korean miso is basicaly soybean miso, made by cooking and mashing soybeans, shaping them into 6-inch balls, tying these with strands of rice straw under the eves or rafters for 1 to 3 months until they are covered with a white bloom of mold. They are then crumbled to make *meju*, which serves as the base of jang or soy sauce.

Early Japanese mention a miso-like product or hishio from Korea. The *Wamyosho* (903-938), the earliest dictionary of the Japanese language referred to a Korean product called *koma-bishio*, a fermented soy and/or grain hishio. This product was further discussed in the *Honcho Shokkan* of 1695. While it is doubtful that miso came to Japan from Korea, it is very likely that Japanese miso and its name were influenced by its Korean forbears.

In 1976 in Korea, per capita daily consumption of soybean jang and red-pepper soybean jang were 15 grams and 10 grams respectively. Some 82% and 76% of each product respectively were produced in farmhouses and urban dwellings, and consumed directly by the families that made them (Wang and Lee 1978, Choe and Song 1960). Lee (1976) has given a detailed description of making Korean soybean jang and soy sauce.

Indonesia: The earliest reference to a relative of chiang in Southeast Asia was by the Dutch scientist Prinsen Geerligs in 1895 and 1896. He described Indonesian taucho, calling it *tao tsioe* in his Dutch article of 1895 and *tao tjiung* (after *tou-chiang*) in his German article of 1896. He indicated that the soybeans were inoculated with hibiscus leaves, called *waroe*. Ochse (1931) gave a detailed description of taucho, which he spelled *taotjo*. Burkill (1935) mentioned "*tao-cho*" saying that the cooked soybeans were mixed with roasted rice flour, then arenga palm sugar and a paste of glutinous rice.

The main soy-based varieties of Indonesian taucho, listed in order of popularity are soft sweet taucho (taucho Chianjur, which contains 25% by weight of palm sugar), salty liquid taucho (also called black bean sauce, a relative of *tausi*), firm dired taucho (*taucho kering*, sold in sun-dried cakes), and smoked dried taucho. Taucho is produced and consumed mainly in West Java, the center of production being the town of Chianjur, located midway between Bogor and Bandung. Figures on production and distribution have been given by Winarno (1976). Popular recipes include Sambal Goreng Taucho and Oseng-Oseng Taucho.

Vietnam: Vietnamese chiang is called tuong. The best and earliest description of tuong and its manufacture in North Vietnam (Tonkin) was given by BUI Quang Chieu (1905) and later summarized by Li (1912). Bui described two basic types of tuong, made with roasted soybeans and either glutinous rice or corn. For that made with glutinous rice: steam glutinous rice, cover on trays with banana leaves, and leave for 2 to 3 days until it molds to form koji *(moc)*. Roast the soybeans, grind to a powder, boil with water, and put in a jar for 7 days until sweet from auto-hydrolysis and fermentation. Then add salt plus 6 parts of the rice koji to 5 parts of the soy, ferment for 15 to 30 days, stirring before sunrise and covering at night; serve without filtering off the liquid. Tuong comes with either a chunky or a very smooth consistency; the chunky *(tuong ban)* is the most popular, while the smooth is made only in Cu-da, North Vietnam. A good tuong is mellow, thick, and brown; it is sweeter and smoother than *nuoc mam* fish sauces. Annamites (from central south Vietnam) say that only prosperous households succeed in making tuong. If tuong begins well but then sours, this is a bad omen. According to Mr. Hoang Van Chi (1981), owner of the first company to make smooth tuong in the West, since about 1950 there has been no soy tuong in North Vietnam because of a shortage of soybeans and rice caused by the protracted anticolonial war, and by the fact that the pre-Communist soy sauce makers were classified as landlords. Starting in the late 1970s efforts began to make soy sauce with peanut or cottonseed presscake.

Other Southeast Asia: Soybean chiang has long been used in Malaysia (where it is called *tau-cheo* or *tau-chio*) and in Thailand (where it is called *tao-chio* or *tau-cho cheaw*), but little is known of the history or present status of these products.

HISTORY OF MISO IN JAPAN

The origins of miso are not clear, although most scholars agree that its earliest progenitor came from either China or Korea. Some set the date of arrival in Japan at shortly before the introduction of Buddhism (540-552 A.D.), whereas others feel that the lack of definite records demands the more conservative estimate of 663 A.D. The miso transmitted from Korea is thought to have been prepared using the *miso-dama* technique whereby cooked soybeans were mashed, shaped into balls, and inoculated with wild mold spores to form the koji. Crushed and mixed with salt and water, the balls were then fermented in crocks to make a variety of soybean miso. This special tradition, though largely unrecorded, is thought to have been the origin of much of Japan's earliest farmhouse miso. The product brought from China, on the other hand, is believed to have gained its first acceptance among the nobility and in monasteries.

Early Non-Soybean Hishios (Before A.D. 700): There is evidence that long before the arrival of miso-like foods from China and Korea, the Japanese had independently developed their own varieties of fermented sauces, resembling Chinese chiang and based on fish, shellfish, and meat. The earliest inhabitants of Japan were hunters and gatherers who are said to have arrived about 20,000 years ago. Long before the Chrisitan era, they learned to extract salt from sea water, and their earliest seasonings consisted of this natural salt, together with *sansho* pepper and ground shellfish. Starting in the late Jomon period and continuing through the succeeding Yayoi period (200 B.C.-25 A.D.), however, fish and meat sauces basically similar to chiang were independently developed, as attested to by pickling crocks recently excavated in the northeastern provinces and dating back 3,000 to 4,000 years. The Japanese word for these primordial seasonings was *hishio* (or *hishiho*), and when the first writing system was introduced from China, it was written with the character for chiang.

A number of these Japanese hishios (each made without the use of koji) can still be found: *shiokara* is squid, squid intestines, or bonito pickled in a mixture of mirin and salt; *shottsuru* (from Akita) is sardines and hard-finned *hatahata* pickled in salt; *shuto* is salted bonito intestines pickled in sake; and *gyoeki* is fermented fish liquid. Two lesser-known relatives are *ikanago shoyu* from Kagawa and *kurozukuri* from Hokuriku. (Ancient Rome had a similar fermented sauce called "garum," an ancestor of anchovie sauce.) All are aged for one week or more and served as toppings for rice or as hors d'oeuvres. Throughout the northerly regions characterized by long snowy winters and severe flooding, they have also long been used as emergency food staples (Kawamura 1972).

Today, the northeastern provinces are known as the "miso heartland" of Japan; the per-capita consumption there is the highest in the nation and the ancient homemade-miso tradition is still very much alive. These facts, combined with the archeological evidence indicating early mastery of salt-pickling and fermentation, move some scholars to go so far as to trace the origins of miso (and shoyu) to this part of Japan rather than to China or Korea.

The Nara Period (A.D. 710-784): The first written records of miso and hishio date from the Nara period; no documents or legends from before this time mention any varieties of fermented foods. And, strangely enough, no mention is made of them in either the *Kojiki* (712 A.D.)

or *Nihonshoki* (720 A.D.), which do mention soybeans and were written more than ten years after miso and a closely related variety of hishio are known to have been produced at the Imperial Palace.

One of the first references to this hishio appears in the *Man'yoshu*, an extraordinary collection of thousands of Japan's earliest songs and poems recorded from as early as the year 315 A.D. and compiled circa 760. In most of the poems, the Japanese words are elaborately spelled out with Chinese characters used phonetically. The character for hishio (chiang) appears in scroll 16 in a poem by Imiki Okimaru (686-707), a humorous bard who improvised at banquets for the court nobility. We and Pierson (1929) translate this as:

I want to eat red snapper *(tai)*
With a dressing of minced garlic and vinegar-hishio
So do not offer me a leek soup.

Another poem describes two comic crabs happily making themselves into crab hishio seasoned with pounded elm bark. Mention is also made of hishio containing wild game and deer meat. Unfortunately we are not told exactly what type of product this hishio was nor how it differed from miso and chiang, yet it is now generally believed that all of these products were well known at this period among the nobility and, to a lesser extent, the common people.

During the first several centuries of contact with the continent, miso and hishio were probably very similar to chiang, and many of the basic raw materials and complex fermentation techniques were undoubtedly acquired largely from the Chinese. However, Japanese and Chinese taste preferences have always been fundamentally different, the Chinese preferring to use relatively large amounts of spices, oil, and meat in their strongly flavored cookery and the Japanese preferring the simpler, more sublte flavors inherent in the foods themselves. Gradually, therefore, by altering the basic ingredients and preparatory techniques, the Japanese began to transform chiang into foods uniquely suited to their own tastes. Soybeans—used alone or together with rice or barley—came to be preferred to fish or meat as the basic ingredient, while wine and spices were generally reduced in quantity or omitted. Hishio probably retained much the same applesauce-like texture as chiang, but miso slowly evolved into a firmer product with a shorter aging time. Of the two foods, hishio was probably the more important and more varied. Both were initially served primarily as toppings for rice; the hishio still widely prepared in country farmhouses continues to be served mostly in this way.

Perhaps the most important event in the early development of miso and hishio was the establishment in 701 of the *Hishio Tsukasa* or Bureau for the Regulation of Production, Trade, and Taxation of Hishio and Miso, which was originally an annex of the emperor's kitchen *(kunaicho daishokuzen)*, where hishio was made. Inaugurated by the Emperor Monmu in the *Taiho Ritsuryo* (Taiho Law Codes, one of Japan's earliest constitutions, which went into effect in 702), this bureau was located in the Imperial Palace. Using methods very similar to those developed in China, it transformed soybeans into high- and low-quality hishio, miso, and soy nuggets. These foods were consumed by the Imperial Household.

Another early reference to hishio, perhaps a soy-based product, appeared in the *Yoryo Ritsuryo*, written by Fujiwara Fuhito in 718. It mentioned various types of chiang and soy nuggets, plus *misho,* the second character of which was *chiang* (Ichiyama 1968).

The most detailed information to date on the early relatives of miso and the first clear reference to a soybean hishio appeared in the Todaiji Shosoin documents, written between 730 and 748, and still preserved in excellent condition in the Imperial Treasury of the Shosoin, connected with Nara's Todaiji temple. It records that in 730 taxes were being paid on hishio and on misho (a variety of hishio and an early relative of miso). A document from the next year mentions the same foods again. A document written prior to 748 clearly referred to soybean hishio (Ichiyama 1968). In a document of 740, first mention is made of *kasu hishio*, which may have been the lees remaining after the extraction of tamari. Records of about 750 show the following relative prices: highgrade hishio 15 *mon*, hishio 10.7 *mon*, ara-bishio 10 *mon*, and miso 7 to 8 *mon*. They also indicate that miso and hishio were sold in the markets of Nara; prices calculated on the basis of 1 *sho* (about 1.8 liters or 2 quarts) reveal that they were relatively inexpensive. These various fermented foods were most commonly written with the following characters; note that even the word "miso" contains the ideograph for hishio (chiang), indicating both origin and relationship:

| Miso | Rice Hishio | Ara-bishio | Soy Nuggets |

Much of Nara's miso was used at temples to provide free meals for the monks and laymen who donated their time to hand-copy Buddhist scriptures. Small quantities were used in side dishes and *aemono* (mixed salads) as well as with pickles, noodle dishes, *mochi,* and soups. Many of these preparations were served to the laborers who built Todaiji temple, then the largest wooden building in the world, and its immense cast statue of Buddha, the *Daibutsu,* which was completed the year 752.

One of the most colorful chapters in the history of miso concerns the great Chinese T'ang dynasty Buddhist master Chien-chen (Japanese: Ganjin). The founder of the Japanese Ritsu or "precepts" sect and of the well-known Toshodaiji temple in Nara, Ganjin spent over eleven years trying to reach Japan. After being blocked by pirates, shipwrecks, and storms, and having lost his eyesight during one of his six attempted crossings, he finally reached the

Buddhism-dominated Japanese court in 754 at the age of 66. The records of his ship's cargo show that in addition to 185 monks, sailors, and craftsmen, he brought with him 1,428 gallons of salt-free soy nuggets *(kan shih).* Later records show that this same fermented soyfood was prepared at his temple in Nara, carried by foot to Kyoto, and peddled there in the streets.

It is not clear exactly what type of food Ganjin's salt-free soy nuggets were. They probably resembled soybean koji, but it is not clear what kept them from spoiling or how they were served or used in foods. Nevertheless, Ganjin is widely reputed to have brought the progenitor of Japanese miso to Japan from China. Yet records show that something called "miso" was already being sold in Nara's markets more than 20 years before Ganjin's arrival. Hence, some scholars have concluded that the popular "Ganjin theory" probably reflects more of a desire on the part of early miso makers and Buddhist priests to link their product to Ganjin's lofty reputation than to historical fact.

One of the key links in the transmission from China to Japan of the techniques for preparing the different varieties of chiang was the *Ch'i-min yao-shu,* the 6th-century encyclopedia mentioned above, which arrived in Japan during the late 700s. Its ten fascicles describe the preparation of koji, soy (and barley) nuggets, and numerous varieties of chiang. From it, the Japanese learned how to prepare red-snapper miso, crab miso, *yuzu* miso, savory soy nuggets (Hamanatto), and products closely related to Kinzanji miso. A veritable treasurehouse of accurate and detailed information, this tome had a profound effect on the development of Japanese farming methods and crafts as well as food preparation.

One of the historical puzzles concerning the early development of miso in Japan concerns the origin of sweet white miso, which is still the favorite in the area of Japan's earliest capitals (Nara and Kyoto) and along the northern shores of the inland sea. The pattern of miso consumption in this area is very different from that of the rest of Japan: miso soup is relatively uncommon, only about one-third as much miso is consumed per capita as in Japan as a whole, and white miso's sweet flavor and light color are preferred to regular miso's dark saltiness. These facts have given rise to the theory that at a very early period, sweet white miso was brought from China to the ancient Japanese capitals where it continued to preserve its aristocratic mein and distinctive usage in cookery.

Documents written near the end of the Nara period describe more than 22 varieties of hishio, miso, and soy nuggets. Of these, hishio was by far the most diversified, yet all its 15 or more varieties were generally grouped into three basic types:

1. *Fish, Shellfish, and Wild Game Hishio (Shishibishio):* Generally prepared by pickling crabs, sea urchins, or shrimp in a mixture of salt, water and sake. Deer meat, eggs and, occasionally, fowl were also used.

2. *Vegetable and Fruit Hishio (Kusa-bishio):* Foods such as *uri* melon, eggplant, *daikon,* green leafy vegetables, *kabu* turnips, *udo,* fresh green soybeans, *mizunegi* onions,

peaches and apricots pickled with salt and fermented. In some cases, vinegar and/or *mizuamé* sweetening was used with or in place of the salt. These preparations later evolved into *tsukemono* (salted pickles) and the various types of finger lickin' miso. During this period the first miso pickles were made using *uri* melons and eggplants.

3. *Soybean and/or Grain Hishio (Koku-bishio):* The last type of hishio to develop, these products contained soybeans, grain (rice, wheat, or barley), salt, and often sake or sake lees. The Chinese equivalent of this fermented soyfood was called *kara hishio* and that from Korea was called *komabishio* ("high-elegant hishio"). These three foods evolved into today's miso and shoyu.

The Heian Period (A.D. 794-1160): One of Japan's great Buddhist pioneers was Kukai (best known by his posthumos title Kobo Daishi). He went to T'ang China from 804 to 806, and in 816 founded a great Shingon monastery on Mt. Koya. In 811 he wrote a letter to Emperor Saga which concluded, "I made a mess writing on this white cloth you gave me, so please use it as a lid for your hishio." This indicates that hishio was widely popular at that time.

At the beginning of the Heian period, the word "miso" suddenly began to be written with a new combination of characters, which is used to this day. The character for "mi" meant "flavor" and the one for "so" meant throat. This second character was, itself, a Japanese invention and is presently used in no other words. It first appeared in an official Japanese document of 806 in connection with a food called *enso,* a salt seasoning. According to Kawamura (1972), the modern word "miso" made its first appearance in the *Sandai Jitsuroku,* a history book by Ogura Yoshiyuki that was published between 901 and 908 but had been widely circulated in manuscript form since 886. Ichiyama (1968), however, says that the modern word for miso first appeared in the *Fuso Ryakuki* of 938. The new word was written like this, just as it is to this day:

味 噌

We may well inquire why the Japanese of this period deliberately invented a new character to replace the character chiang (hishio) that had been used during the previous two centuries, and why they introduced the character meaning "flavor" into the combination. It seems likely that by this time the Japanese had so thoroughly transformed chiang into a food suited to their own culture and tastes, that they felt it deserved a uniquely Japanese name. In fact, the *Sandai Jitsuroku* portrays miso as a truly Japanese food rather than as simply a Chinese import. But there were broader cultural changes too behind the change in characters. In 894, at the beginning of the Heian period, Japan essentially cut off contact with the outside world, and began an extended period of assimilating and transforming Chinese cultural imports. During this period, Japan also developed the *hiragana* and *katakana* writing styles, which were completed in the 10th century. It was as part of this larger cultural transformation that the change in miso and its characters took place.

Scholars generally agree that miso finally achieved its own identity during the 100 years prior to the emergence of its new name. Yet traditional writing habits were slow to change, and as late as the 18th century, the word miso was still written most frequently using the character for hishio or chiang, rather than the new Japanese *so*. The combination would have meant "hishio with a lot of flavor *(mi)*." The character for hishio could also have been pronounced *sho*, as it is in the word "shoyu." Thus if the combination were pronounced *misho*, it could have been the forerunner of the word "miso." The word "shoyu" would not appear for another 700 years.

Some scholars believe that the pronunciation "miso" originated with the *Wamyosho* (also called *Wamyo Rui-jusho*), the earliest dictionary of the Japanese language, encyclopedic in scale and written between 903 and 938 by Minamoto no Shitagau. It was modeled after Chinese dictionaries and listed many types of hishio including ones pronounced *"miso," "misho,"* and *"kara hishio."* It also mentioned soy nuggets.

The earliest Japanese document to contain information about the production of miso and hishio was the *Engi Shiki*, an elaboration of old law codes, compiled in about 927 by Fujiwara Tokihira and others. In it we are told that miso was a fermented food with soybeans as its main ingredient, but also containing rice, rice koji, wheat, salt, and saké. The *Engi Shiki* gave detailed information about the Hishio Tsukasa government bureau, stated that hishio was given to the Emperor's civil and military officials as part of their annual wage, and listed at least ten different types of miso and hishio. Among these, the word "miso" was written using at least five different character combinations, all of which were pronounced "miso," or perhaps occasionally "misho."

It is not always clear whether each of these names refers to a different food, or whether the name of a single variety was simply being written with different character combinations. The book gives the amounts of basic raw materials used in preparing numerous different types of miso and hishio, but most of the quantities appear quite inaccurate

and cannot be used experimentally to make the products they describe.

Although notebooks dating from as early as the 8th century reveal that miso was bought and sold in the marketplaces of the former capital at Nara, the first shops specializing in its sale are said to have originated in about 925 in the new capital at Kyoto. The *Engi Shiki* records the presence of a miso retail shop in Kyoto's western market and a hishio outlet in the eastern market. Moreover, 50 other shops are reported to have carried hishio, and 32 miso, as one among numerous other foods. Thus by the middle of the 10th century, it seems that hishio and miso were becoming basic staples.

The *Engi Shiki* also mentions *kasu-hishio* and *hishio-kasu*. Perhaps the former was lightly pressed, yielding a smaller amount of the shoyu-like liquid, so that the moist residue could be used as a seasoning. And perhaps the latter was very firmly pressed, yielding more liquid and a dry presscake, which was discarded.

The *Utsuho Monogatari* (911-983) mentioned *kasu miso*. In the *Utsubo Monogatari* of 969, the word "miso" was first written in kana script, thus clearly indicating the pronunciation.

Records from the year 980 show that monks in Nara's Todaiji temple were provided with a large daily supply of miso which was used in mixed salads *(aemono)*, foods simmered in seasoned broths *(nimono)*, and soups. Meanwhile, Chinese-educated monks in other Nara temples had begun to prepare Kinzanji, abalone, and red-snapper miso.

In the epics of the Heian period, such as the *Tale of Genji* and *Konjaku Monogatari*, are found descriptions of all-night parties held by the court nobility in the Imperial palace. A typical dinner consisted of seven courses, each served consecutively on separate trays. Popular foods included abalone miso and red-snapper hishio, *uri* melons and eggplants pickled in miso, and red snapper, carp or other sea foods lightly marinated with miso sauces. Both hishio and miso were also apparently widely used as table seasonings. Among the palace women, miso was known as *ko*, meaning "fragrance or incense," or *higurashi* meaning "a clear-toned summer cicada" whose song is said to be able to penetrate even the hardest stone. Likewise the rich fragrance and fine flavor of miso were said to penetrate and season other foods. For this reason, in the Kyoto area miso is still occasionally called *mushi* or *bamushi* meaning "insect or honorable insect."

By the middle of the 10th century, miso-making had spread from the capital to the countryside. The *Wamyosho* (903-938) tells us that miso was being produced in the prefectures and usually bore the name of the area in which it was made: Shiga miso and Hida miso, still enjoyed to this day, were among the early favorites.

The Kamakura Period (1185-1333): In 1185, with the beginning of the Kamakura period, a great revolution occurred in Japan. A new and vital government, composed largely of samurai, took away control of the country from the degenerate and effete ruling aristocracy in Kyoto, and established its capital in remote Kamakura, just south of present-day Tokyo. Buddhism awoke as a new spiritual force, aimed at showing the common people how they could attain enlightenment by a simple life based on daily religious practice, faith, and meditation. Out of the basic, lean Buddhist lifestyle evolved a simple yet healthful way of eating which became the standard Japanese diet. A typical meal consisted of a large serving of cooked grain (rice, barley, or millet) accompanied by the newly discovered *takuan* (salt-pickled *daikon*) and miso soup containing tofu and vegetables.

Thus among miso historians the Kamakura period is famous as the the period in which miso soup developed. A preparation then unknown among the Japanese aristocracy and still unknown in China, it came to be a symbol of the "food of the people." Miso, tofu, and deep-fried tofu *(agé)* became the basic, favorite foods both among the ruling Shoguns (Generalissimos) and in the Zen temples. Many Zen temples established shojin vegetarian restaurants within their own compounds as a way of making contact with the common people; here meatless meals, generally including a soup containing miso made at the temple, were served at reasonable prices in a quiet atmosphere of refined simplicity and beauty. Almost all temples made their own miso and gradually taught the process to people throughout the country, until in the hearts of many, the flavor of miso and the "flavor" of Zen became the same. In times of famine, the miso stored in large quantities in most farmhouses and city homes served as a lifesaving staple. Soon the saying *miso sae areba*, "Everything's all right as long as there is miso," came to be heard everywhere. Hence it was under the new Buddhist influence of the Kamakura period that the consumption of hishio containing fish or animal-derived products steadily declined, and that grain-and-soybean-based miso began to play its important role in the Japanese diet.

One new type of miso introduced to Japan during the Kamakura period was Kinzanji miso. In about 1255 A.D. the Japanese Buddhist monk Kakushin returned to Japan from China, where, according to the most widely held theory, he had learned to make this miso at Kinzanji, the Temple of the Golden Mountain, one of China's five great Sung dynasty Zen centers. This delectable, chunky, rather sweet miso contained a large percentage of barley koji plus minced eggplant, gingerroot, white *uri* melon, *kombu* (sea vegetable) and burdock root. Kakushin taught the method of Kinzanji preparation to the people of Yuasa in Wakayama prefecture, where the same ancient technique is used to this day. Yuasa has since become a famous center of shoyu production as well, and legend has it that shoyu's earliest progenitor, tamari, was discovered as the dark, fragrant liquid left over at the bottom or top of the Kinzanji barrel. A second theory holds that Kinzanji was transmitted to Japan by the *Ch'i-min yao-shu* in about 1650. A third theory suggests that it originated from the practice of soaking vegetables in hishio to make "vegetable hishio" *(kusa bishio)*.

The historical connection between miso, tamari, and shoyu that started in Japan in about 1200 in Yuasa bears further examination. The term *tamari* derives from the verb *tamaru*, meaning "to accumulate," as "water accu-

Making miso-damari

mulates in ponds." Originally the word *tamari* was written with the two characters shown below. The character on the left, *to*, means "soybean," and the one on the right, *yu*, means "a liquid extracted by filtering or pressing."

Later, however, a new character, the one used today, was adopted; it is the right-hand character in the word miso-damari, shown below. By 1260 tamari was being prepared for home consumption in the nearby towns of Yuasa and Hiromachi, and by 1290 the first Yuasa tamari, still a by-product of Kinzanji miso, is said to have been sold commercially, although no early documents exist. The tamari was always removed by either filtering or ladling, never pressing, as that would ruin the miso. Pressing the miso originated during the Muromachi (1336-1568), a period noted for its opulence. The term *miso-damari*, referring to the rich liquid tamari removed from miso, seems to have originated during the 1500s, when it came to be prepared and prized by the monks living in the five major temples of Kyoto.

Miso-damari

The word *shoyu* did not appear until a very late date, being first mentioned in a Japanese dictionary (*Ekirin Honsetsu Yoshu*), published in 1597, but thought to have been written by a priest sometime between 1469 and 1503 and widely circulated in manuscript form.

Shoyu

The Muromachi Period (1336-1568): During the Muromachi period, the seat of government returned to the Kyoto area and some of the formality, splendor, and aristocratic feeling of the Heian period was revived. But the period as a whole was characterized by social chaos and civil war. The famous samurai Takeda Shingen (1521-1573), lord of a large fief in the Shinshu area north of Tokyo, was the first to recognize miso's full potential as a soldier's food. Long-lasting, inexpensive, and highly nutritious, it took only minutes to make it into a warming soup. To ensure that his men had a large supply of it wherever they went, Takeda taught farmers throughout Shinshu to plant soybeans and process them into miso. The preparation of homemade miso soon flourished throughout the area and gradually spread to other nearby provinces. During the 16th century miso shops attached to private homes appeared in urban areas and gradually every region developed its own techniques and new varieties, which often came to be called by such lofty names as "morality" or "Bodhidharma" miso. Documents of this period show frequent references to miso in plays, stories and songs, indicating that it was not only a popular food but an integral and intimate part of the social fabric.

The Muromachi period saw the development of two new varieties of miso; Hatcho and sweet white. Oral tradition has it that Hatcho was first prepared as early as 1370, but scholars generally place the date somewhere between the late 1400s and early 1500s. A kabuki drama tells of how Hideyoshi Toyotomi (1536-1598), the child of poor farmers in central Japan's Aichi prefecture, rose to become one of Japan's most powerful feudal lords. When only ten years old, the child is said to have fallen asleep one night on a bridge near his home, wrapped only in a straw mat. A famous robber passing over the bridge scornfully kicked the urchin, who awoke and intrepidly grabbed the man's spear commanding him to stop such cruelty. The robber, impressed with the boy's courage, decided to raise him as his own son. In the play, the straw mat bears the trademark of one of the nearby Hatcho miso shops where it was used to prepare koji. Historians cite the incident to prove that Hatcho miso was being made as early as 1546. (The shop uses the same trademark to this day.) Later records show that by 1590, when Tokugawa Ieyasu left for the frontier town of Edo to found his new capital, both of Japan's present Hatcho miso makers were doing a thriving business.

Although some scholars support the previously mentioned theory that sweet white miso was transmitted from the Chinese to the Japanese capital during the Nara period, most believe that the present product was developed by Kyoto craftsmen during the 14th and 15th centuries to suit the tastes of the indolent court nobility. It is interesting to note that both Hatcho and sweet white miso still

The child Hideyoshi on a mat bearing the Hatcho miso mark (circa 1546).

retain a certain high-class image, a reflection, perhaps, of the era in which they originated.

In the late 1300s one of Japan's most famous miso recipes, Dengaku, is said to have originated, probably in rural villages. Miso spread on tofu was broiled over an open fire, as described in Chapter 6. Dengaku first became popular throughout Japan in the early 1600s and by 1775 was served in fashionable tea shops in Kyoto and Tokyo.

By the 15th century, the most widely available varieties of miso are said to have finally lost their luxury status and made their way into the homes of the common people. Yet at the same time, miso emerged as an essential and esteemed ingredient in the more famous schools of Japanese haute cuisine. Under the wise guidance of Senno-Rikyu, *shojin* cookery was carried to its peak of refinement and subtlety in Tea Ceremony Cuisine *(Kaiseki Ryori)*. It was in these newly emerging schools of fine cookery that sweet simmered, broiled, *yuzu,* and *kinomé* miso, together with many other of Japan's finest miso preparations, were first developed. From its earliest beginnings in simple peasant fare, miso now rose to attain the same level of honor among the people that it had enjoyed among the Japanese palace nobility eight centuries earlier, and that its predecessor *chiang* had enjoyed in China's Imperial Household twelve centuries before that.

Mention of miso was made in many cookbooks during this period. A work (the pronunciation of whose title is unknown) of 1467 discussed miso soup and its popularization. The *Hocho Kikigaki* (1487) discussed tarémiso. The *Shijoryu Hocho-gaki* (1489) talked of tarémiso, usutaré, and surimiso. The *Ogusaden Yori Soden no Kikigaki* (1504) described sumashi miso, tarémiso, and suri hishio.

The year 1593 is usually given as the year in which Sendai miso originated. Originally it was made for the soldiers of the great feudal lord and soldier Ida Masamune, and as a reserve food during times of famine. That same year they took Sendai miso to Korea (Ichiyama 1968).

The Edo or Tokugawa Period (1603-1867): In 1603 the capital of Japan was moved from Kamakura to Edo (later renamed Tokyo), where the Tokugawa Shoguns establsihed Japan's longest period of stability and peace. Miso made commercially in the towns of Shimousa and Saitama was sold in the huge markets of the new capital city. Because supply was insufficient to meet demand, however, the Shogun, Tokugawa Ieyasu, imported his favorite soybean and Hatcho miso by boat from his native town in central Japan. Although miso was consumed in increasingly large amounts, several factors prevented the many small miso makers of the period from growing into large-scale companies. First, miso, generally packed into large wooden kegs, was heavy and bulky, and the lack of good roads or river routes made long distance distribution difficult and expensive. Second, and perhaps more important, people enjoyed preparing their own miso at home at very little cost, making it difficult to price commercial miso competitively. Indeed, there was a saying popular at the time that a family that did not make its own miso would never have its own treasury-storehouse *(kura)*, and many considered it a source of embarrassment if they had to use miso which they had not made themselves. Furthermore, most people preferred the flavor of the homemade or locally made product. Nevertheless, urbanization sped miso's commercialization and many of Japan's larger cities developed their own varieties. Here miso was first sold at saké stores; only later did outlets specialzing in miso and miso pickles come into existence.

It was during this period that many farmers and small miso-shop operators, who had formerly made only soybean miso, began to experiment with the use of barley or rice koji in order to obtain a wider variety of flavors. In the capital at Edo during the 1600s, the three most popular varieties were Sendai red miso, barley miso made in nearby Saitama prefecture, and the hometown specialty Edo sweet red miso. Salty rice miso was developed throughout the northeastern provinces and in the Shinshu area north of the capital. Both salty and sweet barley miso were produced in Kyushu and at the southern tip of Japan's main island, and new varieties of sweet white miso emerged in the Kyoto-Nara area. As grain koji became more widely used, the traditional practice of forming cooked soybeans into balls was abandoned in many areas and the grain koji was fermented in wooden trays.

By the early Tokugawa period, the first reports of Japanese miso had begun to reach Europe. The Italian Carletti mentioned it in 1597, the German Kaempfer gave a detailed account of its production in 1691-92, and Thunberg mentioned it in passing in 1795.

When the Chinese Zen master Ingen (founder of the famous Obaku sect) came to Japan in 1661, he was surprised to find miso totally different from the chiang he had known in his native country. Becoming extremely fond of it, he is said to have enjoyed miso soup each day and used it as an effective substitute for a Chinese herbal medicine that he had taken for many years.

In the early 1800s, Hokusai (1760-1849) did a nice woodblock print of a cedar vat, the type widely used until the 1970s for making miso and shoyu.

A Brief Overview of Origins: Before proceeding, it might be interesting, and indeed provocative, to reflect briefly on the origins and genealogies of miso and shoyu. The most widely held opinion among Japanese researchers and fermented-food historians is that both miso and shoyu trace their ancestry to Chinese chiang. However, Dr. Kinichiro Sakaguchi, Professor of Fermentation Science at Tokyo University, in his "Searching for the Roots of Shoyu" (1979) argues convincingly that today's miso traces its ancestry back through early Japanese misos and hishio to chiang, whereas shoyu traces its ancestry back through early shoyu, then through the four products of tamari shoyu, tamari miso, Hatcho miso, and savory soy nuggets (Hamanatto), and ultimately to Chinese soy nuggets *(shih)*. In the shoyu lineage, the koji is always made from either soybeans alone or a mixture of soybeans and cracked wheat, whereas in the miso lineage the koji is always made from grain. Sakaguchi believes that the fundamental biochemical consequences of this difference are of much greater importance than the more superficial differences of form that have led researchers up until now to group solid or semisolid products in the miso lineage and liquid products in the shoyu lineage. Thus, in shoyu, the *Aspergillus oryzae* molds act directly on the soybeans during the koji fermentation, then their enzymes continue to act on the soybeans during the subsequent brine fermentation. This leads to the formation of more complicated metabolic compounds, a higher degree of protein hydrolysis and liquefaction, and the production of a sharper and stronger flavor in shoyu than in miso. Sakaguchi argues that miso has a 3,000-year history dating from the development of chiang during the Chou dynasty in China, whereas shoyu has a 2,000-year history dating from the development of soy nuggets *(shih)* during the Han dynasty. It is important to note here that most Chinese would probably disagree with Dr. Sakaguchi. They clearly trace the lineage of their soy sauce to *chiang*, not to *shih*, as evidenced by the Chinese word for soy sauce, *chiang-yu*, meaning "the liquid extracted from chiang." Moreover, most of their *chiang* and *shih* have always been made from a soy-based koji. We would say that both miso and shoyu trace their lineage back to both soy nuggets *(shih,* which existed prior to 206 B.C.) and to soybean chiang (which existed prior to A.D. 500).

Dr. Sakaguchi considers there to be three main reasons that shoyu and miso were not developed in the West: (1) Westerners did not know how to make koji using molds; (2) they had no soybeans until the 20th century; and (3) the basic flavoring components of shoyu and miso, especially natural L-glutamic acid and inosinic acid, were traditionally unknown in the West.

The Meiji and Pre-War Periods (1867-1939): From 1635 until 1854 Japan had lived in relative seclusion and isolation under the Tokugawa shoguns. The great advances made in Western science during this 220-year period passed largely unnoticed. There were few important developments in the production of miso or other fermented foods, and those which were made by local craftsmen were based on an empirical, trial-and-error process. In 1854 the American

Commodore Perry forced Japan to end its self-imposed isolation and begin trade with the West. In 1868 the Emperor replaced the declining Tokugawa shoguns as the political head of state, ushering in the Meiji Restoration. Openness, modernization, westernization, scientism, positism, and the ideal of progress all formed the dominant ethos of the Meiji Period, which lasted until 1912. In 1877 Tokyo Imperial University, the most famous of the new breed of government colleges and universities, was established, primarily for teaching western science and technology. By paying princely salaries and offering high positions, the Japanese were able to attract top European scientists to staff the new universities.

The imported European scientists and professors (mostly Germans and Englishmen) caused an almost immediate revolution in the field of Japanese food fermentations, for they brought with them the powerful tools of the Western scientific method and a host of new discoveries in the fields of fermentation and microbiology. Prior to 1870, makers of miso and other fermented foods were unaware of the basic nature of the fermentation process, of microorganisms, enzymes, and their respective interactions. Makers of koji had no idea what caused grains and/or soybeans to become covered with a fragrant white mycelium after several days incubation in a warm koji room, or what later transformed the koji almost magically into delicious, savory miso or shoyu. The microscope was essentially unknown in East Asia prior to the 1880s.

The pioneering first generation of European scientists in Japan studied the country's many fermented foods with great curiosity and enthusiasm. One of their first subjects for research was the koji mold, now known as *Aspergillus oryzae,* and the various foods in which it was used: saké, shoyu, and miso. In 1874 the German professor Dr. J.J. Hoffman wrote the earliest known description, detailed and scientific, of the process for making rice koji—although he did not use the word *koji.* In 1878 Korschelt, also a German, gave a long, detailed description of exactly how koji and koji starter were made. Although Hepburn had mentioned koji (and miso) in his Japanese-English Dictionary of 1867, Korschelt was the first western *scientist* to use the terms *koji* and *tané koji.* In a section of Korschelt's article and in a Japanese article written with Matsubara in 1878, Ahlburg, another German, who taught natural history at Tokyo University, gave the first detailed description of the koji mold, which he called *Eurotium Oryzae* Ahlburg. In 1884 the Polish botanist and mycological taxonomist F.J. Cohn first gave the koji mold its present name, *Aspergillus oryzae.* After 1884 the koji mold was referred to as *Aspergillus oryzae* (Ahlburg) Cohn, in recognition of Ahlburg's earliest accurate description. Other early pioneering research on koji and saké was done by the Englishman Atkinson (1878, 1881), the German Kellner (1889), and the Dutchman Wehmer (1895, 1901).

The first scientific study of miso in Japan was published, not by a Japanese, but by a German, Dr. Oscar Kellner, in conjunction with two Japanese scientists, M. Nagaoka and Y. Kurashima. In their "Researches on the Manufacture and Composition of Miso," published in English in 1889 in the *Bulletin of the College of Agriculture, Tokyo Imperial University,* they devoted 24 pages to miso's history, raw materials, manufacture, and chemical changes during fermentation, plus a description of eight types of miso and an analysis of three of these. The authors stated that miso was widely consumed by the lower classes and was especially favored in the northeastern provinces. In the countryside it was made by families in their homes, with special miso works being established only in large communitiies. Noting that no statistics on miso consumption were then available in Japan, Kellner made the rough estimate (which he was sure was on the low side) that since the smallest amount of miso consumed per day by one person was about 37.5 grams (10 monme or 2.16 tablespoons) and since an estimated 20 million of Japan's 39,000,000 inhabitants (51%) ate miso every day, the yearly miso consumption was nearly 30,000,000 kilograms. Actually Kellner's arithmetic was mistaken; even assuming that the remaining 49% ate no miso (an impossible but most conservative assumption), his figures show an average per capita consumption of 19.1 gm per day or 6.98 kg per year, for a total production of 274,000 metric tons per year, a more probable figure, but still probably much too low. He then concluded, whether by calculation or from original data is not known, that more than half of Japan's yearly production of soybeans (335,800 metric tons in 1883) were used to make miso.

In 1905 Oshima in Japan reported statistics showing that Japanese living in areas other than in the countryside consumed an average of 43 gm of miso a day, with a range of 13 to 100 gm; average rural consumption was estimated at 40 gm per person per day. Given that 80% of the population was rural, this would give an average daily consumption figure of 40.6 gm, or 14.8 kg per capita per year.

In 1911 Shaw, a British customs official in Manchuria, reported that, according to the latest statistics, the Japanese consumed 724,656 metric tons of soybeans and that the majority (393,768 metric tons or 54%) were used to make miso. Given that 1 kg of soybenas in those days yielded 2.5 pounds of miso, this would give an annual production of 1,984,419 metric tons of miso. The population of 49.85 million would then consume 19.7 kg per capita per year. These figures seem much too high.

In 1913 Takahashi and Abe estimated annual Japanese miso consumption at 45,000,000 kg or 45,000 metric tons, equivalent to 0.88 kg per capita per year. These figures are so far below the other estimates that they are highly suspect.

The figures of Kellner and Oshima show a rapid growth in total production and per capita consumption of miso from 1889 to 1911. Kawamura (1972), however, estimated Japanese per capita miso consumption to be roughly constant from the start of the Edo period (1600) to the beginning of World War II, at 35 gm per person per day or 12.78 kg per person per year. This assumption shows production increasing directly with population as indicated on page 226. The various production statistics (excepting Shaw's) from 1889 to 1940 show roughly similar trends. During this period, more than 50% of all Japanese miso was

THE MISO MARKET IN JAPAN (1930 - 1980)

Number of Manufacturers (1,000 plants)
Per Capita Consumption (Kg per person per year)
Production (100,000 metric tons)

Sources: Pre 1930, journal articles, as noted. 1930 on, Japanese National Miso Association, personal communication, 1983.

THE BOOK OF MISO

made noncommercially in people's homes or farmhouses, where it was consumed by the family; in 1940 some 35 to 55% was made in homes and farmhouses.

Most of the early scientific research on miso and miso koji, during the period from the mid 1870s to 1905, was done by Europeans, as will be discussed later at "Europe." In 1889, however, Mori and Nagaoka assisted the German Kellner in an article "On the Manufacture, Composition and Properties of Koji," and Nagaoka and Kurashima assisted Kellner that same year in his classic article on miso. Starting in the early 1900s Japanese researchers began to write a number of articles on miso in European languages (primarily English and German) for both Japanese and European publications. Oshima (1905) discussed miso's nutritional value and its consumption in Japan. Takahashi (1908, in Japanese) wrote "A Preliminary Note on the Chemical Composition of Miso." Takahashi and Abe (1913, in English) published "Preliminary Notes on the Chemical Composition of Miso," containing an analysis of miso's amino acids. Akaghi and co-workers (1915) wrote "Researches on Hatcho-Miso." In 1921 Kinoshita wrote a 480-page tome entitled *Practical Miso Fermentation*, the most complete work on miso production to date. In 1924 Nishiwaki (in German) wrote about Hatcho miso koji and *tomé koji*. In 1935 and 1936 I. Iwamura wrote three articles in Japanese about miso in *Nippon Nogei Kagaku Kaishi*. He was one of the first to investigate the use of warming the miso during fermentation to shorten the fermentation time. The extent of other research articles on miso published in Japanese prior to World War II is not known.

During the late 1800s, paralleling the pioneering research on miso in Japan, was some extremely innovative research on koji by Jokichi Takamine. He was the person most responsible for introducing the koji process to the Western world and giving it important commercial applications there. As an early Japanese student of microbiology and fermentation science, Takamine had come to learn of the malting process in the West. He decided ambitiously to try to introduce the koji process in its place. After making considerable increases in the diastatic activity of the koji mold, he went to America in 1880, but met with opposition from the malt makers. He then undertook a new project to extract the enzymes from the koji mold for commercial use. In 1894 he was granted two U.S. Patents (No. 525,823 and 525,825) for a process for making diastatic enzyme, which was very successfully marketed as Taka-diastase. This product, derived from the traditional miso and shoyu processes and containing a rich variety of enzymes, came to be widely used in the field of enzymology; it brought international fame to both Takamine and the koji mold.

The result of all this research was that the Japanese gained a better understanding of and control over the miso fermentation. One of the earliest major advances came in 1904, when the Japanese prepared their first pure-culture koji starters for use in miso.

Beginning in the early 1930s, the world of Japanese miso-production underwent a series of drastic changes which have continued to affect it up until the present.

With the rise of Japanese militarism, the conquest of new overseas territories in Korea, China, and Manchuria, and the development of Hokkaido and the islands to the north, many new markets for miso appeared and stimulated the growth of miso factories with international scope. By 1936, commercial miso production had soared to an all time estimated high of 600,000 tonnes (metric tons) or 600 million kg—a figure that would not be equalled again until the mid 1970s. But in 1936, most basic Japanese foodstuffs—including miso—were suddenly subjected to strict government price and quality controls. For purposes of standardization, government authorities grouped all miso varieties into three types (rice, barley, and soybean) and two grades (excellent and medium). Each type and grade had a fixed price. Although the designation of special varieties—such as Edo, Shinshu, or Hatcho miso—was allowed, the brand names of individual makers were outlawed. This system delivered a mortal blow to the production of many fine miso varieties and tended to encourage makers to lower their quality to the minimum, since they were assured that whatever they made would be sold.

World War II and the Postwar Period: Modern Times (1940-1983): To counter the growing threats to miso quality from oppressive controls, Japan's first nationwide miso trade association, the Japanese National Miso Association *(Zenkoku Miso Kogyo Kumiai Rengokai)* was founded in January 1940. In 1944 it came under government control, but in 1948 regained its original independence; in November 1960 it was rechartered under its original name and today it is very active with large offices and several publications in Tokyo.

With the founding of the Japanese National Miso Association in 1940, the provincial miso trade associations were unified under its leadership. Although its representatives worked with determination for the repeal of the oppressive controls, they were unsuccessful. During the war years, miso production decreased considerably, and although the control system was abolished after the war in 1946, the damage it did to the consciousness of both miso producers and consumers was never fully repaired. Many makers had lost pride in the quality of their product and had begun to adapt themselves to faster, lower-cost methods of production. And many consumers had begun to lose their sensitivity to and appreciation for fine natural miso as they grew accustomed to standardized, lower-quality products.

During the War, with the massive food shortages and dislocations throughout the Japanese food system, miso consumption and production inevitably dropped, and they continued to fall until about 1950 during the period of postwar austerity, but rebounded sharply with recovery, rising to a postwar peak in about 1955. Thereafter, however, miso consumption and production began a steady decline, that has continued to the present (page 226). There were various reasons for this trend.

After World War II, the entire value system of the Japanese people underwent a dramatic change. The process of Westernization that had begun in 1868 was suddenly accelerated in the areas of food, clothing, and housing. Western-style diets with higher contents of animal products, sugar, and refined foods, with white bread partially replacing white rice, gradually became the norm, partially replacing traditional Japanese eating patterns in which miso played a more important role. At the same time, mechanization in agriculture and other areas and the resulting more urban, sedentary lifestyle, greatly reduced physical labor, and with it both salt consumption and total food intake. This Westernization of the diet and mechnization with less physical labor were the main factors leading to reduced miso consumption. During the 1960s concern among Japanese over their excessive salt consumption (then twice that of most other nations) further accelerated the decline. Between 1955 and 1980, per capita miso consumption fell from 10 kg per person down to 6, a drop of 40%. The 1980 figure was still, however, 11.2 grams or about 1 tablespoon per day. During the 1970s, the per capita miso consumption of urban businessmen was only 58% of the national average.

With this decline in per capita miso consumption, total miso production also fell. Actually commercial or factory miso production after 1955 stayed quite constant, even rising slightly after 1965, in part because of slowly rising population. The main drop came in home miso production, as the country became more urbanized, commercial miso became more widely available at low prices, and people generally found less time or inclination to make their own. Thus from a peak of 336,000 tonnes in 1945 (homemade miso increased during the war), it fell to a mere 75,000 tonnes in 1980, a decline of 78%. The drop in total production combined with the larger proportion of rice used in miso led to a decline of total soybean usage in miso from about 288,000 tonnes in 1960 to 226,000 tonnes in 1980.

During the postwar period, dramatic changes in the structure of the miso industry also took place, in part because the entire economy was shifting from a rural-agricultural to an urban-industrial base, but more specifically because of government postwar taxes and incentives designed to stimulate modernization, mechanization, and amalgamation. Within the space of one generation, the primary center of miso production shifted from farmhouses and private homes to commercial shops; just before and during the war, 55% fo the country's total miso output was homemade, whereas in 1980 less than 11% was homemade. As shops grew into small factories and moved nearer to cities, the higher costs of land and labor demanded increased profitability from each unit of capital, space, and time; this led to extensive mechanization of the miso process including quick temperature-controlled fermentation, development of fast-maturing sweeter misos, and machine-paced packaging methods. As a result, the number of commercial manufacturers decreased from 5,500 during the 1930s (at which time they were mostly small and medium-sized shops) to 4,800 in 1950, then down to 1,900 in 1980, a 60% drop in 30 years. Meanwhile, the number of highly mechanized, large factories showed a steady increase. By 1958 a number of miso plants had a capacity of up to 10 tons per day. By 1965 a number of the larger traditional manufacturers had amalgamated to form

huge modern companies; 23 factories had a yearly capacity of at least 4,100 tons each, and the ten largest made 154,000 tonnes per year, or about 26% of the nation's total miso output. By 1974 the latter statistic had climbed to 30% and individual factories were then turning out 15,000 to 20,000 tons a year. The names of the "top ten" miso companies (see App. E) had become household words in Japan. In 1980 Japan's 1,900 commercial miso manufacturers employed 10,600 workers and made miso with a net ex-factory value of $573 million.

During the postwar period Japanese research on microbiology and its application to food fermentations advanced rapidly; soon the Japanese became world leaders in this field. Important early publications on these subjects, all in Japanese, include the works of Tomoda and Sakaguchi (1956), Nakano, Ebine, and Ota (1967), Yoshii and Kaneko (1972), and Sakaguchi et al. (1974).

Research on miso and its fermentation increased substantially, along with the advances in applied microbiology. One of the first Japanese scientists to apply these new advances to miso production was Dr. Masahiro Nakano, Professor of Microbiology at Meiji University and the dean of modern miso researchers in Japan. Nakano (1967, 1976) published extensively in Japanese, and he taught many other fine miso researchers, including Dr. Hideo Ebine and Dr. Tsutomu Mochizuki. Dr. Ebine worked at the Japanese National Food Research Institute. Between 1966 and 1976 he and his co-workers published many miso studies; seven of the most important of these (a number of which are in English) are cited in our Bibliography. After April 1982 Dr. Ebine worked at the National Miso Association's Central Miso Research Institute. Dr. Mochizuki, director of the prestigious Shinshu Miso Research Center, also published extensively. In 1972, for example, Mochizuki and co-workers showed the importance of *Pediococcus halophilus* bacteria (which produced lactic acid) and *Saccharomyces rouxii yeasts* (which produced ethyl alcohol and higher alcohols) in the miso making process.

By the mid 1960s, various new "Advances in Miso Production" were being proudly hailed by Japanese food scientists. Halophilic (salt tolerant) lactic acid bacteria (*Pediococcus halophilus* and *Streptococcus faecalis*) and yeasts (*Saccharomyces rouxii* and *Torulopsis* species) were being used commercially as inocula by some miso makers. They remarkably reduced the fermentation time required to obtain a well-fermented miso with a pleasing flavor. Batch type rotary pressure cookers, which heated to 120°C, replaced traditional steel or iron caldrons; the rotary action gave even cooking. Mechanized rotary fermenters (huge horizontal-axis rotating drums), with regulated temperatures and humidities, and purified circulating air, were used in large plants to replace the traditional, labor-intensive koji rooms. Epoxy-lined steel and concrete tanks came to be used in place of the hugh, traditional cedar vats; coopers gradually were put out of business. Miso prepackaged in polyethylene bags rapidly replaced that sold out of wooden kegs. The combination of the sealed bags, nationwide distribution, supermarket retailing, and sweeter misos with less salt led to the use of pasteurization and preservatives (sorbic acid to keep the bags from bursting). Some research was done on the use of enzyme preparations to replace koji for hydrolysis of miso's protein and carbohydrates. They did not give satisfactory results except for soybean miso, for which they reduced the fermentation time by 33% and the yield by 8% (Watanabe 1969, 1971, 1974; Ebine 1971). By the late 1970s huge koji incubation rooms, with perforated stainless steel floors, had replaced the rotary fermenters in large factories; koji filled the room to a depth of 12 inches or more and was stirred and harvested mechanically. Ethyl alcohol preservatives began to replace sorbic acid.

Ingredients also changed after the mid 1960s. In 1971 Ebine wrote that Japanese soybeans were the best for making miso, followed by those from China and then the U.S.A. U.S. soybeans were generally considered "not suited for making miso of high quality." Extensive research by Shibasaki, Ebine, and others, however, located three U.S. varieties (Kanrich, Mandarin, and Comet) which were considered comparable to the best Japanese ones. Being less expensive, the U.S. soybeans soon became widely used. During the 1960s quite a bit of low-cost defatted soybean meal was also used in miso, but this resulted in an inferior product and the practice was largely abandoned; less than 0.5% was used after 1975. In addition, more rice and less barley and soybeans were used in miso to accelerate the fermentation process and give a lighter-colored, sweeter product. Water, previously drawn from deep wells was partially replaced by the chlorinated product supplied by municipal pipelines. Natural sea salt was abandoned for sodium chloride—the only product now produced by the Government Salt Monopoly Corporation. Japanese grown soybeans gave way to lower-cost, generally lower-quality American soybeans. And a wide variety of chemical additives, in addition to preservatives, came to be used quite uncritically in miso: coloring agents, MSG, rice anti-clumping agents, artificial sweeteners, bleach, and the like. Yet the basic ingredients remained the same. Ebine (1972) reported that in 1969 some 180,000 tons of soybeans, 9,200 tons of rice, 19,000 tons of barley, and 75,000 tons of salt were used to make 552,000 tons of various types of commercial miso. Note that, on average, 1 ton of soybeans yielded 3.06 tons of miso, and 4.8 times as much rice as barley was used.

One major and very unfortunate result of the modernization, mechanization, and concentration of control in Japan's miso industry was the gradual loss of the local and regional character of traditional misos. Nevertheless a considerable number of provincial (and some urban) miso masters continued to value the ancient way and the distinctiveness of their local, unique products. Like the many thousands of small European wine or cheese makers who have successfully resisted modern standardization by showing that real quality is found in tradition, individuality, and naturalness, these Japanese miso masters chose to view the modern rush toward uniform factory miso as a passing fad. Keeping in touch with the great natural cycles and with their own traditions and intuitions, they held on to their fine wooden tools and vats, searched for sources of natural

ingredients, and never forgot the true meaning of "culture." Nourishing the secrets and wholeness of their craft, they worked hard—and waited. Some (such as Sendai Miso Shoyu and the major Hatcho miso companies) exported their misos to a growing market demanding such products in North American and Europe. In addition, there were efforts to revive traditional and unique misos. Mogi (1946) described the preparation of misos using unconventional carbohydrate sources, such as potatoes, chestnuts, buckwheat, millet, etc. Misumi Kan, a Kyushu-born novelist, worked to resuscitate homemade miso. Upon retirement he turned his spacious Tokyo home into a center for the study and preparation of miso and miso pickles. His two books about his work, *Miso University* and *Pickle University*, written in a highly literary and personal style, contain a wealth of information about the preparation of these two fermented foods in the traditional, natural way, plus many color and monochromatic photographs.

An important and colorful figure in the movement to revive traditional regional diversity of miso types and uses, explore miso history, and stamp out mass-produced uniform, modern misos was Wataru Kawamura, who became known throughout Japan as "Miso Sensei" (Miso Professor). In 1958 he wrote *Historical Chronicles of Miso*, an 815-page tome that was the first definitive work on the subject. In 1972 he and Ms. Hamako Tatsumi teamed up to write Japan's first *Book of Miso* (320 pages). In part I he discussed miso history in China and Japan (upon which we have drawn heavily), miso production and varieties, and the role in miso in the various Japanese provinces. In part II Ms. Tatsumi presented several hundred of Japan's best known miso recipes. In 1973 he wrote *Miso Soups Throughout the Provinces*, in 1974 *Encyclopedia of Miso Soups*, and in 1976 (with the Japanese National Miso Association), *Miso Digest*, a booklet of basic information about miso in Japan. Mr. Kawamura followed with delight the rising interest in natural miso in America and reported developments to the Japanese public.

Paralleling the revival of interest in traditional, natural misos was an interest in the ability of miso to promote long life and good health. One of the first publications in this area was the provocative *Physical Constitution and Food* (1965), written by Dr. Shinichiro Akizuki, a physician and hospital director in Nagasaki. He felt that miso had saved his life and that of his co-workers after the atomic blast at Nagasaki and that it could be used by anyone to help build a strong physical constitution. Other publications in this field included Kondo's *Japanese Long-Life Villages* (1972, showing a relationship between longevity and regular miso consumption), Morishita and co-workers' (1972*) investigations indicating that miso contained dipicolinic acid, which might protect the body from the effects of radioactivity, Iwadare's (1976) work on miso nutrition and healthful recipes, and *Asahi Simbun's* 1981 report of Dr. Hirayama's 13-year research project showing that people who drink miso soup regularly have the lowest rates of stomach cancer in Japan. For details on the above, see Chapter 2.

In 1960 aflatoxins (carcinogenic toxins produced by

two species of *Aspergillus* molds) came to the public attention when 100,000 turkeys and ducks died suddenly in England after consuming a poultry feed containing moldy Brazilian peanuts that had been contaminated with *Aspergillus flavus*. There was great concern that since miso and shoyu were fermented with another species of *Aspergillus*, (*A. oryzae*) they might also contain aflatoxins. Extensive investigations on samples of commercial koji, miso, and shoyu were conducted and from 1966 many reports were published on the subject. In Japan, for example, Manabe and Matsuura (1968) detected no aflatoxin on 238 samples of koji from koji makers, 28 koji samples from miso factories, 108 industrial miso samples, 30 homemade samples, and 20 shoyu samples collected nationwide. Other important early Japanese research showing that miso and shoyu were free of problems from aflatoxin contamination was done by Murakami et al. (1967-68), Matsuura (1970), Manabe et al. (1972), and many others.

Likewise, starting in about 1970, substances called nitrosamines, found in a number of Japanese protein foods (especially broiled, dried, or smoked fish and red frankfurters containing nitrites) were shown to be carcinogenic. Many foods (including fresh bread crumbs, spinach, green salads, miso, and shoyu) have low levels of nitrosamines, that are considered well within the limits of safety. Nagahori (1980) found that substances in miso and shoyu suppress formation of nitrosamines by 62 to 79%, keeping them at levels generally below 1 part per billion, which is of no concern.

During the 1960s, largely unnoticed in Japan, a major event in the history of Japanese miso was taking place; it was being transmitted to the West, largely by Japanese Macrobiotic teachers. By the mid to late 1960s, for the first time in history, large numbers of Caucasian Americans had begun to buy imported Japanese miso and use it in their cooking. A few Westerners began making miso, and more and more information about it began to appear, as described in the next section.

In Japan, by the early 1970s, a popular reaction had begun to set in against the processes of standardization and increased use of chemicals in traditional foods. People began to grow nostalgic for the taste of fine, natural miso and shoyu, and to speak out against the widespread use of preservatives, bleach, and other synthetic additives. In city apartments and communes, the tradition of preparing fine natural homemade miso began to be revived. Traditional miso and shoyu producers found that their products sold better if they advertised the fact that they were made from whole soybeans, fermented slowly at the natural temperature of the environment, and were free of chemical preservatives and other additives. In 1975 most larger producers stopped using chemical preservatives and switched instead to ethyl alcohol, a more natural preservative. Whereas in the 1960s traditional miso and shoyu were considered by many to be old fashioned, by the early 1980s they were increasingly viewed as the highest quality fruits of Japan's ancient tradition of fine craftsmanship.

Starting in the late 1960s a flood of cookbooks featuring miso began to hit the market. Among the better ones were the Women's College of Nutrition's 1969 seasonal miso cookbook, Lima Ohsawa's *Macrobiotic Cookery* (1971, with many miso recipes), Shufu-no-tomo's 1972 *Encyclopedia of Japanese Cookery*, Tsuda and co-workers' 1974 *Zen Temple Cookery*, and Egami's 1975 *Miso Soup and Miso Cookery*—to mention but a few.

Ichiyama's extremely interesting, 804-page *History of Kikkoman Shoyu* (1968), throws a great deal of light on the history of miso and fermented foods in general in Japan. Tamura's derivative 294-page *Book of Shoyu* (*Shoyu no Hon*, 1971) is more condensed, covering Ichiyama's key historical developments.

During the 1960s and 1970s dehydrated miso, both freeze-dried and spray dried, started to become quite popular in Japan, especially as the main ingredient in instant miso soups. First developed in 1959 by Ebine and Oguri, some 10,000 to 15,000 tons were made each year during the 1970s; this was roughly 2½ to 3½% of Japan's total miso production. Of the dehydrated product in 1979, an estimated 80% was freeze dried and the remainder was spray dried. By the mid 1970s instant miso soup, sold in small packets, was widely available.

Another new variety of miso was low salt (6.3% NaCl) or salt free miso. Early reports on this subject were published by Sano (1960*), Kobatake et al. (1964), Ito et al. (1965*), and Ebine (1966). Low salt miso was introduced commercially during the mid 1960s in response to the concern over high Japanese salt consumption (30 gm per capita per day in northern Japan and 18 gm in the rest of Japan, compared with 11 gm in the United States) and the corresponding high rates of stroke and high blood pressure (hypertension). A campaign throughout Japan to reduce salt intake was almost surely a key factor in lowering the death rate from strokes from 175 per 100,000 people in the period 1963-1970 down to 145 per 100,000 people in 1977, a 17% decrease. Low salt miso had become extremely popular by 1979, when most of the large manufacturers began to reduce the percentage of salt in their basic misos by 10 to 25%. In 1980 standards had been set for three low-salt products: mild-salt (*usujio*) miso had 10 to 25% less salt than normal; low-salt (*gen-en*) miso had less than half the normal amount of salt, and very-low salt (*tei-en*) had less than 1 gram of salt per 100 grams of miso. Thus standard Japanese misos came to contain only 9 to 12% salt. Ethyl alcohol was typically added as a preservative.

In 1977 Nagano Miso Company was the first to introduce a salt-free miso; in 1978 it started to be marketed as Jepron, and in 1982 the name was changed to GOLD 'N RICH. The first patent on such a product was issued to Nagano Miso Co. on 28 May 1981 (Japan Patent 1,048,853). By early 1983 Nagano Miso had applied for patents in nine countries; U.S. Patent No. 4,311,715 had been granted. Nagano Miso Co. also introduced a low-salt miso in 1979. For more details, see Chapter 4.

Starting in the early 1970s Japanese fermentation scientists began to investigate the possibility of using commercially available purified enzyme preparations in place of koji in the miso making process. This might allow greater control over the process, accelerate and simplify it, and eliminate the 10% loss of raw materials consumed by the mold during its growth. Kitaoka (1972) used protease enzymes to make a soybean miso, but the flavor of the resulting product was rather "flat and unbalanced." Saito et al. (1973) used a combination of protease enzymes with decreased amounts of koji to bring about a considerable reduction in miso aging time. Other research in this area during the 1970s has been reviewed by Aboise (1982). As of the early 1980s, purified enzyme preparations were not widely used in commercial miso manufacture, probably because their increased cost does not pay for itself in reduced fermentation time.

As of 1983, miso continued to be a basic part of the Japanese diet. An estimated 80 to 85% was used to make miso soup, with most of the rest used in sauces and simmered dishes, or as a topping for tofu. The three basic types of regular miso were rice miso, barley miso, and soybean miso. The six varieties of rice miso comprised about 81% of all regular miso made in Japan; the two varieties of barley miso comprised about 11%, and the two varieties of soybean miso comprised about 8%. There were also two types of special miso (Finger Lickin' and sweet simmered miso) and three varieties of modern miso (akadashi, dehydrated, and low-salt miso).

The various types of miso, though used largely as a seasoning, make a very substantial contribution to the protein intake of the Japanese. Rice misos contain an average of 115 gm of protein per kg of miso and Hatcho miso contains 217 gm per kg; shoyu contains 78 gm of protein per kg of shoyu. Thus in the late 1970s, miso contributed about 66,000 tonnes of vegetable protein to the Japanese diet, and shoyu contributed about 112,000 tonnes.

Starting in the mid 1970s, exports of miso from Japan began to increase steadily. In 1975 total miso exports were 828 metric tons (tonnes), with the largest importers being the U.S.A. (459 tonnes, 25% of which was for the natural food trade), EEC/Europe (156 tonnes), Brazil (58 tonnes), and Canada (36 tonnes). The net value in Japan was $680,000. Natural foods exporters shipped 117 tonnes, Mitoku shipping 67 tonnes and Muso 40. Of this roughly 22 tonnes were Sendai red miso, 50 tonnes were barley miso, and 35 tonnes were Hatcho or soybean miso. By 1981 miso exports had increased dramatically (by 84%) to 1524 tonnes. Of this 834 tonnes were exported to the U.S., 95 tonnes to Singapore, and 67 tonnes to the Netherlands, the three leading miso importing nations.

HISTORY OF MISO IN EUROPE

Miso has a surprisingly long history in Europe and the West. Miso was known to Europeans for almost 300 years before it was known in America. The earliest reference dates from the late 1500s, just before the beginning of the Edo period in Japan.

Early European References (1597 to 1899): The first known reference to miso (or to any soyfood) by a European or Westerner appeared in 1597, when the Florentine Francesco Carletti, a most literate and observant traveler who was very interested in Japanese cookery, visited Nagasaki during a two-year stay in Japan and wrote in his memoirs (first published in Italian in 1701): "They prepare various sorts of dishes from fish, which they flavor with a certain sauce of theirs which they call *misol*. It is made of a sort of bean that abounds in various localities, and which cooked and mashed and mixed with a little of that rice from which they made the wine already mentioned, and then left to stand as packed in a tub—turns sour and all but decays, taking on a very sharp, piquant flavor. Using this a little at a time, they give flavor to their foods . . ." (Carletti, 1701, 1964; first cited by Hymowitz and Newell, 1981).

The next reference to miso, which contained a much more detailed description of how it was made, was written in 1691-92 by Englebert Kaempfer, a brilliant self-educated German scientist and traveler who lived and traveled in Japan during these two years. His description, first published in Latin in his *Amoenitatum Exoticarum* in 1712 read:

> To produce miso, one takes one measure of *mamé* or *phaseolus daidsu* which is cooked with water for a long time then brayed or ground and mixed into a soft pap. Under continued braying, common salt is added, in summer four parts, in winter three. If less salt is added, one gets the product quicker, but shelf life is shorter. After reducing is repeated, one mixes the pap with *koos* or dehulled rice, and mixes the total by repeated braying. This rice in preparation has been boiled a little in the steam of unsalted water. One lets the mixture cool down and remain in a warm cellar one or two days and nights to ripen.
>
> This mixture, which has the texture of a pap or spread, is put into a bowl that has recently contained the popular *sacki,* a rice wine. Before using, one lets the bowl stand one or two months untouched.
>
> Koos lends to the product an agreeable taste, and its production requires like that of the Germans' "polenta," the experienced hand of the master. Those therefore who make it are held in high esteem, and they sell it ready made (Bening 1951).

Thereafter Kaempfer gave an equally detailed description of the shoyu making process. Prior to Kaempfer, numerous Western travelers had made mention of soyfoods (such as miso, tofu, and shoyu) but none of them had understood that these were made from soybeans. Through Kaempfer's description and illustration of the soybean and his descriptions of how miso and shoyu were made, the Western world first understood the relationship between soybeans and soyfoods.

In 1776 the Swedish doctor and botanist C.P. Thunberg mentioned miso in his famous *Travels,* which were published in English in 1795 and in French in 1796, based on his 14-month journey to Japan. In the chapter on "Japanese Foods" he wrote: "Three times a day, with each meal, the people eat miso soup prepared with fish and leeks. These miso closely resemble lentils. They are the small *dolic* beans of Japan. (He apparently thought soybeans were called "miso.") Miso or soy sauce constitute the principal food of the Japanese. People of all levels, great or small, rich or poor, eat them several times a day, year-round." He then described the method for making shoyu.

In 1783 the English botanist Charles Bryant discussed miso, apparently thinking that it was used as the basis for making soy sauce. Although some of his terminology was adapted from Kaempfer (1712), his observations were apparently original, although not very detailed or accurate: "The sauces prepared from miso are known under the name of 'Sooju or Soy.' The preparation of miso is rather complicated. A mass of soybeans are cooked in water until they become completely soft. These are then pounded several times with the addition of an approximately equal quantity of salt. This mass is mixed with a rice preparation called Roos *(koji)*. It is filled into a wooden vat and allowed to stand for several months. It is used in place of butter." He noted that the preparation of koji was a secret known to only a few people, who sold it in the streets to miso makers.

The earliest reference to Chinese chiang in Europe was in 1855 in a letter from Stanislaus Julien to the Society for Acclimatization in Paris. In discussing soyfoods, he mentioned in passing that "They also make *tsiang* (chiang), a sort of seasoning sauce."

When Japan began to introduce European scientific techniques during the Meiji period (1868-1912), one of the first areas of food research was the koji mold. The history of this early research and identification of the mold, *Aspergillus oryzae*, is described earlier at "Japan." Pioneering researchers included Hoffman (1874), Korschelt (1878), Ahlburg (1878), Atkinson (1878, 1881), Cohn (1884), Kellner (1889, 1895), and Wehmer (1895, 1901). The word *koji* was first mentioned by a Western scientist in 1878.

The most detailed early description of the process for preparing koji and koji starter was given in 1878 by the German Korschelt. He noted that all koji for sake was made only during the period from November to February. The steamed rice was inoculated with koji starter *(tané koji)* in the form of a fine yellow powder made by the koji maker, wrapped in straw mats, and incubated for three days in an underground chamber. On the evening of the third day it was put into wooden koji trays and incubated, with occasional mixing, until the morning of the fifth day. The koji starter was made at the end of the koji season using as a substrate a mixture of rice and wood ash. After a seven to ten day fermentation, in the same room with the koji, the trays were inverted and the spores tapped off on clean paper, then stored in a sealed crock until the next year.

In 1880 Paillieux of the Society for Acclimatization in France noted that the soybean "lends itself particularly well to the preparation of a puree, resembling puree of peas . . . According to my experience, one could also mix this paste, which the Japanese call miso, with other ingredients to keep them over the winter in barrels, for use in provisioning ships, etc." Paillieux had apparently tasted miso and conceived of miso pickles, long popular in East Asia.

In 1882 Prof. Edward Kinch of Cirencester, England, published the first chemical/nutritional analysis of miso; figures were given for both red miso and white miso. It is not known how he obtained this information.

The first European to publish a detailed scientific study of miso was the German Dr. Oscar Kellner (1851-1911). One of the great pioneers of German agricultural chemistry (along with Liebig and Hellriegel), Kellner accepted an invitation in 1880 to teach his specialty at Tokyo Imperial University. He stayed in Japan for 12 years, married a Japanese woman, and helped lay the foundations of agricultural chemistry and animal nutrition in Japan (Breirem 1952). In 1889 he and Japanese co-workers Mori and Nagaoka published "Researches on the Manufacture, Composition and Properties of Koji," which contained a chemical analysis of koji and noted that "The ferment of koji transforms gelatinized starch into maltose and dextrose, and also converts maltose to dextrose. It has strong diastatic properties." Also in 1889 Kellner, Nagaoka, and Kurashima wrote their classic "Researches on the Manufacture and Composition of 'Miso.'" Both these studies were in English. The latter 24-page work discussed miso's history, raw materials, manufacture, chemical changes during fermentation, and numerous miso varieties. It also contained chemical/ nutritional analyses of four types of miso, whose fermentation time Kellner reported varied from as little as three to four days up to one to one and a half years. The various types of miso discussed by Kellner included Shiro Miso, Yedo Miso, Inaka Miso, Sendai Miso, Kinzanji Miso, Sakura Miso, Tekka Miso, and Kogo Miso. Kellner even discussed miso's early history: "The *Sandai Jitsuroku*, one of the oldest Japanese records, tells us that a Chinese priest named *Jingo* transmitted more than 1000 years ago a small quantity of miso to the then emperor of Japan . . . And the name '*Korei Shiwo*' sometimes, though not frequently used instead of the word 'miso,' points to its introduction from Korea." Kellner's remarkably detailed study is still one of the best ever published by a Westerner. It was long the main source of information for other Western articles on miso. Kellner continued his publications on miso with excellent articles in German, "Die Bereitung von Miso in Japan" (1895, in response to an inquiry that year), and "Ueber die Bereitung von Sake, Shoyu, und Miso" (1895).

Also in 1886 and 1889 the German Rein gave brief descriptions of miso and its production, with an analysis of its nutritional composition done by the College of Agriculture at Komaba, Tokyo. He said that miso "is said to be at its best when three years old."

Bretchneider (1893) cited numerous references to chiang in early Chinese literature.

The first descriptions of Indonesian miso-like foods (*taucho* or *tao tsioe* and *tao tjiung*) were given by Prinsen Geerligs, in Dutch in 1895 and in German in 1896. Both articles included nutritional analyses.

Prior to 1897 Europe's first commercial miso started to be manufactured in Switzerland. In 1897 the American Langworthy (using data from an unknown source) published a nutritional analysis of this miso; it must have been a dried product since it contained only 12.5% moisture (versus 48 to 50% for traditional Japanese misos), plus 26.4% protein and 13.9% fat. Langworthy also mentioned that numerous East Asian soyfoods had been made in

Switzerland but, again, unfortunately, he did not cite the source of his information. In 1907 Senft of Germany stated, "Recently the firm Jul. Maggi & Co. in Kempthal (Switzerland) has begun to make and market a type of miso." Maggi was also the first company in Europe to develop hydrolyzed vegetable protein (HVP), from which they are said to have made a type of unfermented soy sauce.

1900 to 1949: Senft (1907) in Germany called miso a "vegetable cheese" and described its preparation and composition, using information from Kellner. He also gave the first report on miso pickles *(misozuke)* then noted, as mentioned above, that Maggi in Switzerland had begun to make and market miso.

In 1910, Li Yu-ying, the Chinese soyfoods pioneer in Paris, discussed Chinese chiang in his book on *Soybeans.* In 1912, in French, Li discussed Chinese chiang and Vietnamese *tuong,* based on the work of Bui (1905). In 1911 the Englishman Shaw in Manchuria described the manufacture of two types of Chinese chiang and reported that 54% of all soybeans consumed in Japan were used to make miso. In 1914 Winkler gave a description of miso making. Then in 1917 Fuerstenberg repeated information about miso from Kellner and Winkler. He, too, called miso a "vegetable cheese." Surprisingly, after Fuerstenberg, there was no reference to miso or chiang in scientific literature in Europe for over 40 years.

1950 to 1982. The late 1950s saw a rebirth of interest in miso in Europe. The person responsible for this was a remarkable Japanese gentleman named George Ohsawa, whose life and work are discussed later at "U.S.A." He began teaching a little about miso during his first stay in France from 1929 to 1935, then again more seriously and to a growing audience from 1956 (Kotzsch 1981). As a result of his teachings about Macrobiotics and Japanese natural foods, the first commercial miso company since Maggi in the early 1900s was started by the Gevaert family in Belgium in 1959. They continued to make traditional, natural barley miso from 1959 until 1966, then re-started in January 1981. In late 1981 they were making 1,200 kg a month of barley miso at plants in France and Belgium. The French miso plant was powered by hydropower. The macrobiotic community in Europe has continued to be the pioneering force in introducing, distributing, teaching about and using miso. By 1975 the European Economic Community (EEC) was importing 156 tonnes of miso from Japan; England, the largest importer, was importing 28 tonnes. By 1981 EEC miso imports from Japan had jumped to 230.7 tonnes; the leading importing nations were the Netherlands (67.8 tonnes), England (40.4 tonnes), West Germany (40.0 tonnes), and France (28.0 tonnes). Much of this miso was specially made in Japan using traditional, natural methods for the European natural-food and macrobiotic markets. Also in 1981 there were five miso plants in Europe: four in France and one in Belgium. In July 1980 *The Book of Miso* by Shurtleff and Aoyagi was published in Germany as *Das Miso Buch*; by December 1982 some 3,200 copies had been sold. For the first time in European history, largely because of macrobiotic influence but also

because of emigration from and travel to East Asia, Europeans were beginning to use and enjoy miso.

Starting in the late 1970s the Department of Microbiology at the University of Strathclyde in Glasgow, Scotland began to do research on miso. Dr. Brian Wood, Sumbo Abiose (from Africa), and co-workers published numerous scientific papers on miso in prestigious journals. Abiose's 1979 PhD dissertation was entitled *Studies on Miso Fermentation,* and her 1982 journal article "Microbiology and Biochemistry of Miso Fermentation" is the best review to date of the world's research literature on this subject; it cites 137 references. Other important publications from the Glasgow group were by Wood and Yong (1975) and by Wood (1977, 1982).

HISTORY OF MISO IN THE UNITED STATES AND CANADA

Early Developments (1896-1929): The earliest known reference to miso in the U.S. was by Trimble in 1896. Writing about "Soybeans and Soybean Products" in the *American Journal of Pharmacy,* he gave a detailed and accurate account of miso, based on three earlier publications by Kellner. In 1897 in "Soy Beans as Food for Man," Langworthy mentioned miso briefly and published a collection of earlier nutritional analyses of red, white, and Swiss misos; he did not cite the source of his information. These nutritional analyses were also reprinted by Abel of the USDA in 1900.

During the period from 1900 until the early 1960s, virtually no important research and very few original publications related to miso appeared in the United States (or in Europe). The various reports from Japan written in English by Oshima (1905), Takahashi and Abe (1913), and Akaghi et al (1915) were presumably read by a few interested Americans. Piper Morse (1916) referred briefly to miso, calling it a "soybean cheese," apparently after Sawa (1902) or Senft (1907). Piper and Morse (1923) gave four pages of information on miso from earlier sources, plus three excellent photographs showing miso manufacture in Japan, the first such photographs published in the West. In 1927 Horvath summarized much of the earlier research on miso and mentioned chiang tofu, made in China by pickling tofu in chiang; it resembled a sharp cheese and could be used in the West in sandwiches.

Starting in the early 1920s pioneering research on the *Aspergillus* molds was done by Dr. Charles Thom and Dr. Margaret Church, both of the Microbiological Laboratory of the USDA Bureau of Chemistry. Thom, one of America's USDA culture collection, now housed at Peoria, Illinois. 1904 to 1942; in 1904 he started what later became the USDA culture collection, now housed at Peoria, Illinois. In 1921 Thom and Church wrote "Aspergillus Flavus, A. oryzae, and Associated Species," in which passing mention was made of miso, shoyu, and tamari shoyu. In 1923 Church wrote "Soy and Related Fermentations," which focused on Japanese shoyu but gave a short description of miso production and referred to the miso mold as *Aspergillus flavus oryzae.* Thom and Church's research culminated in 1926 with the publication of their classic 272-page monograph *The Aspergilli*. This was expanded by Thom's co-worker Kenneth Raper into *Manual of the Aspergilli* (1945), then by Raper and Fennell in 1965 into *The Genus Aspergillus*. The work of Thom and Church laid the foundation for much of the important work on miso done at the USDA Northern Regional Research Center in Peoria, Illinois, starting in 1959. Thom's culture collection, transferred to Peoria in about 1940, was the largest such collection in the world by 1983, containing some 55,000 cultures. . . . including those used for miso, shoyu, tempeh, and other fermented soyfoods.

In the early 1900s exports of miso from Japan (mostly to the West) began to increase, rising from 2.2 million pounds (1,000 tonnes) worth $34,647 in 1903 to 6.9 million pounds (3,130 tonnes) worth $135,800 in 1907 (Piper and Morse 1923). By 1930 some 308,104 pounds (140 tonnes) of Japanese miso were being imported to Honolulu. These foreign markets began to attract Japanese miso makers.

According to Wilcox (1909), miso was being made in Hawaii by 1908 and most of the soybeans were imported from Japan. The leading (and perhaps only) manufacturer was the Hawaiian Soy Company, with Mr. M. Yamakami as manager. They probably also made soy sauce (Kraus 1911). By 1911 the manufacture of both miso and soy sauce were being rapidly expanded in Hawaii, which was then a U.S. Territory; it was annexed in 1911 and became a state in 1959. The next miso company in Hawaii, the Kanda Miso Factory, was started in Honolulu in 1920 by Mr. Takejiro Kanda, and in 1921 the Takei Miso Factory was started on Maui by Mr. Shuji Takei. Other early Honolulu miso manufacturers were Ueno Miso Factory (1920s), Fukuda Miso Factory (1920s). Over the years a new and unique style of miso was developed in Hawaii. It originated in Okinawa, whence came many of Hawaii's early miso makers. The Hawaiian-style miso was sweeter and less salty than most Japanese misos, containing typically 70% rice and 30% soybeans. It was prized mostly for use with seafoods, rather than in miso soups or with vegetables. Many of the first miso makers in the continental USA were from Hawaii or had learned to make miso in Hawaii, and most of the miso made or used on the American mainland prior to World War II was this sweeter Hawaiian-style product.

The earliest known miso plant in the United States, the Fujimoto Miso Company, founded by Mr. Genpei Fujimoto, began operation in San Francisco in 1917. During World War II, about 1943 or 1944, because of the Japanese evacuation, the company was shut down and moved to 302 South Fourth West, Salt Lake City, Utah. It was re-established after the War by the son of the founder, Edward Kanta Fujimoto, and his wife Shizue. Edward died in 1958 and Mrs. Fujimoto continued to run the business until 1976, when she sold her equipment and the Kanemasa brand to Miyako Oriental Foods, which was established that year in Los Angeles.

The next commercial miso plant in the U.S. was the Norio Company, started in 1919 in San Francisco at 1531 Geary St. by Mr. Masaichi Norio; he made only *shiro miso* (probably sweet white, mellow white, or light yellow miso)

and exported most of it to Hawaii. In about 1932 the company was moved to 1532 Post St., where it was run by relatives, Mr. and Mrs. Minoru Arikawa and son. The U.S. government forced the family to close the business (then making about 82 tonnes of miso a year) when World War II started in 1941. They resumed after the War but retired in 1972 and the business was closed to make room for construction of a high-rise condominium (B.W. 1971; Arikawa 1982, personal communication).

According to George Tsuchiya, manager of T. Amano Co., there were several semi-commercial makers of miso and shoyu in Canada, in the Vancouver area, prior to World War I, and at least one commercial miso manufacturer was in the area prior to 1927. In that year, Mr. T. Amano, who stemmed from a family that made commercial miso and shoyu in Hiroshima, started a company called Amano Brothers on East Powell Street in Vancouver. He made his first miso in 1927 and his first shoyu in 1931. In 1982 the T. Amano company was making a red miso and a sweet white miso, as well as fermented shoyu.

Sometime between 1927 and 1932 the Tsuruda Miso Company was started in San Jose, California, by Mr. and Mrs. Tsuruda; it was shut down during World War II and never resumed.

1930 to 1959: When William Morse visited East Asia from 1929 to 1931 he wrote a lot about Japanese miso in his journals and included numerous photographs. He mentioned that Hatcho miso was then aged for 20 months and had been made in the same Hayakawa Kyuemon plant for about 300 years, that all miso was sold in wooden casks with braided bamboo hoops and, when retailed, was wrapped in the outer sheaves of bamboo shoots, that sweet white miso was most widely used for pickling fish, beef, etc., and that in making Sendai miso the steamed beans were still cooled by spreading them in wave patterns on the plant's wooden floors.

Miller (1933) discussed the use of miso in pickling vegetables such as eggplant, cucumbers, and the Oreintal pickling melon. A.K. Smith (1949) gave a good update on the manufacture and use of miso in Japan. This important article was partly responsible for the first real research on miso done in the West, at the USDA in Peoria, Illinois.

During this period a number of new miso manufacturers started production in Hawaii: Yamaju Miso Factory (1936, purchased by George Higa from Mr. Fukuda), American Hawaiian Soy Co. (1941; George Higa and coworkers), Fujii Miso Factory (c. 1941-54), Honolulu Miso Factory (c. 1942-50), and Hawaiian Miso & Soy Co. (1947; George and William Higa). In Los Angeles, the Yamaizumi Co. started making miso in about 1948 under the direction of Mr. Nagai, a craftsman from Fukuoka, Japan. During the 1960s their business declined, and in 1972, they started repacking Marufuku-brand miso, imported from the Hawaiin Soy Sauce Company in Honolulu, and selling it in America under the Yamaizumi brand. In 1975 Miyako Oriental Foods bought the rights to the Yamaizumi brand from Mrs. Nagai and the Yamaizumi company ceased operations.

In February 1942, shortly after the outbreak of

World War II, President Roosevelt signed Executive Order 9066, which permitted internment of 120,000 West-Coast Japanese-Americans in ten detention camps. All of the miso shops on the West Coast of the U.S. were forcibly shut down and their owners and workers sent to the camps. At that time Fujimoto was the largest miso company in the U.S. and Arimoto, making 82 tonnes a year, was probably second.

After the war there was little or no interest among non-Oriental Americans until the early 1960s.

Growth of Interest in Miso (1960-1982): The first real research on miso fermentation done in the Western world was carried out at the USDA Northern Regional Research Center in Peoria, Illinois, by Dr. Kazuo Shibasaki (a Japanese professor of agricultural chemistry, well trained in microbiology) and Dr. Clifford W. Hesseltine (Director of the NRRC fermentation laboratory and an eminent American microbiologist). Work began when Shibasaki arrived at the NRRC in 1957. Funded by various American groups promoting soybean exports, the team hoped to find new soybean varieties and processing methods to overcome some of the objections to American soybeans voiced by miso makers in Japan. But the research went much farther than anticipated; between 1960 and 1962 Shibasaki and Hesseltine published six pioneering scientific journal articles about miso and its fermentation and in 1961 a public service patent on "Preparation of Miso," was issued to Smith, Hesseltine, and Shibasaki. In 1959, in part because of this research, the first U.S. soybeans imported to Japan started to be used in making miso. And the NRRC miso research found other practical applications in Japan. It led to (1) the use of pure culture yeast inocula in the second stage of the miso fermentation, in place of the traditional mixed culture taken from a previous miso fermentation, (2) the development and use of solid substrate fermentations for the industrial production of enzymes and secondary metabolites, and (3) the development of the large-scale trommel (horizontal-axis tumbler) system of making koji, which produced more enzymes. Later, in April 1974, another Japanese researcher, Mr. Ichiro Ouchi, arrived at the NRRC then spent one year with Dr. Hesseltine developing new uses for miso in Western-style foods (such as barbecue sauce, spaghetti sauce, pizza, miso mayonnaise, and potato chips) to be introduced into the increasingly westernized diet of the younger generation in Japan. While the ultimate aim of this work, like Dr. Shibasaki's, was to increase soybean exports to Japan, some of the new recipes attracted interest in America as well. Hesseltine liked the barbecue sauce, thickened and seasoned with miso, and enjoyed introducing miso to visitors, served on a cucumber slice. From the early 1960s on, Hesseltine and co-workers at Peoria published information on miso in a wide variety of books and presented papers at many symposia. The early research at Peoria plus these publications on miso led to considerable interest in this savory fermented soyfood among western microbiologists and food scientists (an interest dormant since the 1880s), and helped to "legitimize" this ancient seasoning. As of early 1983 the NRRC was working with the University of Wisconsin to investigate the safety and storage life of low-salt misos, testing for possibilities of food poisoning from *Staphylococcus, Yersinia,* or botulism.

As noted previously at "History of Miso in Japan," the subject of aflatoxins came to the public attention in 1960 when contaminated peanuts killed 100,000 poultry in England. Despite the fact that by 1969 Japanese researchers had proved conclusively that aflatoxins were not a problem in miso or shoyu, in May of that year *TIME* magazine published a half-page article titled "Cancer: A Clue from Under the Eaves," about possible aflatoxins in homemade East Asian miso and soy sauce. Although the article's conclusions were highly speculative and the analytical techniques used strongly criticized, some Americans unfamiliar with the details and background of the issue became alarmed and wondered if it was perhaps unsafe to consume miso and soy sauce. In response to these concerns and much larger concerns with aflatoxins in U.S. livestock feeds, peanuts, and corn, researchers at the NRRC in Peoria began extensive investigations of aflatoxins. In 1979 Wang and Hesseltine, top American researchers on the subject, reviewed the literature, which showed repeatedly that soybeans are a poor substrate for aflatoxin production. The koji mold is completely different from molds of the same *Aspergillus* genus that produce aflatoxins, just as edible and poisonous mushrooms come from the same genus. Moreover, aflatoxins are most commonly found on peanuts, corn, cottonseeds, and copra. In short, then, fears concerning aflatoxins in miso are totally ungrounded, for none have ever been found in any commercial miso or soy sauce. The same is true of nitrosamines, as discussed previously at "History in Japan."

The single most important force in introducing miso to America and popularizing its use was the macrobiotic movement, founded by a remarkable Japanese couple, George and Lima Ohsawa. Their work began at about the same time as that at the USDA/NRRC in Peoria, although the two knew nothing of one another. In the early 1950s several of Ohsawa's macrobiotic students had arrived in New York City to prepare a beachhead and as early as March 1952 Herman Aihara was selling miso, imported from Ohsawa in Japan, in New York City. Ohsawa first arrived in America in December 1959. From January to March, 1960, he presented 30 lectures on macrobiotics and published a mimeographic edition of *Zen Macrobiotics,* which was sold for $0.50 at the lectures. The booklet contained ten miso recipes (perhaps the first published in the U.S.) and introduced miso and shoyu as key components of a macrobiotic diet. Shoyu was spelled "syoyu;" Ohsawa did not call it *tamari,* as he later would. Soon Ohsawa's small but dedicated group of American students were using these new foods as part of their daily fare. During the late 1950s and early 1960s, two restaurants (Zen Teahouse and Musubi) and a macrobiotic food store (Ginza) were started by Ohsawa's Japanese students in New York City. They served and/or sold miso and natural shoyu, which Ohsawa had sent from Japan. In about November 1963 Michio Kushi opened the Genpei Restaurant in the Diamond Jim Building on 46th St. in

New York. In the basement, Junsei Yamazaki, just arrived from Japan via Chico, California, made his own barley koji then made about 100 pounds of miso in three 18-liter soy sauce vats. This was the first "macrobiotic" miso made in America; it was later moved to the basement of the Kushi home in Boston, where it finished its aging, then was enjoyed by the Kushis and their students.

For Ohsawa, as for all subsequent teachers and students of macrobiotics, miso was far more than just a savory high-protein seasoning and a source of natural digestion-aiding enzymes and bacteria. According to macrobiotic philosophy, it was, above all a very *yang* food (since it contained salt and was fermented under pressure for a long time) and, as such, it had intrinsic healing, almost medicinal effects that could be used to combat various diseases (the result of an excessively *yin* constitution) and aid in maintaining a balanced constitution or body/mind. For this reason most macrobiotic followers recommended the more *yang* barley and Hatcho misos for daily and healing use, rather than the various rice misos, which were considered more *yin*. It was primarily because of this belief in a deeper dimension to miso's value that Ohsawa and the macrobiotic movement took such a deep interest in miso. Indeed brown rice, cooked land and sea vegetables, and miso soup were considered the primary ingredients, to be used daily, in a healthful and healing macrobiotic diet.

From 1960 to 1966 Ohsawa lectured repeatedly about the virtues of miso and shoyu. In 1964 and 1966 editions of his popular macrobiotic cookbook, *Zen Cookery*, were published. It contined an entire chapter on "Miso Soy Bean Paste," including 13 recipes, which generated growing interest in this largely unknown soyfood. In 1965 a second edition of *Zen Macrobiotics* contained numerous miso recipes. At the time of Ohsawa's death in 1966 (he was 72), a rapidly growing number of young Caucasian Americans, interested in natural foods and macrobiotics, were using miso and shoyu regularly.

Ohsawa's students, both Japanese and American, actively continued his work. In late 1961 a group of students from New York had migrated to Chico, California, and in March 1962 they founded a new food company called Chico-San. They imported traditional miso from Japan and had it widely distributed under their label. Herman Aihara and Bob Kennedy lectured widely on miso and macrobiotics. In 1964 Junsei Yamazaki began experimental production of miso and shoyu at Chico-san and over the years he made 20 whiskey barrels full of 320 pounds miso each. When this miso matured, it was generally mixed with miso imported from Japan. In mid 1970 Yamazaki began to make large batches. Tragically in September 1972, when he had 4,500 to 5,000 pounds aging in wooden vats, the building burned down and all the miso was destroyed. After that Yamazaki taught miso making to small groups of students. In mid 1968 *Health Food Business Review* wrote an article about Chico-San's miso, calling it "Soy Bean Puree." This was the first popular article or health-food article about miso written in the U.S. In 1972 Aihara wrote and published *Miso and Tamari*, the first booklet about these foods in the West. It contained

the first recipes for making miso and miso pickles at home; recipes for making barley, rice, and Hatcho miso were also given. In 1974 a revised and expanded edition of the book entitled *Soybean Diet* was published. Herman and Cornellia taught about miso extensively and published a number of other macrobiotic cookbooks containing miso recipes, such as the *Chico-San Cookbook* (1972). Chico-San continued to import, advertise, and distribute fine natural miso, expanding their efforts in the early 1980s. As of 1983 Chico-San had a three-stage plan to make miso in Chico. Working with a Japanese miso company they would first import bulk miso to Chico and practice aging it, then make miso at Chico using koji imported from Japan under refrigeration, and finally make the entire miso (including the koji) at Chico. They also hoped to make shoyu. In 1980 Yamazaki bought land in Orland in Northern California, where he hoped to start making high-quality miso using the finest natural ingredients, and to grow *ume* plums for *umeboshi* salt plums

Another center of activity for macrobiotics and miso was Boston, where Michio and Aveline Kushi taught, starting in September 1963. In April 1966 they opened Erewhon, a small macrobiotic food store that carried, among other things, natural miso and shoyu. The miso was purchased from Infinity Foods in New York, Chico-san in California, and a little from Lima Foods in Belgium. Hatcho miso was ordered from local Japanese trading companies, Japan Foods Corp. or Nishimoto. These misos were among the store's best-selling items. In 1968 Sanae, a macrobiotic restaurant, was started in Boston; it served miso and other soyfoods, as did all subsequent macrobiotic restaurants in Boston. Also in 1968 Erewhon started to import foods, including miso and shoyu, from Japan. A wholesale and distribution company was started that year and soon it was trucking a line of fine imported Japanese red, barley, and Hatcho misos to a growing number of natural food stores. The natural foods boom hit America in 1970, carrying Erewhon (and miso) along with it. Sesame miso and tekka miso were added to the Erewhon line. Other macrobiotic and natural food distributors sprang up across America and they too all carried and strongly promoted miso. In 1980 Erewhon sold roughly 150,000 pounds of its three basic misos. The *East West Journal*, founded in Boston in January 1971, soon became America's leading macrobiotic magazine. It played a major role in popularizing miso, with many excellent articles and recipes, as described later. Autumn Press, whose founder Nahum Stiskin studied macrobiotics in Boston, translated and published Lima Ohsawa's *The Art of Just Cooking* (1974), which contained many miso recipes, then in 1976 published the original edition of *The Book of Miso* by Shurtleff and Aoyagi. In 1978 Aveline Kushi wrote *How to Cook with Miso*, which was widely read. In 1980, after about a year of eating a strict macrobiotic diet and receiving consultations from Michio Kushi, Dr. Anthony Sattilaro, a physician and then chief administrator at Methodist Hospital in South Philadelphia, experienced an almost miraculous complete recovery from terminal cancer that had riddled his body. The dramatic story was published in the *East*

West Journal (March 1980 and March 1981), the Saturday Evening Post (August 1981), and LIFE magazine (August 1982) and eventually in a best-selling major book Recalled By Life (Sattilaro 1982). Through these publications miso, in the form of miso soup, which was a key part of his daily macrobiotic diet, was introduced to millions of Americans. In these and a host of other ways, the Boston macrobiotic community played a leading role in introducing miso to America.

During the 1960s New York remained active as a center of interest in macrobiotics and miso. Howard Rohr's Infinity Foods, established in the mid 1960s, imported fine miso from a macrobiotic exporter in Japan and distributed it to natural food companies in the U.S. Michael Abehsera, a young Jewish French Moroccan who began studying and practicing macrobiotics in 1961, arrived with his wife in New York from Paris in 1964. Thereafter the couple ran a number of highly successful macrobiotic restaurants in New York City, all of which served miso and he wrote two macrobiotic cookbooks, Zen Macrobiotic Cooking (1968) and Cooking for Life (1970), which sold very well and each contained four miso recipes. In 1969 the Abehseras toured the entire U.S., lecturing about macrobiotics, including miso.

Another key macrobiotic miso teacher was Noboru Muramoto, who immigrated to America from Japan in 1971. In his popular book Healing Ourselves (1973) he suggested a number of medicinal uses for miso. From 1976, at his Asunaro Institute near Glen Ellen, California, he set up a regular shop for making miso and shoyu, developed (with his students) various American-style miso recipes, and taught many students these food crafts, including at least one (Elwell) who went on to open a commercial miso company (Lachman and Elwell 1978). His newsletter Asunaro Notes published several articles on miso mkaing. In late 1979 Muramoto relocated his Institute in Escondido, California, where he continued to give classes on miso and other Japanese foods.

The first four non-Oriental miso companies in America were all founded by students of macrobiotics: Thom Leonard of Ohio Miso Co., John Belleme of American Miso Company in North Carolina, Christian and Gaella Elwell of South River Miso Co., in Massachusetts, and Dale Deraps of Imagine Foods/Montaeu Farm in Missouri. Strangely, many macrobiotic companies, teachers, and publications persisted in the use of Japanese names for miso (saying mugi for "barley," genmai for "brown rice," kome for "rice," etc.) which gave miso a slightly exotic image and probably slowed its introduction to America. They also were slow to accept the growing medical advice that less salt consumption is better. Despite these minor points, the macrobiotic community unquestionably played the leading role in introducing miso to the Western world.

Although students of macrobiotics were the first Caucasians seriously interested in miso and in using it daily, and although they opened the first Caucasian miso shops, they were not the very first Caucasians to make their own miso for food use. Students at Tassajara Zen Mountain Center in California have that distinction. In the fall of either 1968 or 1969 Kobun Chino-sensei, a Japanese Zen priest, worked with Ed Brown (head cook), William Shurtleff, and several other Americans in making miso. They obtained koji starter from Japantown in San Francisco, made rice koji which was incubated in handmade wooden trays above the Tassajara kitchen stove, cooked soybeans in large pots and ground them in a Corona hand mill, then mashed together the koji, soybeans and salt in a large brandy barrel (the charred interior had been scraped clean) using a wooden mochi pounder. After being aged in the basement for 12 months, the 35 to 50 gallons of excellent-quality miso was used in the community's meals — mostly in soups. It is interesting to note that the transmission of this ancient art was made by Buddhist priests, just as it had been in Japan 1200 years earlier.

After 1973 a growing number of Caucasian Americans, mostly students of macrobiotics, began to make their own miso. In about 1973 Aveline Kushi in Boston held some informal miso making classes using ready-made storebought koji; one 18-liter keg of miso was made. In 1974 Blake Rankin, freshly returned from studying miso shops in Japan, worked with George Gearhart at Janus Foods in Seattle making small batches from storebought koji. By 1975 they were making their own barley and wheat koji in redwood koji trays during 3-day workshops and teaching six students from the Seattle Zen Center. Eventually they made 500 pounds and published a description of the process. By 1976 Gearhart was teaching miso making classes in Washington and California, as was Bob Gerner at Westbrae Natural Foods in Berkeley. In the fall of 1974 Thom Leonard made his first batch of barley koji and barley miso in Lawrence, Kansas, using a recipe in Aihara's new book Soybean Diet. The 80-pound batch of miso was aged in a soy sauce keg from Hong Kong. He then made 80-pound batches of chunky wheat miso in the fall of 1975 (he later pickled tofu in it) and of barley miso in early 1976. After moving to Fayetteville, Arkansas, he and Jim Hemminger made larger scale miso equipment and on 15 April 1977 packed their first 35-gallon cedar vat with brown-rice miso. Soon over 1,000 pounds were aging in the vats (Leonard 1977). This miso was sold to and distributed by the Ozark Cooperative Warehouse. In the summer of 1980 Leonard taught miso classes at the macrobiotic Moniteau Farm in Missouri. Then from late 1980 on he taught about 15 classes on making miso and other soyfoods at the Kushi Institute and at his home in Boston. In 1983 he went to Ireland to start a miso plant in County Killkenny. Others who made miso on a home or community scale in the mid 1970s included Charlie Kendall, Robert Johnson, David Tucker, and The Farm in Tennessee.

In May 1974 William Shurtleff and Akiko Aoyagi, then living in Japan, started to write The Book of Miso. Shurtleff had been introduced to miso by poets Allen Ginsberg and Gary Snyder on a Circumambulation of Mt. Tamalpias in February 1967 (it was served with sesame tahini as a spread on crackers), had frequently used and twice made miso after June 1968 while working as a cook at Tassajara Zen Mountain Center near Big Sur in California, and in the spring of 1973 had made miso on Suwanose Island in southern Japan, then studied miso-like products in Taiwan and Korea. *The Book of Miso*, published in September 1976 by Autumn Press, was the first major book on miso in the West, and Shurtleff was the first westerner since Kellner in 1889 to do extensive research on miso in East Asia and the first ever to apprentice to a Japanese miso master. The book contained information on miso varieties, nutrition, history, production (on a home, community, traditional shop, or modern factory scale), and microbiology, plus 400 recipes and a lengthy bibliography. In 1981 an updated mass market edition was published by Ballantine Books; by late 1982 the two editions had sold 70,000 copies. In 1977 the Shurtleffs' self-published *Miso Production*, describing how to start and run a commercial miso plant, which was used in starting a number of such plants in the following years. These books helped to establish and standardize the English names of miso varieties and, in general, to introduce miso to the West.

With the growing demand for fine miso, a new wave of miso manufacturers started in America. The last company had been started in 1932. The first of the new companies was Miyako Oriental Foods, which opened in an 11,000-square-foot plant in Los Angeles (404 Towne Ave.) in June 1976, as a division of Yamajirushi Miso Company in Japan. The company was founded by Mr. Noritoshi Kanai, who had come to the U.S. in 1955 from Japan and noticed that no Japanese miso was being imported, so that only Hawaiian-style miso was available. He started to import Japanese miso to meet a growing demand from new Japanese immigrants. In 1975, to expand his line, Mr. Kanai bought the rights to the Yamaizumi brand of Hawaiian-style miso, then being imported to Los Angeles, and in 1976 his Miyako Oriental Foods began making this product in Los Angeles. Also in 1976 he bought the Kanemasa brand and some of the equipment from the former Fujimoto Miso Company and began to make a Japanese-style miso to supplement his imports. His main competitors were in Hawaii; in the early 1970s about 200 tons a year of Maruhi brand miso was being made and 100 tons a year of Murafuku brand (made by Hawaiian Soy Sauce Co.). During its first year of production in Los Angeles, Miyako made 150 to 200 tons of miso. Its bestseller was Yamajirushi brand (65%), followed by Kanemasa (25%) and Yamaizumi (10%). Most of the company's miso was sold in California. In 1978 Miyako introduced the Cold Mountain brand, marketed to the natural foods trade and started selling firm granular rice koji under that brand in tubs of 12 or 20 ounces, or 25 pounds for people wishing to make their own miso. By 1981 Miyako was producing four brands of miso plus rice koji, and also doing some private labeling. Ninety percent of their miso was sold to the Oriental trade; the remaining 10% was their Cold Mountain brand, with four varieties sold to the natural and health food trades. Eighty percent of their total sales were in California. Their production capacity was reported to be 454 tonnes (500 U.S. tons) a year in 1979, up 300% in five years and growing with the market at 15 to 25% a year. By late 1982 Miyako, now making 544 tonnes (600 U.S. tons) of miso a year, had outgrown its original plant.

In September the operation was moved into a sparkling new 20,000-square-foot plant with an annual capacity of 1,800 tonnes in Baldwin Park, California. The grand opening, costing $15,000, drew 500 miso enthusiasts. With sales now growing at 10 to 15% a year Miyako is considering production of powdered misos (Leviton 1983).

THE OHIO MISO COMPANY, INC.
ROUTE 2 MONROEVILLE, OHIO 44847
419/668-9512

The first Caucasian-run miso company in North America was Ohio Miso Co. in Monroeville, Ohio, founded by Thom Leonard and Richard Kluding; they began production on 13 March 1979. Thom had been making miso on a small, noncommercial scale since late 1974, as described earlier. By January 1980 Ohio Miso was making several varieties of miso: brown rice, barley (one or two year), mellow brown rice, mellow red, and black soybean; output was 2,400 pounds a week (Whole Foods 1979; Carr 1980; Leviton 1980).

Other early companies were Shin-Mei-Do Miso (opened April 1979 by Lulu Yoshihara; Denman Island, B.C., Canada); American Miso, Inc. (October 1981 by John Belleme; Rutherfordton, North Carolina); South River Miso Co. (having bought out Ohio Miso Co. in November 1980, Christian and Gaella Elwell started their own production in October 1982 in a beautiful traditional shop at Conway, Massachusetts). The founders of Shin-Mei-Do and American Miso, Inc. had both apprenticed with makers of traditional miso in Japan (Belleme 1981, 1981a). American Miso was the largest of the new Caucasian-run companies. Located on 100 acres of rural land, the company spent $325,000 for two buildings (3,500 square feet) and unique equipment, which combined both traditional and modern-mechanized components. The plant's capacity was 227 metric tons (500,000 pounds) of miso a year. Production grew steadily from 1,250 pounds a week in April 1982, to 3,000-4,800 pounds a week in late summer 1982, up to 6,000 pounds a week in early 1983, the latter being the equivalent of 131 tonnes a year. A detailed cover story by Leviton in the summer 1981 issue of *Soyfoods* magazine described the company's operations; it was making red (rice), mellow barley, and mellow white misos of excellent quality, with plans for miso dips and dressings, and from 1983, natural shoyu (see also Greenwood 1982). In 1982 Dale Deraps of Imagine Foods/Moniteau Farm in Jamestown, Missouri, and Mr. Chong of General Oriental Foods (225 tonnes a year capacity) in Holmdel, New Jersey, both began making miso. Most of these companies made naturally fermented, unpasteurized miso. As of 1983 a number of new companies and individuals were seriously considering starting miso plants in the U.S., which will certainly help create an expanding market.

The American media, and especially the macrobiotic and natural foods media, took a strong interest in miso. Major articles included "Soy Bean Puree: Miso. Ancient Oriental Health Food" (*Health Food Business Review*, July 1968), "Recipes from Aveline Kushi's Book of Miso" (*East West Journal* 1971), "Making Miso in America" (B.W. 1971, *EWJ*, a visit to the Norio Company in San Francisco), "How to Make Miso: An Excerpt from *The Book of Miso*" (*EWJ*, Nov. 1976), "Cooking: From the Book of Miso" (*EWJ*, June 1977), "Making Miso in America" (*EWJ*, Sept. 1978), "Cooking with Miso" (*Alternatives*, Nov. 1978), "Down-Home Miso" (*Whole Foods*, Oct. 1979), "Miso: Made in the U.S.A."(*EWJ*, Jan. 1980), "Make Way for Miso" (*Bestways*, July 1980), "The Miso Master's Apprentice" (*EWJ*, April 1981), "American Miso Makes a Big Move Down South" and "Miso-Cup" (*Soyfoods*, Summer 1982), and "Smokey Mountain Miso" (*EWJ*, Nov. 1982, about American Miso Co.). After the near nuclear reactor catastrophe at Three Mile Island in March 1979, a number of media articles recommended that Americans use miso since the dipicolonic acid it contains may partially protect the body from ingested radioactive materials.

Starting in the 1960s, there was a growing interest in Chinese and Japanese cooking in the U.S. Gloria Miller's *The Thousand Recipe Chinese Cookbook* (1966) was one of the first to have good information on and recipes for Chinese chiang. Good early Japanese cookbooks with many miso recipes included *Japanese Country Cookbook* (Rudzinsky 1969), The *Cookery of Japan* (Steinberg, 1969; a magnificent work), and *Zen Tastes in Japanese Cooking* (Tsuji 1971; the finest work available on Tea Ceremony Cuisine).

After the pioneering scientific research on miso and its fermentation by Shibasaki and Hesseltine in the early 1960s, there was surprisingly little such research subsequently. In 1974 C. Kao at Kansas State University published a PhD dissertation on miso (and other fermented foods) made from chickpeas, fava beans, and soybeans, then in 1977 Robinson and Kao wrote a jounral article summary of that research. In 1979 and 1981 Fukushima gave general information on miso and its status in Japan. Also, a number of Japanese patents for miso and koji began to be granted in the U.S. (Koyama 1976; Hayashi 1977).

American miso makers and marketers were innovative, developing a number of new products suited to American tastes. In the mid 1970s most of the miso in America was sold as such, in bulk or plastic bags, imported from Japan. The most popular varieties were red, barley, and Hatcho miso. A Finger Lickin' miso was also quite popular on the West Coast. America's first widely distributed product in which miso was used as an ingredient in a popular preparation was Instant Aka Miso Soup, introduced by Kikkoman in a foil packet in 1968 and sold in the Japanese food section at many West Coast supermarkets, as well as Japanese food stores. By 1983 Kikkoman was offering an Instant Aka Miso Soup, Instant Shiro Miso Soup, and Instant Tofu Miso Soup, each in a large, colorful foil packet. In the fall of 1978 Edward & Sons Trading Co., under the direction of Joel Dee, introduced Miso-Cup, an instant natural dehydrated miso soup, packaged in foil pouches. By 1980 two flavors were available: golden light and rich savory with seaweed. Miso-Cup soon became the most widely advertised miso product in America (Leviton 1982). Year after year, full-page color or black-and-white ads in many U.S. natural and health food publications served to introduce millions of Americans to miso. Some people used Miso-Cup to help them kick the coffee/caffeine habit, finding its aroma and flavor as appetizing as those of coffee. In 1982 Edward & Sons introduced two powdered miso dip mixes, Miso-Plus Chive and Miso-Plus Jalapeno. Mixed with sour cream, yogurt, avocado, etc., they yielded quick and easy party dips or salad dressings. In the late 1970s San-J introduced a powdered soybean miso, containing 33% protein, which they sold to food processors as a natural substitute for MSG. White Wave in Colorado introduced a Yellow Miso Dressing, sold in an 8-ounce jar. In 1980 Marusan started importing two types of instant miso soups with red or white miso and ran full page color ads in trade magazines. In 1982 Fantastic Foods launched a widely advertised Quick Pilaf: Brown Rice with Miso, Health Valley introduced Vegetarian Baked Beans with Miso and Corn Chips with Miso and Wizard Baldour debuted a Hot Stuff with Miso. In early 1983 Westbrae Natural Foods presented their Instant Miso Soup in "white flavor and red flavor." Increasingly, then, miso was used as a key ingredient in other popular American foods.

American miso makers also experimented with using new basic ingredients to make new basic types of miso. Starting in about 1975 craftsmen began getting good results using peanuts, garbanzo beans (chick peas), black soybeans, and natto in place of regular soybeans, making their koji from corn, millet, wheat, or buckwheat, and using powdered kelp as a partial salt substitute. Yet except for the corn-soy miso and moromi wheat miso made by South River Miso Co. and Imagine Foods, relatively little of these new American-style misos were sold commercially.

During the 1970s and early 1980s the miso market in the U.S. grew steadily, with the growth coming from both increased imports and increased domestic production. Imports of miso from Japan to the U.S. grew from 219 tonnes in 1970 to 959 tonnes in 1982, for a 4.4-fold increase in just 12 years and a compound growth rate of more than 12% a year. Note that the growth rate increased markedly after 1968 (page 240). An estimated 20 to 25% of this imported miso was the traditional, natural style sold to the natural foods trade, with most of the rest going to Oriental food stores. Imported miso was subject to a 14% import duty. Interestingly miso and soy sauce were the only two soyfoods imported in large quantities to America; smaller quantities of soymilk and tofu in Tetra-Pak were also imported.

Despite the rapid increase in miso imports, it appears that production of miso in America grew at an even faster

U.S. MISO IMPORTS, PRODUCTION AND CONSUMPTION

Source: Japan Exports & Imports: Commodity by Country

$4.9 million. The total retail value of domestically made and imported miso was about $8.2 million.

This miso was consumed by both Asian and Caucasian Americans, both in growing numbers. During the 1970s the population of Asian and Pacific Americans grew by leaps and bounds, from 1,369,000 in 1970 to 3,500,000 in 1980, up 2.5-fold. The leading miso consumers in 1980 were probably Japanese-Americans, which numbered 700,747, up from 591,000 in 1970. The 806,000 Chinese-Americans and 774,000 Filipino-Americans were also important consumers. The main centers of Asian-American population, in order of importance, were Honolulu, New York, Los Angeles, San Francisco, Chicago, San Jose (California), Seattle, and Houston.

Caucasian miso consumers came from several groups. The great majority came from the closely related natural foods, macrobiotic, or vegetarian movements, but some came from the growing number of people interested in Japanese, Chinese, and other Asian cuisines. The prime consumer age group was 25 to 40. To each of these meatless or largely meatless diets, miso added its savory rich flavor plus some protein. Although the percentage of all miso in America consumed by Caucasians grew rapidly during the 1970s, as of 1983 it was probably still somewhat less than that consumed by Oriental Americans (primarily Japanese Americans).

From the mid 1970s to 1983 major changes took place in the miso market in America. Total miso consumption tripled and miso was increasingly sold as an *ingredient* in other popular foods rather than as miso itself. Misos with a lower salt content, lighter color, and sweeter flavor passed the darker, more traditional misos in popularity as Americans looked to reduce their salt intake. The market share of American-made misos steadily increased, even though they were generally more expensive than imports. The sale of domestically made misos in a cottage-cheese style round plastic tub with a pop-off lid made them easier to use than those in a sealed plastic bag and allowed them to be sold unpasteurized. Packaged miso (in tubs and bags) rapidly replaced the lower cost but messier bulk, self-serve misos. Important importers who distributed miso to the prime Caucasian markets (most also carried domestic misos) were, in approximate order of size, Westbrae Natural Foods in California, Tree of Life in Florida, Eden Foods in Michigan, Erewhon in Massachusetts, Chico-San in California, and Marusan in New Jersey. Major Japanese distributors, which serviced Oriental food stores and supermarkets, are listed in Appendix E. In 1982 a survey of 60,000 readers of *New Age* magazine showed that 36% purchased miso at least once a month. Yet more important, a steadily growing number of typical Americans were starting to use miso, usually as an ingredient in other popular foods. More and more natural foods restaurants (including soy delis, restaurants, and cafes) included miso dishes on their menu. The most popular use, at home and in restaurants, was in soups, followed by dips, dressings, sauces, and spreads. Most Americans greatly enjoy the flavor of a well-made miso soup.

In late 1982 JETRO, a Los Angeles based organization promoting Japanese exports, published a 32-page study

rate, although precise, prior to 1975, statistics are not availabe. Reliable estimates, however, indicate that between 1975 and 1982 miso production in the contiguous 48 states jumped from 120 to 750 tonnes, a remarkable 525%, while production in Hawaii grew steadily from 543 to 640 tonnes, some 18%. Thus total U.S. miso consumption (imports plus domestic production) grew from 756 tonnes in 1970 to 1,122 tonnes in 1975, up to 2,349 tonnes in 1982. By late 1982 Americans in the continental U.S. were consuming *three times* as much miso as they had in 1975 and the market was growing at about 17% a year!

As of 1983, the miso industry in the U.S. consisted of eight manufacturers (three in Hawaii), plus two more in Canada (see Appendix D). The largest producers were Miyako Oriental Foods (544 tonnes a year), Hawaiian Miso & Soy Co. (512 tonnes a year), American Miso, Inc. (125 tonnes a year), and American Hawaiian Soy Co. (125 tonnes a year). The U.S. miso industry used about 463 tonnes of soybeans and employed about 27 workers to make this miso, which retailed for about (in Japanese) on the American Miso Market. Surveys done in Los Angeles showed that 63% of miso buyers in stores were Asian Americans and 37% were Caucasians; the predominant buyers were in their thirties or fifties; there were seven major miso importers in Los Angeles; and in 20 of Los Angeles' 450 Japanese restaurants, the main dishes in which miso were served were miso soup (19), Ishikari Nabe (one pot cookery, 5), Tofu Miso Dengaku (5), Steak Grilled with Miso (4), and Salad with Vinegar Miso Dressing (2).

Miso was introduced to Caucasian Americans from the 1960s on as food that fostered good health. Starting in the late 1970s there was a rising concern by a growing number of Americans over their excessive consumption of salt (sodium). At least initially, this probably hurt miso's image as a healthful food, since it contains an average of 12% salt. The low-salt trend definitely led to a shift toward lower salt misos. Yet in the process more and more people came to realize that miso is actually and excellent food to help *reduce* salt intake (as explained in detail in Chapter 2). Research has shown that people who season their food with miso instead of straight salt typically end up using 50% less salt, since miso adds its own rich flavor. The extensive research done in Japan on the relationship between miso consumption and good health is described in Chapter 2. And finally, there is a growing consensus among nutritionists and physicians that diets containing less saturated animal fats and cholesterol (as are widely consumed in red meats) are healthier. As interest in meatless diets grows among those interested in good health, reduced food bills, world hunger, and animal rights, miso is increasingly being used to provide the savory flavors and protein once obtained from meats.

It is interesting to compare consumption of miso and soy sauce in both Japan and the United States. In 1980 in Japan the per capita yearly consumption of miso was 6.0 kg (13.2 lbs.) whereas that of shoyu was 11.86 kg or 10.1 liters (26.1 lbs. or 2.67 gallons). Thus Japanese consumed almost twice as much shoyu by weight as miso. In America the figures were, of course, much lower. Per capita yearly consumption of soy sauce in the U.S. was 254 gm or 0.254 kg or 0.216 liters or 14.7 tablespoons, roughly 2% of the per capita consumption in Japan. Per capita yearly consumption of miso in the U.S. was 7.37 gm or 0.007 kg or 1.3 teaspoons per year, roughly 0.1% of the per capita miso consumption in Japan. Thus the average Japanese consumes 50 times as much shoyu and 800 times as much miso as the average American, and the average American downs 35 times as much shoyu as miso.

One might be inclined to ask why, if both miso and shoyu are so widely used in Japan, miso is not nearly so well known nor widely used in the West. The reason for this unusual development lies, we feel, more in the difference in structure between the miso and shoyu industries, than in the basic appeal of the two foods. Most Japanese shoyu is produced by a few huge companies which have had the capacity and foresight to engage in international advertising and commerce. By comparison, the largest miso companies are quite small and have only a few decades of modern business experience. Therefore they have not yet

been able to make their product known or available throughout the world. Nor, perhaps, have they become fully aware of the genuine interest in and potential market for fine miso in the United States and Europe. We are convinced that if a large (Japanese) miso company believed in the potential of miso as much as Kikkoman believes in that of shoyu (Japanese style soy sauce) and would promote miso as extensively and effectively as Kikkoman has promoted shoyu, miso's popularity would grow dramatically.

Miso's Future in the West: As of 1983 miso would seem to have a bright future in the West, as indicated by all major market trends except the concern with excess salt consumption, which can be turned to miso's advantage. In much the same way that the Japanese, over a period of 1,000 years, gradually transformed Chinese soybean chiang into unique and truly Japanese-style misos, so may we also expect that Westerners will continue the creative process, adapting miso to their own tastes, technology, and cuisine. There are many reasons to believe that miso will play an increasingly important role in America's evolving cuisine and become a standard household seasoning, just as soy sauce now is, as people discover the great variety of delicious flavors and aromas found in the many and varied types of fine miso.

MISO IN OTHER COUNTRIES

Miso has not yet attracted the attention it deserves in most Third World countries. We know of miso reasearch in only two countries not already mentioned:

Israel: Using United States P.L. 480 funds, Ilany-Feigenbaum and others (1967, 1969) and Diamant and Laxer (1967, 1968) developed misos from defatted soybean flakes and alternate carbohydrate sources such as corn, oats, potatoes, and sweet potatoes. Diamant and Laxer also developed a low-salt miso (4%), which had twice the P.E.R. of regular miso when fed to rats. Apparently the excess salt suppressed rat growth.

India: Rao et al. (1968, 1972) have done research on miso-like foods based in Indian oilseeds and pulses.

Latin America: The only Third World country we know of where miso is widely available is Brazil. However much of this miso is imported from Japan and most of it is consumed by the country's large Japanese population.

Friends of miso from Mexico have suggested that miso there might be marketed as "Super Miso," a play on words with *"Con su permiso,"* or "With your permission, I'd like some please."

Africa: The earliest known work on miso in Africa is very recent. In 1979 and 1982 Ms. Sumbo Abiose of Nigeria, working in Glasgow, Scotland, published excellent works on the miso fermentation process. Hopefully this will serve as an impetus to introduce miso to Africa, where soybean production is expanding rapidly and protein shortages are widespread.

Appendix B
Other East Asian Misos: Chinese Chiang, Korean Jang, and Indonesian Taucho

DEVELOPED IN China long before the Christian era, chiang was the progenitor of the many varieties of miso and soy sauce that are now used throughout East Asia. As chiang was assimilated by various cultures, its name and basic character gradually changed to suit local conditions. In Korea it was transformed into *jang*: in Japan, it became miso and shoyu; in Indonesia and Thailand, *taucho;* and in Malaysia, *taucheo.*

Chiang in courtyard

CHINESE CHIANG

Although all varieties of Chinese-style miso are known collectivey as *chiang* (pronounced jiang), this term actually encompasses a remarkably wide range of foods, most of which are fermented with *Aspergillus oryzae* molds but many of which contain neither soybeans nor grain koji. Sharp in flavor, chaing often contains large amounts of fiery red peppers, plus small amounts of other spices such as garlic. Basic ingredients include nuts and seeds, broadbeans, flour or steamed bread, vegetables, and many sea foods. The most common varieties in China are Chunky Chiang (*tou-pan chiang*), Sweet Wheat-flour Chiang (*t'ien mien chiang*), and Red-pepper Chiang (*la-*

chiao chiang). In the West, the most widely available varieties— generally known by the Cantonese pronunciation of their names—are Bean Sauce (*yun-si* or *yuen-shi chiang*), Hoishin Sauce (*hoisin chiang*), Bean Paste or Chunky Chiang (*to-pan chiang*), and Sweet Wheat-flour Chiang or Soy Jam (*t'inmin chiang*); they are usually sold in 1-pound cans at Chinese food markets.

Whereas most Japanese miso is presently prepared commercially by professional craftsmen, the majority of Chinese chiang is prepared at home is much the same way that we in the West make our own jams, canned fruit, or pickles. Following centuries-old methodologies, both chiang and chiang-yu (the liquid pressed from chiang, i.e., soy sauce) are usually started in March or April; packed into 1- to 10-gallon earthenware crocks that are placed in courtyards or on rooftops or apartment balconies, they are allowed to ferment for 6 to 12 months. Most varieties are stirred daily, with rice wine added during the fermentation. The total production of chiang-yu is considerably larger than that of chiang. The Chinese have various terms for koji: *niang*, meaning "mother" is the general one, but it is often combined with the name for the type of fermentation for which it is used: *chiu niang* ("mother of alcohol") is koji used in making grain-based wines and *ts'u niang* ("mother of vinegar") for vinegar.

The flavor of homemade chiang varies greatly from household to household, and in many cases the strong aroma, high salt content, dark color, and extreme spiciness combine to create a product which appeals to only a small percentage of the population. In recent years, however, more uniform-tasting and universally appealing varieties have come to be prepared commercially on a large scale for distribution throughout the world. We find that sweet wheat-flour chiang—known to many Westerners as the basis for the delicious chocolate-brown sauce served with Peking Duck—is especially well suited to Western tastes.

In Taiwan and China, both homemade and commercial chiang scooped from open-top wooden kegs are sold at stores called "chiang gardens," which also deal in salt-pickled vegetables and soy sauce. Most shops sell only the three main varieties mentioned above, plus one or two local ones. Chiang is used in all of the major schools of Chinese cookery, usually as the base for sauces served with meat, seafood, or poultry

Fig. 47. Composition of Nutrients in 100 Grams of Chiang and Jang

Source: *Food Composition Tables for Use in East Asia (USDEW 1972) and Wang, (1979)*

Type of Chiang	Food Energy	Moisture	Protein	Fat	Carbohydrates (incl. fiber)	Fiber	Ash	Sodium	Calcium	Phosphorous	Iron	Potassium	Vit. B₁ (thiamine)	Vit. B₂ (riboflavin)	Vit. B₃ (niacin)
	Calories	Percent	Percent	Percent	Percent	Percent	Percent	Mg	Mg	Mg	Mg	Mg	Mg	Mg	Mg
Chunky Chiang (tou-pan chiang)	194	48.6	11.6	5.2	27.2	2.1	7.4	761	55	365	1.3	334	.07	1.19	1.2
Hot Chunky Chiang (la tou-pan chiang)	185	52.7	8.1	4.1	30.2	3.5	4.9	680	126	72	13.6	280	.35	.35	1.5
Sweet Wheat-flour Chiang (t'ien mien chiang)	192	47.0	5.4	1.2	40.1	2.7	6.3	570	32	104	5.7	183	.18	.80	0.9
Korean Soybean Jang (doen jang)	—	59.4	10.6	8.4	5.7	2.6	16.0	—	—	—	—	—	.002	.01	1.8
Korean Red-pepper Jang (kochu jang)	—	49.3	9.3	4.2	23.4	2.3	13.7	—	—	—	—	—	.08	.11	1.2
Korean Soybean Koji (meju)	—	23.2	43.0	17.8	11.9	5.7	4.1	—	—	—	—	—	—	—	—

dishes, and less commonly, with stir-fried tofu and vegetable preparations. (The Chinese have never adopted the Japanese practice of using chiang in soups.) At Chinese restaurants in the West, it can be sampled in a wide array of dishes listed as containing "bean sauce" or "bean paste."

The most common classification divides all chiang into four basic types: red or regular chiang, black chiang, assorted chiang, and chiang sauces. The varieties within each type are listed below in order of popularity. All Chinese names are written using the Wade-Giles system of romanization and standard Mandarin pronunciation, which has the following unique conventions: ch is pronounced like the j in jam, ch' like the ch in chard; k like the g in game, k' like the k in Korea; p like the b in bean, p' like the p in pea; t like the d in dough; t' like the t in tea.

Red or Regular Chiang

Chunky Chiang (*tou-pan chiang, topan chiang, or do-ban jiang*): Literally "bean petal chiang" or "board chiang" and also known as "Chinese soybean paste," this is a variety of wheat miso made with either soybeans or broadbeans and usually containing wheat flour. Soft in texture and very chunky due to the presence of unmashed beans, it ranges in color from warm chocolate to dark russet. Most varieties contain as much as 18 percent salt, and hence have a strong salty flavor, although modern commercial varieties are lower in salt and have a distinctive, yet milder taste. Prepared in basically the same way as the common Chinese soy sauce called *toyu* except that the percentage of liquid is much smaller, this chiang is fermented outdoors in large earthenware crocks and stirred daily for 7 to 12 months. Some varieties contain whole roasted sesame seeds, oil, or fish. Typical proportions by weight of raw materials are: soybeans 10, barley 3.3, wheat flour 3.3, salt 5.

A well-known seasoning made by dissolving chunky chiang in water is called *huang-hsi chiang*.

Hot Chunky Chiang (*la tou-pan chiang* or *tou-pan la-chiang*): Also known as "hot bean paste," this hot-and-spicy variety is made by adding *togarashi* red peppers to chunky chiang. If dried red-pepper powder is also added, the product is known as *tou-pan yu la-chiao*.

Szechwan Red-pepper Chiang (*ssu-ch'uan tou-pan chiang*): Sharper in flavor than hot chunky chiang but not as hot as red-pepper chiang (see below), this spicy variety is specially prepared in Szechwan and renowned for its abundant use of red peppers. Often known in English as Szechwan Hot Soybean Paste, it plays a key seasoning role in Szechwan's fiery cuisine.

Hamanatto Chiang (*tou-ch'ih chiang*): Resembling a combination of chunky Japanese red miso and *hamanatto* (p. 42), this savory product is closely related to Chinese-style hamanatto (*tou-ch'ih* or *shang-ch'ih*), a seasoning made by fermenting lightly-salted soybeans. If hot red peppers are added, the product becomes Red-pepper Hamanatto Chiang (*tou-ch'ih la-chiao chiang*).

Cantonese Red Chiang (*mien-ch'ih chiang*): Made from beans particular to Canton, this variety also contains wheat flour.

Great Chiang (*ta chiang*): A variety using soybeans as the key ingredient.

Yellow-red Chiang (*huang chiang*): Literally "yellow chiang," this variety is made primarily with soybeans.

Black Chiang

Sweet Wheat-flour Chiang (*t'ien mien chiang, mien chiang,* or *t'ien chiang*): This chocolate-brown, sweet preparation, also called "sweet (soy)bean paste," "sweet flour paste," or "flour jam," is made from wheat flour, salt, and water. Its consistency is smooth and soft—like that of melted chocolate—and its flavor somewhat resembles that of Japanese akadashi miso (p. 44). When prepared commercially, the flour and water are combined to form a dough which is either shaped into 4½-inch-diameter dumplings (*man-t'ou* or *manju*) and steamed, or flattened into ¾-inch-thick sheets, dried until firm, then broken into pieces about 5 inches in diameter. The steamed buns or flat pieces are arranged on 4-foot diameter bamboo trays and allowed to ferment in an incubation room for about 4 days. (Or in some areas, the steamed buns are arranged on sorghum stalks in an outdoor shed and allowed to mold for 3 weeks during the month of May.) The molded buns or sheets are then transferred to large earthenware pots located in an outdoor courtyard or on a rooftop. Mixed with a small amount of water and about 5 percent salt, the steamed dough soon begins to soften and dissolve. The mixture is stirred daily and allowed to ferment for at least 3 to 4 months, and sometimes as long as 6 to 8 months. A small amount of additional water is sometimes added each day during the first week of fermentation. During the day and sometimes at night the lids of the pots are left open to give access to the supposedly beneficial effects of dew and moonlight.

When this variety of chiang is prepared at home, the steamed bun or moist dough (often inoculated with a yellow storebought koji starter mold) is placed on a platter in a warm, damp place for 7 to 15 days until mold forms. The molded product is then transferred to a small earthenware crock and covered with salty water; left uncovered under the sun and night sky for 5 days, the mixture is squeezed daily by hand. For the next 15 days the mixture is stirred with a bamboo pole, after which time the chiang is ready, although its fermentation may be continued for 2 months more to give a mellower flavor and darker color. In some areas, soy sauce pressing-residue is added to the mixture to make it saltier.

In Chinese restaurants, sweet wheat-flour chiang is often combined with small amounts of sugar, sesame oil, and rice wine to make the dipping sauce served with Peking Duck (p. 129) or Pancake Rolls (p. 128). In Japan, where chiang is not widely available, a similar sauce is prepared using Hatcho miso as the basic ingredient (p. 70). Sweet wheat-flour chiang is also served as a dip with thinly sliced meat hor d'œuvres or as a spread for steamed buns or baked bread topped with sliced leeks; as the basis of the sauce served with Mabo-doufu (tofu cooked with ground beef and red pepper); as a topping, mixed with ground beef, for the noodle dish Cha-chiang Mien; and as a seasoning with sautéed chicken or pork dishes. It is also widely used as a pickling medium.

Prepared commercially with the addition of plenty of minced red peppers, this variety becomes Red-pepper Wheat-flour Chiang (*la-mien chiang*).

Black Chiang (*hei chiang* or *he do-ban jiang*): Actually dark chocolate brown, black chiang (often sold as Black Bean Paste) is made from black soybeans, as is its close relative Bean Chiang (*tou chiang*). A well-known seasoning made by dissolving black chiang in water is called *hei-hsi chiang*.

Assorted Chiangs

The earliest varieties of chiang are said to have been sauces made by fermenting salted fish, shellfish, and meats. Similar to the well-known, strong-smelling *nuoc-mam* of Vietnam and *shiokara* or *shottsuru* of Japan, the modern descendents of these ancient foods are still widely used as both seasonings and sauces.

Red-Pepper Chiang (*la-chiao chiang* or *la-chiang*): An all purpose seasoning used like tabasco sauce, this hot-and-spicy preparation is made by fermenting salted red peppers. Containing no soybeans, it is vermilion red and has a soft, semi-liquid consistency similar to that of a thick chili sauce. At restaurants, it is often placed on the table in small bottles.

Canton Sweet Simmered Chiang (*hai-hsein chiang*): A close relative of Japanese Sweet Simmered Miso (p. 60). A variety made in the Fo-shan region near Canton containing fennel and spicy powder is called *chu-hou chiang*.

Dried Chiang (*kan chiang*): A general term for all chiang that has been dried after fermentation, this unique product has no counterpart among traditional Japanese misos.

Other Varieties, none of which contain soybeans or grain koji, include:

> *Sesame Chiang (chih-ma chiang):* The Chinese equivalent of Western-style sesame butter
> *Peanut Chiang (hua-chih chiang):* Chinese-style peanut butter
> *Umeboshi Chiang (shun-mui chiang):* With tart, salted *ume* plums
> *Shrimp Chiang (hsia chiang):* Often served with meat dishes
> *Cockle Chiang (hsien-chien chiang):* Featuring tiny salt-cured shellfish
> *Tangy Chiang (kuei-hua chiang):* Made from minced garlic, tangerine rind, and sesame seeds
> *Semi-fermented Chiang (chiang-p'i):* Made in large bun-shaped lumps

Chiang Sauces

Most of these sauces, which have a consistency similar to that of thick gravy, are presently available in cans at Chinese grocery stores in the West.

Bean Sauce (*yuan-shih chiang* or *yun-si-* or *yuen-shi chiang*): This chocolate-brown sauce, made from soybeans, flour, salt, and water has a thick consistency and rather salty flavor. The regular variety has a slightly chunky texture, whereas that labeled "ground bean sauce" (*mien-shih chiang* or *min see jeung,* i.e. flour and soy nugget sauce) is smooth. Also known as "soy jam or soybean condiment," this product is also called "yellow bean sauce" when yellow beans are used in place of the usual soybeans. In making soy sauce, the Chinese filter off the liquid from chiang. The lees or residue that remain are used as the basic ingredient in bean sauce. (Note that Japanese shoyu producers press the residue and then discard it.) Some varieties of bean sauce contain added sesame seeds, sugar, or caramel coloring, molasses, MSG, vinegar, and/or preservatives. Bean sauce is an essential seasoning with the famous Cha-chiang Mien (Soy Jam Noodles) and is also widely used in stir-fried preparations, as a pickling medium, and mixed with gingerroot and minced green onion as a seasoning atop steamed fish.

Hoisin Sauce *(hai-hsien chiang):* The Chinese name means "sea fresh chiang," i.e. "chiang to be eaten with fresh seafoods," which however, it usually isn't! Also known as "soy jam," this jet black paste is creamy smooth and very sweet; it looks and tastes quite like melted chocolate or like Sweet Wheat-Flour Chiang (above). After the light soy sauce is drawn off of chiang, the soybean lees are lightly pressed to extract some remaining soy sauce, ground to a smooth paste, then mixed with flour, sugar, vinegar, salt, chili powder, and water; some varieties also contain garlic, food coloring, and preservatives. Sold in the West in 1-pound cans or 14-ounce jars, it is a favorite sauce for Peking Duck or Mu Shee Pork, and Chinese style spareribs. It is prized for its spicy sweetish flavor when used as a barbecue sauce, especially with *yakitori* (Japanese-style grilled chicken).

Oyster Sauce *(hao-yu chiang* or *hao-wei chiang):* A widely-used seasoning made from the liquid that rises to the surface of salt-pickled, fermented oysters.

Barbecue Sauce *(sha cha chiang):* Known also as "shacha jam," this Cantonese or Taiwanese barbecue sauce is used mainly with *sukiyaki* and *yakitori* (grilled chicken), but is also served as a topping for rice, noodles, sea cucumber, pork, and fried beef.

Other Chiang Sauces, none of which contain soybeans or grain koji include:

> *Shrimp Sauce (hsia-yu* or *lu hsia-yu):* Features tiny shrimps
> *Chinese Worcestershire Sauce (suan-la chiang, la-chiang yu,* or *chi-ch'ih):* A close relative of its English counterpart
> *Chinese Ketchup (fan-ch'ieh chiang):* Similar to Western tomato ketchup

Chunky Chiang *(tou-pan chiang):*	豆瓣醬, 豆板醬, 豆弁醬;
Huang-hsi Chiang:	黄稀醬
Hot Chunky Chiang *(la tou-pan chiang):*	瓣豆辣醬
Tou-pan Yu La-chiao:	豆瓣油辣椒
Szechwan Red-pepper Chiang	
(ssu-ch'uan tou-pan chiang):	四川豆板醬, 豆瓣醬
Hamanatto Chiang *(tou-ch'ih chiang):*	豆豉醬
Red-pepper Hamanatto Chiang	
(tou-ch'ih la-chiao chiang):	豆豉辣椒醬
Cantonese Red Chiang *(mien-ch'ih chiang):*	麵豉醬
Great Chiang *(ta chiang):*	大醬
Yellow-red Chiang *(huang chiang):*	黄醬
Sweet Wheat-flour Chiang *(t'ien mien chiang):*	甜麵醬
Red-pepper Wheat-flour Chiang *(la-mien chiang):*	瓣麵醬
Black Chiang *(hei chiang):*	黑醬
Bean Chiang *(tou chiang):*	豆醬
Hei-hsi chiang:	黑稀醬
Red-pepper Chiang *(la-chiao chiang):*	辣椒醬
Canton Sweet Simmered Chiang	
(hai-hsien chiang):	海鮮醬, 柱候醬
Dried Chiang *(kan chiang):*	干醬
Sesame Chiang *(chih-ma chiang):*	芝麻醬
Peanut Chiang *(hua-hsien chiang):*	花生醬
Umeboshi Chiang *(shun-mui chiang):*	酸梅醬
Shrimp Chiang *(hsia chiang):*	蝦醬
Cockle Chiang *(hsien-chien chiang):*	蜆介醬
Tangy Chiang *(kuei-hua chiang):*	桂花醬
Semi-fermented Chiang *(chiang-p'i):*	醬坯
Bean Sauce *(yuan-shin chiang):*	原豉醬
Hoisin Sauce *(hai-hsien chiang):*	海鮮醬
Oyster Sauce *(hao-yu chiang):*	蠔油醬, 蠔味醬
Barbecue Sauce *(sha cha chiang):*	沙茶醬
Shrimp Sauce *(hsia-yu):*	蝦油, 滷蝦油
Chinese Worcestershire Sauce	
(suan-la chiang):	酸辣醬 辣醬油 喼汁
Chinese Ketchup *(fan-ch'ieh chiang):*	番茄醬

KOREAN JANG

Korea's three main fermented soyfoods are soybean miso *(doen jang)*, soy sauce *(kan jang)*, and red-pepper miso *(kochu jang)*. These three products accounted respectively for 18.3 percent, 10.6 percent, and 6.6 percent of total Korean soybean utilization in 1976. In that year, the daily per capita consumption of the three products was about 15 grams, 20 grams (ml), and 10 grams respectively. As in China, most of the soybean miso (82 percent), soy sauce (64 percent) and red-chili miso (76 percent) are produced in farmhouses and urban dwellings, and consumed directly by the families that make them; each family is allotted 6 pounds of free salt per year for just this purpose. A typical downtown high-rise apartment in Seoul will have six to eight brown earthenware crocks containing homemade *jang* and *kan jang* on 80 to 90 percent of its balconies. For this reason, jang is sold on only a relatively small scale at the miso-and-pickle sections of outdoor markets and food stores. Jang is widely used in hot spicy soups *(chigé)* which are generally thicker than Japanese miso soups. Kan jang, sweeter and stronger than Japanese shoyu, is made with soybeans, salt, and water, without the use of koji grain.

Retailing Korean jang

The various types of Korean miso and soy sauce are made from a dried soybean koji called *meju*, which is prepared in much the same way as Japan's *miso-dama* (p. 193). To make *meju*, soybeans are soaked, cooked, pounded until well mashed in a mortar, shaped into balls and wrapped in rice straw (or put unshaped into rice straw sacks), then hung under the rafters or eaves for 1 to 3 months, until each ball is covered with a natural bloom of white mold. The material is then broken into chunks, dried in the sun, and generally ground to a fine powder, usually in a hand-turned stone mill. The resulting *meju* (dried and ground soybean koji) has a composition of nutrients as shown in figure 47; it contains almost no sodium chloride (0.2 percent). At present ready-made *meju* is sold in marketplaces and used as the basis for some homemade jang. And some families have recently begun to inoculate their cooked soybeans with koji starter *(Aspergillus oryzae* or *A. sojae)*, which is also sold in the markets. The starter is mixed with a little wheat flour and sprinkled over the cooked, air-dried soybeans. The beans are then incubated in a warm place (79-86°F) for 24 to 48 hours, or until they are covered with white mold. They are then dried, crushed, and mixed with salt and water as above.

Korean Soybean Jang *(doen jang):* The only traditional Korean jang, this variety is light grayish brown and slightly chunky from the small proportion of uncrushed soybeans it contains. Two varieties of this salty and very strong-flavored jang are found in traditional markets; neither contains grain koji and one is slightly more salty and lumpy than the other. Most of this jang is still made in private homes, even that which is sold commercially, since most Koreans prefer the homemade product.

To prepare Korean soybean jang, *meju* is mixed with an 18- to 22-percent salt brine (and sometimes with sesame seeds or sesame leaves) in an earthenware container of 1 to 10 gallons capacity. The container is covered (but has no pressing lid) and placed outdoors on a balcony or rooftop, or in a courtyard. Traditionally the fermentation lasted for six months, from March to September. If a commercial starter is used to make the *meju*, the fermentation may be reduced to 2 to 3 months, and even less if the *meju* is soaked in warm brine and the container kept exposed to sunlight. After the basic fermentation period, the liquid that has accumulated in the container is filtered off and pasteurized by simmering to make *kan jang* (Korean soy sauce). The remaining nonliquid portion left in the vat is allowed to age for at least a few months longer, until it is good quality *doen jang* (soybean miso).

In the United States, a commercial variety is now available in 1-pound cans at Korean and Japanese food markets. Labeled "Bean Mash" *(doen jang)*, it contains soybeans, wheat, salt, and water. Nutrient composition is shown in figure 47, page 243.

Red-Pepper Jang *(kochu jang):* This spicy hot Korean miso is bright brownish red, has a smooth texture, and is somewhat softer than Japanese miso; each of the three main varieties contain slightly different amounts of red pepper. To make red-pepper jang, dried, finely ground *meju* is mixed in crocks with cooked glutinous rice, ground red pepper, and either salt brine or Korean soy sauce. Typically the fermentation takes 2 to 3 months; however, it may be accelerated by placing the crocks in sunlight. A good red-pepper jang contains a combination of sweet, hot, sour, and salty flavors. In some areas, rice flour is mixed with water to form dumplings, which are dropped into boiling water and cooked, then mashed together with *meju* and ground red pepper. One-third of the salt is added daily for three days; the red-pepper jang may be served on the fourth day, but it is usually fermented for 6 months. It is said that some varieties are also prepared from rice koji and wheat flour, or from a mixture of cooked soybeans and mochi or glutinous rice. Red-pepper jang is the favorite base for a thick soup or stew containing thinly sliced or ground meat and a little sugar.

In the United States, a commercial variety is now available in 1-pound cans at Korean and Japanese food markets. Labeled "Hot Bean Mash" *(kocho jang)*, it contains rice, red peppers, soybeans, salt, and water.

Mild Red-Pepper Jang *(mat jang):* This variety is similar to red-pepper jang but it contains more *meju*, less ground red pepper, and less salt. Glutinous rice is generally used to add natural grain sugars and a sweet flavor. The jang is wrapped in blankets and fermented in a warm place for a relatively short time (about 2 weeks). Like Japanese Finger Lickin' Miso, it is often served with fresh vegetables or tofu as a dip, topping, or garnish.

Chinese Sweet Black Jang *(cha jang* or *chungkuk jang):* This soft, jet black miso is a close relative of Chinese Sweet Wheat-flour Chiang (p. 244). Most of the Korean varieties are made by Chinese in Korea or imported from China. It is most popularly served with noodles in a dish called Cha Jang Mien (p. 126). The words *cha* and *chungkuk* both mean "Chinese."

Japanese Red Jang *(wei jang* or *ilbon jang):* This is a salty red rice miso similar to Japanese Sendai miso but with a flavor adapted to Korean tastes. It is saltier than the Japanese product. A smooth, reddish brown jang, it originated in Japan and was sold during the 36 years of Japanese occupation. It is now produced in large quantities in Korea. The words *wei* and *ilbon* both mean "Japanese."

Korean Jang

INDONESIAN TAUCHO

Formerly spelled tao-tjo (and now spelled tauco in Indonesia), this is a fermented soybean paste or chunky sauce, a variety of soybean miso with a long history that is produced and consumed mainly in West Java, the center of production being the town of Chianjur. There are four different flavors and consistencies of taucho, all of which are dark brown in color and usually known simply as *taucho:* 1) *Sweet soft taucho* (also called *taucho Chianjur*) is the most popular variety. It has a consistency of porridge or apple-sauce, interspersed with prominent soybean chunks. Its pronounced sweetness is due to the addition of 25 percent by weight of palm sugar. 2) *Salty liquid taucho* (also called black bean sauce, salted soybeans, or salted black beans) is a non-homogeneous mixture of firm reddish to black soybean halves immersed in a soy-sauce-like concentrate. It is extremely strong, pungent, and salty (much saltier than Japanese miso or shoyu). 3) *Firm dried taucho (taucho kering)* is a relatively new product made by sun-drying cakes of either of the previously mentioned taucho types. 4) *Smoked dried taucho* is a relatively uncommon product prepared mostly by Chinese.

The various types of taucho are used primarily as a seasoning in soups, vegetables, seafood, and noodle preparations, especially Lodeh, Taucho Ikan, Ikan Goreng Taucho, Sambal Taucho, Sambal Goreng Taucho, Oseng-Oseng Taucho, Mie Goreng Taucho, Tempeh Maska Taucho, and Tumis Udang.

Taucho differs from Japanese miso in that it is either sweeter or saltier and softer or firmer, is prepared by a much shorter natural fermentation, and contains a large proportion of glutinous rice flour. An estimated 84 cottage-industry shops produce taucho in Indonesia and 77 of these are located in West Java.

Taucho is traditionally made by a two-part fermentation process; a mold fermentation followed by a brine fermentation. One hundred kilograms of dry soybeans are washed and soaked in excess water for 15 to 20 hours, brought quickly to a boil, then dehulled underfoot or by hand. The beans are rinsed and the hulls usually floated off, boiled for up to 5 hours, drained, spread on 3-foot-diameter woven bamboo trays, where they are allowed to cool for 12 hours to air temperature (82°F). The beans are inoculated with a starter prepared by pounding to a powder 10 grams of sundried tempeh and mixing it with 190 grams of roasted glutinous rice flour. The active organisms in the starter are *Rhizopus oligosporus, Rhizopus oryzae,* and *Aspergillus oryzae.* This mixed culture inoculum has been shown to give taucho with the best flavor and aroma. Two hundred grams of this starter are mixed with 50 kilograms of roasted glutinous rice flour, mixed thoroughly with the soybeans, spread in a 1¼-inch-deep layer in the bamboo tray, sometimes covered with cheesecloth, and incubated in racks at 81°F for 3 to 4 days (traditionally as long as 7 to 14 days) until the beans are covered with a dense white mycelium. This koji-like substance is then broken into small pieces and put into 2½-gallon earthenware crocks with an 18 percent brine solution in the ratio of 100 kilograms koji to 200 liters brine. The resulting mash is allowed to stand outdoors in the sun for an average of 4 weeks and is mixed each morning. The crocks are covered each night. Beneficial bacteria and yeasts such as *Lactobacillus delbruekii* and *Hansenula spp.* become active and aid the brine fermentation. The finished product may be sold in small plastic bags as salty liquid taucho.

To make sweet soft taucho, 100 kilograms of the original taucho is combined with 25 kilograms each of palm sugar and water; the mixture is cooked until a homogenous, viscous consistency is obtained. Firm dried taucho is then prepared by sun-drying or smoking this product.

Taucho is the least important of Indonesia's four basic soyfoods, which include tempeh tofu, and kechap (soy sauce). It accounts for less than 1 percent of all Indonesian soybean utilization and the annual per capital consumption of all types of taucho is only 7.2 grams.

There are a number of publications on taucho. The best is F.G. Winarno's *Research on Taucho* (Phases I-III) published by FATEMETA, Bogor Agricultural University, Jalan Gunung Gede, Bogor, Indonesia, 1975. Additional information about this Indonesian miso is found in Winarno's *The Present Status of Soybeans in Indonesia* and *Indonesian Fermented Foods.* Publications by his colleagues include Nurhajati *et al.* (1975), Swastomo *et al.* (1975), and Zaenuddin *et al.* (1975).

For more details on taucho and a list of researchers, see the professional clothbound edition of our *Book of Tempeh* (Harper & Row).

A close relative of Indonesian taucho is Malaysian *taucheo.*

The Microbiology and Biochemistry of Miso Fermentation

THE PREPARATION of miso involves two consecutive fermentation processes. In the first, olive-green "koji starter" (*tané koji;* literally "koji seeds") consisting of dried mold spores is mixed with cooked rice, barley, or soybeans; the mixture is then incubated to produce the mold grain or soybeans called "koji." In the second, the koji is mixed with cooked soybeans, salt, water, and usually a little mature miso. Packed into vats, the ingredients are allowed to age while the dual processes of enzymatic digestion and fermentation transform them into the finished miso.

Let us enter this unfamiliar world, learn the names of its main dramateurs, and follow the interrelated processes of transformation. We will begin by discussing the nature of the basic molds used to prepare the koji starter, then go on to study the two fermentation processes mentioned above.

Koji Starter Molds

Select varieties of mold spores are the chief actors in the fermentation process, just as other varieties are used in the production of delicious natural cheeses, or yeasts are used in the making of wines or bread. What exactly are molds? Botanically, they are a family of lower plants which is part of a larger group known as fungi. The latter includes molds, mushrooms, yeasts, and mildews. All fungi lack chlorophyll, may be as small as a single cell, and can reproduce abundantly by the process of sporulation. Mycology—derived from the Greek stem *myco-* or *myc-* meaning fungus—is a special branch of botany dealing exclusively with the study of this vast world.

All molds and fungi grow on other organic substances called substrates. Bread, fruits, and vegetables allowed to stand too long in the cupboard often become the substrates for unwanted varieties. In the miso shop, cooked rice, barley, or soybeans are used intentionally as substrates. In addition to a suitable substrate, molds require a particular environment for hearty growth. For good miso, it must be fairly warm (about 80°F to 95°F), moist but not wet, and aerobic (i.e. containing plenty of free oxygen). Yeasts and anaerobic bacteria, however, can thrive in moist environments containing little or no free oxygen.

Molds are present in large numbers almost everywhere. Up until several decades ago, these wild spores were used as the "starter" for most of Japan's commercial miso, and they are still used in the preparation of some farmhouse varieties. Gradually, however, miso makers discovered that some mold varieties seemed to produce better quality miso than others; resorting largely to intuition and personal experience, they began to cultivate select strains in much the same way that prospectors nourished their sourdough cultures, Balkan peasants their yogurt starters, or cheesemakers their molds for mold-ripened cheeses such as Roquefort, Brie, Camembert, Blue or Bleu, Stilton, and Goronzolla. isolated pure cultures of miso molds, they discovered that virtually all varieties belonged to the single species *Aspergillus oryzae.*

The genus *Aspergillus* is part of the class Fungi Imperfecti, which also includes *Penicillium* molds. These fungi reproduce only asexually and are hence "imperfect." Their reproduction is by means of specialized spores called conidia (from the Greek meaning "fine dust"), which are born at the tips of special fungal filaments (modified hyphae) called conidiophores ("spore bearers"), shown in the figure on page 250.

The genus *Aspergillus* derives it's name from the term "aspergillum," which refers to a brush or small perforated container with a handle used, usually by priests or nuns, for sprinkling holy water in a liturgical service. The species name *oryzae* is probably derived from the Latin genus name for "rice" (*Oryza sativa*) since this mold was widely grown on rice by early East Asian cultures.

A close relative of *Apergillus oryzae* is *Aspergillus flavus,* (ass-per-JIL-us FLAY-vus), the main mold that produces aflatoxins on peanuts, corn, and a few other foods that are not stored properly. Aflatoxins, highly carcinogenic liver toxins, came to the public attention in 1960 when 100,000 turkeys and ducks suddenly died in England from consuming moldy Brazilian peanut presscake, contaminated by *A. flavus.* Since that time extensive tests around the world have been conducted to see if similar toxins might be produced in soyfoods such as miso, shoyu, tamari, or Hamanatto fermented by other species of *Aspergillus.* Dr. C.W. Hesseltine, one of the world's foremost authorities on aflatoxins (and on miso), has shown repeatedly that soybeans are a poor substrate for aflatoxin production, and there have been no reports of aflatoxins in miso or any other soyfoods fermented by *Aspergillus.*

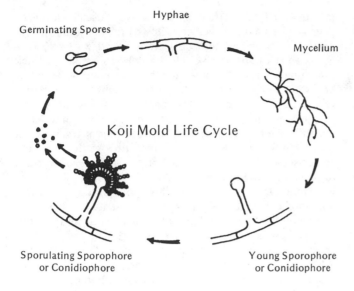

Germinating Spores

Hyphae

Mycelium

Koji Mold Life Cycle

Sporulating Sporophore
or Conidiophore

Young Sporophore
or Conidiophore

Within the single species *Aspergillus oryzae,* just as within the world of roses, there are a vast number of strains or subspecies—estimates range from 10,000 to 100,000— each with its own unique physical properties and name! Some mycologists, in fact, devote their entire lives to the study of *A. oryzae* and often specialize in the study of one or more of the important strains, those, that is, which yield koji with good fermentation "strength" and produce miso characterized by excellent flavor and aroma. Some strains are valued for their ability to produce large amounts of the enzyme amylase which digests or breaks down starches; these might be used in sweet white miso containing a large proportion of grains. Other strains are prized for their abundant production of the enzyme protease which breaks down proteins; these might be used to prepare the koji for soybean miso. Some molds have long "hairs" that create a firmly interlocking mycelium, excellent for commercial koji such as the soft mat variety available in grocery stores. Others have short "hairs" suited to modern factory koji production. Some molds have white "hairs" that give ready-made koji an attractive appearance. Others generate heat quickly and are used to make koji in short periods of time.

Most Japanese miso makers do not cultivate their own *A. oryzae* starter molds since the process requires extensive technical know-how and fairly complex equipment. Rather, this work is entrusted to a small number of specialty shops (fewer than ten), each of which tends a number of carefully bred strains, some of which may have been in their possession for centuries. These molds are bred and cross-bred over a period of many years as carefully as racehorses and chosen to give exactly the desired flavor and aroma to the miso. A shop's stock of molds is its most valued asset and the owner goes to great lengths—storing samples in vaults or caves—to guarantee their protection from fire or theft. Those portions of the stock in daily use are kept in their pure-culture state inside carefully sealed bottles in spotlessly clean laboratories to prevent even the slightest contamination by alien strains.

At the specialty shops, the molds are used to make "koji starter" (*tané koji*), later sold by special order to miso makers who use it in small amounts to make *koji,* the preparation of which precedes the making of miso itself.

Koji starter is prepared in basically the same way as koji itself except that the trays of inoculated steamed rice are allowed to stand for five (rather than just two) days in the warm incubation room until the mold turns from white to olive green indicating sporulation. The mycelium-bound grain is then dried in large rooms and sold in small sealed packages.

The substrate for koji starter is a mixture of cooked brown rice (or barley) and a small amount (about 2%) of the ash of a deciduous tree such as camellia or oak. Brown rather than white rice is used because the latter lacks the necessary nutrients for hearty mold growth. The alkaloid ash, in addition to preventing the excessively rapid generation of heat, provides the young mold with nutritious potassium and phosphorous salts, manganese, and other trace elements, and helps bring about the RNA/DNA balance required for proper sporulation. (It also prevents the rice from clumping.) After the warm rice-and-ash substrate is inoculated by mixing in pure-culture spores of a selected strain of *A. oryzae* mold, it is incubated for five days at 76°F in shallow wooden trays in a large humid room. Naturally, great care is taken to see that no contaminating microorganisms enter the culture during this time.

Soon after incubation begins, the mold spores send out hairlike shoots called hyphae. These growing filaments make the body of the mold, the white mycelium. Many hyphael cells make long erect shoots called "conidiophores" or "sporophores," which terminate in a bulbous head. After three to four days, these heads have formed bud clusters, which begin to sporulate luxuriously. It is at this stage that the color of the mold turns from creamy beige to soft olive green, the color of the spores themselves. Eventually each spore will have multiplied over 10 million times. The finished mats of mycelium-bound rice are transferred (in the trays) to drying rooms (113°F) for three to four days. Here the koji starter develops a tantalizing aroma similar to that of roasting chestnuts or almonds. Delicious as a snack, its flavor is richer and sweeter than that of regular koji.

Koji starter is made available commercially in three forms. The mycelium-bound grains are sometimes only lightly crumbled and sold as "whole-grain" starter. Or the spore-covered rice may be ground and sold as a "meal." About 50 percent of all koji starter sold today comes in the form of "spore powder" made by sifting whole-grain starter, discarding the mold-free rice grains, and collecting the olive-green spores; one gram of this pure powder contains from 6 to 10 billion spores. It is usually mixed with a powdered starch extender to make it easier to package and use.

Most modern starters contain not just one but several mold strains in a mixture carefully formulated to produce the right balance of enzymes needed to produce the particular type of koji desired. Some are also enriched with yeasts such as *Saccharomyces rouxii* or bacteria such

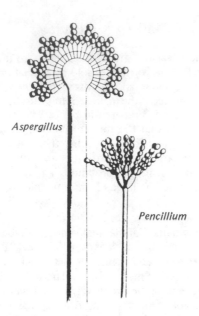

Conidiophores of Aspergillus and Penicillium

as *Pedicoccus halophilus* and *Lactobacillus delbrueckii* which play important roles after the miso ingredients begin the second stage of their fermentation. A typical shop selling koji starter will offer eight or more basic types as explained on page 178.

Making Koji: The First Fermentation

Once in the miso-maker's hands, the starter is used to make koji in what is perhaps the most difficult but crucial part of the miso-making process. Koji (or "mold rice") is cooked grains or beans which have been inoculated with starter and allowed to ferment for about two days until covered with and bound together by a fragrant white mycelium. This mold produces the enzymes that eventually break down the complex molecules of protein, starch, and lipids (oils and fats) in the substrate, reducing them to simpler, more readily digestible products which are later fermented by yeasts and bacteria. Enzymes, complex substances produced by living cells, are actually only catalysts; they simply promote chemical reactions (such as hydrolysis or oxidation) without themselves undergoing marked change in the process. In the process of beer fermentation, malt is prepared by sprouting barley (without the use of molds) in order to develop enzymes. Thus, koji is to miso what malt is to beer.

The nature of koji is embodied in the very characters with which the word is written. In the more traditional form—used with most miso koji and especially with barley koji—the ideographs for "barley" and chrysanthemum" are placed side by side. In the more recent form—used especially with ready-made rice koji—the ideographs for "rice" and "flower" are conjoined. The first form is said to have originated in China, whereas the latter was developed in Japan about 1,000 years ago. In both, the notion of grain covered with a bloom of mold is vividly expressed.

To make koji, about one part by weight of starter is mixed with 1,000 parts substrate, cooked (usually steamed) grains or beans that have been allowed to cool to body temperature. The inoculated substrate is placed in a large, well-insulated, cloth-lined box called a crib, covered with thick insulating mats, and allowed to stand overnight. After a few hours, the temperature inside the crib begins to rise as heat is generated by the process of fermentation. Briefly uncovered the next morning, the ingedients are well mixed in order to replenish the oxygen supply, release carbonic acid gasses, and blend the warmer substrate at the crib's center with the cooler substrate near the sides, bottom, and top. The crib is re-covered, only to be opened several hours later. The young koji is then transferred into shallow wooden trays where it is mounded to help it retain the heat of fermentation. However, a small hollow—like the crater of a volcano—is dug at the top of each mound to prevent overheating. The koji trays are arranged in a special incubation room where the temperature is kept at 82°F to 86°F and the humidity at 90 to 95 percent. The koji's temperature rises slowly as shown in figure 36 on page 181.

To protect against the intrusion of contaminating microorganisms, the craftsman's hands and tools must be kept spotlessly clean and the koji kept within the required range of temperature and moistness. (Special care must be taken during the warm months when alien microorganisms are abundant and propagate more rapidly.) If the koji temperature is allowed to rise above 104°F, the production of enzymes decreases and undesirable bacteria (such as black and *natto* varieties) begin to flourish; as these bacteria multiply, additional overheating results and free water condenses on the substrate causing even more rapid bacterial growth. Koji containing black molds develops an unpleasant odor and may have to be discarded. If the koji temperature is allowed to rise above 113°F, the koji begins to die of its own heat; if it drops below about 77°F, fermentation gradually comes to a halt and non-toxic bluish-green molds (usually related to *Penicillium*) may flourish giving the koji and resultant miso a poor flavor.

If temperature and humidity are kept within the ideal range, only the *Aspergillus oryzae* molds propagate. To prevent overheating as the first fermentation progresses, and to remove carbon dioxide, provide oxygen, and help the mold penetrate the substrate more deeply, the mycelium is broken up at regular intervals and the koji is well stirred. After the second stirring, the mounded koji is spread in even layers over the trays.

The energy required to support the growth and metabolism of the molds and create the essential enzymes is supplied by the grain or soybean substrate. During the first fermentation, about 5 to 10 percent of the food energy in the substrate is consumed by the mold and is therefore ultimately lost as nutritional energy available to human beings from the finished miso. This is the small price we pay to obtain enhanced flavor, aroma, and digestibility.

After 40 to 50 hours, depending on the "speed" of the starter and the incubation temperature, the burgeoning molds will have thoroughly covered the substrate and bound it into a solid cake. The koji must be harvested while the conidiophores of the mold are still forming, before the olive-green color typical of sporulation has appeared. At this stage, there is maximum availability of desirable enzymes; further mold growth would result in an undesirable (moldy) flavor in the finished miso. Thus, the finest koji is characterized·by a felt-like white mycelium, a fragrant aroma, and—when tasted—a sweet delicious flavor.

Removed from the trays, the finished koji is now crumbled, cooled, and usually mixed with just the right amount of salt to prevent further mold growth. The first step of miso's two-step fermentation process is now finished.

Cooking the Soybeans

As the koji fermentation nears completion, soybeans are boiled or steamed until they are soft enough to be crushed easily between the thumb and ring finger. Thorough cooking makes their protein more receptive to enzyme activity and helps to inactivate the trypsin growth inhibitors present in uncooked beans. Cooking time and temperature influence the color and flavor of the finished product; the longer the cooking, the darker the miso. The soybeans for white and light-yellow miso are boiled under high pressure for a short time (30 to 60 minutes) and the cooking water then discarded. Sweet red miso is given its dark-red color by simmering the beans for six to eight hours, allowing them to stand overnight in the caldron and then returning the beans to a boil the next morning. After steaming or boiling, the beans for all types of miso are partially or completely crushed to facilitate the permeation of enzymes from the koji. Whereas koji is said to provide most of miso's aroma and sweetness, soybeans are thought to contribute most of its flavor.

Preparing the Miso:
The Second Fermentation

The second fermentation is divided into four stages: the mixing of the basic ingredients; the digestion of protein, starch, and lipids in these ingredients by koji enzymes; the fermentation of the digested products by bacteria and yeasts; and the aging of the miso until it is fully mature.

The mashed soybeans are mixed with the salted koji, water or soybean cooking liquid, and "seed miso." The water—comprising about 10 percent of the total miso weight—is used to give the miso a moisture content of 48 to 52 percent. Regular water is almost always boiled before being added to eliminate contaminating microorganisms. A small amount of (unpasteurized) "seed miso" from a previous fermentation improves the miso aroma and flavor while decreasing the fermentation time by up to 50 percent by introducing hearty yeasts and bacteria. In modern miso factories the seed miso is often replaced by a pure-culture inoculum consisting of halophilic (salt resistant) yeasts such as *Saccharomyces rouxii* or *Torulopsis* and lactic acid bacteria such as *Pediococcus halophilus*, *Lactobacillus delbrueckii* or *Streptococcus faecalis;* the latter species are also used in cheese production. About 100,000

of these microorganisms are added for each *gram* of miso and, when used in temperature-controlled fermentation, they are kept at a maximum of 86°F, where they do their optimum work. Modern miso makers insist that the use of good inoculum is one of the secrets of preparing fine miso. The same type may be used for many different miso varieties.

Before packing the mixed ingredients into a huge wooden vat, the interior of the container is thoroughly scrubbed with boiling water and then sprinkled or rubbed with salt. In addition to removing contaminating microorganisms on the wood's surface, this serves to ferret out any mites or other tiny insects that can enter the chinks between the planks of vats which are allowed to stand empty. For broader protection, many producers now disinfect their entire buildings once or twice each year and sterilize (by steaming) all small kegs that enter the shop and the various cloths used in preparing the miso and koji. Although such insects cannot live in the miso and are not believed to represent a health danger, food inspectors and miso makers take every precaution to ensure that miso shops are free of them.

In the same way that grapes were traditionally treaded to make wine, the mixture in the vats is now mashed underfoot to remove air pockets in which alien molds might grow or liquid might accumulate. Its surface is carefully leveled and covered first with a cloth sealing-sheet and then a pressing-lid which fits snugly down inside the vat's mouth, thereby preventing the growth of surface molds. While not actually harmful, such molds cause a decline in the miso's aroma and flavor. The lid is then weighted with heavy stones to force a small amount of liquid (*miso-damari*) to the surface, creating a sealed, airtight (anaerobic) environment. This is ideal for the activity of the anaerobic bacteria and yeasts which will later gain predominance; it also prevents the entry of contaminating microorganisms. In many shops, a second sheet is tied over the the vat's mouth to keep out dust, insects, and the like.

During the first fermentation, the number of molds per gram of substrate had increased from about 13,000 to 295,000. Now, with the work of these molds finished the highly sensitive mycelium dies from the lack of oxygen and high salinity in the environment. But the work of enzymes left behind is about to begin.

Inside the vat, the enzymes begin breaking down—actually digesting—the nutritional components of soybeans and grains. Three basic enzymes are active: protease works on protein, amylase on carbohydrates, and lipase on lipids (oils and fats) (fig. 48). In this chemical process—technically known as hydrolysis—the reaction of water ions with the basic food nutrients produces a weak acid which transforms complex molecules into simpler ones that can be more easily assimilated by the body.

The enzyme protease converts soy protein molecules first into polypeptides and peptides, and then into more than 18 simple amino acids. The main soy protein is glycinin (80% to 90%) and the predominant resulting amino acid is glutamic acid, the active ingredient in the refined chemical seasoning known variously as MSG, monosodium glutamate, *aji-no-moto*, or Accent. These natural amino acids—and particularly glutamic—give the miso much of its flavor and some of its color, while also softening and mellowing the inherent sharpness of the miso's salt.

The enzyme amylase—with the help of a small amount of maltose—reduces starches in the koji to simple sugars and polysaccharides, primarily glucose, but also maltose, dextrose, and dextrin. These in turn serve as fermentable sugars for yeasts and bacteria which are soon to come upon the scene. About 80 to 90 percent of the proteins and starches in the soybeans and koji grains are broken down into simpler substances by the action of these microorganisms.

Since a large part of the starch is saccharified, miso that initially contained a large percentage of grain koji is sweet, whereas miso made from soybean koji (which is low in starch) is not.

The enzyme lipase transforms the 18 percent lipids contained in soybeans into simple free fatty acids, which assume a variety of different forms in the finished miso. The esters of some of these contribute to the miso's aroma.

At each stage of its development, miso is teeming with multitudes of living microorganisms. Continuous and multiple changes in the fermentation call forth different and specialized varieties one after another, each with its own part to play. These microorganisms are all *plants* (more specifically fungi and bacteria) that are halophilic (salt tolerant) and, in many cases, osmophilic (thriving in a medium of high osmotic pressure). Although anaerobic bacteria and yeasts are favored by the airtight environment, aerobic bacteria also manage to survive on the oxygen incorporated into the basic ingredients before they were packed into the vats.

As the process of enzymatic digestion nears completion, fermentation by yeasts and bacteria (many of which were supplied by the seed miso or pure-culture inoculum) assumes predominance. Working in a sealed environment with plenty of nutrients, the anaerobic bacteria suddenly increase in number from 10 million to 930 million per gram of substrate. One of the most important and abundant of these is *Lactobacillus*, the lactic acid bacteria used as yogurt, cheese, and butter starters. After the miso ingredients have been in the keg for two to three months under natural conditions, these bacteria assume dominance and begin to transform sugars into various acids (especially lactic and acetic); the acids in turn impart a subtle mellow

Fig. 48. The Interactions of Basic Miso Components (Adapted from *Miso Fermentation*, Shibasaki & Hesseltine, 1962)

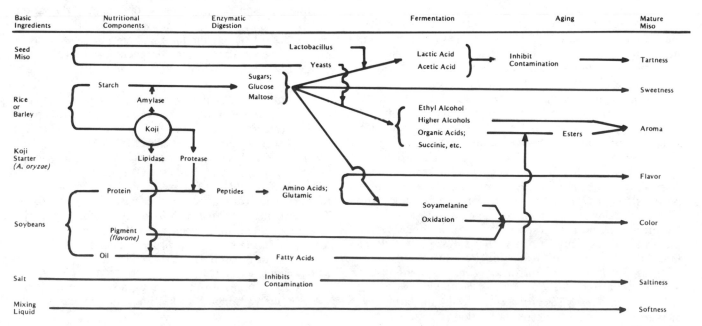

sourness to the finished miso and also assist in preventing spoilage.

Soon various yeasts begin their work of alcoholic fermentation. Consuming sugars, they produce alcohols (ethyl and higher varieties) and organic acids (especially succinic); the higher alcohols contribute to miso's pleasant bouquet and the organic acids to its flavor. Some varieties of yeasts make a film on the miso surface, while also contributing to the aroma.

As various substances are created by enzymatic digestion and bacterial or yeast fermentation, they begin to react chemically with one another. The full complexity of this interaction is illustrated in figure 48. Organic acids react with ethyl- and higher alcohols, with free fatty acids, or with acetic acid to produce esters (a primary aromatic element in fruits and flowers), which become the chief components of miso's bouquet. In quick miso, the distinctive fragrance of esters and alcohols often appears after only eight to ten days of fermentation. Amino acids react with sugars to produce red or brown pigments (soyamelanine), which combine with the soybean pigment flavone and deepen in color due to oxidation as the miso matures. Since amino acids play the dual role of enhancing flavor and deepening color, it is often said that miso with the richest color also has the richest flavor.

The cooking and fermentation processes deactivate trypsin inhibitors and other unfavorable substances such as hemagglutins and saponins, while simultaneously eliminating carbonyl compounds such as hexanol that sometimes carry a beany flavor. As these successive chemical changes continue quietly and leisurely inside the apparently dormant vats, the individual particles, first of the koji and then of the soybeans, slowly break down and merge to form the unique miso texture. Students of the biodynamic teaching of Rudolph Steiner feel that cosmic rays entering the miso during lengthy natural fermentation also have subtle but very beneficial effects.

When miso is fermented in the traditional natural way, the vats or kegs are placed in a covered area out of direct sunlight and left to experience the rhythmic temperature changes of the four seasons. These call forth, accelerate, or slow the changes occurring in the miso mixture. Most natural miso starts its fermentation during the colder months, undergoes most of its transformation during the warmer ones, and is finally removed in the fall. Thus, it experiences a rise and fall of temperature in the form of a bell curve. When quick light-yellow miso is prepared by modern temperature-controlled fermentation, the vats are placed in large heated rooms. Over a period of about one week, the temperature is gradually raised from roughly 80°F to a high of 90°F, where it is kept for several weeks or months before being lowered back to 80°F (fig. 49). Thus, the miso experiences the same rise and fall of temperature but over a shorter period of time and at a somewhat higher temperature than that found under natural conditions. For sweet white or sweet red miso, the unfermented ingredients are packed into insulated vats while still quite hot (86°F to 90°F), then aged at the natural temperature or slightly warmer. For mellow beige, they are placed in a heated room until their interior temperature rises to 90°F, and then allowed to cool of their own accord.

Fig. 49. Temperature Control Curves for Four Quick Misos

Whereas natural miso is usually allowed to stand untouched in the kegs or vats during the entire second fermentation, quick miso is generally mixed and transferred to a new vat or epoxy-lined steel tank once or twice during the process. Supplying the yeasts and aerobic bacteria with oxygen in this way hastens the fermentation process and raises the internal temperature. In some farmhouses, too, the miso is mixed at regular intervals or at least once during the summer for the same reason. After quick miso has been removed from its heated fermentation room, it is often allowed to stand for several weeks at room temperature; this final ripening (shown on the above graphs) further improves the flavor and aroma.

The Finished Miso

Unhurried aging in rhythm with the cycle of the seasons is one of the traditional secrets for evoking the finest miso flavor. Thus, natural miso is generally found to be of higher quality than its quick modern counterpart—and it therefore commands a premium price.

When natural miso is ready, each gram contains an immense number of active and beneficial microorganisms: 4,000 molds, 6,000 yeasts, 1.5 million aerobic bacteria, and 2 million anaerobic bacteria. Remarkably, the salt in miso exerts a selective action on the full range of microorganisms present, favoring those which are beneficial to human beings and which contribute to the miso flavor. If salt were not present, a toxic anaerobic bacterial fermentation would occur. Furthermore, because only the heartiest microorganisms can survive the rigors of months and years in miso's largely anaerobic, saline environment, they are very well suited to continue their ceaseless activity of breaking down complex food molecules after they have entered the human digestive tract. Thus the salt, in addition to acting as a preservative, also functions as a "sentient" agent for the human palate and digestive system. In the same way, lactic acid inhibits the growth of many contaminating bacteria, and most of the beneficial microorganisms present are actively antagonistic to the few dangerous varieties *(Staphylococcus aureus* and *Escherichia coli)* which cause food poisoning. Consequently, repeated tests conducted at laboratories throughout the world have shown that miso is free of all toxins, including those called aflatoxins.

The finest miso is sold in wooden kegs in the same form in which it emerges from the fermentation vats with all its microscopic flora alive and vital. Indeed, the principal reason miso is usually cooked only briefly—if at all—is precisely because the beneficial microorganisms (especially lactic acid bacteria) and enzymes they contain are easily destroyed by prolonged exposure to high temperatures. Unfortunately, much of the miso sold today in sealed polyethylene bags is pre-pasteurized by means of prolonged heating (140°F) in order to stop the microorganisms from producing carbon dioxide which causes the bags to swell. In some cases, preservatives are also added for the same purpose. Both of these newly-invented processes cause a definite decline in the miso fragrance and flavor—while also reducing its value as a food. Hence the best miso is that prepared by traditional natural fermentation methods and sold without additives or pasteurization. Many such varieites are now available throughout the West.

Edo period shoyu production

Appendix D
Miso Manufacturers in the West

USA AND CANADA

CALIFORNIA

Baldwin Park 91706—Miyako Oriental Foods, 4287 Puente Ave. Ph. 213-962-9633. Teruo Shimizu. America's largest miso company. Makers of Cold Mountain brand red miso, light-yellow miso, mellow white miso, and rice koji, distributed by Mutual Trading Co. and various natural-food distributors. A division of Yamajirushi miso company in Japan.

HAWAII

Honolulu/Oahu 96819—American Hawaiian Soy Co. 274 Kalihi St. Ph. 808-841-8435. Harry Morita. Produces white miso, sometimes sold in cans, distributed by Mutual Trading Co. in Los Angeles.

Honolulu/Oahu 96817—Parks Brand Products, 145 N King St., Stand 53. Ph. 808-536-4074. A small producer of Korean miso/jang.

Oahu 96819— Hawaiian Miso & Soy Co. 1714 Mary St. Ph. 808-841-7354. William Higa. Hawaii's largest miso maker. Emphasizes traditional, natural miso made without any additives. Produces mainly mellow white miso but also a small amount of red. Sold under the brand name "Maruhi," this miso is widely distributed by Nishimoto Trading Co. in Los Angeles and some natural-food companies.

MASSACHUSETTS

Conway 01341—South River Miso Co. South River Farm. Ph. 413-369-4057. Christian & Gaella Elwell. Beautiful traditional shop.

MISSOURI

Jamestown 65046—Imagine Foods/Moniteau Farm, RR 1 Box 11. Ph. 816-849-2583. Dale Deraps and David Carlson. Small homestead miso shop.

NORTH CAROLINA

Rutherfordton 28139—American Miso Inc, Rte 3 Box 541. Ph. 704-287-2940. John Belleme. America's second largest miso company. Traditional and modern nicely blended.

NEW JERSEY

Holmdel 07733—General Oriental Foods, 20 Longview Dr. Ph. 201-264-8754. Mr. Chong.

WASHINGTON

Belleview 98005—Junsei Yamazaki Miso Co. 13440 SE Eastgate Way. Ph. 206-747-6939.

WISCONSIN

Gays Mills 54631—Cottage Miso, RR 2, Box 83. Ph. 608-872-2135. David McGovern.

CANADA

Denman Island BC V0R1T0—Shinmei-Do Miso, Wren Rd. Ph. 604-335-0253. Yasuo & Lulu Yoshihara.

Vancouver BC 6—T Amano Co Ltd, 1139 E Hastings St. Ph. 604-254-3943. George Tsuchiya. Also makes shoyu.

EUROPE

AUSTRIA

Merzg 34—Weg Der Natur, A2380 Perchtoldsdorf. Lawrence Dreyer.

BELGIUM

Bruxelles—Takanami Miso Shop, 128 Rue Des Treffles. Ph. 025228192. Takanami. Red miso.

Sint-Martens-Latem 9830—Lima Foods, Edgar Gevaertdreef 10. Ph. 09-52-4176. A macrobiotic for three generations, Pierre is head of the Lima Factory and one of the founders of the first miso shop in Europe.

ENGLAND

E Sussex BN71XH—Full of Beans Wholefoods, 97 High St Lewes. Ph. 079162627. John & Sara Gosling.

FRANCE

Baillestavy 66320—Miso, Mas Miquelet. Ab & Paulien Schaft.

Herault—Communante De L'arche. La Boire Noble, 34260 Le Bousquet D'orb.

Ris Orangis—Jacquot Roland, 10 Rue Bretagne 91390.

Mezin 47170—Lima-Andiran, Moulin D'andiran. Ph. 58651002. Pierre Gevaert. Barley Miso.

Poisy 74330—Les Sept Marches. Les Cruesettes, Chemin Des Mouille.

SWEDEN

19063 Orsundsbro S19063—Aros Sojaprodukter. Bergvagen 1. Ph. 017160456. Ted Nordquist & Tim Ohlund.

SWITZERLAND

Nyon CH-1260—Soy Joy, Chemin De La Prelsz 1. Ph. 022619312. Marty Halsey.

LATIN AMERICA

BRAZIL

Campinas, S.P.—Tozan, Bairro Carlos Gomes.

Mogi das Cruzes, S.P.—Industria & Comercio de Molhos Leguvita Ltda, Rua Heliotropos 595. Tel: 469-0320. Leguvita miso

Ribeirao Pires, S.P.—Masakazu Takai, Rua Venceslau Braz S/N C.P. 136. Tel: 459-3303. Marutaka miso.

Sao Paulo, S.P.—Maruviti, Rua Ibituruna 264, Jabaquara. Tel: 275-4533.

Sao Paulo, S.P.—Sakura-Nakaya Alimentos, Rua Ordenacoes 151, C.P. 16131. Tel: 295-4117.

Vila Idelandia Suzano, S.P.—Takai & Cia Ltda., Estrada de Suzano a Ribeirao Pires Km 11. Tel: 476-1447. Kikko miso.

Appendix E
People and Institutions Connected with Miso

PEOPLE AND INSTITUTIONS IN JAPAN

In the following references, all Japanese personal names are written in the standard Japanese manner, last name first. All addresses are given in the Western style (street, ward [ku], city [shi], prefecture [ken], and zip code), rather than in the reverse Japanese style.

Miso Research Scholars and Institutes

Akizuki Shinichiro: St. Francis Hospital, Hongen Machi 2-535, Nagasaki, Japan. A practicing physician and hospital director, Dr. Akizuki has experimented widely using miso and miso soup to prevent radiation sickness and maintain health (p. 26). His findings are presented in a pamphlet entitled *Physical Constitution and Food* (p. 248).

Ebine Hideo: Norinsho Shokuhin Sogo Kenkyujo, Shiohama 1-4-12, Koto-ku, Tokyo 135. Tel: 03-645-9911. Head of the fermentation division of the prestigious National Food Research Institute, Dr. Ebine is also the author of many English-language articles about miso.

Japanese National Miso Association: Zenkoku Miso Kogyo Kyodo Kumiai Rengokai, Shinkawa 1-26-19, Chuo-ku, Tokyo 104. Tel: 03-551-7161. Mr. Fujimori Denei, director; Mr. Miyachi Kazuo, executive vice president, and Mr. Matsushita Zenichi, fact finder. The coordinating body for all miso shops and factories in Japan. Also operates a large miso research lab.

Kawamura Wataru: Kugenuma 2373, Fujisawa-shi 251. Tel: 0466-22-1351. Author of several of Japan's most popular books about miso, widely known as Japan's "miso sensei" (teacher), and former director of publicity for the National Miso Association, Mr. Kawamura describes himself as a scholar (and lover) of miso soup.

Mochizuki Tsutomu: Director of the Shinshu Miso Research Institute in Nagano city (see below), Dr. Mochizuki is the leading expert on modern Shinshu miso.

Morishita Keiichi: Morishita Eiyo Kyoshitsu, Bunkyoku, Hongo 2-3-10, Tokyo. Tel:03-814-6786. An expert on the nutritional and health-given value of miso. Dr. Morishita is an M.D. who heads a hospital and nutritional research center in Tokyo. The author of more than 30 books, he has for many years advocated the value of traditional Japanese fermented soyfoods.

Murakami Hideya: Kokuritsu Jozo Shikenjo, Takinogawa, Kita-ku, Tokyo. Director of the National Fermented Foods Research Institute and a well-known scholar of *A. oryzae* molds.

Nakano Masahiro: Meiji Daigaku, Ikuta Kosha, Ikuta 5158, Kawasaki-shi, Kanagawa-ken 214. Tel: 044-911-8181. The dean of miso scholars and teacher of Drs. Ebine and Mochizuki, Dr. Nakano is professor of microbiology at Meiji University where he directs a laboratory engaged in the study of miso and other fermented foods.

Ouchi Ichiro, c/o Yamajirushi, Komome 3-15-1, Itabashi-ku, Tokyo. Tel: 03-972-3151. Formerly of the Shinshu Miso Research Institute, he spent one year in the U.S. at the Northern Regional Research Center developing new foods incorporating miso as a flavoring agent.

Sakaguchi Kinichiro: Takabon 3-17-4, Meguro-ku, Tokyo 152. Tel: 712-7033. A retired scholar of koji molds, Dr. Sakaguchi received the Emperor's medal of honor for his research work. He now publishes a magazine on foods with frequent articles on miso and shoyu.

Shibasaki Kazuo: Tohoku University, Nogaku-bu, Shokuhin Kagaku-ka, Kita 6 Banchi. Sendai-shi. Dr. Shibasaki spent 1958 and 1959 in the U.S. doing research on miso at the NRRL. He has co-authored many English-language articles on miso with Dr. Clifford Hesseltine and other researchers, and is now a consultant for the Sendai Miso-Shoyu Company.

Shinshu Miso Research Institute: Shinshu Miso Kenkyujo, 469-6 Nakagosho, Nagano-shi 380. Tel: 0262-28-1221. Under the directon of Dr. Mochizuki, this large and prestigious organization is doing basic scientific and technological research on miso production.

Exporters of Natural Miso and Koji to the West

Muso Co. Ltd., Export Dept. Otedori 2-5-1, Higashi-ku, Osaka 540 Japan. Tel: 06-945-0511. Yuko Okada.

Mitoku Co. Ltd., C.P.O. Box 780, Tokyo 100-91; Marunouchi Bldg., Marunouchi, Tokyo. Tel: 03-201-6706 thru 8. Mr. Akiyoshi Kazama, director.

Traditional or Semi-traditional Shops Making Natural Miso

Amanoya: Makers of Finger Lickin'- and sweet red miso, as well as koji and *amazaké* (see p. 240).

Arai Miso Ten: Suwa, Mitsukaido-shi, 2765, Ibaragi-ken. Tel: 0297-2-0274.

Fuchu Miso: Honmachi, Fuchu-shi, Hiroshima-ken. Tel: 0847-41-2080. Mr. Kanemitsu Yanosuke, director. The main supplier of natural barley miso to the West via Muso Shokuhin. Fuchu also produces natural Kinzanji miso and quick rice miso.

Hayakawa Kyuemon Shoten (also called Hatcho Miso Kakkyu Goshi-kaisha): Aza, Okan-dori 69, Hatcho-cho, Okazaki-shi, Aichi-ken 444. Tel: 0564-21-0151. Mr. Kaneko, director; Mr. Hayakawa Kyuemon, 18th proprietor. Located near Nagoya in Central Japan on the banks of the Yahagi river (once famous for its fine artesian wells and *Yahagi* soybeans), this company is the largest and best known of Japan's two very old makers of natural Hatcho miso—both of which are located on the same block. Said to have been established in 1362 (but thought by scholars to have originated in its present form about 350 to 400 years ago). Hayakawa is the proud supplier of the Imperial Household Agency. They presently transform about 50 percent of their Hatcho miso into akadashi miso.

Horikawa-ya: Gobo-shi, Toyota-shi, Aichi-ken. A traditional maker of natural Kinzanji miso.

Ikeda Kojiro Miso Shoten: Motogo 4-8-24, Kawaguchi-shi. Saitama-ken 332. Tel: 0482-22-6766. A traditional maker of natural barley miso located near Tokyo, Ikeda now exports to the U.S. and also produces quick rice miso.

Kantoya Shoten Matsumoto-cho 582, Ebisugawa Noboru, Gokochodori, Nakagyo-ku, Kyoto. Tel: 231-1728 or 211-4371. A maker of traditional red miso, this shop has a fine koji incubation room.

Kawasaki Shoten: Nishi Arie-cho, Minami Takagi-gun, Nagasaki-ken, Kyushu. A maker of traditional, natural Finger Lickin' (natto miso) and sweet barley miso.

Kawasho Miso Shoten: Kaizan-cho 3-145, Sakai-shi, Osaka 590. Tel: 0722-33-1061. A maker of delicious, traditional Kinzanji miso.

Meiji Seifun, Fuchu-machi 536, Fuchu-shi, Hiroshima-ken 726. Tel: 0874-41-2255. A maker of natural barley and red miso.

Nagata Tozaimon: Hatonaka 133, Aza, Taketoyo-cho, Kita-gun, Aichi-ken 470-23. Tel: 05697-2-0341. A maker of natural soybean miso and shoyu.

Ota Shoten: Okan-dori 52, Hatcho-cho, Okazaki-shi, Aichi-ken 444. Tel: 0564-22-0222. Mr. Kato Choichi, director. The second largest maker of Hatcho miso in Japan, Ota produces 1,000 tons annually and an additional 1,500 tons of one-year soybean miso (*waka Hatcho*). Their prices are relatively low.

Sendai Miso-Shoyu Inc.: Furujiro 1-5-1, Sendai-shi, 982. Tel: 0222-86-3151. Mr. Sasaki Kenichiro, director; Mr. Sasaki Shigeo, managing director; Mr. Haga Hiroshi, production director. The largest miso maker in the northeast provinces and the largest producer of Sendai-type red miso in Japan, this company produces much of the natural red miso (and shoyu) now imported into the United States. Their miso is aged 18 to 24 months, and their shoyu (made from whole soybeans) 18 months. They also make a natural brown-rice miso and a 6-month red miso using the most modern techniques of temperature-controlled fermentation. The company is now thinking about starting to produce miso in the United States. They have recently developed an excellent color film about the commercial production of miso and shoyu, available direct from Sendai or via Mitoku (above), and they hold an exclusive patent on the process of packaging (pasteurized) miso in sealed bags without the use of alcohol or other preservatives.

Shiromizu Shoten: Meihama-cho 3135, Nishi-ku, Fukuoka-shi, Fukuoka-ken 814. Tel: 092-881-0413. A maker of natural barley miso.

Suyamo Shoten: Ashida 2618, Tateshina-cho, Kitasaku-gun, Nagano-ken 384-23. Tel: 02675-6-1001. A maker of traditional Shinshu miso.

Tsuchiya Miso-shoyu: Higashi Yokomachi 383, Susaka-shi, Nagano-ken 383. Tel: 02624-5-0259. A producer of natural Shinshu miso.

Tsujita Miso Shoten: Kojiya Saburo Uemon, Nakamura 2-29-8, Nerima-ku, Tokyo 176. Tel: 03-999-2276. Mr. Tsujita Kiyoshi, master. A very old shop using traditional, natural methods, this firm makes 18- and 24-month brown-rice miso, 3-year chunky barley miso, ready-made dried koji, and brown-rice *amazaké*. Tsujita uses organic rice, natural sea salt, and the finest Hokkaido-grown *tsurunoko* soybeans. The producer of all brown-rice miso now sold in the West, this shop was the source of much of our information about making miso in traditional shops.

Yamatoya: Adzusa Kawamura, Adzusa, Nagano-ken. Tel: 026378-2280. Producer of natural miso using *miso-dama*.

Japan's Ten Largest Miso Factories

The following, listed in order of size (using 1974 production statistics), generally prepare light-yellow miso using quick temperature-controlled fermentation methods. Details are given in Chapter 9.

1. *Miyazaka Jozo* (Shinshu ichi), Nogata 2-4-5, Nakano-ku, Tokyo 165. Tel: 03-385-2121. Mr. Watanabe Yojuro, production director. This Tokyo factory produces about 15,000 tons per year; the Nagano and Yamanashi plants produce 9,300 and 3,300 tons respectively. All make Shinshu-type light-yellow miso. Tokyo makes freeze-dried miso.

2. *Hanamaruki:* Hirade 1560, Tatsuno-cho, Oaza, Kamiina-gun, Nagano-ken 399-04. Tel: 02664-2-1321. Also produce a mellow beige miso imported to the U.S.

3. *Takeya:* Kogan-dori 2-3-17, Suwa-shi, Nagano-ken 392. Tel: 02665-2-4000.

Busy Making Dengaku (from the "Tofu Hyaku Chin")

4. *Marukome:* Amori 833, Nagano-shi, Nagano-ken 380. Tel: 0262-26-0255. Yamamoto Yasuo, production mgr. The biggest single miso factory in Japan. Makes dehydrated miso.

5. *Kanesa:* Tamagawa 202, Hamada-aza, Aomori-shi 030. Tel: 0177-39-5211.

6. *Marudai:* Ohashi, Hamochi-machi, Sado-gun, Niigata-ken 952-05. Tel: Hamochi #3 or #4. Makers of Sado-style rice miso.

7. *Marusan:* Aza-arashita 1, Jingi-cho, Okazaki-shi 444-21. Operates 3 factories.

8. *Yamajirushi:* Komome 3-15-1, Itabashi-ku, Tokyo. Tel: 03-972-3151. Other factories in Maruko City (Nagano) and Moriya City (Ibaragi). Total output is 18,000 tons per year. The Moriya plant produces 6,000 tons of *shikomi-miso* (p. 167) yearly which is sold in 20-pound quantities to farm cooperatives, whence it is distributed to farm families.

9. *Ichibiki:* Shinto-machi 14, Atsuda-ku, Nagoya-shi. Also operates a factory in Toyohashi.

10. *Kaneko:* Aizumi-machi Okuno, Itano-gun, Tokushima-shi. Output is 11,000 tons per year.

Other Makers of Fine Miso

Abumata Miso Co.: Honmachi 3-32-19, Nakano-ku, Tokyo. Tel: 372-5211. Mr. Takeyama, director of production. A large producer of sweet red miso.

Amadaya: Nakamura Fujio, Gobo 1, Gobo-shi, Wakayama-ken. Tel: 07382-2-0455. A maker of delicious Kinzanji and moromi misos, containing lots of koji and uri melons.

Ebiya: Azumbashi 1-15-55, Sumida-ku, Asakusa, Tokyo. Tel: 03-625-0003. A producer of high-quality Peanut and Tekka Miso.

Echigo Miso Jozo, Yoshida 5884, Yoshida Machi, Nishi Tanbara-gun, Niigata-ken, Tel: 02569-2-4805. A maker of natural Kinzanji miso.

Ezaki Honten: Ebisu machi 902, Shimbara-shi, Nagasaki-ken 855. Tel: 2-3161. Mr. Shibata. A large and well-known producer of natural miso pickles.

Hagoromo Miso: Fuchu-machi 533-3. Fuchu-shi, Hiroshima-ken 726, Tel: 0847-41-2010. A main source of the natural barley miso sold in the U.S. Also makes a sweet white miso.

Hamamoto: Osaki 1-19-6, Shinagawa-ku, Tokyo. Tel: 03-493-0885. A maker of Kinzanji miso.

Hinode Miso Brewing Co., 3567 Shimo-Oyamada-Machi, Machida-shi, Tokyo 194-01. Mr. Tetsuo Fumoto. Tel: 0427-97-2311. Makers of Peanut Miso, Peanut & Raisin Miso, and Glutinous-rice Miso *(Mochigome miso),* each sealed in small plastic packets for easy export and sale.

Honda Miso Honten: Ichijo Agaru, Muromachi-dori, Kamikyo-ku, Kyoto 558. Tel. 075-441-1121. Mr. Honda Shigeru, fourth generation owner. One of Japan's best known makers of sweet white miso, Honda is a relatively traditional shop and is unique in preparing one natural variety without the use of preservatives (ethyl alcohol is used) or bleach. Honda's sweet white miso is sold under the registered brand name "Saikyo Miso" meaning "Western Kyoto Miso." Honda also produces akadashi and red miso.

Ichikyu Miso: Tokiwacho 2-15, Higashi-ku, Osaka. Tel: 941-09-4154. A maker of moromi miso.

Ishino Miso Co.: Ishiizutsu-cho, Shijo Kudaru, Aburakoji, Shim-okyoku, Kyoto. Tel: 075-361-2336. One of Japan's two large producers of sweet white and akadashi miso. At present they do not export.

Ishiyama Miso Shoyu: Nigata-shi. Tel: 0252-28-2034. Mr. Kinji Ishiyama, exec. v.p. A maker of low-salt miso.

Iwanaga Shoyu Gomei-gaisha: Sashiki, Ashikita-machi, Ashikita-gun, Kumamoto-ken. A maker of natural chunky barley miso.

Kageju Shokuhin, Yawata 1-4-41, Shizuoka-shi, Shizuoka-ken. A maker of natural Kinzanji miso.

Kame-gen Jozo: Suwa 2-4-8, Suwa-shi, Nagano-ken. A maker of buckwheat miso containing buckwheat groats, soybeans, salt, and alcohol preservative.

Kirishima Food Co.: Okubo 65-1, Kirishima-cho, Kagoshima-ken. Japan's primary maker of Yubeshi Miso.

Marui Jozo: Azuma-cho 56, Iida-shi, Nagano-ken. Tel: 0265-22-6363. A maker of miso pickles. Uses wild mountain vegetables and Shinshu miso.

Nagano Miso Co.: Tenjin 3-9-29, Ueda-shi, Nagano-ken 386. Tel: 02682-4-7771. Mr. Hideki Oka, president. A maker of salt-free and traditional misos.

Nakamuraya Shoten: Yaji 3225, Tokuyama-shi, Yamaguchi-ken. Tel: 0834-62-3108 or 9. The maker of the delicious Hana-bishi brand sweet white miso now widely available in the U.S. both in 1-pound cartons or 35-pound kegs.

Sanjirushi Jozo: Meisei-dori 1-572-1, Kuwana-shi 511. Tel: 0594-22-3333. Tokyo office: 03-722-4433. Japan's largest maker of soybean miso. A larger maker of natural real tamari.

Sanman Kajimaya Shoten: Chuo 3-1-5, Okaya-shi, Nagano-ken. A maker of brown-rice miso.

Shinsho Miso Jozo: Sanjo-machi 3-12-23, Hiroshima-shi, Hiroshima-ken. A maker of Eiyaku brand brown-rice miso.

Shinshu Miso K.K.: Aramachi, Komoro-shi, Nagano-ken 384. Tel: 02672-2-0007. Mr. Koyama Masakuni, director. Head office: Shimo Ochiai 3-17-38, Shinjuku-ku, Tokyo 161. Tel: 03-951-1141. Mr. Koyama Kunitomo. A large producer of Shinshu miso, sold in the U.S. and Japan under the brand name "Yamabuki."

Shinshu Sennichi Miso K.K.: Kamimachi 82, Susaka-shi, Nagano-ken. Tel: 02624-5-0958. One of the first makers of natural miso to use natural (unrefined) salt.

Shoman K.K.: Nagisa 2-32, Matsumoto-shi, Nagano-ken. Makers of instant miso soup sold in a box with dehydrated tofu, leeks, wakame, dashi; and a tiny packet of fresh miso.

Yamanaga Miso: Hyakunin-cho 2-8-1, Shinjuku-ku, Tokyo. Tel: 03-371-9146. A maker of traditional-type miso.

Yorosho Honpo: Yuasa-machi Yokocho 519, Arita-gun, Wakayama-ken. Tel. 07376-2-2318. A maker of Kinzanji miso.

Yoshida Shohachi: Takashima-cho 382, Shimabara-shi, Nagasaki-ken 855. Tel: 09576-2-4107. The sole supplier of the natural natto (finger lickin') miso now sold in the U.S.

Yoshino-ya Jozo (Zenkoji Miso): Nishi-no-mon, Nagano-shi, Nagano-ken, Japan. Tel: 34-1171. A famous old maker of Shinshu light yellow miso.

MAKERS OF KOJI STARTER AND KOJI

Amanoya Kojiten: Soto Kanda 2-18-15, Chiyoda-ku, Tokyo. Tel: 03-251-7911. Mr. Amano Yaichi. A very old, traditional and beautiful shop preparing ready-made koji, some of which they use in the *amazaké* sold in their restaurant. The koji is fermented in long, earth-walled tunnels 20 feet beneath the streets of Tokyo. They also make delicious, natural Finger Lickin', and sweet red miso.

Hishiroku: A traditional Kyoto maker of koji starter. Tel: 075-541-4141.

Kojiya Sanzaemon Roho: Shimotachiuri-sagaru, Omiya-dori, Kami-kyo-ku, Kyoto. A traditional koji maker.

Amanoya Kojiten: Soto Kanda 2-18-15, Chiyoda-ku, Tokyo. Tel: 03-251-7911. Mr. Amano Yaichi. A very old, traditional and beautiful shop preparing ready-made koji, some of which they use in the *amazaké* sold in their restaurant. The koji is fermented in long, earth-walled tunnels 20 feet beneath the streets of Tokyo. They also make delicious, natural Finger Lickin', and sweet red miso.

Hishiroku: A traditional Kyoto maker of koji starter. Tel: 075-541-4141.

Kojiya Takahashi: Agebocho, Toyota-shi, Aichi-ken 471. Tel: 0565-32-1323. A traditional maker of Kinzanji koji.

Nihon Jozo Kogyo: Sales office: Koishigawa 3-18-9, Bunkyo-ku, Tokyo 112. Tel: 03-816-2951. Factory: Higashiori-ue, Iishi-aza, Oaza, Juo-machi, Taga-gun, Ibaragi-ken. Tel: 0293-32-2307. Mr. Niimi Yasu, director; Mr. Chiba Akira, ass't. director. The Japan Brewing Co. is a large, reliable producer of koji starter used for both miso and shoyu and sold under the brand name of Marufuku Moyashi. This company was the source of much of our information on preparing koji starter.

Tokai Hakko Kagaku Kenkyujo: Ichigen 1712, Toyoda mura, Iwata-gun, Shizuoka-ken. A traditional maker of miso koji starter.

*Cutting tofu for Dengaku
(from the "Tofu Hyaku Chin")*

JAPANESE RESTAURANTS SPECIALIZING IN MISO CUISINE

Dengaku: Komachi 1-6-5, Kamakura-shi, Kanagawa-ken. Tel: 0467-23-2121. Dengaku cookery at its best in a charming atmosphere.

Nakamura-ro: Yasaka Jinja-nai, Higashiyama-ku, Kyoto. Tel: 075-561-4589. Delicious Dengaku and *amazaké.*

Shiru Hatchi: Ginza 8-chome, Tokyo. Tel: 571-0456. Popular and inexpensive miso soups.

PEOPLE AND INSTITUTIONS IN NORTH AMERICA

MISO RESEARCHERS AND INSTITUTES

Hesseltine, Clifford W.: Known for his outstanding research as a mycologist, Dr. Hesseltine has had a lifelong interest in miso and has written many articles on the subject. Past President of the Mycological Society of America, he is presently director of the fermentation laboratory of the NRRC (below).

Northern Regional Research Center (USDA/NRRC): 1815 North University St., Peoria, IL 61604. Tel: 309-685-4011. The main center for miso research in North America, the NRRC offers a good selection of scientific-journal articles on miso fermentation as well as pure-culture koji starters. Directed by Dr. Clifford W. Hesseltine, who is assisted by Dr. Hwa L. Wang, the fermentation laboratory has sponsored miso researchers from Japan, including Dr. Kazuo Shibasaki and Dr. Ichiro Ouchi.

Wang, Hwa L.: A woman working at the NRRC fermentation research lab, Dr. Wang has extensive experience in the field of miso and has written articles on the subject.

COMPANIES IMPORTING JAPANESE MISO, KOJI, OR KOJI STARTER

American Pacific Trading International Inc.: 2309 East 8th St., Los Angeles, CA 90021. Tel. 213-622-0422. Importers of Yamabuki brand miso from the Shinshu Miso Company in Komoro, Nagano prefecture.

Chico-San, Inc., P.O. Box 810, Chico, CA 95927. Tel: 916-891-6271. Importers of koji and various natural misos.

Eden Foods Inc., 701 Clinton-Tecumseh, Clinton, MI 49236. Tel: 517-456-7424. An importer of natural miso and shoyu.

Edward & Sons Trading Co., Route 1 Box 153, Saluda, NC 28773. Tel: 704-749-9666. Importers of instant freeze-dried miso soup sold as "Miso-Cup."

Erewhon Inc., 5 Waltham St., Wilmington, MA 01887. Tel: 617-657-8120. Importers of all basic miso types.

GEM Cultures, 30301 Sherwood Rd., Ft. Bragg, CA 95437. Tel: 707-964-2922. Gordon McBride. Presently America's best source of koji starters for many types of miso and shoyu. Their starter is imported from Japan's finest producers.

JFC International, Inc.: 445 Kaufman Ct., So. San Francisco, CA 94080. Tel: 415-873-8400. Or 1131 So. Mateo St., Los Angeles. Tel: 213-627-6534. Importers of more than 15 varieites of Japanese miso.

Kagemuri, T., 8578 Birnom St., Montreal, Quebec H3M 2V3, Canada. An importer of natural miso.

Kikkoman International, 50 California St., Suite 3600, San Francisco, CA 94111. Tel: 415-956-7750. Mr. Terumitsu Hattori. Importers of red miso which they dehydrate (and mix with dehydrated tofu plus land-and-sea vegetables) to make their instant miso soup, now sold in many supermarkets.

Lifestream, 12411 Vulcan Way, Richmond, B.C. Canada V6V 1J7. Tel: 604-278-7571. Or 91 Esna Park Dr., Markhah, Ont, Canada L3R 2S2. Tel: 416-475-6836. An importer of natural miso.

Manna Foods Inc., 112 Crockford Blvd., Scarborough, Ontario, M1R 3C3 Canada. Tel: 416-759-4108. An importer of natural miso.

Marusan Foods Corp., 8780 E. Valley Blvd., Rosemead, CA 91770. Tel: 213-571-8997. Importer of instant miso soups.

Mutual Trading Co., 431 Crocker St., Los Angeles, CA 90013. Tel: 213-626-9458. Mr. Noritoshi Kanai. Importers of light-yellow miso and distributors of miso and koji made by Miyako Oriental Foods, their subsidiary.

Nishimoto Trading Co.: 1884 E. 22nd St., Los Angeles, CA 90013. Tel: 213-747-4111. Importers of Hawaiian mellow white miso.

Soken Trading Co., Box 1705, Sausalito, CA 94965. Tel: 415-332-2313. Importers of various misos.

Tree of Life Inc., 315 Industrial Drive, St. Augustine, FL 32084. Tel: 904-829-3284. Importer of miso.

Westbrae Natural Foods, 4240 Hollis St., Emeryville, CA 94608. Tel: 415-658-7518. Importers of brown-rice, red, barley, Hatcho, and Finger Lickin' (natto) miso. Also distribute U.S.-made koji and miso.

INDIVIDUALS INTERESTED IN MISO

The following list of names, although quickly outdated, may prove helpful in bringing together people interested in miso.

Aihara, Cornellia and Herman: c/o GOMF, 902 14th St. Oroville, CA 95965. Tel: 916-533-7702 or 9900. Cornellia has given classes in miso making and miso cookery, and has prepared barley koji commercially. Herman has written and spoken extensively about miso; his books include *Miso and Tamari* and *Soybean Diet*.

Kendall, Charlie: Kendall Food Co., P.O. Box 69, Ashburnham, MA 01430. Tel: 617-827-6236. Research.

Kerrigan, Rick: 688 Capp St., San Francisco, CA 94110. Tel: 415-282-9909. Doing miso research.

Kushi, Aveline and Michio, 62 Buckminster Rd., Brookline, MA 02146. Tel: 617-232-6869. Aveline has taught miso making and cookery. Michio has taught thousands of people about the many virtues of miso, and numerous members of his macrobiotic community have experience making miso at home.

Muramoto, Noboru: 145 W. El Norte Parkway, Escondido, CA 92026. Tel: 714-743-6890. Teacher of many students now active in making miso. Note that his first name is spelled Noboru, not Naboru.

Shrift, Eric: P.O. Box 25, Andes Land Project, Andes, NY 13731. A student of N. Muramoto who plans to produce miso and teach miso-making classes.

Truslow, Will: 36 Hempstead Rd., Jamaica Plain, MA 02130. A student of N. Muramoto who makes miso at home and gives miso-making classes through the Kushi Institute in Boston.

Yamazaki, Junsei: See address at miso manufacturers, App. D. A highly skilled miso craftsman, he has taught miso-making classes throughout the U.S.

PEOPLE AND INSTITUTIONS IN EUROPE

Imported natural miso is now available throughout Europe. Macrobiotic teachers have played a major role in its popularization, and have already built one large miso production center in Belgium. Please send us other names if you know of them. For names of miso manufacturers, see Appendix D.

ENGLAND

Ceres, 269 Portabello Rd., London W.11, England. Attn. Craig Sams. An importer of natural miso and shoyu.

Harmony Foods, 1 Earl Cottages, Earl Rd., London S.E. 1, England. Tel: 01-237-8396. An importer of natural miso and shoyu.

Sunwheel Food Ltd., 12 Orpheus St., Camberwell, London S.E. 5-8RT, England. Tel: 01-701-7160. Attn. Peter Bradford or Robert Harropp. An importer of natural miso and shoyu.

FRANCE

Le Bol en Bois, 35 rue Pascal, 75013 Paris, France. Tel: 707.2724. Attn. Mr. Noboru Sakaguchi. A natural-food center and tofu shop that imports natural miso.

Mittler, Jacques: Route de la Montagne d'age, F-74330 Le Lechat, Poisy, France. Makes miso.

Roland, Jacquot: 10 Rue Bretagne, 91 390 Ris Orangis, France. Makes miso.

Yoshimi, Clim: Institute Yin/Yang-Tenryu of Paris, 8 rue Rochebrune, Paris 75011, France. Tel: 805-9135. Chief editor of the macrobiotic monthly magazine *Principe Unique*. Tenryu imports natural miso and shoyu.

GERMANY (WEST)

Nakamura, Jiro: Ubersetzung und Verlag, Münsterstrasse 255, 4 Düsseldorf, West Germany. Tel. 632-443. A translator, publisher, and teacher, he is one of the key figures introducing miso to Europe.

Rabenau, Detlef von: Am Seenfer 15, D-8194 Ambach, West Germany. Tel: 08177-8488. Interested in miso.

Weghaupt, Mascha and Thomas Lüttge: 800 Munchen 2, Theresienstr, 68, West Germany. Interested in miso.

ITALY

Blanchini, Gilberto: Centro Macrobiotico, Via Cuoco 9, 47037 Rimini, Italy. Tel: 0541-33670. Interested in miso and tofu production.

D'angella Giuseppe: V. Pasubio 16, 21047 Saronno (Varese), Italy. Making miso.

La Via Macrobiotica: C.P. 12032, 00135 Roma, Belsito, Italy. An importer of natural miso.

Romano, Silvio: Casale "Sosselva," 05010—Prado n. 123 (Terni), Italy. Interested in miso.

NETHERLANDS

Loo, Dr. Thio Goan: Dept. of Agricultural Research, Royal Tropical Institute, 63 Mauritskade, Amsterdam-Oost, Netherlands. Microbiologist interested in miso.

Manna Natural Foods, Meeuwenlaan 70, 1021 JK Amsterdam, Netherlands. An importer of natural miso and shoyu.

Nelissen, Adelbert: Stichting Oost West Centrum, Achtergracht 17-19, 1017 WL, Amsterdam, Netherlands. Tel: 020-240-203. A great place to learn about miso and natural foods.

Nelissen, Thomas: Overboslaan 13, Heemstede, Netherlands. Working with miso.

PORTUGAL

Edvardo Galamba de sa Pires: Apartado 5, Torres Novas, Portugal. An importer of natural miso.

UNIMAVE: Rua de Boa Vista. 55-2°, Lisbon-2, Portugal. Tel: 607283. An importer of natural miso.

PEOPLE AND INSTITUTIONS IN LATIN AMERICA

BRAZIL

Kikuchi, Tomio: Praca Carlos Comes 60, Sao Paolo, Brazil. A macrobiotic teacher who makes his own miso.

Zanatta, Flavio: Rua Almte Alexandrio, 3226/801, Rio G.B., Brazil. Interested in tofu and miso.

COSTA RICA

Prana: Av. Central Calles 21-23, San Jose, Costa Rica. A macrobiotic food store and importer of natural miso.

MEXICO

American Soybean Association: Rio Sena #26-201, Col. Cuauhtemoc, Mexico 5, D.F. Tel: 905-535-0659. Attn. Gil Harrison. The ASA is a source of information about buying and growing soybeans.

Takata, Maestro Ejo: Zen A.C., Avenida Revolucion #2036. San Angel, Mexico 20, D.F. A Japanese Zen priest teaching the local people about miso and other soyfoods.

Tovar, Dr. Raul: Faculty of Chemistry, Dept. of Food Science, University of Mexico, Mexico 20, D.F. An expert on miso.

Appendix F

Miso with Seafoods, Chicken and Meat

Although this is a meatless cookbook and we wholeheartedly support all the basic tenets of vegetarianism, the following information has been included for three reasons: 1) Fish and shellfish taken from un-polluted waters, barnyard fowl and hogs allowed to forage or fed scraps, and cattle or sheep grazed on land that cannot be used to grow crops can each serve as key sources of protein and other nutrients (especially in hungry countries) while also providing manure for the fields; 2) This book is, in part, a study of miso's role in Japanese cuisine and culture, and the omission of preparations using animal products would leave an incomplete picture; 3) Those moving toward a meatless diet (or away from meats and poultry toward seafoods) may like to use miso with small quantities of animal products (as most Japanese usually do) during the transition.

The various Japanese recipes fall into six basic categories, listed in the order they appear in the book. Within each category the preparations are listed in order of popularity.

Miso Toppings

Red-snapper Miso *(Taimiso):* Steam red snapper (or cod or salmon) until tender, then simmer briefly in a little sake. Add an equal weight of red or white Nerimiso and a little grated gingerroot; simmer until mixture is amber to reddish brown.

Clam Miso *(Shiguré Miso):* The word *shiguré* means "late autumn rains," reminiscent of the seashore weather at clam-digging time. Sauté clams in oil until just tender, then simmer for several minutes in a mixture of *mirin* and shoyu. Remove clams, add dashi, miso and sugar, and proceed as for Nerimiso. Add back clams and simmer briefly. Serve chilled, topped with *sansho* pepper, parsley, or grated gingerroot.

Oyster Miso *(Kaki Miso):* Combine sweet white miso, *mirin*, shoyu, and grated gingerroot in a saucepan. Add an equal volume of stock or dashi and bring to a boil. Add oysters and simmer for 5 minutes.

Pork- or Chicken Miso *(Buta- or Tori Miso):* Sauté ground or torn bits of pork or chicken in oil until tender. Add sweet white miso, sugar, *mirin* or sake, and shoyu; proceed as for Nerimiso. Serve as a topping for noodles, Cha-chiang Mien, Furofuki Daikon, Sang-chu, taro, or sweet potatoes.

Shrimp-, Abalone-, Bonita-, or Sweetfish Miso *(Ebi-, Awabi, Katsuo-, or Ayu Miso):* Prepare and serve as for Clam- or Oyster Miso.

Aemono

Nuta: Mix steamed or parboiled fish, shellfish, or squid with Vinegar Miso and one or two lightly cooked vegetables (especially leeks, wakame, or cucumbers).

Squid & Kinomé *(Ika no Kinomé-ae):* Combine fresh or lightly steamed squid with thinly-sliced, parboiled bamboo shoots. Mix with Kinomé Dressing.

Octopus & Gingerroot *(Tako no Shoga Miso-ae):* Broil octopus (or squid or abalone), slice, and mix with Gingerroot Miso Dressing.

Carp & Mustard-Vinegar *(Koi no Karashi Sumiso-ae):* Parboil whole (regular or Crucian) carp. Skin, bone, and tear into small bits. Mix with Mustard-Vinegar Miso Dressing.

Shrimp & Egg Yolk-Vinegar: Mix parboiled shrimps with Egg-Yolk Vinegar Miso.

Miso Soups and Stews

Carp Soup *(Koi Koku):* One of the few Japanese soups requiring the lengthy simmering of miso, this preparation is said to stimulate milk-flow in nursing mothers and is often used to invigorate the weak or sick. Sauté slivered burdock root in oil until tender. Add water to cover and bring to a boil. Add creamed miso and chopped carp and simmer for 2 hours (or pressure cook for 40 minutes). Stir in grated gingerroot and serve topped with slivered leeks and *sansho* pepper.

Chicken & Vegetable Miso Soup *(Satsuma-jiru):* Pre-cook chicken in water until tender. Strain stock and use to cook sliced carrot, burdock root, *daikon*, mushrooms, and leek. Add chicken and creamed miso; simmer until thick.

Pork & Vegetable Miso Stew *(Buta-jiru):* Simmer cubed pork in lightly salted water until tender. Add sliced spinach and leeks, and grated gingerroot. Stir in creamed miso and bring just to a boil.

Oyster or Fish Miso Soups *(Kaki or Sakana no Misoshiru):* Simmer seafoods in dashi until tender, then add vegetables and creamed miso. Bring just to a boil. Traditional Akadashi (p. 104) often featured oysters.

Simmered Dishes & Nabémono

Boston Mackerel Simmered with Miso *(Saba no Miso-ni):* Combine sweet white miso, sake, dashi, sugar, and grated gingerroot; bring to a boil. Add cutlets of unskinned mackerel and simmer for 15 minutes.

Oyster Nabé *(Kaki Nabé):* Combine miso, *mirin* and dashi, and bring to a boil. Add spring chrysanthemum leaves, chopped scallions, shelled oysters, and tofu; cook 3 to 4 minutes. Serve hot, dipping oysters in beaten raw eggs.

Doténabé with Oysters *(Kaki no Doténabé):* Substitute oysters for the tofu in Doténabé.

Salmon Nabé *(Ishikari Nabé):* Simmer chunks of salmon in a rich miso broth together with tofu, *konnyaku*, leeks, Chinese cabbage, carrots, *daikon*, green beans, and sliced leeks.

Chicken Nabé *(Tori Nabé):* Simmer chicken, green peppers, sliced onions, and mushrooms in dashi until tender. Add miso, *mirin*, sake, and sugar, and simmer several more minutes.

Grilled Preparations

Fish Dengaku *(Gyoden):* Sprinkle horse mackerel, sweetfish, or trout with salt, skewer, and broil over high heat tilt speckled. Spread both sides with Sweet Simmered Miso and rebroil briefly. Or sandwich the miso between broiled fish slices and steam in cherry or oak leaves.

Foods Pickled in Miso

Red Snapper, Mackerel, or Salmon *(Tai-, Saba-, or Sake no Misozuké):* Sprinkle fish lightly with salt, wrap in cheesecloth, and embed in a mixture of sweet white miso and a little sake or *mirin* for 2 to 3 days (or in red or barley miso for 1 to 2 days). Rub off excess miso and broil on both sides until cooked through. Serve as a topping for rice, an hors d'œuvre, a sandwich filling, or an ingredient in miso soups.

Pork *(Buta no Misozuké):* Arrange sliced pork on a plate and top with gingerroot slices. Sprinkle with sake and allow to stand for 1 hour, then steam for 40 minutes. Cool and embed with gingerroot in red or barley miso for 5 to 7 days. Rub off miso with fingertips, cut pork into thin strips, and serve as for red snapper above.

Chicken *(Tori no Misozuké):* Cut chicken into thin strips, sprinkle with sake, and allow to stand for 10 minutes. Wrap in cheesecloth and proceed as for red snapper.

Beef *(Gyuniku no Misozuké):* Pound meat lightly, cut into thin strips, and wrap in cheesecloth. Embed for 2 to 4 days in sweet white miso. Broil for 3 minutes on each side.

Traditional shoyu seller

TEMPERATURE

C = Celsius or Centigrade; F = Fahrenheit
$C = 5/9 (F-32)$
$F = (1.8 \times C) + 32$
Freezing point of water = $32°F = 0°C$
Boiling point of water = $212°F = 100°C$
Body temperature = $98.6°F = 37.0°C$

WEIGHT (MASS)

1 ounce (avoirdupois) = 28.3495 grams = 16 drams = 437.5 grains
1 pound (avoirdupois) = 16 ounces = 453.59 grams = 0.45359 kg
1 (short or U.S.) ton = 2,000 pounds = 0.907 tonnes or metric tons = 33.33 bushels of soybeans (used chiefly in the U.S. and Canada)
1 tonne or metric ton (MT) = 2,204.6 pounds = 1.1025 (short) tons = 36.75 bushels of soybeans
1 long ton = 2,240 pounds = 1.12 (short) tons = 1.016 tonnes or metric tons = 37.33 bushels of soybeans (used chiefly in England)
100 grams = 3.527 ounces
1 kilogram = 1,000 grams = 2.2046 pounds
1 quintal (qt) = 100 kg = 220.46 pounds
10 ppm = 0.01 gm/kg = .0045 gm/lb.

CAPACITY (U.S. LIQUID MEASURE)

1 teaspoon = 60 drops
1 tablespoon = 3 teaspoons = 14.75 ml or cc
1 fluid ounce = 2 tablespoons = 29.57 ml = 0.0296 liters = 1.8047 cu. in.
1 cup (U.S.) = 16 tablespoons = 8 fluid oz. = 236 ml
1 quart = 2 pints = 4 cups = 32 fluid oz. = 0.946 liters
1 gallon (U.S.) = 4 quarts = 231 cu. in. = 0.8333 imperial gallon = 3.785 liters
1 gallon (imperial) = 1.20 gallons (U.S.) = 4.456 liters
1 liter = 1,000 ml or cc = 1.0567 liquid quarts = 4.237 cups = 61.03 cu. in. = 33.814 fluid ounces = 0.264 gallons = 0.220 imperial gallons
1 kiloliter = 1,000 liters = 264.18 gallons (U.S.)= 33.315 cu. ft. = 2200.6 lb. water
10 ppm = 0.01 ml/liter = 0.38 ml/gallon

CAPACITY (U.S. DRY MEASURE)

1 quart = 2 pints = 67.20 cu. in. = 1.1012 liters
1 peck = 537.605 cu. in. = 9.309 quarts = 8.809 liters
1 bushel (bu) = 4 pecks (approximately 8 gallons) = 2,150.42 cu. in. = 35.2390 liters

CAPACTIY (JAPANESE)

1 *go* (Japanese) = 10 *shaku* = 180 cc = 0.763 cups (U.S.)
1 *sho* = 10 *go* = 1,903 quarts = 0.476 gallons = 1.800 liters
1 *koku* = 10 *to* = 100 *sho* = 47.6 gallons = 180 liters
1 tablespoon = 15 cc = 3 teaspoons
1 cup = 200 cc = 0.847 U.S. cups = 13.5 U.S. tablespoons

LENGTH (LINEAR MEASURE)

1 inch = 2.540 cm = 1,000 mils
1 foot = 12 inches = 30.48 cm
1 yard = 3 feet = 91.44 cm
1 mile = 5,280 feet = 320 rods = 1.609 km
1 mm = 0.03937 inches
1 cm = 0.3937 inches
1 meter = 39.37 inches = 3.2808 feet = 1.094 yards
1 km = 1,000 m = 0.621 miles = 3,280.8 feet

AREA (SQUARE MEASURE)

1 sq. in. = 6.452 sq. cm
1 sq. ft. = 144 sq. in. = 929.03 sq. cm = 0.0929 sq. m
1 sq. yd. = 1296 sq. in. = 0.836 sq. m
1 sq. mile = 640 acres = 2.593 sq. km
1 acre = 43,560 sq. ft. (208.7 ft. on a side) = 4840 sq. yds. = 4047 sq. m = 0.405 hectares
1 sq. cm = 0.1549 sq. in.
1 sq. meter = 1550 sq. in. = 10.764 sq. ft. = 1.196 sq. yd.
1 sq. km = 0.3856 sq. miles = 247.1 acres = 100 hectares
1 hectare (ha) = 10,000 sq, m (100 m on a side) = 2.471 acres

VOLUME (CUBIC MEASURE)

1 cu. in. = 16.387 cc
1 cu. ft. = 1728 cu. in. = 0.028 cu. m = 7.48 gallons
1 cu. yd. = 46,656 cu. in. = 0.765 cu. m
1 cc = 0.061 cu. in.
1 cu. m = 35.315 cu. ft. = 1.308 cu. yd. = 1 kiloliter

NATURAL AND SOY EQUIVALENTS

Atmospheric pressure = 14.7 lbs./sq. in. = 1.036 kg/sq. cm
1 gallon (U.S.) of water weighs 8.33 lbs. = 3.78 kg
1 cup of soybeans weighs 6.5 ounces = 182 grams
1 quart of soybeans weighs 1.62 lbs. = 0.736 kg
1 gallon of soybeans weighs 6.47 lbs. = 2.94 kg
1 bushel of soybeans weighs 60 lbs. = 27.24 kg; it yields 10.7 lbs. (17.8%) crude soy oil plus 47.5 lbs. (79.2%) defatted soybean meal plus 1.8 lbs. (3%) manufacturing loss
1 metric ton of soybeans contains 36.75 bushels; it yields 400 lbs. of oil and 1850 lbs. of meal
For equivalent weights of basic miso ingredients, see p. 184.

ENERGY, WORK & PRESSURE

A BTU (British Thermal Unit) is the quantity of heat required to raise the temperature of 1 pound of water one degree Fahrenheit (near $39.2°F$)
A watt is a unit of power equal to the rate of work represented by a current of 1 amp under a pressure of 1 volt.
A horsepower (H.P.) = 746 watts = 0.746 kilowatts = 550 foot pounds per second
1 lb./sq. in. = 70.45 gm/sq. cm. = 0.070 kg/sq. cm.
1 kg/sq. cm. = 14.19 lb./sq. in.

Appendix H
So You Want to Study Miso in Japan?

A growing number of people have recently begun to consider the possibility of going to Japan to study miso making at its source. The traditional art and craft is best studied in depth under the guidance of a master. The problems to be expected in undertaking such an adventure are definitely not insurmountable.

1. *Time:* A basic apprenticeship will probably last at least 2 years, the first half of which will be devoted primarily to learning the language. A more thorough study might take three to four years. Or you could simply apply for a three-month tourist visa (which is readily obtainable and requires no letter of guarantee; see below), visit a number of shops to watch and get a feeling for the whole process, and make one good contact who would be willing to serve as your guarantor for a longer visit. You could then either go home, begin to practice what you have learned, and return later for a longer stay, or go to Korea with your letter of guarantee and return to Japan with a six-month visa.

2. *Money:* You will need money for your round trip transportation, daily food and housing, language study, and incidental expenses. As of this writing, a round-trip charter flight costs about $500. Living expenses range from $120 per month on up. Remember that Japan—and particularly any of its larger cities—is one of the most expensive places to live in the world. Monthly language school costs may average $100 per month or more. And incidentals including travel, entertainment, etc., usually go no lower than $25 per month. Before you start your trip, make sure you have enough money to last as long as you plan to stay—the Embassy will ask you to prove that you do. Do not expect to get an income from the miso master with whom you study. In fact, you should probably provide him with gifts from time to time as tokens of thanks.

3. *Visa:* Phone or write your nearest Japanese Consulate (offices in Anchorage, Atlanta, Chicago, Honolulu, Portland, New Orleans, New York, San Francisco, Seattle, and Vancouver) and ask them to send you the necessary application forms for a general-study visa No. 4-1-16-3 which is good for six months and can be renewed indefinitely. They will ask you to provide an explanation of the purpose of your trip, how long and where you intend to stay, and how you intend to support yourself. They will ask to see your passport, a letter of guarantee, your round-trip ticket, and perhaps your bank balance.

4. *Letter of Guarantee:* Obtaining this letter is the hardest part of getting a non-tourist visa. Your guarantor may be any Japanese or foreigner living in Japan who has lived there for one year or more. Send this person the form which explains exactly what information his letter of guarantee must contain together with a description of the purpose of your visit. If you are unable to locate a guarantor, explain this to the consulate and they will probably allow your parents or an American friend to serve as a substitute.

5. *Housing:* This problem is easiest to solve if you have a friend living in Japan who can lodge you when you arrive and then help you to find a place to stay. Travelers without a friend often start by staying in an inexpensive hotel or hostel. Many language schools have facilities for locating student housing. Living with a Japanese family will be a great aid to learning the language. Rent will range from about $30 per month on up.

6. *Language:* In order to study with a miso master, you will have to be able to speak some Japanese. The easiest and quickest way to learn is in an established language school. Some of the best include:

Tokyo Japanese Language School (Naganuma Tokyo Nihongo Gakko): Nanpeidai-machi 16-26, Shibuya-ku, Tokyo 150. Tel: 03-463-7261. They offer four semesters beginning in early January, April, July, and September.

Kyoto Japanese Language School (Kyoto Nihongo Gakko): Ichijo-dori, Muromachi Nishi, Kamikyo-ku, Kyoto 602. Tel: 075-414-0449. They offer three semesters beginning in early April, July, and September.

International Christian University (Kokusai Kirisutokyo Daigaku): Osawa 3-10-2, Mitaka-shi, Tokyo 181. Tel: 0422-31-3131. Yearly registration for the 3 successive semesters begins in early September.

At all three schools, classes are held three hours each morning five days a week at a cost of $300 to $365 per semester. At the first two schools, beginners may enter without previous application at the beginning of each semester. At the third school, admission applications (including numerous documents) must be at the school before May 1; not all applicants are accepted. After 6 months of intensive study, you should be able to carry on a conversation without difficulty; after one year, you should be fluent enough to continue language study on your own.

7. *Finding a Master:* If you were sponsored by an organization affiliated with miso, it should be able to assist you in finding the type of master you are looking for. If not, the list of names in Appendix D may well be of help. Or you may simply wish to begin visiting miso shops in your area and talking with the craftsmen until you find a situation that is mutually agreeable. Remember that you should generally call and make an appointment before visiting and take a small present with you when you go. Be careful not to be a nuisance and don't wear out your welcome. At first, you may wish to ask to visit the shop only once or twice each week while continuing your language studies. Later, you may be permitted to serve a full-time apprenticeship. At some time during your study, it would probably be helpful to visit a number of other shops throughout Japan to get a better perspective on your own work situation.

8. *Help from Your Friends:* Let us know if we can be of help to you in establishing contacts. We will probably be able to put you in touch with other people like yourself studying miso in Japan.

Miso Additives

All traditional miso was prepared using only natural ingredients, and all of the varieties available today are prepared by at least some makers without the use of chemical additives. Following World War II, however, a number of additives began to be used in order to make miso more suited to mass distribution, to create whiter colors and sweeter flavors, and to counteract the negative effects of temperature-controlled quick fermentation. The use of additives increased steadily until about 1975 when consumer reaction developed momentum and a government law was passed requiring producers to list all ingredients and additives contained in packaged miso. Remember that most red, barley, and Hatcho miso is completely free of additives (except perhaps ethyl alcohol), whereas many varieties of sweet or white miso are not. The following, listed in order of frequency of occurrence, are presented here for the benefit of those who prefer natural foods and have developed the valuable habit of reading labels. Japanese equivalent terms are given to help natural-food importers double-check that no additives have been used.

Ethyl Alcohol Preservative *(shusei):* Also known simply as alcohol (C_2HO_5), this is the substance that occurs naturally in wine and liquor. Used to prevent sealed polyethylene bags from swelling, while halting fermentation and surface-mold growth, it is allowed at the legal limit of 2 percent by weight and is mixed with the miso just before packaging. Some companies use it only with miso packaged during the summer months. In Japan, it is legal to advertise miso as containing no additives even though it contains ethyl alcohol. For this reason it has recently replaced sorbic acid as the mostly widely employed preservative. It is most often used in misos which are relatively sweet, packaged in sealed bags or jars, and/or are prepared by quick temperature-controlled fermentation. Nevertheless, it is also frequently found in relatively salty, bulk-packed varieties prepared by natural fermentation. Traditional shops generally use it with unpasteurized miso, while modern makers may add it to reinforce the effects of pasteurization.

Food Coloring *(chakushokuzai):* Riboflavin (vitamin B_2) is occasionally used in light-yellow and semi-sweet beige misos. Added to the miso before fermentation, it improves the luster and gives a more natural yellow color which is lost during bleaching and quick fermentation.

Chemical Seasoning *(kagaku chomiryo):* Quick sweet white, light-yellow, and akadashi miso may contain monosodium glutamate (MSG, *aji-no-moto, gurutamin-san,* Accent) which appears to enrich the miso flavor by actually sensitizing the taste buds in the tongue. Unfortunately, many people find that MSG causes unpleasant physical and mental sensations if ingested in even moderate amounts. MSG is used because quick temperature-controlled fermentation and the discarding of the cooking water from light-colored varieties yield miso with a less than satisfactory flavor.

Non-clumping Agent: A chemical mixture with the brand name *Eimaruji* is sometimes cooked with the rice to prevent clumping.

Artificial Sweeteners *(kanmiryo):* Virtually all akadashi miso contains refined *mizuamé* (millet jelley) or malt sugar *(bakuga-to)*. In a few cases, these are added to sweet white and sweet barley miso. Honey and sugar are virtually never used in miso of any type.

Vitamins: Vitamin B_1 is often added to the steamed rice together with the koji starter, and is meant to restore the nutrients in light-colored miso which are lost when the cooking water containing water soluble vitamins is discarded in order to give the miso a lighter color. In some misos methionine or its derivatives are added to miso at the end of fermentation to supplement the lack of sulfur-containing amino acids in soybeans. Other fortifiers occasionally added at the beginning of fermentation include vitamins A and B_2, plus calcium carbonate.

Sorbic Acid Preservative *(sorubin-san* or *sorubin-san kari):* This preservative or its potassium salt is allowed at the level of 1 gram per 1,000 grams of miso. Although still occasionally used in the same ways as ethyl alcohol, it is rapidly being replaced by the latter which is now generally considered safer and more natural.

Sodium Thiosulphate Bleach *(jiaryusan natorium* or *jiaryusan soda):* This bleach (also known as hyposulphite, SO_2) was used up until the late 1970s to bleach soybeans when making light-colored misos; at present its use has been discontinued.

Caramel: Used in most akadashi miso to add color and sweetness.

Shoyu: Often used in small amounts in akadashi miso to add color and flavor.

Bibliography

PUBLICATIONS ABOUT MISO

Additional publications relating to the manufacture of miso will be found in *Miso Production* by Shurtleff and Aoyagi.

Abbreviations: FSTA = Food Science and Technology Abstracts. *Chem. Abstr* = Chemical Abstracts.

Abehsera, Michel. 1968. *Zen Macrobiotic Cooking.* New York: University Books/Avon. 224 p.

Abehsera, Michel. 1970. *Cooking for Life.* New York: Swan House/Avon. 364 p.

Abel, Mary H. 1900. Beans, peas, and other legumes as food. *USDA Farmers Bulletin* No. 121. p. 9-11.

Abiose, Sumbo H. 1980. *Studies on Miso Fermentation.* Glasgow, Scotland: PhD thesis, University of Strathclyde.

Abiose, S.H., Allan, M.C. and Wood, B.J.B. 1982. Microbiology and biochemistry of miso (soy paste) fermentation. *Advances in Applied Microbiology* 28:239-65.

Ahlburg, H. 1878. (About Eurotium oryzae). In Korschelt 1878. p. 252-55.

Aihara, Cornellia. 1972. *The Chico-san Cookbook.* Chico, CA: Chico-san Inc. Reissued as Macrobiotic Kitchen by Japan Publications in 1982. 140 p.

Aihara, H. 1972. *Miso & Tamari.* San Francisco, CA: George Ohsawa Macrobiotic Foundation. 34 p.

Aihara, H. 1974. *Soybean Diet.* Oroville, CA: George Ohsawa Macrobiotic Foundation. 164 p.

Ajinomoto Inc. 1972. Dried miso preparation. Japanese Patent 26,719/72 (cited in FSTA 1973, No. 1J80).

Akaghi, T., Nakajima, I. and Tsugane, K. 1915. Researches on "Hatsucho-Miso." *Journal of the College of Agriculture,* Tokyo 5(3):263-69.

Akizuki, Shinichiro, 1965. *Taishitsu to Shokumotsu* (Physical Constitution and Food). Nagasaki: Self published. 40 p. An abridged edition, edited by Kawamura Wataru, is available from the Japanese National Miso Assoc. under the title *Taishitsu wa Shokumotsu de* (Your Physical Constitution Depends on What You Eat).

Akizuki, S. 1980. How we survived Nagasaki. *East West Journal.* Dec. p. 10, 12-13.

Aonuma, T. 1973. Soy and miso paste. U.S. Patent 3,764,708. By Kikkoman Shoyu Co.

Asahi Shimbun. 1981. Miso shiru igai na koyo. Tokyo. Sept. 27.

Atkinson, R.W. 1878. Brewing in Japan. *Nature* 18:521-23 (Sept. 12).

Atkinson, R.W. 1881. On the diastase of koji. *Proceedings of the Royal Society of London* 32:299-332.

Atkinson, R.W. 1881. The chemistry of sake brewing. *Memoirs of the Tokyo Imperial University Science Department* (Tokio Daigaku). No. 6. pp. 1-73.

Belleme, J. 1981a. The miso master with big heart. *Soyfoods.* Sum-April:50-54.

Belleme, J. 1981. The miso master with a big heart. *Soyfoods.* Summer. p. 64-66.

Biot, Edouard, trans. 1851. *Le Tcheou-Li ou Rites des Tcheou.* 3 Vols. Paris. Reprinted 1969, Taipei.

Breirem, K. 1952. Oscar Kellner. *J. of Nutrition* 47:3-10.

Bretschneider, Emilii Vasilevich. 1881-95. *Botanicon Sinicum.* Notes on Chinese Botany from Native and Western Sources. London: Trübner & Co. 3 Vols. Issued originally in the Journal of the Royal Asiatic Society, North China Branch. Series 2, Vols. 16, 25, 29.

Bryant, Carl. 1785. *Verzeichniss der zur Nahrung dienenden so wohl einheimischen als auslandischen Pflanzen.* Part 1. Leipzig: Weidemanns Erben und Reich. p. 378-80.

Bryant, Charles. 1783. *Flora diaetetica: or History of esculent plants, both domestic and foreign . . .* London: B. White. 379 p.

Bui, Quang Chieu. 1905. Les cultures vivrieres au Tonkin. *Bulletin Economique de l'Indo-Chine.* New Series 2. No. 48. p. 1152-53, 1157-68.

Burkill, I.H. 1935. *A Dictionary of the Economic Products of the Malay Peninsula.* London: Crown Agents. p. 1080-86. (The work is 2 volumes, 2400 p.)

Carletti, Francesco. [1701] 1964. *My Voyage Around the World.* Trans. by H. Weinstock. Pantheon Books, New York. p. 110. (Orig. Ragionamenti, 1594-1606).

Carr, B. 1980. Miso (Made in the U.S.A.). *East West Journal.* January. p. 68-69.

Chang, K.C. ed. 1977. *Food in Chinese Culture.* New Haven, CT: Yale University Press. 429 p.

Cheryan, M. 1980. Phytic acid interactions in food systems. *CRC Critical Reviews in Food Science & Nutrition* 13(4):297-335.

Choe, C. and Song, P. 1960. Fermented soybeans of Korea. *Bulletin of the Scientific Research Inst. of Korea* 5:29.

Church, M.B. 1923. Soy and related fermentations. *USDA Department Bulletin* No. 1152, May 12. 26 p.

Cohn, Ferdinand. 1884. Ueber Schimmelpilze aus Gaerungserreger. *Jahresberichte Schles. Ges. Vaterland Kultur.* 61:226. Breslau.

D.B. 1979. Down-home miso. *Whole Foods.* October. p. 62.

Diamant, Y., Ilany-Feigenbaum, J., Pinsky, E., Laxer, S., and Shor, F. 1963. "The preparation of Japanese miso for human consumption by fermentation of defatted soybean meal." *Israel J. of Chemistry* 1:184.

Diamant, E.J. and Laxer, S. 1968. Nutritional evaluation of miso. *Israel J. of Chemistry* 6:147.

Dyson, G.M. 1928. Mould food of the Far East. *The Pharmaceutical Journal and Pharmacist* 121:375-77. (Oct. 20, London).

Ebine, H. 1966. Manufacturing digestible proteinous foods from oilseeds and pulses by enzymatic treatment. *Japan Agricultural Research Quarterly,* Vol. 1, No. 1.

Ebine, H. 1967. Evaluation of dehulled soybean grits from United States varieties for making miso. *USDA Final Technical Report.* Public Law 480. Project UR-ALL-(40)-2.

Ebine, Hideo. 1968. *Fermented Soybean Foods in Japan.* Tokyo: Tropical Agricultural Research Center, Ministry of Agric. and Forestry. 20 p.

Ebine, H. and Yamamoto, K. 1968. Miso manufacturing from dehulled soybeans. 2. Evaluation of dehulled soybeans for miso making. *Shokuryo Kenkyusho Kenkyu Hokoku* No. 23:1.

Ebine, H. 1972. Miso in *Conversion and Manufacture of Foodstuffs by Microorganisms.* Proceedings of the sixth international fermentation symposium held in Kyoto, Japan, Dec. 5-9, 1971. p. 127-32.

Ebine, H. et al. 1972. Evaluation of U.S. soybeans as raw materials for making miso. *Report of the Central Miso Institute.* No. 7. July. 66 p. In Japanese with 4-page English summary.

Ebine, H. 1976. Fermented soybean foods. In Expanding the Use of Soybeans. *INTSOY Series* No. 10. pp. 126-29.

Egami, Tomi. 1975. *Miso Shiru to Miso Ryori.* (Miso Soup and Miso Cookery). Tokyo: My Life Series No. 46.

Fuerstenberg, Maurice. 1917. *Die Soja.* Berlin: Paul Parey. 43 p.

Fukushima, D. 1979. Fermented vegetable (soybean) protein and related foods of Japan and China. *J. of the American Oil Chemists' Society* 56(3):357-62, 379-80.

Fukushima, D. 1981. Soy proteins for foods centering around soy sauce and tofu. *J. of the American Oil Chemists' Society* 58(3):346-54.

Greenwood, R. 1982. Smokey Mountain miso. *East West Journal.* Nov. p. 50-53.

Hayashi, K. 1977. Process for producing koji for fermented food products. U.S. Patent 4,028,470.

Health Food Business Review. 1968. Soy bean puree: Miso. July. p. 44-45.

Hepburn, James C. 1867. *A Japanese and English Dictionary.* London: Treubner & Co. 558, 132 p. 2nd ed. 1872; 3rd ed. 1886; 4th ed. 1888. 5th ed. 1894; 7th ed. 1903.

Hesseltine, C.W. and Shibasaki, K. 1961. Miso: III. Pure culture fermentation with Saccharomyces rouxii. *Applied Microbiology* 9:515-18.

Hesseltine, C.W. 1962. Research at Northern Regional Research Laboratory on fermented foods. In *Proceedings of Conference on Soybean Products for Proteins in Human Foods.* USDA ARS-71-22. p. 74-82.

Hesseltine, C.W. 1965. A millennium of fungi, food, and fermentation. *Mycologia* 57:149-97.

Hesseltine, C.W. 1967. Fermented products—Miso, sufu, and tempeh. In *Proceedings of International Conference on Soybean Protein Foods.* USDA, ARS-71-35. p. 170-80.

Hesseltine, C.W. and Wang, H.L. 1972. Fermented soybean food products. In A.K. Smith and S.J. Circle. 1972. *Soybeans: Chemistry and Technology.* Westport, CT: AVI Publ. Co. p. 389-419.

Hesseltine, C.W., Swain, E.W. and Wang, H.L. 1976. Production of fungal spores as inocula for Oriental fermented foods. In *Development in Industrial Microbiology* 17:101-15.

Hesseltine, C.W. and Wang, H.L. 1977. Contributions of the Western World to Knowledge of Indigenous Fermented Foods of the Orient. Presented at *Fifth Intl. Conference on Global Impacts of Applied Microbiology,* Nov. 1977, Bangkok, Thailand. 32 p.

Hoang, Van Chi. 1981. *The Vietnamese and their favorite sauces.* Unpublished manuscript. 7 p.

Hoffmann, J.J. 1874. Ueber die bereitung von schoju, sake und myrin. *Mitteilungen der Deutsche Gesellschaft fur Natur- und Volkerkunde Ostasiens* 1(6):8-11.

Horvath, A.A. 1927. The soybean as human food. Peking: Chinese Government Bureau of Economic Information. *Bulletin Series* No. 3. 86 pp. Also published as a series in Chinese Economic Jnl. Sept. 1926 to April 1927.

Hymowitz, T. and Newell, C.A. 1981: Taxonomy of the genus Glycine, domestication and uses of soybeans. *Economic Botany* 35(3):272-88.

Ichiyama, M. 1968. *Kikkoman Shoyu-shi.* Noda, Japan: Kikkoman Shoyu K.K. 804 p.

Ilany-Feigenbaum, J. and Laxer, S. 1967. Color development in Israeli miso type products and its possible use for quality control. *Food Technology* 21:1527-28.

Ilany-Feigenbaum, J., Diamant, J., Laxer, S., and Pinsky, A. 1969. Japanese miso-type products prepared by using defatted soybean flakes and various carbohydrate-containing foods. *Food Technology* 23:554-56.

Ito, E., Ebine, H. and Nakano, M. 1965. About miso. *Report of the Food Research Inst.,* Tokyo. 20:127.

Iwadare, Shoji. 1976. *Miso, Tofu, Natto no Kenkoho* (Miso, Tofu, and Natto: The Way to Health). Tokyo: Yomiuri Shimbun.

Iwamura, I. 1935. Miso, a fermented soybean paste. *Nippon Nogei Kagaku Kaishi* (Bulletin of the Agricultural Chemical Socy. of Japan) 11(1):1-7.

Iwamura, I. 1936. Miso, a fermented soybean paste. *Nippon Nogei Kagaku Kaishi* 12:78-88.

Japanese National Miso Assoc. 1976. *Miso Digest.* Tokyo: Zenkoku Miso Kogyo Kyodo Kumiai Rengokai. 48 p.

JDAC: Japan Dietetic Assoc. Corp. 1964. *Standard Composition of Japanese Foods.* Tokyo: Daiichi Shuppan K.K. Bilingual: Japanese/English.

Julien, S. 1855. (Comments on tsiang/chiang in China). Cited in Paillieux 1880, p. 417.

Kaempfer, E. 1712. *Amoenitatum Exoticarum Politico—Physico—Medicarum.* Fasculi V. Lemgoviae, Germany: H.W. Meyerei. p. 837-40.

Kao, C. 1974. *Fermented Foods from Chickpea, Horsebean and Soybean.* Kansas State University. PhD thesis. 143 p.

Kawamura, W. 1958. *Miso Enkakushi* (Historical Chronicles of Miso). Tokyo: Zenkoku Miso Rengokai. 815 p.

Kawamura, W. and Tatsumi, H. 1972. *Miso no Hon* (The Book of Miso). Tokyo: Shibata Shoten. 320 p.

Kawamura, Wataru. 1973. *Miso Shiru Fudoki* (Miso Soups Throughout the Provinces). Tokyo: Mainichi Shimbun.

Kawamura, Wataru. 1974. *Miso Shiru Hyakka* (Encyclopedia of Miso Soups). Tokyo: Kosei Shuppansha.

Kellner, O., Mori, Y. and Nagaoka, M. 1889. Researches on the manufacture, composition, and properties of "koji." *Bulletin of the College of Agriculture, Tokyo Imp. Univ.* 1(5):9-33.

Kellner, O., Nagaoka, M. and Kurashima, Y. 1889. Researches on the manufacture and composition of "miso." *Bulletin of the College of Agriculture, Tokyo Imperial Univ.* 1(6):1-24.

Kellner, O.J. 1895. Die bereitung von miso in Japan. *Chemiker-Zeitung* 19(13):265.

Kinch, Edward. 1882. Die sojabohne. *Biedermann's Centrall-blat fur Agriculturchemie* 11:753-55.

Kinoshita, Asakichi. 1921. *Jitsuyo Miso Jozo* (Practical Miso Fermentation). Tokyo: Meibundo. 480 p.

Kitaoka, K. 1972. Soybean miso manufacturing with enzyme preparations. *Miso no Kagaku to Gijutsu* No. 218. p. 19-24. Cited in *Chem. Abstr.* 80 (1974), 81,090.

Kobatake, Y. et al. 1964. Nutritional value of protein in Japanese soybean products. *Eiyogaku Zasshi* 22(5):27-31.

Kondo, Akitani. 1972. *Nihon no Chojuson, Tanmeison* (Japanese Long-Life and Short-Life Villages). Tokyo: Sanrodo.

Korschelt, O. 1878. Ueber sake. *Mitteilungen der Deutsche Gesellschaft für Natur und Volkerkunde Ostasiens* 2(16):240-58.

Kotzsch, R.E. 1981. *Georges Ohsawa and the Japanese Religious Tradition.* PhD Thesis, History of Religions, Harvard University. 360 p.

Koyama, M. 1976. Process for producing processed low-salt soybean paste. U.S. Patent 3,937,844. Assigned to Shinshu Miso Co.

Krauss, F.G. 1911. Leguminous crops for Hawaii. *USDA Ag. Expt. Sta. Bull.* No. 23. p. 23-26.

Kushi, Aveline, 1971. Recipes from The Book of Miso. *East West Journal* 1(8):7.

Kushi, Aveline. 1978. *How to Cook with Miso.* New York: Japan Publications Trading Co. 127 p.

Lachman, G. and Elwell, C. 1978. Making miso in America. *East West Journal.* Sept., p. 54-58.

Langworthy, C.F. 1897. Soybeans as food for man. *USDA Farmers Bulletin* No. 58. p. 20-23.

Lau, D.C. 1979. *Confucius: The Analects.* New York: Penguin.

Lee, C-H. 1976. The effect of Korean soysauce and soypaste making on soybean protein quality. *Korean J. of Food Science and Technol* 8(1):12-32.

Leonard, T. 1977. Making brown rice miso in Arkansas. *Soycraft.* Autumn. p. 1.

Leviton, R. 1980. The Ohio Miso Company. *Soyfoods.* Summer. p. 26-31, 63-68.

Leviton, R. 1982. Miso-Cup. *Soyfoods.* Summer. p. 34-35.

Leviton. R. 1982. American Miso makes a big move down south. *Soyfoods.* Summer, p. 18-22.

Leviton, R. 1983. Cold Mountain Miso expands. *Soyfoods.* Winter. p. 7.

Li, Shih-chen. 1597. *Pen ts'ao kang mu.* 1965 ed. Hong Kong: Commercial Press (in Chinese). p. 360-71.

Li, Yu-ying. 1910. *Ta Tou: Le Soja.* Paris: Societe biologique de l'Extreme Orient. 65 p.

Li Yu-ying and Grandvoinnet, L. 1911-12. Le soja. *L'Agriculture Pratique des Pays Chauds* 11:177-96, 270-94, 360-75, 459-74. 12:28-38, 120-32, 213-23, 302-08.

Li Yu-ying and Grandvoinnet, L. 1912. *Le Soja. Sa Culture. Ses Usages Alimentaires, Therapeutiques, Agricoles et Industriels.* Paris, France: A. Challamel. 141 p.

Lockwood, L.B. and Smith, A.K. 1952. Fermented Soy Foods and Sauce. *Yearbook of Agric.*, 1950-51. p. 357-61.

MacDonald, W.C. and Deuck, J.W. 1976. Long term effect of shoyu (Japanese soy sauce) on the gastric mucosa of the rat. *J. of the National Cancer Inst.* 56(6):1143-47.

Manabe, M. et al. 1972. Fluorescent compounds in fermented foods: II. Tests on aflatoxin contamination of miso and miso-koji in Japan. *Nippon Shokuhin Kogyo Gakkai-shi* 19(2):76-80. Cited in *Chem. Abstr* 81 (1974), 167,973.

Matsuura, S. 1970. Aflatoxins and fermented foods in Japan. *Japan Agricultural Research Quarterly* 5:46-51. (Cited in FSTA 1971. 4066).

Miller, C.D. 1933. Japanese foods commonly used in Hawaii. *Hawaii Agric. Exp. Station. Bulletin* No. 68. p. 1-10, 28-43.

Miller, Gloria B. 1966. *The Thousand Recipe Chinese Cookbook.* New York: Antheneum.

Misumi, Kan. 1969. *Miso Daigaku* (Miso University). Tokyo: Bungeisha. He also wrote Tsukemono Daigaku (Pickle University).

Mochizuki, T. et al. 1972. Changes of several components during miso making. *Ferment. Technol. Today.* Proc. 4th Intl. Ferment. Symp. 663-68. (Cited in *Chem. Abstr.* 1976. 84, 29,405F).

Mogi, Masatoshi. 1946. *Taigai Miso* (Making Miso with Nongrain Koji). Tokyo: Seikatsu-sha.

Morohashi, Tetsuji. 1955-60. Daikanwa Jiten. Tokyo: Taishukan Shoten. 12 vols + Index.

Morse, W.J. 1929-31. *Log of the Dorsett-Morse Expedition to East Asia.* Typewritten manuscript in 17 volumes and handwritten notebooks. Only copy located at offices of American Soybean Assoc., St. Louis, Missouri. 6,000 p.

Motoyama, T. 1958. *Inshoku Jiten* (Encyclopedia of Food and Drink). Tokyo: Heibonsha. 604 p.

Murakami, H. et al. 1967-68. Non-productivity of aflatoxin by Japanese industrial strains of Aspergillus. *J. of General and Applied Microbiology* 13:323-34; 14:97-110, 251-62.

Muramoto, Noboru and Abehsera, Michel. 1973. *Healing Ourselves.* New York: Avon/Swan House. 150 p.

Nagahori, T. et al. 1980. On the substances in shoyu to suppress the nitrosation of dimethylamine. *Eiyo to Shokuryo* 33(3): 151-60.

Nakano, M., Ebine, H. and Ota, T. 1967. *Hakko Shokuhin* (Fermented Foods). Tokyo: Korin Shoin.

Nakano, M., Ebine, H. and Ito, H. 1976. On miso, a Japanese traditional fermented food. In *Proceedings of the Fifth International Fermentation Symposium* (held in Germany). p. 363.

Nakayama, Tokiko. 1973. *Chugoku Meisaifu* (Chinese Cuisine: Famous Recipes). Tokyo: Shibata Shoten. 4 Vols.

National Academy of Sciences. 1980. Recommended Dietary Allowances, 9th ed. Washington, D.C.: NAS.

Nishiwaki, Y. 1924. Biologische untersuchungen uber den koji-pilz des Okazaki-Hatchomiso-Koji und der kabocha-bana des tome-koji. *Centralblatt fur Bakteriologie* 63:25-28.

Norinsho. 1964. *Nihon Shokuhin Hyojun Seibunhyo.* (Standard Composition of Japanese Foods). Tokyo: Norinsho (Japanese Ministry of Agriculture and Forestry).

NRRC. 1976. Removal of phytic acid in soybeans to increase utilization of trace elements in soybeans and also the solubility of soybean protein. Peoria, IL: *Report of the USDA Northern Regional Research Center.* p. 11.

Ochse, J.J. 1931. *Vegetables of the Dutch East Indies.* Buitenzorg (Bogor), Java: Archipel Drukkerij. p. 366, 372, 389-93, 398, 407-08, 732, 943-71.

Ohsawa, G. 1960. *Zen Macrobiotics.* New York: Ohsawa Foundation. 103 p.

Ohsawa, Georges. 1965. *Zen Macrobiotics: The Philosophy of Oriental Medicine*, Vol. I. Los Angeles, CA: Ohsawa Foundation. 128 p.

Ohsawa, G. 1966. *Zen Cookery:* Practical Macrobiotics. Los Angeles, CA: Ohsawa Foundation. 84 p.

Ohsawa, Lima. 1971. *Makurobiotiku Ryori* (Macrobiotic Cookery). Tokyo: Nihon CI Kyokai. 199 p.

Ohsawa, Lima. 1974. *The Art of Just Cooking.* Brookline, MA: Autumn Press. 216 p.

Oshima, Kintaro. 1905. A digest of Japanese investigations on the nutrition of man. *USDA OES Bulletin* 159. p. 23-33, 145-53, 168-73.

Paillieux, A. 1880. Le soya, sa composition, chimique, ses varietes, sa culture et ses usages. *Bulletin de la Societe d'Acclimatization* 27 (or 3rd Series vol. 7): 414-71, 538-96.

Pierson, J.L. trans. 1929-63. *Man'yoshu.* Leiden (Leyden): E.J. Brill Ltd. 20 vols. 16:44. The only translation of the entire Man'yoshu.

Piper, C.V. and Morse, W.J. 1916. The soybean, with special reference to its utilization for oil, cake, and other products. *USDA Bull.* 439. 20 p.

Piper, C.V. and Morse, W.J. 1923. *The Soybean.* New York: Mc Graw-Hill. 329 p.

Prinsen-Geerligs, H.C. 1895. Eenige Chineesche voedingsmiddelen uit Sojaboonen bereid. *Pharmaceutisch Weekblad Voor Nederland* 32(33):1-2. Dec. 14.

Prinsen Geerligs, H.C. 1896. Einige chinesische Sojabohnenpräparate. *Chemiker-Zeitung* 20(9):67-69 (Jan. 29).

Rao, N.N., Dwarakanath, C.T. and Rao, T.N.R. 1968. Development of predigested protein-rich food based on Indian oil seed cakes and pulses. *J. of Food Science and Technology* (Mysore). Part I, 5:198-201. Part II (1972) 9:57-62.

Rao, N.N., Rao, T.N.R. and Shanthamma, M.S. 1972. Development of pre-digested protein-rich food based on Indian oilseed meals and pulses. II. *J. of Food Science and Technology* (Mysore) 9(2):57-62.

Raper, K.B. and Fennell, D.I. 1965. *The genus Aspergillus.* Baltimore, MD: Williams & Wilkins Co. 686 p.

Rein, J.J. 1899. *The Industries of Japan.* London: Hodder and Stoughton. p. 105-07. A translation of volume II of his *Japan nach reisen und studien.* publ. 1886.

Robinson, R.J. and Kao, C. 1977. Tempeh and miso from chickpea, horse bean, and soybean. *Cereal Chemistry* 54:1192-97.

Rudinsky, Russ. 1969. *Japanese Country Cookbook.* San Francisco: Nitty Gritty Productions. 192 p.

Saito, Y. et al. 1973. Miso manufacturing using enzymic preparations. *Miso no Kagaku to Gijutsu* 236:20-30. (Cited in *Chem. Abstr.* 1975. 82:169,030p).

Sakaguchi, K. 1972. Development of industrial microbiology in Japan. In *Proceedings of the International Symposium on Conversion and Manufacture of Foodstuffs by Microorganisms.* Kyoto, Japan. 5-9 Dec. 1971. p. 7-10.

Sakaguchi, Kinichiro, et al. 1974. Miso. *Shoku no Kagaku.* December.

Sakaguchi, Kinichiro. 1979. Shoyu no ruutsu o saguru. *Sekal.* Jan. p. 252-66.

Sawa, S. 1902. Note on Hamanatto, a kind of vegetable cheese. *Bulletin of the College of Agriculture, Tokyo Imp. Univ.* 4:419-20.

Senft, E. 1906-07. Ueber einige in Japan verwendete vegetabilische nahrungsmittel, mit besonderer berüchsichtigung der japanischen militärkonserven. *Pharmazeutische Praxis* 5(12):481-91, 6(3):81-89, 6(4):122-24.

Shaw, Norman. 1911. The Soya Bean of Manchuria. Shanghai: Statistical Dept. of the Inspectorate General of Customs. II. *Special Series No. 31.* 32 p.

Shibasaki, K. and Hesseltine, C.W. 1961. Miso I. Preparation of soybeans for fermentation. *J. of Biochemical and Microbiological Technology and Engineering* 3:161-74.

Shibasaki, K. and Hesseltine, C.W. 1961. Miso II. Fermentation. *Developments in Industrial Microbiology* 2:205-14.

Shibasaki, K. and Hesseltine, C.W. 1962. Miso Fermentation. *Economic Botany* 16:180-95.

Shih, Chi-yien. 1918. *Beans and Bean Products.* Shanghai: Soochow Univ. Biology Dept. 13 p.

Shih, Sheng-han. 1962. *A Preliminary Survey of the Book Ch'i Min Yao Shu: An Agricultural Encyclopedia of the 6th Century.* Peking: Science Press. 107 p.

Shinoda, Osamu. 1974. *Chugoku Shokumotsu-shi* ("History of Chinese Foods"). Tokyo: Shibata Shoten. 389 p.

Shufu-no-tomo. 1972. *Ryori Hakka* (Encyclopedia of Japanese Cookery). Tokyo: Shufu-no-tomo.

Shurtleff, W. and Aoyagi, A. 1976. *The Book of Miso.* Brookline, MA: Autumn Press. 256 p. Revised edition. 1981. New York: Ballantine Books, 620 p.

Shurtleff, W. 1977. Beikoku ni okeru miso. *Miso no Kagaku to Gijutsu.* No. 289, March, p. 11-15.

Shurtleff, W. and Aoyagi, A. 1977. *Miso Production.* Lafayette, CA: The Soyfoods Center. 62 p. Revised edition. 1979. 80 p.

Shurtleff, W. and Aoyagi, A. 1979. *The Book of Tempeh.* New York: Harper & Row. Paperback, 160 p. Professional hardcover, 248 p.

Shurtleff, W. and Aoyagi, A. 1980. *Das Miso Buch.* Soyen, W. Germany: Ahorn Verlag. 266 p.

Shurtleff, W. 1982. Miso soup-Safeguard against cancer. *East West Journal.* January. p. 42-43. Translation of *Asahi Shimbun* article.

Shurtleff, W. and Aoyagi, A. 1983. *Soyfoods Industry and Market: Directory and Databook.* Lafayette, CA: The Soyfoods Center. 116 p.

Smith, A.K. 1949. Oriental use of soybeans as food. *Soybean Digest.* Feb:15-17, March:26-34, April:23-31, May:24-30, June:15-22.

Smith, A.K. Hesseltine, C.W., and Shibasaki, K. 1961. Preparation of Miso. U.S. Patent No. 2,967,108.

Stahel, G. 1946. Foods from fermented soybeans as prepared in the Netherlands Indies. I. Taohoo, a cheese-like substance, and some other products. *J. of the New York Botanical Garden* 47:261-67.

Steinberg, Raphael. 1969. *The Cookery of Japan.* New York: Time-Life Books.

Sun Yi-jang, ed. 1966. *Chou-li Cheng-yi* (Ssu Pu Pei Yao edition). 6 Vols. Taipei.

Takahashi, J. 1955. Studies on sources of vitamin B-12. *Eiyo to Shokuryo* 8(2): 25-27.

Takahashi, T. 1908. A preliminary note on the chemical composition of miso. *J. of the Tokyo Chemical Socy.* 29(2).

Takahashi, T. and Abe, G. 1913. Preliminary notes on the chemical composition of miso. *J. of the College of Agriculture. Tokyo* 5(2):193-98.

Tamura, Heiji and Hirano, M. 1971. *Shoyu no Hon* (The Book of Shoyu). Tokyo: Shibata Shoten. 294 p.

Thom, Charles, and Church, M. 1921. Aspergillus flavus, A. oryzae, and associated species. *American J. of Botany* 8:103-26.

Thom, C. and Church, M. 1926. *The Aspergilli.* Baltimore, MD: Williams and Wilkens. 272 p.

Thom, Charles and Raper, Kenneth B. 1945. *Manual of the Aspergilli.* Baltimore, MD: The Williams and Wilkins Co. 373 p.

Thunberg, C.P. 1795. *Travels in Europe, Africa, and Asia, Made Between the Years 1770 and 1779.* London: F and C Rivington. 4 vols.

TIME magazine. 1969. Cancer, a clue from under the eaves. May 9. p. 81.

Tomoda Noritaka and Sakaguchi Kinichiro, ed. 1956. *Hakko Shokuhin: Biseibutsu Kogaku Koza* (Fermented Foods: Microbial Technology Course). Tokyo: Kyoritsu Shuppan.

Trimble, H. 1896. Recent literature on the soja bean. *American J. of Pharmacy* 68:309-13.

Tsuda, Tadao et al. 1974. *Shojin Ryori* (Zen Temple Cookery). Tokyo: Fujokai Shuppansha. 242 p.

Tsuji, Kaichi. 1971. *Zen Tastes in Japanese Cooking.* Tokyo: Kodansha. 207 p.

U.S. Dept. of Health, Education, and Welfare. 1972. Food Composition Table for Use in East Asia. Nutrition Program, Center for Disease Control, HEW, Atlanta, GA 30333. 334 p.

Waley, Arthur. 1938. *The Analects of Confucius.* London: George Allen & Unwin Ltd. U.S. ed. 1966 Random House, New York. 257 p.

Wang, H.L., Ellis, J.J. and Hesseltine, C.W. 1972. Antibacterial activity produced by molds commonly used in Oriental food preparations. *Mycologia* 64(1):218-21.

Wang, H.L. and Hesseltine, C.W. 1979. Mold-modified foods. In *Microbial Technology.* 2nd ed. Vol. II. H.J. Peppler ed. New York: Academic Press. p. 95-129.

Wang, Mrs. J.R. and Lee, Y.H. 1978. Traditional soybean foods in Korea. In *International Soya Protein Food Conference Proceedings.* Singapore, Jan. 25-27. p. 43-47.

Watanabe, T. 1969. Industrial Production of Soybean Foods in Japan. Presented at *Expert Group Meeting on Soya Bean Processing and Use,* Peoria, IL 17-21 Nov. 1969. United Nations Industrial Dev. Org. 38 p.

Watanabe Tokuji, Ebine Hideo, and Ota Teruo. 1971. *Daizu Shokuhin* (Soyfoods). Tokyo: Korin Shoin. 270 p.

Watanabe, T., Ebine, H. and Okada, M. 1974. New protein food technologies in Japan. In *New Protein Foods. Vol. 1A. Technology.* (A.M. Altschul, ed.). New York: Academic Press. p. 414-53. Ebine wrote the part of miso.

Wang, H.L., Swain, E.W. and Hesseltine, C.W. 1980. Phytase of molds used in Oriental food fermentation. *J. of Food Science* 45(5):1262-1266.

Watson, Burton, trans. 1961. *Records of the Grand Historian of China: From the Shih Chi of Ssu-ma Ch'ien.* 2 vols. New York: Columbia University Press.

Wehmer, C. 1895. Aspergillus oryzae, der Pilz der Japanischen Sake-Brauerei. *Centralblatt fur Bakteriologie und Parasitenkunde.* Series 2. 1(5):150-160 and 1(6):209-220.

Wehmer, C. 1901. *Die Pilzgattung Aspergillus.* Societe de Physique d'histoire Naturelle de Geneve, Memoirs. 23:1-157.

Wilcox, E.V. 1909. Soy Beans. *Hawaii Agric. Exp. Station Annual Report for 1908.* p. 83-84.

Winarno, F.G. et al. 1976. *The Present Status of Soybean in Indonesia.* Bogor, Indonesia; FATEMETA, Bogor Agricultural University. 128 p.

Winkler, G. 1914. *Die Sojabohne der Mandschurei.* Frankfurt am Main.

Women's College of Nutrition. 1969. *Tofu, Mame, Miso Ryori: Ju-ni Kagetsu* (Tofu, Soybean, and Miso Cookery Throughout the Twelve Months). Tokyo: Joshi Eiyo Daigaku.

Wood, B.J.B. and Yong, F.M. 1975. Oriental food fermentations. In *The Filamentous Fungi,* Vol. 1. J.E. Smith and D.R. Berry eds. London: Edward Arnold Ltd. p. 265-80.

Wood, B.J.B. 1977. Oriental food uses of *Aspergillus.* In *Genetics and Physiology of Aspergillus.* J.E. Smith and J.A. Pateman, eds. New York: Academic Press. p. 481-98.

Wood, B.J.B. 1982. Soy sauce and miso. In *Economic Microbiology,* Vol. 5, p. 39-86. (Academic Press).

Yoshi Hisao, Kaneko Yasuyuki, and Yamaguchi Kazuo. 1972. *Shokuhin Biseibutsu-gaku* (Food Microbiology). Tokyo: Gisho-do.

Yong, F.M. and Wood, B.J. 1974. Microbiology and biochemistry of soy sauce fermentation. *Advances in Applied Microbiology* 17:157-94.

Yoshihara, L. 1980. Shinmei-do Miso Company. *Soyfoods.* Summer. p. 10.

ABOUT WORLD HUNGER

The three most important works are starred.

Berg, Alan. 1973. *The Nutrition Factor*. The Brooklings Institute, 1775 Massachusetts Ave., N.W., Washington, D.C. 20036. A nutrition expert on the staff of the World Bank, Berg discusses the way hunger in the third world is linked to underdevelopment and malnutrition.

Borgstrom, Georg. 1974. *The Food/People Dilemma*. New York: Duxbury Press.

_____. 1973. *World Food Resources*. New York: Intext.

_____. 1972. *The Hungry Planet*. New York: Collier-Macmillan. A professor at Michigan State Univ., Borgstrom examines the food/population problem from an environmentalist's point of view, focusing on the effects of uneven food distribution between the rich and poor nations.

Brown, Lester R. 1974. *By Bread Alone*. New York: Praeger. One of the best books on the world food crisis. Head of the newly formed Worldwatch Institute in Washington, D.C., Brown is a highly articulate agricultural economist with a clear vision of the present problem and its solutions. His other recent writings include *In the Human Interest* (1973), *World Without Borders* (1972), and *Seeds of Change* (1970).

*Brown, Lester R. 1978. *The Twenty-Ninth Day: Accommodating Human Needs and Numbers to the Earth's Resources*. New York: W.W. Norton. 363 p. Outstanding!

Brown, Lester R. 1981. *Building a Sustainable Society*. New York: W.W. Norton & Co. 433 p. A great work.

George, Susan. 1977. *How the Other Half Dies: The Real Reasons for World Hunger*. Montclair, NJ: Allanheld, Osmun & Co. 308 p.

Lappé, Frances M. 1982. *Diet for a Small Planet* (Revised Edition), San Francisco: Ballantine/Friends of the Earth, 498 p. A two million-copy bestseller and one of the most influential books ever written concerning the world food crisis and basic nutrition. Emphasis on protein complementarity, meatless meals, and the wisdom of eating low on the food chain.

*Lappé, F.M., and Collins, J. 1978. *Food First: Beyond the Myth of Scarcity*. New York: Ballantine Paperback, Revised edition. 619 p. The finest and most up-to-date book on the world food crisis. A must! Available at reduced rates from the Institute for Food and Development Policy, 2588 Mission Street, San Francisco, CA 94110.

Lerza, Catherine, and Jacobson, Michael, ed. 1975. *Food for People Not for Profit*. New York: Ballantine. This official handbook for Food Day 1975 contains a wealth of up-to-date information concerning every aspect of the food crisis; each chapter written by an authority in the field.

Manocha, Sohan L. 1975. *Nutrition and Our Overpopulated Planet*, Springfield, Ill: Charles C. Thomas. An extensive and up-to-date treatment of the population/food crisis and means for its solution.

*Mesarovic, M., and Pestel, E. 1974. *Mankind at the Turning Point: The Second Report to the Club of Rome*. New York: Signet. The successor to *The Limits of Growth*, this highly readable and condensed book, based on sophisticated computer models, spells out clearly what we can and must do to avoid worldwide famine and catastrophe in the near future.

Miller, G. Tyler. 1975. *Living in the Environment*. Belmont, CA: Wadsworth. An excellent ecology textbook with extensive material concerning the population/food crisis and the means for its solution.

Glossary

Since the companion volume to this work, *The Book of Tofu*, has a lengthy and highly detailed glossary, this one will be kept short to avoid repetition. Basic ingredients are described in Chapter 5, and preparations (such as dashi) are listed in the Index. Most of the following foods are avilable in the West at Oriental grocery stores listed in the yellow pages under "Japanese (or Chinese) Food Products." Main outlets are listed on page 49.

Agar *(Kanten):* A sea-vegetable gelatin sold in light bars, strands, or flakes.

Amazaké: Literally "sweet sake"; see page 162.

Aona: Specifically a Chinese rape, generally all vegetable greens.

Asatsuki: A cross between a wild onion and a chive with a hint of garlic flavor.

Azuki beans: A small red bean, generally cooked with rice or used in desserts, and respected for both its nutritional and medicinal properties.

Bamboo shoots *(Takenoko):* Usually sold fresh in Japan, they appear in April and May and require lengthy cooking.

Bean sprouts *(Moyashi):* The sprouts of the mung bean, easily grown at home.

Beefsteak plant *(Shiso):* The fragrant green leaves *(aojiso)*, aromatic red leaves *(shisonoha)*, richly-flavored seeds *(shisonomi)*, and tiny pink buds *(mejiso)* are each used fresh. The mint-like plant is now cultivated throughout the United States.

Bonito flakes *((Hanakatsuo):* The hard-as-wood dried, fermented bonito *(katsuobushi)* is shaved into paper-thin flakes and used as the basis for dashi or as a garnish.

Burdock root *(Gobo):* A long, dark-brown tapering root vegetable ½ to 1 inch in diameter and 18 to 24 inches long.

Butterbur *(Fuki):* The 4-foot-long, ½-inch-diameter stem of this spring vegetable has a flavor resembling that of celery. The young buds *(fuki-no-to)* are widely served with miso.

Carob: The chocolate-like brown powder made from the seed of a tree-borne pod; also called St. John's bread.

Chinese cabbage *(Hakusai):* A mild-flavored delicacy that may be used either like lettuce in salads or cabbage in simmered preparations. Very inexpensive.

Chrysanthemum leaves *(Shungiku):* Fragrant greens resembling spinach or trefoil.

Cloud-ear mushroom *(Kikuragé):* A delicate variety with a wavy cap, it grows on trees and has virtually no stem. Sold dried, it is also known as Dried Black Fungus or Wood Ear.

Daikon: The marvelously versatile Japanese giant white radish is often as thick as a man's arm and 18 to 24 inches long. Dried slivered *daikon (kiriboshi)* is sold in 4-ounce bags.

Eggplant *(Nasu):* The Japanese variety, sweeter and more tender than its American counterpart averages 4 inches in length, 1½ inches in diameter, and weighs 2 ounces.

Garbanzo beans: Also called chickpeas, this 3/8-inch-diameter tan variety is a favorite in Near Eastern cookery.

Gingerroot *(Shoga):* The 4-inch-long knobby tan root is peeled and freshly grated. Two parts powdered ginger may be substituted for 1 part fresh grated gingerroot.

Gingko nuts *(Ginnan):* These tender, ½-inch-long delicacies are sold fresh or canned.

Glutinous rice *(Mochigomé):* The natural unpolished form is also sold in the West as Sweet Brown Rice; the flour *(shiratamako)* is widely used for making the steamed balls called *dango*.

Glutinous yam *(Tororo imo):* When rubbed on a fine metal grater, these yams develop a highly cohesive, glutinous quality. Available fresh in many varieties.

Green nori flakes *(aonori):* A sea-vegetable seasoning made by crumbling the fragrant, bright-green fronds of dried *Enteromorpha prolifera;* delicious on noddles.

Hamanatto: A fermented, raisin-like soybean product with a mild flavor. Called "soy nuggets" in the West.

Hijiki: A stringy black sea vegetable *(Hizikia fusiforme)* sold in lengths about 1½ inches long. Often misspelled "hiziki" in the West.

Horsetails *(Tsukushi):* A wild spring plant the size of one's little finger.

Junsai: A "water shield" *(Brasenia purpurea)*, this tiny wild pond plant, surrounded by a gelatinous slippery coating, is popular in soups.

Kabocha: Also called Hokkaido pumpkin, this delectable fall vegetable, with its dark-green edible skin, looks like a 6- to 8-inch-diameter acorn squash. Substitute winter squash or pumpkin.

Kampyo: Strips of shaved dried gourd used for tying foods into rolls or bundles.

Kinako: The delicious flour made by grinding roasted soybeans; widely used in confections.

Kinomé: The fragrant, bright-green sprigs of the *sansho (Xanthozylum piperitum)* tree, plucked in the spring.

Koji: Cooked rice, barley, or soybeans inoculated with *Aspergillus oryzae* mold and incubated in a warm, humid room for 45 hours until bound together with a fragrant white mycelium.

Kombu: A sea vegetable *(Laminaria species)* sold in leathery olive-brown sheets 3 to 6 inches wide and 2½ to 6 feet long. *Tororo kombu* is prepared by spraying the sheets briefly with a dilute vinegar solution, shaving them finely, and then shredding.

Konnyaku: Eight-ounce gray cakes made from the starch of *Amorphophallus konjac*, or devil's tongue plant, a member of the yam family. Konnyaku threads *(ito konnyaku)* and noodles *(shirataki)* are used in soups and *nabé* dishes.

Kudzu Powder *(Kuzu):* A high quality, rather expensive starch used somewhat like arrowroot or gelatin or as a highly effective medicine, and made from the root of the "kudzu" plant which grows throughout the United States. For details see *The Book of Kudzu* listed in the Bibliography.

Leek *(Negi):* The Japanese variety is milder and more slender than its Western counterpart.

Mandarin orange *(Mikan):* Japan's most popular and least expensive domestic fresh fruit, it is available from November until March. Delicious.

Matsutaké: The most expensive and most delicious of Japanese mushrooms, *Armillaria matsutake* grows a cap up to 8 inches in diameter.

Mirin: Also called sweet sake, mirin tastes like a mildly alcoholic mixture of sugar and water. Substitute for each tablespoon ½ teaspoon honey and 2 teaspoons sake or pale dry sherry. Or substitute 1½ teaspoons honey and 2½ teaspoons water.

Mizuamé: A natural grain sugar extracted from rice, millet, or barley, it looks like a solid pale-amber resin and may be softened by heating. Also sold as Amé, Rice Honey, or Millet Jelly. Close relatives are barley malt syrup and sorghum molasses.

Mochi: Cakes of steamed, pounded glutinous rice, each about 3 by 2 by ½ inches.

271

Myoga: The pinkish white buds of the *Zingiber mioga* that emerge from the plant's base each August.

Nameko: Tiny yellowish-brown mushrooms with a slippery coating; sold fresh or canned.

Nanohana: Rape blossoms; a springtime favorite in miso soups.

Natto: Sticky fermented whole soybeans.

Niboshi: Dried 2½-inch-long sardines used to make dashi.

Nira: A relative of the chive, *Allium odorum* has flat, dark-green leaves about 10 inches long and a rich fragrance, especially when sautéed.

Nori: A sea vegetable sold in paper-thin purplish-black sheets about 8 inches square and packaged in bundles of ten. The Japanese presently consume about 9 *billion* sheets each year. Other species of *Porphyra* are known in the West as laver. For details, see *The Book of Sea Vegetables*, listed in the Bibliography.

Osmund fern (*Zenmai*): The slender young fiddlenecks are a springtime delicacy.

Ramen: Crinkley yellowish-white Chinese noodles.

Red pepper (*Togarashi*): The Japanese variety are slender, 2½ inches long, and usually sold dried.

Rice flour (*Joshinko*): A fine-textured product usually made from white rice and widely used in the preparation of steamed desserts.

Sake: Rice wine contains about 15 percent alcohol and is widely used in cooking. The lees (*sake-no-kasu*) are used in dressings and soups.

Sansho pepper (*Kona-zansho*): A fragrant brownish-green pepper made from the seedpods of the *sansho* tree, the same tree which bears *kinomé* sprigs.

Sesame seeds (*Goma*): The delicious calcium-rich seeds come in white and black varieties and are usually lightly roasted then ground before use. Substitute one-half the amount of sesame butter or *tahini*.

Seven-spice red pepper (*Shichimi togarashi*): A zippy blend of red peppers and other spices including sesame, *sansho*, grated dried orange peel, green nori flakes, and white pepper.

Shiitaké: Japan's most popular mushroom, *Cornellius shiitake* is sold fresh or dried and widely used as the basis for stocks.

Shimeji: Small mushrooms with tan caps 1 to 1½ inches in diameter, *Tricholoma conglobatum* are usually sold fresh.

Shochu: A popular and very potent type of inexpensive spirits related to gin.

Shoyu: Japanese all-purpose soy sauce (see p. 49).

Snow peas (*Saya endo*): Also called edible-pod peas, these are the paper-thin type often associated with Chinese cookery.

Soba: Japanese buckwheat noodles.

Spinach (*Horenso*): Milder and slightly sweeter than its Western counterpart.

Sweet potato (*Satsuma imo*): One of Japan's most delicious and beloved foods, this variety has no exact counterpart in the West. About 1½ to 2½ inches in diameter and 4 to 8 inches long, they have a pale red skin and light-yellow richly-flavored meat.

Tahini: A smooth creamy paste made from unroasted (or very lightly roasted), hulled white sesame seeds. Due to the removal of the calcium-rich hulls, tahini is not as nutritious as sesame butter, and some commercial varieties use caustic soda in the cleaning and hulling process. Contains 19 percent protein.

Takuan: Dried whole daikon pickled for a long time in salted rice bran.

Tamari: A seasoning liquid resembling shoyu (p. 49).

Taro: A 2½-inch-diameter root vegetable also known in the West as dasheen or albi; the most popular of the many Japanese varieties are *Sato imo*, *yatsugashira*, and *akame imo*. Rich, creamy, and delicious.

Tempeh: Cultured soy cakes, see p. 50.

Tofu: For a description of the many types, see page 50.

Tororo imo: see Glutinous yam.

Trefoil (*Mitsuba*): Prized for its unique pungent aroma and handsome green leaves, *Crytotaenia japonica* is most widely used as a garnish.

Turnip (*Kabu*): The Japanese variety is a heart-shaped, white root about 3 inches in diameter having a mild, slightly sweet flavor.

Udo: Neither quite celery nor asparagus, *Aralia cordata* is a crisp and tender oddity with a unique hint of lemon flavor that is enjoyed fresh or cooked. The best varieties grow wild.

Udon: Fat white wheat-flour noodles similar to a No. 2 spaghetti.

Umeboshi salt plums: Salt-pickled plums from the *Prunus mumé* tree.

Uri melon: Also called "white melon" or "white gourd melon," this is a pale green fruit shaped like a cucumber, about 12 inches long and 3 inches in diameter.

Wakame: A dark-green sea vegetable (*Undaria pinnatifida*) with fronds about 3 inches wide and 12 to 18 inches long, it is sold both fresh and dried; widely used in soups and salads.

Wasabi: A hot green horseradish-like paste made from the grated root of the *wasabi* plant which is cultivated in terraced mountain stream beds.

Wheat gluten (*fu*): Both fresh and dried varieties sold in a multitude of different shapes are widely used in Japanese cookery.

Yuzu: A citrus fruit similar to a citron, lime, or lemon having a green and refeshingly fragrant rind which is slivered or grated; widely used in miso preparations, broths, and dipping sauces.

Index

William Shurtleff and Akiko Aoyagi Shurtleff spent their formative years on opposite sides of the Pacific. Born in California on 28 April 1941. Bill received degrees in engineering, honors humanities, and education from Stanford University. He taught physics for two years in Nigeria in the Peace Corps and has lived and traveled extensively in East Asia and Third World countries. He speaks seven languages, four fluently, including Japanese.

Akiko Aoyagi Shurtleff, born in Tokyo on 24 Janaury 1950, received her education there from the Quaker-run Friends' School and the Women's College of Arts. She has worked as an illustrator and designer in Japan's modern fashion industry and America's emerging soyfoods industry.

Since 1972 Bill and Akiko have been working together, doing research and writing books about soyfoods. They lived for six years in East Asia, mainly in Japan, studying with top soyfoods researchers, manufacturers, nutritionists, historians, and cooks. Over 500,000 copies of their eleven books on soyfoods are now in print. The titles and publishers are listed on the copyright page at the beginning of this book.

In 1976 Bill and Akiko founded The Soyfoods Center, and since that time they have worked to introduce soyfoods, especially traditional low-technology soyfoods, to the Western world. They feel that soyfoods can play a key role in helping to solve the world food crisis while providing high-quality low-cost protein and healthier diets for people everywhere. Their work has led to the establishment of hundreds of soyfoods businesses making tofu, soymilk, miso, tempeh, and other soyfoods, and to the publication by others for more than 33 books about these foods. Their nationwide tours and many lectures, demonstrations, and media appearances have drawn widespread acclaim.

Their global view and uniquely holistic, interdisciplinary approach are aimed at presenting the best of both traditional lore and modern scientific knowledge about soyfoods in a language accessible to both laymen and professionals.

By constantly addressing the problems of world hunger, the suffering of human beings and animals, and the perennial longing for good health and liberation, they hope to make their work relevant everywhere and a force for planetary renaissance.

If you would like to help in the larger work related to soyfoods and world hunger, if you have questions or suggestions related to this book, or if you would like to receive a free copy of their Soyfoods Center Catalog, the authors invite you to contact them.

MISO PRODUCTION
The Book of Miso, Volume II

The authors have prepared this craft and technical manual describing how to start and run your own miso shop or factory on any of various scales and budgets. It contains detailed information on equipment, ingredients, making red, yellow, mellow white, barley, and Hatcho miso, producing koji and koji starter, and sources of miso-making equipment and ingredients. Contains over 100 illustrations. To order, send $11.95 (postpaid) to:

THE SOYFOODS CENTER
P.O. Box 234
Lafayette, CA 94549 USA
(Phone: 415-283-2991)

The Soyfoods Center

THE SOYFOODS CENTER, founded in 1976 by William Shurtleff and Akiko Aoyagi, has offices in California. Our basic goals and activities are related to soyfoods and world hunger.

Soyfoods: Our center is, above all, a source of information about soyfoods, especially tofu, soymilk, tempeh, and miso, about which we have done extensive research and written books and recipe pamphlets. Like a growing number of people, we feel that soybeans will be one of the key protein sources of the future on planet Earth, and that both traditional and modern soyfoods from East and West will serve as important sources of delicious, high-quality, low-cost protein in the diets of people everywhere, regardless of their income. We are interested in each of the following soyfoods, listed here in what we consider to be their approximate order of potential worldwide importance: tofu (soybean curd), soy flour, soymilk, tempeh, shoyu (natural soy sauce), textured soy protein (TVP), miso, whole dry soybeans, soy protein isolates and concentrates, roasted soybeans or soy nuts, fresh green soybeans, roasted full-fat soy flour *(kinako)*, soy sprouts, yuba, and natto. We have developed hundreds of tasty and nutritious Western-style recipes for the use of these foods and compiled extensive, up-to-date information on their nutritional value, history, and production.

World Hunger: Presently more than 15,000,000 people die each year of starvation and malnutrition-caused diseases; three fourths of these are children. We constantly relate our work to this urgent problem of world hunger by studying and developing creative, low-cost, village-level methods for soyfood production using appropriate technology, by traveling and speaking in less developed countries, and by sending complementary copies of our publications to and communicating with key soyfoods researchers and producers in these countries.

Meatless Diets: Over half of all agricultural land in the United States is now used to grow crops (such as corn, soybeans, oats, and wheat) that are fed to animals. The affluent American diet is emerging as a major cause of world hunger as well as of degenerative diseases such as heart disease and cancer. Soyfoods, which are low in cost, high in protein, low in saturated fats, free of cholesterol, and relatively low in calories, can be used as delicious replacements for meats and dairy products as part of meatless or vegetarian diets. We encourage the adoption of such diets which help to make best use of the planet's precious food resources, are conducive to the development of a healthy body and clear mind, kind to animals, economical, and ecologically sound.

Commercial Soyfood Production: We encourage and aid people throughout the world in starting community or commercial production of soyfoods by providing technical manuals, technical advice, materials, and equipment. We have helped to establish the *Soyfoods Association of North America* (SANA) and its international publication *Soy-*foods, to found *Bean Machines, Inc.* (a company selling tofu and soymilk equipment), and to develop catalogs of large and small scale equipment. We have compiled varous technical manuals and presently serve as consultants for a wide variety of companies.

Lecture Demonstrations: We have done more than one hundred programs relating to soyfoods for natural food groups, research scientists, food technologists, nutritionists, commercial producers, university audiences, international symposia, home economists, and cooking schools. We have also done numerous television and radio programs and cooking classes throughout the world. We welcome invitations.

Soyfoods Center Network: Our main Center in California is devoted primarily to research and publication about soyfoods. We have the world's largest library (more than 3,500 documents) on soyfoods. Our growing International Soyfoods Center Network, with branches around the world, is helping to introduce soyfoods around the world. Our Centers do not presently provide residence accomodations.

New Lifestyles: Our work is deeply involved in the development of lifestyles conducive to the welfare and survival of all beings on planet Earth. Thus we encourage voluntary simplicity, self-sufficiency (particularly food self-sufficiency on personal, regional, and national levels), right livelihood, a deeper understanding of selfless service, and of daily life and work as a spiritual practice, ecological awareness, wholistic health, appropriate technology, the rapid development and adoption of solar energy, and the phasing out of nuclear energy.

Publications and Catalog: Our Center has published a number of full-sized specialty books on soyfoods including *Tofu & Soymilk Production, Miso Production, Tempeh Production, Soyfoods Industry and Market: Directory and Databook*, and *History of Soybeans and Soyfoods*. We also provide a free catalog listing our other widely distributed books on tofu, miso, and tempeh, materials such as pamphlets, tofu kits, and slide shows related to soyfoods and a list of soycrafters in North America and Europe.

Your Financial Support and Help: Our work, now reaching people throughout the world, is not supported by government or corporate funds. We do, however, welcome contributions of any size from individuals and private foundations to aid us in furthering the soyfoods revolution and helping to put an end to world hunger. We have established *Friends of The Center* for supporters willing to contribute $35.00 or more; smaller contributions are also welcomed. If you would like to contribute your time and energy to our work, please contact us:

Bill Shurtleff & Akiko Aoyagi Shurtleff
The Soyfoods Center
P.O. Box 234
Lafayette, CA 94549 USA
Tel. 415-283-2991